The Sickle
   under the Hammer

STUDIES OF THE RUSSIAN INSTITUTE
COLUMBIA UNIVERSITY

The Sickle
under the Hammer

THE RUSSIAN SOCIALIST REVOLUTIONARIES
IN THE EARLY MONTHS OF SOVIET RULE

By OLIVER HENRY RADKEY

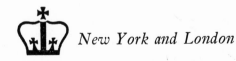 *New York and London*

COLUMBIA UNIVERSITY PRESS 1963

The system of transliteration from the Russian employed in this book is based on that of the Library of Congress with certain modifications. Familiar names of German or Jewish origin are given in the German form (Rosenblum, Richter), whereas less familiar ones or names the original form of which is doubtful are transliterated from the Russian (Gendelman, Shreider); in a few instances names are simply given in the form most familiar to the author. The soft and medial hard signs and the two dots over the stressed *e*, pronounced *yo* in Russian, have been confined to Russian text or titles and do not appear in the case of proper names in the English text or in the citation of authors, the only exceptions being names of some significance that are frequently mispronounced (Slëtov).

Dates are given in the Old Style.

The Russian Institute of Columbia University

The Russian Institute was established by Columbia University in 1946 to serve two major objectives: the training of a limited number of well-qualified Americans for scholarly and professional careers in the field of Russian studies, and the development of research in the social sciences and the humanities as they relate to Russia and the Soviet Union. The research program of the Russian Institute is conducted through the efforts of its faculty members, of scholars invited to participate as Senior Fellows in its program, and of candidates for the Certificate of the Institute and for the degree of Doctor of Philosophy. Some of the results of the research program are presented in the Studies of the Russian Institute of Columbia University. The faculty of the Institute, without necessarily agreeing with the conclusions reached in the Studies, believe that their publication advances the difficult task of promoting systematic research on Russia and the Soviet Union and public understanding of the problems involved.

The faculty of the Russian Institute are grateful to the Rockefeller Foundation for the financial assistance which it has given to the program of research and publication.

STUDIES OF THE RUSSIAN INSTITUTE

TO THE MEMORY OF MY AUNT AND UNCLE

Hattie W. and David G. Hewlett

Foreword

In revolution as in war it is inevitable that the victor should receive more attention than the vanquished. A lost cause is soon overlaid by the dust of neglect, and its surviving image is grossly distorted by prejudice and purposeful misrepresentation. The adherents of "agrarian" socialism in Russia, and more particularly the Socialist Revolutionaries, who had made the peasant cause their own, experienced the common fate of losers, but neither this fate nor the exceptional vindictiveness of the "industrial" socialists who came to power in Russia can altogether account for the barrier of ignorance and error behind which the truth has been concealed.

As related in *The Agrarian Foes of Bolshevism*, to which this book is the sequel, the Socialist Revolutionary movement had, by the fall of 1917, disintegrated into three warring factions—right, center, and left—not one of which has received its due in history. Their role in the revolution as well as their essential character has been misinterpreted, willfully distorted, or simply ignored, and the stereotype of error, once created, has been endlessly copied by uncritical writers, either from the source or from one another. The Bolsheviks are only partially to blame for this situation. In part the SR's themselves are responsible, since in the heat of factional strife they did not hesitate to malign one another. As for the rest, the fault lies in the way in which history is written, or, rather, with those who write it.

The right SR's have fared best so far as friendly treatment is concerned. They backed the Provisional Government and so have been considered exponents of democracy, they inveighed endlessly against the evils of Prussian militarism and endlessly extolled the virtues of Allied unity, they were against violence and bloodshed everywhere except at the front. Hence the indulgence granted them by Western writers. But indulgence leads to superficiality, and the true role of the right SR's inside and outside their party has remained obscured behind the screen of virtue erected by themselves and accepted by others.

The left SR's, on the other hand, have been viewed as irresponsible people who helped the Bolsheviks into power, then belatedly broke with them when the terms of the treaty of Brest Litovsk were disclosed. As a matter of fact, they were far more independent of the Bolsheviks than were the right SR's of the Constitutional Democrats, and Brest Litovsk was merely the occasion, not the cause, of their break with Bolshevism. The martyrs of Social Revolutionism were more often than not the left SR's, since they stayed and took it while other SR's were finding refuge in Paris and in Prague. Their competition was peculiarly unwelcome to Bolshevism because of the combination of genuine revolutionary fervor with championship of the peasant cause. As a result, they were smashed by a regime which always insisted on having its left flank clear, and this smashing, together with the reluctance to flee abroad and the absence in exile of outlets for publication (aside from one small firm in Berlin), has helped to make left-wing Social Revolutionism a dark province of the revolution and to excuse in some measure the ignorance concerning its aims and its actions, its fate and its character.

The center SR's have fared worst of all, since not only their role in the revolution but their very existence has been disregarded. The Bolsheviks are doubtlessly responsible for the conventional division into right and left SR's, but the practice of speaking in these terms has spread to non-Soviet sources, with the result that numerically the largest segment of the movement and by rights its dominant faction has been deprived of its identity and classified under the name of numerically the weakest segment. As this study will show, the lumping together of right and center SR's is not wholly devoid of logic; yet when all is said and done, the center had its own position, distinct from either wing. If it did little to defend that position, the explanation is to be found in the quality of its leadership and in the grievous conditions of the times, which were allowed to deflect it from its purpose. Its influence on the course of events is important, but, unfortunately, only in an indirect or negative sense.

To set things in their proper perspective, both within the SR camp and outside, in relation to other movements, to determine the part played by the SR's in the October Revolution, and to analyze the causes of their failure have been the purpose of this study. Two related matters that have merited a large amount of attention are the fate of the peasant movement in the months immediately following the October Revolution and the makeup, record, and potentialities of the All-Russian Constituent Assembly. The significance of these matters has not preserved the first from oblivion nor the second from falsehood and error, so that the information herein presented, whether once known and then forgotten or never known and left in darkness, will help to reveal the true situation and overcome two generations of neglect and misconception.

Secondary sources have contributed virtually nothing to this study. With two or three notable exceptions, primary sources have contributed only in piecemeal fashion. Always it has been necessary to reconstruct the story, with aid from some of the participants, and then interpret it in the light of long years of study. These alone make possible the uncovering and analysis, which distinguish historical scholarship from an exercise in writing, of deeper-lying threads of development and causal relationships. To compare the book to a building, the factual framework is the foundation and the interpretation the superstructure; never have preconceived notions been allowed to influence the selection or marshaling of material. But wherever the author has felt himself to be on firm ground as a result of thorough investigation and seasoned judgment, he has not hesitated to make evaluations and present his conclusions in unequivocal language, doubtless to the displeasure of those who begin with objectivity as a principle and end by erecting it into a fetish.

It is fitting to acknowledge the help I have had from certain individuals and institutions. The inner working of the political society being studied were first revealed to me by V. M. Chernov, ostensibly the head of that society and undoubtedly its chief intellectual force. The innate kindness that came out as weakness on the revolutionary stage in 1917 was a priceless boon to a struggling student. The criticism of Chernov's actions and character voiced in this study has been dictated solely by historical necessity and in no way reflects a lack of gratitude for services rendered; rather, it betokens regret that he failed to defend a position which in the author's opinion was the correct one in 1917 (excepting always the refusal to admit compensation for landowners). In passing it may be noted that few critics of Chernov have been more unsparing than Chernov himself.

From my friend Alexander F. Izjumow, once director of the archives in the Russian collection at Prague and now dead as a result of the callousness of the Soviet government, I have learned the valuable lesson that while it is no part of a scholar's duty to please readers or critics, it is his duty, from the vantage ground of mastery of his subject, to draw out the threads of development and point up the issues, clearly and unmistakably, without the endless equivocation that is the refuge either of the timorous scholar or of the one who has not been scholarly enough.

Boris Nicolaevsky has given advice on certain bibliographical matters and has placed several rare and valuable materials from his private collection at my disposal.

To my friends at the Hoover Library, where much of the research and most of the writing were done, I wish to express my appreciation for favors too numerous to mention, as well as for a congenial and stimulating atmosphere in which to work.

The Russian Institute of Columbia University, with which I have had the good fortune to be associated as a Senior Fellow and as a visiting professor, has assumed the main burden of publishing this study. I wish to thank its members, severally and collectively, for all that they have done. The plan of publication was suggested by Professor Philip E. Mosely, to whom a special word of thanks is owing, now that it has at last been carried out.

The Research Institute of the University of Texas has rendered substantial assistance on more than one occasion as a result of the good offices of Dean W. Gordon Whaley and his staff. Their kindness in working out arrangements amid considerable difficulty is gratefully acknowledged.

Finally, a word of appreciation is due my friend Henry H. Wiggins, Executive Editor of the Columbia University Press, for his patient and persistent efforts to convert this manuscript into a book. Many things have fallen into place under his competent direction, and he has never failed to understand the problems of an author who is also a teacher.

My wife Jakoba and daughter Ingrid have assumed a major share of the drudgery connected with a task of this kind. That they have done so as a matter of course does not mean that their services should be overlooked or their kindness left unacknowledged.

OLIVER HENRY RADKEY

Hoover Library
Stanford, California
July 6, 1962

Contents

The Sickle
under the Hammer

I

The October Revolution:
The Attempt at Armed Resistance

Among the groups raised to power in Russia by the February Revolution of 1917, the largest, though by no means the strongest, was the Socialist Revolutionary. This political movement had retained the essence of old-line Populism while discarding or modifying certain of its more utopian features. Its neo-Populism found expression in a form of "agrarian" socialism that was set off against the "industrial" socialism of the Marxists. Although labor in factories and "intellectual labor" had from the first held an honored position in the SR system of values (even though the older Populists, or Narodniks, had viewed the former with something akin to horror), more solicitude had been lavished on the peasants than on other components of the army of toil. The peasant-centered character of the movement had not, however, prevented it from amassing a following in the towns, recruited in part from the proletariat and in part from the white-collar element, but success in these social categories had proved detrimental to effective organization, since the workers gravitated leftward and the intellectuals leaned toward the right. Centrifugal tendencies had been greatly strengthened by the strains of war, especially since the cleavage over social questions coincided with the division over war, and by the latter part of 1917 the ranks of the party had fallen into disarray.

The Socialist Revolutionaries entered the period of the second upheaval of 1917 under the handicap of their record in the first.[1] Since the February overturn, they had achieved nothing beyond a regime of political liberties, and these had yet to bear fruit in the form of a constituent assembly. The constriction of the February Revolution within the narrow limits of political reform had en-

[1] This record has been set forth in my book *The Agrarian Foes of Bolshevism.*

gendered great tension in Russian society and not least within the Socialist Revolutionary Party. There, a considerable segment of the peasantry and the bulk of the worker and soldier support had become dissatisfied with a leadership which either acclaimed or acquiesced in this limitation. The party had never possessed the organizational strength to hook up its mass following with its intellectual leadership; now, with discord between adherents of political reform on the upper levels and of social revolution on the lower, even a superior organization would not have availed to transform paper strength into reality. Only by reverting to the tradition embodied in its name, only by firmly taking again the path of social revolution, could the party hope to recover lost ground. It could never do this in coalition with the Constitutional Democratic and Menshevik parties, one of which abhorred social revolution on principle and the other, at this stage of historical development. It is true that Menshevism had presented no model of unity in 1917 and was now undergoing a shift to the left, but its ideology would always have impeded bold solutions—or attempted solutions—of basic problems.

There was within the PSR itself an element for which coalition was not an expedient but a way of life. This element constituted the right wing of the party. It was small in numbers but large in influence, and clung to the partners in coalition as a protection against all the evils—chief among them, some gesture in favor of peace—into which the majority of its own party might conceivably have forced it but for the compulsions of a partnership to which that majority had adhered, less because of conviction than because of inability to choose anything else. Now if these compulsions were removed through collapse of the coalition under some external blow, the question would arise whether the freedom of action thus restored to the majority SR's through no virtue of their own would be used to set the party on a more promising course or whether the majority would again default on its obligations and expose the party to a recurrence of the malady which had laid it so low. The October Revolution would first remove the compulsions and then provide the opportunity for the SR's to answer the question.

For the experiment in coalition, strained in conception and barren in consequence, the hour of reckoning was at hand. Ever since General Kornilov's abortive coup had disarmed the right and cracked open the center, it had been evident that the left would bid again for power, this time in earnest, and with much better prospects for success than it had had in July. The influence of defensist elements in the moderate socialist parties and the tenacity with which the Provisional Government held to its caretaker role, together with the uncompromising nature of Bolshevism itself, decreed that no accommodation would be sought or offered and that the issue would be settled by force of arms. There was no great mystery about the timing of the stroke. With the Second All-Russian Congress of Workers' and Soldiers' Soviets set for the latter part of October and the election of the Constituent Assembly for the middle of November, the period for maneuvering was circumscribed, and it seemed probable that sometime within the limits fixed by these dates Lenin would move against the Provisional Government. The Socialist Revolutionaries, having failed to grapple with the conditions nourishing Bolshevism, now faced the task of containing its swollen power. The protection of their peasant following against the deceptive advances and destructive designs of Bolshevism was now, apart from sentiment, the sole remaining bond of union among the Socialist Revolutionaries, though one not strong enough to withstand the strain which the October Revolution would impose.

How did the Socialist Revolutionaries prepare to meet the onslaught of their Marxist adversaries? The man who came closest to playing the role of party boss, the right-centrist leader A. R. Gotz, has made the astonishing statement that the October Revolution caught the PSR unawares and obliged it to assemble its scattered forces after taking the field.[2] On the face of it, this is an absurd contention. If there was anything secret about what the Bolsheviks were preparing in St. Petersburg, it was the worst kept secret in Russia. The Socialist Revolutionaries could not help but know as well as anyone else what was going on. Already at the end of September the central organ of the party had noted the danger of an uprising in conjunction with the Second Soviet Congress.[3] V. M. Chernov had

[2] See his testimony at the SR trial in Moscow in *Izvestiia*, No. 171 (August 2, 1922).
[3] "Novaia revoliutsiia ili Uchreditel'noe Sobranie?" (A New Revolution or the Constituent Assembly?), *Delo Naroda*, No. 168 (September 30, 1917).

gloomily prophesied in the paper's columns that more "days" were in the offing.[4] On the 16th of October, from the tribune of the Petersburg Soviet, Trotski had openly avowed the purpose of his party.[5] The SR Central Committee itself had on two occasions, the 15th and 21st of October, given formal consideration to the question of a Bolshevik uprising.[6]

But when we consider the state of the party mind and the spirit which dominated its councils, the statement of Gotz becomes understandable. Many of the members were living in a sort of dream world where fears of counterrevolution mingled with scorn of Bolshevism, where small groups of monarchists, now more out of favor than ever with the armed masses, were blown up to menacing proportions and Bolshevism was dismissed as an effervescent phenomenon confined to the army and a few large towns with no roots in the country at large. Eight months' experience in power had not corrected the distorted vision of these people; their old tendency to underestimate the extreme left and quake before the Black Hundreds possessed them as before. As they saw it, the Bolsheviks were uttering bold words, but their ability to make noise exceeded their capacity for mischief. Probably they would not go beyond verbal threats, and if they did resort to arms, the only result would be a repetition of the July Days. Even if they seized power, they could hold it but a few days. Less than three weeks before the extinction of the Provisional Government, one of the prominent SR leaders, N. I. Rakitnikov, expressed the opinion that the Bolsheviks did not really want to seize power, their game being to force the moderate socialists to take over the government so that these would discredit themselves in the eyes of the masses.[7] Too much attention was paid to the frozen attitudes of elected representatives and not enough to the shifting mood of those who elected them. *Delo Naroda* took comfort in the unanimous stand of army committees against a Bolshevik rising; yet only a week previously the same paper had printed a warning of delegates from the front that the army committees had

[4] See unsigned editorial in *ibid.*, No. 180 (October 14, 1917).
[5] *Revoliutsiia 1917 goda*, V, 101.
[6] Protokol Zasedaniia Tsentral'nago Komiteta PSR for the dates indicated.
[7] "Voina i zemlia" (The War and Land), *Delo Naroda*, No. 174 (October 7, 1917).

lost their influence over the soldier mass.[8] In the words of Kerenski, the degree of complacency pervading circles loyal to the Provisional Government, and foremost among them his own party, defies comprehension.[9]

There was one SR leader who did not misjudge the situation, but it was the misfortune of his party that in the person of V. M. Chernov depth of intellect and breadth of vision were combined with inferior qualities of leadership. Alone among his colleagues Chernov had taken the measure of Lenin. He had discerned from the first elements of greatness in the Bolshevik captain—that "Anti-Christ of the Philistines"—though he considered these qualities to have been stunted by the abnormal conditions of tsarist times, which blocked the development of real political parties and of seasoned leadership, condemning Lenin to remain the type hero of an epoch when each tiny sect had its prophet, each ant bed its pope. Chernov respected the enterprise and unbending purpose of this man hewn from a "single block of granite," but at first had not believed the new Russia to be imperiled by the "hatchet socialism" which Lenin preached. Writing in the rosy dawn of the revolution, he had dismissed as absurd the fears that Lenin would "break to pieces the new Russian life." [10] The capacity of the skeleton army created by Lenin to attract and subordinate to itself a mass following amid the special conditions of 1917 had not entered into the calculations of the SR leader. By autumn, however, after months of steadily increasing tension between the upper and lower levels of Russian democracy, Chernov's optimism had changed to despondency, and he had little hope either that Bolshevism's triumph could be averted or that its sway would prove short-lived.[11] Indeed, he had so keen an appreciation of its dangers that he could see how it threatened to engulf in a common ruin not only the main body of his party but its schismatic left wing as well.

[8] See Nos. 186 (October 21, 1917) and 181 (October 15, 1917). The warning was addressed to a joint session of the All-Russian Soviet Executive Committees.

[9] "Gatchina," in *Izdalëka*, p. 201. The above exposition of the mood of the party on the eve of the October Revolution is based in part upon the oral statements of V. M. Zenzinov (interview in Paris, September, 1935).

[10] "Lenin," *Delo Naroda*, No. 26 (April 16, 1917).

[11] Chernov, manuscript commentary on the minutes of the Central Committee, p. 55.

Yet aside from his press campaign to hasten agrarian reform, the SR leader awaited developments with resignation. Since the Provisional Government refused to do anything to take the wind out of the sails of Bolshevism, Chernov refused to do anything to save the Provisional Government. Essentially his strategy and that of the large segment of party opinion which looked to him for leadership was to combat Bolshevism without linking their fortunes to those of the Kerenski regime.[12] The left-centrist SR's correctly saw in Bolshevism a popular phenomenon which could not be overcome by coercive measures alone, but even they failed to realize how hard it would be to repossess the apparatus of state once the Bolsheviks had seized control, forgetting that Chernov himself had once said that when Lenin grasped something, he held it like a rope holds a man who is hanged.[13] For the left center to have rallied actively to the side of the Provisional Government in the closing days of October it would have been necessary for the Central Committee to force concessions in foreign and agrarian policy; but the committee would not act as long as the right and right center remained in control, and Chernov saw no way of changing this situation until the next party congress, short of a breach of discipline on his part which would probably wreck the organization.

So great was the tension within the party by the latter half of October that Chernov decided to leave the capital. When queried at the Fourth Congress by delegates who expressed the amazement of the provinces at his absence from St. Petersburg during the decisive days of the October Revolution, he replied that he had not wished to be present at the Second Soviet Congress: as a disciplined member of the party he had no right to defend his personal point of view and to defend that of the Central Committee was out of the question.[14] He had determined to spare himself a repetition of the humiliating experience at the Democratic Conference.[15] Reluctantly he had agreed to remain through October 22 lest his departure be construed

[12] Stankevich, *Vospominaniia*, pp. 279–80.
[13] "Lenin," *Delo Naroda*, No. 26 (April 16, 1917).
[14] *Kratkii otchët*, p. 108.
[15] Chernov, manuscript commentary on the minutes of the Central Committee, p. 67; for the incident in question, see my book, *The Agrarian Foes of Bolshevism*, p. 417.

as withdrawing support from the opposition to Bolshevism, but when that day passed without untoward developments, he left in the evening on a speaking tour of Moscow and the Western Front.[16] The Gotz-Zenzinov faction, dominant in the Central Committee and grossly deceived in its estimate of Bolshevism, now had a clear field in which to pursue its course to the end, and the end was near at hand.

With party unity hopelessly shattered and the spirit of the organization at its lowest ebb since the Azef affair of the years around 1905, when party leadership was entrusted to a traitor, it is not surprising that no serious preparations were made to meet the Bolshevik challenge. It is doubtful whether any could have been made. The SR's in the Petersburg Soviet tried to block the formation of a military revolutionary committee, seeing in it the nucleus of insurrection, but they were now too weak to offer any effective opposition. In the soldiers' section, where once they had held undisputed sway, the motion to form the committee passed by a vote of 283 against one with 23 abstaining (October 13).[17] The Left SR's had made common cause with the Bolsheviks, one of their number, P. E. Lazimir, having sponsored the proposal, and their participation in the military revolutionary committee would soon become one of the grounds for their exclusion from the PSR. If the moderate SR's could no longer influence the garrison in a positive sense, they could still speculate with its overwhelming aversion to combat duty by offering resolutions designed to hold the troops in their barracks, some of which were accepted by the same meetings which approved the Bolshevik slogan of "ALL POWER TO THE SOVIETS." The ephemeral effect of such resolutions, however, may be judged from the action of the assembly of regimental committees in first banning armed demonstrations at the behest of the SR-Menshevik bloc[18] and then refusing a few days later even to listen to the spokesmen of these parties.[19] The SR's also did their best to keep arms out of the hands

[16] Chernov, manuscript commentary on the minutes of the Central Committee, p. 55.
[17] *Revoliutsiia 1917 goda*, V, 76–77. For adoption by the whole soviet, see pp. 100–1; *Delo Naroda*, No. 182 (October 17, 1917).
[18] *Delo Naroda*, No. 183 (October 18, 1917).
[19] *Ibid.*, No. 187 (October 22, 1917).

of the working class, knowing that the Red Guard units being formed would become instruments of the Bolshevik Party, now much the strongest in proletarian quarters. In league with the Mensheviks, by a vote of 151 to 123, they defeated at the Second Moscow Regional Congress of Soviets the proposal to create a Red Guard,[20] but the soviets were changing complexion so rapidly as a result of reelections that the Bolsheviks were only momentarily embarrassed in their plans. Dwindling SR strength in these organs also nullified the effort to postpone the Second All-Russian Congress of Workers' and Soldiers' Soviets,[21] in which the SR's had been quick to discern a dangerous rival of the Constituent Assembly.

All such tactics, however, merely skirted the edge of the problem without getting to its core. On October 15 the Central Committee squarely faced the issue of what to do about the impending coup. With an imperturbability matched only by its capacity for self-delusion, the committee decided to take the matter "under advisement" (*priniat' k svedeniiu*) and to draft a manifesto for consideration at its next meeting. No other act in its unfortunate history is more revealing than this decision to take the October Revolution "under advisement." On October 21 the manifesto was approved by a vote of eight to two and published the next morning in the *Delo Naroda* (No. 187). It reminded the workers and soldiers that the Constituent Assembly was only a month away and that nothing must be done to interfere with its task of giving land and liberty to the people. The manifesto also invited them to refuse every call to action, even if made by the Bolshevik Party, and to restrain others from responding, if need be by force, since the Black Hundreds were only awaiting an explosion in the revolutionary camp to destroy the republic and restore the old order. And there the matter rested, aside from a charge to a subcommission to hasten the drafting of a bill turning the land over to the land committees so that it could be introduced into the Council of the Republic.[22] The Central Committee was more taken up with preparations for electing the Con-

[20] *Ibid.*, No. 172 (October 5, 1917); *Revoliutsiia 1917 goda*, V, 8–9, 219–20.
[21] For the SR attitude, see editorial, "Sovety i Uchreditel'noe Sobranie" (The Soviets and the Constituent Assembly), *Delo Naroda*, No. 173 (October 6, 1917); Bykhovski, *Vserossiiskii Sovet Krest'ianskikh Deputatov*, p. 271.
[22] Protokol Zasedaniia Tsentral'nago Komiteta PSR, October 21, 1917.

stituent Assembly than with warding off a threat to its existence.[23]

Under the Central Committee there was a body known as the Military Commission, entrusted with supervision of SR elements in the army and presumably capable of mustering a fighting force in case of need. A member of the committee presided over its sessions, either L. Ia. Gerstein or, in his absence, A. Iu. Feit. The secretary of the Military Commission was M. Rakitin-Broun. It appears to have had a fluctuating membership (a list is not available), but among the names more prominently identified with it were those of Alexander A. Bruderer and Lieutenant Colonel A. A. Krakovetski. Another officer of the tsarist service belonged to the commission at this time,[24] probably the Lieutenant Colonel A. N. Kuropatkin who perished in the cadet uprising of October 29.[25] Lesser figures included Kashin, Paevski, and Nikanorov. Like other party organs, the Military Commission never functioned properly, having neither the men nor the means for the performance of its important task: its work was badly organized; it failed to establish ties with the army; it received almost no financial support from the Central Committee; and it could boast of a permanent staff of but three or four workers. Dissension in the party and the absence of a clear and definite policy which could be interpreted to the rank and file had injured the Military Commission no less than other agencies.[26]

On the eve of the October Revolution, despite an awareness of what was impending, the Central Committee issued no instructions to the Military Commission. This we have on the authority of Broun, who describes the committee's position as "not especially firm." [27] His language veils the state of near prostration in which that body found itself as it sat amid the wreckage of its policy of coalition at

[23] This is apparent from a study of the minutes; moreover, Chernov asserts that the committee centered its attention on the election campaign (manuscript commentary on the minutes of the Central Committee, p. 51).

[24] Testimony of Feit in *Izvestiia*, No. 130 (June 14, 1922).

[25] See below, pp. 27 ff.

[26] Report of Nikanorov to the military section of the Fourth Party Congress, *Partiinyia Izvestiia*, No. 5 (January 20, 1918), pp. 14-15; M. Broun, "Ocherk deiatel'nosti voennoi komissii pri Tsentral'nom Komitete PSR" (An Account of the Activity of the Military Commission of the Central Committee of the PSR), *ibid.*, No. 3 (October 19, 1917), pp. 10-15; testimony of Keller in *Izvestiia*, No. 131 (June 15, 1922).

[27] Testimony in *Izvestiia*, No. 129 (June 13, 1922).

any cost, without knowing which way to turn, with an unrealistic view of the situation, and with the most authoritative of SR leaders having virtually seceded from its ranks. Elsewhere things were no better. The SR caucus in the Council of the Republic threw down resolution after resolution on the crisis—five in the course of a single session [28]—and in the All-Russian Peasants' Executive Committee the left SR minority battled the rightist majority at every turn.[29] Inaction, indecision, and mutual recriminations were the order of the day in party circles.

By the night of October 24 the revolution was under way, not in the form of rioting and mob action but swift and organized seizure of one strategic point after another. Never did the contrasting natures of the rival parties stand forth in clearer relief, the cohesion and hardness of Bolshevism against the lassitude and formlessness of the PSR. All night long the SR Central Committee remained in session without ever coming to a decision.[30] No plan of resistance, no concerted action with other groups opposed to the coup came from its nerveless hands. Nor did the high command on the following day recover its presence of mind to the extent necessary to undertake defensive measures on behalf of the perishing Provisional Government—in party circles as in those of allied groups the time passed in outbursts of helpless indignation, in lamentations, and, of course, in endless palaver.[31] Kerenski tells us that the Bolsheviks tied the socialist opposition in knots by negotiating over formulas for the peaceful liquidation of the rising even as they struck at the nerve centers of power. He adds that fear lest the speedy downfall of Bolshevism play into the hands of reactionaries also helped to lame the opposition.[32] Actually, these judgments apply more to the Mensheviks than to the SR's, who were hamstrung not so much by the treachery of the Bolsheviks as by their own contradictions, as will presently be shown.

The minister-president had awaited developments with confidence,

[28] Stankevich, *Vospominaniia*, p. 259.
[29] Bykhovski, *Vserossiiskii Sovet Krest'ianskikh Deputatov*, p. 274.
[30] Semenov, *Voennaia i boevaia rabota PSR*, p. 5.
[31] Ignatiev, *Nekotorye fakty i itogi chetyrëkh let*, I, 3.
[32] "Gatchina," in *Izdalëka*, pp. 198, 201, 211–12.

believing that he could do in October what he had done in July.[33] This time he would finish with Bolshevism. This time, he told Stankevich, the Chernovs were not going to save the Kamenevs and Zinovievs.[34] Kerenski had misread the situation as badly as his friends in the Central Committee: the whole ground swell of extremism seems to have been lost on him, and instead of weak-kneed Bolsheviks like Kamenev and Zinoviev, he should have singled out as objects of wrath Lenin and Trotski, the real architects of his doom. Kerenski had entrusted the defense of the capital to Colonel G. P. Polkovnikov, commander of the Petersburg military district, and General Ia. G. Bagratuni, chief of staff for the district, refusing to make any changes even after some of the ministers had expressed dissatisfaction with Polkovnikov's dispositions.[35]

Kerenski soon had cause to regret his decision. According to Miliukov, Polkovnikov owed his position to the favoritism shown officers who paraded their loyalty to the revolution,[36] but according to Kerenski, Polkovnikov in fact had belonged to that rather numerous category of officers who conspired to overthrow the Provisional Government by withholding aid when the Bolsheviks struck so that the ensuing breakdown could be exploited in the interests of an authoritarian regime. Kerenski portrays the whole tragedy of his situation in terms of a struggle on two fronts, against the Bolsheviks of the left and against the Bolsheviks of the right (the reactionaries), who for the moment were acting in collusion. He had received daily reports of an optimistic nature from Polkovnikov and was wholly unprepared for the situation which had developed by the early morning of the 25th, with the garrison lost to the government, the Cossacks still saddling their horses (as they had been all through the night), and the promised reinforcements from the front nowhere in evidence. Kerenski tells us that he and A. I. Konovalov now became convinced of the colonel's untrustworthiness, but what he does not tell us is that Konovalov for some days previously had been

[33] Bykhovski, *Vserossiiskii Sovet Krest'ianskikh Deputatov*, p. 265.

[34] Stankevich, *Vospominaniia*, p. 258; see also Miliukov, *Istoriia*, I, Part III, 200.

[35] Miliukov, *Istoriia*, I, Part III, 199–200; Maliantovich, "V Zimnem Dvortse," *Byloe*, VI (June, 1918), 112.

[36] *Istoriia*, I, Part III, 194.

highly critical of Polkovnikov, in whom he reposed not a particle of confidence.[37] In his extremity Kerenski bethought himself of the "rather numerous" military forces of the PSR, but here again he was doomed to disappointment, for the overconfidence pervading party circles and the belief in a peaceful solution had prevented it from mobilizing its strength.[38] In desperation Kerenski decided to leave the capital and seek out the detachments moving up from the Northern Front, the first echelons of which had been due to arrive on the 24th. Supreme military authority in the city passed to the Kadet minister N. M. Kishkin, who used it to remove Colonel Polkovnikov from his post.[39]

The extent of treason in the military entourage of Kerenski is not easily determined. Leaving the matter for future historians to decide, Miliukov suggests that the disaffection around Kerenski may have sprung less from motives of betrayal than from the sincere belief that his elimination would improve the chances of successful resistance. He goes on to explain that right-wing elements had lost all desire to assist the regime after Kerenski's appeal to the revolutionary parties [40]—a charge of dubious validity in view of the readiness of these same elements to act under SR auspices only four days later, at the time of the cadet uprising. On the eve of the revolution the staff of the military district had repeated to Commissar Stankevich the assurance of adequate strength so often given the minister-president. Later, with hostilities in progress, Stankevich says it was impossible to get a clear answer from the military authorities as to what was being done.[41] Loyal officers told Kerenski it was a case of purposeful sabotage, and Kerenski adds that later he learned that Polkovnikov himself had touched off the agitation for his arrest.[42] Yet it is doubtful whether more is involved than the last

---

[37] Nabokov, "Vremennoe Pravitel'stvo," in *Arkhiv Russkoi Revoliutsii*, I, 83.

[38] This is Kerenski's explanation ("Gatchina," in *Izdalëka*, p. 201). Actually, more is involved than he realized (see below, pp. 15–17).

[39] "Iz zapisnoi knizhki arkhivista: Poslednie chasy Vremennogo pravitel'stva v 1917 g." (From an Archivist's Notebook: The Last Hours of the Provisional Government in 1917), in *Krasnyi Arkhiv*, LVI (I, 1933), 137; Miliukov, *Istoriia*, I, Part III, 227; Kerenski, "Gatchina," in *Izdalëka*, pp. 194–204.

[40] *Istoriia*, I, Part III, 201, 219–20.   [41] *Vospominaniia*, p. 261.

[42] "Gatchina," in *Izdalëka*, p. 202.

desperate flailings of a cause that was lost. Perhaps it was not so much a story of treason as of incompetence or impotence, or of both combined. General Alekseev, who must certainly be reckoned among the reactionaries, apparently was willing to assume a command on the 25th if only there had been something to command.[43] And the impression one gets from the jumbled notes of Kishkin's assistant, P. I. Palchinski, is that the military authorities were hopelessly at sea and were looking to Kerenski for the leadership which they themselves could not furnish,[44] just as Kerenski seems to have relied upon their judgment and dispositions until it was too late for his personal intervention to achieve any results. Each failed the other, probably less because of incompetence than because of the whole hopelessness of the situation in which they found themselves.

Whatever the personal culpabilities may be, the doom of the Provisional Government was no longer a matter of doubt. From the besieged quarters of the cabinet in the Winter Palace, the minister of agriculture, S. L. Maslov, sent a despairing message to his party colleagues in the Peasants' Executive Committee, advising them of the determination of the ministers to die at their posts and adding that his last words would be a curse upon the democracy which had delegated them to official positions only to betray them in their hour of need. Greatly moved, the Executive Committee thereupon proposed to the city council a joint procession to the Winter Palace, either to rescue the entrapped ministers or to perish at their side. The death march got under way with Mayor Shreider in the van, but it did not end in death nor did it march very far, being halted and turned back by a detachment of Baltic sailors. Even so, it represents the main achievement for the day of the PSR, whose membership had furnished most of the demonstrants.[45] Nothing

---

[43] Miliukov, *Istoriia*, I, Part III, 227. Though the chronology is not certain, the reference is apparently to the afternoon of the 25th. It seems that on the preceding night Savinkov had found the general without any plans, and peacefully asleep in his apartment (*Boris Savinkov pered voennoi kollegiei verkhovnogo suda SSSR*, p. 30).

[44] "Iz zapisnoi knizhki arkhivista: Poslednie chasy Vremennogo pravitel'stva," in *Krasnyi Arkhiv*, LVI (I, 1933), 136–37.

[45] Bykhovski, *Vserossiiskii Sovet Krest'ianskikh Deputatov*, pp. 276–78; *Istoriia grazhdanskoi voiny v SSSR*, II, 271–74; Ignatiev, *Nekotorye fakty i itogi chetyrëkh let*, I, 3–4.

more could be done to lift the siege of the Winter Palace [46] and once the Bolsheviks had coordinated their movements they had little difficulty in taking the last citadel of the Provisional Government. As the arrested ministers proceeded under guard to the Petropavlovsk Fortress, narrowly escaping death on the way, they experienced at first hand, in the threats and imprecations of the mob, how intense was the feeling against the war and how evanescent the popularity of A. F. Kerenski.[47]

While these events were transpiring in St. Petersburg, the head of the government was scouring the countryside for troops, finding none until he had gone all the way to Pskov. Here at headquarters of the Northern Front he got in touch with General P. N. Krasnov, commander of the III Cavalry Corps of Kornilov fame, and together they assembled units of the corps as a striking force over the protests of the SR commissar Semenov who felt that the notoriety of the corps and its known aversion to Kerenski made it a dubious asset.[48] By the evening of the 26th Kerenski was again in the vicinity of the capital with a force of about 600 Cossacks and a few guns. The next day he occupied Gatchina and gained a position from which to launch an attack upon the victorious Bolsheviks. Necessary to the morale of the Cossacks, however, was the support of infantry, and this was not forthcoming. The firm grip that Bolshevism already had upon a large portion of the army, the aversion to fighting of the entire army, the "Italian strike" or "slowdown" practiced by the railroad workers, and the neutrality of some of the commanding officers, particularly of General V. A. Cheremisov, chief of the Northern Front, prevented the reinforcement of Krasnov's small detachment. General Cheremisov, who harbored a personal grudge against Kerenski because of a slight once offered him,[49] had gone so far as to countermand, on the night of October

[46] Later Shreider made an attempt at the head of a small party and with the consent of the Bolsheviks to get through to the Winter Palace and arrange a cease-fire. But he could not get clearance across the square and abandoned his efforts. See V. M. Molotov, "Smol'ny i Zimnii (Otryvok iz vospominanii)" (Smolny and the Winter Palace [A Fragment from Memoirs]), in *Oktiabr'skoe vooruzhënnoe vosstanie v Petrograde* (*Vospominaniia uchastnikov*), pp. 187–91.

[47] Maliantovich, "V Zimnem Dvortse," *Byloe*, VI (June, 1918), 134 ff.

[48] *Voennaia i boevaia rabota PSR*, p. 5.

[49] Chernov, *The Great Russian Revolution*, pp. 333–34.

25, the order for the dispatch of troops to the capital.[50] His attitude was that the army must not be drawn into the political struggle, and he made it quite plain, even to Kerenski, that he placed the effort of the Provisional Government to retain power on the same level as the ambition of the Bolsheviks to seize it.[51] Aside from an armored train and a lonesome regiment from Luga, Kerenski's strength remained as before—so small that neither friend nor foe suspected the true state of affairs, crediting him with thousands of troops instead of the hundreds at his disposal.[52]

By the time Kerenski had returned to the approaches of St. Petersburg, the SR leadership had recovered from the shock of the successful uprising. That it had so palpably underestimated Bolshevism only added to its determination never to accept the result of the October Revolution. There is no evidence of clear-cut, decisive action to sustain the Provisional Government while it still held the reins of power, yet no sooner was Petersburg in the possession of the Bolsheviks than the PSR, or a part of it, decided to fight. It is true that on October 25 Doctor Feit of the Central Committee had tried to call out units of the garrison supposedly loyal to the Provisional Government, only to discover the futility of relying on the word of soldiers whose mood by the hour became more favorable to Bolshevism.[53] However that may be, the failure of the party to lend effective support to the Provisional Government on the decisive day of the revolution can be explained only in part by the confusion reigning in the high command and the deception practiced by the Bolsheviks in stringing out negotiations when they had no intention of seeking a peaceful solution. In other words, neither

[50] He claims to have done this with the consent of Kerenski, who later reverted to the original plan. See "Oktiabr' na fronte" (October at the Front), in *Krasnyi Arkhiv*, XXIV (V, 1927), 100; see also Vol. XXIII (IV, 1927), p. 161. This is not Kerenski's version (see "Gatchina," in *Izdalëka*, p. 206).

[51] "Oktiabr' na fronte," in *Krasnyi Arkhiv*, XXIII (IV, 1927), 176, 194; "Dokumenty: Stavka 25–26 Oktiabria 1917 g." (Documents: General Headquarters, October 25–26, 1917), in *Arkhiv Russkoi Revoliutsii*, VII, 297–303, 309–12; *Istoriia grazhdanskoi voiny v SSSR*, II, 274; Kerenski, "Gatchina," in *Izdalëka*, pp. 206–7.

[52] Kerenski, "Gatchina," in *Izdalëka*, p. 211; Stankevich, *Vospominaniia*, p. 270.

[53] See his testimony at the SR trial in 1922 in *Izvestiia*, No. 130 (June 14, 1922); see also Trotski, *History of the Russian Revolution*, III, 251.

the explanation of Broun, Semenov, and others nor that of Kerenski is adequate.

The deeper explanation lies in the ebbing strength of the PSR and the special nature of its Petersburg organization, which prevented mobilization in support of the Kerenski regime. The bulk of the membership in the capital consisted of workers and soldiers, and these were precisely the elements among which the party had lost the most ground as a result of its policy of coalition. With this proletarian and military base to build upon, the radical intellectuals, more numerously represented here than elsewhere, had seized control of the organization after a prolonged tussle with the moderates, who themselves stood to the left of center in this furnace of revolution. Expressed in terms of factional allegiance, the left SR's had taken over in September after displaying marked strength since the beginning of the revolution. When they broke away in November, the membership that remained adhered to the Chernovian line. In the words of Vysotski, the Petersburg organization had always been leftist in orientation and continued so even after the schism.[54] Such an organization would never go to the rescue of the third coalition. At best it would stand aside,[55] letting the crash of the regime pave the way for the all-socialist ministry which the Bolsheviks would be induced or compelled to accept, so they thought, and at worst some of its membership would join the assault, as in the case of the Kolpino SR's. Here in an industrial suburb, a stronghold of left-wing sentiment, the rank and file consisted of radical workingmen who would not stand aside when they saw Kerenski marching with Cossacks against their class brothers. At the trial in 1922 when one of the central committeemen, the intellectual Likhach, asked how it was that members of the party could have fought on the side of the Bolsheviks against Kerenski, the worker Usov replied:

There is nothing hard to understand about it. The explanation is quite simple. Our Kolpino organization did not consider Kerenski, whom Chernov himself had criticized, a Socialist Revolutionary, and the Provisional Government which he headed enjoyed no confidence whatever in our ranks. In as much as Kerenski went with the Cossacks against the

[54] *Kratkii otchët*, p. 94.
[55] For expressions in this vein see speeches of M. P. Kapitsa and Milchik in the city council on October 24 (*Delo Naroda,* No. 188 [October 25, 1917]).

workers—and we know what Cossacks are like—we were against him. There was complete bewilderment in our party center. I saw the Cossacks coming and, as a worker of prerevolutionary times who more than once had felt the sting of the Cossack whip on his back, I rose with the workers against Kerenski.[56]

Here is an excellent illustration of the difference in point of view between the national organization and its Petersburg branch, between the intellectual upper crust and the plebeian rank and file. The SR's of the capital and its industrial suburbs were not willing to take up arms in defense of the Provisional Government, though some were willing to take up arms against it.

On the day after the revolution a party conference consisting of the Petersburg municipal district or ward committees and the delegations in the city council and the soviet met to consider the situation. A resolution denouncing the overturn and excommunicating the usurpers, but significantly passing over the claims of the Provisional Government in favor of a new and purely socialist ministry, nevertheless failed of adoption.[57] The left, in other words, had voted down a resolution of the left center; the right and the right center, constituting the backbone of Kerenski's support in the party, had so little strength in the Petersburg organization that they did not even figure in the proceedings.

The right and right center, however, controlled the Central Committee and would do their utmost to reverse the decision of October 25, now that the initial shock of the upset had been overcome. The disrupting influence of events upon the conduct of business in high party circles is seen in the gap in the minutes of the Central Committee from October 21 to November 14, indicating that deliberations eventuating in formal decisions had given way to fly-by-night conferences between individual members. According to Chernov, the gravest decisions were taken without formal action of the Central Committee.[58] Yet there is evidence of a definite policy, consistently adhered to, in the conduct of the right-centrist majority. The whole

[56] Pokrovski, *Chto ustanovil protsess "sotsialistov-revoliutsionerov"?*, p. 18, quoting from the proceedings of the trial.
[57] *Delo Naroda*, No. 190 (October 27, 1917).
[58] Manuscript commentary on the minutes of the Central Committee, pp. 55–56.

Central Committee, now that Natanson was gone, opposed as one
man the "criminal Bolshevik venture, ruinous alike to country and
revolution." But when Zenzinov says that all sympathy was on the
side of Kerenski, he is not speaking for the entire body but only
for the right-centrist majority of which he was part. Faced by the
overthrow of everything for which it had contended and convinced
that it was acting on the defensive against a movement responsible
for the outbreak of civil war,[59] the dominant clique in the Central
Committee decided on an armed struggle with Bolshevism in support of Kerenski's effort against the capital. For this purpose the
committee vested full authority in A. R. Gotz, empowering him to
act in its name and leaving to his discretion the details of execution.
The decision was made informally and is not a matter of record. In
fact, it was not until some years later, at the time of the Moscow
trial of 1922, that the story could be pieced together from the
testimony of Gotz [60] and others. For security reasons these matters
had been muted at the Fourth Party Congress (December, 1917),[61]
though the spokesman for the Central Committee left no doubt that
it had favored suppression of the Bolshevik revolt "by the most
decisive means." [62]

The delegation of authority to Gotz for the purpose of organizing
a counteroffensive ushered in the first stage of the SR struggle
against the Soviet regime—the stage of armed resistance. The man
chosen to direct the enterprise was not only the most authoritative
personage in the Central Committee but also one of the most determined opponents of Bolshevism: in an open letter assuming responsibility for the events now to be described, Gotz declared it to

[59] For an opposing point of view, see Pokrovski, *Chto ustanovil protsess
"sotsialistov-revoliutsionerov"?*, p. 21. Here Kerenski's decision, a week in advance of the revolution, to bring in troops from the front is cited as an act
provocative of civil war.

[60] *Izvestiia,* No. 136 (June 22, 1922); *Revoliutsionnaia Rossiia,* No. 21–22
(October-November, 1922), p. 7.

[61] See evasive replies of Rosenblum (Firsov) to questions about the role of
Gotz and the attitude of the committee toward Kerenski's campaign in *Kratkii
otchët,* p. 110.

[62] *Volia Naroda,* No. 185 (December 5, 1917); softer paraphrasing in *Kratkii
otchët,* p. 106. Information regarding the stand of the Central Committee is
drawn in part from the interview with V. M. Zenzinov in Paris (September,
1935).

be his belief that "the rule of Bolshevism is a great menace to all of the gains of the revolution, a mortal danger to the integrity and independence of Russia . . . each additional hour of its existence works irreparable harm to the people's cause." [63] In the motivation of this SR leader, as in that of so many others, hatred for the peace policy of Bolshevism was at least as strong as concern for political freedom. Gotz naturally turned to the Military Commission of the Central Committee as the instrument for his design. Though badly organized, it was the only agency through which he could work.

The question in whose name the effort would be made occasioned a difference of opinion between the members of the commission, who wanted to fly the party banner, and Gotz, who preferred to act under nonpartisan auspices so that in case of failure responsibility could be diverted from his party. At least that is the charge brought by the Bolsheviks and supported by the testimony of Broun and Krakovetski.[64] Gotz, however, disclaimed any intent to erect a screen behind which his party could hide and maintained that he had sought to broaden the appeal of the movement by placing it under a super-party agency, the newly formed Committee to Save the Fatherland and Revolution, which had as its nucleus the Petersburg city council and included representatives of all of the democratic organizations.[65] Actually this committee was largely an SR enterprise, for Mayor Shreider had taken the initiative in its formation, Avksentiev was its chairman, and Boris Flekkel, its acting director. Branded by the Bolsheviks as the first in a long series of counterrevolutionary organizations, the committee was so loosely put together that the main body did not even know of the plan for armed resistance, and it was Gotz, acting in its name and working through the Military Commission of his own party, who engineered the blow at the Soviet government from within the city as Kerenski was striking at it from without.[66]

[63] "Bol'shevistskie rytsari bez strakha i uprëka" (Bolshevik Knights Without Fear or Reproach), *Delo Naroda*, No. 200 (November 5, 1917).

[64] *Izvestiia*, No. 129 (June 13, 1922) and No. 130 (June 14, 1922).

[65] *Ibid.*, No. 171 (August 2, 1922); *Revoliutsionnaia Rossiia*, No. 21–22 (October–November, 1922), p. 7.

[66] Vladimirova, *God sluzhby "sotsialistov" kapitalistam*, p. 21; Ignatiev, *Nekotorye fakty i itogi chetyrëkh let*, I, 4–6; testimony of Ignatiev in *Izvestiia*, No. 129 (June 13, 1922); Bykhovski, *Vserossiiskii Sovet Krest'ianskikh Deputatov*, p. 278.

What forces could Gotz and his associates count upon in their venturesome undertaking? The sad truth was that they had none of their own. Certainly they could expect no support from the Petersburg organization, the dissolution of which would be decreed by the Central Committee on November 2. Nor was there any use in looking to the rank-and-file membership, which was permeated with maximalism and scarcely less hostile to Kerenski's regime than the Bolsheviks themselves. Not only in the capital but throughout the Northern Region party opinion was predominantly averse to the line of the Central Committee, and where it was favorable, the factors of distance and disorganization would have prevented a mobilization of strength even if the sentiment had represented the heartfelt conviction of the workers and peasants rather than the will of the intellectuals at the head of the local committees. Only Petersburg and its immediate vicinity counted for the time being, and the men in charge of the enterprise knew well enough that the official party leadership had lost the last vestige of influence among the troops of the garrison and could expect no support from the party's still rather substantial working-class following. In explaining why no appeal was made to this following, Broun said that "workers could hardly be expected to go against workers," and Krakovetski asserted that the SR's, "primarily a party of the intelligentsia," had stood in fear of the proletariat.[67] While these witnesses at the trial of 1922 were scarcely free agents, there can in general be no doubt that the revolution meant one thing to the intellectuals who made up the party bureaucracy and quite another to the peasants and workers who constituted its sinews of power.

Unable to count upon their own resources, Gotz and his associates were obliged to fall back upon two forces, neither of which could be considered as dependable from the socialist point of view and either of which in case of victory would probably have caused embarrassment. These were the students of the officer training schools, the "junkers" or cadets, as we shall call them, and the Cossack regiments stationed in St. Petersburg, whose political thinking was supposedly dominated by men like A. I. Dutov, chief of

[67] *Izvestiia*, No. 129 (June 13, 1922) and No. 130 (June 14, 1922); see also testimony of Feit in No. 130.

the Orenburg Cossacks, and Boris V. Savinkov of Kornilov fame—
names that would have given pause to most revolutionists but that
now were welcome to the outraged patriots of the PSR, who were
desperate for help. The cadets were drawn from the privileged
classes of the population, the *haute bourgeoisie* and the aristocracy.
Politically they seem to have been rather sharply divided between
those who accepted the February Revolution and those who would
have preferred a more traditional order, but they were united in
their hatred of the October Revolution, for virtually all were
strongly nationalist in sentiment and disposed to look upon the
Bolsheviks as "German agents" or at least as rabble who would
destroy the elements of Russian statehood. No estimate can be made
of the relative strength of the two currents, but the cadets of the
Nikolaev Engineering School, for example, had had an elective committee evenly divided between socialists and nonsocialists until the
Bolshevik seizure of power disturbed the balance by throwing many
cadets to the right.[68] Though the Military Commission of the SR
Central Committee had ties with party-minded elements in all of the
leading schools, the SR's were in no position to claim the main body
of cadets as their own. In fact, they were playing with fire when
they evoked a force over which, in the hour of victory, they would
have had little control.

If the PSR had its cells in the military schools, so also did the
monarchist society of V. M. Purishkevich. Organized on the Masonic
model in groups of five with no contact save through a single
trusted individual in each institution, this movement claimed many
cadets among its adherents. The October Revolution had produced
a split in its ranks between the faction headed by a Captain Shatilov,
which believed that in view of the discouraging prospects in St.
Petersburg the scene of operations should be shifted elsewhere, and
the activists under Purishkevich—one of those rare individuals who
sensed that Bolshevism would grow stronger with the passage of
time and that now was the time to strike it down before it had consolidated its position by vanquishing the socialist opposition. The

[68] "Iz zapisnoi knizhki arkhivista: Zagovor monarkhicheskoi organizatsii
V. M. Purishkevicha" (From an Archivist's Notebook: The Conspiracy of the
Monarchist Organization of V. M. Purishkevich), in *Krasnyi Arkhiv*, XXVI
(I, 1928), 184–85.

monarchist leader, realizing that his own forces were unequal to the
task, desired a working agreement with other movements favoring
dictatorial rule, particularly with the right-wing fringe of Social
Revolutionism (the Savinkov group), in which he sensed the affinity
of chauvinism. Purishkevich, of course, intended to exploit a victory
for his own purposes, in the hope of preventing the return of
Kerenski or the elevation to power of any group opposed to the
restoration of the monarchy. With these considerations in mind, it is
easy to understand how a rising being prepared under SR auspices
should have attracted the support of an organization which had
nothing in common with Social Revolutionism except a hatred of
Bolshevism.[69]

If the cadets of the military schools were definitely a counterrevolutionary force, the three Cossack regiments stationed in the
capital no longer could be ranked in that category. The Cossack
officers might yearn for the times when the Orthodox tsar wielded
his autocratic power and the Jews were kept in the Pale, but uppermost in the minds of their soldiers was the thought of returning to
the quiet meadows of the Don—a thought incompatible with the
prospects of dying on the streets of St. Petersburg in combat with
the Bolshevik hordes. The chieftains themselves had lapsed into
passivity and made no effort to lead their troops into action. Purishkevich would later complain of the "strange policy" of Dutov in
letting the moment go by when decisive action might still have
saved the day.[70] Whether because of confidence that Bolshevism
would soon outlive itself or because of a spirit of defeatism, the
Cossack leaders remained on the sidelines, from which in any event
the spirit of their troops would have forbidden them to stir.[71]

At a conference before the uprising the SR leaders, as a member

[69] Statements based on confession of Staff Captain A. B. Dushkin, *ibid.,* pp.
179–81; summary in *Istoriia grazhdanskoi voiny v SSSR,* II, 324–25.
[70] Letter to General A. M. Kaledin, dated November 4, 1917 ("Iz zapisnoi
knizhki arkhivista: Zagovor monarkhicheskoi organizatsii V. M. Purishkevicha,"
in *Krasnyi Arkhiv,* XXVI [I, 1928], 171).
[71] There is now documentary evidence that by early October Ataman
Kaledin had already made several efforts to have the regiments removed from
the capital on the ground that if they remained there longer they would completely succumb to Bolshevism. The Fourth Regiment, he said, already had
gone to pieces. See *Oktiabr'skoe vooruzhënnoe vosstanie v Petrograde* (*Velikaia
Oktiabr'skaia revoliutsiia*), No. 299, p. 257.

of the Military Commission expressed it, were obliged "to trump only with cadets and Cossacks." [72] Strange trumps for Socialist Revolutionaries! To such a pass had their addiction to coalition and default on their promises brought them. With the party in control of the municipality since the election of August 20, it should have been able to count upon the police, but N. V. Ivanov, the "March Socialist Revolutionary" who had been named chief of militia, largely because of his party affiliation, had displayed no administrative talent nor any will and initiative, and had confined himself to signing papers.[73] The Bolsheviks had no trouble in removing the militia from the hands of the city administration,[74] though Mayor Shreider and the council were vociferous in opposing the revolution. Apparently the SR's were still looking everywhere for assistance except to themselves. A Soviet source suggests that Avksentiev's visit to the British ambassador on October 27 involved more than a desire to report on current developments.[75] However that may be, it is interesting to note that Sir George Buchanan's appraisal of the situation was more realistic than N. D. Avksentiev's, having in it none of that easy optimism which would soon be so rudely dispelled.

On the morrow of the overthrow of the Provisional Government, when the Military Commission assembled at party headquarters, it learned that the cadets were the only force that could be relied upon. Accordingly, the commission centered its attention upon establishing ties with the military schools and bringing them to a state of readiness. The shock of the fall of the Provisional Government, the sharpening of the class struggle as a result of the initial decrees of the Soviet government, and the news of Kerenski's advance on the capital, together with the weakening of the garrison by the dispatch of troops to the front, raised the spirit of opposition and helped the commission in its work.[76] Through the party

[72] Testimony of Kashin, *Izvestiia*, No. 131 (June 15, 1922).
[73] Z. Kelson, "Padenie Vremennogo Pravitel'stva" (Fall of the Provisional Government), *Byloe*, VI (1925), 192–93.
[74] *Delo Naroda*, No. 190 (October 27, 1917).
[75] *Istoriia grazhdanskoi voiny v SSSR*, II, 325–26; Buchanan, *My Mission to Russia*, II, 208–9.
[76] Vladimirova, *God sluzhby "sotsialistov" kapitalistam*, p. 25; Stankevich, *Vospominaniia*, p. 267; confession of Colonel B. M. Muffel in "Iz zapisnoi knizhki arkhivista: Zagovor monarkhicheskoi organizatsii V. M. Purishkevicha," in *Krasnyi Arkhiv*, XXVI (I, 1928), 185.

cells existing in all cadet units it succeeded in laying a basis for action in the Vladimir and Pavlov Infantry Schools and the Nikolaev Engineering School, and in receiving less definite commitments from several others. Furthermore, certain elite groups like the battalion of shock troops quartered in the palace of the ballerina Kshesinskaia could be expected to join in when the time came; and among the officers of the garrison, though not among the troops, there were numerous sympathizers, including a compact group in the Armored Division. One of the detachment commanders in this division, a man named Keller, had for some time been in close contact with the Military Commission and had, in fact, urged it to take action ahead of the Military Revolutionary Committee of the Petersburg Soviet while the garrison had not yet completely succumbed to Bolshevism.[77]

So far, the Military Commission had acted on its own initiative, though, of course, with the knowledge of the Central Committee, particularly of Gotz, Gerstein, and Avksentiev. The committee had placed Colonel Krakovetski, with Kashin as his assistant, in command of all party military units. At the conference on the morning of October 26, the proposal of A. A. Bruderer for armed action against Bolshevism had met with the approval of Krakovetski and of Rakitin-Broun, secretary of the Military Commission. The 26th, 27th, and 28th were days of feverish activity, spent in lining up the support noted above.[78] On the 27th the commission and the Central Committee issued a joint manifesto,[79] proclaiming their determination to bring about a "decisive liquidation of the mad act" of October 25 in union with the Committee to Save the Fatherland, which would then proceed to organize a government of the revolutionary democracy on the basis of immediately transferring landed property to the land committees and immediately proposing to all belligerent powers a general democratic peace. The significant features of the manifesto are the tacit rejection of any separate approach to Germany and the failure to come out for restoration of the

[77] Testimony of Keller in *Izvestiia*, No. 131 (June 15, 1922); testimony of Krakovetski in *Pravda*, No. 129 (June 13, 1922); Vladimirova, *God sluzhby "sotsialistov" kapitalistam*, p. 26; *Istoriia grazhdanskoi voiny v SSSR*, II, 343, 346.
[78] *Obvinitel'noe zakliuchenie*, pp. 7, 58.
[79] *Delo Naroda*, No. 191 (October 28, 1917).

Provisional Government, which the right wing of the party in its heart still favored,[80] despite everything that had happened. So unpopular had the Provisional Government become, even in the judgment of its supporters, that the Committee to Save the Fatherland would not hear of Stankevich's proposal to conduct its struggle in the name of that authority.[81] Nevertheless an effort was to be made, under cover of the reigning confusion, on the part of SR and Menshevik elements in the garrison of the Petropavlovsk Fortress, to free the incarcerated ministers, presumably in order to sustain the legal fiction of the unbroken succession of power if not to restore the Provisional Government. This effort was geared to the projected uprising.[82] Whether the SR leadership and its allies really meant to throw off the incubus of the discredited regime may be doubted.[83]

Just when the Military Commission seemed to be in a position to enjoy the fruits of its labor, Gotz intervened to announce that not only would the fight not be waged in the name of the party but that command of the enterprise would be transferred to nonpartisan hands. And whom had Gotz picked for this post? None other than Colonel Polkovnikov, ex-commander of the troops of the Petersburg Military District, whom Kerenski had accused of treachery on the morning of October 25 and whom Kishkin later in the day had summarily dismissed. A man obviously derelict in his duty and suspect in the eyes of a Kadet minister had now been chosen by the head of the Socialist Revolutionary Party to lead its offensive against Bolshevism. The reaction of the members of the Military Commission may well be imagined: Krakovetski felt that he had been slapped in the face, and Broun uttered a stiff protest against such ungrateful treatment of the commission, whereupon Gotz summoned them to submit to party discipline and accept Polkovnikov's direction.[84]

---

[80] See *Volia Naroda*, No. 159 (October 31, 1917). Argunov in his paper was always more forthright than such politicians as Avksentiev who held the same views but wanted to consort with the right center.

[81] *Vospominaniia*, p. 272.

[82] See G. Blagonravov, "Oktiabr'skie dni v Petropavlovskoi kreposti" (October Days in the Peter-Paul Fortress), in *Oktiabr'skoe vooruzhënnoe vosstanie v Petrograde (Vospominaniia uchastnikov)*, pp. 129, 130, n. 1.

[83] See further discussion of this point below, pp. 63 ff.

[84] Testimony of Broun in *Izvestiia*, No. 129 (June 13, 1922); *Obvinitel'noe zakliuchenie*, pp. 58–59.

Gotz then graciously designated Krakovetski as Polkovnikov's assistant and brought in the Menshevik Sinani to serve on the staff of the insurrection. According to Krakovetski, Polkovnikov rejected the commission's plan and put through his own with the support of Gotz,[85] while according to Broun, the commission had drawn up a plan in two variants, one of which Polkovnikov accepted.[86]

What possessed Gotz, with two SR lieutenant-colonels (Krakovetski and Kuropatkin) at his disposal, to appoint a discredited officer of comparable rank whom the Soviet historian terms a monarchist [87] and whom Krakovetski himself describes as standing "to the right of the Kadets?" Though done in the name of the Committee to Save the Fatherland, the decision was actually Gotz's. In general, this committee was little more than a front behind which the SR's operated; it had no part in organizing the insurrection, of which its main body had been kept in ignorance, and it issued no orders save the final one to cease fire. It may be that Gotz had been won over by Polkovnikov's promises—boastful promises, Krakovetski calls them —to bring the Cossack regiments into line. At least this is the explanation of Broun, adopted by the prosecution at the trial of 1922. The Cossack officers had refused to commit themselves beyond a vague promise of aid in case infantry support were forthcoming,[88] and anyone who could induce them to take a more positive stand obviously would have been a great asset to the cause.[89]

But Gotz himself denied that the Cossack angle dictated his choice. It is not necessary to assume that the exigencies of defense prompted him to make such a denial, for he bore himself defiantly throughout the trial, making no attempt to conceal his hostility to the Soviet regime or to disclaim responsibility for the rising of October 29. According to Gotz, if Polkovnikov awakened doubts in the minds of the socialist opposition, it was not because of any reactionary leanings but because of his reputed softness toward Bolshevism. Gotz had looked upon such reproaches as unfounded and had dismissed them from his calculations. Krakovetski, of course, would have been a more natural choice as a party man

[85] *Pravda*, No. 129 (June 13, 1922).   [86] *Izvestiia*, No. 129 (June 13, 1922).
[87] Vladimirova, *God sluzhby "sotsialistov" kapitalistam*, p. 26.
[88] *Istoriia grazhdanskoi voiny v SSSR*, II, 343.
[89] See proceedings of the trial in *Izvestiia*, No. 130 (June 14, 1922).

"but we felt he was not energetic and decisive enough, and so he was slated merely as chief of staff, as Polkovnikov's closest assistant. We had still another colonel at our disposal, the SR Kuropatkin, who would have been a more fitting person to head the movement, but he refused the leading role out of humility and took upon himself merely the execution of one of the most important tasks—the seizure of the Petropavlovsk Fortress." In this situation Polkovnikov received the assignment "because we considered him the ablest and most outstanding military leader." [90]

This is a remarkable statement. How Gotz could entertain such an opinion of Polkovnikov after the spectacle of October 25 defies comprehension. One is tempted to conclude that Gotz, in avowing so much at the trial, still could not bring himself to admit the weakness of his cause by conceding that the quest for Cossack aid had overridden all other considerations in his mind. But how could he have been so confident that Polkovnikov would deliver the Cossacks on the 29th when four days earlier he had signally failed to do so? What new element had intruded into the situation to suggest that the opposition could now do what it had not been able to do when it constituted the government, with the whole apparatus of power at its command? The answer is "none." There is another possible conclusion, namely, that here we are confronted with an example of the bad judgment not infrequently displayed by the leadership of this party, beginning as far back as 1905 with the designation of Azef and Savinkov to prepare the uprising of that year.[91]

Neither conclusion, however, is wholly satisfying. There remain some elements of obscurity in the background of the cadet uprising of October 29. Not only are there two contradictory opinions about the ability of Colonel Polkovnikov but there are also two regarding his political views, which inclined in one direction, according to Gotz, and in precisely the opposite direction, according to Kerenski and everyone else. During the cross-examination at the trial in 1922, Krakovetski declared, amid laughter in the courtroom, that it was possible "to suspect Polkovnikov of anything,

[90] From the speech of Gotz at the trial, morning session, August 1, 1922, in *Revoliutsionnaia Rossiia*, No. 21–22 (October–November, 1922), p. 8.
[91] See my book, *The Agrarian Foes of Bolshevism*, pp. 77–78.

only not of Bolshevism." [92] To shed light on all aspects of the matter, we would have to unlock the character of this man, and very little can be found concerning it. One thing we do know, refuting to some extent Gotz's estimate and pointing in the direction of the predominant opinion: along with members of his staff, Colonel Polkovnikov could often be seen in the gambling dives of St. Petersburg.[93]

The Polkovnikov appointment strongly suggests that liaison between the plotters in the city and Kerenski's advancing force was not at all what Soviet sources credit it with being.[94] In fact, it hardly existed. After an earlier attempt with Avksentiev had failed, Zenzinov and Gotz tried to get through to Gatchina as members of a delegation from the city council—in order to gather information and stop the fighting, according to the *Delo Naroda*,[95] but actually, as Zenzinov admits,[96] to help Kerenski assemble an army. Nothing came of the attempt, however, for the two men were arrested at the Baltic Station, manhandled and cursed by the sailors, and very nearly lynched by them. We shall come back to this episode,[97] as nothing else points up quite so well the state of affairs in the PSR. The next day, on the 28th, contact was finally established when Stankevich succeeded in reaching Kerenski. But Stankevich left Gatchina without having ascertained how many troops Kerenski had with him. Restrained by the presence of onlookers during the interview, he had simply assumed that Kerenski stood at the head of the whole III Cavalry Corps instead of a few detachments.[98] The archives reveal that Kerenski's adjutant, SR Captain A. I. Kozmin, tried to get in touch with the Military Commission of the Central Committee through Krakovetski in order to concert measures inside and outside the city—Gerstein on the way to Luga had evidently informed Kozmin of the projected rising—but what, if anything, came of this attempt to communicate by courier we do not know.[99] As for the charge in the *Novaia Zhizn'*, based on reports from Left SR circles,

[92] *Izvestiia*, No. 130 (June 14, 1922).

[93] Kelson, "Padenie Vremennogo Pravitel'stva," *Byloe*, VI (1925), 194.

[94] Vladimirova, *God sluzhby "sotsialistov" kapitalistam*, pp. 31–32.

[95] No. 191 (October 28, 1917).   [96] Interview in Paris (September, 1935).

[97] See below, pp. 95–96.   [98] *Vospominaniia*, p. 270.

[99] "Iz zapisnoi knizhki arkhivista: Podgotovka k nastupleniiu na Petrograd" (From an Archivist's Notebook: Preparation of the Advance on Petrograd), in *Krasnyi Arkhiv*, XXIV (V, 1927), 205, document no. 9.

that Kerenski had conferred with the Central Committee on the day he left the capital and that everything which followed had been based on its directives, the *Delo Naroda* is probably correct in branding this as a fabrication.[100] Things were not that well organized in the anti-Bolshevik camp. Though mindful of the crucial importance of avoiding isolated action, the Committee to Save the Fatherland had largely failed in the endeavor to coordinate plans for action inside the city with the advance of Kerenski's troops from without. But for an untoward circumstance, however, it would have come measurably closer to success than it did.

On the evening of October 28 when Stankevich returned from the interview with Kerenski to report to the counterrevolutionary staff, the situation was as follows. Kerenski's small force, grossly overdrawn in the imagination of both the Soviet government and his supporters within the city,[101] and hence endowed with an effectiveness out of all proportion to its numbers, was not yet ready to enter St. Petersburg. It had momentarily stalled at Gatchina and would only occupy Tsarskoe Selo toward midnight instead of twelve hours earlier, as Kerenski insists it might have done.[102] The Petersburg Soviet, through its Military Revolutionary Committee, was making great exertions to repel the attack and was denuding the city of the best fighting forces, thereby presenting the SR's and their allies with a golden opportunity. And the SR's were now ready to take advantage of it.

Among the papers of Colonel Polkovnikov there is a list showing the location, strength, and equipment of the forces on which he was counting. The total of 830 men, including 300 without rifles at the recently disarmed Pavlov Infantry School, the question marks after the names of several other institutions, and the absence of artillery strength suggest that the organizers of the uprising were banking heavily on the element of surprise and on the preoccupation of Soviet authorities with the danger before the city gates.[103] At any

[100] No. 198 (November 3, 1917).

[101] One report to the Military Revolutionary Committee credited Kerenski with 5,000 troops—nearly ten times the actual number. See *Istoriia grazhdanskoi voiny v SSSR*, II, 358–59; see also Piontkovski, *Oktiabr' 1917 g.*, p. 29.

[102] "Gatchina," in *Izdalëka*, pp. 213–15.

[103] *Istoriia grazhdanskoi voiny v SSSR*, II, 343–44.

rate, Polkovnikov pronounced the forces at hand adequate to the task,[104] repeating to Gotz the assurance that had sunk Kerenski. The plan was to establish headquarters in the Nikolaev Engineering School, in the grim castle where the Emperor Paul had been strangled to death, and from there to seize the telephone station and the Mikhailov Manege with its armored cars. Meanwhile, on the other side of the river the cadets of the Vladimir and Pavlov Infantry Schools were to effect a junction and reduce the Petropavlovsk Fortress, preparatory to a general advance upon the nerve center of Bolshevism in the Smolny Institute.[105] In order to gain a little more time, and also because Stankevich advised that General Krasnov was not quite ready to resume the offensive, the secret conference on the night of October 28 between the military section of the Committee to Save the Fatherland and the Military Commission of the PSR decided against an immediate uprising and in favor of waiting at least one more day. Because of the need for action, however, orders were drawn up at once and commissars despatched to the military schools with instructions to place them on a war footing. The conference then turned to technical matters and many of those in attendance dispersed to their quarters.[106]

At this juncture fate intervened to change the decision and precipitate the uprising before it could be coordinated with the thrust from Gatchina. Among the commissars appointed to key positions was Alexander Arnoldovich Bruderer, prominent member of the Military Commission of the Central Committee though not of the Central Committee itself, as Soviet histories state.[107] He was to be

[104] Testimony of Broun in *Izvestiia*, No. 129 (June 13, 1922).

[105] Vladimirova, *God sluzhby "sotsialistov" kapitalistam*, p. 26.

[106] Stankevich, *Vospominaniia*, pp. 270–71; *Istoriia grazhdanskoi voiny v SSSR*, II, 345; Kerenski, "Gatchina," in *Izdalëka*, p. 216; Miliukov, *Istoriia*, I, Part III, 284*n*. Krakovetski and Broun both state that Avksentiev signed the orders (*Izvestiia*, No. 129 [June 13, 1922] and No. 130 [June 14, 1922]). But Gotz says that he, and not Avksentiev, signed them (*Revoliutsionnaia Rossiia*, No. 21–22 [October–November, 1922], p. 8). This is borne out by the signature on Bruderer's papers (*Istoriia grazhdanskoi voiny v SSSR*, II, 345) and by the statement that Avksentiev, though present in the same building, did not attend this conference, whereas Gotz was certainly there (Miliukov, *Istoriia*, I, Part III, 284*n*). Since Miliukov had his information directly from Avksentiev, his account is preferred to others affirming the latter's participation (see Vladimirova, *God sluzhby "sotsialistov" kapitalistam*, p. 26).

[107] *Istoriia grazhdanskoi voiny v SSSR*, II, 345; *Petrogradskie bol'sheviki v Oktiabr'skoi revoliutsii*, pp. 407, 423.

the commandant of the Vladimir Infantry School on one side of the Petropavlovsk Fortress (the citadel or *Burg* of St. Petersburg), and it was also his duty to alert the shock battalion in the Kshesinskaia Palace on the other side. Late that night, as he was leaving the pretentious dwelling of the Polish ballerina (the foundations of whose fortune, according to Trotski,[108] had been laid by the male members of the Romanov dynasty), he was accosted by a patrol from the fortress, placed under arrest, and taken to the commandant's quarters. One look at the papers found on Bruderer's person convinced the commandant that he had big quarry, and he set out in person to bring them to the Military Revolutionary Committee.[109] In this way the Soviet authorities learned in some detail of the plans of the opposition and were able to proceed against the centers of disaffection without groping in the darkness. But the opposition, also, had kept abreast of developments and Colonel Polkovnikov burst in upon the conference—or what was left of it—to announce that the Bolsheviks had decided to disarm the military schools [110] the next day and that in order to preserve the nucleus of the rising it was necessary to act at once. The conference thereupon decided to shoot the works: Polkovnikov and his staff (mainly the Military Commission of the PSR) moved from the building of the All-Russian Peasants' Soviet to the Engineer's Castle, and at 2 A.M. on October 29 issued an order calling on the units of the garrison to throw off the yoke of the Military Revolutionary Committee or be branded as "enemies of the country and traitors to the cause of revolution." [111]

At first things went not unfavorably for the insurrection. The cadets of the Nikolaev Engineering School rose in response to orders transmitted through their colonel, B. M. Muffel, and seized with

[108] *History of the Russian Revolution*, II, 58.
[109] Blagonravov, "Oktiabr'skie dni v Petropavlovskoi kreposti," in *Oktiabr'skoe vooruzhënnoe vosstanie v Petrograde* (*Vospominaniia uchastnikov*), pp. 130–33.
[110] According to Krakovetski, it was specifically the Bolshevik decision to proceed against the armored car units which touched off the rising (*Pravda*, No. 129 [June 13, 1922]).
[111] *Istoriia grazhdanskoi voiny v SSSR*, II, 345–46; Stankevich, *Vospominaniia*, p. 271; testimony of Broun in *Izvestiia*, No. 129 (June 13, 1922); Vladimirova, *God sluzhby "sotsialistov" kapitalistam*, pp. 26, 29. The last source treats the Bruderer episode solely from the standpoint of disclosing the plot and does not see in it the circumstance which forced the hand of the conspirators. Kerenski, who did not have all the facts at his disposal, ascribes the haste to provocation ("Gatchina," in *Izdalëka*, p. 216).

little difficulty the central telephone station and the Mikhailov Manege, partially disrupting the communications system of the Smolny Institute and providing the insurrectionary staff with five armored cars—all that were fit for service. Encouraged by these initial successes and hoping to start a bandwagon rush, Rakitin-Broun published a manifesto [112] in which he made it appear that the Bolsheviks had been forced back upon their two remaining places of refuge, the fortress and the institute. The manifesto bore the signatures not only of Broun and his Menshevik collaborator, Sinani, but also of Gotz and Avksentiev, their names having been affixed by Broun in their absence.[113] Meanwhile, across the river Colonel Kuropatkin with some companions from a wounded veterans' detachment arrived at the Vladimir Infantry School and roused the sleeping cadets with orders to disarm the soldiers stationed there. This was the beginning of the projected action against the Petropavlovsk Fortress.

It was also the high water mark of the insurrection. Already there were disheartening tidings: the Cossacks had refused to come out despite frantic backstage efforts by the ringleaders of the plot. Polkovnikov had boasted that he could deliver the Cossacks and now went in person to their barracks, but his importunities were of no avail—Krakovetski states that he met with a categorical refusal.[114] Avksentiev as chairman of the Committee to Save the Fatherland made the rounds of the First, Fourth, and Fourteenth Don Cossack regiments, beseeching them to come to the aid of the cadets, but his entreaties and those of his companion, the Populist patriarch N. V. Chaikovski, were equally unavailing.[115] The military schools them-

---

[112] Text in *Istoriia grazhdanskoi voiny v SSSR*, II, 347; Sukhanov, *Zapiski*, VII, 285; see also Vladimirova, *God sluzhby "sotsialistov" kapitalistam*, pp. 27–28, and *Revoliutsiia 1917 goda*, VI, 24. See also *Oktiabr'skoe vooruzhënnoe vosstanie v Petrograde* (*Velikaia Oktiabr'skaia revoliutsiia*), No. 1195, pp. 818–19.

[113] For controversy on this point, see below, pp. 35–36. Either through ellipsis or intent, the official Soviet history has Broun sign as a member of the Central Committee of the PSR, whereas other sources, including the earlier Soviet ones, state that he signed with his correct title of member of the Military Commission of the Central Committee.

[114] *Pravda*, No. 129 (June 13, 1922).

[115] Testimony of Gotz in *Izvestiia*, No. 129 (June 13, 1922); Vladimirova, *God sluzhby "sotsialistov" kapitalistam*, p. 30; Ignatiev, *Nekotorye fakty i itogi chetyrëkh let*, I, 6; Melgunov, *N. V. Chaikovskii v gody grazhdanskoi voiny*, pp. 31–32. Their pleas were not addressed to A. I. Dutov, as stated in the last two sources, because he had already left the city (*Istoriia grazhdanskoi voiny v SSSR*, II, 324). Gotz was in doubt as to Dutov's presence on the night in question.

selves had continually sought contact with the Cossacks, hoping to acquire an ally for the impending struggle, but the attitude of the leaders when the showdown came is foreshadowed in the words of a representative of the Petersburg Cossack Union whose telephone conversation with the front the Bolsheviks had intercepted. Speaking of Kerenski, he said, "Let Cossackdom beware of tying its fortunes to this swindler. Behind the front he has lost all influence. To be sure, we should take him unto ourselves as bait for a certain kind of fish." [116]

Though the Military Revolutionary Committee had few regular units left in the city, the Cossack defection spared it any serious embarrassment. In the proletarian levies, stiffened with small detachments of sailors, and the active sympathies of some elements of the demoralized garrison, the Bolshevik government possessed far greater resources than the SR Central Committee could muster against it. Before the day was over it is estimated that 10,000 Red Guards were set in motion against the several hundred cadets who constituted the core of the uprising. So great was the disparity of forces that the Military Revolutionary Committee found it possible to isolate the centers of rebellion, smothering the separate fires before they could merge in a general conflagration. Its levies enveloped the Vladimir Infantry School even as Colonel Kuropatkin was preparing the students for action, so that instead of marching out to effect a junction with the Pavlov contingent, they had to stand siege in their quarters. Here the most stubborn engagement of the day took place, with the numerical superiority of the Red Guard offset by its poorly coordinated movements and inferior marksmanship until such time as the Bolsheviks played their trump card in the form of artillery. The roar of the cannon and the damage they wrought shattered the nerves of the brave defenders. The SR colonel sought to prolong their resistance by shouting the deception that Kerenski was already within the city and that the Cossacks were near. But the Soviet troops battered the school into submission, killing the colonel and overbearing his youthful charges.

With the fall of the Vladimir academy went the last hope of effective resistance. Elsewhere the fighting was either nipped in

[116] "Vokrug 'Gatchina'" (Around Gatchina), in *Krasnyi Arkhiv*, IX (II, 1925), 175, 193; Sukhanov, *Zapiski*, VII, 277. Though the date is not revealed, the conversation probably took place on the 26th.

the bud or assumed only a desultory character. There is evidence of
the same confusion in rebel headquarters as had prevailed in the
offices of the General Staff when the Provisional Government expired. Polkovnikov's performance on October 29 in no wise differed
from his default on October 25. The staff in the Engineer's Castle
could not make up its mind to reinforce the centers of resistance
with the meager means at its disposal (230 cadets, 50 shock troop
volunteers, and 5 armored cars), and presently found itself surrounded by a mass of poorly organized but determined workers
against whom there was little point in struggling in view of the
obvious lack of success in other parts of the city. Polkovnikov in
the name of the Committee to Save the Fatherland gave the order to
surrender, and by late afternoon nothing remained for the Bolsheviks to do except mop up a few pockets of resistance. When
Lieutenant Colonel Krakovetski emerged from staff quarters, the
impression he received was one of a small island surrounded by a
raging sea; and while a professional soldier could only disdain the
armed rabble, he no longer could harbor any illusions as to where
the sympathy of the populace lay.[117]

So ended in fiasco the uprising of October 29. It is appropriately
called the "junker uprising" because no one but cadets took part
in it, even though it was staged under the auspices of the Committee
to Save the Fatherland and directed by the Central Committee of the
Socialist Revolutionary Party in the person of A. R. Gotz. How
much of the fiasco must be attributed to faulty execution and how
much to the inherent weaknesses of the sponsoring party and, indeed,
of the whole opposition to Bolshevism, it is difficult to say. The uprising was too long delayed from one standpoint and too soon provoked from another. Touched off on the spur of the moment, without adequate technical preparation and with no possibility of using
the wealth of volunteer material which was at hand, the effort could
have been made with much better prospects of success a few days

[117] *Istoriia grazhdanskoi voiny v SSSR*, II, 346–51; Vladimirova, *God sluzhby
"sotsialistov" kapitalistam*, pp. 27–31; testimony of Krakovetski in *Pravda*, No.
129 (June 13, 1922), and *Izvestiia*, No. 130 (June 14, 1922); confessions of Baron
de Bode, of the Duke of Leuchtenberg, and of Colonel Muffel in "Iz zapisnoi
knizhki arkhivista: Zagovor monarkhicheskoi organizatsii V. M. Purishkevicha,"
in *Krasnyi Arkhiv*, XXVI (I, 1928), 174, 176–78, 185; Blagonravov, "Oktiabr'skie
dni v Petropavlovskoi kreposti," in *Oktiabr'skoe vooruzhënnoe vosstanie v
Petrograde (Vospominaniia uchastnikov)*, pp. 133–39.

earlier when the Provisional Government was still alive and the Bolsheviks had not yet taken over the apparatus of state.[118] Yet in as much as the party had not even realized the need for action at that time, such considerations are nothing more than an afterthought.

For the PSR the affair of October 29 would have an aftermath only less damaging than the debacle itself. The circumstances of the rising reflected little honor on its sponsor. In the first place, its leaders certainly displayed no courage comparable to that of the youthful cadets who rose at their command and paid the price of their misjudgment. Colonel Kuropatkin died bravely at his post, but the other leaders dropped the enterprise and dispersed in all directions—Polkovnikov to the Don Region, Krakovetski to Siberia, and Gotz with the core of the Central Committee to Gatchina—leaving the stranded cadets to their fate, which was not so merciful as one would gather from later Soviet accounts.[119] The party leaders, moreover, had permitted the cadets to be misled by promises of support from Kerenski's force when they knew well enough it could not be expected in the city on that day. It is not surprising that conservative officers who participated in the uprising were incensed at the conduct of the instigators.[120]

The impression of faintheartedness was strengthened when Gotz and Avksentiev disclaimed any knowledge of the manifesto bearing their signatures which the Military Commission had issued after the initial successes on the morning of the 29th.[121] While technically correct, their statement had the effect of dissociating the ring-

---

[118] Stankevich, *Vospominaniia*, pp. 271–72.

[119] Miliukov quotes two sources (both bitterly anti-Bolshevik, it is true) as to the barbarous punishment meted out to the cadets (*Istoriia*, I, Part III, 285–86), and Trotski, without going into details, frankly concedes that excesses occurred as an unavoidable consequence of the intensification of the class struggle (*Oktiabr'skaia revoliutsiia*, p. 81). The report in *Novaia Zhizn'* alludes to the lynching of several cadets; see *Oktiabr'skoe vooruzhënnoe vosstanie v Petrograde (Velikaia Oktiabr'skaia revoliutsiia)*, No. 1220, p. 839. It is only fair to point out, however, that had the insurrection succeeded the cadets would probably have behaved in similar fashion. Krakovetski had not taken seriously Gotz's admonition against lynch justice—both knew the mood of the cadets made excesses inevitable in the event of victory (*Izvestiia*, No. 130 [June 14, 1922]).

[120] "Iz zapisnoi knizhki arkhivista: Zagovor monarkhicheskoi organizatsii V. M. Purishkevicha," in *Krasnyi Arkhiv*, XXVI (I, 1928), 174, 178, 185. See also Sukhanov, *Zapiski*, VII, 287.

[121] See letters to the editor, *Delo Naroda*, No. 195 (October 31, 1917). For reference to manifesto, see above, p. 32.

leaders from the enterprise and profoundly shocked the members of the commission, who felt they were being thrown to the wolves.[122] It was only after a merciless flagellation in the Bolshevik press,[123] followed by a decree placing him outside the law, that Gotz published a frank avowal of his responsibility for the events of October 29, claiming for himself and his party the right to rise in arms against the violence and ruin which the Bolsheviks were visiting on the country.[124]

In the second place, it ill became a party which prided itself on being "the sovereign of the country's thoughts" to have raised an action which enlisted no popular support and remained from start to finish the affair of a small circle of conspirators. The SR mountain had labored and brought forth a puny plot instead of a broad popular insurrection against "the ravishers of the people's will." And, finally, to accomplish even this little, the SR high command had not scrupled to consort with elements which compromised the whole venture in the eyes of many party members, to say nothing of their political opponents.

While the Bolsheviks are wrong in charging that the SR Central Committee on this occasion served as the tool of reaction, there is no doubt that the activist wing of the counterrevolution, the monarchist organization of V. M. Purishkevich, was mixed up in the events of October 29. One does not have to accept the extravagant statement that Baron de Bode was actually in charge at the Engineer's Castle until Polkovnikov and the SR Military Commission moved in [125] to find convincing evidence of monarchist participation in the uprising. Purishkevich in his confession states that "cadets who were in our organization and subject to Bode's direction

[122] *Obvinitel'noe zakliuchenie*, p. 8; testimony of Broun in *Izvestiia*, No. 129 (June 13, 1922).

[123] See especially the article "Kak oni izvorachivaiutsia" (How They Turn and Twist), *Pravda*, No. 178 (November 3, 1917).

[124] "Bol'shevistskie rytsari bez strakha i uprëka," *Delo Naroda*, No. 200 (November 5, 1917); see also testimony of Gotz and his cross-examination by Lunacharski at the Moscow trial in *Izvestiia*, No. 129 (June 13, 1922). For statement of Military Revolutionary Committee regarding order for arrest of Gotz, see *Delo Naroda*, No. 207 (November 12, 1917).

[125] See confession of Staff Captain A. B. Dushkin, "Iz zapisnoi knizhki arkhivista: Zagovor monarkhicheskoi organizatsii V. M. Purishkevicha," in *Krasnyi Arkhiv*, XXVI (I, 1928), 181.

were sent to occupy the telephone station, the Mikhailov Manege, and the Engineer's Castle in spite of his and my own instructions, and in obedience to the provocative orders of Colonel Polkovnikov and the Committee to Save the Fatherland and Revolution, with neither of whom I personally had any relations whatever." [126] One notes that the monarchist leader, though a prisoner of the Bolsheviks, could not deny the complicity of his followers. The assertion that they participated against the will of their leaders is disproved by Bode's own account of how he went to headquarters in the castle "for information" and spent the rest of the day furthering the cause of the insurrection.[127] Another member of the organization says that a large number of Purishkevich's adherents were involved in the uprising as a consequence of their leader's stand for immediate action,[128] and Broun is quoted in a Soviet source as testifying that the military figures who gathered around Polkovnikov after the start of hostilities were definitely of a monarchist cast.[129] On the day of the insurrection Colonel F. V. Vinberg went to the city council and offered his services, receiving the command of one of the districts into which the capital was divided; this gentleman belonged to the Society of the Archangel Michael and also to the Union of Landowners.[130] Finally, it might be mentioned that the man who commandeered the armored cars and took them out of the garage was the officer Wildenkreuz, a convinced monarchist later shot by the Bolsheviks as a bandit.[131]

The association of monarchist elements with the enterprise, however, does not mean that it was primarily their affair or that its direction slipped into their hands after the action was launched. Naturally, that is the impression the Bolsheviks have sought to create, either by direct assertion or by innuendo, in order to discredit their SR rivals, but the record is clear that the initiative proceeded from the Central Committee of the PSR and that the threads were held in its hands, or rather in those of its plenipotentiary, Gotz, to the very end. Whatever the political views of Polkovnikov may have been, he derived

[126] *Ibid.*, p. 172.   [127] *Ibid.*, pp. 173–74.   [128] *Ibid.*, p. 181.

[129] Vladimirova, *God sluzhby "sotsialistov" kapitalistam*, p. 27.

[130] "Iz zapisnoi knizhki arkhivista: Zagovor monarkhicheskoi organizatsii V. M. Purishkevicha," in *Krasnyi Arkhiv*, XXVI (I, 1928), 181–82.

[131] Testimony of Keller, *Izvestiia*, No. 131 (June 15, 1922).

his authority from Gotz, about whose judgment and discretion, of course, there can be divergent opinions. Polkovnikov directed the whole uprising, according to Broun,[132] the role of his staff being a nominal one, and Polkovnikov took his orders from Gotz. Just how these orders were transmitted is not clear. Gotz himself says he was at staff headquarters in the Engineer's Castle, where he confirmed all orders issued during the day,[133] but the commandant of the Nikolaev Engineering School in the castle states that Polkovnikov got his instructions from Gotz over the telephone.[134] There is documentary evidence that the directives sent to the military schools by Polkovnikov had been countersigned by Gotz.[135] In his summation at the Moscow trial of 1922 the Bolshevik prosecutor, Krylenko, was correct in asserting that conservative officers rallied to the SR standard because they needed a protective coloration under which to strike at Bolshevism,[136] but adherence does not constitute appropriation, and the difficulty the SR leaders would have experienced in restraining their reactionary allies in case of victory does not mean that on the 29th of October they had surrendered control of the movement.

The hopelessness of the venture and the association with monarchist elements left a bad taste in the mouth of many Socialist Revolutionaries. V. M. Chernov, especially, condemned the course of the Central Committee, though not in public.[137] From a cryptic entry in the minutes of the Central Committee,[138] we know that a party commission had been set up to investigate the affair and that the Central Committee found it necessary to ask this body to speed up its labors "in view of the categorical demand" of its own Military Commission —probably a reflection of dissatisfaction over Gotz's and Avksentiev's disavowal of the Broun manifesto. But unfortunately there is no

[132] Testimony of Broun, *ibid.*, No. 129 (June 13, 1922).

[133] *Revoliutsionnaia Rossiia*, No. 21-22 (October–November, 1922), p. 8.

[134] "Iz zapisnoi knizhki arkhivista: Zagovor monarkhicheskoi organizatsii V. M. Purishkevicha," in *Krasnyi Arkhiv*, XXVI (I, 1928), 185. Colonel Muffel confirms Broun's assertion that Polkovnikov was in complete command of the enterprise.

[135] See *Oktiabr'skoe vooruzhënnoe vosstanie v Petrograde (Velikaia Oktiabr'skaia revoliutsiia)*, Nos. 1189, 1190, 1225, pp. 816, 841.

[136] *Izvestiia*, No. 169 (July 30, 1922).

[137] Manuscript commentary on the minutes of the Central Committee, p. 56.

[138] Session of November 14—the first for which there is a record since October 21.

record of the outcome of the investigation, if, indeed, it was pursued in the course of the further disasters which overtook the party. Besides increasing the tension in the PSR, the abortive uprising lifted the spirit of the Bolshevik camp and caused the Petersburg working class, hitherto hopeful of a compromise among all of the socialist parties, to harden its attitude and accept the ultimate conclusions of the October Revolution.[139] The Bolsheviks now had a free hand, as far as the city was concerned, to turn their attention to Kerenski, since they had disrupted the opposition strategy of taking them between two fires, one from without the city and one from within, which alone could have saved his small force from destruction or capture.

Immediately after the suppression of the uprising, certain prominent Socialist Revolutionaries hastened to the camp of Kerenski to attempt from without what they had been unable to do from within. Foremost among them was A. R. Gotz, still acting under the powers vested in him by the Central Committee. In addition to Gotz, Avksentiev, Gerstein, and Feit slipped away from the city, so that if we include Chernov, who was already at the front on a speaking tour, no less than five members of the Central Committee were out seeking troops who would actively oppose the October Revolution, even though they differed as to reinstatement of the Provisional Government. Gotz headed straight for the headquarters of General Krasnov to report that the Cossack units in Petersburg could not come out because Soviet troops were surrounding their barracks [140] (as though they wanted to come out!) and to inquire whether the force at Krasnov's disposal was large enough to permit an immediate advance on the capital. He now learned that Kerenski's venture represented daring and desperation rather than physical strength, and that unless infantry support were forthcoming, the small Cossack band would yield to the conviction that it was marching in isolation. To provide infantry support now became the chief purpose of the

[139] Sukhanov, *Zapiski*, VII, 289; Kerenski, "Gatchina," in *Izdalëka*, p. 216.
[140] Miliukov, *Istoriia*, I, Part III, 255. The Kadet historian, relying on the original—and more dependable—version of Krasnov's story, places this interview on October 30, but other sources indicate that it probably occurred on the 29th, though Gotz did confer with Krasnov the following day.

SR leader as he pressed on to join Kerenski and lend the weight of his authority to the military orders which the prime minister was dispatching in all directions.[141]

Infantry could be obtained from two sources: either from the armies at the front or, closer at hand, from the large and inactive garrisons of towns near the capital such as Luga, Gatchina, and Tsarskoe Selo, where many thousands of troops were stationed (12,000 to 16,000 in Tsarskoe alone). Let us follow briefly the frantic efforts of Gotz and his confederates to enlist aid from both quarters and redeem a situation which even these smug and self-confident men now realized was desperate.

The situation at the front was reasonably clear. The mass of the soldiery was Bolshevik in spirit if not in fact, whereas the military committees, top-heavy with officers and other intellectual forces (ex-teachers, clerks, scribes, physicians, and so on), were dominated by the SR-Menshevik bloc, partly as a result of the blurred political consciousness of the rank and file and partly because in many cases these bodies had not had new elections since the early months of the revolution. Thus army committees might pass resolutions condemning the Bolshevik seizure of power, but it was quite another matter to induce the troops they represented to take up arms against "the ravishers of the people's will." Gotz had been apprised of this situation in mid-October but had brushed the warning aside; [142] he was now to experience its force in full measure.

The most strategically located of the fronts with reference to political developments in the capital was the Northern, and the most strategically located of the three armies comprising this front was the Twelfth, which covered the Livonian and Esthonian approaches to the Russian capital. In the whole enormous organization of this army (numbering some 800,000 men, if the rear be included) there was but one first-class fighting force—the two divisions of Lettish Riflemen, distinguished alike by their fervent Bolshevism and their order and discipline. The proximity of St. Petersburg had intensified political strife in the Twelfth Army, and the tension increased as the

[141] Testimony of Gotz in *Izvestiia*, No. 136 (June 22, 1922); Stankevich, *Vospominaniia*, pp. 272–73.
[142] See my book, *The Agrarian Foes of Bolshevism*, p. 445.

date drew near for its fifth congress, which would decide whether the army's existing executive committee, a typical combination of Menshevik generalship with SR voting strength, would retain its power or be swept aside in the Bolshevik flood. Both sides prepared as though for a general engagement, the Bolsheviks under the leadership of S. M. Nakhimson, and their opponents under the SR Likhach and the Menshevik Kuchin, chairman of the executive committee. Then came the October Revolution, two days before the opening of the congress. The stakes were now higher than ever and the leaders of the governing bloc, not trusting in local talent, decided to bring in from the outside the heaviest gun they could find. The name of V. M. Chernov was still one to conjure with in army circles; the "Zimmerwaldism" which rendered him odious to Russian liberalism endeared him to the Russian soldier, and he was near at hand, in Pskov.

On the first day of the congress, in this dramatic setting, Chernov opened up on the October Revolution in one of the major oratorical flights of his career. In the words of a hostile chronicler, the SR nightingale sang sweetly and listeners drank in the message for four and one-half hours. Under the spell of Chernov's oratory wavering SR's were pulled back into line, Likhach was chosen as presiding officer over Nakhimson, and on the initial ballots the Bolsheviks found themselves thirty or forty votes in the hole. But later, on the crucial test of the army's relation to the October Revolution, their demand for a recorded vote intimidated some of the moderates and the resulting abstentions permitted the Bolshevik resolution to go through by a vote of 248 against 243. By the next day the faint-hearts had recovered their courage and the decision to count them in caused the left bloc [148] to bolt the congress until a compromise was effected: a new congress was called for the middle of November, the executive committee then in office agreed to resign, and a pro-

[148] Chernov claims to have found the left bloc in control at the time of his arrival and to have split it by reforming the ranks of his party (he admits this cost him great difficulty), but the indications are that some of the left SR's, at least, continued to ally themselves with the Bolsheviks. Unfortunately, in this instance, as in so many others, it has not been possible to reconstruct the role of the left SR's, which in the early days of the October Revolution is often of crucial significance. Bolshevik sources give as little credit as possible to their allies; usually they are mentioned only to be damned.

visional committee was chosen on the basis of parity between the extremist and moderate blocs. The Fifth Congress of the Twelfth Army thus ended in a drawn battle, but less because of the announced desire to preserve the unity of the front than because of the arrival in Wenden of two regiments of Lettish Riflemen, which overawed the Menshevik-SR coalition. The Bolsheviks easily secured control at the next congress—the decisive vote was 396 to 123 with 26 abstentions—but they had already achieved their purpose of preventing the Twelfth Army from being used as a reservoir of strength for their enemies.[144]

The SR leaders in the vicinity of Petersburg could have been only imperfectly informed about these developments when they tried to draw on the Twelfth Army in order to build up Kerenski's force. We know that Gotz and Avksentiev entered into negotiations with the outgoing executive committee and that the members of the committee bestirred themselves on behalf of Kerenski, but all that came of their efforts was the movement of certain units as far as the town of Valk, where the news that they were to take part in the "fratricidal civil war" caused the troops to sit down on their haunches and refuse to move another step.[145] The official indictment of SR leaders at the trial in 1922 relates the Wesenberg enterprise of the Central Committee to this period, but press accounts of the testimony on which the indictment is based link it with the later effort to assemble strength in defense of the Constituent Assembly.[146] The Twelfth Army contributed nothing to the SR offensive against Petersburg.

The political situation was even more unfavorable in the other two armies on the Northern Front, for the SR's in the First Army were mainly leftist in point of view and joined hands with the Bolsheviks to impose a ban on assistance to the Provisional Government, while

[144] V. Denisenko, "Piatyi i chrezvychainyi s"ezdy 12-i armii (oktiabr'-noiabr' 1917 g.)" (The Fifth and Extraordinary Congresses of the XIIth Army [October–November, 1917]), *Proletarskaia Revoliutsiia,* XXXV (XII, 1924), 191–207; Chernov, manuscript commentary on the minutes of the Central Committee, pp. 58–59; *Istoriia grazhdanskoi voiny v SSSR,* II, 469–73; *Revoliutsiia 1917 goda,* VI, 45, 147, 152, 159; P. Dauge, "Oktiabr'skaia revoliutsiia v Latvii" (The October Revolution in Latvia), *Istoricheskii Zhurnal,* XI (November, 1940), 36–37.
[145] T. Draudin, "Generaly bez armii: Istor. spravka" (Generals Without an Army: A Historical Inquiry), *Izvestiia,* No. 132 (June 16, 1922).
[146] *Obvinitel'noe zakliuchenie,* p. 57; see below, p. 345.

in the Fifth Army the Bolshevik-dominated committee wanted to send troops to fight against Kerenski.[147] On the front as a whole the SR's encountered the steady obstruction of General Cheremisov, whose animus against Kerenski extended to the whole party of which he was at least nominally a member. This is what Cheremisov thought of the PSR:

The celebrated "Committee to Save the Revolution" belongs to a party which for eight months has governed Russia and has slandered us, the commanding staff, as counterrevolutionaries; now it comes slinking to us like a beaten dog and demands that we save it. While the Bolsheviks are successfully propagandizing the troops, these gentlemen have nothing better to do than to quarrel among themselves and demand help from the commanding staff. It is a disgusting spectacle.[148]

One notes that Cheremisov, in common with many other people, imputes to the SR's a power they did not have or at least had never taken. That was the penalty for assuming responsibility while permitting others to wield the substance of power.

Too much should not be made of the obstruction of one general, however. When Miliukov magnifies this factor in the collapse of Kerenski's campaign,[149] he merely betrays his unwillingness to recognize how great was the gulf between the war policy of his party, communicated with such ease to successive coalitions, and the will of the Russian people. Other commanders did try to execute the orders received from Kerenski but with results which differed in no essential particular from the performance of General Cheremisov. The class consciousness of the rank-and-file railroad workers which led them, often in contradiction to their formal political ties, to impede in every way the dispatch of troops to the Gatchina front was a more weighty factor, but in the last analysis it was the temper of the troops themselves which doomed all efforts to bring up substantial reinforcements.

The SR leaders had long closed their eyes to what was happening at the front. Now they were to experience at first hand the fruits of their stand on war and peace. When Feit and Gerstein, acting on

[147] *Istoriia grazhdanskoi voiny v SSSR*, II, 474-79.
[148] "Oktiabr' na fronte," in *Krasnyi Arkhiv*, XXIV (V, 1927), 78; also quoted in *Istoriia grazhdanskoi voiny v SSSR*, II, 482.
[149] *Istoriia*, I, Part III, 246, 250-51, 257, 261, and esp. 281-82.

instructions from the Central Committee to mobilize units loyal to the Provisional Government and concentrate them in Gatchina, entered into negotiations with a given unit, they generally secured a pledge of support, but when they asked the unit to honor the pledge, they were invariably disappointed.[150] Probably some organ at the top with an SR majority and a Menshevik chairman would make the commitment, only to have the Bolshevik or left SR rank and file throw it down when the moment for action arrived. The result was everywhere the same: either the unit never moved at all or else it quickly succumbed to the general contagion and went to pieces as a fighting force. This was true of the 42nd Infantry Division, to which Gotz repaired in person; [151] it was true of the shock troop batallion at Pskov when Gerstein's emissary arrived to speed its progress; [152] and it was true even of the 17th Corps, a body recently moved up from a remote front where the Bolshevik contagion was at a minimum. Miliukov makes much of the 17th Corps (or a part of it) as having finally beaten its way through to Luga in spite of Cheremisov, the Bolshevik garrison at Pskov, and the railroad workers, but it is apparent from his own account that its will to fight melted like ice in the sun the closer it approached the furnace of revolution.[153]

In order to provide the infantry support without which Krasnov could not sustain the morale of his small Cossack force, the SR leaders should not, of course, have been compelled to look so far afield —there was plenty of infantry in the towns of Gatchina and Tsarskoe Selo. But this infantry had declared its "neutrality" in the "fratricidal civil war," and it was not so much a question of whether it could be brought over to the side of Kerenski as of whether it could be prevented from gravitating in the opposite direction. In fact, it was only with the utmost difficulty that Gotz and others averted a catastrophe at the time of the decisive engagement at Pulkovo by dissuading a section of the Tsarskoe Selo garrison from falling on

[150] Testimony of Feit in *Izvestiia*, No. 130 (June 14, 1922).

[151] Chernov, manuscript commentary on the minutes of the Central Committee, p. 60.

[152] *Ibid.; Obvinitel'noe zakliuchenie*, p. 59.

[153] *Istoriia*, I, Part III, 260–62; *Istoriia grazhdanskoi voiny v SSSR*, II, 318, 372–73. Miliukov's account has special value because it is based on an unpublished manuscript prepared for him by the corps commander, General Schilling.

the Cossack rear. The rude reception accorded him by the soldiery seems finally to have awakened the SR leader to the magnitude of the task before him and to have shaken his confidence in the feasibility of subduing Bolshevism by force of arms.[154] Apart from this incident, however, the stumbling block was not so much hostility as inertness. Not even a handful of men could be recruited from these bulky garrisons to fight on the side of the Cossacks—in the words of Stankevich, the troops would stand and patiently listen to exhortations, persuasions, and calls to duty and would then disperse, not disputing, not agreeing, and not acting.[155]

All attempts to provide Kerenski with a real fighting force, whether made at the front or in the garrisons of the rear, had ended in failure. The party which a few short months before had dominated the soldiers' councils almost without exception could not muster a corporal's guard when its political life was at stake, now that the consequences of its refusal to pursue an active peace policy had finally caught up with it.

On October 30 General Krasnov, spurred on by reports of excesses in the capital in the wake of the cadet uprising, attempted a reconnaissance in force beyond Tsarskoe Selo against an entrenched foe twenty times stronger than himself. This action at Pulkovo ended in a repulse for the Cossacks and impelled them to beat a retreat, evacuating Tsarskoe Selo and falling back to Gatchina in order to avoid envelopment. Once started backwards, there was no stopping. The unsuccessful engagement and the continued absence of infantry reinforcements demoralized the Cossacks and gave free rein to the centrifugal tendencies already at work within their ranks. Their officers attributed the skilled handling of the Baltic sailors at Pulkovo to German intervention [156] and their own sad plight to the presence

---

[154] Semenov, *Voennaia i boevaia rabota PSR*, p. 6.

[155] *Vospominaniia*, p. 276.

[156] Both Miliukov and Kerenski charge that the sailors had German instructors, basing their accusation on the testimony of General Krasnov (*Istoriia*, I, Part III, 254; "Gatchina," in *Izdalëka*, p. 217). Miliukov, in fact, becomes quite specific in asserting that Lieutenant Otto Bauer commanded the red forces and that "disciplined Lettish riflemen" took part in the action. Here Miliukov ceases to be a historian and becomes a Kadet propagandist, eager to depict Bolshevism as a non-Russian phenomenon and prone to look for its mainsprings anywhere except where they actually were—in the soul of a people tortured by war and devoid of a property consciousness.

of A. F. Kerenski, whom they had previously hated as the author of Kornilov's downfall [157] and had now selected as the scapegoat of their ill fortune. The men, on the other hand, began to fraternize with the Bolsheviks in the hope of returning to the quiet Don. As the officers unbridled their reactionary passions, the ordinary Cossacks slid into Bolshevism, leaving the hapless Kerenski with no ground to stand on. By November 1 the situation had deteriorated to the point where Kerenski was in imminent danger of being seized by the Cossacks and handed over to the Kronstadt sailors.

From this fate his party would rescue him. Gotz and Avksentiev had joined Kerenski in signing an order on October 31 to the effect that each army was to send at least one infantry regiment by express train to the environs of St. Petersburg,[158] but fast-moving events compelled the SR leaders on the following day to spirit their comrade, disguised in the clothes of an SR sailor, out of the palace and into a waiting automobile, which bore him off in the direction of Luga. Commissar Semenov organized the flight and commander Keller of the Armored Division furnished the automobile, perhaps unwittingly, as he would later claim that it was used without his knowledge.[159] For a part of the way Kerenski's party was trailed by a Studebaker driven by Staff Captain A. B. Dushkin, who had been tipped off as to the identity of those in the car ahead. When asked at

---

It is significant that Krasnov does not repeat the German canard in the later version of his memoirs ("Na vnutrennem fronte" [On the Home Front], in *Arkhiv Russkoi Revoliutsii*, I, 165–69). The Soviet troops at Pulkovo were commanded by a tsarist colonel, Valden or Walden, of whom Trotski observes that he could never fathom what prompted this old-line officer to place his sword at the disposal of the Bolsheviks. "It couldn't be that he embraced our cause, for he had no understanding of what was transpiring. Apparently his hatred of Kerenski was so intense that it inspired him momentarily with sympathy for our side" ("Vospominaniia ob Oktiabr'skom perevorote" [Reminiscences of the October Revolution], *Proletarskaia Revoliutsiia*, X [1922], 61–62). In other words, there was an affinity between Colonel Walden's reaction and that of General Cheremisov. Still other officers simply went along with their men, not wishing to be separated from them and accepting their Bolshevism as something against which it was useless to struggle. See Trotski, *Oktiabr'skaia revoliutsiia*, pp. 86–87.

[157] Krasnov says all of his officers were Kornilovists. See "Na vnutrennem fronte," in *Arkhiv Russkoi Revoliutsii*, I, 163; Miliukov, *Istoriia*, I, Part III, 251 (Miliukov's study is based on the original, less embellished, and more authentic version of Krasnov's memoirs).

[158] "Oktiabr' na fronte," in *Krasnyi Arkhiv*, XXIV (V, 1927), 82.

[159] *Izvestiia*, No. 131 (June 15, 1922).

his trial why he did this, Dushkin replied that he wanted to see the expression on the face of the absconding minister-president. But the muzzle of a rifle thrust out of the rear of Kerenski's car whenever he approached too close discouraged excessive intimacy on the part of the monarchist captain.[160] Kerenski made good his escape and dropped out of sight. For once an SR enterprise had not miscarried. For the party a major disaster had closed with a humble success.[161]

With Kerenski's disappearance on the road to Luga the Provisional Government had passed into history. Henceforth there could be no thought of its restoration but only of establishing a new center of power to dispute the rapidly expanding authority of the Council of People's Commissars. Before discussing the efforts of the SR leaders along this line, however, it is necessary to examine briefly the course of events in the second city of the empire, for not until the October Revolution had triumphed in Moscow could the Bolsheviks feel themselves masters of the situation.

Developments in Moscow did not conform to the same pattern as in St. Petersburg. The outcome was the same in both cities, and in both the SR's headed the political opposition, but there the similarity ends. Bolshevism had attained power in the capital with relative ease, and if the cadet uprising of October 29 has claimed a large share of our attention, it is not because of its scale or consequences but because it so clearly demonstrates the weakness of the Socialist Revolutionary Party and the bankruptcy of its Central Committee. Quite different was the story in Moscow. The ancient capital was the scene of a prolonged and bloody struggle which may have claimed as many as five thousand victims, according to Bukharin's estimate. Bolshevism

[160] *Delo Naroda,* No. 244 (December 30, 1917) (report of proceedings before the Revolutionary Tribunal); "Iz zapisnoi knizhki arkhivista: Zagovor monarkhicheskoi organizatsii V. M. Purishkevicha," in *Krasnyi Arkhiv,* XXVI (I, 1928), 180.

[161] On the flight see Semenov, "Vospominaniia byvshego esera," *Prozhektor,* No. 9 (June 17, 1923), pp. 29–31; V. A. Weiger-Redemeister, "S Kerenskim v Gatchine" (with Kerenski at Gatchina), *Proletarskaia Revoliutsiia,* XXI (IX, 1923), 92–94; "Vokrug 'Gatchiny,'" in *Krasnyi Arkhiv,* IX (II, 1925), 173–77; Miliukov, *Istoriia,* I, Part III, 271–77; Kerenski, "Gatchina," in *Izdalëka,* pp. 222–25 (Kerenski tells very little); Vladimirova, *God sluzhby "sotsialistov" kapitalistam,* p. 37; Trotski, *Oktiabr'skaia revoliutsiia,* pp. 90–91 (text of Krasnov's original report); Krasnov, "Na vnutrennem fronte," in *Arkhiv Russkoi Revoliutsii,* I, 173–74 (this later version must be rejected).

had great strength in Moscow, as great as in St. Petersburg, but the city committee did not have the districts well in hand and the leadership displayed little of the skill and singleness of purpose which Lenin and Trotski had imparted to the Petersburg organization. As a result matters tended to take their course instead of conforming to plan, particularly in the first stage of the insurrection.

The character of the local SR organization likewise influenced the course of events. Extremism in Moscow took the form of Bolshevism and did not express itself in left-wing Social Revolutionism. There were, of course, left SR's in Moscow, as in virtually every other locality, but they carried little weight in an organization whose center of gravity lay as far to the right as it did to the left in St. Petersburg. Hence the greater cohesion of the Moscow SR's and their more determined resistance to the Bolshevik seizure of power, even though in point of numbers or of popular following they could not compare with the large but hopelessly riven Petersburg organization.

The tone in Moscow party circles was set by men like V. V. Rudnev, whom the sweeping electoral victory of June had lifted into the mayor's chair. Rudnev was an honest and forthright man, with firm convictions that could readily be translated into resolute actions. In 1905 he had fought on the barricades; but by the outbreak of revolution in 1917 he had moved so far to the right, particularly under the influence of the war (which had awakened in him the nationalism latent in so many revolutionists of the Populist vein), that if the ties of sentiment binding him to the PSR had been less strong or if the Constitutional Democratic Party had been less exclusive and more popular in character, he might perhaps have renounced a social-ist coloration and openly embraced the liberal faith from which little or nothing separated him save the memory of the past. When he became mayor, Rudnev ceased to attend the sessions of the local SR committee, feeling that his office required him to set an example of nonpartisanship,[162] but since men of the same stamp dominated the committee, no friction arose. Nowhere in Russia was the party leadership more firmly committed to the principle of collaboration with the Kadets at home and the Allies abroad; nowhere in Russia,

---

[162] Interview in Paris (September, 1935). Another reason was the pressure of business.

therefore, would it offer more strenuous resistance to the Bolshevik assumption of power.

On the eve of the October Revolution the substance of power was divided locally between the two chief protagonists. The city government was in the hands of the Socialist Revolutionaries as the result of their triumph in the June election of an all-city council,[163] but the reversal of this trend a few months later had placed the majority of district or ward councils in the hands of the Bolsheviks.[164] The Soviet of Workers' Deputies was now a stronghold of Bolshevism, as in most other industrial centers, but the Soviet of Soldiers' Deputies, whose identity the SR's had maintained to offset their loss of influence among the workers, still eluded Bolshevik control. From a low of seven deputies out of a total of 400 in the original soldiers' soviet,[165] however, the Bolsheviks had steadily increased their strength until on September 5 they had managed to put through a resolution which entailed the resignation of the Executive Committee. In the new committee they secured 16 seats against 26 for the SR's, 9 for the Mensheviks, and 9 for those without party, so that control remained in moderate hands. Yet within a few days 90 percent of the soldiers of the garrison who voted would cast their ballots for the Bolshevik candidates in the election of the city district councils, thereby demonstrating that the SR's owed their dominant position in the Executive Committee solely to the fact that it had been chosen by the soldiers' delegates in the soviet instead of directly by the soldiers themselves. This discrepancy prompted the Bolsheviks to inaugurate a vigorous campaign for the reelection of company and regimental committees, and by the latter half of October most of these lower organs had come under their sway. In both the municipal and soviet sectors, therefore, the superstructure of power in SR hands had been undermined by Bolshevik gains at the base until the advantage of those who would lead the resistance to the October Revolution had become more apparent than real.[166]

[163] See my book, *The Agrarian Foes of Bolshevism*, pp. 240–42.

[164] *Ibid.*, pp. 432–35.

[165] O. Varentsova, "Oktiabr'skie dni v Moskve" (October Days in Moscow), *Istoricheskii Zhurnal*, X (October, 1937), 69.

[166] On the soldiers' soviet see especially *Istoriia grazhdanskoi voiny v SSSR*, II, 62, 65–67.

When the news of the overthrow of the Provisional Government reached Moscow, neither the Bolsheviks nor their opponents were ready to fight and, if the truth be told, neither wanted to fight. The apparatus of civil war had first to be created, and spirits raised to a fighting pitch. The mobilization of forces took place around the rival centers of authority, the soviet and the city council, the soviet setting up a Military Revolutionary Committee as in Petersburg and the council serving as a base for the Committee of Public Security. The Socialist Revolutionaries boycotted the soviet organ and threw their energies behind the rival body, but a minority broke away, either to collaborate as individuals with the Bolsheviks in the Military Revolutionary Committee or, as a group, to take up an intermediate position for joint action with the Mensheviks in an attempt to reconcile the differences between the opposing camps.[167] But the SR schism did not knock the bottom out of the organization as in Petersburg, nor did the rightist majority in Moscow share the doubts and hesitancy which paralyzed the left-centrist residue in Petersburg.

Hence when Mayor Rudnev determined to resist the October Revolution, even at the cost of civil war, he had his party solidly behind him. To such an extreme had he carried his aversion to partisan action that the decision was made without consulting the Moscow committee, and only on the day after did he notify it of the stand he had taken.[168] Yet the committee offered no objection, even though, in approving the mayor's initiative, it had entered a path on which there was no turning back short of violence and bloodshed. As the spokesman of the committee told the Ninth City Conference, which had assembled to sit in judgment upon its actions, "we render this accounting with a quiet conscience, for we had no other course than to defend with arms in hand the rights of the people." The rightist inclination of the Moscow organization is clearly seen in the vote of confidence it gave the committee on this occasion (55 in favor and 1 against, with 11 abstentions),[169] as also in the fact that the SR dele-

---

[167] *Protokoly pervago s"ezda PLSR*, p. 9; *Oktiabr'skoe vosstanie v Moskve*, pp. 8, 11–12, 20.

[168] Interview in Paris (1935).

[169] *Partiinyia Izvestiia*, No. 5 (January 20, 1918), pp. 53–55. The conference was held on November 23.

gation in the city council never wavered in support of the mayor's stand.

The Committee of Public Security was formed in the mayor's office, in accordance with the SR wish for institutional rather than partisan representation. Among the public bodies included were soviet organs under SR or Menshevik domination, particularly the Soldiers' Executive Committee referred to above and the Peasants' Executive Committee for Moscow province. Though formed to defend the existing order against subversion on the eve of the supreme manifestation of the will of the Russian people in the election of the Constituent Assembly, the Committee of Public Security refused to be associated in any way with the Provisional Government, lest the unpopularity of that regime become a millstone about its neck. And when S. N. Prokopovich, the only minister to escape arrest, arrived in Moscow with the proposal to co-opt the members of the committee into the government as a surrogate for the imprisoned ministry, he met with a reception that was "more than restrained." Paradoxically, the Committee of Public Security felt obliged to hold at arm's length the emissaries of an authority which, in effect, it was striving to restore, at least in the first stage of the conflict in Moscow. The committee did not presume to take over the direction of military operations, which it left in the hands of the garrison commander, Colonel K. I. Riabtsev, a man who has often been accused of weakness simply because in his uncertainties and hesitations he so faithfully reflected the state of the public mind. Beyond the basic decision not to give in to the Bolsheviks, the committee imposed no restrictions upon Riabtsev either in negotiating with them for a peaceful settlement or in serving them with an ultimatum when he determined the time had come for action. It cannot be said that the SR's in Moscow were spoiling for civil war, though they did not shrink from it when it came.[170]

Despite the greater cohesiveness and more resolute spirit of their Moscow organization, the SR's made scarcely a better showing than

[170] Interview with Rudnev (1935); Voznesenski, *Moskva v 1917 godu*, pp. 158–59; Miliukov, *Istoriia*, I, Part III, 288–89, 292–93, 295–97; *Istoriia grazhdanskoi voiny v SSSR*, II, 389, 395–96; *Samoupravlenie*, No. 14–15 (November 5, 1917), pp. 35–36.

in St. Petersburg when it came to mobilizing popular forces against the October Revolution. The appeal of the Moscow committee to all party members to come out and defend the city council with arms in hand met with a feeble response, and the effort to organize volunteer groups under the party banner ended in fiasco when not more than thirty or forty men appeared on the scene.[171] The workers and soldiers had deserted the PSR, either to fight on the other side of the barricades or to occupy a neutral position as the battle unfolded. "I know," said one member of the party on a later occasion, "that not a single military unit supported the city council though some organ continued to speak in the soldiers' name" [172]—a reference to the Executive Committee of the Soldiers' Soviet. "In Moscow," Bukharin told the All-Russian Central Executive Committee, "not one regiment, not one company of soldiers, not one detachment of workers was to be found on the side of the counterrevolution." [173] The loss of its proletarian and military following had reduced the party in Moscow to an organization of intellectuals and radical-democratic elements that were not minded to fight in the streets, aside from an undetermined number of students who joined their classmates of other persuasions in a volunteer movement said to have been initiated by Constitutional Democrats.[174] The attempt of the SR's to fashion a dependable fighting force of their own, without which they could not banish the specter of counterrevolution in the event of victory, had failed as lamentably in the ancient capital as on the banks of the Neva.

They were, therefore, thrown back upon elements with which they had little or nothing in common save an aversion to Bolshevism. The officer-training schools,[175] here as elsewhere, constituted the backbone of the forces resisting the October Revolution, but in Moscow these institutions represented an element of exceptional strength, not only because of their number but also because they were better in

---

[171] Testimony of Gregory Ratner in *Izvestiia*, No. 136 (June 22, 1922).
[172] *Ibid.*
[173] Quoted in Vladimirova, *God sluzhby "sotsialistov" kapitalistam*, p. 62.
[174] *Istoriia grazhdanskoi voiny v SSSR*, II, 403; Miliukov, *Istoriia*, I, Part III, 303, where the total number of students volunteering is set at 600.
[175] Two schools of cadets ("junkers") and six of ensigns (*praporshchiki*) from the front were of significance. The Alexandrov Military School was headquarters for the counterrevolution.

hand and moved as a unit in response to orders transmitted by the military command under the authority of the Committee of Public Security. In addition to the youthful officers-to-be, one section of the right wing of the officers' corps was activist-minded and disposed to strike at Bolshevism without waiting for it to run its course after ousting the Provisional Government. The mood of these officers placed a sharp sword in the hands of the committee, but the edge of the weapon was dulled by the apprehension of the SR's and of democratic groups in general about what these officers might do in the event of victory.[176] The other section of traditionally minded officers preferred to stand aside and let Lenin's wrecking crew do its work in the expectation that it would thereby be paving the road to reaction,[177] while the rest of the officers' corps was either inert in a political sense or simply conformed to the temper of the troops, whether these elected to stay on the sidelines or throw in their lot with the Bolsheviks. The statement Rudnev made to this writer that the officers in Moscow responded poorly to the call of the city administration, and that many of them held off or even preferred to see the Bolsheviks win,[178] must be balanced against the assertion of the spokesman for the Military Revolutionary Committee that only a small number of officers rallied to the side of the Bolsheviks,[179] leaving one to conclude that a great many of the 15,000 officers present in Moscow [180] must have held aloof from the fray.

According to Rudnev, the greatest disappointment of all was not the default of the officers but the passivity of the population. The election of the Constituent Assembly a few weeks later would reveal that half the citizens of Moscow supported the October Revolution and half opposed it. But the quarter of a million voters who stood behind the Constitutional Democrats and the hundred thousand others who still adhered to the PSR or backed some intermediate group [181] were nowhere in evidence during the street fighting which was going to deprive this national referendum of any practical signifi-

[176] Miliukov, *Istoriia*, I, Part III, 294–95.
[177] Testimony of Eugenia Ratner, *Izvestiia*, No. 137 (June 23, 1922).
[178] Interview in Paris (1935).   [179] *Oktiabr'skoe vosstanie v Moskve*, p. 19.
[180] See *Istoriia grazhdanskoi voiny v SSSR*, II, 63.
[181] See the author's study, *The Election to the Russian Constituent Assembly*, pp. 34–35.

cance. The mass of civilians opposed to Bolshevism left the burden of armed resistance to their representatives in the officers' corps or their children in the military schools. They themselves did virtually no fighting, aside from some individuals and small groups of the home guard who sniped at the Soviet forces from buildings and private residences and slowed down their advance, but otherwise exerted no influence on the course of the struggle.[182] Even this small bit of participation on the part of the citizenry, which apparently regarded military action as strictly a professional matter, had been lacking in St. Petersburg. The civilian arm of the law, the police, made no better showing than the civilians themselves. Either they occupied a position of neutrality, or they were easily overborne by the Red Guard [183] —a deficiency that must be attributed to the SR municipal adminis-tration, which had been in power for several months and ought to have been able in that time to assemble at least the nucleus of a dependable police force.

The Bolsheviks drew more support from the half of the population which sided with them, some thousands of Red Guardsmen taking part in the hostilities, but it was more the green proletarian youth than the average workingman who answered the call and fought with fanaticism and cruelty.[184] To offset the elite guard of officers and cadets the Bolsheviks had with them virtually the entire garrison, though much of this sympathy was passive rather than active and, even if active, was often less than wholehearted. Besides their numeri-cal superiority the Bolsheviks had one special advantage which told heavily in their favor—they alone had artillery. It was a feature of the October Revolution that this arm of the service was generally controlled by the Bolsheviks, and its effect on the street fighting in Russian cities proved decisive. By the fourth year of the war the artillery personnel of the old army had been watered down by re-cruits from the working class, who possessed the mechanical skill needed for the upkeep and use of the guns but shared the suscepti-

---

[182] Voznesenski, *Moskva v 1917 godu*, p. 146; *Istoriia grazhdanskoi voiny v SSSR*, II, 64, 446; Vladimirova, *God sluzhby "sotsialistov" kapitalistam*, p. 60; Miliukov, *Istoriia*, I, Part III, 302.

[183] Miliukov, *Istoriia*, I, Part III, 303n; *Istoriia grazhdanskoi voiny v SSSR*, II, 394.

[184] Miliukov, *Istoriia*, I, Part III, 303–4.

bility of their comrades in factories and plants for the message of Lenin's party. In Moscow, on the day the fighting began (October 27), the Military Revolutionary Committee secured its grip on the First Reserve Artillery Brigade, located on the Khodynka Field, by having all the soldiers' committees reelected and a replica of itself installed in office.[185] This was a signal triumph, one which permitted Bukharin later to boast that the Bolsheviks had had everything in Moscow, even eleven-inch cannon and airplanes.[186] They also possessed the inestimable advantage of being able to draw on the garrisons and proletarian centers of the whole industrial region around Moscow as a reservoir from which to build up their strength and widen the already great disparity of forces in their favor.[187] The five to ten thousand effectives of the Committee of Public Security with an abundance of machine guns and a high level of consciousness confronted forty to fifty thousand troops of the Military Revolutionary Committee with both light and heavy artillery and a reservoir of strength at their backs.[188]

Perhaps under these circumstances Mayor Rudnev and his colleagues in the city government would not have thrown down the gage of battle had their resolution not been strengthened by assurances of support from General Baluev, commander in chief of the Western Front.[189] They had permitted Colonel Riabtsev to spend the 26th and 27th of October in negotiations with the Bolsheviks but had decided to authorize the use of force if no agreement could be reached securing their position against usurpation.[190] Accordingly, when the commandant of the garrison sent an ultimatum on the evening of the 27th, demanding the evacuation of the Kremlin, the dissolution of the Military Revolutionary Committee, and notifica-

[185] *Istoriia grazhdanskoi voiny v SSSR*, II, 67, 401–2.

[186] Vladimirova, *God sluzhby "sotsialistov" kapitalistam*, p. 62.

[187] On conditions in the Moscow or central industrial region see especially *Istoriia grazhdanskoi voiny v SSSR*, II, 73–79.

[188] For varying estimates of the strength on both sides see Voznesenski, *Moskva v 1917 godu*, p. 170; Miliukov, *Istoriia*, I, Part III, 302–3.

[189] Interview with Rudnev (1935); Voznesenski, *Moskva v 1917 godu*, pp. 165–66; *Istoriia grazhdanskoi voiny v SSSR*, II, 404–5. The assurance was confirmed by General Dukhonin, chief of staff of the supreme commander (Kerenski) and actual head of the entire army.

[190] *Istoriia grazhdanskoi voiny v SSSR*, II, 396, 410–12; Voznesenski, *Moskva v 1917 godu*, p. 161.

tion of acceptance within the next quarter of an hour, he acted with the authority vested in him by the Committee of Public Security. Just as the committee backed up the military commander, so did the party stand behind the committee—one of its leaders affirmed at the trial of 1922 that the PSR had sanctioned the ultimatum, but reminded the court that it had been sent only after the Bolsheviks had seized the arsenal and in general had set themselves up in place of the duly constituted authorities.[191]

The fat was now in the fire, for the Military Revolutionary Committee, though still disposed to temporize, could not think of accepting such terms. Heavy fighting broke out and raged for two days. The seizure of the Kremlin on the 28th by the troops of the Committee of Public Security established the pattern of struggle: the center of the city in the hands of the counterrevolution girdled by a ring of fire from the industrial suburbs. Efforts to break into the outlying districts ended in failure; the Bolsheviks were too strong, the proletariat too solidly behind them. Rudnev attempted to ease the constrictive pressure of the industrial provinces adjacent to Moscow by stirring up local governments everywhere to resist the encroachments of the soviets and engage them in battle.[192] The Executive Committee of the Moscow Soldiers' Soviet, controlled by the SR's, attempted to win over the troops by contrasting its own authority as a bona fide soviet institution with the narrowly partisan complexion of the Military Revolutionary Committee, but the Bolsheviks countered this maneuver by proclaiming the dissolution of the Executive Committee and organizing a rival organ on the basis of the newly reelected company committees.[193] It was not this countermeasure, however, but deeper-lying factors such as the pro-war leadership of the PSR and the peace declaration of the Soviet government which bound the soldiers so firmly to the chariot of the Bolshevik Party. To offset the authority of the city council, upon which the Committee of Public Security rested, the Bolsheviks set up an interdistrict council of representatives from the municipal bodies (ward or district councils) chosen in September, claiming that

---

[191] Testimony of Eugenia Ratner, *Izvestiia*, No. 137 (June 23, 1922).

[192] *Istoriia grazhdanskoi voiny v SSSR*, II, 420.

[193] *Ibid.*, pp. 397–98, 422; *Oktiabr'skoe vosstanie v Moskve*, pp. 19, 218; Voznesenski, *Moskva v 1917 godu*, p. 177.

since this creation of theirs was based on a fresher mandate from the people, it should supersede the central council elected in June.[194]

Things were at a deadlock on the night of October 29 when a truce of twenty-four hours was agreed upon as a result of the mediative efforts of the Mensheviks and Left SR's powerfully reinforced by the intervention of Vikzhel (All-Russian Executive Committee of Railway Employees), which threatened to halt all movements by rail unless the fighting were stopped. Each side assented to the truce in anticipation of reinforcements [195] which would decide the issue in its favor. The Bolshevik calculation proved to be correct; that of the Committee of Public Security did not. From the garrisons and industrial towns of the central region came a steady stream of Soviet partisans. The Socialist Revolutionaries of Tula, one of the few industrial centers where the wave of Bolshevism had not yet engulfed the working class, succeeded in blocking a movement of troops from the Orel garrison,[196] but elsewhere they possessed little influence and could do nothing to halt the dispatch of partisans from the Bolshevik stronghold in Vladimir province, two thousand of whom under the command of M. V. Frunze saw action in the later stages of the Moscow conflict.[197] Substantial, also, was the contribution of St. Petersburg: 500 sailors from there detrained on the evening of October 30, a detachment of workers came the next day, and on November 1, 2,000 Red Guardsmen and sailors, flushed with success over the cadets and Kerenski, arrived in the ancient capital.[198] With sure instinct Lenin had recognized the implications of defeat or victory in the struggle at Moscow. The flow of reinforcements continued after the denunciation of the truce, despite the decision of the Moscow branch of Vikzhel to support the Com-

---

[194] *Istoriia grazhdanskoi voiny v SSSR*, II, 388, 406–8.

[195] Interview with Rudnev (1935).

[196] "Po Rossii" (Around Russia), *Delo Naroda*, No. 211 (November 16, 1917).

[197] See D. Baevski's review of M. I. Zelenski, *M. V. Frunze v Ivanovo-Voznesenskom raione v 1917 godu* (M. V. Frunze in the Ivanovo-Voznesensk Area in 1917), in *Voprosy Istorii*, II (February, 1948), 128; P. Ekzempliarski, "Ivanovo-Voznesensk v period podgotovki i provedeniia Oktiabr'skoi sotsialisticheskoi revoliutsii" (Ivanovo-Voznesensk at the Time of the Preparation and Carrying Out of the October Socialist Revolution), *Istoricheskii Zhurnal*, X (October, 1937), 129; *Oktiabr'skoe vosstanie v Moskve*, p. 33; *Istoriia grazhdanskoi voiny v SSSR*, II, 454, 457.

[198] *Istoriia grazhdanskoi voiny v SSSR*, II, 444, 457.

mittee of Public Security, because the lower ranks of the railway-men's organization refused to impede the transportation of Bolshevik units.[199]

To the swelling hosts of the enemy the Committee of Public Security could oppose but one modest accretion of strength: 176 members of a "battalion of death" from the front.[200] It was not the fault of Generals Baluev and Dukhonin that they could not make good on their assurances of support. They did what they could, but their dispositions were either countermanded by Kerenski in his desperate search for assistance, or were not fulfilled because of the temper of the troops, or were set at naught by the intervention of Bolshevik garrisons in towns through which the trains had to pass (Orsha, Smolensk, Viazma).[201] In one notable instance the SR's made matters worse instead of improving them: their representatives in the Committee for the Western Front at Minsk agreed to halt the transit of troops as long as hostilities continued in the metropolitan centers, in return for a Bolshevik commitment not to press for recognition of the Soviet order, either locally or nationally. Yet within a few days the partisans of the new regime gained the upper hand at the front while the opportunity to send aid to Moscow had vanished forever. Thus in effect the SR's in Minsk bound the hands of General Baluev while their comrades in Moscow were losing the fight.[202]

The truce agreed upon worked to the advantage of no one except the Bolsheviks, who were in the stronger position to begin with. The Mensheviks and Left SR's, borrowing a leaf from the book of Chernov, attempted to build up a "third force" which would supplant both the Military Revolutionary Committee and the Committee of Public Security with a new center of authority in which the balance of power would belong to these intermediate groups.[203]

[199] *Ibid.*, pp. 431, 448; Vladimirova, *God sluzhby "sotsialistov" kapitalistam,* pp. 59–61.
[200] *Istoriia grazhdanskoi voiny v SSSR,* II, 439.
[201] *Ibid.,* pp. 432, 435–36, 448, 500–5.
[202] Interview with Rudnev (1935); *Istoriia grazhdanskoi voiny v SSSR,* II, 496–500. It is doubtful, however, that even if the SR's in the army committee had pursued a different policy they could have influenced the course of events in Moscow because of the situation at intervening points.
[203] *Istoriia grazhdanskoi voiny v SSSR,* II, 441–42, 454; Miliukov, *Istoriia,* I, Part III, 298.

Vikzhel exerted such effective pressure upon the Committee of Public Security that the Moscow SR's, notorious for the tenacity with which they had clung to the principle of coalition, capitulated and agreed to a purely socialist government without in any way being convinced in their hearts that it was a desirable expedient. Having made this concession, they insisted on the dissolution of the Military Revolutionary Committee and on the evacuation of its troops from the positions occupied.[204] But neither the efforts of the in-between groups nor the agreement to exclude the class enemy from the government could save the situation now. The Bolsheviks in the Military Revolutionary Committee, feeling solid ground beneath their feet and encouraged alike by the stream of reinforcements and the victorious trend of events in the capital, reverted to the original demand of all power to the soviets and denounced the expiring truce. On the evening of October 30, in a setting of stillness and gloom, Rudnev announced to the council that a resumption of hostilities was inevitable because of the bad faith and intransigence of the Bolsheviks.

From October 30 to November 3 the streets and public squares of Moscow were the scene of stubborn and protracted fighting such as has often marked the course of Russian history, whether the people face a foreign invader or turn upon one another. The renewal of action caught the anti-Bolshevik forces at a serious disadvantage: they had plenty of officers but not enough foot soldiers, plenty of machine guns but nothing in the way of artillery, and there had been no reinforcements to speak of. Now strictly on the defensive, they were reduced to the extremity of using officers to fill in the ranks as privates.[205] Yet barricades and buildings were held with a tenacity matched only by the grim persistence of the Bolsheviks in pressing the defenders back upon the Alexandrov Military School and the city hall, and finally upon the Kremlin alone. The one-sided arrival of reinforcements and the inability to reply to the artillery fire of the Reds, which was becoming steadily more intense and "German"

[204] Miliukov, *Istoriia*, I, Part III, 298–301; see also speech of Rudnev on November 15 in "Moskovskaia Gorodskaia Duma posle Oktiabria" (The Moscow City Duma after October), in *Krasnyi Arkhiv*, XXVIII (III, 1928), 71–73.

[205] See report on the situation at the telephone station in *Oktiabr'skoe vosstanie v Moskve*, p. 241.

(that is, accurate), depressed the spirit of the defenders and snapped their overwrought nerves.[206] Recriminations broke out in the camp of the besieged, the scorpion-stinging-itself-to-death psychology began to manifest itself on the weaker side, and Rudnev concluded that the time had come to discontinue armed resistance and fall back upon political action in the hope that the masses would outlive their infatuation for Bolshevism when they saw that its level of performance did not measure up to its promise. He therefore sent a letter to the Military Revolutionary Committee, asking for an end to hostilities.[207] The terms he received were more magnanimous than either the nature of Bolshevism or the character of the fighting would have suggested. The vanquished were spared the humiliation of having to recognize the Soviet regime and the disarmed combatants were set free, many of them to make their way to the Don, where the elements of the White or Volunteer Army were slowly assembling. The Committee of Public Security, of course, was dissolved. All of the socialist parties had a hand in drafting the terms of pacification, which were more a matter of negotiation than of dictation.[208]

The fighting in Moscow during the October Revolution was more sustained and larger-scale than elsewhere in the country. Circumstances had placed the Socialist Revolutionaries at the head of the resistance movement because the city administration was in their hands, but the armed forces which fought under their nominal leadership did not represent the party and it is an open question whether, in the event of victory, the SR's could have stayed in the saddle. An unusual concentration of professional fighting men had created a formidable spearhead with which to pierce the enemy's armor, but the SR's had not commanded enough of a popular following to provide a shaft for the spearhead. Once again, they had been obliged to rely on an alien force without the means of building it up to the

[206] On the effect of artillery fire see especially *Istoriia grazhdanskoi voiny v SSSR*, II, 445, 454–55; Miliukov, *Istoriia*, I, Part III, 305.

[207] In this as in other matters, Rudnev acted with the consent of the military authorities. See Miliukov, *Istoriia*, I, Part III, 305–6 and *passim*.

[208] *Ibid.*, p. 306; *Istoriia grazhdanskoi voiny v SSSR*, II, 454–62; Vladimirova, *God sluzhby "sotsialistov" kapitalistam*, pp. 60–63; *Delo Naroda*, No. 199 (November 4, 1917); see also statement of Rudnev before the Petersburg city council in *Delo Naroda*, No. 204 (November 9, 1917); text of agreement in *Oktiabr'skoe vosstanie v Moskve*, pp. 236–37.

requisite proportions or of controlling it in case of victory. In this respect the events in Moscow differed in no essential particular from those in St. Petersburg. If they confirmed the debility of the PSR they also, and in still greater measure, attested the strength of its rival, for the Bolsheviks had now demonstrated that there was nothing isolated or accidental about their triumph in the capital. They had given up the heart of Moscow to a skilled professional force numbering in the thousands and yet had won through in the end. Especially disheartening to the opposition was the fact that Bolshevism had established itself as an all-Russian phenomenon, by no means restricted to the metropolitan centers, and with sufficient strength in the provinces to redress the balance in the city.[209] Even more than the ease with which the cadet uprising had been smothered in St. Petersburg, it was the hard and bloody fighting in Moscow which finally destroyed the illusion of Bolshevik weakness in SR minds.

[209] In his conversation with this author, the former mayor stressed the initially defensive attitude of his side as a fateful handicap in the struggle; yet there is no assurance that a sudden onslaught while the Bolsheviks were gathering their forces would have led to anything more than a slightly enlarged island in a hostile sea. The SR's themselves were troubled by this consideration. In the words of Eugenia Ratner, "We understood that by the strategic occupation of Moscow alone we would not be able to free all of Russia from the Bolshevik contagion." See her testimony at the SR trial in *Izvestiia*, No. 137 (June 23, 1922).

II

The October Revolution:
The Search for an Alternative

By the first days of November the Socialist Revolutionary Party had sustained three shattering defeats in the centers of authority, its already modest influence at the front was ebbing fast, and workers' soviets all over the country were seizing power with the assistance of local garrisons. The combination of workers imbued with Leninist doctrine and of soldiers tired of war was everywhere stripping the PSR of the power and influence it had enjoyed in the early months of the revolution. It was now apparent that the party would not succeed in overcoming Bolshevism by force of arms, particularly so long as it left the impression that it meant to restore the Provisional Government or at least offered nothing concrete to take its place. There remained the possibility that, in conjunction with other social-ist groups, the PSR could oppose to the Council of People's Com-missars (Sovnarkom) a new government free of the bourgeois taint and perhaps enable it to repossess the central authority, especially if the election of the Constituent Assembly turned out in its favor. A less desirable but more feasible alternative would be to force the Bolsheviks to share their authority with the moderate socialist parties, for the slogan of a "homogeneous socialist government from the Bolsheviks to the Popular Socialists" enjoyed great popularity among workers and soldiers whose class consciousness or aversion to war impelled them to throw in their lot with the Bolsheviks without by any means agreeing that this party should exercise a monopoly of political power. In fact, "broad masses" of workers and soldiers who had drifted away from the moderate socialists but were not yet owned body and soul by the extremists regarded Lenin's council of commissars as simply a stopgap, bridging the interval between the overthrow of Kerenski's regime and the formation of an all-inclusive socialist ministry. With the left-wing Socialist Revolutionaries this was not merely an attitude but a conscious policy. The question of power was an open one for some days after the October Revolution. How did the SR party stand on the issue of restoring the Provisional Government, and what role did it play in the efforts, first of Vikzhel in St. Petersburg and then of the General Army Committee in Mogilev, to set up a new government free of both bourgeois and Bolshevik domination?

Contrary to what might be expected, the SR leadership studiously avoided a commitment to bring back the fallen regime. Only the small Argunov circle championed this course.[1] As we noted earlier, the Central Committee in a public statement on October 26 and again on October 27 pronounced in favor of a "new government exclusively of the revolutionary democracy" which would be pledged to the immediate transfer of the land to the land committees and the immediate proposal of a *general* democratic peace to *all* of the warring powers.[2] When Stankevich moved that the Committee to Save the Fatherland and Revolution conduct its struggle in the name of the deposed regime, no one supported him; all declared that in view of the government's unpopularity it would be better to say nothing at all about it.[3] Similarly in Moscow, the Committee of Public Security kept the emissaries of the government at arm's length and accepted the principle of a purely socialist government at the dictation of the railwaymen's union. It is also worthy of note to recall that when Gotz addressed the turbulent garrison at Tsarskoe Selo he made no effort to defend the Provisional Government; he admitted its mistakes and declared that he himself was not an adherent of Kerenski's policy.[4]

The October Revolution, therefore, had freed the PSR from the spell of coalition and brought it to acceptance of a purely socialist ministry. All this had happened overnight, as though the step the

[1] "Pravitel'stvo Kerenskago ne svergnuto" (The Kerenski Government Has Not Been Overturned), *Volia Naroda*, No. 160 (November 1, 1917); see also the appeal in *ibid.*, No. 159 (October 31, 1917), and several other numbers.

[2] Text of statements in *Delo Naroda*, No. 191 (October 28, 1917). Italics are mine.

[3] *Vospominaniia*, p. 272.

[4] Semenov, "Vospominaniia byvshego esera," *Prozhektor*, No. 8 (May 31, 1923), p. 28.

party had so long refused to take was now the most natural thing in the world. "We are witnessing a unique spectacle," remarked a Social Democrat of the left, "when SR's and Mensheviks begin to talk of an all-socialist ministry, for this is something about which they did not even think three or four days ago." [5] Unique, also, was the way in which such a ministry should come into being, according to the SR's and their allies: "Adhering to the principle of continuity of power, we propose that Kerenski shall enter Petrograd as a victor and restore the former government, after which it will be possible to form a socialist ministry, but without the Bolsheviks." These were the words of representatives of the Committee to Save the Fatherland at a session of the railwaymen's executive committee (Vikzhel) on October 28.[6] An even more authoritative indication of the course the party intended to pursue is found in its official organ, which acknowledged the need of replacing a government so weak that it could be brushed aside by a "soap bubble," yet demanded a thoroughly legitimist approach to the problem: "As soon as the self-styled dictatorship of the proletariat is liquidated and the government appears before the Council of the Republic, the question of confidence in the bankrupt coalition and of forming a purely democratic regime should be posed as the first order of business." [7]

The proposed course of action, put forward on the very day of the cadets' insurrection, is very typical of Social Revolutionism. A party with enough strength to seize the government was to have its venture "definitively liquidated"—the language is the Central Committee's [8] —by a party with no strength at all, and after Kerenski had been restored to power he was to be asked to stand aside in favor of an exclusively socialist regime which would bar the most vigorous socialist party in the country. But what if Kerenski refused to stand

[5] Vompe, *Dni oktiabr'skoi revoliutsii i zheleznodorozhniki*, p. 30. On the other side of the fence, the right-wing SR organ pointed out that only a week beforehand the majority of the revolutionary democracy had considered such a course "dangerous and harmful." See "Pravitel'stvo Kerenskago ne svergnuto," *Volia Naroda*, No. 160 (November 1, 1917).

[6] Vompe, *Dni oktiabr'skoi revoliutsii i zheleznodorozhniki*, p. 28, n. 1. From what is said later, it may be inferred that the representatives were Skobelev and Zenzinov. See pp. 79–80.

[7] "Nuzhna li novaia vlast'?" (Is a New Government Needed?), *Delo Naroda*, No. 193 (October 29, 1917).

[8] See its manifesto of October 27 in *ibid.*, No. 191 (October 28, 1917).

aside in favor of an order which he would undoubtedly consider ruinous to the country? In that case the Committee to Save the Fatherland would proceed to isolate Kerenski and struggle against him "with the strength of its moral authority and also with other means." In any event Kerenski had been stricken from the list of prospective ministers in the new government. This was the assurance which the Menshevik Skobelev gave to Vikzhel,[9] but one wonders how effective the "other means" would have been and also whether Skobelev's associate, Zenzinov, would have supported the demotion of his friend and party comrade after Kerenski had entered the capital in triumph. It is not to be wondered that the Russian people did not find their way around in this maze of fine distinctions and regarded the struggle of the Socialist Revolutionary Party simply as one waged in behalf of the restoration of the Provisional Government.

The SR position was enunciated by Gendelman at the first conference of democratic organizations convoked on October 29 by the All-Russian Executive Committee of the Railwaymen's Union (Vikzhel) under imminent threat of a strike that would tie the country's rickety transportation system completely in knots. Of the forty-odd members of this committee nearly a fourth were Left SR's [10]—the largest single element—and in its determination to bring the squabbling parties into agreement on a ministry which would shut out the bourgeoisie and yet deny a dominant position to any one socialist party, Vikzhel was pursuing essentially the same policy as the Left SR's,[11] who wanted to have done with coalition and war and yet dreaded being left alone in the government with the redoubtable Lenin and his strong and disciplined party. On the occasion in question Gendelman spoke in the name of the Central Committee of the Socialist Revolutionary Party.[12] Rejecting out of hand any

[9] Vompe, *Dni oktiabr'skoi revoliutsii i zheleznodorozhniki*, p. 80.

[10] See list of members and breakdown by parties in *ibid.*, p. 10.

[11] On the community of interest between them and Vikzhel, see especially p. 81 of Vompe's account.

[12] A mistake in Vompe, repeated in later accounts based on his study (see Vladimirova, *God sluzhby "sotsialistov" kapitalistam*, p. 42, and *Istoriia grazhdanskoi voiny v SSSR*, II, 532), is the statement (p. 26) that one Iakobin also represented the Central Committee at this conference. There was no person by this name on the committee. Gendelman's party name was "Iakobii"; he probably inscribed both names on the register and thus gave rise to the confusion.

thought of treating with the usurpers, he conceded the necessity of a socialist ministry but said the railwaymen erred in thinking that agreement was always possible: "Even in the democratic camp there are moments when a quarrel must be settled by force of arms, and for us a government with Bolsheviks participating is unthinkable." [13] The country would not forgive Lenin's party the bloodshed it had occasioned, and no government could breathe easily as long as one component was free to dictate its will to others by force of arms. So first of all the Bolshevik venture must be "liquidated"—that is, the power of the Bolshevik Party must be broken. Gendelman advised the railroad employees to get in touch with Kerenski and if he agreed to turn over his authority to a new government after finishing with the Bolsheviks, they should abandon their neutrality and rally to his support.[14]

It was a strong position to take for a party which on this very day had sustained one disaster and would on the morrow sustain another. One wonders why the SR's even bothered to appear at the conference. The answer lies in their healthy respect for the railwaymen's union and the threat a strike would pose to the arrival of reinforcements at Kerenski's Gatchina headquarters.

What was unthinkable on the evening of October 29, however, became quite conceivable by the evening of October 30. The full-dress conference on the latter occasion had been preceded by the work of a commission and by a morning conference at which the SR's and Mensheviks had amplified their position by demanding, 1) that the Red or Workers' Guard be disarmed, 2) that the garrison be placed under orders of the city council, and 3) that an armistice be declared, offering for their part to secure a pledge that the troops

---

[13] Vompe, *Dni oktiabr'skoi revoliutsii i zheleznodorozhniki*, pp. 27–28.

[14] "Prekrashchenie grazhdanskoi voiny?" (Cessation of Civil War?), *Delo Naroda*, No. 195 (October 31, 1917). Here the summary of Gendelman's statement is toned down in comparison to the direct quotation in Vompe, and the reference to a settlement by force is omitted. As this is thoroughly in line with the policy of the central organ, however, and as the inference from the summary is that force was necessary, there is no reason to doubt that Gendelman used the words in question, particularly since other speakers referred to them with indignation (see Vompe, *Dni oktiabr'skoi revoliutsii i zheleznodorozhniki*, pp. 29–30) and since they merely reflect the fundamental policy of the Central Committee in commissioning Gotz to break the revolution.

of Kerenski on entering the city would not fire a shot or engage in search and seizure. A socialist government would then be constituted, but without Bolshevik participation.[15] At least the SR's were now ready to negotiate, having been forced into this position by Vikzhel.[16] The evening conference marked a further recession on their part, whether because the lesson of the cadet uprising had now sunk in or because the true situation at the front was already known in the city.[17] At this conference, Rakitnikov of the left center replaced Gendelman of the right center as representative of the Central Committee, which now urged a three-day armistice, effective throughout the country, and the construction of a socialist ministry on a personal rather than a party basis. According to one source, Rakitnikov proposed a government of experts rather than of politicians.[18] The new government must not be rooted in the Bolshevik coup d'état nor could that party be officially represented in it, but individual Bolsheviks who had not offended the sensibilities of the country could be admitted on a personal basis, and in this manner satisfaction would be given their party.[19] In other words, Rakitnikov kept the front door closed to the Bolsheviks while opening the back door to their admission. Major culprits like Lenin and Trotski would be excluded, but certain less prominent members might enter from the

[15] "Prekrashchenie grazhdanskoi voiny?", *Delo Naroda*, No. 195 (October 31, 1917); Vladimirova, *God sluzhby "sotsialistov" kapitalistam*, p. 44. The latter source adds several other demands.

[16] See Kamenev's report to the Petrograd Soviet, *Revoliutsiia 1917 goda*, VI, 31–32; see also statement of the Central Committee, *Delo Naroda*, No. 198 (November 3, 1917), where the influence of Vikzhel is acknowledged. The Mensheviks and SR's, according to Kamenev, had demanded dissolution of the Military Revolutionary Committee.

[17] Vladimirova, *God sluzhby "sotsialistov" kapitalistam*, p. 47. This source assumes that the Bolshevik success at Pulkovo and the recapture of Tsarskoe Selo softened the SR attitude. It is very dubious, however, whether the conferees had a clear picture of the day's developments at the front. Tsarskoe Selo was not completely occupied until midnight (*Revoliutsiia 1917 goda*, VI, 29), and Trotski did not send his victory message over the radio until 2:10 A.M. the next day; see his *Oktiabr'skaia revoliutsiia*, p. 88.

[18] S. An-ski (S. A. Rappoport), "Posle perevorota 25-go Oktiabria 1917 g." (After the Overturn of October 25, 1917), in *Arkhiv Russkoi Revoliutsii*, VIII, 47.

[19] Vompe, *Dni oktiabr'skoi revoliutsii i zheleznodorozhniki*, p. 36; "Prekrashchenie grazhdanskoi voiny?", *Delo Naroda*, No. 195 (October 31, 1917); statement of the Central Committee, *ibid.*, No. 198 (November 3, 1917).

rear if the workers wished it. This backhanded compromise origi-
nated with the SR's, who then induced the Mensheviks also to recede
from their stand for total exclusion, if we are to believe the anonymous reporter in the *Delo Naroda*,[20] although this assertion contra-
venes the general rule that the Mensheviks were less irreconcilable
toward the October Revolution than the SR's. It is certainly not true
of party attitudes in the city council, where the Mensheviks accused
the SR's of spoiling the prospects for an armistice by their intransigence.[21]

The Central Committee, in fact, did not carry the whole party
with it in conceding unofficial representation to the Bolsheviks in
the projected government. Not only did Mayor Shreider and the SR
delegation in the city council continue to oppose a compromise [22]
but the All-Russian Peasants' Executive Committee with its top-heavy
right-wing representation refused to have any part in a government
which should be contaminated by the presence of Bolsheviks or their
Left SR accomplices. The committee would only promise not to
obstruct such a combination if other organizations found it possible.
As for itself, it disclaimed any responsibility for so reckless a venture
and washed its hand of the matter. The growing Left SR opposition
in the committee gave fierce battle on this issue at the session of
November 1, and the majority stand was deprived of much of its
moral authority by the narrowness of the division (33 to 26 with 4
abstentions). The reasoning of the majority was tortuous, for coupled
with an appraisal of the October Revolution as a "soap bubble" which
would soon be pricked was the fear that Bolshevism would devour
those who compounded with it.[23] The Central Committee could
usually count upon the Peasants' Executive Committee and the city
administration, but not in this instance. The Central Committee itself

---

[20] "Prekrashchenie grazhdanskoi voiny?", *ibid.*, No. 197 (November 2, 1917).
[21] See report on proceedings of the council in *ibid.*
[22] See Shreider's speech in *ibid.*, No. 196 (November 1, 1917), and declaration of Trupp, No. 197 (November 2, 1917).
[23] Bykhovski, *Vserossiiskii Sovet Krest'ianskikh Deputatov*, pp. 283–86. Only
under the whip of adversity had the Executive Committee put aside its aversion
to an all-socialist government. The day after the overthrow of the Provisional
Government, when the Central Committee had already conceded this point,
the Executive Committee still hung back, speaking only of the "re-creation of a
generally recognized authority." See its manifesto, "Ko vsem krest'ianam" (To
All Peasants), *Delo Naroda*, No. 191 (October 28, 1917).

was divided, with the Avksentiev faction fighting any suggestion of compromise.[24]

Having modified their original stand with respect to collaboration with Lenin's party, the Socialist Revolutionaries also ceased to insist on a legitimist solution to the crisis of power. An editorial in the central organ on October 31 admitted that the old government had passed from the scene and urged that since all socialist parties had agreed on a ministry excluding the bourgeoisie there was no further reason for bloodshed.[25] Indeed, the SR's were pushing hard for an armistice at this moment, making a virtue out of necessity, for the Vikzhel historian is probably right in thinking they wanted to gain time for Kerenski to strengthen his position.[26] The SR's, moreover, did not stand on Rakitnikov's proposal at the conference of October 30 that the new government be made responsible to the resurrected Council of the Republic.[27] They were willing to constitute a new organ of control, but insisted on watering down the representation of the workers' and soldiers' soviets by alloting many seats to the peasants' soviets and the municipal organs of self-government so that the Bolsheviks would be in a minority. Here they collided not only with the Bolsheviks, who were determined to assert the supreme authority of the Central Executive Committee growing out of the Second Congress of Workers' and Soldiers' Soviets (October 26), but also with the Left SR's in their effort to supplant the existing Peasants' Executive Committee with the much more radical organ expected to arise from the forthcoming Second Congress of Peasants' Soviets (see chapter 5).[28]

In the last analysis, it was the Bolshevik commitment to the soviet form of government which wrecked the negotiations. The Bolsheviks

[24] *Volia Naroda,* No. 159 (October 31, 1917).

[25] "Nemedlennoe peremirie!" (An Armistice at Once!), *Delo Naroda,* No. 195.

[26] Vompe, *Dni oktiabr'skoi revoliutsii i zheleznodorozhniki,* p. 33.

[27] "Prekrashchenie grazhdanskoi voiny?", *Delo Naroda,* No. 195 (October 31, 1917). This account is preferred to another and later one which has Rakitnikov proposing a consultative organ of representatives of all the socialist parties. See An-ski, "Posle perevorota 25-go Oktiabria," in *Arkhiv Russkoi Revoliutsii,* VIII, 47.

[28] "Prekrashchenie grazhdanskoi voiny?" *Delo Naroda,* No. 196 (November 1, 1917) and No. 197 (November 2, 1917); Vladimirova, *God sluzhby "sotsialistov" kapitalistam,* p. 47.

could not yield to the SR's without sacrificing the dictatorship of
the proletariat and the SR's could not accept the hegemony of the
soviets without doing violence to their belief in universal suffrage as
the sole legitimate source of state authority. The majority Socialist
Revolutionaries always rejected the soviets as organs of state since
these represented a particular class rather than the citizenry as a
whole, and the most they were willing to concede under the circumstances was equality between the soviets and the local organs of self-
government in setting up a supreme council to which the government
would be responsible pending the convocation of the Constituent
Assembly.[29] The ideal solution from the SR point of view would
have been for the Bolsheviks to retire from the scene and permit the
constitution of a new government without either themselves or the
bourgeoisie, now that their face had been saved by the death of the
old coalition. Coalition in the narrower sense of an agreement among
the socialist parties was impossible as long as they insisted on being
the dominant partner and clung to their shibboleth of the dictatorship of the proletariat.[30]

At the night conference of October 31 it seemed that an understanding had been reached, with the Bolsheviks accepting a council
which they would not control, but Lenin overruled the peacemakers
in his party and on the following day the supreme soviet organ, in
a resolution devoid of any suggestion of compromise, reverted to
the original demand of "all power to the soviets." [31] The SR Central
Committee thereupon declared that the basis of agreement had been
destroyed and broke off negotiations, recalling its representatives
from the Vikzhel conference.[32] The action sounded the death knell
of the efforts at conciliation, as neither the milder resolution subsequently passed under the prodding of the Left SR's nor the resignation of five members of the Bolshevik Central Committee in opposition to Lenin's course availed to bring the SR's back to the confer-

[29] "V chëm raznoglasie?" (Wherein Lies the Difference?), *Delo Naroda*, No.
200 (November 5, 1917); Bykhovski, *Vserossiiskii Sovet Krest'ianskikh Deputatov*, pp. 283–84.
[30] "Tupik" (A Dead End), *Delo Naroda*, No. 197 (November 2, 1917).
[31] An-ski, "Posle perevorota 25-go Oktiabria," in *Arkhiv Russkoi Revoliutsii*,
VIII, 50, 53–54; *Revoliutsiia 1917 goda*, VI, 46–48; Vladimirova, *God sluzhby
"sotsialistov" kapitalistam*, pp. 47–48.
[32] Text of announcement in *Delo Naroda*, No. 198 (November 3, 1917).

ence table.[33] Each side, of course, blamed the other for the rupture, the SR's by citing the refusal of the Bolsheviks to conclude an armistice or modify their stand in favor of a soviet government, and the Bolsheviks by accusing the SR's of a desire to behead their party through the exclusion of Lenin and Trotski from the list of ministers.[34] Some days later *Pravda* announced that the effort of the Mensheviks and SR's to disarm the proletariat had constituted for the Petersburg Soviet an insuperable barrier to any kind of agreement.[35]

Abram Gotz later disclaimed for his party any responsibility for the failure to arrive at an understanding which would have healed the breach in the revolutionary democracy and ended the civil war. It was the irreconcilability of the Bolsheviks, he said, which had wrecked the Vikzhel negotiations.[36] Sources that cannot be suspected of partisan bias confirm this charge. The victory of the Bolsheviks over Kerenski had made them unwilling to conclude an agreement, the chairman of Vikzhel, the Left SR Malitski, informed his Moscow bureau.[37] Later, at the railwaymen's convention, Malitski once again laid the burden of responsibility upon the dominant party.[38] The Bolsheviks themselves have never bothered to conceal their insincerity in entering upon these negotiations. Lenin characterized them as a diplomatic screen for military operations [39] and Molotov told the Petersburg committee that only part of the comrades had assigned any significance to them.[40]

Yet there can be little doubt that the Socialist Revolutionaries

[33] Except for informational purposes. After the Bolsheviks had to some extent backed water, the SR Central Committee once more "categorically denied the possibility of an agreement," citing the other party's insistence upon a majority in the government, upon arming the workers all over Russia, and upon soviet control of the Petersburg and Moscow military districts. See the information furnished V. M. Chernov by the Central Committee in the General Army Committee's bulletin No. 9 (November 5, 1917), on pp. 33–34 of appendix to Lelevich, *Oktiabr' v stavke.*

[34] Speech of Sokolnikov in the Petersburg Soviet, *Delo Naroda,* No. 197 (November 2, 1917).

[35] Vladimirova, *God sluzhby "sotsialistov" kapitalistam,* p. 54.

[36] *Izvestiia,* No. 136 (June 22, 1922); *Revoliutsionnaia Rossiia,* No. 21–22 (October–November, 1922), p. 8.

[37] Vompe, *Dni oktiabr'skoi revoliutsii i zheleznodorozhniki,* pp. 38–39.

[38] *Delo Naroda,* No. 245 (December 31, 1917).

[39] *Revoliutsiia 1917 goda,* VI, 46.

[40] *Ibid.,* p. 57; Vladimirova, *God sluzhby "sotsialistov" kapitalistam,* p. 42.

were equally insincere in attending the conferences, and that if the shoe had been on the other foot, if the preponderance of force had been on Kerenski's side, they, or at least the majority of the Central Committee and the section of party opinion behind it, would have refused to treat with the Bolsheviks. Writing at the moment when an agreement seemed likely, the unknown commentator in the central organ of the PSR, doubtlessly a personage of authority, had predicted that the new government would likely be stillborn, as the SR's and Mensheviks were entering it against their will in order to save the revolution from the danger to which it had been exposed by the very party they would have to accept as a partner.[41] The Central Committee, in announcing the breaking off of negotiations, made the bald statement that it "had not deluded itself with the hope that an agreement with Bolshevism was actually feasible" but had felt obliged to exhaust the possibilities of ending the civil war at the behest of so potent an organization as the railwaymen's union.[42] The representative of the city council admits frankly that it was the unfavorable military situation which impelled the opponents of Bolshevism to seek an agreement,[43] and the willingness of Kerenski after Pulkovo to accede to whatever the Central Committee found advisable [44] stands in sharp contrast to his refusal to make any kind of commitment to the Vikzhel delegation which visited him before Pulkovo.[45] The PSR at the outset had taken an intransigent stand, departing from it only under the spur of disaster and even then demanding that their adversaries come around by the back way to share in power the plenitude of which they already possessed. A compromise was possible only at the very first, before a trial of strength; once the fortunes of the battlefield were allowed to intrude upon the council chamber, the negotiations were doomed. The Chernov wing of the

[41] "Prekrashchenie grazhdanskoi voiny?", *Delo Naroda*, No. 197 (November 2, 1917).

[42] Proclamation in *ibid.*, No. 198 (November 3, 1917).

[43] An-ski, "Posle perevorota 25-go Oktiabria," in *Arkhiv Russkoi Revoliutsii*, VIII, 50.

[44] *Ibid.*, p. 49; "Prekrashchenie grazhdanskoi voiny?", *Delo Naroda*, No. 197 (November 2, 1917).

[45] Vompe, *Dni oktiabr'skoi revoliutsii i zheleznodorozhniki*, pp. 41–43; *Delo Naroda*, No. 195 (October 31, 1917); Kerenski, "Gatchina," in *Izdalëka*, p. 219; Stankevich, *Vospominaniia*, p. 274. Kerenski errs in placing the visit on October 30 instead of the day before.

PSR and the Kamenev faction of the Bolshevik Party could perhaps
have reached an agreement, but there was never any chance that the
element opposing any move toward peace in the one party and the
Leninist core of the other could come to terms. Their quarrel could
be settled by force alone.

Although a government of compromise was now out of the question, the moderate socialists could still try to set up a countergovernment outside the immediate reach of Bolshevik power which
would serve as a point of crystallization for whatever strength they
still possessed in the country. The focal point of this endeavor was
the General Army Committee, the top organ of the hierarchy of
soldiers' committees which had grown out of the February Revolution. The scene now shifts from St. Petersburg to Mogilev on the
Dnieper, and the principal actors on the stage are once again the
head men of the PSR, Gotz and Chernov, whose absence from the
capital had prevented them for taking part in the Vikzhel negotiations.

The army committee system resembled many other institutions
of the post-February era in that it consisted of Menshevik shepherds
and SR sheep: the qualities of intellect and leadership of the one
party formed a natural graft on the amorphous mass gathered under
the banner of the other. The Menshevik chairman of the General
Committee, Staff Captain S. V. Perekrestov, had taken stock after
the collapse of the Provisional Government and come to the conclusion that in order to oppose Bolshevism with any prospects of
success a new government must be formed with its center of gravity
decisively to the left of the fallen regime. Perekrestov and his
fellow committeemen, the majority of whom were Social Democrats,
considered Kerenski a finished man, the last straw, as far as the
army was concerned, having been the designation of the Kadet
Kishkin as his substitute in St. Petersburg. A new man must be
found, and since the Mensheviks had no one in their own ranks
with sufficient authority to enlist the support of the peasant army,
it is not surprising that the members of the committee should have
settled on V. M. Chernov as the logical choice for minister-president.
Chernov's reputation as a foe of imperialism and as a champion of

peasant interests, his break with the Provisional Government and dissociation form Kerenski's policies, had preserved for him, alone among SR leaders, a measure of his original popularity, affording hope that a government under his presidency could find real support in the army.

At the moment Chernov was in Pskov, whence he had returned from Gatchina, convinced that Kerenski's hand was played out and that only the concentration of serious forces in the vicinity of St. Petersburg would make the Bolsheviks amenable to reason. In order to provide the physical power needed to put the moderate socialists on an equal footing with the extremists in the Vikzhel negotiations, Chernov had fallen in with the plan of the Kerenski circle [46] to remove the obstructive General Cheremisov as commander of the Northern Front. On November 1 he and his colleague Dr. Feit informed General Dukhonin of the latest political decisions, of how Kerenski would retire and Avksentiev would become prime minister, and asked the chief of staff to get Cheremisov out of the way so that troops could be dispatched to the capital.[47] While Dukhonin was temporizing, Chernov accepted an invitation of the General Army Committee to come to Mogilev, where he met with an appraisal of the situation which opened up before him entirely new perspectives. Instead of Avksentiev, Chernov himself should become the head of a government formed in opposition to the Council of People's Commissars, and the committee asked his permission to sound out the army as to whether it favored such an enterprise and would form special volunteer units to enforce the authority of the new government.[48]

According to Chernov, the Bolshevik Party would have been excluded from the projected coalition,[49] but the documents leave no

[46] See "Oktiabr' na fronte" (October at the Front), in *Krasnyi Arkhiv*, XXIV (V, 1927), 86, 95–97.

[47] *Ibid.*, pp. 97–98.

[48] Manuscript commentary on the minutes of the Central Committee, pp. 60–61.

[49] *Ibid.*, pp. 61, 64. That this was not an afterthought, written into the commentary years after the events in question, is shown by the record of a conversation Chernov had with Lunkevich at the time (November 7), in which he defined the strategy being pursued as the isolation of the Bolsheviks and the formation of a democratic government without them. See *Izvestiia Tiflisskogo Soveta* (News of the Tiflis Soviet), No. 183, as quoted in *Revoliutsiia 1917 goda*, VI, 96.

doubt that the General Army Committee envisaged an all-inclusive socialist ministry from the Popular Socialists to the Bolsheviks.[50] Gotz stated some years later at his trial that the SR view had been that Bolsheviks responsible for plunging the country into civil war were beyond the pale but elements in the party which had opposed the rule-or-ruin policy of Lenin could have a voice in the government.[51] Perhaps the best explanation of the discrepancy lies in the admission of SR leaders on November 10 that, while the Bolsheviks ought to be debarred from participation in the government, the temper of the troops made it impossible to take a firm stand on this issue.[52] Another aspect of the plan was to leave General Headquarters out of the political struggle so that it could concentrate on holding the front against the enemy. The army committees themselves would form the special volunteer units required for the protection of the General Staff and the coercion of the usurpers.[53] The planners did not dare to breast the tidal wave for peace; in fact, the General Army Committee, in promising an "immediate approach to peace negotiations," branded the government of Lenin and Trotski as the "sole obstacle to the conclusion of peace," since it stood in the way of the formation of a generally recognized government with which friend and foe alike would treat.[54] The defensists on the committee had at last awakened to the consequences of leaving the Bolsheviks a free hand in exploiting the antiwar sentiments of the army.

The nomination of Chernov as minister-president is evidence in itself that moderate socialists, at least on the front, had been shaken out of their complacency. A political figure standing to the left of center would now have the opportunity to show whether he could succeed where more conservative colleagues had failed. Chernov reacted to the committee's proposal in characteristic "yes-

[50] See declarations of November 7 and 11 (Lelevich, *Oktiabr' v stavke*, p. 62, and bulletin No. 16 [November 12, 1917], p. 58 of appendix to *ibid.*).
[51] *Izvestiia*, No. 136 (June 22, 1922).
[52] Bulletin of the General Army Committee, No. 15 (November 11, 1917), on p. 52 of appendix to Lelevich, *Oktiabr' v stavke*.
[53] Chernov, manuscript commentary on the minutes of the Central Committee, p. 64.
[54] "Nakanune peremiriia" (On the Eve of the Armistice), in *Krasnyi Arkhiv*, XXIII (IV, 1927), 196; text of declaration of November 7 in Lelevich, *Oktiabr' v stavke*, p. 62; *Istoriia grazhdanskoi voiny v SSSR*, II, 518–19.

and-no" fashion: he had no right to refuse the role thrust upon him, but as an obedient soldier of his party he must first of all have its sanction; then the program of the government should be approved by a special soldiers' congress and by the approaching Second All-Russian Congress of Peasants' Soviets; after the blessings of the front and the peasantry had been bestowed, an effort should be made to win the support of the urban working class. As there was more "yes" than "no" in this answer, the General Committee went ahead and submitted its proposal to the army organizations, while Chernov himself began the spadework of forming a cabinet.

First of all, through the courtesy of Vikzhel, he got in touch with the capital to inform the Central Committee of what was going on and to ask the All-Russian Peasants' Executive Committee to transfer the seat of the approaching congress from Petersburg to Mogilev, where it could deliberate calmly and cloak the new government with its authority. The opinion of the Central Committee—if it had any at this time—does not appear to have been communicated to Chernov, but the right SR majority in the Peasants' Executive Committee acceded to his request, overriding by the slender margin of four votes the protests of the left opposition that Mogilev was a nest of counterrevolution, and of some members of the majority that it was too late to make a change without creating confusion and risking the disruption of the congress.[55] Chernov negotiated with the Vikzhel delegation at Mogilev and claims it agreed to place the railroads at the disposal of a "third power," formed in opposition to both the Provisional and Bolshevik governments and headed by Chernov as the only man who could swing such a venture. But a Vikzhel official asserts that the delegation lodged a categorical protest against the Mogilev enterprise under instructions from the central office to obstruct by every means in its power the formation of a government outside the capital.[56] The response of the army organizations was prevailingly favorable, and Chernov began to fill the posts in his cabinet by securing the promise of General Verkhovski to return to the war ministry, whence he could enforce the

---

[55] Bykhovski, *Vserossiiskii Sovet Krest'ianskikh Deputatov*, pp. 288–89; *Delo Naroda*, No. 204 (November 9, 1917).

[56] Vompe, *Dni oktiabr'skoi revoliutsii i zheleznodorozhniki*, pp. 47–48.

authority of the new regime in both big cities, and by sending an invitation to Iraklii Tsereteli in the Caucasus to become minister of foreign affairs—a bid that went unanswered, since Tsereteli had already left for St. Petersburg.[57]

But just when things seemed to be going well and the program on the verge of fruition, the whole business crashed to the ground. On November 7 the General Army Committee had proclaimed its design; on November 11 it announced its abandonment. What had happened in four days' time to thwart its purpose and wreck its plan? Two reasons were assigned by the committee for the disaster sustained. First, the political parties, outwardly apprehensive of anything that smacked of "Praetorianism" and inwardly jealous of the committee's initiative, had taken the position that the formation of a new government must proceed from a civilian instead of a military authority, and that it could not be done immediately but must be preceded by a conference of party representatives, democratic organizations, and regional authorities (Ukrainian Rada, etc.), to be convoked at some uncertain date in an unspecified location. Second, the response of the army organizations, while favorable in the great majority of instances, had been unsatisfactory in the case of the First, Third, Fifth, and Tenth armies (the most Bolshevik on the front), and the altered balance of forces in the committees beneath it had compelled the General Committee to curtail its political activity.[58] In short, the attempt to set up a government under the auspices of the front organizations had foundered on the obstruction of the parties and the wave of extremism which was cutting the ground from under the soldiers' committees, changing the complexion of those at the base of the structure and foreshadowing the recall of the SR and Menshevik spokesmen at the top. The words of the General Committee indicate where the trouble lay but do not reveal what was going on behind the scenes—and plenty was going on, for in a complete reversal of his initial attitude, V. M. Chernov had suddenly announced the withdrawal of his candidacy as prime

[57] Manuscript commentary on the minutes of the Central Committee, pp. 61–62.

[58] Lelevich, *Oktiabr' v stavke*, pp. 59–61, 71; bulletins No. 15 (November 11, 1917) and No. 16 (November 12, 1917) of the General Army Committee, on pp. 51–52, 57–58 of appendix to *ibid.*

minister, thereby ending any thought of establishing a new center of power at army headquarters.

The change in his attitude is startling, and behind it lies an interesting story. On the evening of November 8 Chernov declared his willingness to assume the burdens of state in an address [59] to a local party conference which brought him the acclaim and backing of the peasant and party organizations of Mogilev province. "Heavy, endlessly heavy, is the burden of power. . . . But if it is necessary, if the party commands, if it will help, I would not dare to refuse." [60] And he went on to praise, as equally binding on all, the party's stringent discipline, which had never existed except in his imagination and which now less than ever was equally binding on all. To this same night,[61] apparently, relates the story of an eyewitness who depicts Chernov in a jovial and expansive mood, full of the joy of life, as he whiled away the time in the communications room of General Headquarters, trying to conceal the eagerness with which he followed reports from the front on the reaction to his candidacy.[62] What a contrast to the Chernov of November 10, whom another eyewitness describes as lying in a state of complete moral and physical collapse with a compress on his head! [63]

What had plunged Chernov so abruptly from the heights of anticipation to the depths of despair? What had destroyed his dream of heading, and, indeed, of saving the Russian republic, and reduced him to the level of a bankrupt politician? Surely not the evidence of Bolshevik strength in the army; he had known of that all along, and his whole course of action was based on the calculation that by restoring to his party its long-lost freedom of action in matters of land and peace, he could wean the peasant soldiers away from the unnatural Marxist connection. As was so often the case, the answer lies within the intimate circle of party relationships. It was the arrival on the scene of Gotz and Avksentiev that spiked the plans of

[59] *Mogilëvskaia Zhizn'* (Mogilev Life), November 11, 1917, as quoted in Lelevich, *Oktiabr' v stavke*, pp. 64–66.

[60] *Ibid.*, p. 66.

[61] The date is not given, and may only be inferred. It would have to be either the 8th or the 9th, and the 8th is more probable.

[62] A. Dickhof-Derental, "Siluety oktiabr'skago perevorota" (Silhouettes of the October Revolution), in *Perezhitoe*, I, 54–55.

[63] Semenov, *Voennaia i boevaia rabota PSR*, p. 8.

Chernov. These two leaders came from their fruitless mission in quest of troops, Gotz in military clothes, Avksentiev minus his beard, and with two disasters already to their credit, they proceeded to wreck the Mogilev combination. After listening to Perekrestov and Chernov, they pronounced the venture foolhardy and fore-doomed to failure, asserted it would meet with no support in party circles, and predicted that not one of the leading soviet figures (that is, of the pre-October era) would enter such a government. The Menshevik leader Skobelev, who was their traveling companion and, like Gotz, a member of the now defunct but once all-powerful "star chamber," threw the weight of his influence in the same direc-tion. Chernov declares that it never entered anyone's mind to doubt that these men accurately reflected the sentiment of the highest party and soviet circles, from which they had so recently come. A second blow was the news from the capital that the Peasants' Executive Committee had lost its nerve in the matter of transferring the peasants' congress to Mogilev, and that it would be convened after all in Petersburg. This was seized upon by the newcomers as evidence of the lack of support in capital circles for the Mogilev plan.

Chernov thereupon announced that he would not go against the will of the party and the allied peasants' organization in forming a government to counterbalance the regime of commissars. To use one of his own favorite expressions, his candidacy withered on the vine without having come to bloom. If there were going to be no follow-through to the SR-Menshevik bolt from the Second Soviet Congress,[64] which Chernov had logically interpreted as a declara-tion of war, then he proposed to return to St. Petersburg on the next train for the purpose of conducting a purely verbal struggle against Bolshevism from the platform of the peasants' congress.[65] He therefore parted company with Gotz and Avksentiev—none too amicably, we may suppose—in order to head for the capital, while they proceeded southward in search of troops as yet untouched by Bolshevism, leaving in their wake the wreckage of the Mogilev plan.[66]

[64] See below, pp. 101–103.   [65] See ch. 5.
[66] Manuscript commentary on the minutes of the Central Committee, pp. 62–64.

Only later did Chernov learn that Avksentiev was carrying with him a letter from Kerenski, which conferred the supreme authority, received in "unbroken" succession from the last representative of the Romanov dynasty, on the bearer, and which empowered him to form a new government if Kerenski were incapacitated or otherwise removed from the scene. Kerenski had drawn up the letter in triplicate at the behest of Gotz and Stankevich, either on October 29 or 30, and had given a copy to each of his advisers.[67] Most probably Avksentiev had received his copy from Gotz, and this had been the basis of the plan to proclaim Avksentiev minister-president. Chernov seems to have known of the plan on November 1 when he was trying to speed reinforcements from Pskov.[68] The initiative of the General Army Committee had posed the alternative of a ministry headed by Chernov, with the result that the personal ambitions of the SR leaders were brought into head-on collision. It is obvious that Avksentiev would not propose to step aside in favor of Chernov, and obvious, also, that Gotz, in following the line traced by Kerenski's letter and in accompanying his colleague southward to feel out the situation on fronts more insulated against the Bolshevik contagion, had sided against Chernov. Replies to the General Army Committee's proposal from three armies on the Rumanian Front (Sixth, Eighth, and Ninth) had doubtlessly whetted Avksentiev's appetite by favoring him instead of Chernov as minister-president.[69] But when the SR leaders arrived on the spot, they found that the opinion of committees which were essentially a holdover from the day when the pro-war socialists ran the show no longer corresponded to the mood of the troops, even on these more remote fronts. Thus the SR high command had reposed much hope in the Extraordinary Congress of the Southwestern Front (November 18–24), but when Avksentiev arrived to line up support, he met with such an unfriendly reception in the caucus of his own party that he left with-

---

[67] Stankevich, *Vospominaniia*, pp. 274–75; Kerenski, "Gatchina," in *Izdalëka*, pp. 219–20.

[68] See above, p. 74.

[69] Bulletin of the General Committee, No. 15 (November 11, 1917), on p. 53 of appendix to Lelevich, *Oktiabr' v stavke*. In contrast to this stand, the Executive Committee of the Western Front and the Peasants' Executive Committee for the armies on that front pledged their wholehearted support to Chernov's candidacy.

out daring to appear before the congress as a whole.[70] In December the Rumanian Front succumbed to Bolshevism.[71]

Chernov has accused Gotz and Avksentiev of misrepresenting the will of the Central Committee, which had decided to send a delegation to Mogilev to take part in the conference on organizing a new center of power. The committee's decision was never communicated to Mogilev, he says, for one of the delegates named, L. Ia. Gerstein, was led away by Gotz to help in finding troops for Kerenski, and the other, V. G. Arkhangelski, simply defaulted on his obligations and remained in the capital.[72] It is readily apparent, however, that here Chernov has confused developments, for the Central Committee did not adopt this motion until November 14,[73] several days after the collapse of the Mogilev plan, and Gotz could not have sidetracked Gerstein in the manner described because the General Army Committee did not broach or even formulate its design until Kerenski's game had been played to the end.[74] In fact, several sources attest to Gerstein's presence in Mogilev, and Semenov says Gerstein accompanied him back to Petersburg.[75] Yet Chernov is right in his accusation of misrepresentation against Gotz and Avksentiev in the sense that the Central Committee appears to have taken no stand against a ministry headed by himself. That sorely tried and badly

[70] *Revoliutsiia 1917 goda*, VI, 172; *Istoriia grazhdanskoi voiny v SSSR*, II, 509. Of the 213 members of the congress who were SR's, about fifty adhered to the left wing. There were 267 Bolsheviks, 47 Mensheviks, 73 Ukrainians, and 42 nonpartisans.

[71] See report of the Southern Regional Congress of Soviets (including the Rumanian Front), *Delo Naroda*, No. 241 (December 24, 1917); "Delegaty Petrogradskogo garnizona na fronte" (Delegates of the Petersburg Garrison at the Front), in *Krasnyi Arkhiv*, LXXXV (VI, 1937), 55; A. Manusevich, "Istoriia zakhvata Bessarabii Rumyniei" (The Story of the Seizure of Bessarabia by Rumania), *Istoricheskii Zhurnal*, VIII (1940), 83.

[72] Manuscript commentary on the minutes of the Central Committee, pp. 62–63.

[73] Protokol Zasedaniia Tsentral'nago Komiteta PSR.

[74] At first the General Committee backed the Gatchina offensive and only began to shift its position on October 31—after Pulkovo. Kerenski fled Gatchina on November 1, Chernov did not arrive in Mogilev until November 4, and the committee's plan was submitted to the army on November 7. On initial attitudes of the General Committee, see Vladimirova, *God sluzhby "sotsialistov" kapitalistam*, pp. 63–64; Vompe, *Dni oktiabr'skoi revoliutsii i zheleznodorozhniki*, pp. 43–46.

[75] *Voennaia i boevaia rabota PSR*, p. 8; N. Karzhanski, "Verkhovnye glavnokomanduiushchie" (Supreme Commanders in Chief), in *Perezhitoe*, I, 153.

disorganized body, which, as we have seen, did not even keep a record of its proceedings between October 21 and November 14, had wavered between a compromise solution that would stop the civil war (the Vikzhel plan) and a countergovernment under Chernov that would fan it more vigorously than before (the Mogilev plan), without being able to make up its mind in favor of either.[76]

It was not the Central Committee which vetoed the ambitions of V. M. Chernov by raising the specter of party discipline, always a frightening thing to him; this was the work of A. R. Gotz, acting on his own initiative. Gotz represented authority to Chernov, the authority of the right center which had placed him in a minority position within the Central Committee, forced him to acquiesce in one distasteful combination after another, and thwarted his whole conception of how the party should deal with the urgent problems of the revolution. So accustomed had he become to yielding to Gotz that he gave up the struggle and surrendered his convictions and aspirations rather than commit an offense against what he considered party discipline, a discipline which actually was nonexistent and had become the laughingstock of all Russia. Better to lie with a compress on his head, amid the wreckage of his plans, than to defy the man who had in effect become the evil genius of the party and, more than any other, the author of its doom.

How easily Chernov gave in is apparent in two incidents which occurred at the time. On the night of November 10, the date when the plan was abandoned, a consultation by direct wire was held between Chernov, Gotz, and Skobelev in Mogilev and Zenzinov and Tsereteli in St. Petersburg. We do not know what the men in the capital said but a summary of the remarks of the three leaders in Mogilev has been preserved.[77] The sentiments expressed as to the inadmissibility of forming a government at this time, the impropriety of army sponsorship in such a matter, and the inevitability of a period of breakdown until the sobering-up process had run its course, are all those of Gotz and Skobelev and stand in flagrant contradiction to

---

[76] Manuscript commentary on the minutes of the Central Committee, p. 64; Ignatiev, *Nekotorye fakty i itogi chetyrëkh let*, I, 6.

[77] In the bulletin of the General Army Committee, No. 15 (November 11, 1917), on pp. 51–52 of appendix to Lelevich, *Oktiabr' v stavke*.

the views of Chernov; yet they are set forth as the opinions of all three men. The two "star chamber" bosses had successfully blanketed Chernov and made him subscribe to judgments against which he inwardly rebelled but outwardly was too weak to protest. Instead of being the leader of his party, Chernov was more like a prize bird, exhibited on occasion because of the brilliance of its left-centrist plumage and the attraction this had for soldiers and peasants, but caged again as soon as it gave indications of independent flight. And on the night of November 10 Chernov was very definitely in the cage. The real leader of the party, as this incident conclusively demonstrates, was A. R. Gotz.

Similarly with respect to the cancellation of plans for transferring the Second All-Russian Peasants' Congress to Mogilev, which Chernov lists as the second blow to his hopes and ascribes to the flabbiness of the Executive Committee: what happened was that the delegates began to arrive in the capital, and it was resolved to call a conference at which all present would decide the question of location. The decision went by default, for Chernov telegraphed his assent to holding the congress in Petersburg and the moderate SR's no longer saw any purpose in making an issue of the matter.[78] So not the Executive Committee but Chernov himself had capitulated on this point.

The whole course of our study shows that Gotz was strong willed and Chernov was not, that Gotz was the wirepuller behind the scenes and Chernov merely a figure on the stage. The Mogilev episode, therefore, fits into the general picture without adding anything new to it. But there is still the question of why Gotz vetoed the Mogilev enterprise and particularly why he vetoed it with such vehemence. Stankevich, who was on the spot, says Gotz reacted against the plan with "wrathful indignation," feeling it had no chance of success and would so discredit the party that it could not play the decisive role which fate and the will of the Russian people had reserved for it in the Constituent Assembly.[79] Other

[78] Bykhovski, *Vserossiiskii Sovet Krest'ianskikh Deputatov*, pp. 290–92; Lelevich, *Oktiabr' v stavke*, p. 67; *Revoliutsiia 1917 goda*, VI, 108; *Delo Naroda*, No. 206 (November 11, 1917).

[79] *Vospominaniia*, p. 288.

sources confirm Gotz's pessimism as to the means at the disposal
of the General Army Committee.[80] It may be, of course, that Gotz
discerned the true situation at the front—it would be the first time
he had done so—and it may be, also, that his feathers were drooping
after the disasters at Petersburg and Gatchina. He himself dates the
change in the party's tactics from the failure of the cadet uprising,
which convinced the leadership that it did not command enough
strength to upset the Soviet regime by force of arms.[81] Yet defeatism
and concern for the Constituent Assembly do not alone explain his
conduct at Mogilev, if only because he appears to have done what
he could to advance the fortunes of Avksentiev, whose ambitions
to become the successor of Kerenski were even more chimerical
than Chernov's. Probably something more was involved; the clue as
to what it was is furnished by press reports of the Vikzhel negotiations at the end of October, when discussion of Chernov as prospective head of state had brought forth the objection that the Allies
would not approve.[82]

Here, as the Russians say, was where the dog lay buried. According
to Stankevich,[83] the Mogilev plan died because of the negative reaction in Petersburg circles, and we do not need to be told that these
anonymous "circles" consisted of those same half-socialist, half-
Kadet elements who for eight months had fought each and every
step in the direction of peace and whose opposition to a government
headed by Chernov, already manifested in the Vikzhel negotiations,
was now reinforced by the decision of the Menshevik leaders to
shun the "adventure." A similar reaction greeted Stankevich's effort
to convene a conference at General Headquarters for the purpose
of working out terms of peace, even though no action separate from
the Allies was contemplated and even though Stankevich himself
had an unimpeachable pro-war past.[84] Against this evidence of

[80] Semenov, *Voennaia i boevaia rabota PSR*, p. 8; Lelevich, *Oktiabr' v stavke*,
pp. 67 ff.

[81] *Revoliutsionnaia Rossiia*, No. 21–22 (October–November, 1922), p. 8.

[82] "Prekrashchenie grazhdanskoi voiny?", *Delo Naroda*, No. 197 (November
2, 1917).

[83] *Vospominaniia*, p. 288.

[84] *Ibid.*, pp. 293–94. That it was not only the influence of Petersburg circles
which defeated Stankevich's initiative is shown by Dukhonin's emasculation of
his memorandum on this subject. See "Nakanune peremiriia," in *Krasnyi
Arkhiv*, XXIII (IV, 1927), 220–22.

sabotage, which was certainly in line with the whole temper of these circles, must be set the statement of Ignatiev that the leaders of the Committee to Save the Fatherland finally agreed on a Chernov ministry and left to organize it at General Headquarters.[85] In any event, it is unlikely that Gotz needed either the prodding of his friends in Petersburg or the example of his Menshevik associates to determine his course of action. For him the source of authority was near at hand in the form of the Allied missions attached to General Headquarters, and whatever may have passed between him and the missions, he could have been under no misapprehension as to their distaste for a ministry under Chernov. It is not from the veiled language of Stankevich, hinting at strenuous, if confused, activity in Allied quarters,[86] but straight from the lips of General Dukhonin that we learn of the very strong line adopted by these missions in combating the threat of a separate armistice.[87] The British ambassador himself considered the joint Allied note of November 10 [88] to have exceeded the bounds of propriety in speaking of the "gravest consequences" to follow a breach of treaty obligations on Russia's part.[89]

In the absence of knowledge of what went on behind the scenes, it is not possible to say whether Allied influence killed outright the idea of a Chernov ministry or whether it merely created an atmosphere in which that idea could not live. But that it was one or the other, there can be no reasonable doubt. The visit which Skobelev paid to the British ambassador on November 7, just before leaving for Mogilev, must have had an intimate connection with the fate of the project. With Skobelev came Chaikovski—a combination of rosewater Menshevism and faded Populism, claiming to speak in the name of the workers and peasants of Russia and deceiving no one

[85] *Nekotorye fakty i itogi chetyrëkh let,* I, 6. As Ignatiev gives no details or dates, it is impossible to know to what he is referring. If to the Gotz-Avksentiev mission, then, of course, he is in error, whatever may have been the understanding in Petersburg.

[86] *Vospominaniia,* pp. 288–89.

[87] "Nakunune peremiriia," in *Krasnyi Arkhiv,* XXIII (IV, 1927), 225–26.

[88] Text in *ibid.,* pp. 201–2.

[89] Buchanan, *My Mission to Russia,* II, 224. The official Soviet history tries to pass off the note as a political maneuver, directed at the Bolshevik Party (see *Istoriia grazhdanskoi voiny v SSSR,* II, 520–21), but its acceptance at face value by Buchanan and Dukhonin demonstrates the falsity of this approach.

but themselves. They told Buchanan that a socialist government was about to be formed, that the Bolsheviks would be suppressed by force, and that in order to strengthen their hand with the soldiers they must have the assurance that the Allies would move in the direction of peace. Sir George gave them no satisfaction whatever in regard to an early peace: there must be guarantees for the future, he said, and Russia must try to hold out. With a touch of British magnanimity which had been conspicuously absent on an earlier occasion in June, he suggested that the ruined and broken country need not assume the offensive. The visitors then made a much more modest request. Skobelev informed the ambassador that he was leaving that evening to confer with other socialist leaders at General Headquarters and asked whether he could give provisional assurance that the Allies would hold a conference and endeavor to agree on terms of peace. All Buchanan would promise was to refer the matter to London.[90] Skobelev went empty-handed to Mogilev, where he joined Gotz and Avksentiev, not in forming a new government, but in destroying the only combination in sight. On November 10 occurred the joint démarche of the Allied military representatives, and on that same day the General Army Committee announced the abandonment of its effort to construct a cabinet about Chernov as minister-president.

We do not know whether the new government which the "star chamber" clique was all set to inaugurate on November 7 before the fateful visit to the British ambassador was to be headed by Avksentiev or Chernov. Ignatiev may have referred to Skobelev and Chaikovski when he wrote that the Committee to Save the Fatherland had at length agreed on a Chernov ministry and had dispatched a delegation to bring it into being. On the other hand, Skobelev had told Buchanan that the new regime would have Kadet support, and it is very difficult to envisage this in the case of a man whom the Kadet Party had been shamelessly baiting for the better part of a year. Perhaps the claim of Kadet support belongs in the same category as the claim of Skobelev and Chaikovski to represent the workers and peasants of Russia. It is conceivable that in their extremity the dethroned soviet camarilla and the Petersburg "circles" toyed with the idea

[90] *My Mission to Russia,* II, 220–22.

of a Chernov ministry, in which he would be a figurehead and they would have the substance of power, only to abandon the idea when they learned the Allies were not going to permit a gesture in favor of peace, without which a Chernov ministry would have no meaning. Gotz and his associates would certainly have preferred the Avksentiev candidacy, but by this time even their self-confidence must have been shaken. The SR boss was ready to try anything, from clutching at the support of the Ukrainian Rada and the Don Cossacks [91] to haranguing shock troops who marched through the streets of Mogilev with monarchist hymns on their lips,[92] but he stubbornly refused to sanction any step which might have reclaimed for his party some of its forfeited authority in the ranks of the Russian army. On the night of November 10, when the Allied attitude was well known to him and had already decisively influenced his actions, Gotz and his friend Skobelev could still speak of the necessity of preliminary negotiations with the Allies on the subject of an armistice.[93] No wonder the army had lost confidence in such leaders. For them to act independently of the Western powers was as unthinkable as for Chernov to assert himself in the presence of men who in the fullest sense of the word were the gravediggers of the Russian Revolution in its moderate phase.

If the socialist leaders had been less sensitive to foreign influence—or less submissive to foreign dictation—and had gone ahead with their plans, they would have benefited from a change of attitude on the part of the British ambassador. Concluding that no purpose was to be served by flogging a dead horse, Sir George Buchanan advised the Foreign Office on November 14, only a week after the above-mentioned interview, of his opinion that the best course would be to release Russia from her obligations and allow her freely to decide the question of war and peace, for in this way the national resentment over continuation of the war could be diverted from the Allies onto the heads of the Germans.[94] A foreign diplomat had at last

[91] See bulletin of the General Army Committee, No. 15 (November 11, 1917), on p. 52 of appendix to Lelevich, *Oktiabr' v stavke.*

[92] Lelevich, *Oktiabr' v stavke*, pp. 72–73.

[93] Bulletin of the General Army Committee No. 15 (November 11, 1917), on p. 52 of appendix to *ibid.*

[94] *My Mission to Russia*, II, 225–26; Knox, *With the Russian Army 1914–1917*, II, 727.

hit on the means of taking the wind out of the sails of Bolshevism, which Russian socialists had been either too shortsighted to perceive or too timid to grasp. But by then the Mogilev design was as dead as a dodo and Buchanan's change of heart had come too late to undo the mischief of eight months of unrelenting pressure upon weak but willing friends. As for the French, they never wavered in their stand against "criminal negotiations," and proceeded to strip the last pound of flesh from the carcass of the horse.[95] When Lloyd George seemed disposed to accept Buchanan's formula, Clemenceau exclaimed: "Alors, vous voulez que je remercie les gens qui me volent mon porte-monnaie?" (So you want me to be gracious to people who have robbed my purse?) [96] It is doubtful whether M. Clemenceau ever used more self-revealing words.

No claim can be made, of course, that if the SR leaders had been less fainthearted and the Allies more amenable to reason, the results would have been any different. In all probability the time had passed for a Chernov ministry, which would have had to be inaugurated before the October Revolution, or perhaps as far back as the Kornilov rebellion, in order to have had any prospects of success. By November the Bolshevik flood was rising higher and higher, washing the defensists out of one position after another and threatening to engulf at any moment the General Army Committee. The campaign to reelect the soldiers' committees yielded a succession of Bolshevik victories [97] and the election of the Constituent Assembly, which began on November 12, offered conclusive evidence of the change in army sentiment by revealing that on the Northern Front the Bolsheviks were already twice as strong as the SR's and on the Western Front more than three times as strong.[98] Even on the more

[95] See Noulens, *Mon Ambassade en Russie soviétique 1917–1919*, I, 145–48; General Niessel, *Le Triomphe des bolchéviks et la paix de Brest-Litovsk*, pp. 101–4; "Nakanune peremiriia," in *Krasnyi Arkhiv*, XXIII (IV, 1927), 214–15; Lelevich, *Oktiabr' v stavke*, pp. 53–54. Earlier rumors that the Mensheviks and SR's had approached the Allied embassies on the subject of an Allied conference to discuss war aims had brought forth a denial from the French embassy. See *Delo Naroda*, No. 197 (November 2, 1917).

[96] Poincaré, *Au Service de la France*, IX, 395.

[97] Karzhanski, "Verkhovnye glavnokomanduiushchie," in *Perezhitoe*, I, 153; Trotski, *Oktiabr'skaia revoliutsiia*, p. 92; Stankevich, *Vospominaniia*, p. 290; *Istoriia grazhdanskoi voiny v SSSR*, II, ch. 8 *passim*.

[98] See my book, *The Election to the Russian Constituent Assembly*, p. 80.

remote fronts (Southwestern, Rumanian, Caucasian) the large SR majorities inspired no confidence in their ability to withstand the general contagion.[99] In fact, a member of the Central Committee had warned on the eve of the election that the SR influence generally predominant on the Caucasian Front was not proof against the war weariness and thirst for peace which had produced turbulent conditions elsewhere.[100]

Even if Chernov's ministry had not been swept away within a few days of its inception, the policies it would have pursued would scarcely have been bold enough to capture the imagination of the country, particularly of the soldiers, whose favor would determine the outcome of any contest for power. When Chernov invited Tsereteli to assume the portfolio of foreign affairs, he was acting, not as a statesman intent on coming to grips with the problem of peace, but as a personal friend, as a man with a political debt to pay. For months Tsereteli as the key figure in the "star chamber" web of power had tolerated the presence of Tereshchenko in the foreign office, permitting this exponent of dilettante imperialism to run the external policy of the revolution into the ground. And while he differed from Tereshchenko in honestly desiring a general pacification, Tsereteli would never have pursued an active peace policy in the face of Allied disapproval. The October Revolution had made some impression upon the Georgian Social Democrat but not to the extent of weakening his determination to cleave to the Western powers. He now acknowledged the necessity for an effort to end the war as the only way out of the existing situation, and in the same breath affirmed the possibility of taking this step in agreement with the Allies.[101] Here again was the old inability to distinguish between the victor's peace desired by the Western powers and the peace of conciliation sought by the Russian socialists, the

---

[99] *Ibid.*, pp. 36–37.

[100] *Revoliutsiia 1917 goda*, VI, 110; *Delo Naroda*, No. 206 (November 11, 1917). O. S. Minor made the statement.

[101] "Protokoly zasedanii TsIK i biuro TsIK S.R. i S.D. 1-go sozyva posle oktiabria: Iz deiatel'nosti uchrezhdeniia, v deistvitel'nosti ne sushchestvovavshego (Minutes of Post-October Sessions of the Central Executive Committee and Bureau of the Central Executive Committee of the First Soviet of Workers' and Soldiers' Deputies: From the Activity of an Institution Which in Reality Did Not Exist)," in *Krasnyi Arkhiv*, X (III, 1925), 102; *Revoliutsiia 1917 goda*, VI, 117; *Delo Naroda*, No. 206 (November 11, 1917).

same illusion of advancing toward peace in the company of powers bent upon continuing the war until they had achieved the aims even now being exposed by the Bolsheviks through the publication of secret treaties. Not only had the moderate socialists failed to progress beyond the point where their external policy had been snagged for eight months but they had failed even to establish the basic incompatibility of war aims which left them no alternative except to surrender their own or adopt an independent course. Not wishing to face the alternative, they did nothing at all, and from this morass of inaction neither the October earthquake nor the vision of a new government had rescued them.

Whatever might have been done in respect to the land question, the Tsereteli appointment [102] would probably have spoiled Chernov's fundamental strategy of reclaiming the peasant soldiers from Marxist influence by reuniting them with the village, as through the medium of the Peasants' Congress which he had tried to have transferred to Mogilev.[103] Only a simultaneous assault on the problems of land and peace could have prevented the front from sliding further into the embraces of Bolshevism and Lenin from acquiring the ally he needed to impose a proletarian dictatorship upon a peasant country. There was nothing wrong with Chernov's strategy. It was sound and well conceived, and had he possessed the will power and the combative energy to match his breadth of vision he would have struck Bolshevism at its most sensitive spot—the link between the peasant and proletarian movements. Chernov could survey the enemy's line and see where a blow should fall, but in powers of execution he was sadly lacking. To judge from the record, the other SR leaders could neither see nor act. Yet the instinct of self-preservation, if nothing else, should have caused them to rally behind the

---

[102] On November 12 Tsereteli had taken a definite stand against forming a ministry at this time; he said it would be a pure adventure and could not even be thought of ("Protokoly zasedanii TsIK S.R. i S.D. 1-go sozyva posle oktiabria," in *Krasnyi Arkhiv*, X [III, 1925], 103). Whether this represented his original view or reflected the decision of Gotz and Skobelev, imposed upon Chernov and communicated to Tsereteli by direct wire on the night of November 10 (see above, p. 82), is not clear. Certainly Tsereteli was far less positive in his address of that date before the town and zemstvo conference, judging from the report in *Delo Naroda*, No. 206 (November 11, 1917).

[103] See Bykhovski, *Vserossiiskii Sovet Krest'ianskikh Deputatov*, p. 289.

Mogilev plan and at least make an effort to save the situation through a fresh approach. But that they did not do.

For the PSR the October Revolution had been a succession of disasters unrelieved by a single act of foresight and good judgment. The role that inferior leadership played in these events is so evident as to require no further comment. The susceptibility of the leadership to foreign influence contributed a vast deal to bringing on the crisis and blocked the only way out. The appraisal of Bolshevism as a "soap bubble" which soon must burst, leaving the masses a prey to some bogey man from the right, merely shows how far these SR intellectuals were from the heartbeat of the revolution and how little they understood the country in whose name they presumed to speak. The Socialist Revolutionaries had long purchased unity at the expense of action but the October events put an end to their temporizing and forced upon them a division between moderates and extremists such as many years before had come to the Social Democrats. Within the moderate group itself there was not enough cohesion to confront Bolshevism with any serious opposition as it seized control of the state, dissolved the Constitutent Assembly, subordinated the peasant to the proletarian movement, and dug deeper the grave which history and their own errors had prepared for the Socialist Revolutionaries.

Fundamentally, the October Revolution admitted of only two courses of action: either the SR's must wage war upon Bolshevism or they must take advantage of the widespread desire, equally shared by the workers and soldiers and also by a section of the Bolshevik Party, for an all-inclusive socialist government which would saddle Lenin with a divided authority and perhaps defeat his dictatorial purposes. Yet once again, as on the question of peace, the SR's refused to choose between the alternatives and accepted disaster while standing still, since everyone to the right of center could not bear the thought of working with a party of "ravishers" who would make a separate peace in preference to no peace at all, and everyone to the left of center could not enter wholeheartedly upon a struggle with Bolshevism as long as it feared the advent of counterrevolution in the wake of a Bolshevik defeat. Hence the working at cross-purposes, the "yes-and-no" attitude which caused the SR's to throw out slogans of combat to the public while themselves hanging back in the hope of a peaceful solution.[104] The rank-and-file party members did not respond to a leadership which itself was divided. Zenzinov might denounce the neutrality of the railwaymen's union,[105] but the SR workers on the Petersburg system strongly approved of the Vikzhel policy.[106] Those observers who could detect little inclination in SR circles for an armed struggle against Bolshevism[107] are, of course, correct. It could not have been otherwise in view of the left-centrist state of mind and the strength of this element in the party.

The left center was against Bolshevism and against the Provisional Government. It could muster no enthusiasm for a fight against the one as long as success threatened to restore the other. Hence Chernov's failure to give a clear lead to the party following on the Western Front and his sanction of neutrality in the case of the Luga SR's. At the peasant soldiers' congress on the Western Front he had everything his own way, yet he feared to talk as was necessary, "keeping the matches out of the children's hands" and leaving his followers in such a confused state of mind that when news came of the October coup d'état they did not know what his position was in relation to it.[108] When a delegation of party members from the important communications center of Luga came to Chernov at Gatchina to ask for guidance in respect to the civil war, he approved their decision to let through reinforcements from the front to both sides, blandly turning aside the protest of Stankevich with the remark that, apparently, no units would be dispatched to the aid of the Bolsheviks.[109] The attitude of the left center and its sharp divergence from the right center are very clearly registered on the pages of the central organ. There, side by side with Zenzinov's execrations of Bolshevism, foreshadowing a resort to force, appear editorials urging a peaceful solution of the crisis in the consciousness that "the

---

[104] See Ignatiev, *Nekotorye fakty i itogi chetyrëkh let*, I, 6–7.

[105] See his article, "Vikzhel'," *Delo Naroda*, No. 197 (November 2, 1917).

[106] See report of conference on November 12 in *ibid.*, No. 210 (November 15, 1917).

[107] Stankevich, *Vospominaniia*, p. 291.   [108] *Kratkii otchët*, p. 47.

[109] *Vospominaniia*, pp. 278–79.

soldiers and workers who follow the Bolsheviks are our brothers, with whom we began the revolution and with whom, when their fever has passed, we hope to complete it." [110] In making it clear that SR hostility toward Lenin did not extend to the workers behind him and that the masses must not be made to expiate the crimes of the leaders, the editors had warned Kerenski against entering upon the path of repression.[111] After the fighting was over, they took a firm stand against further attempts to oppose Bolshevism by force and contended that the proper course was to isolate that party and draw off its following through exposing its "whole inner falseness." With Bolshevism triumphant in the north and Cossack reaction ascendant in the south, the SR's must pound the counterrevolution on both its heads, though not in the same way: against Lenin they must fight with strength of word and organization; against Kaledin, with strength of arms.[112] This formula discloses the essence of the left-centrist position.

If that position rendered futile all efforts to defend the Provisional Government or overthrow the Council of Commissars, the attitude of the right center, in turn, had barred recourse to a mixed government of moderates and extremists—the Vikzhel solution—or to a countergovernment with a program radical enough to reclaim at least some of the following lost to Bolshevism, as was envisaged under the Mogilev plan. The Chernov wing of the party would not extend itself on behalf of the Provisional Government and Gotz and his friends would not permit the experiment of a left-centrist ministry. The cleavage in the party and the pulling at cross-purposes had left the Socialist Revolutionaries with no solution to the crisis except to mark time in the hope that Bolshevism would discredit

[110] See editorial, "Ne poddavaites' na provokatsiiu" (Don't Succumb to Provocation), and Zenzinov's article, "Krovavyi fars" (A Bloody Farce), in the evening edition of the *Delo Naroda* for October 28 (No. 192). See also the article "Kto oni?" (Who Are They?), by the same author in *ibid.*, No. 190 (October 27, 1917).

[111] "Izoliatsiia, no ne rasprava" (Isolation, but Not Retribution), *ibid.*, No. 193 (October 29, 1917).

[112] "Nashi zadachi" (Our Tasks), *ibid.*, No. 198 (November 3, 1917); see also "Razryv" (Rupture), in the same number, "Kto za grazhdanskuiu voinu?" (Who Is for Civil War?), No. 200 (November 5, 1917), and " 'Rabochee i krest'ianskoe pravitel'stvo' " (The Workers' and Peasants' Government), No. 201 (November 6, 1917).

itself before it could fasten the instruments of tyranny upon the unhappy land. And the party had done little except mark time since the Third Congress. From this point of view the October Revolution merely repeats, in more concentrated form and with more tragic consequences, the whole agonizing experience of the preceding era.

Yet the revolution was too far-reaching an event to have passed without introducing some movement into the stagnant pool of Social Revolutionism. The left center might continue the old waltz with the right center, round and round and round again, but the vigorous left wing of the party, whose rise has elsewhere been noted,[113] now at last emancipated itself from the fetters of sentiment and ideology and broke away from the parent body, carrying with it much of the party's youth and zeal and—even more seriously— a substantial portion of its peasant following. Thus far in sketching the history of the party during the October Revolution we have traced its debacle on the front and in the big cities. The question remains whether it could mobilize enough strength in the provinces to redress or at least partially offset the adverse trend in the towns and the trenches, since the peasantry was now the sole remaining reservoir of strength after the defection of the workers and soldiers. The answer to this question lies with the new party of the Left Socialist Revolutionaries.

[113] See *The Agrarian Foes of Bolshevism, passim.*

III

The Formation of the Left SR Party

The best illustration of the state of affairs in the PSR at the time of the October Revolution is an incident that occurred on October 27 near the Baltic Station in St. Petersburg. Gotz and Zenzinov with several companions had intended to leave for Gatchina, ostensibly as envoys of the city council to collect information and mediate in the civil war, but actually as plenipotentiaries of the Central Committee to help Kerenski assemble a force for his march on the capital.[1] They were not permitted to depart. Worse still, after being turned back at the station, they were arrested by a group of sailors and soldiers who roundly cursed them and threatened to shoot them down. Quite possibly the sailors would have done so but for the warning cry of one of their number: "Don't shoot, boys, we might hit one another!" Some of the men were drunk and gave free rein to their anti-Semitic feeling, swearing that "the soviets had fallen into the hands of the Jews." Whether because he was Jewish or because of his self-assurance, Gotz fared worst of all: he was beaten with rifle butts and twice a sailor pointed a gun at him and pulled the trigger, only to have the weapon misfire.[2]

As party leader, Gotz must have been considerably embarrassed to learn that his youthful assailant was also a Socialist Revolutionary. He turned to the sailor and asked:

"Aren't you ashamed to do this to a senior comrade who has worked in the party from the day of its founding?"

"This is revolution—all are now equal," was the grim reply. The simple people had taken the party teachings at face value. Their socialism may be questioned, but not their leveling instincts. When

---

[1] See ch. I.

[2] " 'Zheleznaia rukavitsa' " (The Iron Gauntlet), *Delo Naroda*, No. 193 (October 29, 1917); Zenzinov, *Iz zhizni revoliutsionera*, pp. 96–97.

Gotz told another of his captors, who was holding a pistol against his head, that he had spent ten years of his life in tsarist prisons, he received the answer: "Isn't that something—my father was in for twenty." [3]

The sailor who raised his gun against the leader of his party was a left SR, certainly by instinct if not by conscious affiliation. All the SR genius for deferring decisions and evading issues could not withstand the strain of the October Revolution, which put an end to the fiction of unity and led to the formation of a new party on the left flank. The break came at the Second All-Russian Congress of Workers' and Soldiers' Soviets (October 25–26).

The official SR line on the congress had wobbled in unison with that of the Mensheviks. At first averse to the idea of holding a congress, the moderate socialists had lifted the ban when they saw that the extremists would succeed in forcing the pace of events and in convoking a congress which would have authority in the eyes of the masses and in which the moderates would be left without representation. But the reversal of policy came too late to dispel the negative attitude hitherto prevailing, and participation in the election of delegates appears to have been governed by local circumstances: where they had a chance of winning, the SR's took part, and where they did not, they found a pretext for standing aloof. On the Western Front, where things were going badly for them, the party conference decided against seeking representation in the congress on the ground that such activity would distract from the work of preparing for the Constituent Assembly, into which all available forces had been thrown. [4]

Hence the poor showing at the congress is to be explained only in minor degree by these abstentionist tactics, by the half-boycott of the soviet elections, as one observer has termed it. [5] By far the main cause for the party's debacle was the ground swell of extremist sentiment [6] which had wiped out the earlier SR and Menshevik majorities in the local soviets and replaced them with equally

---

[3] See Gotz's letter entitled "Klevetnikam" (To My Slanderers), *Delo Naroda*, No. 198 (November 3, 1917).

[4] Knorin, *Revoliutsiia i kontr-revoliutsiia v Belorussii*, I, 69.

[5] Mstislavski, *Piat' dnei*, p. 121.

[6] See *The Agrarian Foes of Bolshevism*, ch. 10 and 11.

top-heavy margins for the Bolsheviks and left SR's. In Odessa the moderate socialists did not stand aside but entered the lists in a bid to retain their influence, predominant as late as the middle of September. They even talked themselves into agreeing to a purely socialist ministry, but all in vain—they were routed and only extremists were returned from Odessa to the Second Soviet Congress.[7] In general, Menshevik delegates at the First Congress were replaced by Bolsheviks at the Second, and SR delegates either by Bolsheviks or by left SR's.[8] The Izhevsk Soviet of Viatka province had been represented in June by a Menshevik and an SR, whereas in October it sent one Bolshevik and one left SR;[9] the Helsingfors Soviet, one of the most radical in the country because of the concentration of soldiers and sailors, switched from an all-SR delegation of three moderates and one extremist to a representation evenly divided between the Bolsheviks and the left SR's.[10]

In view of the general mood of the workers and soldiers, who alone were represented in the soviets, and in view of the energetic campaigning of the left SR's, sometimes in league with the Bolsheviks,[11] it is not surprising that the Central Committee should have despaired of controlling the SR delegation and should have regarded its prospective majority as lost children against whom disciplinary action of the sternest kind was in order.[12] This time the calculations of the Central Committee were correct. While the statistics of the Second All-Russian Soviet Congress are in what might be termed a fluid condition, and neither the strength of the SR delegation nor the factional divisions within it can be determined with exactitude, a plausible estimate is that 200 SR's were present at the opening of the congress as against twice that number of Bolsheviks and their sympathizers.[13] A breakdown of the SR

[7] *Oktiabr' na Odeshchine*, pp. 15–16; "Vtoroi Vserossiiskii S"ezd Sovetov (Ankety bol'shevikov-delegatov II S"ezda Sovetov)" (The Second All Russian Congress of Soviets [Questions Submitted to Bolshevik Delegates at the Second Congress of Soviets]), in *Krasnyi Arkhiv*, LXXXIV (V, 1937), 98–102.

[8] See in this connection the comment of Sukhanov, *Zapiski*, VII, 191.

[9] *Krasnyi Arkhiv*, LXXXIV (V, 1937), 32–33.

[10] *Ibid.*, p. 94. Another typical example is afforded by Zlatoust in the Urals, where a left SR and a Bolshevik replaced two SR defensists (*ibid.*, p. 91).

[11] As in Odessa. See *Oktiabr' na Odeshchine*, pp. 15–16.

[12] Mstislavski, *Piat' dnei*, p. 123.

[13] *Vtoroi Vserossiiskii S"ezd Sovetov*, pp. 170–71, n.15; Sukhanov, *Zapiski*, VII, 179–80.

representation on the basis of questionnaires filled out at the congress, which are neither complete nor free of error, shows 98 left SR's, 40 SR's of the center, 16 right SR's, 4 Ukrainian SR's, and 32 others without indication of factional allegiance.[14] At the caucus on the eve of the congress, with some 150 party members attending, the left mustered 92 votes in opposition to the resolution of the Central Committee as against the 60 that were cast in its favor.[15] Mstislavski's statement that extreme right-wingers of the Zenzinov stripe did not exceed fifteen in number [16] is further evidence that the figures given above are not too far wide of the mark. Yet at the end of the congress, after the moderate socialists had withdrawn, a new count disclosed that as many SR's were in attendance as before, only now 179 of them were classed as left SR's and 21 as Ukrainian SR's.[17] This sweeping revision of figures on factional preference is confirmed by Kamkov's assertion that 169 party members had fallen under the ban of the Central Committee because of their refusal to leave the congress.[18] Just where all of these left SR's had come from is not readily apparent. A number of moderates had refused to bolt and so automatically were ranked as leftists, and there were some dozens of late arrivals to be distributed among the parties,[19] but presumably many of the new recruits had also come from that element in the congress whose party affiliation had for some reason not been previously established.[20]

Whatever the exact figures may have been, the lesson of the congress is clear: the left wing of the party had achieved a decisive majority and the Central Committee had sustained a crushing de-

[14] *Vtoroi Vserossiiskii S"ezd Sovetov*, pp. 108–9, 171. Miliukov is hopelessly confused in reporting 69 left and 159 right SR's (*Istoriia*, I, Part III, 236). Shliapnikov's estimate is also inaccurate ("K Oktiabriu" [Toward October], *Proletarskaia Revoliutsiia*, X [1922], 22).

[15] *Delo Naroda*, No. 189 (October 26, 1917). See below, p. 102.

[16] *Piat' dnei*, p. 122. Zenzinov, as we know, was a right centrist but in so radical a setting it is proper to speak of his type of SR as being of the extreme right.

[17] *Vtoroi Vserossiiskii S"ezd Sovetov*, pp. xxxi, xxxv, 170–71; *Istoriia grazhdanskoi voiny v SSSR*, II, 289, 295–96.

[18] *Protokoly pervago s"ezda PLSR*, p. 17.

[19] *Istoriia grazhdanskoi voiny v SSSR*, II, 288.

[20] Brief mention of this element is made in *Vtoroi Vserossiiskii S"ezd Sovetov*, p. 170, n. 15; see also pp. 111–12, where the factor of inadequate registration is further discussed.

feat. A collision was now inevitable, for the October Revolution left no room for temporizing and raised issues concerning which no agreement was possible. We are already familiar with the position of the Central Committee in the initial stage of the revolution: it was not yet ready to abandon the principle of coalition and meant to defend the Provisional Government as its embodiment.

More complex was the position of the left SR's. They desired neither the continuance of the existing regime nor the installation of a new one in which the Bolsheviks would have a free hand in implementing their doctrines, particularly in respect to the peasantry. Having as their objective the transformation of society through the independent initiative of the toilers rather than state intervention, the left SR's hoped to avert a political crisis so acute as to bring on civil war, for in that case the revolutionists would be driven to create an apparatus of power beneath the weight of which the spontaneity of the toilers would be crushed, the nature of the parties perverted, and the soviets transformed from free agencies into organs of state. The right-wing socialists should not be excluded from office but should be allowed to participate in the government as representatives of the most advanced section of the bourgeoisie, in order to prevent the social struggle from boiling up into a political crisis, but they must be impelled to move in the right direction through mass pressure directed by the Bolsheviks and the left SR's.[21] The Petrograd Soviet should not undertake the seizure of power but should leave the initiative to the All-Russian Congress, confining its role to gathering a force which would be placed at the disposal of the congress. The purely socialist government organized by the congress of workers' and soldiers' soviets in conjunction with a sister congress of peasants' soviets would enjoy so much authority in the eyes of the Russian people that the Kerenski regime would either voluntarily resign or else be painlessly removed from power. That is how the left SR's would have liked to see the October Revolution develop, without a violent upheaval and with the Petrograd Soviet bridled by the All Russian Congress, and this congress by a peasant counterpart.[22]

[21] Mstislavski, *Piat' dnei*, pp. 113–15.
[22] See Kamkov's report in *Protokoly pervago s"ezda PLSR*, pp. 38–40. This report was made on November 22. Another left SR leader, I. Z. Steinberg, has

One may say that the left SR's were semi-anarchistic in their approach to the problems of revolution. One may also say they were utopian—how could a showdown with the bourgeoisie be averted by leaving rosewater socialists in office and how could any amount of mass pressure induce a Zenzinov to move in the direction of peace if France and Great Britain were unwilling?—but one cannot deny these men the gift of foresight. They saw quite clearly, at the outset of the revolution, how civil war and the "dictatorship of the proletariat" would stifle the freedom of the soviets and kill the people's initiative.

Since the revolution was not developing according to their wishes, and since the Bolsheviks were obviously bidding for one-party rule in order to give free rein to their bias against the peasantry and in favor of state coercion, what did the left SR's propose to do? Their answer was that if they were plunged into civil war against their will, they would range themselves with the Bolsheviks on the left side of the barricades, despite their misgivings over such an alliance. As Karelin told the Second All-Russian Congress, the fate of Bolshevism was now tied to the fate of the revolution, and the ruin of the one would involve the ruin of the other.[23] Though the left SR's liked neither the way in which the revolution had been precipitated nor the course it was taking, they knew their duty to a movement which might have been touched off by one political group but otherwise was thoroughly popular in character, dictated by the heartfelt interests of the people and inflamed by the apostasy

---

given a somewhat different version of his party's purpose, based upon an earlier statement of Kamkov's before the fall of the Provisional Government (the source and date are not given). According to this version, the Kerenski regime would not immediately be replaced but would operate under the shadow of the soviet congress, which would indicate to the local soviets what measures to accept and what to reject; the showdown over power would be deferred until the Constituent Assembly had demonstrated its unwillingness to obey the toilers' wishes (*Ot fevralia po oktiabr'*, p. 123). It would not be surprising if there were this discrepancy in Kamkov's utterances, though Steinberg may here be merely voicing his own point of view. Yet another left SR leader, A. L. Kolegaev, was calling on October 24 for the immediate removal of the coalitional government and the constitution of a new authority by the soviet congress, provided representatives of the peasantry were included. See *Revoliutsiia 1917 goda*, V, 171.

[23] *Vtoroi Vserossiiskii S"ezd Sovetov*, p. 82.

of the moderate socialists.[24] The left SR's acknowledged the sovereignty of the workers' and soldiers' congress, with which they associated the congress of peasants' soviets now being convoked as a result of their efforts.[25] They would never bolt the congress at the behest of a Central Committee under whose dictation they long had smarted. Another more practical consideration was that the left SR leaders had no choice but to stay at the congress if they wished to keep in step with their rank and file,[26] for the workers and soldiers who marched under their banner were making common cause with those who followed Lenin, unmindful of the differences that divided their high commands.

Thus the stage was set for a showdown with the Central Committee, which was determined to impair the legitimacy of the congress by ordering party forces to withdraw from its deliberations. The showdown came on October 25, just before the opening of the congress, at the caucus of the SR delegation. During most of the day the tide of battle swayed back and forth as the left SR leaders fought to wrest the whole delegation, and with it the party organization, from the grasp of the Central Committee. They played for high stakes in the knowledge that locally the membership of the party had moved well beyond the point where the May Congress had stood in confiding the direction of affairs to men who believed that the party must not overstep the bounds of the February Revolution. Though unable to realize their maximum objective of unhorsing the Central Committee, the extremist leaders easily won the upper hand at the caucus and placed in the chair one of their number, S. Mstislavski. They had the satisfaction of needling the spokesmen of the Central Committee—Gotz, Zenzinov, and Gendelman—by making them wait their turn as ordinary members of the party before addressing the assembly. The numerically impotent right could only protest this lack of deference to authority.

The committeemen went through the motions of defending the

---

[24] *Protokoly pervago s"ezda PLSR*, pp. 41–42; Steinberg, *Ot fevralia po oktiabr'*, pp. 123–24; see also pronouncements by the left SR's in *Znamia Truda*, No. 58 (October 31, 1917).

[25] See ch. 5.

[26] This is indirectly admitted by Mstislavski (*Piat' dnei*, p. 131); see also report of Kamkov, in *Protokoly pervago s"ezda PLSR*, p. 42.

principle of coalition and condemning the Bolshevik coup, but
their arguments sounded hollow, as though they expected defeat
and had resigned themselves to the inevitability of a split in the
party. Without backing water, they apparently toned down their
utterances in keeping with the mood of their audience, and the
resolution proposed by Gendelman in the name of the Central
Committee, while irreconcilable in essence, was less provocative
than might have been expected in view of the known attitude of
Gotz and his lieutenants. But the left was determined to preserve
contact with Bolshevism as long as there was any possibility of an
understanding. In general, it sought not to thwart but merely to
restrain the October Revolution through associating other groups
with the Bolsheviks in the exercise of power; and when Gendelman's
resolution was put to a vote, it was lost by the decisive margin of
92 against 60. The minority then withdrew to a separate chamber,
where it arrogated to itself the title of "SR delegation" and continued its deliberations under the presidency of V. N. Filippovski,
a veteran soviet figure who in February had been Mstislavski's associate in directing the military dispositions of the infant revolution,[27] and who now in October became the counterchairman of a
delegation hopelessly divided by the further course of the revolution.[28]

With the split in the party thus precipitated by action of the
Central Committee, further measures soon deepened it into a schism
which neither common interest nor mutual adversity could heal.
The decision to leave the congress had been taken before the opening session,[29] but it was not until after the election of the presidium
and consideration of another matter that Gendelman arose—as
always, in the wake of the Mensheviks—to announce the withdrawal

[27] See *The Agrarian Foes of Bolshevism*, pp. 132–33.

[28] Mstislavski, *Piat' dnei*, pp. 121–23; *Delo Naroda*, No. 189 (October 26, 1917).
These are the only sources. The *Novaia Zhizn'* and *Volia Naroda* add nothing.

[29] This is definitively established by the postscript to the report of the caucus
in the *Delo Naroda*, No. 189, except that here the prediction is made that the
"so-called left" would join in the walkout. The SR action, therefore, was entirely independent of what transpired at the congress. See also Mstislavski,
Piat' dnei, p. 123; Sukhanov, *Zapiski*, VII, 195–96. Miliukov is in error when
he writes (*Istoriia*, I, Part III, 238) that the decision was not taken until after
the opening of the congress.

of the SR delegation,[30] or rather of that lesser part of it which obeyed the Central Committee. On this occasion he minced no words, branding the Bolshevik seizure of power as a "crime before country and revolution," as a "mad and iniquitous act" provocative of civil war and destructive of the Constituent Assembly; yet his attack on the legitimacy of the congress came with ill grace from the spokesman of a group which had permitted, if belatedly, its followers to take part in the election of delegates and now was proclaiming its intention to bolt after the congress had been constituted with the bolters participating. Gendelman justified his contention on the ground that the front and many soviets were not sufficiently represented at the congress. But then the next day the Central Committee would use the bolt itself as the pretext for denying recognition to a body in which only Bolsheviks and SR dissenters continued to sit.[31] The plain fact of the matter is, however, that the SR's and their Menshevik allies had been roundly beaten in the contest for delegates and so had picked up their marbles and gone home.[32] The staged withdrawal was anything but impressive—of the 130-odd moderates present,[33] only about seventy actually walked out,[34] the others apparently fearing their soviet constituents more than the whip of party discipline—and the left SR's further spoiled the effect of the demonstration by sending Kamkov to the platform to announce that they were staying on at the congress.[35]

No other action of the left SR's so infuriated the Central Committee as their taking the edge off the chosen weapon of isolating

[30] *Vtoroi Vserossiiskii S"ezd Sovetov*, pp. 37–38; *Delo Naroda*, No. 190 (October 27, 1917).

[31] See its statement of October 26 on page 2 of the *Delo Naroda*, No. 191 (October 28, 1917).

[32] Sukhanov, *Zapiski*, VII, 191–93, 199–200; Miliukov, *Istoriia*, I, Part III, 238–39; Vladimirova, *God sluzhby "sotsialistov" kapitalistam*, p. 87.

[33] Roughly seventy Mensheviks and sixty SR's of the center and right (those who had supported Gendelman in the caucus of October 25).

[34] *Vtoroi Vserossiiskii S"ezd Sovetov*, pp. xxxv–xxxvi, 171; Mstislavski, *Piat' dnei*, p. 131; Sukhanov, *Zapiski*, VII, 201. The best surmise is that the SR's of the center who were closely connected with the party organization bolted, and those whose first allegiance was to their local soviets remained.

[35] *Vtoroi Vserossiiskii S"ezd Sovetov*, p. 45. The announcement was greeted with applause, showing the relief felt by the congress at not having to buck the whole of the PSR.

the Bolsheviks from other sections of the revolutionary democracy. Zenzinov would later reproach the Left SR's with having saved the October Revolution by breaking the ranks of the opposition and providing the Bolsheviks with enough additional support to enable them to hold to their course.[36] On October 26 the Central Committee summoned all party members to get out of the Military Revolutionary Committee,[37] the nerve center of the successful insurrection, and when this injunction was disregarded, excluded the offenders from membership in the party. But the ban of excommunication, issued on October 27, was much broader than would have been required for the purpose: "All those members of the party who have taken part in the Bolshevik venture and who did not leave the Soviet Congress after the bombardment of the Winter Palace, the arrest of party members, and other acts of violence committed by the Military Revolutionary Committee against the democracy, are expelled from the party for gross breach of discipline." [38] This shotgun measure thus was leveled at those who had merely refused to leave the congress as well as at those who had actively assisted the Bolsheviks in staging their coup.[39] In this manner a number of moderate-minded individuals unsympathetic to the Bolshevik venture, yet loyal to the soviet congress, were cast out of the party.

The men in control of the Central Committee were now on the warpath, striking out in all directions. From expelling individuals they passed on to disbanding entire party organizations, including the one at St. Petersburg, the largest in the country, with some 45,000 members. From striking at the head of the serpent in the capital they proceeded to belabor its coils in the provinces. On November 8 the excommunication decree of October 27 was extended to localities throughout the country, and members of the

[36] "Na zapiatkakh" (On the Footboards), *Delo Naroda*, No. 219 (November 26, 1917).

[37] See notice in *ibid.*, No. 189 (October 26, 1917).

[38] *Ibid.*, No. 191 (October 28, 1917).

[39] Zenzinov flatly stated that by remaining at the congress the left SR's had cut themselves off from the party; see " 'Levye s.-r.-y' samoopredelilis' " (The "Left SR's" Have Exercised Their Right of Self-Determination), *ibid.*, No. 196 (November 1, 1917). See also below, pp. 170–71 for treatment of this problem at the Fourth Party Congress.

party who had in any way been involved in the Bolshevik seizure of power or had worked on the local organs of the new regime found themselves ejected and specifically deprived of the right to vote for delegates or to serve as delegates to the forthcoming party congress.[40] In numerous instances SR's had entered local military revolutionary committees which, unlike the Petersburg prototype, were not under Bolshevik domination, only to find their party status compromised as a result.[41] On November 11 the venerable Mark Natanson was dropped from the Central Committee, where he long had been isolated.[42] Three days later the round of exclusions came to an end when the Provisional Central Bureau of the left SR's fell under the ban.[43] By this time, however, the Central Committee had reached the point of diminishing returns, for all members of the bureau had already been read out of the party on other grounds.

At the Fourth Party Congress the spokesman of the Central Committee would not venture an estimate of the number of members lost to the party as a result of these sweeping exclusions.[44] His assertion that only in the case of St. Petersburg had an organization been dissolved, and it only after having split in two,[45] does not accord with Kamkov's statement that the Helsingfors and Voronezh locals likewise had been disbanded.[46] The Helsingfors SR's had long engaged in hostilities with the Central Committee, and in Voronezh the SR workingmen had grown restive under the sway of the city committee and had ousted it in favor of a new one with a leftist majority, whereupon the provincial committee had proclaimed the dissolution of the city organization.[47] There was a good deal of dissatisfaction in the party, outside the ranks of those who were being expelled, at the way in which the Central Committee had dealt with the matter, and many felt that a policy of mass exclusions in accordance with the doctrine of collective guilt ill became a party

[40] *Delo Naroda*, No. 203 (November 8, 1917).   [41] *Kratkii otchët*, p. 96.
[42] *Delo Naroda*, No. 207 (November 11, 1917).
[43] Protokol Zasedaniia Tsentral'nago Komiteta PSR, November 14, 1917; *Delo Naroda*, No. 211 (November 16, 1917).
[44] *Kratkii otchët*, p. 111.
[45] *Delo Naroda*, No. 224 (December 5, 1917). The statement is not contained in this form in the official report of the congress (see *Kratkii otchët*, p. 110).
[46] *Protokoly pervago s"ezda PLSR*, p. 17.
[47] *1917i god v Voronezhskoi gubernii*, pp. 108-9, 118.

which had always stressed the individual approach in matters of theory and practice. The Ekaterinoslav provincial conference demanded the adoption of a more discriminating policy which would admit of individual exceptions.[48]

The Central Committee in the person of V. M. Zenzinov—the key figure in organizational matters, along with A. R. Gotz—defended its action on the ground that the leftist movement was a cancerous growth which had bitten deeply into the vitals of the party, requiring excision before the organism could be restored to health. It was not as though the party was losing something of its own, he argued, for the left SR's were essentially an alien element, most of them being maximalists, syndicalists, or anarchists who not only had built up their own organization within the party, flouting its discipline at will, but also had committed acts of aggression against it in serving as accomplices to the Bolshevik crime.[49] While Zenzinov refrains from analyzing the basic attitudes involved, it is likely that his own and his colleagues' course was dictated primarily by the old antagonism between the "defensists" entrenched in positions of leadership and the "internationalists" seeking a change of policy with respect to the war. Certainly no other issue had so inflamed passions nor produced a more irreconcilable clash of opinion. Spiridonova saw in the desperate resolve of the right SR's to block the peace efforts of their opponents the cause of their readiness to split even the peasant movement.[50] Not all members of the party agreed that the war was the main issue at stake; some held that the seeds of schism had been planted when the left wing came to regard the revolution as socialist in nature instead of intermediate between private ownership and a collectivist economy, as party doctrine had hitherto maintained.[51] This was a point of view current in left-centrist circles, where some issue besides the war was needed to justify the break with the left. As between the left and every-

---

[48] *Kratkii otchët*, p. 92.

[49] " 'Levye s.-r.-y' samoopredelilis'," *Delo Naroda*, No. 196 (November 1, 1917); see also Rosenblum's statement at the Fourth Congress, *ibid.*, No. 224 (December 5, 1917).

[50] Speech to the peasants' congress, *ibid.*, No. 225 (December 6, 1917).

[51] Report of Kaplan (LC) to the refounded Petersburg organization, *ibid.*, No. 203 (November 8, 1917). The symbol in parentheses indicates the factional allegiance of the party member after whose name it is placed; see below, p. 176.

thing to the right of center, the war undoubtedly was the chief plane of cleavage.

The question remains whether the Central Committee also had some more practical end in view when it expelled the left wing. The extremists always maintained that control of the approaching party congress was the prize at stake, and that the official leadership faced certain defeat unless it could distort the congress by throwing out of the party so large a number of dissenters as to leave its henchmen in control. The committee pursued its purpose both from above and from below, depriving local organizations of leaders they most likely would have sent to the party congress by expelling those who had already been sent to the soviet congress, and striking at the rank and file of dissent by dissolving whole organizations. According to Kamkov, a freely chosen congress, untrammeled by the decrees of expulsion, would have found the left in possession of three fourths of the seats.[52] While this estimate is badly overdrawn, the purge undoubtedly played into the hands of the Central Committee in its attempt to keep the direction of party affairs out of the hands of the antiwar faction, and the question is to what extent, consciously or subconsciously, the committee was influenced by this consideration in framing its policy. The decree extending to the entire country the excommunication of party members associated with the Bolshevik seizure of power specifically debarred them, as we have seen, from serving as delegates to the congress or from taking part in the selection of delegates. Chernov took cognizance of what was afoot in right-wing circles when he predicted that the scheme to obtain an artificial majority at the congress through amputation of the left wing would not be realized, for it would be proved that the element eliminated actually stood to the left of the party instead of being its authentic left wing.[53] In other words, he meant that with the extremists gone—and he welcomed the purge of elements that could not be relied upon in a crisis—the left center would still be strongly enough represented at the Fourth Congress to settle accounts with the right and right center. And in

[52] *Protokoly pervago s"ezda PLSR*, pp. 17, 78–79; *Kratkii otchët*, pp. 35–36.
[53] "Ochishchenie partii" (Purging the Party), *Delo Naroda*, No. 218 (November 24, 1917).

this prediction he was essentially correct. The calculation in right-wing circles as to the political advantage of a purge does not, of course, in itself establish the complicity of the Central Committee, yet the Gotz-Zenzinov core of that organ may well have been moved by its conception of patriotic duty to weight the scales at the congress in favor of those for whom a separate peace was the worst of all conceivable evils growing out of Kerenski's fall.

Simultaneously with cutting off the left wing the Central Committee had proceeded against the effort on the opposite extreme to rally hard-shelled defensists behind the "Organizational Council of the Petrograd Group of SR's," a society which had established branches elsewhere and which in some provinces, notably in Simbirsk and Kharkov, had put forth competing lists of candidates for the Constituent Assembly. The schismatics in question having failed to desist from their activities, the Central Committee on November 14 proclaimed the expulsion of members of the Organizational Council and its provincial affiliates.[54] This action, however, does not demonstrate the impartiality of the committee nor redress the balance sheet of exclusions, for, as Zenzinov himself pointed out, the right-wing dissenters were a staff without an army, whereas those on the left had wide popular backing.[55]

The reaction of the left SR's to the disciplinary proceedings against them varied from assuming an air of aggrieved innocence to striking back with vengeful vigor. The favor of the Soviet government gave them an advantage, and in a number of soviets they wielded power in their own right. In the Finnish capital left SR's filled many soviet offices and commanded a strong following among the Russian soldiers and sailors stationed there. In point of fanaticism Proshian and his colleagues did not lag behind their Bolshevik allies and may even have exceeded them. The Helsingfors Soviet, acting in concert with the regional soviet and the supreme organ of the Baltic Fleet, suppressed the local SR newspaper, arrested its editor, and turned its property over to the regional SR committee in Finland. In its broader aspect, this action marked a resort to force by the antiwar majority against a defensist organ;

[54] Protokol Zasedaniia Tsentral'nago Komiteta PSR; text of decree in *Delo Naroda*, No. 211 (November 16, 1917).

[55] *Kratkii otchët*, pp. 70-71.

more specifically, it marked a gain for the left SR's at the expense of the Central Committee. The motion to close down the newspaper had been introduced in the local soviet by Shishko, a left SR.[56] Other strong-armed actions on the part of the extremists are mentioned by Zenzinov, who accuses the left SR's of waging a veritable war upon their erstwhile comrades.[57] The All-Russian Peasants' Executive Committee, with its core of old-line Populists, was a natural target for impatient revolutionaries of the younger generation. The left SR Ustinov joined the Bolsheviks in action against the committee's newspaper, and the left SR Spiro inspected its correspondence at the behest of the Military Revolutionary Committee. Everywhere, the left SR's seemed to be working hand in glove with the Bolsheviks as far as assaulting the PSR was concerned. A tendency to appropriate the party label could be noted: in opening a campaign to discredit the Central Committee, Mstislavski wrote in the *Znamia Truda* (Banner of Labor) that the masses must be freed from the influence of the apostate center, for only the left had the right to call itself Socialist Revolutionary.[58]

How much of the old organization did the Left SR's carry away with them into a separate party? The scope and character of the schism can be determined only by examining its local aspects, for there are no data pertaining to the party as a whole, and the crisis that had overtaken the PSR was not confined to spheres of leadership but extended down to the bottom of the organizational structure. Unfortunately, the chaotic conditions of the time, the looseness of organizational ties, and the vastness of the country leave many gaps in the record, but there is enough information to serve as a basis of judgment.

The banner organization of the country, and the one about which we are best informed, was the St. Petersburg local. At the peak of its development, the registered membership hovered in the vicinity of 45,000. As we have seen, the left wing was strongly represented in Petersburg from the outset and had vigorously challenged the of-

[56] *Delo Naroda*, No. 191 (October 28, 1917).
[57] " 'Levye s.-r.-y' samoopredelilis'," *ibid.*, No. 196 (November 1, 1917).
[58] See extract reprinted in *Delo Naroda*, No. 193 (October 29, 1917).

ficial line of the party at the Second or April Conference; [59] by the
Seventh or September Conference it had won a majority,[60] and
the Eighth Conference in October confirmed it in control of the
city committee. That was the state of affairs when the Provisional
Government was overthrown. In the light of the new situation the
committee felt impelled to summon a fresh conference for October
29, after the Central Committee had already fulminated its bull of
excommunication against the element of the party dominant in the
local organization.[61]

With the stage set for a fight to the finish, the Ninth City Conference opened with 194 voting delegates in attendance. At least
that was the figure announced in the *Znamia Truda*,[62] the official
organ of the city committee and subsequently the mouthpiece of
the new party. It was now a case of the extremists against the field,
including the left center, whose following up to the present had not
been sharply marked off from that of the left. The Ninth Conference drew a clear line between these two sectors of party opinion
by forcing the left center to choose between entering the path of
schism or breaking with the left wing. The test came on a resolution of no confidence in the Central Committee for its policy of
exclusion. Although the left center had been at odds with the Central
Committee over general policy, it could not bring itself either by
conviction or in party conscience to condemn that body for its
stand on the October Revolution. The Chernov group was not
going to give aid and comfort to Bolshevism, even in an indirect
or left-handed manner, and was determined to preserve its party
status unimpaired for the reckoning with the right deviation at the
Fourth Congress. The resolution of no confidence, therefore, cut
like a knife through the as yet imperfectly differentiated following

[59] See *The Agrarian Foes of Bolshevism*, pp. 152–55.

[60] See *ibid.*, pp. 440–42.

[61] On October 26 a preliminary conference of the city district committees
and of party members in the soviet and city council had demonstrated the
ascendancy of the left by burying a resolution which condemned the Bolsheviks and pledged support to the Committee to Save the Fatherland and Revolution. See report in *Delo Naroda*, No. 190 (October 27, 1917).

[62] "Zhizn' partii: 9-ia Petrogradskaia konferentsiia partii s.-r." (Party Matters:
The 9th Petrograd Conference of the PSR), No. 58 (October 31, 1917). In
addition, 103 delegates attended with the right to be heard but not to vote.

of the left and left center, and the result was a wide-open split. The "group of the center" announced that it would take no part in the vote. The resolution was declared adopted with 99 votes in its favor, three against, and six abstaining, but two delegates from the Liteiny district immediately raised charges of irregularity on the ground that the left-wing presidium had allowed Kalegaev to serve as chairman even though his name was not listed on its rolls, and had fixed the voting strength of the conference at a figure below 200 even though these delegates personally had been issued tickets numbered 202 and 213—an indication that the resolution had failed to secure an absolute majority.[63]

The conclusion to be drawn from the outcome of the conference is that on the issue of the October Revolution the city organization was not far from evenly divided. Other evidence points in the same direction. When the Central Committee responded to the challenge by proclaiming the dissolution of the Petersburg local and appointing a commission to reconstitute it from elements amenable to party discipline, the first conference of the new organization—it was called the Tenth to maintain the semblance of unbroken succession—announced that 25,850 party members were represented,[64] as against the 20,600 members who had constituted the base of the Left SR organization at the outset of its independent career.[65] The sum of the two figures is not widely at variance from the last an-

[63] "Netochnosti otchëta" (Inaccuracies in the Account), *Delo Naroda*, No. 196 (November 1, 1917). I. Romanov and Mark Miasoedov were the delegates who published this criticism. Otherwise the *Delo Naroda*, in keeping with its habit of shunning embarrassing developments, contains only scattered references to the Ninth Conference. Kamkov's resolution for mutual concessions, an all-socialist government, and against isolation of the Bolsheviks had drawn more support (122 against 3 with 6 abstentions)—perhaps because it was more popular or (more likely) because it had been voted on earlier when a larger number of delegates were in attendance. See account of the proceedings together with the texts of the resolutions and the vote on each in the *Znamia Truda*, No. 58 (October 31, 1917). The most reliable Soviet source errs in asserting that the left had a big majority at this conference (see Vladimirova, *God sluzhby "sotsialistov" kapitalistam,* p. 97). From the defeat of certain amendments offered by the center and its subsequent refusal to take part in the voting, it may nevertheless be concluded that the left did have a majority.

[64] *Delo Naroda,* No. 212 (November 17, 1917). The conference convened on November 15.

[65] "Krasnorechivyia tsifry" (Eloquent Figures), *ibid.,* No. 221 (December 1, 1917). The initial Left SR conference was held November 7-10.

nounced pre-schism total of 44,500.[66] The basis of dividing the membership is not stated. Apparently the strength of district organizations was totaled according to the side they took, in disregard of the fact that in each instance there must have been a seceding minority.

As time went on each side became more sanguine in estimating its own strength and belittling that of its rival. Thus the Left SR's claimed to have carried away from the crumbling edifice of the PSR 30,000 [67] or even 40,000 [68] of its former numbers, while the regulars progressed from claiming a mere majority of the district organizations [69] to asserting that more than three fourths of them had returned to the fold.[70] But it was the outcome of the November elections in Petersburg which gave the regulars a club with which to belabor the Left SR's. Although the schism had taken place before the election of the Constituent Assembly, there had been no time to disentangle the two wings of the SR movement from the composite list bearing the party label, and the 152,230 votes cast for it in the capital represented both factions. A few weeks later, however, in the special election for the city council which the Bolsheviks had called after forcibly dissolving the old council, an election that was boycotted by all of the moderate socialist parties as well as by the Kadets, the Left SR's, now on their own, polled only a handful of votes. The SR's hailed the discomfiture of their rivals in not being able to draw a vote in excess of their registered membership, and when later dispatches revised the figure downward (from 26,194 to 16,000), Chernov ridiculed the Left SR's before the Fourth Congress as an organization that claimed an actual membership of 30,000, yet could produce only 16,000 votes from both membership and following.[71] The moderates interpreted the results to mean either that the Left SR's had had no strength to begin with

[66] At the Eight City Conference on October 8 (*ibid.*, No. 176 [October 10, 1917]).

[67] Statement of A. Shreider, cited in "Krasnorechivyia tsifry," *ibid.*, No. 221 (December 1, 1917).

[68] Statement attributed to Kamkov (see Vladimirova, *God sluzhby "sotsialistov" kapitalistam*, p. 98).

[69] See under heading "Iz zhizni partii s.-r." (From Party Life), *Delo Naroda*, No. 205 (November 10, 1917).

[70] *Kratkii otchët*, p. 94 (statement of Vysotski).

[71] *Ibid.*, p. 116.

or that it had quickly been dissipated.[72] But the soviet organ tells us that "because of technical difficulties" the Petersburg Left SR Committee had been able to make up and publish its list of candidates only on the last day. Most of the district organizations had not been informed in time of the decision to participate in the election, and the Left SR's had staged no electoral campaign whatever. Hence the handful of votes (19,194 as against 358,184 for the Bolsheviks).[73]

There is much to be said in favor of the latter contention. The Left SR's had not approved of the manner in which the dominant party in the soviets was riding roughshod over the opposition, arresting the mayor, dissolving the council, and in general displaying such intolerance that even its allies could not trust its intentions.[74] The election of November 29 was widely regarded as a fig leaf to conceal the naked violence of the regime, and the turnout of 395,-844 stood in marked contrast to the 942,333 votes cast in the election of the Constituent Assembly. The rank-and-file Socialist Revolutionaries were bewildered at the turn of events, at the spectacle of an extremist group which first blew hot and then blew cold to the October Revolution, and at its acrimonious controversy with the kindred left-center group which had moved into control of the regular party organization as a result of the wholesale exclusion of the left and the local weakness of the right.[75] Nearly all of the SR's, extremists as well as moderates, remained away from the polls, while some on the fringe may already have made the transition to Bolshevism. Certainly the influence of the Left SR movement on the political life of the capital cannot be measured in terms of a

---

[72] *Ibid.*, p. 99; *Delo Naroda*, Nos. 221, 222 (December 1, 2, 1917).

[73] *Izvestiia TsIK i petrogradskago soveta*, Nos. 241, 242 (December 1, 2, 1917).

[74] See especially reports in the *Delo Naroda*, Nos. 204, 214, 215 (November 9, 19, 21, 1917); *Protokoly pervago s"ezda PLSR*, pp. 45–46. Only a few days before the municipal election the Left SR spokesman in the Central Executive Committee had moved to revoke the edict dissolving the city council, without offering any defense of the council itself (see *Delo Naroda*, No. 219 [November 26, 1917]; *Revoliutsiia 1917 goda*, VI, 203). The "technical difficulties" referred to above are an euphemistic phrase to cloak the vacillation of the Left SR leadership in the face of the impending election. If the leaders could not make up their minds as to a course to follow until the last moment, how could their followers have been other than confused and apathetic?

[75] The Petersburg organization had always been considered leftist in tendency; it still was, said Vysotski, but it was determined to remain within the party. See *Kratkii otchët*, p. 94.

paltry figure like 19,194. The best estimate that can be made from so confused a situation is that the October Revolution had rent the SR city organization in twain.

In the provinces lines were not so sharply drawn and the pace of events lagged behind developments in the capital. The provincial organizations in left-wing strongholds like Kharkov and Kazan went over bodily to the new party, though not without some wavering and delay in severing connections with the rest of the PSR. At Kharkov the middle-of-the-road element, master of all it surveyed in the near-by provinces of the Central Black-Earth Region, did not exist, and only a small group of fervent nationalists in the SR fold disputed the sway of the left. The strength of this group may be judged from the fact that in the provincial party congress it had mustered but seven votes against the resolutions of the left. It is said to have numbered only a hundred adherents among the 3,000 members of the city organization and to have been nonexistent in Izium *uezd*.[76] Nevertheless, it thoroughly muddied the waters and managed to touch off the schism by entering a rival list of candidates for the Constituent Assembly, at a time when the Left SR's were still divided over the issue of whether to attend or boycott the Fourth Party Congress. The dissident list, headed by Breshkovskaia and V. I. Lebedev, drew 33,913 votes against 650,386 for the official slate,[77] which in this province represented a fusion of the Left and Ukrainian SR's, kindred elements that would soon merge their organizations.[78]

Similarly in Kazan, the center was lacking, and while the right may have been stronger in the city, it was as weak in the country as in Kharkov. Here, also, the left drew its strength directly from the Russian peasantry and indirectly from the influence it exerted over the agrarian movement which had sprung up among subject

[76] *Protokoly pervago s"ezda PLSR*, pp. 6, 9–10, 13. An *uezd* was an administrative subdivision of a province.

[77] See my book, *The Election to the Russian Constituent Assembly*, p. 79; N. V. Sviatitski, "Itogi vyborov vo Vserossiiskoe Uchreditel'noe Sobranie" (The Results of the Election of the All-Russian Constituent Assembly), in *God russkoi revoliutsii*, p. 114. The latter source gives 44,110 for the dissident list, but because Sviatitski's figures for this province leave something to be desired, I have preferred another source.

[78] *Novaia Zhizn'*, No. 214 (December 31, 1917).

peoples. The Chuvash and Tatar elements in Kazan formed a reservoir of support like the Ukrainian in Kharkov, though not to the same extent, for the rival current of nationalism had more appeal to a Turkic or Moslem population than to a branch of the Russian people. Hence the absence of joint lists in Kazan. The city organization had split for the second time on the eve of October,[79] but the left had everything its way in the rural areas, and the effort of the "old SR's," as the defensists were called, to win over the rank and file came to nought when their splinter list collapsed in the election, with only 10,000 votes to its credit against 260,000 for the Left SR's.[80]

In other provinces where the left predominated it is not possible to gain a clear impression of the schism, except in Ufa, which closely resembled Kharkov and Kazan. Elsewhere only bits of information are available. At Pskov the town organization was in the hands of the right-wing *Volia Naroda* group, probably because the industrial element was not strong enough here to break the grip of the prowar intellectuals inscribed on the party rolls. The less articulate social groups with strength in the soviets had not taken the same precautions with reference to registration and the intellectuals were disproportionately represented on the party organs.[81] But the provincial organization must have been dominated by the left, for Pskov was one of those provinces which returned an extremist delegation to the Constituent Assembly. The same is true of Kaluga. There the repressions [82] against the soviet instituted in October by the SR provincial commissar Galin had split the party, and the left SR's inveighed loudly against their rightist brethren with the charge that even the Kadets had been more correct in their conduct.[83]

[79] See *The Agrarian Foes of Bolshevism*, p. 439.
[80] K. Shnurovski, "Kazanskii Sovet Krest'ianskikh Deputatov i levye es-ery pered chekhami" (The Kazan Soviet of Peasants' Deputies and the Left SR's before the Czechs Came), in *Bor'ba za Kazan'*, I, 61; *Kazanskii Oktiabr'*, I, 198–220; see also my book, *The Election to the Russian Constituent Assembly*, pp. 27–28. Where the left controlled the provincial organization, as in Kharkov and Kazan, its list was official and had the advantage of the party label, since the ax of the Central Committee had fallen too late to alter the electoral arrangements. See ch. 6.
[81] *Protokoly pervago s"ezda PLSR*, p. 10.
[82] See *Istoriia grazhdanskoi voiny v SSSR*, II, 77–78.
[83] *Protokoly pervago s"ezda PLSR*, p. 11.

Kherson province was one of the bailiwicks of the left; the Odessa organization had been in its hands since May. The right-wing intellectuals had split off to form their own group but a limited collaboration had been the practice until the decree of expulsion by the Central Committee destroyed any semblance of harmony.[84] Even so, the left in Kherson was not prepared to leave the party in November and held aloof from the schismatic congress in Petersburg, apparently in the hope that the Fourth Congress would reverse the Central Committee.[85] Presumably it went over when the Chernov faction, triumphant at this congress, refused to make any concessions. In Poltava province the left was also in the saddle, but the steed it rode was smaller, for in this opulent and homogeneous region, where Great Russian influence was at a minimum, it was the Ukrainian SR's who really counted.[86] For Riazan there is no information whatever, aside from Chernov's allusion to left-wing strength [87] and the fact that in the election of the Constituent Assembly the SR delegation was evenly divided between moderates and extremists.[88] In all these provinces it must be assumed, in the absence of evidence to the contrary, that the dominant left-wing faction, however great its initial reluctance may have been, sooner or later withdrew from the PSR and carried with it the bulk of the local membership.

Looking now at the country as a whole, and first at the central and northern regions, we can say that outside of the Petersburg sector, the provinces of Pskov, Kaluga, and Riazan, and certain scattered localities, the schism does not seem to have gravely impaired the party organization. Serious losses were sustained, it is true, but more to the Bolsheviks than the Left SR's. The right-centrist organization in Moscow had not experienced anything like the bloodletting in Petersburg when the schism occurred. According to Eugenia Ratner,[89] it had sheared off the extremists without appreciable numerical loss, and had retained its conscious following while losing all of its mass support to the Bolsheviks. The left was stronger in

---

[84] *Ibid.*, pp. 11–12.   [85] *Ibid.*, p. 113.
[86] See *The Election to the Russian Constituent Assembly*, pp. 29–31.
[87] Manuscript commentary on the minutes of the Central Committee, p. 53.
[88] See p. 295.
[89] *Delo Naroda*, No. 220 (November 30, 1917).

Moscow province than in the city, and had sternly contested the September provincial conference with the center, losing out on the crucial resolution by a vote of 90 to 63; but it had been loath to push matters to the breaking point because of the hope of getting a majority at the Fourth Congress, from which it was now excluded by decision of the Central Committee.[90] The situation in Kostroma presented a different pattern: here the left had the city, and the center—branded by the opposition as "right"[91]—the outlying districts. Voted down in the provincial party congress, the left had bolted and set up its own establishment, contending that the provincial committee had manipulated the congress so as to secure a majority for its own supporters. The schism was complete in the towns by the end of November but not as yet in the *uezds*, though the existing friction was dissolving the bonds of union.[92] Matters had not progressed so far in Nizhni Novgorod, where the split between the dominant center and the left-wing opposition had not yet come to a head, either in the city or in the province. The extremists were sufficiently active, however, to render party work ineffective.[93] They were evidently weaker in Smolensk and Novgorod provinces,[94] having achieved no organization in the latter and in both places betraying a tendency to throw in with Bolshevism rather than stand on their own feet. For the Left SR's in Smolensk *uezd* a definite figure of 300 exists. In Novgorod province the list of candidates for the Constituent Assembly had been a bitter pill for the minority to swallow, with a name like Avksentiev's heading the list.

If the schism had not shredded the fabric of organization in the middle and northern sections of the country, still less damaging were its effects in the Central Black-Earth Region and the provinces along the Volga, the cradle and stronghold of Social Revolutionism. Over

[90] *Protokoly pervago s"ezda PLSR*, pp. 9, 10; *Delo Naroda*, No. 220 (statement of Mukhin on the eve of the Fourth Congress).

[91] In general, the Left SR's are only less bad than the Bolsheviks in refusing to distinguish between center and right. One must always be on the lookout for willful confusion.

[92] *Protokoly pervago s"ezda PLSR*, p. 7; *Delo Naroda*, No. 220; "Iz zhizni partii s.-r.," *ibid.*, No. 242 (December 28, 1917).

[93] See report on the eve of the Fourth Congress in *Delo Naroda*, No. 220 (November 30, 1917).

[94] *Protokoly pervago s"ezda PLSR*, pp. 8, 12.

this granary of Russia the center held sway, and it was not so much a question of the left center or the right center as of dead center. Factionalism had made less headway here within the dense, homogeneous mass of the Great Russian peasantry than in areas where the party following was more largely made up of intellectuals and of workers and soldiers—elements that were less enthralled by the vision of land redistribution and responded more readily to the divisive influences of the big cities, the front, and the cockpits of national strife. From the extremist point of view the only leaven in all this dough was the city of Voronezh, with a war-inflated proletariat some ten thousand strong. These workers had become thoroughly radical in outlook and formed the basis not only for a thriving Bolshevik organization but also for a vigorous left SR movement which in September had seized control of the local party machinery. Its dominion did not extend beyond the city limits, however, for the moderates easily maintained their grip on the provincial organization, and the extent to which the peasantry remained proof against the blandishments of the extremists may be judged from the fact that at the Third Provincial Congress of Peasants' Soviets (November 21– 23) there were 487 SR's and three Left SR's.[95] Furthermore, in the election of the Constituent Assembly the Left SR's, despite their bloc with the Ukrainian SR's and the Polish Socialists (PPS), could muster but 11,871 votes for their separate list against 875,300 for the official slate.[96] Hostilities had begun in September and well before the October Revolution the provincial committee had completed the break by reading the leftist leaders out of the party and dissolving the city organization. The next provincial congress (party convention) had confirmed this action by a heavy majority. Henceforth everything was in duplicate—committees, newspapers, and electoral candidacies. The Left Socialist Revolutionaries, and Soviet writers after them, regularly refer to the majority in Voronezh province as "right" SR, in willful disregard of the clear-cut preponderance of the center and the impotence of the right. The extent of the distortion can be appreciated from the fact that the SR's themselves

<hr/>

[95] *1917i god v Voronezhskoi gubernii*, pp. 148–49.
[96] *Ibid.*, pp. 142–43, 157; Radkey, *The Election to the Russian Constituent Assembly*, pp. 78, 80.

classified the organ of the provincial committee, the *Golos Truda* (Voice of Toil), as left-centrist in tendency.[97]

In this banner province the PSR claimed one hundred thousand members.[98] If the actual strength fell below this mark it was because of the inertness of many inscribed on the rolls rather than because of the losses occasioned by the schism. Elsewhere in the Central Black-Earth Region the party was equally entrenched and comparably powerful. Little is known of the other provinces but nowhere does the November schism appear to have assumed serious proportions. Even in Tambov province, the scene of widespread disorders in September,[99] little sympathy for a breakaway can be detected, and what happened seems to have been due to the spontaneous action of the peasantry, to the dilatory policy of the government and the failure of the moderates to control their followers, rather than to the efforts of the left to stir them up. The new party did have adherents in Tambov, Kursk, Orel, and Penza provinces,[100] as well as in Voronezh, but it was only amid the chaotic conditions of 1918, after the crumbling of party bastions under the blows of fortune and the Bolshevik dictatorship, that the Left SR's acquired real strength in this fertile region.

Similar conditions prevailed in the Volga provinces. Samara was another stronghold of the center, and more of the right than of the left center, if one is to judge from the tenor of resolutions on the war, the complexion of the delegation sent to the Constituent Assembly, and the events of 1918 in this region. The extremists were quite weak, numbering by their own admission only about one sixth of the total membership.[101] Their dissent was more natural and their imputation of rightist leanings to the majority more justified than in other cases. In Saratov province the left was stronger,

[97] *Partiinyia Izvestiia*, No. 5 (January 20, 1918), pp. 25–26; *1917i god v Voronezhskoi gubernii*, pp. 115–16. On this province see also the latter source, pp. 108–9, 118, 128, 140; *Protokoly pervago s"ezda PLSR*, p. 5; *Partiinyia Izvestiia*, No. 4 (December 10, 1917), pp. 65–66.

[98] Alekseev, *Oktiabr' i grazhdanskaia voina v TsChO*, p. 38.

[99] See *The Agrarian Foes of Bolshevism*, pp. 437–39.

[100] Kursk returned twelve SR's to the Constituent Assembly and Penza nine; in each case one of the deputies elected adhered to the new party. See below, p. 295.

[101] *Protokoly pervago s"ezda PLSR*, p. 6. It is not clear whether the estimate refers to the whole province or only to the Buguruslan district.

having enough influence among the peasantry to force the dominant center to take it into account in choosing candidates for the Constituent Assembly, with the result that two of the nine seats won by the party were lost in the schism.[102] Apparently the intelligentsia was less defensist-minded and the peasants more radically inclined than in Samara, for the new party had support in both classes, drawing to its side some of the eminent leaders in the city [103] and taking strength from the SR's in the villages,[104] though the exact proportions of the schism are as indeterminable as in other areas. Astrakhan, the southernmost province on the Volga, had a contingent of SR's whose outlook could be ascribed to the remoteness of their habitat had it not been so representative of a large segment of party opinion that was by no means confined to areas that were far removed from the centers of political life. Here on the threshold of Asia the party had a membership of about three thousand, very unevenly divided into a leftist group some two hundred strong, an even smaller rightist group of a hundred or a hundred and fifty, and in between, a swamp of confused thinking in which most of the members, particularly those in the villages, were mired. The left had lacked both the numbers and the militancy to dispel habits of mind associated with an earlier stage of the revolution, and Astrakhan remained a domain of the center, less from conviction, it would seem, than from inertia and bewilderment.[105]

If the schism had damaged the party least in the Central Black-Earth and Volga regions, its worst effects were experienced in the Ukraine. Gravely weakened as it had been from the beginning by the powerful competition of its nationalist offshoot, the PSR went to pieces when the left wing became an independent party, carrying away the organizations in Kharkov and Poltava provinces, presumably also in Kherson province, and subtracting elsewhere a minority of undetermined strength. Only in the Kievan district did the party more or less hold together behind the Central Committee,

---

[102] *Ibid.*, p. 9. The provincial peasants' congress had dictated the inclusion of the two leftists (A. M. Ustinov and G. K. Ulianov).

[103] Antonov, *Pod stiagom proletarskoi bor'by*, I, 226.

[104] M. Levison, "Krest'ianskoe dvizhenie v Saratovskoi gubernii" (The Peasant Movement in Saratov Province), in *1917 god v Saratove*, pp. 78–82.

[105] *Protokoly pervago s"ezda PLSR*, p. 7.

but the Southwestern Region, comprising the provinces of Kiev, Volynia, and Podolia and constituting the hotbed of Ukrainian nationalist sentiment, had witnessed the virtual extinction of the PSR as a mass organization.[106] More flesh was left on the bones in Ekaterinoslav and Chernigov provinces, but the party organisms here were anything but solidly behind the Central Committee, blaming it as much as the extremists for the civil war in the SR camp.[107] The correlation of forces in the Ukraine as a whole after the left had departed can be seen in the decisions of the December party congress, which chose a regional committee of three left-centrists, three centrists, and two rightists.[108]

Midway between the Ukraine, the area of maximum disintegration, and the Black-Earth provinces of Great Russia, the scene of minimum damage, stands the Ural region. Here the PSR suffered grievous defections but managed to keep its head above water. Ufa province resembled Kazan in being a stronghold of the left and in having a large native population amenable to radical influence. Like Kazan, also, it was wholly lost to the party as a result of the schism. The number of Left SR's in Ufa province is placed at from 15,000 to 20,000 on the basis of convention reports, but actually the membership did not exceed 7,000 or 8,000, according to a Bolshevik authority, whose testimony is the more credible in that it deflates to the same extent the claims of his own party (4,000 to 5,000 members instead of 10,379).[109] Other political groups, including, presumably, those SR's who followed the line of the Central Committee or stood to the right of it, are dismissed as of no consequence. Where the Zlatoust SR organization fits into this picture is difficult to say, for its membership of 2,500 (much of it dead wood, no doubt) is reported to have been wavering between allegiance to the Central Committee and acceptance of the leftist point of view dominant in other parts of the province.[110] In general, the workers of this in-

---

[106] The best evidence is the general election in November and December; see my book, *The Election to the Russian Constituent Assembly*, p. 79.

[107] *Kratkii otchët*, p. 92; *Protokoly pervago s"ezda PLSR*, p. 14.

[108] Erde, *Gody buri i natiska*, I, 103, n. 2.

[109] Podshivalov, *Grazhdanskaia bor'ba na Urale*, p. 109.

[110] *Protokoly pervago s"ezda PLSR*, p. 25. To credit a Soviet source, little remained of an organization that in the summer had counted 3,000 members, yet by September could scarcely bring together 150 to 200 as a result of the

dustrial center seem to have lagged behind other sections of the Ural proletariat in revolutionary spirit,[111] being for a long time SR's rather than Bolsheviks and SR's of the swamp rather than Left SR's. Particulars as to other local branches are lacking, but the presence of a radical intellectual group headed by Steinberg and Brilliantov had helped to make the provincial capital of Ufa, as previously noted, one of the chief bases in the country for the leftist struggle against the Central Committee.

To the north of Ufa lay the province of Perm, heart of the Ural region and hotbed of partisan conflict. With a more complex social structure than other provinces, Perm had become the scene of a three-cornered struggle among the Bolsheviks, the SR's, and the Constitutional Democrats, each being rooted in some element of the population—the Bolsheviks in a working class numerically strong and steeped in the party tradition, the SR's in a peasant mass more steadfast in its loyalty than elsewhere, and the Constitutional Democrats in a bourgeoisie numerous enough to exert some influence on the general population, particularly on the propertied element in the villages. The activity of a powerful Bolshevik organization had not seduced the peasantry from its SR ties, and in the elections for the Constituent Assembly the party of Lenin sustained a thumping defeat in a district it had expected to carry.[112] Perm went into the SR column, 664,883 to 267,577, with the Kadets mustering enough strength to lift their poll over the hundred thousand mark—the only district in all of Russia, outside the two metropolitan areas, where they did so well.[113]

For the SR's however, it was a Pyrrhic victory, the last triumph of

---

inroads of Bolshevism (*Istoriia grazhdanskoi voiny v SSSR*, II, 99). But from another Soviet source we learn that as late as the spring of 1918 the Bolsheviks were having trouble bridling the Zlatoust workers. The provincial congress of the Bolshevik Party received a report to the effect that all industrial plants in the southern Urals were now solidly Bolshevik with the exception of Zlatoust, where the workers had not yet freed themselves from the deception of the "petty bourgeois" parties. See *Rabochii klass Urala v gody voiny i revoliutsii*, III, 8.

[111] *Istoriia grazhdanskoi voiny v SSSR*, II, 96; Podshivalov, *Grazhdanskaia bor'ba na Urale*, p. 11.

[112] Vishniak, *Vserossiiskoe Uchreditel'noe Sobranie*, p. 90; Radkey, *The Election to the Russian Constituent Assembly*, p. 70.

[113] See table in appendix of my book, *The Election to the Russian Constituent Assembly*.

a disintegrating movement. The schism that at the end of October had torn the Petersburg organization apart came late but inevitably to Perm, and at the December provincial conference five or six of the local branches withdrew from the party, although all the others renewed their allegiance—clear proof that the left did not have in Perm the strength it possessed in Ufa. The loss was serious enough, however, for at the head of the seceding organizations stood the Ekaterinburg group, probably the largest in the Urals and the only one about which there is any information; Nadezhdinsk also withdrew, while the others are not listed by name. Left-wing sentiment had crystallized only slowly in Ekaterinburg, and when news came of the overthrow of the Provisional Government the party members did not know what to do beyond withdrawing from the local soviet —as though by reflex action. Several days of agitated discussion were necessary before the view prevailed that the events in the capital signified a "spontaneous outburst of revolutionary feeling" instead of a Bolshevik venture. Those who insisted on active opposition, holding that the uprising was a "crime before country, democracy, and revolution," [114] were voted down at the general meeting of October 30, and Ekaterinburg henceforth took its stand with the Left SR's. Of a registered membership of 3,000 and an active membership of half that figure, only a handful of intellectuals (forty-two in all) comprised the seceding right-wing minority.[115] Nothing is said regarding the center, which, after all, formed the core of the provincial organization. Presumably in the city the center had given way under the pressure of the workers and soldiers and had been assimilated to the left, whereas in the country it could hew to the line of party regularity without losing the bulk of its peasant following. From the standpoint of numbers, at least, the Left SR's must have made a respectable showing in Perm, certainly better than in the average province, though not so impressive as in the neighboring stronghold of Ufa. But their corporate activity betrays the same weaknesses as elsewhere, for the local branches functioned independently of each other, with little or no attempt at coordination, while

---

[114] See text of the minority resolution in *Rabochii klass Urala v gody voiny i revoliutsii*, III, 64–65.

[115] *Protokoly pervago s"ezda PLSR*, p. 8.

effective leadership seems to have been restricted to Ekaterinburg (Ustinov, S. Strizhev) and to Nadezhdinsk (Siniarski).[116]

Little is known of developments in Viatka province, a large and rather remote region to the west of Perm, geographically closer to the center of the country but less integrated with its business life and transportation system. Sentiment in favor of the PSR pervaded all parts of the province, according to reports at the September peasants' congress, and the centrist tone of the chief party organ, the *Narodnoe Delo* of Viatka,[117] doubtlessly reflected that of the membership as a whole. In two districts, however, a strong leftist tide was running: in Glazov *uezd*, where only Bolshevism challenged the ascendancy of the left SR's, and in Iaransk, where nearly half the volosts were reported to be leaning in their direction. An unusual situation prevailed at the Izhevsk Arms Plant, one of the largest industrial enterprises in Russia with a labor force of 40,000. Here the moderates had been swept aside and Bolshevism outdistanced by a movement which had found even the left wing of the PSR too tame for its purposes and had seceded in the middle of 1917 to form the Union of Maximalists. Through their appeal to the large peasant element in the Izhevsk proletariat and their anarchist tactics which accorded so well with the mood of the Russian people, the Maximalists created a formidable diversion from other radical movements and weakened the new Left SR party in a province that otherwise might have contributed much to its strength.[118]

In Siberia extremism did not flourish as in the provinces west of the Urals. A simpler and more democratic society bred a less violent reaction to the grievances of the past and the frustrations of the present. The absence of the *pomestie* system (estates held by the nobility), a powerful cooperative movement,[119] politically as

---

[116] *Partiinyia Izvestiia*, No. 6 (March 8/21, 1918), pp. 57–58; *Rabochii klass Urala v gody voiny i revoliutsii*, III, 4–5, 31.

[117] *Partiinyia Izvestiia*, No. 5 (January 20, 1918), p. 26.

[118] *Sovety krest'ianskikh deputatov i drugie krest'ianskie organizatsii*, I, Part II, 131–35; F. P. Makarov, *Oktiabr' i grazhdanskaia voina v Udmurtii*, pp. 37, 43–44; *Izhevsk v ogne grazhdanskoi voiny*, pp. 17 ff. According to Makarov, the Maximalists at one time outnumbered the Bolsheviks three or four to one.

[119] The Siberian cooperatives constituted the backbone and the financial sinews of the SR party and more particularly of its moderate wing. At the All-Siberian Cooperative Congress early in 1918, 75 of the 88 delegates were either

cautious as it was financially solvent, a proletariat less numerous and a peasantry more prosperous than elsewhere were factors impeding the progress of radicalism, without entirely negating its appeal, in a region that was not wanting in combustible material. Besides the soldiers back from the front and the labor element in railroad and mining centers like Krasnoiarsk and Kansk, the tide of immigration from European Russia had introduced into the village a stratum of disaffected newcomers, victimized by the tsarist bureaucracy and debauched by government handouts, envious of the older colonists and certain to differ from them in political outlook. The slogan of land seizure would as surely appeal to the one rural element as it would appall the other, for virtually no privately owned land existed in Siberia;[120] land for distribution must come either from the state properties or from the holdings of the peasants themselves. At the first peasants' congress in Enisei province this question had occasioned a heated controversy between the delegates from Kansk *uezd*, representing the recently arrived recipients of inferior land, and those from Minusinsk *uezd*, where the older settlers were blessed with fertile soil. Political allegiance and economic interest coincided exactly: the Kansk delegates were either left SR's or Bolsheviks; those from Minusinsk were orthodox Socialist Revolutionaries.[121]

Siberia, therefore, was a region in which the left SR's would make some headway without being able to swing majority sentiment in their favor. At first quite weak in most places, they picked up strength until by October they could muster 15 delegates against 45 for the moderates in the soviet congress of eastern Siberia, and 35 against 50 in the general All-Siberian Congress that followed soon after. Aside from the indication of greater strength in western Siberia, these figures reveal very little, for the only peasant soviets

---

party members or sympathizers. See P. S. Parfenov, *Grazhdanskaia voina v Sibiri 1918–1920*, p. 13.

[120] Peasant allotment lands (*nadely*) were vested in the village communities and were entailed in character to prevent them from passing out of peasant hands. Though subject to private use, they were not owned by the households to which they had been assigned, supposedly for a limited period.

[121] E. Kolosov, "Krest'ianskoe dvizhenie pri Kolchake" (The Peasant Movement under Kolchak), *Byloe*, XX (1922), 235–36; Gins, *Sibir', soiuzniki i Kolchak*, pp. 32–34.

represented, with minor exceptions, were those of the urban garrisons.[122] The unevenness of the growth of leftist sentiment is seen in the fact that at the moment of taking over control of the peasant congress in Tomsk [123]—their greatest Siberian triumph—the left SR's were nowhere in evidence at the peasant congress in the adjoining province of Altai.[124] A survey of the SR press at the time of the October Revolution reveals the stand of the various organizations, though less certainly of the membership, since an organization might no longer be in step with the rank and file if the congress that gave birth to it had been held several months before. On the basis of newspaper reaction to the overthrow of the Provisional Government and the question of its successor, the Siberian SR organizations were divided as follows: [125]

Left	*Left Center*	*Center*	*Right Center*
Tomsk	Omsk	Blagoveshchensk	Khabarovsk
	Vladivostok	Chita	Tobolsk
		Eniseisk	
		Irkutsk	
		Minusinsk	

Other information bears out this classification. The most conservative opinion was to be found in Tobolsk province, one of the two districts in the country with enough extreme right-wing Populists to return a Popular Socialist to the Constituent Assembly. Irkutsk province was a citadel of moderate Social Revolutionism—here there was a wealth of leadership with long prison records to appeal to the public and oratorical talents of a high order.[126] The leftist challenge was more serious in Eniseisk province, though the moderates appear to have held the upper hand. In the Transbaikal

[122] A. Abov, "Oktiabr' v Vostochnoi Sibiri (Otryvki vospominanii)" (October in Eastern Siberia [Excerpts from Memoirs]), *Sibirskie Ogni* (Siberian Lights), IV (1924), 111–18; *Khronika grazhdanskoi voiny v Sibiri*, pp. 46–47; *Oktiabr' v zapadnoi Sibiri*, p. 25; *Istoriia grazhdanskoi voiny v SSSR*, II, 109–11.

[123] *Istoriia grazhdanskoi voiny v SSSR*, II, pp. 104–5.

[124] Parfenov, "Predoktiabr'skie dni v Sibiri," *Sibirskie Ogni*, III (1924), 128.

[125] *Partiinyia Izvestiia*, No. 5 (January 20, 1918), pp. 23–26. The organizations listed are of provincial or regional rank, except in the case of Minusinsk which was an *uezd* branch of the Eniseisk provincial organization.

[126] *Sibirskie Ogni*, IV (1924), 110.

Region the PSR had enjoyed the support of the working class as well as the peasantry, but after October the workers warmed up to the slogan of "all power to the soviets" and began to pull away,[127] though whether more to the Left SR's or the Bolsheviks is not clear. The long-standing feud between the radicals entrenched in Vladivostok and the defensists controlling the Khabarovsk and Blagoveshchensk organizations had disrupted the PSR in the Amur Region. Matters had reached a pass where the peasants' soviet refused to be associated with a party so rent with dissension and put up its own slate of candidates for the Constituent Assembly.[128] In the Altai Region, the breadbasket of Siberia and its most populous area, where the left SR's were at first scarcely more in evidence than in neighboring Tobolsk, the coming of fall had brought a radical change in the situation. By that time enough soldiers had returned to crystallize the sentiment of the village for peace, and we find the left SR Kudritski not only standing at the head of Barnaul *uezd* but even arranging for the peaceful transfer of power to the soviets.[129] The other districts may have lagged behind,[130] but the swiftness of the transformation in the region's main organization affords graphic evidence of the harvest awaiting the Left SR's even in a region noted for the affluence of its peasantry.

The harvest was reaped most fully in Tomsk, the only Siberian province where the left held undisputed sway. Why the SR movement in Tomsk should have assumed this character is as difficult to explain as in other areas of leftist ascendancy, but the presence in that provincial capital of a garrison of 76,000 [131] doubtlessly contributed to the growth of radicalism. In Novonikolaevsk, a town in which 90 percent of the party membership is said to have worn uniforms, the defensists had been sloughed off as early as April, leav-

---

[127] V. Sokolov, "Oktiabr' za Baikalom (ianvar'-fevral' 1918 g.)" (October in the Region Beyond Lake Baikal [January–February, 1918]), *Proletarskaia Revoliutsiia*, X (1922), 389–90, 396.

[128] *Volia Naroda*, No. 134 (October 3, 1917); No. 141 (October 11, 1917).

[129] *1917 god v derevne*, p. 350; Parfenov, "Predoktiabr'skie dni v Sibiri," *Sibirskie Ogni*, III (1924), 118, 123–26, 129–30, 132.

[130] This seems to have been true of Slavgorod *uezd;* see *Sibirskie Ogni*, III (1924), 130.

[131] V. Leikina, "Oktiabr' po Rossii" (October over Russia), *Proletarskaia Revoliutsiia*, XLIX (II, 1926), 226.

ing the field to the center and left.[132] Presumably the same process
was repeated elsewhere in the province until the center in turn lost
out to the left at the September peasants' congress (according to the
Soviet version it was the "right SR's" who were vanquished on that
occasion).[133] In any event, the radicals came into control of both
the peasants' movement and the party organization and returned a
solid, or virtually solid, delegation to the Constituent Assembly. The
strange thing about these Tomsk radicals, however, was that they
chose to remain with the parent organization, diverging from it over
the war question but refusing to affiliate with its offshoot, the Party
of the Left Socialist Revolutionaries, because of certain "minor mis-
understandings." [134] What these were can only be surmised, but it
seems safe to conclude that the Tomsk SR's did not vacillate in their
attitude toward the Constituent Assembly—they were convinced
adherents of that institution—and that, even more than their leftist
confreres in other parts of the country, they found themselves at
odds with the Bolsheviks over the peasant question.[135]

The unwillingness of the Tomsk SR's to leave the fold deprived
the new Left SR Party of whatever prospects it might have had of
becoming a mass movement in Siberia. The splinter lists of candidates
for the Constituent Assembly in Tobolsk, Enisei, and the Amur district are evidence that some sort of a split occurred, but the number
of votes they drew—a little over 13,000 in all [136]—indicates that it
amounted to very little. There was a good deal of radicalism in SR
ranks, a growing dissatisfaction with the line of the Central Committee, particularly over the war question, but it was not yet ready

[132] N. Teterin, "Novonikolaevsk v fevral'skuiu revoliutsiiu" (Novonikolaevsk
in the February Revolution), *Severnaia Aziia*, XIII (I, 1927), 27–28. There is a
certain discrepancy between this information and Parfenov's ascription of defensist views to the Novonikolaevsk SR's in July (*Sibirskie Ogni*, III [1924],
109–10). Since his evidence is not conclusive, however, preference is given the
Teterin account.
[133] *Istoriia grazhdanskoi voiny v SSSR*, II, 104–5.
[134] See statement of L. A. Grigoriev in his speech to the Constituent Assembly
(*Vserossiiskoe Uchreditel'noe Sobranie*, pp. 95–96). The fact of nonseparation
was confirmed orally to the author by Chernov and Zenzinov.
[135] *Ibid.*, pp. 56, 95–96; see also Eugene Kolosov's remark to Gins in the
latter's *Sibir', soiuzniki i Kolchak*, p. 182.
[136] Sviatitski, "Itogi vyborov vo Vserossiiskoe Uchreditel'noe Sobranie" (The
Results of the Elections to the All Russian Constituent Assembly), in *God
russkoi revoliutsii*, p. 114.

to assume organizational form. In this respect it was fully in harmony with the general course of developments in Siberia, where even the Bolsheviks and Mensheviks, with all their rigidity of organization and clarity of ideology, did not finally part company until the fall of 1917, long after they had separated in European Russia. The schism in SR ranks eventuated only with the civil war and the competition in excesses that marked the course of the partisan struggle. Then, indeed, did the Left SR's become an important political force in their own right.

Nowhere except in the capital and the half dozen provinces under leftist control were the effects of the schism so grievously felt as in the army. Bolshevism had already won over countless numbers of soldiers who once had made the army the stronghold of Social Revolutionism, and now the Left SR's would claim a great part of what remained, weakening the PSR organization on the more remote fronts, wrecking it on the more immediate ones, and in some cases wiping it clean from the boards. The First Army of the Northern Front held its congress a few days after the October Revolution; of the 268 delegates who assembled in the Livonian hamlet of Altschwannenburg, 134 were aligned with the Bolsheviks, 112 with the Left SR's, 22 with the Menshevik Internationalists, and none with the PSR. By unanimous decision the congress rejected the bid of Kerenski, Gotz, and Avksentiev for assistance in their Gatchina enterprise.[137] Matters had not reached this pass in the Twelfth Army, companion to the First and the only one on the Northern Front not yet under extremist control. Reforming his party's lines in the heat of the October struggle, Chernov had managed to contend on even terms with the leftist bloc in the congress of this army, only to have his victory dissipated a fortnight later when a new congress voted overwhelmingly in favor of the Soviet regime.[138] The million soldiers represented at the November congress of the Western Front had given a three to one preference

[137] *Istoriia grazhdanskoi voiny v SSSR*, II, 474–75; Muratov, *Revoliutsionnoe dvizhenie v russkoi armii v 1917 g.*, pp. 309–10.
[138] *Istoriia grazhdanskoi voiny v SSSR*, II, 472–73; Chernov, manuscript commentary on the minutes of the Central Committee, pp. 58–59; *Revoliutsiia 1917 goda*, VI, 45, 147, 152, 159; *Delo Naroda*, No. 227 (December 8, 1917); see also above, pp. 40–42.

to the Left SR's over the center and right, but all SR groups together had less than a fourth the strength of the Bolshevik party.[139]

Elsewhere the debacle was less starkly revealed, and on fronts
remote from the centers of agitation the SR's seemed to be holding
their own. At the Southwestern Front congress in November only
about fifty of the 213 SR's were leftist,[140] while still further to the
south, on the Rumanian Front, a congress at the end of October
brought together 80 SR's, 40 Mensheviks, and 15 Bolsheviks, no
mention being made of Left SR's.[141] Such figures, however, do not
reflect the conviction of the troops but rather an attitude already
outlived on other fronts and lingering here only because of the distance from the center of developments, as may be seen from a comparison with the alignment of forces at the Southern Regional Congress of Soviets in December, a body made up of civilian as well as
military elements but in large part consisting of delegates from the
Rumanian Front. Here the Left SR's had already won the upper
hand, with 220 delegates to 187 for the PSR, although both had been
outstripped by the Bolsheviks with 396.[142] Everywhere the SR
strength was melting away; the only question was how long it would
take. The Left SR's strove manfully to claim the lost positions for
themselves, but, entering late into their inheritance, they faced the
formidable competition of Bolshevism, their nominal ally. A representative of the First Army put his finger on the whole trouble when
he observed that the left had waited until the soldier mass had gone
over to Bolshevism before disentangling itself from a foundering
cause.[143] With conditions as they were at the front, it was not the

---

[139] Knorin, *Revoliutsiia i kontr-revoliutsiia v Belorussii*, I, 54–55; *Revoliutsiia
1917 goda*, VI, 196.

[140] *Revoliutsiia 1917 goda*, VI, 172; *Istoriia grazhdanskoi voiny v SSSR*, II, 509.

[141] *Istoriia grazhdanskoi voiny v SSSR*, II, 512.

[142] *Delo Naroda*, No. 241 (December 24, 1917). See comment of Sviatitski
(*ibid.*, No. 245 [December 31, 1917]), contrasting these figures with the results
of the general election in November. Apparently the disparity is not to be
accounted for by the imperfections of a soviet election, as Sviatitski implies,
but solely by the isolation of the Rumanian Front from the developments in
St. Petersburg. When the news of October finally seeped into the ranks, the
reaction was the same as on other fronts, and equally disastrous for the PSR.
See the report, "Delegaty Petrogradskogo garnizona na fronte" (Delegates of
the Petrograd Garrison at the Front), in *Krasnyi Arkhiv*, LXXXV (VI, 1937),
55.

[143] *Protokoly pervago s"ezda PLSR*, p. 13.

explosion in the party ranks but the delay in setting it off that had thrown so many soldiers into the Marxist camp.

From all that has been said it can be seen that the schism in SR ranks does not lend itself to statistical analysis. We do not know the strength of the SR organization in October, how many members there were and how many fellow travelers, what proportion of the membership was inactive, or what percentage withdrew to form the new party. We know only that the loss was a major one, that it impaired the spirit as well as the size of the residual party by taking away the ardent revolutionists, and that from both a social and a geographical standpoint it was unevenly distributed. Generally speaking, the schism robbed the PSR of its soldier following, left its intellectual contingent largely intact,[144] and plunged it into a desperate struggle for the retention of influence over the peasantry. In geographical terms, the new party claimed virtually the whole organization in half a dozen provinces, principally in the Ukraine and the Kama-Ural region, half the organization in the city of St. Petersburg, and fragments elsewhere. From the vantage ground of these areas it began to make inroads on the peasant following throughout the country.

As the political expression of the radical-minded peasantry, the party of the Left Socialist Revolutionaries undoubtedly had promise, yet structurally it was never a robust organization and always labored under disadvantages that it shared with the party from which it had come. Though the child had broken away from the parent, it bore within itself the same congenital defects in respect to leadership, discipline, and program of action; it inherited the weakness of a movement that was based primarily upon the peasantry; and from the day of its birth it was as hard put to save itself from dissolution at the hands of the Bolshevik wing of the Social Democracy as the PSR had been to preserve from the Menshevik wing its independence of action.

Leadership was never a strong point with the Left SR's. Youth and impetuosity took the place of maturity and statesmanlike vision. Their leaders included some rabble rousers and a sprinkling of

[144] See below, pp. 158–59.

scoundrels, rather more than the usual quota of prima donnas, and many sincere men and women whose devotion to the revolution exceeded their ability to serve it. An ecstatic cult of revolution flourished among them [145] and an exaltation of spirit more marked than in other groups, with the possible exception of the anarchists. The Left SR leaders reveled in being borne along by the revolutionary current, whereas the Bolshevik leaders from the first were trying to harness the current and make it run in a certain channel. Knowing in their hearts that they were scarcely a match for the hard-bitten core of professionals around Lenin, the men at the helm of the new party nevertheless were sustained by an ideology which subordinated leadership to the spontaneity of the toilers. In contrast to the principle of elite control implicit in Lenin's vanguard theory and his idea of "democratic centralism," they believed that the institutions of the future, instead of being imposed by conscious design from above, would spring from the genius of the toilers themselves. The Left SR's had great confidence in the creative power of the people, liberated from the chains of the past and lifted up by the experience of the present. In a certain sense they were ochlocrats, though not in another, for they had high ethical standards which they were wholly unwilling to compromise for expediency's sake.

The incarnation of their spirit was Maria Spiridonova, whose youth had not prevented her from becoming, like Breshkovskaia, an icon of Social Revolutionism, only a more popular one in the October setting, if we are to judge from the crowds which flocked to hear her "as though she were Chaliapin." [146] Spiridonova was a colorful figure, she was brave and intelligent, and no one fought harder to stop the war or level the old social order; but her nerves were frayed to the breaking point, her judgment of people was not what it should have been, and impartial observers will probably agree that she contributed more inspiration than leadership to the movement she headed. While her services to the revolution, her terrorist past, and the harsh experiences of her youth protected her from the shafts of critics, the immunity she enjoyed did not extend to her colleagues.

[145] See comment of Berezin, in *Kratkii otchët*, p. 64.
[146] *Delo Naroda*, No. 213 (November 18, 1917). Report from Ekaterinoslav.

No sooner had the October Revolution torn away the false façade of party unity than the air was filled with flying dead cats as the left-wing and main-line Socialist Revolutionaries began to hurl in public the charges they had hitherto preferred only in private. A veritable campaign of defamation set in against the leaders of the new party, stoked by Zenzinov, whose position in organizational matters befitted him for the role of prosecuting attorney. The virulence of the attack is a measure of the seriousness with which the SR's regarded the emergence of a competitor with a specifically peasant appeal. Bolshevism had already wrought havoc in the military and proletarian preserves of the hard-pressed party and now it was to be attacked in its inner citadel by a movement kindred to itself in name and ideology. It is not surprising, therefore, that a strenuous effort should have been made to discredit those of the former comrades who were most in the public eye.

Some of them proved to be vulnerable targets. The Dekonski scandal had already broken in early October. Peter P. Dekonski had stood in the front ranks of the extremists; at the Third Congress he had been instrumental in defeating Kerenski's candidacy for the Central Committee;[147] he had become the bosom friend and understudy of Maria Spiridonova, and as much as anyone had sown the seeds of schism. His unmasking as a former agent of the Okhrana who had thought to conceal his services to tsarism under a veneer of ultra-radicalism had greatly embarrassed his associates on the threshold of their independent career.[148] Now they fell under the guns of the party from which they had been expelled. Izaac Z. Steinberg had the inconsistencies of his political career mercilessly exposed. His record on the war was one of zigzags. Why, asked Zenzinov, had he been willing to defend the old Russia in 1915 but not the new in 1917?[149] It seemed odd that even after the February Rev-

[147] See *The Agrarian Foes of Bolshevism*, pp. 226 ff.
[148] On the Dekonski affair see especially *Delo Naroda*, Nos. 175, 180, 184, 189, 209, 213 (October 8, 14, 19, 26; November 14, 18, 1917); *Volia Naroda*, No. 139 (October 8, 1917). Spiridonova made things worse by refusing, in the face of all evidence, to acknowledge Dekonski's guilt. With her, love was stronger than either judgment or political considerations. On her role in the affair see *Delo Naroda*, Nos. 176, 187, 209, 213 (Boldyrev's statement and the report from Ekaterinoslav), 234 (October 10, 22; November 14, 18; December 16, 1917)
[149] "Levyi s.-r. I. Z. Shteinberg" (The Left SR I. Z. Steinberg), *Delo Naroda*, No. 230 (December 12, 1917).

olution so prominent a leftist should have been willing to run on the same ticket with the Moscow rabbi Maze as an exponent of the preservation of Jewish nationality through clerical schools,[150] or that as late as May 15, in defending the Constituent Assembly against soviet encroachments in the Ufa soviet, he should have exclaimed that if that institution "gives us a tsar, I will accept even a tsar." [151] S. Mstislavski was portrayed in the SR press as a military dilettante who had written articles for the *Pravitel'stvennyi Vestnik* (Government Gazette) and dreamed of wide epaulets for his shoulders, preferring not to be seen until after midnight in order to invest himself with an air of mystery. V. Algasov was taxed with concealing his real name in order to avoid connection with some scandal in the past—either service with an employers' society in Kharkov or complicity in a homicide in the North Caucasus. His transgression was not clearly defined but it had debarred him at one time from holding party office. Against Kamkov and Kolegaev the SR's could rake up nothing except their past obscurity. The charges of earlier months against Kamkov, particularly his work on the *Na Chuzhbine* (On Foreign Soil),[152] were not revived because in the October atmosphere they would only strengthen his hand with the soldiers and would do him no harm among the peasants. As for A. A. Shreider, Malkin, Spiro, and others, they were scornfully dismissed as people who had never been heard of, either because of their youth or, inferentially, because they were nonentities. The campaign of defamation leaves one with the impression that the Left SR leaders fell into three categories: those with a very modest record of service to the revolution, those with a shady record, and those with no record at all.[153] Unfortunately, the true record is buried with the movement.

[150] Lieberman, "Otvet, pozhaluista!" (Answer, please!), *ibid.*, No. 229 (December 10, 1917); Zenzinov, "Svet i teni (Iz revoliutsionnykh vospominanii)" (Light and Shadows [From Revolutionary Reminiscences]), *ibid.*, No. 241 (December 24, 1917).

[151] B. Eltsin, "Dni oktiabr'skogo perevorota na Iuzhnom Urale i v Ufe" (At the Time of the October Overturn in the Southern Urals and in Ufa), *Proletarskaia Revoliutsiia*, X (1922), 359.

[152] See *The Agrarian Foes of Bolshevism*, pp. 120–22, 192.

[153] Zenzinov, "Svet i teni," *Delo Naroda*, No. 241 (December 24, 1917); "Oni molchat!" (They Are Silent!), *ibid.*, No. 243 (December 29, 1917); "Bryzgi i oskolki: Geroi levizny" (Spray and Splinters: Heroes of the Left), in the same number. See also editorial attack on Algasov in No. 232 (December 14, 1917).

There is a report in the *Volia Naroda* [154] that the Left SR's would have liked to win over Chernov and put him at the head of their party in order to overcome the deficiency in leadership. It is not clear whether they actually harbored such a notion or whether this was just a canard in the right-fringe press to embarrass Chernov,[155] but in view of the harsh things the suggested partners were saying about each other, and in view of their fundamental disagreement over the role of soviets in the revolution, not to speak of tactical differences, there was never any likelihood that they could come to an understanding. Moreover, though Chernov would have brought the left a wider peasant following, his record in the old party argues against the assumption that he could have improved matters in the new. As it was, the Left SR's were not devoid of talent. Besides his intelligence and honesty, Boris Kamkov had undeniable qualities of leadership, and the head of the Kazan peasant movement, A. L. Kolegaev, combined boldness of spirit with a sober outlook which would have befitted him to conduct the affairs of the ministry of agriculture with benefit to the Russian people if only he had not been saddled with a prime minister like Lenin. After all, it was only against the Bolsheviks that the Left SR's came off so badly, and in such a test what other party shows to advantage?

The new party chose its national leadership in November when its first congress elected a Central Committee of fifteen members and five alternates. Like everything else about the PLSR, this first congress (November 19–28, 1917) bears the stamp of improvisation, and even in the case of delegates elected to the Central Committee there is no indication of the organization they represented. Below are given the names of the successful candidates, together with the vote they received and the organization with which they were usually associated in 1917: [156]

[154] No. 193 (December 14, 1917), under the column heading "Constituent Assembly."

[155] For official denial of the rumor that negotiations were in progress for a reconciliation between Chernov and the Left SR's, see under the heading "Press and Life," *Delo Naroda*, No. 233 (December 15, 1917). The report in the *Volia Naroda* was reaffirmed by the Menshevik *Nash Vek* (Our Age) on the basis of information supplied by an unnamed Left SR who was close to Smolny circles (see *Delo Naroda*, No. 235 [December 17, 1917]).

[156] *Protokoly pervago s"ezda PLSR*, pp. 113–14.

1. M. A. Natanson (Northern Region)   69
2. M. A. Spiridonova (Petersburg)   68
3. B. D. Kamkov (Petersburg)   68
4. A. L. Kalegaev (Kazan)   64
5. V. A. Karelin (Kharkov)   64
6. A. N. Ustinov (Northern Region)   63
7. A. A. Bitsenko (Moscow)   61
8. V. Algasov (Kazan)   57
9. I. Z. Steinberg (Ufa)   55
10. V. E. Trutovski (Ufa)   52
11. I. M. Malkin (Petersburg)   48
12. S. D. Mstislavski (Northern Region) 42
13. P. P. Proshian (Northern Region)   42
14. Shishko (Baltic Fleet)   34
15. A. A. Shreider (Petersburg)   31
16. Cherepanov (Moscow)   27
17. V. M. Kachinski (Kharkov)   26
18. Prokhorov (Petersburg)   21
19. Magerovski (Moscow)   19
20. I. A. Maiorov (Kazan)   18

Sukhanov had observed these men in action at the Second All-Russian Soviet Congress and in other soviet assemblies. Severe critic that he was, he dismisses them as being of no consequence.[157]

In the long run it is true that they could not cope with the situation that confronted them, and one reason is that they were outgeneraled at every turn by Lenin and his associates. But more is involved than leadership. Left-wing Social Revolutionism had crystallized much more slowly than left-wing Social Democracy, in keeping with the general looseness of Populism and the opportunity it afforded discordant elements to go on living together until some cataclysm forced them to deal with specific issues. Even in November, 1917, the Left SR's had advanced no further than the Bolsheviks in 1903, at the time of the London Congress. The cleavage in SR ranks was not underlain by any such fundamental difference as the evolutionary versus the conspiratorial approach to socialism; not basic issues, but tactical divergences had split the PSR,[158] and the left wing had crystallized only from the experiences of war and revolu-

---

[157] *Zapiski,* VII, 258–60.

[158] See Spiridonova, "O Sovete Partii" (About the Party Council), *Nash Put',* No. 2 (no month, 1917), p. 32.

tion, in groping fashion, without a priori decisions and under the compulsion of external events. Right down to the end the leftists had sought to avoid a final break and the initiative in precipitating the schism, as we have seen, came from the Central Committee. While the largely fictitious discipline of the old party had not prevented the drawing together of like-minded elements, the continued association in the public mind of the left and the right SR's had deprived the extremists of some of the strength they might otherwise have held against Bolshevism, particularly in the Northern Region and at the front, where the soldiers and sailors who at first had followed the left SR's were now streaming into the Bolshevik fold.

The Left SR's had waited too long to rear their party structure. With the experience of the war behind them, they should have made a clean break with the pro-war faction at the start of the revolution, disregarding ties of sentiment and displaying more faith in their own slogans, instead of waiting to have independence thrust upon them after Bolshevism had already won the upper hand in the army camps and the cities. Then there was no time to recruit and train the cadres of party workers, to transform public favor into an organized following, and to dig deeper the ditch between that following and Bolshevism.[159] What Lenin's party had accomplished by years of patient endeavor the Left SR's tried to do overnight in the midst of a raging storm. The frail, hastily improvised structure they erected could not withstand the storm and especially could it not withstand the attention of Lenin and his wrecking crew. Many of the Left SR's harped on the danger of a counterrevolution, some evinced faintheartedness over going against the parent organization, but generally they seem to have realized that on their left lay the primary danger, in the form of a movement so superior to their own in leadership and organization and so narrowly partisan in spirit that it threatened as much to devour its allies as to destroy its enemies. From the outset of their independent career the chief problem before them was how to live with this ally, whose intrinsic strength they recognized and whose stand on certain fundamental issues clashed so violently with their own.

[159] *Znamia Bor'by*, Nos. 18–19 (September, 1926), pp. 5–6.

The first of these differences was the attitude toward the village. Like all Populists, the Left SR's favored the peasantry and harbored no illusions as to its fate under a Marxist regime. The attempt in Soviet historiography to portray even the Left SR's as champions of the kulaks [160] has no foundation in fact except that here and there during the period of militant Communism the better-to-do peasants may have taken up with this party, simply because they were being harried like wild beasts and had no other place to go. The truth of the matter is that the Left SR's had no use for the village "rich," [161] any more than they had for the "paupers" upon whom the Bolsheviks lavished so much attention as an element in the village which could be used for the purposes of a party determined in the long run to debase all peasants to the status of factory hands in the field. The Left SR's were par excellence the party of the middle peasantry,[162] favoring the independent tillers of the soil who did not exploit the labor of others but worked their own allotments, individually at present, collectively in the future, after the advantages of toil in common had been disclosed to them and they had freely, of their own will, banded together with their fellows to conduct that type of economy which all socialists, Narodnik as well as Marxist, regard as superior to individual enterprise. That is the way the Left SR's looked at it, and if their views seem naive to Westerners steeped in the concept of private property, it can at least be said of them that they were sincere. They knew the danger that threatened the peasantry from both extremes, from the left as well as from the right. In the words of one of their leaders, "the peasant's interest does not lie close to the heart of the Social Democrat." [163] Viewing with horror Lenin's design of pitting the peasants against one another in order to nullify their political influence, the Left SR's foresaw that the provisioning difficulties of the towns would give the signal for a campaign against the village. Already in Novem-

[160] For an example, see *Istoriia grazhdanskoi voiny v SSSR*, II, 311–12.

[161] On the policy toward kulaks, see Shnurovski, "Kazanskii Sovet Krest'-ianskikh Deputatov," in *Bor'ba za Kazan'*, I, 64.

[162] This is admitted in certain Soviet studies published in the 1920s, which are less distorted than those that came out later; see Morokhovets, *Agrarnye progrommy rossiiskikh politicheskikh partii*, p. 130; Vladimirova, *God sluzhby "sotsialistov" kapitalistam*, pp. 95–97.

[163] Kamkov, *Kto takie levye sotsialisty-revoliutsionery*, p. 8.

ber their spokesman in the All Russian Soviet Central Executive Committee was denouncing talk of *"pomeshchik* grain" as a smoke screen behind which the state would proceed to requisition grain from the peasants, since 90 percent of the harvest was in their hands.[164] The confiscations of 1918, with the committees of the poor serving as an entering wedge for the subjugation of the village, brought the Left SR's and Bolsheviks into violent conflict,[165] but their alliance had been from its inception a *mariage de convenance*, with very little romance on the wedding morn and divorce at the end of the road.

Another major stumbling block in the way of collaboration with the Bolsheviks was the sharply differing conception of the role of soviets in the revolution. For all the lip service paid the soviets, the Bolsheviks regarded them essentially as organs for the mobilization of the working class behind its vanguard, the Communist Party; like all other institutions, they must be dominated by the vanguard. For the Left SR's the soviets assumed an independent value as agencies through which the toilers of Russia could fashion a new order, recognizing in it their own handiwork, accepting it freely, and so making it possible to dispense with those instruments of coercion the use of which had sooner or later always transformed a regime of liberty into one of oppression. Before the Second Peasants' Congress Spiridonova voiced ecstatic approval of the new organs of state: "They ask me: 'What is democracy?' And I answer: 'The soviet system—that is democracy.' "[166] According to V. M. Chernov, the dissident SR's, under the influence of Bolshevism, had scrapped the whole machinery of democracy in favor of a Russified adaptation of Latin anarcho-syndicalism. And the adaptation, moreover, was a bastardization of the model in that the syndicates of the West rested on a solid foundation of tradition and skilled personnel,

[164] *Delo Naroda*, No. 204 (November 9, 1917).

[165] *"Pomeshchik* grain" referred to grain from the estates of the nobility. General comment in Dr. J. Steinberg, The Events of July, 1918, pp. 8–9; N. Murakhver, "Pokhod petrogradskikh rabochikh v derevniu" (The Campaign of the Petrograd Workers into the Village), *Istoricheskii Zhurnal*, X (October, 1939), 40, 47; for the Ural region see Podshivalov, *Grazhdanskaia bor'ba na Urale*, 109–10; for Kazan province, see Shnurovski, "Kazanskii Sovet Krest'ianskikh Deputatov," in *Bor'ba za Kazan'*, I, 72.

[166] *Revoliutsiia 1917 goda*, VI, 218.

whereas soviets were a "revolutionary improvisation," peculiar to a country where sound trade unions and mass political parties could not flourish and where the workers had perforce resorted to small local parliaments in order to meet their political and social needs. These bodies, he argued, were held together only by the exigencies of an abnormal situation, without which they would quickly fall apart into their component elements. To rear a state edifice upon such ephemeral organizations, discarding the normal machinery of democracy, would be simply to provide a façade for the dictatorship of the party which controlled them.[167]

But the Left SR's did not see things that way. For them the soviets were the people's own contribution to the future of Russia, organs which were distinctive and efficacious in implementing the popular will, if only they could be preserved from domination by Lenin's band of disciplined fanatics. The Left SR's were as pleased with the new institutions as the early Populists had been with the village commune, and constituted themselves the guardians of soviet freedom against attempts to subject these organs to the will of any particular party. The best means of blocking Bolshevik designs was to assure parity or better for peasant soviets in all joint bodies so that the non-Bolshevik and nonpartisan elements could be sustained even though the followers of Lenin might gain the upper hand in the workers' and soldiers' soviets. In their struggle for unbossed soviets the Left SR's had a popular cause, for whenever a segment of the Russian people rallied from its helplessness and inarticulate state long enough to throw off the gag of minority rule, the demand for soviets free of Communist dictation came to the fore, as in the Kronstadt rebellion of 1921, the immediate cause for the inauguration of Lenin's New Economic Policy.

With the exception of its attitude toward the peasantry, no other feature of Bolshevism so disturbed the Left SR's as its moral callousness. Populists had never subscribed to the dictum that the end justified the means, and the Left SR's from the first were mindful of what the Russian Revolution itself would so conclusively

[167] Manuscript commentary on the minutes of the Central Committee, pp. 26–28.

demonstrate, that the end may be vitiated by the means employed. So, though advocating a "dictatorship of democracy" in the sense that the revolutionary majority must be free to repress attempts at reaction, the Left SR's condemned any resort to terror as damaging to the moral foundations of the new order and as unnecessary because of the basic correlation of forces.[168] Sensing the direction of soviet policy under Bolshevik control, they resolved to check the drift toward terror by securing for themselves the portfolio of justice. The brief tenure of this post by I. Z. Steinberg is replete with clashes between the two extremist parties over moral issues growing out of the exercise—or abuse—of the police power.[169]

Besides the desire to get on with the revolution, the chief factor counteracting these powerful divisive influences was, of course, the war. The Left SR's owed their origin to the revulsion of feeling against the holocaust. In their moralistic approach to the problems of the day they could find no higher command than to stop the slaughter of peasants and workers in the interests of world imperialism; and throughout 1917 it is probable that no other desire lay so close to their heart as the conclusion of peace. For that purpose they were willing to make a desperate effort to bridge over differences and stand with the Bolsheviks against their former comrades, against the bourgeoisie, against Entente pressure, and also against German imperialism. But when they saw what kind of a peace awaited Russia, and realized that the Bolsheviks would accept even such terms, they recoiled in horror. Had he consciously intended to destroy the basis for collaboration and inflame all the latent differences, Lenin could not have done better than when, in 1918, he accepted the peace of Brest Litovsk, launched a campaign to divide and plunder the Russian peasantry, brought the soviets firmly under party control, and inaugurated the Red terror. The erstwhile allies became mortal foes and the rupture was sealed in the blood of the weaker party.

---

[168] *Protokoly pervago s"ezda PLSR*, p. 104; "Oppozitsiia v stane bol'shevikov" (Opposition in the Bolshevik Camp), *Delo Naroda*, No. 204 (November 9, 1917); Steinberg, *Als ich Volkskommissar war, passim.*

[169] For example, see *Leninskii Sbornik*, XXI (1933), 110–17. See also below, pp. 152–53.

When these considerations are borne in mind, the wavering course
of the Left SR's in the October Revolution will appear not so much
the result of indecision, pusillanimity, or inferior leadership as an
effort to hold the balance even between the exigencies of the revolutionary situation and the dangers of an alliance with Bolshevism. We
shall be disposed to view the record of the Left SR's with more
indulgence if we recognize that, forty years and more after the
Russian Revolution, the world faces the same dilemma of trying to
live with the Bolsheviks without being taken over by them, and
that, to date, the graph of its actions exhibits no straighter line than
that of the group which first attempted this formidable task. Between the zig of teaming up with Bolshevism in the pursuit of common objectives and the zag of drawing back in order to preserve
their independence, the Left SR's described a serpentine course until
well into 1918. "We wavered badly," admitted one of their leaders,[170]
and he did not exaggerate.

With the general outlook of the Left SR's on the eve of October
we are already familiar.[171] Their chief concern was not so much the
elimination of the Provisional Government—that was now little
more than a hollow shell—as the prevention of a Bolshevik coup
that would anticipate the decision of the soviet congress. Only if
the congress were permitted to bring the full weight of its authority to bear upon the solution of the political crisis could civil
war be averted, for the institution of a partisan dictatorship would
surely provoke the right-wing socialists to armed resistance—a
gratuitous favor to the enemies of the revolution, according to the
Left SR's, who disputed the Bolshevik contention that these socialists were counterrevolutionary per se.[172] Back of the insistence
upon a soviet rather than a partisan solution of the crisis lay something more than a distaste for needless bloodshed—the fear of being
confronted with a regime in which the Bolsheviks had already entrenched themselves and in which other elements could exist only
on sufferance.

The Bolsheviks had been willing to give satisfaction—in form

---

[170] *Protokoly pervago s"ezda PLSR*, p. 96. The words are Malkin's.
[171] See above, pp. 99–101.
[172] *Protokoly pervago s"ezda PLSR*, pp. 39–40, 42, 45.

though not in substance. They had contrived to cloak their aggressive designs in the guise of precautions against a counterrevolutionary assault upon the forthcoming soviet congress, and such were the malice and skill of Trotski that he had induced the Left SR's to serve as the means of their own deception: things were so arranged that the initiative in setting up the Military Revolutionary Committee seemed to come from their midst, and a young and inexperienced member of their group had been placed at the head of the bureau that directed the affairs of the new organ, which the more sophisticated Mensheviks recognized at once as the general staff of the revolution.[173] Though young Lazimir was caught more securely in the net than most of his comrades, the contribution he made to the October Revolution did not deviate from the group action until the very eve of the uprising; Kamkov himself is our authority for the statement that during this period the agitation conducted by the Left SR's differed in no respect from the Bolshevik line.[174]

Only at the eleventh hour, when there no longer could be any doubt that the Bolsheviks meant to confront the soviet congress with a *fait accompli,* did the different approach of the two parties manifest itself in divergent tactics. By then it was too late to disentangle the Left SR following from the general revolutionary movement, even had the leadership desired to do so, and as long as there was any danger of a comeback by the hated Provisional Government it would not think of making the attempt. With the Bolsheviks plunging ahead on their predetermined course, the Left SR leaders decided that they would have to support the October Revolution while doing all in their power to prevent its exploitation for partisan ends. To secure the toilers' triumph, they took the same side of the barricades as the Bolsheviks, concerted measures against Kerenski's Gatchina offensive, and stayed on at the soviet congress at the cost of being read out of the PSR. To bridle the

[173] "Vospominaniia ob Oktiabr'skom perevorote: zasedanie uchastnikov oktiabr'skogo perevorota v Peterburge, sostoiavsheesia 7 noiabria 1920 g." (Reminiscences of the October Revolution: A Session of Participants in the October Revolution in Petersburg, Held on November 7, 1920), *Proletarskaia Revoliutsiia,* X (1922), 53, 86; Trotski, *History of the Russian Revolution,* III, 93, 95–96, 109–10.
[174] *Protokoly pervago s"ezda PLSR,* p. 39.

Bolsheviks, they refused to join the first Soviet government, demanded its demission in favor of a ministry representative of all the socialist parties, and insisted upon the principle of peasant parity in the organ before which the reconstituted government would be responsible—the Central Executive Committee of the All Russian Congress of Soviets. Instead of the "dictatorship of the proletariat" they advocated the "dictatorship of democracy," that is, of the whole army of toil, the peasantry as well as the proletariat.

The Left SR's had embarked upon an ambitious program. Running up their banner on middle ground, they thought to restore the unity of the revolutionary democracy by attracting strength from both sides, from moderates who were no longer satisfied to be led by hidebound defensists of the Avksentiev type, and from Bolsheviks who were appalled at the recklessness of Lenin and Trotski. Their resolution was strengthened by a flood of injunctions from the front calling for an end to the civil war, as also by the dissident Bolsheviks who came to them and urged them to persevere in their endeavor. Theirs was the chief partisan influence behind the Vikzhel negotiations, and they had helped to bring about the defection of the Kamenev-Zinoviev group from the Leninist line. The situation was not such but that they had some prospects of success.[175]

In order to preserve unimpaired their status as mediators, in order to reunite the "broken chain" of revolutionary unity, as Kamkov expressed it, the Left SR's had refused to enter the new government when the Bolshevik Central Committee, several hours before its formation, had called in three of their representatives—Kamkov, Karelin, and Spiro—and formally offered them a share of the power. The Left SR's had had their chance, Lenin reminded his restive followers, and though their refusal had been "conditional and temporary," they bore the responsibility for the failure to reach an agreement.[176] Besides their mediational role, there had been other reasons for holding aloof. The Left SR's had been provoked at

---

[175] *Ibid.*, pp. 39 ff., 64, 67, 73, 96–97, especially the reports of Kamkov and Malkin; Vladimirova, "Levye es-ery v 1917–1918 g.g." (The Left SR's in the Years 1917–1918), *Proletarskaia Revoliutsiia*, LXIII (IV, 1927), 103–5.

[176] A. Bubnov, "Odin iz reshaiushchikh momentov" (One of the Decisive Moments), *Proletarskaia Revoliutsiia*, VII (1922), 238–39; *Revoliutsiia 1917 goda*, VI, 57, 426; *Protokoly pervago s"ezda PLSR*, p. 43.

certain actions of the Bolsheviks and were at pains to show their independence. Some of their commissars had been removed from militia posts in the capital, the *Znamia Truda* could not appear because the press had been commandeered for use by the new authorities, the arrant partisanship of the Bolsheviks gave them pause, and they were under some compulsion to show that they would not be pushed around.[177] Underlying everything else, though not acute at the moment, was the rift over the peasantry, unbridgeable and inevasible. As they sat in the soviet congress, listening to Trotski excoriate the kulaks and extol the village pauperdom as though there were nothing in between,[178] the Left SR's must have reflected on how broad a connotation the word "kulak" had in Trotski's lexicon —broad enough to include the whole mass of the middle peasantry.

With the Bolsheviks riding roughshod over civic liberties and beginning to close down the nonsocialist press, the Left SR's moved still further away from collaboration in recalling their representatives from the Military Revolutionary Committee, which had become a national institution as a result of being transferred from the Petersburg Soviet to the All-Russian Executive Committee. Contact was now maintained only through the supreme Soviet organ itself, where the Left SR's constituted the official opposition and employed parliamentary means of struggle against the dominant party. Sharp differences arose over the arrest of Mayor Shreider and the impending dissolution of the Petersburg and Moscow city councils. The Left SR's, in their repudiation of terrorism after the advent of the toilers to power, opposed every one of the strong-armed measures of the Soviet government, in this manner reflecting the difference in point of view—and also in sense of security—between a party that rested its case upon the toilers generally—peasants as well as workers— and a party that trusted only the proletarian minority.[179]

But try as they might the Left SR's could not bridle the Bolsheviks or bring the right-wing socialists into harmony with a move-

---

[177] *Vtoroi Vserossiiskii S"ezd Sovetov*, p. 83. [178] *Ibid.*, pp. 27–28, 84–85.
[179] *Revoliutsiia 1917 goda*, VI, 72–73, 81; "Oppozitsiia v stane bol'shevikov" (Opposition in the Bolshevik Camp), *Delo Naroda*, No. 204 (November 9, 1917); see No. 215 (November 21, 1917) on arrest of Shreider; *Protokoly pervago s"ezda PLSR*, pp. 45–46, 48, 63; Vladimirova, "Levye es-ery v 1917–1918 g.g.," *Proletarskaia Revoliutsiia*, LXIII (IV, 1927), 107–8.

ment that was bent on concluding peace against the will of the
Western Allies. The differences were irreconcilable and the mediators in danger of being ground to dust between the two extremes.[180]
The Left SR's had flouted the law of revolution in trying to build
up strength in the center: a revolution polarizes, it does not augment
the center at the expense of the wings. All the negotiations had
come to nought, and as the Left SR's surveyed the scene their
wrath flared up against the right-wing socialists as the authors of
their discomfiture.[181] Moreover, they were now locked in mortal
combat with the regular Socialist Revolutionaries for control of the
peasant movement, so that their mood began to change, and from
sabotaging the policy of Smolny [182] they veered around to seeking an
accommodation with it, the better to war upon their erstwhile comrades.

Internal pressure worked in the same direction. If the Bolsheviks
were divided by the October Revolution, so were the Left SR's,
and division had always been a more serious matter among Populists,
owing to the premium placed upon individualism and the weaker
sense of discipline. For an offshoot party just setting out on its own
to attempt to drive a wedge between Lenin and Bolshevism [183] was a
daring and even a presumptuous maneuver, equivalent to trying to
separate the Bishop of Rome from the Church of Rome. Even had the
Left SR's been a monolithic party, they would have failed, and they
were far from being monolithic, with factionalism rife in their
midst since before the schism. The October upheaval had crystallized
three more or less distinct factions: a moderate wing that clung to
democratic forms, headed by Karelin and Steinberg; a left wing that
was maximalist in spirit, led by Algasov, Ustinov, and Proshian; and
the Natanson-Kamkov core of leadership in the center.[184] The

[180] Statement of Malkin; see *Protokoly pervago s"ezda PLSR*, pp. 96–97.
[181] *Ibid.*, pp. 41, 44, 96.
[182] One of their spokesmen did not hesitate thus to characterize their line of
action during the period in question (*ibid.*, p. 96). Smolny was the seat of the
Soviet government.
[183] *Revoliutsiia 1917 goda*, VI, 82–83 (summary of Karelin's statement to a
south Russian newspaper).
[184] *Protokoly pervago s"ezda PLSR, passim* (especially the debate on the
Constituent Assembly and relations with the PSR); *Delo Naroda*, No. 215
(November 21, 1917); M. Kogan-Bernstein, "Nashi raskhozhdeniia" (Our Divergences), *Partiinyia Izvestiia*, No. 5 (January 20, 1918), p. 62.

moderates predominated in the Ufa and Kherson organizations and had much influence at Kharkov,[185] where Karelin presided over the city council; the extremists nested in the military organizations of the Northern Region; and the nucleus that held the wings together had its chief base in St. Petersburg. The position of Maria Spiridonova is harder to define. The *Delo Naroda* placed her on the extreme left,[186] but it would be better to think of her as the Holy Ghost of the party, hovering over all factions and committed to none.

The radicals had from the outset favored collaboration with the Soviet regime. Unlike the moderates, they had no reservations about the soviets as organs of government, viewing them as forms which had aroused the toiling masses from their torpor and given fullest expression to their will. The radicals had chafed at the decision not to enter the government and had opposed the recall of representatives from the Military Revolutionary Committee. Algasov pointed out how necessary was membership in this vital institution if one wanted to be in the swim of developments, for it was performing many of the functions of government, in the absence of regular administrative machinery, and was doing so with a minimum of partisan friction. He questioned the whole strategy of trying to bring the socialist parties together in a coalitional ministry, observing that civil war was inevitable, whether the party liked it or not. The people would not understand if the Left SR's boycotted the Soviet regime on such inconsequential grounds as the suppression of two or three bourgeois newspapers.[187] Spiridonova also urged the necessity of working with the Bolsheviks, however crude their actions, because the "masses are with them." [188] And Natanson believed in the feasibility of an agreement since both parties favored transforming the political into a social revolution.[189]

Under the pressure of their own extremists and faced with the hopelessness of getting the right-wing socialists to accept the plat-

---

[185] The sinuous course of the Kharkov organization defies classification. For the flounderings of the official organ (the *Zemlia i Volia*) see comment of A. Grigorovich, "Partiinaia Pressa" (The Party Press), *Partiinyia Izvestiia*, No. 5, p. 23.

[186] No. 215 (November 21, 1917).

[187] *Protokoly pervago s"ezda PLSR*, pp. 47–49, 59–60.   [188] *Ibid.*, p. 36.

[189] *Ibid.*, p. 22.

form worked out in the Executive Committee, the Left SR's abandoned the idea of a broad coalition and agreed to enter the existing government on condition that its social base be broadened by fusing the Peasants' Executive Committee [190] with the Workers' and Soldiers', the combined organ to have sole legislative authority and the Council of People's Commissars (Sovnarkom) to be restricted to executive functions.[191] Their objective, of course, was not only to achieve parity for the peasantry but also to strengthen their influence in the government, since victory in the struggle for control of the rural soviets, now confidently expected, would deliver the peasant representation into their hands. For his part Lenin showed surprising patience in dealing with a group which he had just denounced as not having a spark of true revolutionary spirit,[192] but he desperately needed the peasant *iarlyk* (sanction) for his regime and this was the way to get it. Kamkov had reminded him at the soviet congress that the peasantry, the "infantry of the revolution," would not follow the Bolsheviks,[193] and in order to gain the support of the very considerable number of village toilers who "had broken away from Kerenski but had not yet come over to Lenin," he was willing to compound with elements which were not strictly proletarian in character and which later he would throw overboard.[194]

It was in the middle of November that the deal was made. As late as the 12th the Left SR's had still been passing resolutions in favor of a government embracing all groups from the Popular Socialists to the Bolsheviks,[195] but on the 15th the two sets of soviets were merged at the top. Three days later the commissariat of agriculture was handed over to the Left SR's, who named the head of the peasants' soviet of Kazan province, A. L. Kalegaev, to the coveted post. They also gained the right to have deputies in the other departments of state. Negotiations continued for admitting

[190] Not the old one elected in May and dominated by right SR's but the new one to be chosen in November.

[191] *Protokoly pervago s"ezda PLSR*, pp. 44, 46, 64.

[192] Speech to the trades' union council as reported in *Delo Naroda*, No. 207 (November 12, 1917).

[193] *Vtoroi Vserossiiskii S"ezd Sovetov*, p. 45.

[194] See Foreword by Ia. A. Iakovlev, *ibid.*, pp. xxxii–xxxiii; Vladimirova, *God sluzhby "sotsialistov" kapitalistam*, p. 102.

[195] *Revoliutsiia 1917 goda*, VI, 131.

the new partners to a broader share of power, but they did not proceed smoothly. It was not until December 12, after numerous ups and downs,[196] that the Left SR's attained their second chief objective, the commissariat of justice, together with five other posts of lesser significance, the Bolsheviks retaining eleven for themselves. Steinberg became commissar of justice, Karelin of state properties, Proshian of posts and telegraph, Trutovski of local self-government, Izmailovich, of palaces. The portfolios of justice and agriculture were important but did not bring the Left SR's to the primary sources of power. They might administer the palaces of a vanished monarchy, but the armed forces, finance, foreign affairs, and the presidency of the council were reserved to the party that had staged the October Revolution. Obviously, Lenin had let none of the real power out of his hands. On a qualitative basis the division was even less favorable to the Left SR's than the numerical ratio of seven to eleven. It is true that they had representatives in the collegia of the other commissariats, one of the most significant of the subordinate appointments being that of Peter Alexandróvich as vice chairman of the Extraordinary Commission (Che-ka). But the fact remains that the chief means at their disposal for influencing policy was the threat of resignation. They were the guests in the house; Lenin held the title.

During the first weeks of the partnership, down past the dissolution of the Constituent Assembly, the major questions of land and peace occasioned no difficulty. Bolshevik policy was in its first or Robin Hood stage of giving all the land to all the peasants at the expense of the wicked landowners. Lenin had simply taken over the SR land program, as reflected in the instructions of peasant communities to their national representatives, and promulgated it on October 26 as a decree of the soviet congress.[197] The introduction of the class war into the village, the creation of the paupers' committees,

---

[196] See, for example, the reports in *Delo Naroda*, Nos. 212 and 215 (November 17, 21, 1917); Lenin, *Sochineniia* (2d ed.), XXII, 87–88. Natanson seems to have been in charge of the negotiations for his party. Convocation of the Constituent Assembly as elected, without elimination of any of the component elements, bourgeois or socialist, and representation on the Extraordinary Commission (which later became the GPU) were conditions posed by the Left SR's. See Steinberg, *Als ich Volkskommissar war*, pp. 34–35, 60–61.

[197] *Sochineniia* (2d ed.), XXII, 20–23; *Vtoroi Vserossiiskii S"ezd Sovetov*, pp. 21–22; helpful discussion in Sukhanov, *Zapiski*, VII, 253–58; *Istoriia grazhdanskoi voiny v SSSR*, II, 305–11.

and the grain confiscations were deferred for the time being, and Kalegaev did not have to exert himself to protect the middle peasantry from his partners in power. His policy was addressed to implementing the land decree, which meant, in effect, that the peasants settled the land question in their own way. Though party doctrine had always held that socialization of the land would not involve collectivization of agricultural production, and hence was compatible with capitalism, the commissariat under Kalegaev was obviously moving in that direction, not in accordance with some master plan but simply because of chaotic conditions and the fact that socialization of the land in practice was not what it was in theory. Farm machinery was made a state monopoly,[198] and the Extraordinary Peasants' Congress (which means the intellectuals who ran it) had already proclaimed the necessity for state control over the production and distribution of farm commodities—whatever that might mean.[199]

Members of the old Peasants' Executive Committee, right-wing Socialist Revolutionaries whose separation from power was all the harder to bear in that it came on the threshold of the Constituent Assembly, busied themselves with vilification of the new minister. How could a former railroad agent, asked Bykhovski, presume to occupy the position once held by Shingarev, Chernov, and S. L. Maslov, and how could he propose, as was rumored, to replace an expert like Vikhliaev with a musical comedy actor? Did the Left SR's regard specialists in ministries as a bourgeois prejudice? [200] Kalegaev's reply was not only to withhold protection from the fifteen commissions and subcommissions of the old ministry which had continued to draft agrarian legislation for the Constituent Assembly, but himself to take the lead in driving them apart and reducing them to an illegal footing.[201]

On the question of peace the Left SR's for some time marched shoulder to shoulder with their Bolshevik allies. True, they had displayed from the outset more reluctance in dealing with the Imperial

---

[198] *Revoliutsiia 1917 goda*, VI, 211.   [199] *Ibid.*, p. 187.

[200] "Starina v novizne" (The Old in the New), *Delo Naroda*, No. 224 (December 5, 1917).

[201] Bykhovski, "Razgrom ministerstva zemledeliia" (Ruin of the Ministry of Agriculture), *ibid.*, No. 237 (December 20, 1917).

German authorities,[202] foreshadowing the fateful cleavage over Brest
Litovsk. But since it was not possible to deal with Liebknecht and
Luxemburg, the Spartacist leaders in Germany, one had to make the
best of the situation and see whether a tolerable peace could be
worked out with General Hoffmann and Prince Leopold of Bavaria.
To those who held that an approach to the Central Powers constituted a renunciation of world revolution as a means of bringing about
world peace, Kamkov replied with an argument derived, as he can-
didly admitted, from Martov's reasoning at the Zimmerwald Conference: beyond a certain point war becomes a wholly negative
phenomenon, paralyzing the social movement; the class struggle can
unfold to the fullest extent only when the conclusion of peace has
brought about a recession of national interests and the advance of
social interests into the foreground. Seen in this light the conduct of
peace negotiations even with princes and Prussian generals appears as
a revolutionary act.[203] The Left SR's had accepted Lenin's peace
decree at the soviet congress;[204] they accepted also the conclusion
of a separate armistice. Having gone this far along the road to a
separate peace, they were prepared to go the rest of the way, and
on December 5 Spiridonova absolved the peacemakers of any taint
of shame when she pointed out that the call for a general peace had
gone unanswered and that now it was a matter of keeping faith with
the front. That the Constituent Assembly would have to sanction the
peace was stoutly denied by Kamkov, who maintained that its function was simply to back up the action of the Soviet authorities.[205]

But the peace that Kamkov and the other Left SR's had in mind
was a peace compatible with the revolutionary conscience, and when
the first light began to come through on the nature of the terms
Imperial Germany meant to impose, their reaction was that of
idealists who felt themselves to have been wickedly deceived. Even
before the end of the year the Left SR's were saying that the German
conditions were wholly unacceptable and must lead to a resumption

[202] See Bykhovski, *Vserossiiskii Sovet Krest'ianskikh Deputatov*, pp. 308-9,
for a difference that arose at the Extraordinary Peasants' Congress.

[203] *Protokoly pervago s"ezda PLSR*, pp. 99-100; Bykhovski, *Vserossiiskii
Sovet Krest'ianskikh Deputatov*, p. 336.

[204] *Vtoroi Vserossiiskii S"ezd Sovetov*, pp. 16, 63.

[205] *Delo Naroda*, No. 225 (December 6, 1917); Bykhovski, *Vserossiiskii Sovet
Krest'ianskikh Deputatov*, p. 404.

of war unless modified.[206] There was as yet, however, no rift in the coalition because many Bolsheviks reacted in the same manner and Lenin had not yet disclosed his purpose of seeking peace on any terms that would leave his regime in power.[207]

Nor did questions of lesser significance produce tension within the coalition. The partners saw eye to eye on such matters as placing industrial production under workers' control and nationalizing the banks, though the Left SR's might criticize the haste with which the decrees were drawn.[208] It is surprising that the Ukrainian question did not occasion more trouble, in view of the increasing bitterness of the feud between the Sovnarkom and the Rada, the Left SR stand in favor of national rights, and the desire on their part to maintain good relations with the Ukrainian Socialist Revolutionaries, but no crisis arose and the Left SR's confined themselves to easing the rigor of official measures without deferring overly much to Ukrainian sensibilities. Karelin, the spokesman on Ukrainian affairs, upheld the principle of national self-determination but emphasized that it must not become a screen for counterrevolution.[209] Down in the Ukraine the Left SR's stood shoulder to shoulder with the Bolsheviks against the Rada's attempt to divide the toilers along national lines, and it was not until February of 1918 that trouble arose between the two parties.[210] This resistance to chauvinism, however, does not seem to have disturbed relations with the Ukrainian SR's, probably because of the existence of a kindred extremist current among them known as the Borot'bisty ("Fighters"). In fact, there was even the prospect that the fusion of the local organizations in Kharkov might extend to the whole region.[211]

What did bedevil the relations between Bolsheviks and Left SR's

[206] *Delo Naroda*, No. 238 (December 21, 1917); see also comment in *ibid.*, No. 2 (January 4, 1918), on Kamkov's swift change-over from congratulation of the government on the imminence of a just peace to denunciation of German imperialism and advocacy of measures to arm the population.

[207] See Steinberg, *Als ich Volkskommissar war*, ch. 10, especially pp. 198–201, 206, 246–47.

[208] *Protokoly pervago s"ezda PLSR*, pp. 75–78; *Delo Naroda*, No. 204 (November 9, 1917) (Karelin in the Central Executive Committee), No. 233 (December 15, 1917) (Trutovski in same); *Revoliutsiia 1917 goda*, VI, 343.

[209] *Delo Naroda*, No. 227 (December 8, 1917); Steinberg, *Als ich Volkskommissar war*, ch. 5.

[210] Bosh, *God bor'by*, pp. 26, 62, 80, 88, 98, 154–55, 179 ff.

[211] *Novaia Zhizn'*, No. 214 (December 31, 1917).

in the earlier stages of their collaboration was the incipient terrorism of the Soviet regime, centering in the Extraordinary Commission. One means of keeping things under control was to ask for the commissariat of justice; another was to introduce one's own people into the terrorists' lair. So when the coalition was formed I. Z. Steinberg assumed the portfolio of justice and Peter Alexandróvich, the man of action who had crossed swords with the intellectual leadership of the PSR in the early days of the revolution,[212] gained admission to the Che-ka and presently became, as its vice chairman, second only to Dzerzhinski himself. A small group of party comrades accompanied Alexandróvich into the "hellish fire." Steinberg could not do everything that his party expected of him—he was not able to blow up the Fortress of SS. Peter and Paul, as Spiridonova had demanded (and as she had actually done to the prisons in Chita)—but he was able to accomplish something of his party's purpose of "first throttling and then altering the scope and tempo of the Che-ka's activity." From the initial day of his ministry he was locked in combat with Dzerzhinski. The two men worked always at cross-purposes, in large matters as in small. Alexandróvich likewise adhered faithfully to his party's line. Strange to say, however, Dzerzhinski conceived a liking for this peasant from Riazan, so unwavering and straightforward in his actions, and the two got along very well together, right down to the day in 1918 when they decided to liquidate each other.[213]

The Left SR's did succeed in hobbling the Red terror during their brief tenure of power, yet on the whole their role in the October Revolution was characterized by ineffectiveness. Sukhanov's observation of their actions at the Second All-Russian Congress led him to a devastating appraisal of their character and prospects. These people were like children, he said, and would never serve as a counterweight to Bolshevism; to have them in the government would be a positive advantage, for, lacking in cohesion and leadership as they were, their presence would broaden the base of the regime without in any manner endangering their associate's control.[214] Striking confirmation of his judgment is found in the treatment of the land question, in

[212] See *The Agrarian Foes of Bolshevism*, pp. 133–34, 139–41.
[213] Steinberg, *Als ich Volkskommissar war*, ch. 3.
[214] *Zapiski*, VII, 220, 240, 258–60.

relation to which the Left SR's might certainly have been expected to display initiative. Lenin coolly appropriated the program of socialization and promulgated it as one of the first decrees of a regime in which there were only Bolsheviks. The Left SR's were so taken aback that they could only greet his espousal of their program and request an hour's intermission to caucus on the matter, after which they permitted it to go through without objection.[215] In this way the Bolsheviks got credit in the eyes of the peasantry for something they had not worked out and did not believe in. The theft was at the expense of all SR's—of the left as well as the center and right. They did not even know how to hold on to their program, the source of their popularity, much less implement it.

It was no better in the provinces. Certainly the Left SR's should have been able to dominate the situation in the Southern Urals—Ufa province was one of their major strongholds. Yet they allowed the Bolsheviks to take the initiative in forming a soviet militia, with the result that their rivals were never headed in respect to physical power, and this despite the fact that the Left SR's had nearly an even break in the workers' and soldiers' soviets, a roughly equal following in the military formations themselves, and complete control of the peasants' soviets.[216]

In Kazan, where a division of labor prevailed, the Left SR's taking the country and the Bolsheviks the towns,[217] something of the same disproportion between numbers and influence could be observed, for the Left SR's, with five times the numerical following of the Bolsheviks,[218] do not seem to have carried any more weight. The picture varied little from one part of the country to another—everywhere the Bolsheviks were going forward and the LSR's fighting just to hold their own.

Some of the Left SR's recognized the party's ineffectiveness. When the revolution came, Alexander Shreider told their first congress, the party had stood forth clearly as a third force, seeking to mediate the

---

[215] *Vtoroi Vserossiiskii S"ezd Sovetov,* pp. 75–77.

[216] Podshivalov, *Grazhdanskaia bor'ba na Urale,* pp. 62–63, 68 ff.

[217] Shnurovski, "Kazanskii Sovet Krest'ianskikh Deputatov," in *Bor'ba za Kazan',* I, 61.

[218] Radkey, *The Election to the Russian Constituent Assembly,* p. 27.

civil war, but once the fighting had ceased its line became blurred and its identity submerged. The party had strength, the peasantry was behind it, and yet it did not exert a decisive influence on political developments. "We have still to become a strong, organized force so that we can intervene authoritatively in the revolutionary process." [219]

In these words we find an admission of the movement's structural weakness which prevented it from transforming the good will of the rural mass into political power. The dispersion of the peasantry and its lack of social cohesion made this a difficult task at best, one that was quite beyond the capacity of the frail organization which the Left SR's had managed to put together in the midst of a social upheaval. As for the nerve centers of society, the towns, the appeal of left-wing Social Revolutionism was abating there while still gathering force in the country. The leaders could explain the necessity of playing second fiddle to the Bolsheviks by pointing to the minority status of the Left SR's in the Central Executive Committee and the Council of People's Commissars, but why were they a minority? The answer is that while they were hesitating to break with the mother party, masses of soldiers, sailors, and workers who once had followed the SR banner had been shifting their allegiance to Bolshevism and could not be reclaimed even after the yoke of the SR Central Committee had been thrown off. Nowhere had the shift occurred in such numbers or with such rapidity as in the Petersburg region, though the Bolsheviks generally had the upper hand in military and industrial centers.

At the hearth of the revolution, therefore, where institutions were forged and policies hammered out, the Left SR's found themselves in an inferior position. They could not match the clear line and the full-throated slogans of Bolshevism with their wavering course and their "yes-but" admonitions. Their finely spun reasoning about sharing the power with all the socialist parties was an intellectual argument intelligible only to intellectuals, while the populace was swayed by the blunt, simple phrases of Lenin.[220] The marching together with the

---

[219] *Protokoly pervago s"ezda PLSR*, pp. 61–62.
[220] Mstislavski, *Piat' dnei*, pp. 115–17.

Bolsheviks, then the turning away and turning back once more, were maneuvers that the simple mind could not follow. The chain of command was weakened, and local organizations were thrown into confusion. In contrast, the consistent line of the Bolshevik Central Committee enabled it to keep the local branches firmly in hand, so that in Kazan province, for example, the Left SR's forfeited the advantage of numbers and were hard pressed to maintain equality in a province that should easily have been their own.[221] They were the victims of their intermediate position, being outflanked on the left even as they were outflanking their former comrades on the right.

Chernov had prophesied for the Left SR's the fate of the Maximalists in the sense that they would form a bridge over which unstable elements in the PSR would cross to Bolshevism, even as similar elements in the earlier history of the party had crossed the Maximalist bridge to anarchism. Already he could see evidence for his assertion in the elections to the Constituent Assembly, since the returns indicated that the SR's had sustained a maximum loss of strength in those metropolitan districts where the left had taken over the organization.[222] Regardless of the accuracy of his analysis, it was only too apparent that the fraternization of the Left SR rank and file with the main body of extremism in the towns posed a grave danger of absorption by the stronger movement, especially since the leadership could not afford to fight the Bolsheviks hard enough to keep a clear division between their respective followings because of its belief that the fate of the revolution was now indissolubly bound to the fate of Bolshevism.[223] The danger was pointed up by what had just happened at Kronstadt. On the eve of the second soviet congress the Left SR's had agreed unanimously not to lend any assistance if the Bolsheviks struck before the congress could act, but when the issue was joined, the sailors said that a resolution was one thing and a revolution an-

[221] Shnurovski, "Kazanskii Sovet Krest'ianskikh Deputatov," in *Bor'ba za Kazan'*, I, 61.

[222] Manuscript commentary on the minutes of the Central Committee, p. 28; *Delo Naroda*, No. 212 (November 17, 1917) (speech at the Petersburg conference); see also No. 213 (November 18, 1917) under "Pechat' i zhizn'" (The Press and Life). The schism had occurred on the eve of the election, so that there was no separate Left SR ticket.

[223] See Karelin's statement before the soviet congress (*Vtoroi Vserossiiskii S"ezd Sovetov*, p. 26). Karelin, as we have seen, was spokesman for the more moderate faction of the PLSR—the one most critical of Bolshevism.

other.[224] They had simply been swept along with the tide.[225] Against this mass contagion Spiridonova could oppose nothing better than the prediction that the people would cease to follow the Bolsheviks in the later or constructive phase of the revolution and that the moral virtue of her party would tell in its favor when hatred and destruction had run their course and the people turned for leadership to a movement that emphasized positive values.[226] Her optimism was grounded upon faith, not upon reason, and still less upon experience.

In the fluid situation that prevailed toward the end of 1917 the Left SR's were gaining rapidly at the expense of the PSR but were meeting with much less success in holding their lines against Bolshevism, particularly in the towns. It would never do to permit the strength lost by the SR's to go to the Bolsheviks, for what was gained in respect to the war would be sacrificed in respect to the land. It would never do to become a connecting channel through which coursed a swift current from one lake to another. The engineers of the new party must dam up the current and form a lake of their own. Seemingly their task would be facilitated when the Bolsheviks ceased living off stolen agrarian capital and disclosed their real intentions with respect to the peasantry. But by then the Bolsheviks had gathered enough strength to blast the dam and, with it, the engineers.

There are several aspects of the breakup of the Socialist Revolutionary Party which should be noted in conclusion. In the first place, the cleavage over tactical questions coincided to a remarkable degree with differences in age and professional status. Those who had broken away were noticeably younger than those who remained,[227] and to understand the ardor of the Left SR's, as well as their inexperience, one has merely to note their years of birth. Rarely if ever has a party had such youthful leadership. Only Natanson was old. Spiridonova, Steinberg, and Kalegaev were all under thirty, Kamkov was thirty-two, Karelin twenty-six. On the other hand, Gotz, the youngest of

[224] Mstislavski, *Piat' dnei*, pp. 109–10.

[225] In the November election the Bolsheviks received 17,027 votes in Kronstadt, the Left SR's only 2,080 (here their list was the official one for the PSR). See *Revoliutsiia 1917 goda*, VI, 177.

[226] *Protokoly pervago s"ezda PLSR*, p. 35.

[227] Interview with Chernov in New York (January, 1950); Steinberg, *Als ich Volkskommissar war*, p. 60.

the regular party hierarchy, was thirty-five. Only in a time of up-heaval could such youthful individuals attain to political eminence, and speculation naturally arises in the mind of the investigator as to whether jealousy of the established leadership might not have prompted these young men and women, perhaps subconsciously, to tread the path of schism. Though a statistical analysis is of prohibitive difficulty, it is reasonable to conclude that the average age interval between a Left SR and an SR leader was about the same as the interval between the two revolutions, and certainly the one displayed in 1917 all the ardor, the impetuousness, and freshness of faith of the other in 1905. Whether the same tendency to divide according to age extended into the mass following may be doubted. The new party, for example, had wide support in the army, but would young soldiers have any greater distaste for army life, any greater desire to break away from the front and go home, than older men with family responsibilities?

Besides the youthfulness of its leadership the PLSR was distinguished by its plebeian character. In Petersburg and a few other centers a number of the younger intellectuals sided with it, but the whole mass of Narodnik intellectuals of the elder generation, the whole hierarchy of the peasant movement—all those co-operators, educators, ex-zemstvo employees, and public service people—shunned it as though it were the plague. Natanson's gray beard made him a curiosity among the Left SR's, even an object of veneration, for he was virtually their only link with the formative period of Populism.[228] The reason is not hard to discover. The Narodnik intellectuals, for the most part confessed or concealed nationalists who regarded political liberty as the supreme good, at least for the present, looked with horror on a movement bearing their label which was prepared to desert the Western democracies in order to make peace with the Teutonic and Turkish foe and wage war upon the national bourgeoisie. The local accounts of the schism abound with evidence of this hostility on the part of the intellectuals. In Moscow province the schoolteachers chosen as delegates by local branches had swung the September conference against the left wing.[229] At the time of

[228] See Steinberg, *Als ich Volkskommissar war*, p. 60.
[229] *Protokoly pervago s"ezda PLSR*, p. 10.

the October crisis the Petersburg teachers' and secondary school students' organizations had supported the Central Committee.[230] At Pskov, Voronezh, Taganrog, and Baku the old party had split along professional lines, the workingmen deciding for the Left SR's, the intellectuals against them.[231] The whole intelligentsia in Voronezh is said to have gone against the left, and in Odessa, "when the split came, nearly all the intellectuals deserted us." [232] Kamkov advised his colleagues that in this respect the rump party enjoyed a decided advantage.[233] It is clear that at the breakup of the PSR nearly all of the sailors and a large majority of the soldiers and workers went with the Left SR's, most of the intellectuals and white-collar workers stayed where they were, and the peasantry gradually divided into two warring camps, the larger one loyal to the PSR, but the lesser one already sizable and steadily growing.[234]

From every quarter came complaints of a dearth of intellectual workers which seriously impeded the activity of the new party. Sukhanov termed it the party of the rural plebs and ranked it lower on the cultural scale than the Bolsheviks, the party of the urban plebs.[235] He speaks of its darkness, of its "half-literate" character, and an incident that occurred at the Extraordinary Peasants' Congress no doubt would have confirmed him in his opinion. After the moderates had withdrawn and only Left SR's, Bolsheviks, and nonpartisan extremists remained in the hall, a note was handed to the presiding officer demanding the removal of Jews from the presidium. Spiridonova, chiding those in the assembly who had backslid from revolutionary principles, sought to shift the blame to the right and center SR's, since the *Delo Naroda*, in attacking the congress, had remarked that "in some wondrous way the Radomyslskis and Goldendachs (the real names of Zinoviev and Riazanov) had gotten to be peasants' representatives." [236] But Zenzinov claimed that other reports had

---

[230] *Delo Naroda*, Nos. 202, 203 (November 7, 8, 1917).
[231] *Protokoly pervago s"ezda PLSR*, pp. 5, 8, 10; *Revoliutsiia 1917 goda v Azerbaidzhane*, pp. 205–6; Rathauser, *Revoliutsiia i grazhdanskaia voina v Baku*, pp. 84, 108. The latter author (p. 118) says the skilled workers in Baku favored the SR's.
[232] *Protokoly pervago s"ezda PLSR*, p. 12. [233] *Ibid.*, p. 17.
[234] See ch. 5. [235] *Zapiski*, VII, 259–60.
[236] "Bor'ba za krest'ianstvo" (The Struggle for the Peasantry), No. 209 (November 14, 1917); *Revoliutsiia 1917 goda*, VI, 143.

reached him of anti-Semitic sentiment in the ranks of the extremist parties, and he accused these parties of playing upon the dark passions of the people.[237] In such matters, however, it is not necessary to accuse one socialist group or the other of demagogy or to look for the hidden hand of provocation. The Left SR's aspired to be a people's party; they had become such, quite possibly in a fuller sense than other parties for the very reason that the intellectual element was weaker among them, and now they must take the people as they found them, with their passions and prejudices as well as their thirst for social justice.

Another aspect of the schism is that the Left SR's betrayed the same untidiness in housekeeping as their brethren on the right. Neither succeeded in the course of 1917 in sweeping out the cobwebs and bringing the common program of 1906 up to date. Acknowledging the need for revision, the founding congress of the PLSR put aside basic problems to deal with questions of the hour. With the land already passing into the hands of the peasantry, the agrarian section of the program would either at long last have to be formulated in concrete terms or the idea of equitable distribution would cease to have any meaning—yet matters remained as before. Trutovski secured permission to present his economic theses only on the understanding that they would not be discussed, which left them hanging in air. Organizational problems, vital to a nascent party facing the task of holding its lines against the inroads of a formidable rival, received only a modicum of attention. Relations with the SR's and the stand to be taken on the Constituent Assembly engrossed the interest and consumed the time of the congress.[238]

A final aspect of the schism that should be noted is that it was not as complete as might have been expected. Not only did Chernov's left center remain with the PSR, preserving for it many veterans and a part of its youth,[239] but entire provincial organizations where the left predominated refused to break away, either because of the lagging pace of political development or because of a hope that somehow things might still be straightened out. Tomsk and Kherson

---

[237] "S bolnoi golovy na zdorovuiu" (From a Sick Head onto a Healthy One), *Delo Naroda*, No. 210 (November 15, 1917).

[238] See *Protokoly pervago s"ezda PLSR.*

[239] Manuscript commentary on the minutes of the Central Committee, p. 54.

definitely refused to affiliate with the new party, and Pskov and Chernigov, though sending delegations to its founding congress, had instructed against a definitive split.[240] The further action of these two organizations cannot be established from the records. Much of the wavering at the congress sprang from the knowledge that substantial elements had failed to come over though sympathetic to the views of the secessionists.[241] The question arose, therefore, whether it would be better to go on alone in the hope of detaching these elements at a later date, or better to furl the banner of independence and form, in so far as was possible, a united front within the existing party. The stumbling block of the exclusions already decreed by the Central Committee decided the congress in favor of the first course, but not without considerable misgivings.

With entire provinces of a leftist cast refusing to break away, and with the secessionists looking back over their shoulders at these unredeemed kinsmen, would not a more temperate course on the part of the Central Committee, deferring the decision on discipline to the all-party congress, have preserved the unity of the Socialist Revolutionary movement? The answer is that although real unity had long since ceased to exist, formal unity could have been preserved, and perhaps would have been, had it not been for the war. The war was the nemesis of the PSR as it was of the whole Russian Revolution. It was the great rending force, just as the agrarian question was for the SR's the chief bond of union. It was not, as was sometimes asserted,[242] the divergence over the nature of the revolution that served as the primary cause of disunion, for Kamkov freely conceded that a socialist revolution in Russia was out of the question,[243] nor was it the Left SR espousal of the soviet concept of government, though this renunciation of democracy, as Chernov termed it, formed the watershed between the left and the left center. Above everything else it was the war that separated the left from the dominant right center, and behind the denunciations of the Left SR's as accomplices

---

[240] *Protokoly pervago s"ezda PLSR*, pp. 10, 14, 113. On Tomsk see above, p. 128.
[241] See statements of Kamkov and Karelin (*Protokoly pervago s"ezda PLSR*, pp. 72, 82).
[242] See report of Kaplan to the Petersburg reorganizing convention of the old party (*Delo Naroda*, No. 203 [November 8, 1917]).
[243] *Protokoly pervago s"ezda PLSR*, p. 92.

in the rape of democracy lay the dread that Russia would now be taken out of the war. An observer from the moderate left did not exaggerate when he said that Kamkov and his group would compromise seven times before letting it come to a split,[244] but from the grim patriots in control of the Central Committee no concessions were forthcoming. By the time the complexion of the Central Committee had changed as a result of the Fourth Party Congress, too much water had flowed under the bridge for reconciliation to have any chance. The unity of their movement was but one of the sacrifices that the Narodnik intellectuals laid upon the altar of the Triple Entente.

[244] Kogan-Bernstein, "Nashi raskhozhdeniia" (Our Divergences), *Partiinyia Izvestiia*, No. 5 (January 20, 1918), p. 62.

IV

The PSR after the Schism

With the purging of the left wing it remained to be seen whether the residual party could pull itself together and become an effective organization, now that it had ceased to be "all-embracing." In some quarters it was feared and in others hoped that the amputation of dissident elements would give to the right center undisputed control of the party in place of the tenuous ascendancy it had hitherto enjoyed, more because of the prestige of personalities and confused voting at the Third Congress than because of any real edge in strength. On the other hand, the moderate left under Chernov would be sure to press the advantage which the rout of coalition had given it in an effort to rally all the remaining antiwar and anticollaborationist sentiment against the dominant faction of the Central Committee. The problems which had bred diversity of opinion were still there, in more acute form than ever, and the departure of the left wing hardly lessened the tension among the other factions. A showdown could no longer be averted, even had Chernov's patience in devising elastic formulas not been approaching the breaking point, and it was appropriate that the issue should be fought out before the highest instance of party authority.

From November 26 to December 5 the Fourth, and last, Congress of the PSR met in the Russian capital. The party was still on a legal footing—a status it would not enjoy for very much longer—and the representation at the congress turned out to be almost ideal, in the words of the chairman of the credentials committee, with delegates present from fifty-one provinces.[1] Some familiar faces were missing, since Gotz and Avksentiev, because of their implication in the cadet uprising, could not risk a public appearance, Kerenski was in hiding, and Vishniak in prison,[2] but in general the Fourth Congress was a

[1] *Kratkii otchët*, p. 87.
[2] Gotz, Kerenski, and Vishniak sent letters of greeting to the congress (*ibid.*, pp. 7-11).

fully authoritative body of several hundred delegates in which voting
privileges were restricted to those who had been elected by the
membership for that express purpose. In cases where delegates were
chosen by committee action, without reference to the membership,
floor privileges only were extended.[3] The Fourth Congress, therefore, reflected the state of opinion in party circles at the moment as
accurately as any means that could have been devised.

Reeling from the shock of the double disaster that had overtaken
them, with their official position destroyed and their organization
disrupted in a number of localities, the party members assembled in
St. Petersburg for the decisive fight. Gone was the ecstacy of the
Imatra and Tammerfors congresses, as also the complacency of the
Moscow congress; a somber atmosphere pervaded the hall of the
technological institute as the partisans and critics of the Central Committee prepared to battle it out. One delegate said that the assemblage
produced on him the impression of a group of people who had experienced a political debacle.[4] How much influence the debacle, or
succession of debacles, had on the decisions of the congress, whether
the result would have been different had there been no October
Revolution, is a question that must, of course, be left unanswered. In
any event it soon became clear that the influence wielded by Abram
Gotz in spheres of leadership greatly exceeded the strength of his
popular following, and that the eclipse of V. M. Chernov had been
due to his personal qualities, to an abdication of his position, rather
than to any loss of standing with the general membership, for whom
he was still far and away the party's leading personality. The election
of Chernov as presiding officer and of a left-centrist presidium clearly
revealed the temper of the congress and showed that the hitherto
dominant clique in the Central Committee had lost control of the
party despite the lopping off of its large left wing.[5] The congress was
going to clean house, but in typical SR fashion, with so many Janus-
faced formulas, so many compromises, and so much consideration

[3] *Delo Naroda,* No. 209 (November 14, 1917); *Kratkii otchët,* p. 53. By December 1, 335 delegates were in attendance, 120 of them without voting rights.
[4] *Kratkii otchët,* p. 42.
[5] Chernov, manuscript commentary on the minutes of the Central Committee,
pp. 73–74; *Kratkii otchët,* p. 4. The vote on Chernov as president was 86 for with
11 abstentions. Many delegates arrived after the opening of the congress,
accounting for the thinness of the vote. Rakitnikov and Rusanov were the other
left-centrist members of the presidium and Likhach had no factional ties.

for the feelings of the defeated faction as inevitably to vitiate the effects of the house cleaning.

The first matter to come before the congress was the recent schism. Would the left center in control of the congress confirm the expulsion of a whole segment of party opinion decreed by a Central Committee whose other actions it was now preparing to subject to a searching revision? The Left SR's were not above speculating on the manifest hostility of so many delegates to the organ which had booted them out of the party, and reversed their original decision to ignore the congress after Kamkov had brought the question down from the plane of principle into the realm of tactics with his assertion that the sole consideration should be how to inflict the maximum loss upon the rival organization. The Left SR's decided then to send an able delegation to the Fourth Congress which would read a declaration excoriating the way in which the congress had been convoked and then would slam the door, drawing after it all like-minded elements that still had not made the final break.[6] But the average Socialist Revolutionary, whether of the left or right center, nursed a special animus against his former comrades, either because of the blood shed in October or because of the apostasy from democracy implicit in opposing the soviets to the Constituent Assembly. When the time came for the Left SR's to spring their coup, they met with a reception so hostile as to suggest to one observer the possibility of a lynching.[7]

The declaration of the Left SR's was read by Steinberg, who had been delegated for this purpose along with Trutovski. It raked the party leadership fore and aft because of its "criminal policy" of collaboration with the class enemy, because of its responsibility for shifting the party's center of gravity from the peasants and workers to the petty bourgeoisie, and because of its scheme to perpetuate control by securing a packed congress through the arbitrary exclusion of the left wing.[8] At the words "criminal policy" angry shouts broke in upon the speaker, and at the words "packed congress" a deafening roar shut him off and he was deprived of the floor.

---

[6] See the discussion at the Left SR congress (*Protokoly pervago s"ezda PLSR*, pp. 15–25, 78–85).

[7] *Kratkii otchët*, p. 96.

[8] Text of declaration in *ibid.*, pp. 35–36; see also *Protokoly pervago s"ezda PLSR*, p. 79.

Amidst a hail of imprecations and threats Steinberg and Trutovski made their way out of the hall, accompanied by a handful of delegates—five in all, later joined by two others—and that constituted the response of the congress to the leftist maneuver.[9] The knowledge that the aid of the extremists would not be needed to insure their victory may well have hardened the attitude of the left center—Gerstein, one of Chernov's lieutenants, had earlier exclaimed that the blood of comrades separated these people from the PSR, and that it was shameful even to admit them to the congress.[10] The blood-is-between feeling, however, was also manifest on the other side, and there were Left SR's who condemned the slightest approach to the hateful foe.[11] Indeed, the state of feeling on both sides was such as to suggest that if numbers of SR's and Left SR's were thrown together, even more blood would be in between.

In the back of their minds the Left SR's had not excluded the possibility of taking over the Fourth Congress with the help of all shades of opinion opposed to the Central Committee, in which case they would have come into possession of the apparatus and good will of the mother party. What the good will consisted of was shown by the action of the peasants in casting an enormous number of votes for the ticket with the SR label.[12] But the sharp antagonism of the left center had frustrated this hope, chimerical to begin with in view of the sweeping exclusions which made it impossible for the left to have more than a handful of delegates at the congress. Even the minimum objective of pulling away all leftist sympathizers had certainly not succeeded. A considerable group stayed on at the congress under the leadership of Kogan-Bernstein. It was more radical than Chernov's following but not radical enough to renounce the Constituent Assembly and bolt the party.[13] The Fourth Congress had withstood the wrecking tactics of the separatists.

[9] *Kratkii otchët*, pp. 12–14, 36–37; *Delo Naroda*, No. 220 (November 30, 1917); *Protokoly pervago s"ezda PLSR*, pp. 83–85.
[10] *Kratkii otchët*, p. 4.
[11] See debate on the question at their congress (*Protokoly pervago s"ezda PLSR*, pp. 18–25, 80–82).
[12] *Ibid.*, pp. 19, 78, 81–82 (especially the comments of Kamkov and Karelin).
[13] Kogan-Bernstein, "Nashi raskhozhdeniia" (Our Divergences), *Partiinyia Izvestiia*, No. 5 (January 20, 1918), pp. 62–63; Chernov, manuscript commentary on the minutes of the Central Committee, p. 74.

The right deviation received rather more indulgent treatment from the congress, despite the claim of impartiality in dealing with dissent on either wing. Kogan-Bernstein complained that there was one yardstick for measuring behavior on the left and another for measuring it on the right. While extremists on the left had been cast out of the party, those on the right like Breshkovskaia still were in good standing. She should be excluded, he urged. The PSR was not a society for the veneration of relics and the sooner the accumulation of lifeless forms was swept away the better for the party.[14] But the congress would not raise its hand against the "Grandmother of the Revolution," however much it might disagree with some of her actions. Minor answered that it was shameful to propose the exclusion of one who for sixty years had served the cause of socialism, and the congress applauded his words.[15] When Breshkovskaia herself appeared, however, and gave an address in which she denied having moved away from the party to the right, drily observing that she knew of no right SR's but only of party members who had not approached the Bolshevik position, she drew applause from only a part of the assembly, and a proposal to name her honorary chairman died for want of adequate support.[16]

In general, the right sang in a minor key and tried to gloss over its differences with the center. Men like Argunov and V. I. Lebedev stressed the need for unity in the face of the dangers confronting the Constituent Assembly, and thought that a community viewpoint was now feasible since the main stumbling block, the question of war and peace, had lost its edge with the secession of the "defeatist" element and the definitive collapse of the army. Hitherto the center had made the quest for peace the cornerstone of its program without, however, denying the requirements of national defense, while the right had emphasized defense without renouncing the quest for peace, but now that Bolshevism had ruined any prospect of active defense (that is, of offensive action at the front), the difference in emphasis disappeared and both factions could agree upon a speedy "democratic" peace as the only way out of an impossible situation. The *Volia*

---

[14] *Kratkii otchët*, pp. 42–43; "Raskol ili ochishchenie?" (Schism or Purge?), *Delo Naroda*, No. 218 (November 24, 1917).
[15] *Kratkii otchët*, p. 93; see also S. L. Maslov's defense of her (*ibid.*, p. 57).
[16] *Ibid.*, pp. 54–55.

Naroda group maintained that its struggle had been conducted from within the organization, in obedience to the rules of discipline, and attempted to draw a line between itself and the Organizational Council of SR Defensists, which had been read out of the party. In respect to lists of candidates for the Constituent Assembly competing with the official party lists in certain districts, the right acknowledged its guilt but claimed extenuating circumstances.[17]

The conciliatory and even humble tone of the right-wing deviationists may well have preserved their status in the party and might even have allayed factional rancor had the delegates been able to avoid raking over the painful events of the recent past. But this they could not do, and as soon as the discussion touched upon the Kornilov affair and the relations between the party and Kerenski, the lid blew off and the pot boiled over. Too much bitterness had been stirred in the soul of V. M. Chernov for him to pass over this opportunity to settle accounts with the element in his own party which had echoed the calumnies of the capitalist press in its campaign to drive him from the Provisional Government. The fetish of party unity which explains so much in his conduct did not prevent him on this occasion from smacking those who had "shamefully" joined his external foes in branding him a defeatist. If the right had done less damage than the left, he declared, it was only because its appeal had met with no mass response. It had identified the fortunes of coalition with the fortunes of revolution and taught that the failure of the one would entail the ruin of the other; it had rejected the principle of peace without victors or vanquished in favor of breaking German militarism by military means, and had adopted a strictly defensive position only after the Russian army had lost the capacity for defense. This program had then been foisted upon the party in lieu of its own program adopted at the Third Congress by making Kerenski its executor and placing the party in a position where it had either to accept this program or break with Kerenski, just as a similar stake

---

[17] *Ibid.*, pp. 74–75, 81–82, 99; Chernov, manuscript commentary on the minutes of the Central Committee, pp. 68–69; *Delo Naroda*, No. 223 (December 3, 1917). In a number of instances the right had put up its own lists in districts where the party machinery was in the hands of the element which would shortly secede to form the Left SR Party, as in Kharkov province. Hence the real interest of the party, it was argued, had not been impaired by such independent action. On the subject of these lists see below, ch. 6.

on personalities had forced the party either to overlook the breach of discipline involved in dissident electoral lists competing with its own or to strike the name of Breshkovskaia from the membership rolls. The right had been guilty of playing off personalities against the party to their mutual ruin.[18]

For the right the ex-assistant minister of marine, V. I. Lebedev, arose to answer this scorching attack with a demonstration of loyalty to Kerenski and a denunciation of Chernov's public career. Reminding the delegates that Kerenski could not appear before the congress and defend himself, Lebedev asked why Kerenski alone must bear the blame for the actions of a government of which Chernov also had been a member. The latter had uttered no word of protest against the repressions after the July Days and had even remarked to Lebedev that the Left SR Ustinov should be arrested. This was a charge that always made Chernov squirm, and, according to one version,[19] he broke in upon Lebedev at this point to call him a liar. On the matter of arrests, as also upon the charge of using Kerenski and Breshkovskaia as fronts behind which to operate, Lebedev challenged Chernov to a court of arbitration. Then Lebedev took up the feud [20] between the rightist *Volia Naroda* and the centrist *Delo Naroda* and lumped the latter with *Pravda* and Maxim Gorki's *Novaia Zhizn'* as baiters of Kerenski. The climax came when he attacked Chernov for the fateful articles published in the *Delo Naroda* after the Kornilov affair—the articles that had exploded the unity of the centrist core of the PSR:

"These articles knifed Kerenski in the back; they constituted a betrayal of him; it was these articles that sank him."

"He already was sunk!" cried several of the delegates, among them Chernov himself, who explained that his purpose had been to save the party from being sucked down in the wake of the drowning Kerenski.[21]

There can be no doubt that this outburst strained the unity of what

[18] *Kratkii otchët*, pp. 118–120.
[19] *Russkiia Vedomosti*, No. 268 (December 6, 1917).
[20] The bitterness of the feud may be judged from the comment in the *Volia Naroda* (No. 179; November 24, 1917) on the reaction of the official organ to the arrest of Argunov on November 17. Whereas the public generally had voiced a protest, including the capitalist papers and even Riazanov of the Bolsheviks, the *Delo Naroda* had not even mentioned the arrest until several days later, when it printed a bare notice of the occurrence.
[21] *Volia Naroda*, No. 185 (December 5, 1917); *Kratkii otchët*, pp. 119, 121.

was left of the PSR to the breaking point. The wound had not healed
and now it was torn open again. The small right wing, which
Lebedev himself described as of negligible strength, a group of
intellectuals with no organization behind them,[22] could not have
imposed this strain. The danger lay in the center, for if the Gotz-
Zenzinov and Chernovian factions flew apart, the party was finished,
and it was going to be hard enough to hold them together in the
matter of electing a new Central Committee, even without rehearsing
the original cause of the rupture.

Accounts differ as to what actually took place on this memorable
occasion. *Russkiia Vedomosti,* one of the most reputable journals, in
emphasizing the depth of the split that had developed, says that
Chernov wanted to cut off the whole right wing, including the *Volia
Naroda* group and Breshkovskaia herself, but that a vote on his motion was put off. Conservative Narodnik circles are represented as so
incensed at his attitude as to contemplate the formation of a new
party under Breshkovskaia which would be sharply marked off from
his following as well as from the Left SR's.[23] Nothing like this is
to be found in the SR press or in the official report of the congress,
where Chernov is stated merely to have demanded that the new
Central Committee be empowered to deal sternly with separatist
tendencies of any kind.[24] But we must bear in mind that the official
report is not the stenographic report, which was never published,
and the account in the *Volia Naroda* is notably fuller and the language more impassioned than in the official report. As Chernov himself does not tell us that he demanded the expulsion of the opposing
faction, however, we are forced to the conclusion that the correspondent of the *Russkiia Vedomosti* must have confused the issue,
though it is quite likely there was talk of a new party when it became evident that Chernov would regain his ascendancy in the old.

The upshot of all the discussion at the Fourth Congress about the
left and right deviations was that the amputation of the left wing was
confirmed while no similar operation was performed on the other
side, save to a very minor degree. Two resolutions were laid before

[22] *Kratkii otchët,* p. 99.
[23] *Russkiia Vedomosti,* No. 268 (December 6, 1917).
[24] *Kratkii otchët,* p. 121.

the congress as the basis of its final action in the matter, one by
Zenzinov upholding the action of the retiring Central Committee,
and a second by Revzina, more leftist in tone. Zenzinov's draft prevailed in a thin vote at the end of the congress by 54 to 41, but had
to be modified in the direction of greater leniency for party members
who had been implicated to a slight degree in the October Revolution. All who belonged to the Left SR Party or to the Organizational
Council of SR Defensists in Petersburg—from the standpoint of their
respective numbers, a ludicrous attempt to hold the balance even—
continued to be excluded from the PSR, as also those who participated in the Soviet government, centrally or locally, and those who
acted as plenipotentiaries in negotiations for a separate peace. But
SR's who had stayed on at the second soviet congress or entered
military revolutionary committees, and who accordingly had fallen
under the ban of the Central Committee, were now to have their
cases individualized so that not the action itself, but the degree to
which it indicated a desire to help the Bolsheviks should determine
the offender's status. Conversely, the congress stiffened the line toward the right deviationists by providing for disciplinary action in
cases of competing electoral lists, although none had been envisaged
by the Zenzinov resolution, but here again provision was made for
an individualized procedure.[25]

With the seal of approval set on the schism and the agrarian socialist movement now finally divided into two competing and bitterly
hostile parties, the congress could turn to the problem of leadership.
The outgoing Central Committee had recommended as its last act [26]
that no change be made in its membership, but the prospects were
that it would have to pass through a corridor of fire, in the flames of
which at least some of its members would be consumed. Striving to
put its best foot forward in the crucial matter of rendering an account
to the congress, the Central Committee chose as its chief spokesman
V. M. Zenzinov, most moderate and conciliatory of the right-centrist
hierarchs and always a strong party man. Zenzinov did not deny the

[25] *Ibid.*, pp. 153–56.
[26] Protokol Zasedaniia Tsentral'nago Komiteta PSR (November 22, 1917);
Chernov, manuscript commentary on the minutes of the Central Committee,
p. 65.

imperfections of the Central Committee nor could he conceal the fact that inner tension as well as external adversity had influenced its wavering course. In mitigation of its record he could only urge that its effort to follow the instructions of the Third Congress had been gravely impaired by the growing disorganization of the party and that the Central Committee, as the party in miniature, could not have more unity than its parent, having been chosen on the coalitional principle to give representation to the various points of view. As to policies, the collaboration with other political elements in the Provisional Government and the quest for a general "democratic" peace had followed logically from the committee's belief in a middle course as the only means of saving the revolution and averting a civil war.[27] Zenzinov said that as a consequence he shared the fate of other party members whom the left-wingers regarded as rightist and the right-wingers as leftist. From his report it appears that on one matter— and one alone—the Central Committee had never wavered—its "sharp and decisive" rejection of a separate peace, the cornerstone of the international policy of the people's commissars.[28]

When the floor was thrown open to discussion after the delivery of the report, a hail of criticism descended upon the Central Committee. There was little that it was not reproached for, but the one thing that aroused more general condemnation than any other was the failure to exercise control over party representatives in high places, as a consequence of which Kerenski, Avksentiev, and others had caused the party to assume responsibility for actions and policies which were not its own, in which it did not believe, and which had cost it heavily in popularity with the lower and now sovereign orders of Russian society.[29] There was little the right-centrist spokesmen could do to refute this charge—it was all too true. Zenzinov had to confess that his friend Kerenski had simply disregarded the injunctions of the Central Committee,[30] and Minor said that he did not know of an occasion on which Avksentiev would have subordinated

[27] *Kratkii otchët,* p. 108 (statement of Rosenblum).

[28] *Ibid.,* pp. 64–73, 111–12; Chernov, manuscript commentary on the minutes of the Central Committee, p. 66.

[29] See language of the resolution on the report of the Central Committee (*Kratkii otchët,* p. 143).

[30] *Ibid.,* p. 90; identical statement in No. 224 of the *Delo Naroda* (December 5, 1917).

his opinion to the will of the Central Committee.[31] But it remained for D. S. Rosenblum to make the startling disclosure that since the session in the Malachite Hall of the Winter Palace early in July, when all parties had empowered Kerenski to form a ministry, he had no longer been the representative of the PSR in the government, and that, accordingly, all subsequent actions of his, from the Moscow State Conference to the campaign against Petersburg,[32] had been taken on his own initiative and at his own risk.[33] To the ensuing question whether Kerenski had been expelled from the party the spokesman replied in the negative; for that both a party judgment and the judgment of history would be necessary.[34] The right branded the disclosure as desertion of a comrade under fire [35] and the left wanted to know why it had not been made sooner. Speaking for the remodeled Petersburg organization, which despite the mass exodus of extremists still stood to the left of center, A. D. Vysotski chided the Central Committee for not having had the firmness either to force Kerenski to change his policies or else to end the impression that he acted with party sanction.[36] Judging from the reaction of both the Third and Fourth Congresses, hardly any question so agitated the membership as the abnormal relationship of A. F. Kerenski to the Socialist Revolutionary Party.

The indictment of the Central Committee included other grave charges. Irrespective of factional affiliation, the delegates agreed on the ambiguity of the party's position under its guidance. From the right came the characterization of policy as "wobbling, zig-zagging, and indefinite," [37] from the left the complaint that the people had been confused by not being able to tell where the party stood on the biggest issues of the day.[38] Discipline had suffered under the regime of the Central Committee, which, far from having known how to impart unity to the actions of the party as a whole, had tolerated

[31] *Kratkii otchët*, p. 93.

[32] Our discussion of the October Revolution has shown the falseness of the assertion that the campaign against Petersburg had been made on his own, without sanction of the Central Committee. (See above, pp. 39 ff.)

[33] *Delo Naroda*, No. 224 (December 5, 1917); *Kratkii otchët*, pp. 110–11 (gives less than the newspaper on this point); Chernov, manuscript commentary on the minutes of the Central Committee, p. 66.

[34] *Kratkii otchët*, p. 111.   [35] *Ibid.*, p. 98 (statement of Lebedev).

[36] *Ibid.*, p. 94; *Delo Naroda*, No. 224 (December 5, 1917).

[37] *Kratkii otchët*, p. 91.   [38] *Ibid.*, p. 47.

grievous infractions in its own midst, by the most responsible per-
sonages, and at the most decisive moments.[39] Radical-minded delegates censured the supreme organ for having manifested a consistent
bias against the left, as seen externally in the willingness to collaborate with the bourgeoisie while adamantly rejecting any compromise with the Bolsheviks, and internally by the expulsion of the left
wing while admitting the right to this congress.[40] Another indictment, this time by a member of the Central Committee itself, was that
despite the appeal of the agrarian program, it had not known how to
kindle the enthusiasm of the masses but had let the torch fall into
the hands of the Bolsheviks through a default of leadership so complete that even Chernov's popularity was now gravely compromised.[41] Finally, one delegate found the source of evil in the dominance of the intellectuals: install the workers and peasants in office,
he urged, and they would straighten things out by making a social
revolution, in contrast to the intellectuals, who had been vitally concerned only with political changes.[42]

A straightforward proposal, denouncing the deviation of the Central Committee from the decisions of the Third Congress to the
"immense harm" of the party and instituting a party court to try the
committeemen, failed of adoption at the congress.[43] Instead, a left-
centrist formulation was accepted. Even so, the resolution on the
report of the Central Committee, though softened somewhat in the
final version, expressed the general dissatisfaction with the organ
elected at the Third Congress and called for the choice of a new
committee "more homogeneous" in composition and capable of
putting through a firm policy of revolutionary socialism.[44]

In the light of this resolution and after the flagellation to which
it had been subjected, one would have expected the Central Committee to be sacked completely. But that is not the way the SR mind
worked. Clear-cut decisions were rare in this party and the present
occasion was no exception. In fact, the election of a new Central
Committee came out in such a way as to create a sensation among the
party members themselves. The congress went into executive session

[39] See language of resolution (*ibid.*, p. 143).   [40] *Ibid.*, pp. 47, 97.
[41] *Ibid.*, pp. 78–79. Prilezhaev offered this criticism. He was an independent,
identified with no particular faction.
[42] *Ibid.*, p. 64.   [43] *Ibid.*, p. 142.   [44] Text in *ibid.*, p. 143.

to discuss candidacies,[45] so that what was said does not appear in the official report or in the press, depriving us of some interesting information. Factional lists of candidates did not figure at this congress, perhaps because of the painful memory of what had happened at the preceding one,[46] and electioneering was confined to the corridors of the congress. When the ballots were tabulated, the following were declared to have been elected; their names are listed according to the number of votes received, with an indication of their factional leaning and with the results of the preceding election set down in the adjoining column for purposes of comparison.[47]

IV CONGRESS		III CONGRESS	
Central Committee Members	*Votes*	*Central Committee Members*	*Votes*
1. N. I. Rakitnikov (LC)	167	1. A. R. Gotz (RC)	260
2. D. F. Rakov (LC)	165	2. N. I. Rakitnikov (LC)	258
3. V. M. Chernov (LC)	163	3. N. S. Rusanov (LC)	241
4. V. M. Zenzinov (RC)	161	4. V. G. Arkhangelski (RC)	241
5. N. S. Rusanov (LC)	148	5. V. M. Chernov (LC)	240
6. V. V. Lunkevich (LC)	144	6. M. A. Vedeniapin (X)	237
7. M. A. Likhach (X)	131	7. D. S. Rosenblum (RC) (Firsov)	224
8. M. A. Vedeniapin (X)	126	8. M. A. Natanson (Left SR)	207
9. I. A. Prilezhaev (X)	126	9. V. V. Lunkevich (LC)	202
10. M. I. Sumgin (LC)	120	10. M. Ia. Gendelman (RC)	201
11. A. R. Gotz (RC)	112	11. A. N. Richter (LC)	199
12. M. Ia. Gendelman (RC)	107	12. L. Ia. Gerstein (LC)	193
13. F. F. Fedorovich (LC)	105	13. V. M. Zenzinov (RC)	181
14. A. N. Richter (LC)	104	14. M. P. Zatonski (RC)	177
15. K. S. Sopliakov (L) (Burevoi)	103	15. N. D. Avksentiev (RC)	168
		16. O. S. Minor (X)	157
16. E. M. Timofeev (LC)	100	17. I. A. Rubanovich (X)	156
17. L. Ia. Gerstein (LC)	85	18. I. I. Fundaminski (RC) (Bunakov)	153
18. D. D. Donskoi (RC)	82		
19. V. A. Chaikin (L)	79	19. D. F. Rakov (LC)	146
20. E. M. Ratner (LC)	76	20. I. A. Prilezhaev (X)	142
Alternates	*Votes*	*Alternates*	*Votes*
1. A. B. Eliashevich (RC)	75	1. I. I. Teterkin (LC)	206
2. I. I. Teterkin (LC)	75	2. E. S. Berg (RC)	201
3. N. N. Ivanov (LC)	73	3. A. A. Khovrin * (RC)	130
4. V. V. Sukhomlin (LC)	71	4. N. Ia. Bykhovski (RC)	126
5. M. L. Kogan-Bernstein (L)	65	5. V. Ia. Gurevich (RC)	119

* Initials of Khovrin are not certain.

[45] *Ibid.*, p. 140.   [46] See *The Agrarian Foes of Bolshevism*, ch. 6.
[47] Chernov, *Izbiratel'naia statistika* (appendix to the minutes of the Central Committee, in his possession), pp. 5–8; *Kratkii otchët*, pp. 147–148, 152. The

Five months of adversity and one of unmitigated disaster had
chastened the SR's hardly at all: in place of a Central Committee
composed of eight right-centrists, seven left-centrists, one extreme
leftist, and four waverers they now had one of eleven left-centrists,
four right-centrists, two moderate leftists, and three waverers. The
new body was "more homogeneous," as the resolution had demanded,
but it was not homogeneous. The center of gravity had shifted to the
left of the middle line, the four to one ratio among the alternates had
been reversed, and Chernov's faction had won an undeniable victory,
but not a sufficiently sweeping one to prevent wobbling at the helm
if the new organ should collide with a rival center of authority, as
it soon did in the shape of the party delegation in the Constituent
Assembly.

Why did the congress mix the fruit in this fashion? Why had it
denied the left center a clean sweep? Why did it condemn the
Central Committee only to reelect more than half of its membership
(twelve out of twenty)? According to V. M. Chernov, who plumed
himself on these results, the congress had wanted to teach a hard
lesson to those responsible for steering a rightward course but not to
humiliate them utterly. So it had permitted Gotz, Gendelman, and
Zenzinov to escape the electoral guillotine as the knife descended on
Avksentiev, Fundaminski, Rosenblum, and Arkhangelski.[48] At the
same time it had dropped Gotz from first to eleventh place on the list
of victorious candidates—a measurable decline in the popularity of
his chief rival which undoubtedly gave Chernov a good deal of satisfaction, as did also the failure of the friends of Kerenski even to offer
his name at this congress after his candidacy had rocked the preceding
one to its foundations.[49]

---

following symbols are used: RC for right center; LC for left center; L for
moderate left, between Chernov's left center and the separatist Left SR's;
X for uncertain or wavering, indicating that the individual cannot be assigned
to any one faction. In all cases the oscillation was between right center and
left center.

[48] Zatonski was the other adherent of the right center who failed of reelection, but he was of no significance except that he was the only workingman
in the group. Minor and Rubanovich, who often voted with the conservatives,
were likewise turned down, and, of course, Natanson, who was now the head
of a rival party.

[49] Manuscript commentary on the minutes of the Central Committee, pp.
73-74.

Other evidence suggests, however, a more haphazard procedure without the degree of conscious purpose which Chernov attributes to the action of the congress. An unnamed delegate, pointing to the obvious fact that the votes were scattered over the field, gave as an explanation the coyness of the candidates, many of whom had refused to let their names be put forward, yet had not made their refusal absolute. The congress had further muddied the waters by first deciding to take these declinations at face value and then agreeing with a comrade who urged that no party member could refuse a call to service of this sort. As a result the question was left dangling, and each delegate decided for himself how much or how little weight to assign to these delicate declinations.[50] Such rampant individualism in the matter of electing a Central Committee may have befitted a movement which had always extolled the "critically thinking individual," but in the December darkness of 1917 it ill became candidates for the highest office of a great political party to act like blushing maidens.

If the results were gratifying to V. M. Chernov they aroused the resentment of other delegates on either side of the central aisle. Two members of the old committee, reelected to the new, aired their vexation before the congress. Gendelman announced his refusal to serve any longer on a board the record of which had been roundly condemned without any clear indication as to how the members could comply with the will of the congress.[51] Zenzinov expressed a willingness to remain at his post, but, seeing in the resolutions adopted at the congress no clear line for the Central Committee to follow, he proposed to exercise his own judgment in interpreting them. Both voiced their perplexity at being reelected when their work had been branded as unsatisfactory. These declarations, especially Zenzinov's characterization of the resolutions, much stronger in the press account [52] than in the report which he wrote himself,[53] and the inference that his own discretion was a safer guide than the language of the resolutions, infuriated the radical-minded delegates, who forced a recess to discuss the situation that had arisen. When the

[50] *Kratkii otchët,* p. 148.   [51] *Ibid.,* pp. 149–51.
[52] *Volia Naroda,* No. 187 (December 7, 1917).
[53] *Kratkii otchët,* pp. 151–52.

session was resumed, Zenzinov got up to say that his statement had been misinterpreted and that as a loyal son of the party he meant to abide by the decisions of the duly constituted congress. Gerstein then took the floor to say that while he had often differed with his colleague Zenzinov, their association had convinced him that what Zenzinov said could always be accepted at face value, and that the members of the new committee could be trusted to carry out the decisions of the congress. These reflected, in his opinion, the will of the current previously in the minority in the Central Committee but greatly in the majority at this congress.[54] The left center had once more bestowed a symbolic kiss upon the right center and the old dance could be resumed.

As for Gendelman, the congress turned away from the sensible observation of Kallistov that, if a man could not follow its instructions, his resignation was in order, to adopt by a vote of 46 to 37 (!) a motion inviting Gendelman to reconsider his decision since the congress, in condemning the policy of the Central Committee, had not intended to reflect personally upon any of its members.[55] This in turn was too much for Lisienko of Tomsk, who with several other delegates voiced disgust at proceedings which left the new organ suffering from the same curse of heterogeneity as the old, with the prospect of continued unsteadiness in the direction of party affairs. Proclaiming their intention to remain in the party but calling for a new congress with all expelled organizations represented, and so, in effect, for a reunion with the Left SR's, they bolted the congress. Dismay settled over the assembly in the wake of this renewed evidence of crumbling, and Chernov hastened to brand the demonstration as purposeless, since the rudder had already swung decisively to the left.[56]

The election of a Central Committee was the most important event in the life of a Russian party, in so far as its own actions were concerned, though more important things might be done unto it, as in the case of blows sustained from a hostile force. Small wonder, then, that this election left so bad a taste in the mouth of so many members. The situation was not the same as before, it is true: the left

[54] *Ibid.*, p. 153; *Delo Naroda*, No. 226 (December 7, 1917).
[55] *Kratkii otchët*, pp. 151–52.   [56] *Ibid.*, pp. 158–59.

center had unhorsed the right center, but the delegates knew in their hearts that the fundamental change necessary to save the party had not taken place. Everything was still shrouded in compromise; as always, the sword was dulled before it was used. The tragedy lay in the fact that neither fragment of the broken center possessed the necessary strength or spirit of self-sacrifice to straighten out the line and give the party what would have been at best a fighting chance for survival. And this failing is seen as much in the decisions of the congress on specific matters as in the selection of its directing personnel.

The first problem confronting the congress, and, after its adjournment, the new Central Committee, was the question of power. Rudely ejected from a position of authority in October, the SR's now faced the task of regaining their former eminence so that they would have another chance at doing what they had failed to do in eight months of squandered opportunity. The Constituent Assembly, of course, afforded the best avenue to a return to power, and it was daily becoming more evident that the PSR might control that body; yet every delegate at the congress knew already, a month in advance of its convocation, that the life of the Constituent Assembly hung by a thread. The Soviet regime, which so many SR's had said would prove as ephemeral as the rear garrisons that constituted its chief support, had not faded away but was steadily acquiring more substance. Though it lacked the administrative machinery to implement its decrees, as the SR's never tired of pointing out, it possessed the elemental strength of bayonets, and the network of soviets, roughly and imperfectly but nevertheless in some form, was transmitting its authority to all parts of the land. In the face of its animal vigor and incontestable strength in the towns the PSR had to fight for survival, experiencing at first hand the depth of its fall: nearly all its urban strength had evaporated and in barracks and factories where once the party name had met with acclaim it now evoked only hisses and curses. By the time of the congress the party was on the verge of being driven underground. The delegates had to ask themselves two questions: Why had this situation arisen, and What could be done to overcome it? The first involved fixing the responsibility for the catastrophe, and the second, defining the position to be taken with respect to the Soviet regime.

To say that the party members differed in answering these questions is merely to say that they were still of several minds regarding the revolution, as they had been from the beginning.

One section of party opinion held tenaciously to the view that everything that had been done—or left undone—had been for the best. The Provisional Government had been correct in its policies and the party correct in supporting it, and the breakdown must be ascribed to the lack of devotion to the state in Russian society, to the political immaturity or ignorance of the Russian people. The people had not known how to rise to the level of realization that all else must be set aside in order to wage war on the side of the Western Allies until such time as they should see fit to accede to the Russian desire for peace. These "Populists" had ended by turning on the people when the people proved unable to rise above sufferings and privations from which their educational attainments had freed the intellectuals. In the petulance of their disillusionment some were not above casting a stone at the fallen idol: it was suggested on the floor of the congress that the masses found it easy to accept Lenin because they were accustomed to autocracy.[57] In the face of this national deficiency no government could have succeeded where the Provisional Government had failed, and a ministry without bourgeois representation would all the same have foundered on these same insoluble problems. No matter how the political weights were adjusted, it still would have been impossible to reconcile the demands of the Russian people with the interests of the Russian state.[58]

Such was the justification offered for the coalitional policy, which had been terminated against the will of these SR's by the October Revolution. Even now, after their house had collapsed about them, they clutched at the fallen rafters: two members of the outgoing

---

[57] *Ibid.*, p. 51.
[58] V. Arkhangelski, "O proshlykh takticheskikh oshibkakh" (On Tactical Errors in the Past), *Revoliutsionnaia Rossiia*, No. 42 (April, 1925), pp. 10–14; V. Vadimov (V. Podvitski), "Pod znakom ushcherba (K itogam 4 go s"ezda partii)" (Under an Ill-Fated Banner [On the Results of the Fourth Party Congress]), *Partiinyia Izvestiia*, No. 5 (January 20, 1918), pp. 66–67; speeches of Podvitski, Arkhangelski, and S. L. Maslov at the congress (*Kratkii otchët*, pp. 45–46, 52, 58–59).

Central Committee acknowledged coalition to be no longer feasible, but only because the people would not tolerate it, not because they themselves had experienced a change of heart.[59] In identifying the cause of coalition with the cause of the revolution the right center was at one with the right, and this section of party opinion, influential because of its intellectual following, soon found a new mouthpiece in the SR caucus of the Constituent Assembly.

Agreement among these people on shifting the blame for the present situation to the shoulders of the Russian people did not imply agreement as to a future course of action, at least not at present. The Bolshevik devil had entered the national soul, but opinion differed as to how to cast him out. Some would not only accept, but actively foment, an armed struggle with the usurpers, effecting a common front with all enemies of Bolshevism in a resurgence of the coalitional principle.[60] Bolshakov of Tver reproached the party for knuckling under in the early days of the October Revolution instead of inaugurating a campaign of terrorism which would have wiped the scoundrels from the face of the earth.[61] What these activists were able to do we shall see in the chapters on the Constituent Assembly. Others reacted in quite different fashion. There were the passivists, headed by V. V. Rudnev, formerly mayor of Moscow. Their passivity stemmed from the crushing defeat sustained in that city and from the feeling that Bolshevism was essentially the expression of a self-demobilizing army which could not be restrained short of a disastrous peace, responsibility for which should be left to its authors.[62] No doubt the debacle at the polls in Moscow,[63] where they had controlled the organization, deepened the pessimism of these right-wing passivists. Finally, there must have been a few other sober thinkers like the new committeeman Eliashevich of Samara, wedded to war and coalition, and quite willing to overthrow the new government, but convinced that the time had not come for an armed

---

[59] See speeches of Minor and Gendelman (*Kratkii otchët*, pp. 93, 105–6).

[60] Vadimov (Podvitski), "Pod znakom ushcherba," *Partiinyia Izvestiia*, No. 5 (January 20, 1918), p. 67.

[61] *Kratkii otchët*, p. 44.

[62] Chernov, manuscript commentary on the minutes of the Central Committee, p. 81.

[63] See Radkey, *The Election to the Russian Constituent Assembly*, pp. 35, 52–53.

struggle in view of the arsenal at the disposal of Bolshevism and the
mass contagion of its slogans.[64]

So much for the viewpoint of one broad segment of party opinion,
best described as irremediably pro-coalitional. This segment had
hitherto been in the driver's seat, probably without constituting a
majority of the membership. The other segment of party opinion,
comprising the left center and moderate left, regarded the experiment in coalition, or rather the undue prolongation of it, as the
source of the party's misfortune. Far from seeking a scapegoat in the
Russian people, these SR's found the culprit in their own midst, in
the person of comrades who had insisted on a common front with
the Kadets after it had been demonstrated that this could be purchased only at the price of surrendering the party's position on land
and peace and so of throwing great numbers of its followers into
the embraces of Bolshevism. The second trial of coalition had been
superfluous, said Chernov; the third was inexcusable. Under the
domination of a clique which had no true majority behind it, the SR
concept of a revolution intermediate between a strictly bourgeois
and a thoroughgoing socialist one had been scrapped in order to
perpetuate a sterile union with the bourgeoisie, but the SR masses
would not accept a purely political revolution and, not getting their
own kind, had turned in large numbers to the maximalist utopia of
the extremists.[65]

Now that the mischief had been done, these critics on the left suddenly found their tongue and began to exhibit the vocalness that
notably had been lacking when there was still time to set things
aright. Belatedly they subjected the adherents of coalition to a heavy
shelling. One critic passed over the small right wing and singled out
the right center for especial opprobrium, declaring that a more slavish
fear of standing on one's own feet than had been manifested by it at
the Democratic Conference could not be found in the annals of

---

[64] *Kratkii otchët*, p. 50.

[65] Chernov, "Otkliki pressy" (Echoes of the Press), *Revoliutsionnaia Rossiia*,
No. 32 (December, 1923), pp. 20–21, and "Iz itogov proshlogo opyta" (From
the Results of Past Experience), *ibid.*, No. 23 (December, 1922), pp. 3–4;
Kratkii otchët, pp. 25–26, and see language of resolutions on the current moment, pp. 123, 144–45; see also *Delo Naroda*, No. 212 (November 17, 1917), for
speech of Chernov before the Tenth Petersburg Conference.

socialism.[66] Chernov seized upon Maslov's discourse on the absence of a state consciousness in Russia to brand the whole trend of thinking in right-wing circles as heretical from the standpoint of party doctrine, which had never acknowledged a disjunction between interests of state and the needs of the people and had never elevated the state as an abstraction above the party. This cult of the state, in the name of which the union of classes had been enjoined, the SR concept of revolution buried, and the party program emasculated, had been nothing more nor less than a scarecrow to frighten the democracy away from power. Far from ignoring it, the revolutionists had paid too much attention to it. Now if ever was the time to cast off the hypnosis of Avksentiev's formula of the "union of all live forces" with the "stench of death" that clung to it, for otherwise the Bolsheviks would break up the Constituent Assembly amid the plaudits of such elements of the toiling classes as were yet loyal to the party.[67]

As for the future, this segment of SR opinion believed that since the party had failed to offer the people a positive alternative to Bolshevism, and therefore had been responsible for letting them go astray, it must wait until the negative sides of Bolshevism had manifested themselves to its deluded followers and these had begun to fall away before embarking upon an armed struggle against the Soviet regime. In the language of the SR's of Vitebsk province, care must be taken in combating the Bolsheviks not to war on the masses behind them.[68] Care must also be taken not to play into the hands of the counterrevolution; there would be no truck with reactionaries even at the expense of a two-front war. A further consideration was probably the fear that if the party took up arms prematurely it might be smashed: that the Bolsheviks had much fighting power on their side was generally admitted, and one reelected central committeeman not identified with the left warned of colliding with the healthy enthusiasm which either had been engendered by the Bolsheviks or else

---

[66] Kogan-Bernstein, "Raskol ili ochishchenie?" (Schism or Housecleaning?), *Delo Naroda*, No. 218 (November 24, 1917).

[67] *Kratkii otchët*, pp. 112–13.

[68] *Partiinyia Izvestiia*, No. 5 (January 20, 1918), p. 58 (report of the seventh provincial conference).

had welled up spontaneously.[69] Basically the task was to divest
Bolshevism of its popular following, and also to wean away its allies,
the Left SR's and Menshevik Internationalists, before letting things
come to an open fight. This could be done only if the PSR straightened out its line and provided the country with a thoroughly revolutionary alternative to Bolshevism.[70]

The sobering up and weaning away process would take time. How
could it be facilitated, and how in the meanwhile could the excesses
of the regime be combated? The Fourth Congress was as vague on
these points as on many others. One obvious way of striking at
Bolshevism without hitting its following was to kill the leaders, and
this method was hallowed in party tradition. A good deal of talk
about resuming the terrorist campaign, this time against a Red instead
of a White despotism, could be heard in party circles, and it was
generally agreed that the old slogan, "You shall get it according to
your deeds," should hold in the case of violence against the Constituent Assembly. Both Gotz [71] and Chernov [72] had been broadly
intimating a resort to terrorism, but now Gotz no longer spoke with
his former authority and Chernov had evidently changed his mind
for the present. On December 12 the new Central Committee pronounced terrorism to be "wholly inadmissible" as a means of struggle
at this time, and ordered its decision communicated to all comrades
working on the defense of the Constituent Assembly.[73] Instead, the
committee concentrated on agitation in factories in an attempt to
recover lost ground and drive a wedge between the Bolshevik Party
and its proletarian following.[74]

[69] *Kratkii otchët*, pp. 78–79 (speech of Prilezhaev).
[70] Chernov, "Iz itogov proshlogo oypta," *Revoliutsionnaia Rossiia*, No. 23
(December, 1922), pp. 4–5, and manuscript commentary on the minutes of the
Central Committee, pp. 79, 84–85.
[71] See his letter to the presidium of the congress (*Kratkii otchët*, p. 11).
[72] Speech at the Tenth Petersburg Conference on November 15 as reported
in *Delo Naroda*, No. 212 (November 17, 1917); see also Vladimirova, *God
sluzhby "sotsialistov" kapitalistam*, p. 104. Eugenia Ratner wanted terrorism used
if the Bolsheviks proceeded from arrests to executions (see *Kratkii otchët*,
p. 76).
[73] Protokol Zasedaniia Tsentral'nago Komiteta PSR. The minutes of the
Central Committee from time to time were published in the party press, but
a matter like this would not appear in the printed record. See *Partiinyia
Izvestiia*, No. 5 (January 20, 1918), pp. 45–46.
[74] See below, p. 188.

The left sector of party opinion was as one in regarding coalition with the bourgeoisie as the source of the party's woes and in refusing to engage in an armed struggle against Bolshevism under existing conditions. But in the long run the question of state power would have brought about a divergence within this sector of opinion. While the left center under Chernov envisaged an ultimate showdown with the Soviet regime in which all weapons would be employed, including terrorism,[75] the moderate left proposed to keep the struggle permanently on the ideological plane, avoiding at all costs a blood-letting in the revolutionary camp and bending its efforts toward a peaceful outliving of the Bolshevik contagion on the part of the toilers.[76] This difference over ultimate policy was already important enough at the Fourth Congress to prevent a united front of the left and left center in respect to the resolution on the current moment.

A Janus-faced affair, looking backward at the cause of the disaster that had overtaken the PSR and forward at the means of overcoming it, the resolution on the current moment proved more controversial than any other issue at the congress, aside from the choice of a Central Committee and the question of the schism. Though there were only two broad segments of opinion at the congress, as pointed out in the preceding discussion, there were four draft resolutions.[77] The right-wing point of view found expression in the Arkhangelski resolution, in which one searches in vain for any defense, or even any mention, of the principle of coalition, which had been the chief article of faith of its backers. On the other side no common tongue could be found, and Chernov came forward with one resolution for the left center and Kogan-Bernstein with another for the moderate left. As for the fourth resolution, it was apparently the individual enterprise of Eliashevich of Samara and commanded no group support. The congress threw down Arkhangelski's resolution with only 7 votes in its favor, Chernov's went through, though not gloriously,

---

[75] Chernov, manuscript commentary on the minutes of the Central Committee, p. 85, and "Iz itogov proshlogo opyta," *Revoliutsionnaia Rossiia*, No. 23 (December, 1922), pp. 4–5.

[76] Kogan-Bernstein, "Nashi raskhozhdeniia," *Partiinyia Izvestiia*, No. 5 (January 20, 1918), pp. 63–64.

[77] *Kratkii otchët*, pp. 123–27.

by 99 against 51 with 27 abstentions, and Eliashevich's was rejected without a record vote.[78] The final text [79] followed closely the lines of Chernov's draft but was even less explicit than his had been in fixing the blame for the disaster.

In his private papers, though not on the floor of the congress, Chernov gloats over the failure of the Arkhangelski resolution, calling it an unparalleled drubbing for those circles which had set aside his leadership and presumed to speak in the party's name.[80] But it was not so simple as that. The right center had put Chernov in the hole, but it did not support the Arkhangelski resolution—it was much too devious for that. Instead, it had voted for Chernov's draft or else abstained.[81] There was little reason for it to take issue with him over this matter. Far from initiating any punitive action such as the left had proposed, the resolution merely expressed "regret" that those responsible for the direction of affairs had not upheld the SR concept of revolution. Every blow had been softened, every stand watered down. Even in the hour of his definitive triumph, V. M. Chernov could not avoid building golden bridges for his enemies to retreat over and devising "all-uniting" formulas which united factions that could avoid moving in opposite directions only by standing still. The path of the party in 1917 had been strewn with the wreckage of these formulas, but naught deterred their author, and thanks to this latest feat the right center could hide behind the skirts of the left center even as the left center had formerly hidden behind the skirts of the right center. The spokesman for the left would seem to have

[78] *Ibid.*, p. 128. For Kogan-Bernstein's resolution, see below, p. 192.

[79] *Ibid.*, pp. 143–46.

[80] Manuscript commentary on the minutes of the Central Committee, p. 73.

[81] This is apparent from Podvitski's analysis of the results of the congress and Gendelman's announcement before the balloting on the resolutions. Without giving them a factional label, Podvitski notes that adherents of coalition, because of "tactical" or "diplomatic" considerations, and not because of any change of heart, had voted for the formula condemning it, feeling that in any event they were not bound to anything. See his article, "Pod znakom ushcherba," *Partiinyia Izvestiia*, No. 5 (January 20, 1918), p. 66. We have noted that Minor and Gendelman openly stated that they would still favor coalition were the masses not so dead set against it (see above, pp. 180–81). Gendelman announced his intention to vote for Chernov's resolution because of the strong line it took against Bolshevism and despite the first part gently chiding the party management, the wording of which he would seek to modify (*Kratkii otchët*, p. 128). Though he did not secure its elimination, he does seem to have made the gentle chiding gentler still.

been correct when he said that Chernov's resolution had no political character.[82]

The Fourth Congress, in dealing with the question of power, had not provided the new Central Committee with clear and detailed instructions as to the course it should follow. The congress, to be sure, had asserted the sovereignty of the Constituent Assembly, but it had not indicated how the SR representation in that body was to proceed in organizing an executive authority, nor how—and this was the heart of the whole business—the executive power could be retrieved from the usurpers and lodged in the hands of the assembly. Here the party came into collision with the soviet system. During the period before and after the October Revolution when the Bolsheviks and Left SR's had been taking over one soviet after another, the regular SR's had pretty generally withdrawn from these bodies to sulk in their tents. Their view had always been that the soviets as strictly class organs did not embody the democratic principle as perfectly as elective bodies chosen with much greater care by the entire population and that, accordingly, the public functions of the latter must not be usurped by the soviets.[83] Only the Left SR's recognized the soviets as governmental institutions. The right center had taken a strong line against usurpation, leading to the boycott of offending soviets, the most notable example being, of course, the fateful order to bolt the Second Soviet Congress which had produced the schism. Now at the Fourth Congress with the left center in the saddle, a more conciliatory line was taken without surrendering the party's position that the soviets could not serve as organs of state. The party was to endeavor to straighten out the political line of the soviets, confining them to their proper functions as political mentors of the toiling people and as guardians of the conquests of the revolution, of which the Constituent Assembly was one of the greatest. In other words, the SR's must thwart Lenin's strategy of opposing the soviets to the Constituent Assembly by getting them out of the field of government, the while preserving them as nuclei of class action and, if need be, of defense against counterrevolution.[84]

[82] *Kratkii otchët*, p. 128.
[83] See above, pp. 70, 139–40, and below, pp. 325, 442–43.
[84] See Points 10, 11, and 12 of resolution on the current moment (*Kratkii otchët*, p. 145); "Uchreditel'noe Sobranie i Sovety" (The Constituent As-

But the soviets would never be subordinated to the Constituent
Assembly as long as the Bolshevik Party remained in control, and
the new Central Committee, the "heroic Central Committee of the
Fourth Congress," as Chernov called it, speculating on the inability
of the Soviet government to cope with the economic crisis, sent party
men into the proletarian districts to agitate for the recall of Bolshevik
delegates. When the government, fearing for its grip on the Petersburg Soviet, banned these by-elections, the SR's entered into an
agreement with the Mensheviks to set up a "workers' conference"
parallel to the soviet and with fresher mandates. This body was
actually constituted [85] but failed to strike root. After a flurry of
activity, it fell apart, leaving the soviet alone in the field. The Central
Committee also looked with favor on a general strike as a weapon
against the regime, and appointed a commission to study the expediency of one,[86] but this avenue of attack likewise ended in the
sand. The soviets had sunk too deeply into the workers' consciousness, the Bolshevik Party was too firmly entrenched in them and too
well organized for these maneuvers to succeed. The zigzag course
of the PSR, first withdrawing from the soviets and then striving to
get back in, had worked only harm to the party's cause. Gotz himself, conceding that it was impossible to fight Bolshevism from the
sidelines, described the boycott tactics as suicidal. The party, he
said, had never favored this course of action.[87] That is the way he
talked at the end of December. Formally he may have been right,
in the sense that no blanket instructions were ever issued to SR
members to leave the soviets, but the decree of the old Central Committee ordering withdrawal from the Second Soviet Congress, which

sembly and the Soviets), *Delo Naroda*, No. 228 (December 9, 1917); Chernov,
"Uchreditel'noe Sobranie i 'Sovety,'" *ibid.*, No. 238 (December 21, 1917), and
"Zabytaia azbuka" (The Forgotten ABC's), *ibid.*, No. 239 (December 22, 1917);
see also his speech at the railwaymen's congress, *ibid.*, No. 245 (December 31,
1917).

[85] Chernov, manuscript commentary on the minutes of the Central Committee,
pp. 82–83. Apparently this is the workers' conference referred to in a report in
the *Delo Naroda*, No. 236 (December 19, 1917).

[86] Protokol Zasedaniia Tsentral'nago Komiteta PSR for December 8, 1917;
Chernov, manuscript commentary on the minutes of the Central Committee,
p. 79.

[87] "Uchreditel'noe Sobranie i S"ezd Sovetov" (The Constituent Assembly
and the Congress of Soviets), *Delo Naroda*, No. 243 (December 29, 1917).

had been widely accepted as a guide to action elsewhere, must certainly have had the sanction of Gotz as the most influential member of the committee. Now he was urging his comrades to work within the soviets and strive for a maximum representation at the Third Soviet Congress, in effect acknowledging the failure of his previous policy.

There was a dull realization on the part of many party members that no satisfactory solution of the problem of how to regain power could be found without a solution of the problem of peace. But there was still the same unwillingness to face disagreeable facts that had paralyzed initiative in this direction since the fall of the tsar. With invincible obduracy the SR's held to the thesis that peace must be general as well as "democratic" and that Russia could move only in concert with her allies. Even the extreme right now conceded the impossibility of carrying on the war,[88] and representatives of the armed forces spoke of the vast injury that had been done the cause by the stand on the war. In the words of one delegate from the front, "the party's position and Kerenski's position on the war were a great blunder, and we all know how hard it has made work in the army." [89] Months of experience had revealed alike the hopelessness of this position and the ravages it had wrought, yet the majority of SR's stood exactly where they had in the beginning. No experience was so searing, no catastrophe so overwhelming, as to cause them to budge an inch. And this was true of the whole center, the left as well as the right. Eliashevich expressed the attitude of the right center when he admitted that the country could not continue the war, the party had no following in the army, and the people thirsted for peace, and then went on to say that a separate peace was nevertheless unthinkable and any sacrifice must be incurred in order to conclude peace at the side of the Allies.[90] Similarly Eugenia Ratner for the left center: a separate peace could have no justification, for an internationalist party could sanction only

[88] See statements of Lebedev, Stalinski, and Gukovski in *Kratkii otchët*, pp. 74–75, 82, 132.
[89] *Ibid.*, p. 86. The soldier who said this was named Guchkov—presumably no relation of the ex-minister of war and Octobrist leader A. I. Guchkov.
[90] *Ibid.*, p. 50.

a universal peace.[91] In somewhat weaker terms V. M. Chernov said the same thing.[92] Some years later in exile he would write that although an opponent of a separate peace in 1917, he would have been willing to consider one as a last resort if perseverance in the struggle for a general settlement would have meant the immolation of his country on the altar of the Allied cause.[93] Yet there is no indication of such an attitude in his pronouncements at the Fourth Congress, and if he could not see signs of immolation in the situation of December, 1917, then he would never see them.

The truth is, of course, that if Chernov had mentioned the words "separate peace" he would have been immolated in the holy fire of indignation emitted by the Populist intelligentsia at the mere thought of action separate from the Western Allies. S. P. Postnikov, who belonged to the same faction as Chernov, saw his candidacy for the Central Committee ruined at the congress when Zenzinov dug up his advocacy of a separate peace. Though the workers, the soldiers, and sailors said "so much the better," the intellectuals procured his defeat.[94] A young delegate from the front who had been implicated in fraternization would have had his mandate cancelled had not the congress granted him an indulgence on account of his years.[95] All over Russia it was the same story. The SR Saakian, for instance, put up a fierce struggle at the Transcaucasian Soviet Congress for his formula of a general democratic peace, saying that a peace that was not universal betrayed the workers of other countries and must be rejected even though the carnage continued. The Georgian Mensheviks Zhordaniia and Ramishvili hotly rejoined that to defend a position abandoned as untenable by every other section of the democracy was nothing but a theatrical gesture.[96]

As to the means of getting their general democratic peace, the SR's were as vague as they were definite in rejecting a separate

[91] *Ibid.*, p. 75.   [92] *Ibid.*, pp. 30–31.

[93] "Uroki proshlogo" (Lessons of the Past), *Revoliutsionnaia Rossiia*, No. 42 (April, 1925), pp. 19–20.

[94] Interview in Prague (September, 1935). Postnikov said that he received 73 votes, but in that case he should have placed among the alternates, the lowest of whom (Kogan-Bernstein) got 65.

[95] *Kratkii otchët*, pp. 54, 73. Even so, 7 diehard defensists voted against validation and 15 abstained.

[96] Sef, *Revoliutsiia v Zakavkaz'i*, p. 381.

peace. They never got beyond the point of calling for negotiations with the Allies and organizing an international socialist conference for concerted pressure on the governments of belligerent powers.[97] That is to say, they were talking in December exactly as they had in March. Zenzinov's review [98] of the peace policy of the Central Committee listed a series of halfhearted and wholly ineffectual measures in which there had not been a single resolute step to impress the Allies with Russia's determination to seek the kind of peace the SR's said they wanted. Only in the negative sense had it taken a clear stand: "The Central Committee decisively and sharply protests against a separate peace, which forms the basis of the international policy of the people's commissars." [99] By insisting that only the Constituent Assembly could speak with enough authority to make Russia's will felt in international councils and that only it was empowered to conclude peace in the name of the Russian people, the SR's were predicating the solution of the peace problem on a solution of the problem of power, although many would admit that the problem of power could not be solved so long as nothing was done about the war. In other words, they were caught in a whirlpool, and the only progress they were making was downward, toward the bottom of the stream.

Against this hopeless treading of water, which would assuredly end in drowning, a strong minority raised its voice. The secession of the extreme left had not drained the party of all of its left-wing elements, as we have seen, and a sizable group remained that was more radical than Chernov but less radical or less willing to break away than the Left SR's. At the Fourth Congress this group, which we have named the moderate left or the left unionists, mustered about a third of the voting strength and was most vociferous in respect to war and peace (many of its adherents were from the armed forces), although it also did much to make life miserable for the outgoing Central Committee. What these men said must have shocked and enraged the intellectuals at the party helm, for the speeches were blunt and brutal. One of them told Chernov that his report contained nothing for the men in the trenches, and credited

[97] See editorials in the *Delo Naroda*, Nos. 244 and 245 (December 30, 31, 1917).
[98] *Kratkii otchët*, pp. 65–67.   [99] *Ibid.*, p. 67.

the Bolsheviks with at least having made a bold demonstration for peace.[100] Several of them clamored for immediate peace, not merely a separate peace, but peace at any price,[101] and one said that if this boon were granted the Russian people the Council of Commissars would disappear overnight.[102] Another put his finger on the root of the trouble when he characterized the revolutionary formula for peace as unrealistic because the European democracy (he meant the socialist democracy) was too weak to carry it through. The only effect, he said, had been to undermine one's own position.[103] All warned that it was impossible to continue the war under present conditions and that the Gordian knot must be cut if it could not be untied.

The resolution on the current moment, submitted by Kogan-Bernstein on behalf of the moderate left, proposed as the heart of the SR program in the Constituent Assembly a summons to the Allies to begin negotiations for peace without delay, and in the event of their refusal or failure to answer within the time limit set, the resumption of a free hand by the Russian authorities.[104] How the freedom was to be used, the resolution did not say, but it implied separate action if not a separate peace. The resolution as a whole—there were other provisions, but this was the most controversial—drew the support of 52 members of the congress, while 72 opposed it and 32 chose not to have an opinion.[105] The SR's were great abstainers, and so many of them had on this occasion exercised their cherished prerogative as to impair the effect of the decision.[106] One third of the party representation demanded tangible progress toward peace even at the cost of breaking the alliance, nearly one half clung to the visionary concept of universal peace or none at all, in effect placing the alliance above every other consideration, and a fifth apparently did not know their own mind on the most crucial problem facing the country, after ten months in which to think it over and observe its dire effects.

The only positive action—in a relative sense—taken by the Fourth Congress in respect to war and peace was to vote in favor of in-

[100] *Ibid.,* p. 47. [101] *Ibid.,* pp. 50, 83, 85. [102] *Ibid.,* p. 83.
[103] *Ibid.,* p. 80. [104] *Ibid.,* p. 126. [105] *Ibid.,* p. 128.
[106] There is no explanation as to the identity of the abstainers or the reason for their abstention.

structing the Constituent Assembly to address a note to the Allies proposing a general armistice and the discussion of terms for a general peace in conformity with the principles of the Russian Revolution.[107] Work on this note should begin as soon as the assembly convened. But what if the Allies refused to discuss terms of peace? Would negotiations then be opened with Germany? These questions greatly embarrassed Rakitnikov, head of the commission on drafting a program for the Constituent Assembly, and led to one of the worst exhibitions of floundering seen at this or any other political gathering. Forced to say something and desperately desiring to say nothing, he answered that the Allies, having refused to discuss the subject with the Smolny regime, would react differently to a proposal put forth by the Constituent Assembly, and that in the improved atmosphere the result of the deliberations would "probably be favorable to us." The full scope of this problem, he hastened to add, did not fall within the range of his report.[108] Thus did he ring down the curtain on further attempts to draw him out and elicit from the party leaders at long last a statement as to what they would do if the Allies threw them down. They had for ten months evaded an answer to this question by the simple expedient of not pressing the matter upon the Allies. They never did answer the question—the Smolny regime saved them the embarrassment by dissolving the Constituent Assembly—and they died with their lips still sealed. But the answer they would have given, had it finally been possible to drive them into a corner, was implicit in their whole attitude, just as the reply of the Allies that would have been forthcoming had they ever been seriously pressed was never a matter for doubt: the Allies would have refused to open peace negotiations and the SR leaders would have wanted to continue the war, though by what means is not readily apparent, since the workers and peasants refused to fight any longer and the Narodnik intellectuals were knights of the pen instead of the sword.

In the final analysis, therefore, the Fourth Congress of the PSR

[107] *Ibid.*, p. 157.
[108] *Ibid.*, pp. 130–31. Looking beyond an armistice to the actual terms of peace, Rakitnikov merely implied that the Constituent Assembly would not accept unfavorable terms of peace, nor would this be expected of the Allies (*ibid.*, p. 134).

had registered not a whit of progress in dealing with this basic
problem. And the responsibility for this latest in a long series of
evasions rests squarely upon the shoulders of V. M. Chernov and
his left-centrist colleagues. They had preferred to waltz once again
with the right center rather than join forces with the moderate
left and face squarely the task of salvaging something from the disaster to which their stand on the war had condemned their cause.

The Socialist Revolutionaries made little progress toward the solution of other problems in the interval between the October Revolution and the Constituent Assembly. The land question did not
engage the attention of the Fourth Congress, and the only significant development in that connection was Rakitnikov's disclosure
that "long before the Bolshevik venture" the decision had been taken
at a meeting in Saratov—apparently by the party leaders—to make
the first act of the Constituent Assembly a decree investing the land
committees with the right to administer all landed property and
tracing the lines of the future act of land socialization. The legislation itself could not be rushed but must be worked out patiently
and with great care in the agrarian commissions of the Constituent
Assembly.[109] Now the SR's, as we have seen, had been promising
their supporters since the early months of the revolution that the
land, and especially private estates, would be turned over at once to
the land committees pending the final decision of the Constituent
Assembly. The Rakitnikov statement suggests, though its vagueness
precludes any certainty in the matter, that the SR's had not expected
to see their demand realized until the convocation of the Constituent
Assembly and hence had not pressed for its enactment by the Provisional Government with the vigor they would have employed had
they been in dead earnest—again, they had been prepared to put up
with Kadet obstruction in this as in all other matters.

The nationalities problem did not emerge onto the floor of the
Fourth Congress but remained bottled up in the section devoted to
this question. No concrete proposals were reported out, but the section listened to an account of events in the council of national
socialist parties presented by the SR representative, N. Briullova-

[109] *Ibid.*, p. 130.

Shaskolskaia, and adopted a resolution setting forth the principles the party wished to see incorporated in the constitution of the Russian federal republic. According to this lady, who was the party's specialist on ethnic problems, the non-Russian political groups had been at first well disposed toward the PSR as more trustworthy in respect to national self-determination than the Social Democrats, but the attitude of the Central Committee, which regarded the nationalities problem as of secondary importance, prevented the party from turning this good will to account by taking the lead in an effort to work out a system under which the Russian and non-Russian peoples could live in harmony. The opportunity had passed, the mood had changed, and distrust of the Russian parties, including the PSR, had grown apace, with Bolshevism gathering strength on the one side and separatism on the other. Now the PSR stood in danger of being reduced to a Great Russian party unless it could reorganize itself along federal lines in agreement with kindred national groups. The congress took no action on this matter.[110]

As to re-founding the Russian state, the nationalities section of the Fourth Congress favored a federal republic with a constitution securing to the central authority jurisdiction over the most important fields of political and social legislation. Specifically, the protection of national minorities was to come within the purview of the federal government, and it was to keep Russia an economic whole through control of general finance, transportation, commerce, and communication. The philosophy behind this was the same as Rosa Luxemburg's in her duel with Lenin in the international socialist arena over the problem of national self-determination: the road to socialism lay through the preservation of existing large-scale economies and their gradual fusion rather than through the fragmentation attendant upon economic nationalism. The SR's had drawn appreciably closer to the Menshevik position since the days when non-Russian peoples were promised "unconditional" freedom in choosing their destiny,[111] and consequently had backed away from the Bolshevik position, though the Bolsheviks, of course, had their

[110] N. Briullova-Shaskolskaia, "Natsional'nyi vopros na IV s"ezde" (The Nationalities Question at the Fourth Congress), *Partiinyia Izvestiia*, No. 5 (January 20, 1918), pp. 9–10; *Kratkii otchët*, pp. 139–41.
[111] See *The Agrarian Foes of Bolshevism*, pp. 37–40.

own way of holding the state together. A logical inconsistency seemed to have crept into the SR outlook on the nationalities problem, for the solicitude shown for the integrity of the multinational Russian state did not extend to Austria-Hungary, at least not for the SR's who stood to the right of center. The explanation of this inconsistency is not hard to find—nationalism—and it is idle to deny that it colored the outlook of these people on war and peace.

The sovereignty of the All-Russian Constituent Assembly and the indissolubility of the future federation were reaffirmed once more as cornerstones of SR doctrine. The reconciliation of these principles with that of national self-determination would have troubled earth-bound people but not the SR's, who met the difficulty in typical fashion by closing their eyes and pronouncing an incantation: the All-Russian Constituent Assembly would work out the limits of national autonomy in agreement with the popular will as expressed in national assemblies, and conflicts would be circumvented through the power exercised by the SR's and kindred national groups at both the All-Russian and regional levels. Harmony between the Constituent Assembly and the national assemblies, therefore, depended upon harmony between the SR's and national Populist parties. The SR's were assuming that affinity of agrarian programs would breed affinity on other matters, even in respect to the issue over which the Ukrainians had chosen to form their own party. The rampant separatism in the south they excused as a natural reaction against the destruction of a central authority in St. Petersburg,[112] failing to see, or not wanting to see, in it the logical development of the truculence manifested in Kievan circles all along. When the Bolsheviks began to reassert the prerogatives of the central authority and entered upon the path of coercion, the SR's reacted violently to measures they most likely would have welcomed under the Provisional Government. Chernov set the tone at the Fourth Congress by shouting, "We must gather all our forces and sound the tocsin; the masters in the

---

[112] See resolution of the Central Committee in *Delo Naroda*, No. 241 (December 24, 1917). The approval, of course, was not given to separatism but to "regional self-organization" on condition that the indissolubility of the future federation be recognized, national minorities protected, and democratic procedures observed. The wording of the resolution indicates that the committee was aware of a separatist danger but did not choose at the time to make an issue of it.

Smolny have forgotten there is a limit to our patience!"[113] The SR's even approved of dividing the army along national lines, citing in justification of their change of front the new situation created by the armistice, which swept away the objection to tampering with the army while war was in progress.[114] Thus they were not above using as an argument in favor of another policy the separate armistice which they had so bitterly combated.

In the fury of their reaction against Bolshevism the SR's were storing up plenty of trouble for themselves as the champions of Russian integrity if ever they should return to power. They were engaged in a flirtation with separatism while refusing to recognize it as separatism; they would play with fire and not be burned. It is true they were in desperate straits, badly in need of a common front with the Ukrainian SR's to save the Constituent Assembly,[115] but their stand on the nationalities problem, like their stand on other issues, betrays an inability to be rational or objective, to face reality as it existed. The party was almost like a sleepwalker as it prepared to replace the time-tested administrative divisions of the Empress Catherine with regional units that would give expression to geographical and economic as well as ethnic diversity, and also as it made ready to determine regional boundaries by plebiscites [116] which would place a question mark over areas like the eastern Ukraine, all the while thinking that it was going to maintain by democratic processes the unity of the Russian republic against the disruptive forces unloosed in part by its own actions.[117]

No SR congress could conclude its labors without giving some attention to the party's internal condition and attempting to come to

[113] *Kratkii otchët*, p. 159; "Mezhdousobnaia voina" (Internecine Warfare), *Delo Naroda*, No. 227 (December 8, 1917).

[114] See editorial, "Nasilie nad natsional'nostiami" (Coercion of Nationalities), *Delo Naroda*, No. 237 (December 20, 1917); see also I. Sklovski, "Vlast' na Ukraine" (Power in the Ukraine), in the same issue.

[115] See ch. 6.

[116] I. Sklovski, "K ukrainskomu uchreditel'nomu sobraniiu" (On the Ukrainian Constituent Assembly), *Delo Naroda*, No. 224 (December 5, 1917).

[117] For decisions of the nationalities section of the Fourth Congress, see Briullova-Shaskolskaia, "Natsional'nyi vopros na IV s"ezde," *Partiinyia Izvestiia*, No. 5 (January 20, 1918), pp. 10–12; *Delo Naroda*, No. 229 (December 10, 1917).

grips with the structural defects from which it had never been free. A report from Vitebsk province [118] no doubt reflects the state of local organizations all over the country in the closing months of 1917. With the onset of disaster the inflow of new members had virtually ceased and the ebbing tide carried away many of those who had streamed in earlier when the vogue of membership in the PSR had been strongest. Fair-weather friends deserted the cause, fellow travelers fell away, and the spotlight shifted to another party. In Moscow the organization had been reduced to its hard core of strength and there and elsewhere bordered on an illegal status.[119] Hope for the future seemed to depend more than ever upon a well-integrated structure, but it was just here that there was cause for grave misgivings.

If there was one thing on which all party members agreed, it was the wretched coordination of their activities. Some blamed the Central Committee, others the local branches, but all were as one in attesting a lamentable state of affairs. We are told that the locals stinted the center in funds, neglected to turn in reports at regular intervals, and provided little support for policies decreed in the party's name.[120] We are also told that the Central Committee functioned as a Petersburg office, paying no attention to business referred to it by local branches and providing no real political guidance for the membership.[121] No one denied that the supreme organ charged with coordinating party activities had been out of touch with the provinces [122] and that the cause had suffered as a consequence. Ties had been tenuous, also, between provinces and localities.[123] As one critic put it, all action had been taken post factum, with no realization beforehand of what was brewing in the

---

[118] *Partiinyia Izvestiia*, No. 5 (January 20, 1918), p. 56 (report of the seventh provincial conference).

[119] *Delo Naroda*, No. 220 (November 30, 1917); Chernov, manuscript commentary on the minutes of the Central Committee, p. 78.

[120] *Kratkii otchët*, pp. 90, 108, 122 (statements of Rakov, Prilezhaev, and Vedeniapin).

[121] *Ibid.*, pp. 43, 89–90 (statements of Kogan-Bernstein).

[122] *Ibid.*, pp. 88, 90, 92 (statements of Kallistov and Podvitski; admission of Rakov, a member of the Central Committee).

[123] See reports from Moscow and Kostroma provinces in *Delo Naroda*, No. 220 (November 30, 1917).

depths of Russian society.[124] This was undeniably a just criticism, exemplified most graphically in the case of the armed forces, for the Central Committee had listened to the opinion of committees chosen in the spring or summer without concerning itself with what the soldiers and sailors who had elected them were thinking in October. One wonders, however, whether a body so determined to discount phenomena that did not fit into its conception of the revolution would have profited from a superior type of organization capable of bringing it into intimate contact with the feelings of the people.

The Fourth Congress drafted and adopted a new set of organizational rules [125] with the democratic elective principle effacing all traces of the conspiratorial past. But since the new rules for the most part merely codified existing practices, they promised no radical improvement in the sense of tying things more tightly together and causing the party to function as a single organism. For that it would have been necessary to change, not the rules, but the spirit of organization. It was stipulated, however, that SR delegations in all public bodies, including the soviets and the Constituent Assembly, should be subordinated to the Central Committee.[126] This provision would undoubtedly have had a tightening effect if it could have been enforced, but as our examination will presently disclose, the SR representatives in the Constituent Assembly had a will of their own, different from that of the new Central Committee, and were by no means inclined to defer to the latter, so that this clause in the new code soon became a dead letter. A motion at the Fourth Congress to cut down the size of the Central Committee in the interest of greater homogeneity was voted down.[127] The new rules touched on a sensitive spot in granting to the Central Committee the right to suspend from membership an entire organization, while withholding from it the power of permanent exclusion, which was vested solely in the party congress or council.

Financial stringency was given as a reason for the organizational chaos in the PSR. The party management simply did not have the money to set up and operate administrative machinery on the

[124] *Kratkii otchët*, p. 80; see also p. 43.
[125] *Ibid.*, pp. 135–37; for discussion and amendments, see pp. 138–40, 158.
[126] *Ibid.*, pp. 136, 158.   [127] *Ibid.*, p. 139.

scale necessary to cope with the problems of integration.[128] Finance is often the golden key to an understanding of political conduct, and the Fourth Congress did not pass without some startling disclosures in this respect. Of the total amount of money paid into the treasury of the Central Committee, only 3 percent came from party organizations! "This circumstance, of course," said the committee's spokesman, "did not prove conducive to any sort of broadly conceived work on the part of the Central Committee." [129] He could have said that again. Where, then, had the money come from? From banks, in the form of loans negotiated by the committee. Not much is known about this business, but on September 6 the committee had instructed its financial commission to make plans both for borrowing money from a bank and for floating an internal party loan.[130] O. S. Minor approached the National Bank in Moscow for a loan of one million rubles, and it was agreed that the money should be drawn over a three weeks' period. Then something went wrong and Comrade Zenzinov was sent on October 1 to Moscow to iron out the difficulty.[131] The minutes of the Central Committee say nothing more about the matter. But Minor told the Fourth Congress what had happened. The party management proved dilatory even when it came to taking money and the period of grace had expired with only small sums withdrawn. Meanwhile the political conjuncture had changed, and the bank shut off the credit. "When the SR's held power, we gave money, but now conditions are unsettled and we shall wait," was the laconic comment of the bank director. As reasons for this sudden switch in policy Minor cited reports in the press about the growing influence of the left SR's and the effect of Breshkovskaia's letter announcing her rupture with the Central Committee.[132] But were the bankers actually swayed by the fear that centrifugal forces had rendered the party a bad financial risk, as Minor says, or were they endeavoring to exert pressure on this wobbling party to hold it to the line laid down by the real masters of Russia?

The dependence of a party that called itself socialist and revolu-

---

[128] Statement of Rakov (*ibid.*, p. 90).
[129] Statement of Vedeniapin (*ibid.*, p. 122).
[130] Protokol Zasedaniia Tsentral'nago Komiteta PSR.   [131] *Ibid.*
[132] *Kratkii otchët*, p. 92.

tionary upon the institutions of finance capitalism is interesting, to say the least, and may explain more than one puzzling circumstance in the conduct of this party in 1917. The new Central Committee made a fresh start in exploring the caverns of finance by trying to raise a loan from the trade unions,[133] with what results we do not know, though most likely the effort was unsuccessful, for Bolshevik influence was as rife in the trade unions as conservative influence in banking circles.

The Third Congress of the PSR has been described as a colossal failure. If the Fourth Congress was less so, it was only because the catastrophe then in preparation had now already befallen the party. Probably it was already too late to mend the course and give the party a fighting chance for survival. The Fourth Congress did not even try. It made no effort to heal the breach with the Left SR's in order to be able later to present a united front of peasant defenders against the depredations of a party that never regarded peasants as anything better than stepchildren. It widened the breach and rubbed salt in the open wound. It did not give what was left of the party a unified command; instead, it replaced one fractious Central Committee with another only less badly divided. It did not break cleanly with policies that were linked with disaster. It had no solution for the problem of wresting power from Bolshevik hands, and could not have as long as it insisted on continuing a war which itself it regarded as hopeless. It did not even come to grips with the problem of equitable distribution of the land, which was now being distributed, and inequitably, all over Russia. The nationalities problem it muddied still further. It attested the chaos in the party organization and left it chaotic.

A right-wing and a left-wing delegate appraised the congress from their respective points of view and each beheld in it the ascendancy of the other. Podvitski found the same fissures as before under the surface, since the purge had proceeded along disciplinary rather than ideological grounds and thus had not cleaned out all the anarcho-Bolshevik elements. The "rubber-like" resolutions, devised to en-

[133] Protokol Zasedaniia Tsentral'nago Komiteta PSR for December 8, 1917.

snare votes, on the whole tended to negate the party's past and betrayed a certain readiness to capitulate before Bolshevism.[134] On the
other hand, Kogan-Bernstein could find traces of leftist influence
only in the wording of resolutions. The congress, in his opinion,
leaned psychologically to the right and accepted the inevitability of
an open fight with Bolshevism.[135] In these confused waters only
V. M. Chernov swam happily: he congratulated the congress on having laid down a single line of revolutionary socialism [136] and pronounced its leftist course to be at the same time a sharply anti-
Bolshevik course.[137] An impartial estimate is that the party shifted
its weight from the right to the left center and remained in the
swamp. Neither the congress nor the Central Committee elected by
it proved to be of any assistance to the party in retaining its
hold on the peasantry or in preserving the fruits of its electoral
triumph through a successful defense of the Constituent Assembly—
the two tasks it now must perform or go down in death and
destruction.

[134] "Pod znakom ushcherba," *Partiinyia Izvestiia*, No. 5 (January 20, 1918),
pp. 65–67.
[135] "Nashi raskhozhdeniia," *ibid.*, p. 63.   [136] *Kratkii otchët*, p. 160.
[137] Manuscript commentary on the minutes of the Central Committee, p. 74.

V

The Fight for the Peasantry

The last months of 1917 witnessed an embittered triangular struggle between the two Socialist Revolutionary parties and the Bolsheviks for control of the peasant movement. The stakes were
high and the play was rough. No matter how exclusively Bolshevism
might dedicate itself to the service of the urban working class,
it still had to obtain some sort of peasant sanction in this overwhelmingly peasant land if it wished to give meaning to the inclusion
of the Sickle with the Hammer in the insignia of the new regime,
concealing behind this symbol of the equality of farm and factory
labor its settled purpose of denying an equal status to the peasants
until they had been divested of personal possession of the land and
reduced to the status of workers in the field. The Socialist Revolutionaries had seen their strength melt away in the cities and their
influence banished from the barracks; they now had only their peasant flock, and like the good shepherds they fancied themselves to
be, they had to protect it from this wolf in sheep's clothing and shut
Bolshevism out of the village. The Left SR's agreed that in the long
run the Bolsheviks would betray the rural population, but felt that
the SR's had already betrayed it in order to preserve a truce with
the propertied classes while the war was in progress. As champions
of the peasantry in the Soviet regime, the Left SR's must win control of the peasant movement in order to achieve an equal footing
with an ally who reigned supreme in the barracks and factories.
They hoped that as agrarian socialists who stood for peace they
would succeed in vanquishing both of their competitors. The SR's
had the advantage of the entrenched position which tradition and the
First All-Russian Peasants' Congress had conferred upon them, but
labored under the handicap of their stand on the war and their exclusion from official position. The Bolsheviks controlled the government but faced the problem of weaning the peasants away from the

political influence hitherto dominant in the village, as well as from the radical alternative which the schism in SR ranks had provided. For a brief spell it was not certain who would emerge victorious, and the contest proved to be as exciting as it was desperate.

The question of holding a Second All-Russian Congress had long agitated political circles close to the peasant movement. In fact, it must be reckoned as one of the factors in the breakup of the Socialist Revolutionary Party, for the controversy that rocked the All-Russian Peasants' Executive Committee was exclusively an SR affair—the Bolsheviks had so small a following at the First Congress as to be ignored in the selection of this body. The majority of the Executive Committee, standing well to the right of center in SR political parlance, being strongly in favor of continuing the war, and strongly backing the Provisional Government, had been in no hurry to convene a new congress despite the clamor of a minority consisting of Left SR's, who were conscious of the growing restiveness of the peasantry and knew that another congress would at least strengthen their hand if, indeed, it did not enthrone them in the committee.

Time passed and tempers frayed: August was first mentioned as a likely date for the Second Congress, then September, and finally the matter was postponed till sometime after the election of the Constituent Assembly. The opposition began to charge the majority with bad faith, with a secret determination to delay indefinitely the calling of a new congress in order to preserve the fiction of peasant support for the Provisional Government. It was not so much a matter of saving positions as of upholding policies, Ustinov told the Left SR congress,[1] for the Executive Committee was dominated by extreme defensists who sought to put off as long as possible the evil day when their course of action, already odious to the workers and soldiers, would be repudiated by the class upon which their ideology was founded. When they could no longer use the wholesome, unspoiled mass of rural Russia to overawe the urban radicals, the last prop would be kicked out from under them and their fortress would crumble in ruins.

In his exhaustive study of the All-Russian Peasants' Soviet, which

[1] *Protokoly pervago s"ezda PLSR,* pp. 50, 54–55.

was torn from the press by the Communist authorities after one copy had been sent abroad, the editor of the peasants' *Izvestiia* has denied that the dominant faction of the Executive Committee purposefully delayed the calling of the Second Congress, and affirms the sincerity of its belief in the inexpediency of a congress so long as more pressing matters engaged the committee's attention.[2] The original plan to convene the congress on August 20 had been set aside because of the State Conference in Moscow; September had not been suitable because of the Democratic Conference; and thereafter the election campaign for the Constituent Assembly had first claim on the active workers in the localities, making it inadvisable to withdraw a thousand of them for a mission to the distant capital. Moreover, friction with the cooperative societies[3] had deprived the peasants' soviets of their main source of money, so that the committee did not have the resources to finance a new congress.

But the opposition would not listen to these arguments set forth in Martiushin's report at the session of September 23, seeing in them nothing but excuses for continued inaction, and proceeded to berate the majority for attempting to stifle the voice of the peasantry. Those who were under fire replied in kind and a violent scene ensued; September 23 was henceforth edged in black in the annals of agrarian socialism as the day when the two factions became hopelessly estranged and the whole movement began to fall apart. Hitherto locked within the recesses of the Executive Committee, the feud now erupted into the open. The majority stuck by its guns in the conviction that the bulk of the peasantry was still behind it, and refused to contemplate a date earlier than the end of November, whereas the opposition wanted to convene the congress before the election in

---

[2] Bykhovski, *Vserossiiskii Sovet Krest'ianskikh Deputatov*, p. 251. For the contrary point of view, besides the Left SR sources, see M. Gaisinski, *Bor'ba za krest'ianstvo*, p. 160.

[3] The management of the cooperatives stood even further to the right than the majority of the Executive Committee. After the setting up of democratic organs of local self-government (reformed zemstvos), the cooperatives regarded these as more truly representative of the popular will than the soviets, especially since the growing leftist element in the latter detested the conservatism of the cooperatives and refused to consider them democratic. The left held that if the Executive Committee was short of funds it was its own fault, for if it had been more mindful of the peasants' interest it would not lack funds from the only source from which they should be derived—from the peasantry itself.

order to keep pace with the rival workers' and soldiers' soviets, and not leave their congress on October 25 a clear field in which to resolve the question of power according to their liking.[4] From the standpoint of protecting the peasants' interest the radicals were undoubtedly correct, since the failure to hold a peasants' congress simultaneously with that of the workers and soldiers robbed this class of a voice in the October crisis, and prevented it from wielding a perhaps decisive influence in the first days of the Soviet regime, when the metal was still soft and could conceivably have been diverted from the dictatorial mold which Lenin was preparing. As it was, the cast had already hardened when the Left SR's entered the government and they were unable to change it.

The October Revolution created a new situation. The dominant right-centrist SR faction in the Peasants' Executive Committee now had nothing to lose by summoning a congress, for the simple reason that it had already lost everything. A congress, if it turned out well, might even restore something of what had been lost. But the opposition now had the freedom of maneuver previously denied it. Taking advantage of their position in the new Workers' and Soldiers' Executive Committee, though not yet in the Soviet government, the Left SR's proceeded to set up in the Smolny Institute a bureau for the convocation of the Second All-Russian Peasants' Congress, and began to send out invitations to local peasants' soviets throughout the country. The regular SR's entrenched in the directing organs of the peasant soviets regarded this as an usurpation of their prerogatives and now at last shook the lead out of their shoes in an effort to keep the convocation of the congress in their own hands. Thus the feud between the majority and minority factions in the Peasants' Executive Committee merges with the general fight between SR's and Left SR's after the October Revolution.

For a long while the peasants had not been allowed to have another congress of their own; now it looked as though they might be cursed with two. Both sides agreed that in view of the lateness of the date it would not be possible to assemble a plenary congress before the end of November, but so great was the pressure for action that both strove to convene a preliminary conference in the first

---

[4] Bykhovski, *Vserossiiskii Sovet Krest'ianskikh Deputatov*, pp. 252–54, 265–66.

part of November. The trouble came over who should sit in this conference. While the SR's wanted only representatives of the provincial and army [5] soviets—i.e., of the organs immediately below the Executive Committee—the Left SR's desired to add delegates from the district (*uezd*) and divisional soviets, the whole controversy hinging on the fact that the lower soviets had been more recently reelected than the provincial and army soviets and hence were more radical in outlook. The Executive Committee and the Smolny bureau each issued instructions according to its own conception of how the conference should be constituted. Great was the confusion in peasant circles all over Russia as the wires brought in first one wave of contradictory telegrams and then another.

A second point at issue in this swift maneuvering was where the conference and ensuing congress should be held. At first some SR's had favored Moscow over the capital, only to discover that this meant jumping from the frying pan into the fire. The Executive Committee by a vote of 27 to 23 had then fixed upon General Headquarters at Mogilev, since this was the place where Chernov was trying to form a countergovernment and Gotz was vetoing his initiative.[6] Unexpressed was the hope that the army command could provide some protection for the routed adherents of the Provisional Government. The Left SR's, of course, favored the capital.

Both issues were decided by the peasant delegates themselves, and decided in favor of the opposition. The delegates gravitated naturally to St. Petersburg and the SR's abandoned the attempt to shift the meeting place upon hearing that Chernov, their heaviest cannon, was coming up from Mogilev. The delegates met in fraternal union, those from the district and divisional soviets with those from the provincial and army soviets, and without distinction balloted on the question of credentials. Naturally those representing the lower soviets followed the lead of the Left SR's, who had invited them, and naturally they voted in favor of seating themselves. The forces of the Executive Committee were in retreat all along the line and the Left SR's had won the first round.[7]

[5] Army in the technical sense of the chief subdivision of a front.

[6] See ch. 2.

[7] Bykhovski, *Vserossiiskii Sovet Krest'ianskikh Deputatov*, pp. 280–83, 290–92; Gaisinski, *Bor'ba za krest'ianstvo*, pp. 179–82.

The Left SR's hastened to press home their advantage by broadening the preliminary conference into a full-fledged congress with competence in respect to all matters, including the right to sit as a court in judgment of the Executive Committee. The conference opened on November 10 with from 150 to 200 delegates in attendance. More arrived every day. Desperately the adherents of the Executive Committee fought to hold the conference within bounds, knowing that if they failed they would lose control of the machinery and run the risk of having the real congress at the end of November stacked against them. They pointed out that the First Congress in May had consisted of 1,350 delegates properly elected, whereas the present body numbered about 200, only half of whom under the by-laws of the organization were entitled to vote. Perhaps the presence of some forty-odd Bolshevik intruders into this civil war in the SR camp induced the Left SR's to show forbearance, for they did not force the issue, hoping to avert a schism. But soon the battle raged anew over the question of electing a presidium and the desire of the left to unhorse the Executive Committee while it had the opportunity. This time no compromise was possible. So hot did the battle get that the presiding officer fainted at his post. By a vote of 155 to 85 the right went down in bitter defeat, whereupon it bolted the assembly, leaving the opposition in the saddle.[8]

Out of the hall with the majority of the Executive Committee marched the representatives of twenty-three provincial soviets and four army committees.[9] This was a formidable force and foreshadowed the rending struggle to come. If the bolting delegations included those from White Russian provinces like Vitebsk or Minsk or from central provinces such as Moscow and Tver, where the influence of front and factory was paramount and the complexion of earlier elected organs no longer corresponded to the mood of the people, the same cannot be said of representatives of the black-earth provinces of Tambov and Voronezh, Kursk and Saratov, whose action faithfully reflected the sentiment of their peasant constituents. In these provinces fertility of soil and a dense population that did

[8] Gaisinski, *Bor'ba za krest'ianstvo*, pp. 182, 184; Bykhovski, *Vserossiiskii Sovet Krest'ianskikh Deputatov*, pp. 292–93.

[9] Bykhovski, *Vserossiiskii Sovet Krest'ianskikh Deputatov*, p. 293; list of bolting delegations, p. 293, n. 2.

nothing but farm had bred an exclusively agrarian interest which found its political tongue in the Socialist Revolutionary Party, more deeply rooted and better organized here than anywhere else. The huge gray mass of the peasantry in this part of the country is spoken of as "centrist SR" in its leanings, but it would be more appropriate to think of it as a solid block without any factional fissures. This was the citadel of Social Revolutionism and the Left SR's, to say nothing of the Bolsheviks, had still to crack the citadel. At the present conference, as in all other assemblies of the period, the SR delegates called themselves center SR's and were called by their opponents right SR's. Both terms contained some truth and some distortion. The leadership stood decidedly to the right of center; the following was strictly centrist, fed up with coalition and the delay in land reform, but deeply distrustful of the wrecking tendencies manifested by the left-wing extremists.[10]

V. M. Chernov had more influence with peasant delegates than any other SR leader, and he now arrived in the capital, ready to plunge into the fray. The right-centrist committeemen turned to him as though to a siege cannon with which to shell the newly won position of the Left SR's. Once again Chernov was to fulfill the function most typical of him in 1917, and again in 1918, in the days of the Volga revolt, namely, serving as an instrument of men with whom he did not agree. This cannon could always be brought up and wheeled into position, to belch forth a barrage of left-of-center phrases in the service of a right-of-center cause. Emboldened by his presence and knowing that a lasting split would damage the peasants' cause to the advantage of the Bolsheviks, the Executive Committee decided to lead its delegates back into the conference and offer a motion to elect Chernov honorary chairman as the entering wedge of its return to power. The conference meanwhile had proclaimed itself to be an Extraordinary Peasants' Congress and had chosen a Left

[10] Analysis of the cleavage in *ibid.*, pp. 293–95; Gaisinski, *Bor'ba za krest'ian-stvo*, pp. 183–84. The Soviet author cannot quite bring himself to identify the adherents of the Executive Committee with the kulaks, who, by the very nature of the soviets, had no place in them, according to Bykhovski. But Gaisinski does follow the Bolshevik stereotype in connecting the trench delegates with the village pauperdom—something for which there would seem to be no justification, since a peasant did not have to be landless to be fed up with the war and hence radical in his stand.

SR presidium with Maria Spiridonova in the chair. Chernov's appearance brought him such acclaim from the whole congress that the Bolsheviks threw Gregory Zinoviev into the breach to counteract the effect and hold the Left SR's in line. Amid terrific din Zinoviev berated Chernov as the man who had just been consorting with tsarist generals at Mogilev and as the minister responsible for the dissolution of the Finnish parliament. Admonishing the Left SR's that the masses were with them only because they were with the Bolsheviks, he pointedly inquired of Chernov, "Are you with us, or with these ex-defensists?" Ever an able polemicist, Chernov replied with telling effect, disclaiming any action against Finnish independence or any collusion with the military authorities. "My troops," he said, pointing to the peasant delegates, "are here, in this hall!" The prolonged applause that greeted his sallies showed that the "village minister" still retained his popularity and was a power to be reckoned with. To prevent the motion to elect him honorary chairman from carrying, as seemed quite possible, the Left SR presidium declared an intermission.

At this time the relations between Chernov and the Left SR's, though strained, had not deteriorated to the extent that a few weeks more of this tension would bring. They knew that he also had combated the official line, though far more weakly than had they, and his Zimmerwaldian past caused them to regard him as the fountainhead of the antiwar current, from which he had diverged to their chagrin and sorrow. But now he seemed to have enlisted with the enemy. They could not be sure of his position, and wished to show the Bolsheviks that there would be no backtracking on the path of separation, so, putting aside any lingering tenderness for their former mentor, the Left SR's called on their supporters to vote the motion down, and Chernov was denied the honor. The soldier delegates would have voted against Jesus Christ himself, had he been associated with the Executive Committee.[11]

The climax of the Extraordinary Congress came on the motion of the Left SR's to deprive the members of the Executive Committee

[11] *Znamia Truda*, No. 72 (November 15, 1917); Bykhovski, *Vserossiiskii Sovet Krest'ianskikh Deputatov*, pp. 295–97; Gaisinski, *Bor'ba za krest'ianstvo*, pp. 201–2.

of the right to vote. Thanks to the representatives of the inferior soviets, who welcomed the opportunity to do to the committee what it had tried to do to them, the motion carried by 155 to 137 with 5 abstentions. In an effort to shock the majority with the gravity of the situation and induce a more conciliatory frame of mind, Bykhovski arose to read the telegram announcing the withdrawal of the Allied missions from General Headquarters as a consequence of Russia's infringement of existing treaties by seeking a separate peace with Germany. This was undoubtedly the worst possible approach because it touched upon the sorest point in SR relations. The Left SR's were as hostile to the Allies as the right SR's were deferential, and the only response to the announcement of this "thundering blow," as Zenzinov termed it, was a roar of ridicule punctuated with shouts of indignation.[12] After an intermission, at a midnight session, the ousted leadership of the peasant movement, having asked for reconsideration of the previous decision and having been refused, gathered its flock about it and for the second time marched out of the hall. This time it did not return.[13] So it was that on November 13 this assembly of peasants' deputies preceding the Second All-Russian Peasants' Congress fell apart, into two distinct and hostile bodies: the Extraordinary Congress of the Left SR's and Bolsheviks, and a Conference of the Executive Committee with its supporters, virtually all of whom were SR's of the center and right. Both sides made strenuous preparations for a renewal of the struggle at the Second Congress, which would decide the issue.[14]

At this point it may be well to pause and take stock of what had happened. Statistical information concerning the Extraordinary Congress and its moderate counterpart is as unsatisfactory as in most

[12] "Soveshchanie Sovetov Krest'ianskikh Deputatov: Vpechatleniia" (The Conference of Soviets of Peasants' Deputies: Impressions), *Delo Naroda*, No. 209 (November 14, 1917).

[13] Our Soviet narrator has it coming back when the Left SR's weakened and restored voting privileges, only to bolt again almost immediately (Gaisinski, *Bor'ba za krest'ianstvo*, p. 203). In his eagerness to play up the inconsistency of the Left SR's, however, he neglects to mention that the restoration was conditioned on the resignation of the committee, a demand that was wholly unacceptable to its members. See *Revoliutsiia 1917 goda*, VI, 137–38. The two contending factions henceforth sat apart, though deputations continued to go back and forth down to the Second Congress.

[14] Bykhovski, *Vserossiiskii Sovet Krest'ianskikh Deputatov*, pp. 297–99; Gaisinski, *Bor'ba za krest'ianstvo*, pp. 202–3; *Revoliutsiia 1917 goda*, VI, 131, 137–38.

such instances in 1917. One count, reflecting the situation as of November 18 and stemming from a Left SR source, gave a total of 385 delegates with voting rights, of whom 195 were Left SR's, 65 SR's of the center and right, 37 Bolsheviks, 22 anarchists, 7 SR Maximalists, 6 Social Democrats, 4 Popular Socialists, and 14 nonpartisans.[15] An earlier count reported 169 Left SR's, 100 "right" SR's, 43 Bolsheviks, 15 SR Maximalists, and 9 without party.[16] For one reason or another, neither count reflects the actual division of strength, which was much nearer an even break than these figures suggest. The decisive ballot, depriving the members of the Executive Committee of the right to vote, had been close (155 to 137), and while Chernov was an accomplished orator and his powers of persuasion exceptional, he could hardly have pared down to that extent an advantage for the left of better than two to one. A much more satisfactory statement as to how the delegates divided is to be found in a manifesto entitled "To All the Toiling Peasantry," issued by the conference of moderates, which puts the number of bolters (i.e., their own strength) at around 150 and the number of those who stayed at 175.[17] That is about right.

Bykhovski observes that the approximately even division at the time of the initial bolt held throughout the preliminary skirmishing and also for the Second Congress itself, with the Executive Committee drawing its support from the superior soviet organs in the army and the provinces, and the opposition from the inferior organs. A large majority of the provincial soviet executive committees backed the Executive Committee, as did also the army committees, while fewer of the district or *uezd* soviets and very few of the army divisional soviets gave it support. On the other hand, the Left SR's had the great bulk of the army divisional delegates and a considerable portion of the representation of the *uezd* soviets.

For this distribution of strength Bykhovski gives a plausible explanation but one that is not quite all of the story and is not quite fair to the other side. The delegates of the lower military organs,

---

[15] Gaisinksi, *Bor'ba za krest'ianstvo*, pp. 182–83. The figures do not add up to the announced total, as is the case more often than not.

[16] *Revoliutsiia 1917 goda*, VI, 138.

[17] Bykhovski, *Vserossiiskii Sovet Krest'ianskikh Deputatov*, Appendix, No. 17, pp. 398–400.

he says, were usually privates, thirsting for peace and hating war, for whom the defensist position of the Executive Committee had long been as a red flag is to a bull. Their wrath had been fanned by the Left SR's, who told them that the Executive Committee was dragging out the war, and they were further incensed by its failure to expropriate the landowners. The members of the higher military organs, on the other hand, those who served on committees for entire armies, were usually revolutionists of some rank and experience who shared the defensist views of the official SR leadership. Similarly with delegates from the provinces. Those who were sent by provincial soviet executive committees were for the most part peasants with a revolutionary past, confirmed party members who were influenced by the local party organizations. They no longer toed the line as in the early months of the revolution, it is true, as they were disaffected over the delay in land reform and the coalition-at-any-cost policy of the Central Committee, but they were still loyal Socialist Revolutionaries, still faithful to the Executive Committee, and still distrustful of extremism in any form. Delegates of the district or *uezd* (i.e., subprovincial) soviets, on the contrary, were men whose past was usually a blank, who had come up with the revolution itself, oftentimes because of their extremist views. Many were soldiers. As a rule, they had joined the PSR, but the affiliation had been a formality, devoid of organizational pride or interest, and the friction that soon developed between these foot-loose but violent revolutionists, who cared little for theory and much for action, and the intellectuals in party office, who were long on phrases and short on deeds, caused the former to turn instinctively to the Left SR's as soon as these began to form an organization of their own.[18]

Economic status also helped to determine the way in which the peasant delegates lined up, according to the sources, though partisan viewpoint governs the correlations that are made. Bykhovski identifies the supporters of the Executive Committee from the villages with the middle peasantry and the opposition with the agricultural labor and pauper elements; the soldier delegates he does not divide by economic status. Soviet writers always depict the Executive Committee and its following as kulaks or at least as representative of

18 *Ibid.*, pp. 293–95.

kulak interests, while the middle and poor peasantry are assigned to the opposition.[19] There is agreement, therefore, in respect to the position of the village pauperdom. The difference comes in placing the middle and upper layers of the peasantry. Bykhovski denies the Communist thesis linking the well-to-do peasantry with the SR wing of the soviet movement—this alone would have guaranteed suppression of his book—on the ground that the kulaks could have no place in the peasants' soviets, which embraced the SR agrarian program and so claimed their surplus land without compensation.[20]

These analyses must be given their due weight but cannot satisfy the impartial observer. In the first place, Bykhovski fails to point out that the radicalism of the lower soviets was due in part to the simple fact that, being closer to the people and easier to reelect, they often had a fresher mandate than the higher, less responsive organs and so reflected the leftward drift of opinion which had set in so strongly after Kornilov's coup and, to some degree, even before. There can be no doubt at all that the army committees on the Northern and Western fronts had ceased to be representative of their soldier constituents, and the same is true of a number of the provincial executive committees, particularly those in areas where the peasantry was strongly influenced by workers and soldiers. In the second place, Bykhovski's explanation of the cleavage within the military representation is incomplete because, in stating that the delegates from the divisional soviets were usually privates, he should have added that those from the army soviets were frequently officers drawn from the intellectual class, who were separated from the delegates of the lower military soviets not only by their revolutionary past and outlook on the war but also by their military rank and social background. In the third place, this eminent member of the Executive Committee is unconvincing when he puts the kulaks beyond the pale of the peasants' soviets. The conservative Peasants' Union made a play for them but never attained the proportions necessary to comprehend their interest. The kulaks must have been in the soviets, for there was nowhere else for them to go unless they wanted to cut themselves off from the mass of villagers and not

---

[19] See, for example, Gaisinski, *Bor'ba za krest'ianstvo*, p. 183.
[20] *Vserossiiskii Sovet Krest'ianskikh Deputatov*, pp. 295, 332, n. 1, 335.

only lose the opportunity of influencing these through their superior social energy but also expose themselves to a dangerous isolation which was not compatible with the habits of the Russian peasantry. Moreover, the kulaks coveted the broad estates of the nobility as much as other peasants and might well hope to come out of all this confusion with something more than an average allotment.

In this connection, Bykhovski's comment on an assertion made by a Bolshevik delegate at the Second Congress is revealing. Kharitonov claimed to have overheard a right-wing delegate say that he had forty *desiatinas* of land (a *desiatina* was 2.7 acres) and no one was going to take it away from him. Bykhovski observes that he did not hear this statement but that if the man who made it were from the Urals or Siberia, then a farm of that size could not be considered a big kulak holding.[21] Probably the Bolsheviks were right in linking the SR's with the kulaks—indeed, the SR's had never considered successful peasants to be the evil that landowners were—but the SR's represented much else besides kulaks, and this the Bolsheviks would never admit.

The analyses of these developments in the fight for the peasantry are least satisfactory in respect to the middle peasantry. While all revolutionary parties abominated the kulaks, all coveted the support of the independent tillers who did their own work without exploiting the labor of others (except that of their wives and children). Of course, the right SR's did not really abominate the kulaks, and, of course, the Bolsheviks had no use for independent tillers of the soil, with or without hired labor. But we are speaking now not of private convictions but of public affectation. Bykhovski claims the middle peasantry for the Socialist Revolutionaries, leaving the poor peasants and the hired hands to be shared by the Left SR's and the Bolsheviks. Soviet analysts assign both the middle and poor peasantry to the extremist parties, reserving a special place of honor for the pauperdom as the village element most susceptible to Bolshevism—or least capable of resisting it. Since soldier delegates succumbed most readily to the blandishments of Bolshevism, an effort is made to equate delegates from the trenches with the village poor and have all eggs in one basket.[22] This effort produces no real evidence and

---

[21] *Ibid.*, p. 335, n. 2.   [22] Gaisinski, *Bor'ba za krest'ianstvo*, pp. 183–84.

is not in the least convincing. Why a middle peasant or even a kulak in the trenches could not experience an equally strong revulsion of feeling as a hired hand against passing another winter in frozen muck is a question that Communist sources neither pose nor answer. Nor does Bykhovski offer any proof for his attribution of the middle peasantry to the SR's after the breakup of the party. The Left SR's defended this type of peasant just as strongly and claimed just as fervidly to have his support.

If there were any real way of establishing the relationship between type of peasant and political inclination, we should probably find that kulaks tended to be conservative (in the revolutionary sense), that paupers tended to yield to whatever influence played most strongly upon them, and that middle peasants were divided primarily according to temperament and local political influence, the slow and cautious ones siding with the SR's and the more forward ones, or those who were imbued with social hatred, adhering to the Left SR's. The bulk of the middle peasantry was undoubtedly center SR in Voronezh province and Left SR in neighboring Kharkov province, in accordance with the influence exerted by the dominant political organization. In Riazan province this group was split wide open, just like the former party itself. Finally, a deluded peasant of any type could be a Bolshevik.

Amid the conflicting claims, one feature of the Extraordinary Peasants' Congress stands out clearly and unmistakably: there was a marked predominance of soldiers over civilians on the left and of civilians over soldiers on the right. The whole contest for the allegiance of the peasantry at the end of 1917, in fact, takes on the aspect of a duel between the front and the village, if allowance be made for a nonconforming minority on either side that cuts across the established pattern. The Socialist Revolutionaries still retained a following in the army, particularly on the more remote fronts, though it was like an ice block that once had been an iceberg and now was melting furiously. And the Left SR's had considerable and growing support in the villages to add to their soldier following. But in the main the course of the struggle for the peasantry was dictated, like everything else, by the war, and the average SR delegate at these congresses was a villager and the average Left SR delegate a soldier.

The war had produced still another effect. Through the delegates from the trenches it had injected a small but headstrong and vociferous Bolshevik element into these peasant gatherings. Some forty-odd delegates of this persuasion—forty-five was their maximum showing of strength [23]—enlivened or bedeviled the proceedings of the Extraordinary Congress. That as much as a tenth of the total number of delegates should have followed the banner of Lenin led Bykhovski to observe drily that this was a considerable number for such an assembly [24] and Kogan-Bernstein to warn that henceforth his party must reckon not only with Left SR but also with Bolshevik competition in peasant affairs.[25] He plainly intimated that if the PSR did not watch its step, it soon would have the wolf right in the house. Certainly this was no misplaced warning, for the Bolsheviks already had their foot in the doorway and were already starting to push with their accustomed vigor until eventually they shoved out both sets of SR occupants and made themselves masters of the house.

Both sides to the heated contest in and around the Extraordinary Congress did their utmost to discredit the other's representation. The Left SR's and Bolsheviks made it appear as though the SR's retained their majority in the Executive Committee and their hold on the provincial soviets only by abusing the position to which they had been elevated by the peasantry in the honeymoon stage of the revolution. Through prolonging their mandate and refusing to authorize new elections, they were denying the peasantry the right to bring its representation into line with its new and more radical point of view.[26] This effort to expose the SR's as a spent force clinging to positions of power that no longer corresponded to the strength of its popular following was perhaps half propaganda and half sincere conviction. The extremists would soon have an object lesson as to the enduring hold of the PSR upon the affection of the rural

---

[23] Gaisinski, *Bor'ba za krest'ianstvo*, p. 183.
[24] *Vserossiiskii Sovet Krest'ianskikh Deputatov*, p. 291.
[25] *Kratkii otchët*, p. 43.
[26] *Protokoly pervago s"ezda PLSR*, pp. 50, 54, 56 (report of Ustinov).

population, particularly in its black-earth bailiwick. On the other side, the SR's, concentrating their fire on the Left SR's as the more dangerous opponent in peasant affairs, "crawled out of their skins," as the Russians say, to convince the public that these had no roots in the countryside and were merely a cat's-paw of the Bolsheviks. Zenzinov wrote that the Extraordinary Congress had more the aspect of a soldiers' meeting than a peasants' congress, disclosing the propaganda line of his group to the effect that Left Social Revolutionism was an evanescent phenomenon, resting upon a horde of self-demobilizing soldiers who soon would be absorbed by the peasant matrix. The Left SR's were guilty of having flooded the congress with holders of fictitious mandates—with representatives of the "toiling peasantry of Finland," with youthful extremists of both sexes "who have seen peasants only from summer residences," with "guests" who were simply invited by the leftist presidium. "They have summoned from the Smolny the Radomyslskis and the Goldendachs, who by some miracle have also turned out to be peasant delegates," wrote the *Delo Naroda*, which, without being anti-Semitic, could not refrain from taking this dig at the presence of Jewish intellectuals like Zinoviev and Riazanov at a peasants' congress.[27]

That the self-demobilizing soldiers who would soon be absorbed by the peasant matrix might change the matrix does not seem to have crossed the mind of the SR's nor did they take to heart the lesson provided by the presence of a considerable number of Left SR delegates from the provinces, particularly from the *uezd* or district soviets. Not all of the radical-minded delegates came from the army, and though the Extraordinary Congress was scandalously organized, reflecting the chaos of the times, the strength of the Left SR's was by no means so fictitious as some of their mandates. Both sides were strong, though neither could see, or else did not wish to acknowledge, the strength of the other.

In addition to belittling the support of the Left SR's, the SR's strove mightily to depict them as servitors of Bolshevism, seizing

[27] "Bor'ba za krest'ianstvo" (The Struggle for the Peasantry), No. 209 (November 14, 1917); Zenzinov, "Soveshchanie Sovetov Krest'ianskikh Deputatov: Vpechatleniia" (Impressions of the Conference of Soviets of Peasant Deputies), in the same number.

upon even their independent actions as evidence of a desire to conceal their fundamental subservience. On two occasions during the Extraordinary Congress the Left SR's had clashed with the Bolsheviks, once in respect to the question of power and once in respect to the question of peace. They had refused to permit Lenin as head of the government to come before the congress and present a report on its activity lest this constitute recognition of the existing regime and predetermine the decision of the congress as to construction of the government.[28] When the armistice was signed, they refused to send a telegram of congratulation to Krylenko on the ground that there was no cause for exultation as long as it was not known what kind of peace terms the representatives of Imperial Germany would insist upon. The Bolshevik minority was so infuriated by this attitude that it bolted the congress. As the SR's had already withdrawn, nothing but Left SR's remained.[29] To the Socialist Revolutionaries these actions were half-hearted attempts to show that the Left SR's could be different from the Bolsheviks, after which they would lapse into their nefarious ways, going on to form a coalition with their masters and continuing to move in the direction of a separate peace. To the Bolsheviks they were evidence of the eternal vacillation of the Left SR's of their inability to break cleanly with their former comrades and stand upright on their own feet.

To see their position clearly one has to remember the character of the Left SR's and the nature of their stand on the great issues of the day. They were a peasant party, deeply suspicious of the intent of Bolshevism with respect to this class (and with what reason!), and sincerely desirous of doing everything they could to avert a final breach in the peasant movement which would ruin the already poor prospects of maintaining its rights on the same level with those of the urban working class. And they were a peace party, outraged at the callousness and blind obstinacy of their former comrades, and fervently determined to end this accursed war, even at the cost of an alliance with a party they profoundly mistrusted on agrarian matters.

[28] Bykhovski, *Vserossiiskii Sovet Krest'ianskikh Deputatov*, p. 296; Gaisinski, *Bor'ba za krest'ianstvo*, pp. 187, 189.
[29] Gaisinski, *Bor'ba za krest'ianstvo*, p. 203; Bykhovski, *Vserossiiskii Sovet Krest'ianskikh Deputatov*, p. 309. The Bolshevik motion was beaten by a vote of 71 to 48 in a thin house. Apparently, the Bolsheviks later returned.

The peasant question brought them closer to the other SR's, and repelled them from the Bolsheviks; the peace question brought them closer to the Bolsheviks and repelled them from the other SR's. The Left SR's were intermediate, not because of weakness and indecision, but because of their convictions. The year 1918 would explode the myth of their subservience to Bolshevism. And Soviet historiography impeaches the revolutionary integrity of the Left SR's because it dares not admit the existence of a party that stood up as stoutly, though less exclusively, for the class that comprised the mass of the Russian people as the Bolsheviks for the class that constituted but a small section of that people. Three contending forces occupied the arena, and for the Left SR's, who were in the middle, it was a two-front war. If the result was the same as the lesson of German history, the reason is to be sought in the difficulty of the position, not in faint-heartedness or the lack of a spirit of independence.

After the disruption of the preliminary peasants' congress and its final falling apart into two rival bodies, the Left SR's in their Extraordinary Congress tackled the problem of power and worked out the solution already noted in connection with their emergence as a party.[30] They began by calling for a government composed of all the socialist parties and responsible to an organ that embodied the democratic rather than the soviet principle—a people's council with representation from the zemstvos and town councils as well as from the soviet executive committees.[31] But during the congress they receded from this position and came to accept a coalition of themselves and the Bolsheviks alone. The government so formed would be accountable to a supreme soviet organ consisting of the two soviet executive committees on a parity basis (108 members of the Workers' and Soldiers' Executive Committee and 108 of the Peasants'), plus a hundred representatives of the army and navy and fifty of professional unions, mainly trade unions, the whole to be known as the All-Russian Central Executive Committee of Workers', Soldiers', and Peasants' Soviets. On this basis the Left SR's, as we have seen, entered the Soviet government. They had realized their cherished objective of gaining nominal equality for the peasantry (the fact that they

[30] See ch. 3.
[31] Gaisinski, *Bor'ba za krest'ianstvo*, p. 192. The author bases his statement on the report in the *Novaia Zhizn'*.

claimed no more for so large a class shows how greatly the workers and soldiers outweighed the peasants in the revolutionary scales); but they had not gained equality for themselves with the Bolsheviks because the representation of the front and the trade unions would overcome to the advantage of the latter the equilibrium between the two executive committees.[32] The Extraordinary Congress proclaimed the deposition of the old Executive Committee and elected a new, predominantly Left SR one as its contribution to the organ of control over the reconstructed Soviet government. It was agreed that this government should stand on the platform of the October Revolution, but the Left SR's caused the Extraordinary Congress to demand in a special resolution the repeal of all exceptional measures and the "restitution in their entirety of the liberties guaranteed to Russia by the February Revolution." [33]

The discussion of the land problem at the congress attested the chaos that had arisen in the wake of peasant seizures under the carte blanche policy laid down by the decree of October 26. Things were

[32] We have seen that the soldier delegates at the peasants' congress were mainly Left SR's. Now we are saying that the delegates of the army soviets in the new, consolidated All Russian Soviet Executive Committee would be mainly Bolshevik. The reader may be puzzled and think he has found a contradiction, but there is none. The key to the puzzle lies in the structure of the military soviets. These were affiliated with the network of workers' and garrison soviets in the rear, the whole constituting the organization whose Second Congress on October 25 had given the signal for the Bolshevik revolution. Parallel to these soldiers' soviets, or forming sections of them, were specifically peasants' soviets in the army which were affiliated with the network of peasants' soviets in the rear, heading up in the All-Russian Peasants' Executive Committee (or Executive Committee of Peasants' Soviets). Now soldier delegates at peasant congresses would be accredited from these specifically peasant soviets, or sections of soviets, in the army, which at this time were controlled by the Left SR's, whereas delegates from the front at workers' and soldiers' congresses or in the new supreme organ would represent the soldiers' soviets per se —that is, the main-line soviets in the army, now predominantly Bolshevik in sentiment. The great majority of soldiers were, of course, peasants, but most were not organized in soviets as peasants but simply as soldiers. If a soldier took the trouble also to be organized as a peasant, he was more likely to be Left SR than Bolshevik—in other words, the higher the degree of peasant consciousness, the greater the resistance to Bolshevism, and that was as it should have been. One other matter requires comment. The soldiers were the lords of this revolution. They had threefold representation in the new supreme organ: through the Workers' and Soldiers' Executive Committee, through the Peasants', and through the delegation from the front, exclusively their own. The peasant counted for least; the worker was more favored; the soldier, most of all.

[33] Bykhovski, *Vserossiiskii Sovet Krest'ianskikh Deputatov*, pp. 299–300; Gaisinski, *Bor'ba za krest'ianstvo*, pp. 188–92.

going very badly for the SR principle of equitable distribution. In the wild scramble for land, village clashed with village and district bumped heads with district; the friction extended even to individual households with the tendency of the stronger to take advantage of the weaker, particularly of those whose labor power was at the front. The Left SR's, in common with other SR's, now cried out for standards of distribution which the PSR in seventeen years of corporate activity had failed to provide, notwithstanding the warning given it as far back as 1906 by the Siberian agronomist Shvetsov.[34] They censured the Bolsheviks for giving the people nothing to go by in taking over the land, overlooking the fact that socialization of the land had never been a Bolshevik tenet and that Lenin and his party were least of all interested in seeing the land equitably distributed lest the second social war in the village—that within the peasantry itself—be hampered thereby.

Lenin came to the congress to speak on agrarian problems. He pledged his party to go along, reluctantly, with land socialization, but in his insistence upon Left SR acceptance of the socialist character of the revolution as the gage of a true partnership he indicated both his determination to extend socialism to the village by pitting one section of the peasantry against the other and his conviction that the Left SR's would never agree to set the peasants at one another's throats. For them, equitable distribution of the land would be the means of keeping the peasantry together; for him, uneven distribution was the means of disrupting that class and paralyzing its influence in public affairs. The undertones of the approaching conflict are already audible, even as the wedding march of the Bolsheviks with the Left SR's sounded in the halls of the Extraordinary Congress. But for the occasion stilettos remained concealed and both sides joined in passing a meaningless resolution to the effect that the central government should provide the land committees with instructions on land distribution (which were left unspecified) and otherwise dump the whole problem into the lap of the Constituent Assembly (which Lenin meant to dissolve).[35]

Meanwhile, the other part of the ruptured assembly, the conference of the old Executive Committee with its supporters, had organ-

[34] See *The Agrarian Foes of Bolshevism*, p. 29.
[35] Lenin, *Sochineniia* (2d ed.), XXII, 81–84, 87–91; Gaisinski, *Bor'ba za krest'-ianstvo*, pp. 196–99.

ized with Chernov in the chair and gone its own way. Naturally, it breathed anathema against the Extraordinary Congress and all of its works and, naturally, the Executive Committee refused to be deposed by an assemblage of 150 people, the majority of whom allegedly had no legitimate credentials, anyway, when the committee itself had a membership of 250. Furthermore, the Second All-Russian Congress was in the offing and the haste of the Left SR's in anticipating its decisions and usurping the functions and title of the committee seemed to be a confession of weakness, as though their cause were too shaky and their support too negligible to win in an authentic congress. So the May or "Avksentiev" Executive Committee stood its ground and clung to its premises, its apparatus, and its paper, the peasants' *Izvestiia*. Its effort to continue to play host to the Committee to Save the Fatherland nearly led to bloodshed. On the question of power the conference demanded above all recognition of the sovereignty of the Constituent Assembly. Until then it would accept an all-socialist government responsible to the same sort of people's council the Left SR's are said originally to have had in mind, with no party having the majority in the council of ministers and with the mutual right of vetoing obnoxious candidacies (by which was meant the right to eliminate Lenin and Trotski from the cabinet). Civic liberties were to be inviolable. The stand of the conference in this respect, therefore, was moderate and not greatly different from the original position of the Left SR's. But then came the inevitable millstone which the SR's always insisted on putting around their own necks and anyone else's who worked with them: the chimera of a "universal democratic peace" was to be pursued more "decisively" than ever. The SR conference took no further action except to remain in touch with the Extraordinary Congress for the dual purpose of seducing members who were not firmly caught in the extremist net and attempting to work out a joint plan for handling credentials at the approaching Second All-Russian Congress of Peasants' Soviets.[36]

The Extraordinary Congress (November 10–25) had provided Lenin's regime with a fig leaf to conceal its proletarian nakedness.

---

[36] Bykhovski, *Vserossiiskii Sovet Krest'ianskikh Deputatov*, pp. 303–6 and Appendix No. 17, pp. 389–400.

The mere fact that an assembly of peasants had joined its voice to that of the workers and soldiers helped to stabilize the regime, for in the general confusion few bothered to examine the title of the congress or the validity of its members' credentials, many of which Spiridonova herself acknowledged to be irregular.[37] By agreeing to merge at the summit the peasants' soviets with the workers' and soldiers', the Left SR's had unwittingly furthered the hegemony of the proletariat and made it easier for the Bolshevik Party, as the vanguard of the proletariat, to combat any sort of SR influence over the peasantry, whether of the left, center, or right. The ultimate advantage, therefore, lay with the Bolsheviks, but for the time being the Left SR's seemed to have come off best, having broken the SR grip on the peasants' soviets by dislodging the old Executive Committee and having introduced, with the unanimous blessings of the congress, their man Kalegaev into the government as commissar of agriculture.

The Extraordinary Congress, however, had been only the first round of hostilities, and it remained to be seen whether the Left SR's could hold their advantage, and the Soviet government its peasant sanction, in a full-fledged congress, where the provinces would be more fully represented and the front would have proportionately less weight. The date of the Second All-Russian Congress had been moved up to November 25, and both the leftist Extraordinary Congress and the SR conference spent the last days of their sessions in feverish preparations for the approaching showdown. The SR's had never regarded the Extraordinary Congress as other than a conference run wild, and even the Left SR's conceded that all of its actions were of a temporary nature pending the definitive decision of the Second Congress.[38] Hence the frenzied maneuvering that preceded the 25th of November and the desperate struggle on the floor of the congress after it convened. The Bolsheviks took a back seat in all of this as they could not hope to control a peasants' congress and did not have to, since a split in the agrarian movement with the Populists arrayed against one another would be sufficient for their purposes. But neither the SR's nor the Left SR's felt they could afford to lose this

[37] *Ibid.*, p. 301. She contended, however, that whether their credentials were in order or not, the delegates faithfully reflected the will of the rural toilers.
[38] *Protokoly pervago s"ezda PLSR*, p. 24; Bykhovski, *Vserossiiskii Sovet Krest'ianskikh Deputatov*, p. 301.

fight. Routed in the barracks and driven from the factories, the SR's had now to defend the inner citadel of their castle, knowing that if the peasantry were lost, everything was lost. V. M. Chernov had assured the Petersburg conference of his party that the peasantry would hold firm and serve as the base for the SR center to build on in staging a comeback.[39] The Left SR's, on the other hand, had to overcome their former comrades in order to contend on even terms with their present allies; unless they could speak in the name of the peasantry, they could not claim a coordinate position in the Soviet government. Spiridonova had told her comrades that class leadership was at stake and that as a young party the Left SR's must conquer the peasantry in order to make it a creative force in the revolution. But the party could not fulfill its functions nor the peasantry come into its own without first vanquishing the right SR's, who for nine long months had stifled the revolutionary spirit of the rural toilers.[40]

The Second All-Russian Congress would decide whether the SR's would remain at the head of the peasant movement or be displaced by the Left SR's, but who would constitute the Second Congress? Matters had reached such a pass that neither side trusted the other and each feared, not entirely without justification, that if it left the spadework to the other, the congress would be stacked against it. Originally the Executive Committee elected by the May Congress claimed exclusive jurisdiction over matters pertaining to the calling of a new congress,[41] but the Left SR bureau operating in the Smolny Institute with the state power at its disposal had gone right ahead and had achieved so much success in turning a preliminary conference into an Extraordinary Congress that the committee came down off its high horse and proposed making the convocation a joint enterprise with a credentials commission composed of an equal number of representatives from both sides.[42] Back of this change of front lay the fear that the Left SR's, now a government party, might use force to shut their opponents out of the picture and distort the complexion of the congress. Their field commander was Maria Spiridonova, high priestess of the cult of revolution, in relation to whom the SR's were

[39] *Delo Naroda*, No. 212 (November 17, 1917).
[40] *Protokoly pervago s"ezda PLSR*, pp. 114–15.
[41] Bykhovski, *Vserossiiskii Sovet Krest'ianskikh Deputatov*, pp. 281–83.
[42] *Ibid.*, p. 304; *Delo Naroda*, No. 213 (November 18, 1917).

ready to paraphrase Frederick the Great on Maria Theresa and say
that the more she talked about morality and civil liberties, the more
she relied on bayonets.[43] But the Extraordinary Congress had decreed the deposition of the Executive Committee and the Left SR's—
according to Bykhovski, under Bolshevik pressure—refused to compound with it, leaving each side free to muster its strength and meet
in head-on collision at the congress. Not until after it had opened did
it prove possible to reach an understanding, and then only on technical matters and for a brief time.

The Second All-Russian Congress met on November 26 and continued in session until December 10. Several hundred fewer delegates
attended it than had assembled for the First Congress in May. The
rising of Ataman Kaledin had severed communications with the Don
and Caucasus regions, and the Ukrainian SR's were now definitely
treading the path of separatism, disengaging their following from the
All-Russian peasants' movement. Of all the Ukrainian provinces, only
Kharkov with its Left SR deviation had more or less normal representation. Nevertheless, the congress was large enough. According to
the report of the credentials commission,[44] on December 1 there
were 789 delegates with voting rights, of whom 489 were from the
provinces and 294 from the armed forces. Materials of the same
commission preserved in the Archives of the October Revolution
and including delegates who arrived too late to figure in the report
give a total of 865: 491 from the provinces and 374 from the armed
forces.[45] The accepted ratio of representation had been 1:150,000 in
the case of the rural population and 1:20,000-25,000 in the case of
the armed forces. Actually the disproportion in favor of the soldiers
(and sailors) was by no means so great as it might seem, for the first
base figure would include many children, whereas the second comprised only adult or near-adult male peasants. Chernov accuses the
left of flooding the congress with delegates from the front, the rear
garrisons, and the navy,[46] yet the proportion of members in uniform

[43] See Bykhovski's comment (*Vserossiiskii Sovet Krest'ianskikh Deputatov*,
p. 300).
[44] *Znamia Truda*, No. 87 (December 3, 1917).
[45] Gaisinski, *Bor'ba za krest'ianstvo*, p. 227. Twenty-two more delegates from
the armed forces had arrived on December 1 alone (*Znamia Truda*, No. 87).
[46] Manuscript commentary on the minutes of the Central Committee, p. 74.

at the Second Congress was considerably less than at the First, where they had constituted virtually half of the assembly (558 out of 1,167).[47] Then, of course, it had not mattered. Now, with the split in the PSR and the lesson of the Extraordinary Congress in everyone's mind, the greater the degree of soldier participation, the gloomier the prospects of the old guard crowd. The poison of the war was working more strongly than ever.

The distribution of seats at the Second Congress has not been published, district by district. But it is evident that the way in which the congress was actually constituted diverged widely from the way in which it was supposed to be constituted. Representation was highly uneven. Archangel province had seven delegates, while Kherson province, with a population seven times as great, had only six. Our Bolshevik analyst attributes this unevenness to a whole system of manipulation practiced by the right and center SR's to secure a maximum representation from areas favorable to their cause, particularly from the Volga region,[48] but in all probability much of it was due to chance, to factors of communication, local turmoil, and so on. Undoubtedly, the Executive Committee made good use of its manifold ties with local soviets to get its supporters to Petersburg, but the opposition was not sleeping, either, and the Left SR's and Bolsheviks did not lack means of insuring a good turnout on their side, especially from the army. The democratic principle of electing the delegates in local congresses instead of having them appointed by the local committees set up by past congresses must have taken a beating at the hands of both factions, for the two hundred-odd delegates from provincial soviets and the three hundred from *uezd* or district soviets had been chosen in mixed fashion, partly by congresses and partly by committees, in what proportion we are not told. Similarly with respect to the military units, where the same unevenness of representation prevailed, only two of the armies, the XIth and the XIIth, achieving full representation at the congress (as of December 1).[49]

Sometimes, of course, the procedure was as blameless and the results as unimpeachable as it was possible to make them. In Voronezh

[47] Gaisinski, *Bor'ba za krest'ianstvo*, p. 49.   [48] *Ibid.*, p. 228.
[49] *Ibid.*, pp. 226–28; *Znamia Truda*, No. 87 (December 3, 1917).

province, for example, a huge concourse of 552 village electors at the third peasants' congress had chosen a delegation of twenty-five Socialist Revolutionaries to go to the Petersburg congress.[50] Probably few of the delegates had been accredited by a body two-thirds as large as the national congress itself, though the principle followed in this populous black-earth province must have been rather widely applied. As unevenly and, in many instances, as undemocratically as the Second Congress had been put together, it nevertheless was about as authentic an expression of the will of the rural toilers as it was possible to assemble amid the chaos of the times, and all shades of opinion regarded its control as one of the major prizes of 1917.

Furious battling attended every step of the congress. The mere manner of opening it led to controversy. The left wanted the presidium of the Extraordinary Congress to declare it in session, the right said this was the function of the old Executive Committee. The left prevailed when its leaders simply occupied the dais and made the declaration. The first order of business concerned the election of a temporary presidium and chairman and the choice of a credentials commission, upon whose decisions, as both sides realized, control of the congress might hinge. The Left SR's and their allies desired to recruit these organs on the basis of party strength at the congress. The SR's, taking refuge behind a screen of nonpartisanship, proposed to constitute them on a regional basis as more in keeping with the fact that most of the peasants did not belong to any party, and as stressing the oneness of the class rather than the divisiveness of political opinion.

Immediately the issue became personalized in the opposing candidacies for the chairmanship of Maria Spiridonova and V. M. Chernov. It was the second of three memorable occasions on which the issues of the Russian Revolution in its advanced stage crystallized about the personalities of the former girl terrorist and her former political mentor. The first had occurred at the Extraordinary Congress, the third would come in the Constituent Assembly. But it was not possible for passions to be more heated than at this peasants' congress as the first test of strength approached. Chernov's name was greeted with shouts of "Doloi!" ("Down with him!") and

[50] *1917i god v Voronezhskoi gubernii,* pp. 148–49.

Spiridonova's with whistling and catcalls. The result was as fore-shadowed by the Extraordinary Congress and as feared by organizers on both sides: this would be a desperately contested congress. Two votes were taken, the first by show of hand, the second by filing out of the hall through separate doors. The count by hand gave Chernov 233, Spiridonova 246. Then the congress divided, and Russia could see how the gray trench coats of the soldiers moved in one direction and the sleeveless undercoats of the muzhiks in the other, graphic evidence of the estrangement between the peasants who had been caught in the net of war and those who had remained in the village. This time the range widened a bit, and Spiridonova was placed in the chair by 269 votes against 230 for Chernov. The victory over the temporary chairmanship was followed by a victory for the principle of organization favored by the left, and the congress was fairly launched on its stormy course.[51]

Nothing had been settled, however, with 500 members voting in a congress that eventually would number more than 800. In so big and badly administered a land it was never possible to get everybody in the right place at the appointed time, and delegates continued daily to arrive, creating an unstable situation in which a small margin of strength might be wiped out overnight. Chernov explains his initial setback and the initial advantage of the left by the greater mobility of the soldiers, who, if nothing were available for their transportation, seized rolling stock wherever they could find it and came on to Petersburg. Perhaps he is right as to the differential of late arrivals, but soldiers continued to come as well as villagers, twenty-two of the former, as previously noted, arriving on the first day of December. An added source of instability was provided by delegates who were unsettled in their allegiance as between the two Narodnik parties and who might vote now with the one and now with the other, depending on the conjuncture and the nature of the issue at stake.[52]

Presiding over the deliberations of the Second All-Russian Peasants' Congress was like presiding over the eruptions of a geyser, and Maria

[51] *Znamia Truda*, No. 83 (November 28, 1917); Chernov, manuscript commentary on the minutes of the Central Committee, p. 75; Bykhovski, *Vserossiiskii Sovet Krest'ianskikh Deputatov*, pp. 230–32.

[52] For reference to this element see Gaisinski, *Bor'ba za krest'ianstvo*, pp. 217, 225–26, 229.

Spiridonova was not the person to lessen the subsurface tensions. Her inaugural address, instead of pouring oil on troubled waters, poured it on an open fire. She began in a lofty vein, speaking of how the peasantry was essentially one and of how its congress must also be one despite the partisan strife that threatened to tear it asunder, and then suddenly she began to lash the Socialist Revolutionaries, who responded with shouts of indignation.[53] What had begun as an impartial plea for cooperation ended in a trumpet blast to battle. Spiridonova's speech demonstrated at once the need for class unity and the hopelessness of achieving it. When the SR's and the Left SR's thought of the interests of rural Russia, they talked of closing ranks, but when they thought of one another, the knives came out and the cutting began. Both sincerely desired a common front of agrarian socialists—if it were compatible with their own domination. To her own party congress [54] Spiridonova lamented the fact that the peasants should be witness to the dreadful strife among SR's, and then in the next breath she proclaimed it to be the duty of her comrades to conquer the "right" SR's so that the revolutionary spirit of the village could be fully awakened. The peasants were the object of this strife just as the war was the cause of it. There was no room for compromise here, and the congress only deepened the cleavage which the war and the October Revolution had produced. Spiridonova said that the right sabotaged everything, even to the extent of stealing the bell with which she rang for order and cutting off the electricity. Feeling ran high on the left side of the hall and it was only natural that the soldier delegates, trained as they were, should think of using violence against the recalcitrant rustics of the rear.[55]

The strategy of the three major groups at the congress confirms the impression that this was not dual but triangular warfare. It was not the unity of the peasant movement in the last analysis that dictated the action of either the SR's or the Left SR's, however much

[53] *Znamia Truda*, No. 83 (November 28, 1917).

[54] The First Congress of the Left SR's, the Fourth Congress of the PSR, and this Second All-Russian Peasants' Congress (or Congress of Peasants' Soviets) were all in session at the same time.

[55] *Protokoly pervago s"ezda PLSR*, pp. 114–15; Bykhovski, *Vserossiiskii Sovet Krest'ianskikh Deputatov*, pp. 320–22.

both might desire it, but the domination of that movement, as a means of finishing off the rival Populist group, as well as protecting the class against the disruptive designs of Bolshevism. The Left SR's did their utmost to link the SR's through the old Executive Committee to the policies of the Provisional Government; the SR's, to depict the Left SR's as dupes of the Bolsheviks. The Left SR's now accepted and supported the October Revolution but desired to stamp it with their own character by demonstrating that they spoke in the name of rural Russia and held the Sickle as firmly as the Bolsheviks the Hammer. The SR's abominated the October Revolution and all of its works but shunned the label "right" as a means of distinguishing themselves from their rivals because of the contagion of the times and especially because of the fury of the soldiers. They insisted as stubbornly on being called "center" as their opponents on branding them as "right." [56] The mass of their delegates probably was strictly centrist in point of view, but the leadership nesting in the Executive Committee was as it had been—right centrist—and more right than centrist, a solid core of coalitionists and partisans of war for whom Chernov was a convenient screen behind which to hide in the struggle to retain their grip on the peasant movement.

Their chief immediate objective was to rally the peasantry to the defense of the Constituent Assembly, which embodied their greatest triumph and offered the last hope of regaining the position lost at the time of the October Revolution. For this purpose they unlimbered Chernov to make a major oration revolving around the theme of the Constituent Assembly as the expression of the peasants' will. The Executive Committee knew that it would rally its maximum strength at the congress in conjunction with the defense of the Constituent Assembly and that it would be weakest in respect to the defense of its own record; hence the strategy of getting the Constituent Assembly into the foreground and putting off as long as possible the accounting for its six months' tenure of power.[57] And it was meeting with some success, for newspaper accounts agree that some of the Left SR's— who might perhaps more properly be classed as waverers—had joined

---

[56] Bykhovski, *Vserossiiskii Sovet Krest'ianskikh Deputatov*, p. 313, n. 2; Gaisinski, *Bor'ba za krest'ianstvo*, pp. 213–14.

[57] Gaisinski, *Bor'ba za krest'ianstvo*, pp. 215–16.

in applauding Chernov's speech.[58] The main body had not, however, and their aloofness was taken as a very bad sign. Commenting on how the peasants in the early days of the revolution had revered the Constituent Assembly, Bykhovski observes: "And now in the tenth month of the revolution, half of the All-Russian Peasants' Congress openly demonstrated its indifference or even its negative attitude to the Constituent Assembly. It became clear that the position of the Constituent Assembly was all but hopeless." [59]

As for the Bolsheviks, their strategy was to attack the SR's in their most vulnerable position, the record of the Executive Committee, and thereafter to split the congress with as little delay as possible.[60] Basically their purpose was to keep the champions of the peasantry battling each other so that the class would be divided and could offer no obstruction to the vanguard of the proletariat in securing the hegemony of the revolution for that class. In view of the state of relations between the two agrarian parties, no Machiavellian touch was required to accomplish this end. It served the purpose of the Bolsheviks at this time to have the peasantry divided vertically, along political lines, just as later, in 1918 and the years following, it would serve their purpose to cleave it horizontally, along social lines, into those who had more and those who had little or nothing. The line of division did not matter so much as long as the class was paralyzed. The Bolsheviks always had the peasantry on the operating table, undergoing dissection, until they devised the straitjacket of collectivization.

Two controversies dominated the proceedings of the congress: the dispute over the order of business, and the contest over credentials. The latter had caused trouble before the congress and obviously would continue to do so in an assembly so closely divided. It was not until December 1, however, that the credentials commission made its report. Meanwhile the congress had resolved the order of business dispute in favor of the left by instituting the trial of the Executive Committee before taking up the question of the Constituent Assembly. Attorneys for the defense were Martiushin and Bykhovski,

---

[58] *Ibid.*, p. 233.   [59] *Vserossiiskii Sovet Krest'ianskikh Deputatov*, p. 315.
[60] Gaisinski, *Bor'ba za krest'ianstvo*, pp. 218–19.

both stalwarts of the right center, with V. M. Chernov in reserve. A member of the Left SR minority on the Executive Committee, N. Rybin, served as prosecuting attorney, assisted by a whole battery of extremist orators, among whom Kamkov and Kalegaev deserve special mention.

Martiushin delivered the report on the stewardship of the Executive Committee and was heard in silence, the left having decided to vent its venom in notes and glances. It may also have been that the auditors were worn down by a speech that lasted for five hours. Much could have been disclosed in this report, yet it adds very little to our knowledge of the events of 1917. Martiushin was decidedly on the defensive and not at all convincing in respect to the motivation of committee policy. In general, he took the line that the committee had only tried to carry out the instructions of the First Peasants' Congress, and blamed the Bolsheviks rather than the Kadets for its failures. The recurrent political crises had broken in upon its constructive labors and prevented it from doing all that it had in mind. Martiushin was constrained to admit that perhaps the Executive Committee had been at fault in not having pressed more vigorously upon the Provisional Government for action in respect to peace and agrarian reform. For the experiment in coalition, he offered a novel defense: after the usual explanation that a refusal to work with conservative elements would have resulted in civil war and the triumph of counterrevolution, he asserted that the Executive Committee, to be sure, had foreseen the resistance of the propertied element in the government to any measure in the interest of the workers and peasants, but had desired to give the downtrodden peasant masses an object lesson in what they could expect from men like Miliukov, Guchkov, and Rodzianko whom they had been ready to regard as their friends. This educational role of coalition, this Machiavellian touch of a partnership with propertied elements in order to show them up before the people, according to Kalegaev,[61] was something brand new that had not been heard of before. Previously the argument had always been that coalition was the only proper form of government. Otherwise Martiushin's report did not contain any new

[61] *Znamia Truda*, No. 86 (December 2, 1917).

arguments. In it we find the familiar fear of going it alone, independently of either extreme, the same overestimation of the danger of counterrevolution and underestimation of the strength of Bolshevism, and the same readiness to dump everything into the lap of the Constituent Assembly without explaining why the assembly itself had been continuously postponed.[62]

The report met with a cool reception and the chill in the hall did not lessen perceptibly with the reading of Bykhovski's report on the activity of the land section of the Executive Committee. The second spokesman was more honest than the first. Where Martiushin had shifted ground on the failure to empower the land committees to take over the land fund, first alleging that the committee, in pushing this law, had not been strongly enough supported from below, and then pleading that the peasants had taken the land anyway, Bykhovski flatly stated that in order to have achieved this objective the Executive Committee would have had to raise an armed insurrection against the coalitional government—something that it was not willing to do.[63] He, too, argued that the land had actually passed into the possession of the peasantry and told how the land section had ceaselessly issued instructions to village emissaries so that the land fund could be preserved against encroachments, pending the action of the Constituent Assembly.[64] In other words, the record of the Executive Committee had been one of ineffectiveness at the center tempered by unlawfulness in the provinces.

The Rybin rebuttal on behalf of the minority or Left SR faction of the Executive Committee opened the floodgates of criticism. Where Martiushin blamed the Bolsheviks, Rybin blamed the coalition. Often the minority had pressed for more vigorous action in respect to the Provisional Government but always the majority had held back for fear of endangering the principle to which it was committed heart and soul. Only when it confronted a Bolshevik regime did the majority harden and begin to exhibit the firmness so notably absent in its dealings with the Provisional Government. Collaboration with the

---

[62] *Ibid.*, No. 84 (November 30, 1917); Bykhovski, *Vserossiiskii Sovet Krest'-ianskikh Deputatov*, pp. 316–17.

[63] *Znamia Truda*, No. 85 (December 1, 1917).

[64] *Vserossiiskii Sovet Krest'ianskikh Deputatov*, pp. 317–18.

bourgeoisie, intransigence toward Bolshevism—these were its distinguishing characteristics. The minority spokesman invited the congress to adhere to the action of the Extraordinary Congress in condemning the record of the Executive Committee.[65]

Months of frustration had bred in the Left SR's a furious resentment against the Executive Committee. They had come to regard it as the citadel of everything they were against—coalition, war, and procrastination in land reform. Now they felt their time had come, and they proceeded to storm the citadel. One line of attack was to charge it with cowardly desertion of local soviet or land committee members who had incurred prosecution because of zeal in furthering agrarian reform before the Constituent Assembly. As a leader of the peasant movement in Kazan province who had experienced this clash with the machinery of repression at the disposal of the Provisional Government, Kalegaev was especially incensed at a national agency that had had, as he saw it, no voice of its own and no manhood or courage. Terming the Executive Committee the chief prop of the Kerenski regime, Kamkov denounced it for having gone hat in hand to intercede for arrested members of the land committees before authorities whom the committee itself was keeping in power, simply because it was too weak to go against a handful of bourgeoisie on behalf of one hundred million peasants whom it was supposed to represent. It was not that it was counterrevolutionary, he said—in contrast to the Bolsheviks [66]—it was just that it did not have any revolutionary guts. Another line of attack, partly with an eye to the soldier delegates, but partly also out of sincere conviction, was to depict the Executive Committee as the helpmate of Tereshchenko in conducting a foreign policy which mocked the desire of the Russian people for peace. The tacit support of the June offensive was another article in the indictment against the committee calculated to appeal to the soldiers, and without laying the Left SR's open to the charge of demagoguery since they had always been rabid on this subject. Blasting the Executive Committee bred a certain community of feeling with the Bolsheviks, and the Left SR leaders, reversing in

[65] *Znamia Truda*, No. 84 (November 30, 1917); Bykhovski, *Vserossiiskii Sovet Krest'ianskikh Deputatov*, p. 318; Gaisinski, *Bor'ba za krest'ianstvo*, p. 235.

[66] For Communist comment see Gaisinski, *Bor'ba za krest'ianstvo*, p. 218.

part their previous stand, defended the Soviet regime both for having infringed civil liberties—on the ground that the Provisional Government had shown the way—and for having copied its land decree from the SR program—on the ground that a copied law was better than no law at all.[67]

To stem the flow of condemnation the Executive Committee had recourse once more to V. M. Chernov. There had been a time, and not so long in the past, when Chernov would have commanded the respect of virtually every member of a peasant assembly. His appearance before the Extraordinary Congress on November 12 had brought him the applause of the whole house.[68] Now, a scant two weeks later, as he mounted the tribune at the Second Congress, he was greeted with shouts of "doloi!" [69] In between lay the final act in the expulsion of the Left SR's from the paternal household, the walkout of their delegation at the Fourth Party Congress with Chernov applauding. In between, also, lay the mounting rage of the soldiers at anyone who still bore the SR label. Chernov, of course, did not defend the coalition in which so many of his clients on the Executive Committee still believed. He merely said that it was a necessary stage in the development of a revolution and reminded his listeners that some months earlier they had by no means been so convinced of its wickedness. An all-socialist government had in any event not been feasible because of the refusal of the Bolsheviks to work with the moderate parties. The Left SR organ has Chernov defending the June offensive on the grounds of necessity, but his own paper does not attribute such a statement to him. Chernov warned against passion-rousing speeches like Kamkov's and, above all, against a rupture between the front and the village. In his usual oblique manner, he indicated that the economic policy of the new regime might involve it in difficulty with the rural population. The peasants might then withhold their produce, and in that event guilt would rest upon the strong-armed minority that had tried to impose its will upon the many millions of rural toilers. This veiled reference to the weapon

[67] *Znamia Truda*, Nos. 85, 86 (December 1, 2, 1917), especially the speeches of Kamkov and Kalegaev; Bykhovski, *Vserossiiskii Sovet Krest'ianskikh Deputatov*, p. 318.

[68] *Znamia Truda*, No. 72 (November 15, 1917). See above, p. 210.

[69] Bykhovski, *Vserossiiskii Sovet Krest'ianskikh Deputatov*, p. 318.

of starvation stung the other side to fury, and a frightful din arose.[70]

After three days of mounting tension the debate on the Executive Committee was broken off, never to be resumed before a united assembly. On December 1 the question of credentials intruded itself, with every prospect that its solution would determine control of the congress. Nerves could not stand this added strain. The congress had borne little enough resemblance to a deliberative body as it was; now it degenerated into a bawling mob. The credentials commission had been constituted on a basis of parity for the three main groups. That is to say, no one party had the majority, but the two leftist parties together outnumbered the SR's two to one.[71] From the first, the latter were disposed to challenge the right of a number of delegates on the other side to sit in the congress. They complained that the leftist members of the commission refused to let them check credentials that had already been given out—presumably to the Extraordinary Congress—before the commission had come into existence.[72] Gradually, however, the SR's began to make headway and a number of credentials were invalidated for one reason or another, oftentimes by a majority of only one vote. The SR's gained ascendancy, we are told, through the presence of Left SR waverers who succumbed to their influence and allowed them to name the chairman of the commission.[73] Spiridonova complained that the commission did its best to "strain out" Left SR's, the result being that few of them were on it.[74] What she meant by this, no one can say. Her party had equal representation and if something were wrong with its representatives, the fault would seem to lie with the party itself. Of course, it is just possible that the Left SR's on the commission may have been not so much waverers as fair-minded people who would not vote to accept bad credentials even though their own side suffered thereby. The SR's contended with a good deal of logic that if a commission in which they were in a minority decided in their favor,

---

[70] *Delo Naroda*, No. 221 (December 1, 1917); *Znamia Truda*, No. 85 (December 1, 1917); Bykhovski, *Vserossiiskii Sovet Krest'ianskikh Deputatov*, pp. 318–19; Gaisinski, *Bor'ba za krest'ianstvo*, pp. 214, 236–37.

[71] Gaisinski, *Bor'ba za krest'ianstvo*, p. 218; *Znamia Truda*, Nos. 83, 84 (November 28, 30, 1917).

[72] Bykhovski, *Vserossiiskii Sovet Krest'ianskikh Deputatov*, pp. 315–16.

[73] Gaisinski, *Bor'ba za krest'ianstvo*, pp. 218, 229.

[74] *Protokoly pervago s"ezda PLSR*, p. 114.

then certainly the delegates whom they had challenged were unworthy of being seated.[75]

The majority report of the credentials commission was presented
by the SR chairman, V. T. Vladykin,[76] who announced that 789
delegates with voting rights were in attendance as of that day
(December 1). The partisan complexion of the congress had not yet
been determined, but he could say that there were about 300 SR's of
the center and right and 90 Bolsheviks, while no figures were available for the Left SR's and the smaller groups (nonpartisan, Popular
Socialist, Menshevik, SR Maximalist, anarchist).[77] A dissenting report
which charged the commission with having disallowed a number of
credentials on trivial grounds by one- or two-vote margins was read
by the Bolshevik Anokhin. He proposed that the holders of such
credentials be accorded the right of appeal to the floor. The Left SR
spokesman backed him up. Thereupon Kobytchenko for the SR's
protested hotly, saying that the commission had been drawn from all
groups and hence should enjoy the confidence of the congress. A
question of order arose, and when Spiridonova's ruling contravened
their sense of proper procedure, the SR's lost any vestige of self-
control. An explosion occurred, and for a while the congress ceased
to function. Accounts differ as to the final disposition of the question
of rejected credentials, but a vote on Anokhin's demand for reelection of the commission, reinforced by a specific and personal charge
against its chairman, was deferred until the next meeting. The congress could now return to its debate on the Executive Committee,
which promised to be exciting enough.

But this was not to be. On November 28 the Soviet government
had outlawed the Constitutional Democrats as "enemies of the people" and four prominent members of this party, two of them members of the Constituent Assembly, had been taken into custody (Shingarev, Kokoshkin, Prince Dolgorukov, and the Countess Panina).
On November 30 the government had dispersed a meeting of depu-

---

[75] Bykhovskii, *Vserossiiskii Sovet Krest'ianskikh Deputatov*, p. 321.

[76] Constituency represented at this congress unknown; elected to the Constituent Assembly from Orel province.

[77] Among the nonpartisans was at least one Tolstoian (see Gaisinski, *Bor'ba
za krest'ianstvo*, p. 222). How Mensheviks landed in a peasants' congress is not
explained; in such times incongruities of all kinds were possible.

ties in the Taurida Palace. To the SR's these actions indicated that
Lenin was already moving toward the dissolution of the assembly. In
order to give him pause, and in accordance with their basic strategy
of focusing attention on the Constituent Assembly, the SR's now
maneuvered to get the question before the peasants' congress. A snap
motion was offered by the Menshevik Moiseev to take up the matter
out of turn, just as the congress was preparing to settle down to its
regular business after the heated controversy over credentials. The
motion had the effect of a second and bigger bombshell before the
excitement from the first had subsided. The Left SR's were placed in
an awkward position. By this time their view on the Constituent
Assembly was beginning to crystallize in favor of letting it convene
with its full membership and waiting to see what it would do. They
opposed the violation of members' immunity from arrest, yet could
not make common cause with the SR's. So when the vote was taken,
the SR's supported the motion, the Bolsheviks opposed, and the Left
SR's abstained—the motion, of course, was carried. The Bolshevik
sailor Rozanov had blasted the right for sabotaging the work of the
congress, his abuse had enraged the SR's, and now after the vote,
with the left in its turn exasperated, it became impossible to transact
any business. Moreover, it was dangerous to try, for the atmosphere
was heavy with threats and the soldiers began to think of their rifles.
From the platform Maria Spiridonova pleaded for peace between the
"peasants in gray coats and those who came from the fields." It was
amid shouts on both sides of "Razdelat'sia!" ("Let's have done with
it!") that Kalegaev arose to move adjournment. The motion carried,
305 to 287, and the session of December 1 went down into history,
leaving the congress a shambles.[78]

The next day brought the climax, though the unity of the congress
had already been undermined. The entire session of December 2 was
given over to debate on the Constituent Assembly, in the midst of
which Lenin appeared to deny that the regime was forcing its will
on the peasantry at the point of the bayonet by reminding his audience that the bayonet was in the hands of the peasantry itself. Both

[78] *Znamia Truda*, No. 87 (December 3, 1917); *Delo Naroda*, No. 222 (December 2, 1917); Bykhovski, *Vserossiiskii Sovet Krest'ianskikh Deputatov*, pp.
320–22; Gaisinski, *Bor'ba za krest'ianstvo*, pp. 229–30, 239; *Revoliutsiia 1917 goda*,
VI, 251.

Lenin and his opponents were correct in their assertions, of course, the key to the paradox lying in the fact that the war had divided the peasants into two camps—those who felt primarily as soldiers and those who had preserved a purely peasant outlook—and this whole congress was a testimonial as to how badly divided they were. After Lenin had exalted the soviets above a Constituent Assembly that was already outmoded because the people could vote for but one SR party, whereas now there were two, Chernov answered him with an appeal to the peasants not to be misled by a feint against a counter-revolutionary party which had already been rendered harmless by the election but to realize that the real purpose of the Bolshevik assault upon the rights of the elected representatives of the people was to destroy an institution three-quarters peasant in its make-up. He called for a ringing vote of nonconfidence in the regime in order to demonstrate that it was not really a soviet regime but rather a dictatorship of commissars over both soviets and Constituent Assembly. The Left SR's stayed on middle ground, desiring the assembly to meet as elected but keeping their fingers crossed as to what it would do and how they would react once it was in session. In fact, they spoke with a forked tongue on this occasion, as Karelin expressed the viewpoint of the more moderate faction, closer to that of Chernov, and Kalegaev championed the stand of the more extreme faction, closer to that of Lenin.[79]

Three resolutions were laid before the congress, reflecting the positions of the SR's, the Left SR's, and the Bolsheviks. So that the left could present a united front, the Bolsheviks withdrew their resolution and accepted the middle-of-the-road text of the Left SR's. It was a solemn occasion, surcharged with passionate feelings. The vote was by roll call, and the number of the credentials card and the soviet represented were entered after each individual's name. Polling the huge assembly took a long time and it was late at night before the result was announced: the SR resolution had prevailed, 359 to 321.[80] The right sector of the congress staged an ovation, the left

[79] Bykhovski, *Vserossiiskii Sovet Krest'ianskikh Deputatov*, pp. 322–26; *Delo Naroda*, No. 223 (December 3, 1917); Gaisinski, *Bor'ba za krest'ianstvo*, pp. 239–44; Lenin, *Sochineniia*, XXII (2d ed.), 113–15.

[80] The vote is sometimes given as 360 to 321 or 359 to 314 (see Gaisinski, *Bor'ba za krest'ianstvo*, pp. 221, n. 3, 245, n. 2). The difference is not worth bothering about.

voiced heated protests, accompanied by threats of withdrawal. Despite the slender margin of victory the SR's exulted, for they had carried a vote of censure against the council of commissars.[81]

But they had reckoned without Spiridonova. The next day (December 3) this feminine firebrand, for whom life was one continuous battle and who never shrank from an issue, threw everything back into the crucible by ruling that the resolution adopted was merely the basis for a final draft, not the final draft itself, and hence open to amendment. The SR's cried out against a ruling which in their eyes not only was improper but would undercut every decision of the congress and render its whole work futile. The house, however, sustained the chair by a vote of 342 to 315,[82] from which we may conclude that this was still a wide-open congress with no stable majority for either side. In the midst of these stormy proceedings, with noise coming now from one side, now from the other, and now from both at once, Trotski appeared to report on the progress of peace negotiations. If the devil from hell had mounted the tribune he would not have set off such an explosion of wrath as the man who was reputed to be partial to the guillotine and who was all the more odious in the eyes of the Narodnik intellectuals pulling the strings on the right side of the house because of his determination to move in the direction of peace. Under the hail of abuse that descended upon him (the fact that he was a Jew may not have helped him in a congress where there was more than a little anti-Semitism), Trotski had to retreat to a neighboring hall along with the left part of the congress before he could make himself heard, whereupon the right took advantage of the situation to repass the resolution on the Constituent Assembly without amendments. It then adjourned to gird itself for renewed battle on the following day.[83]

The session of December 4 produced the schism that had long since become inevitable. After an initial breakdown over the refusal of the soldiers to listen to the Menshevik Kuchin, former head of the XII

---

[81] Bykhovskii, *Vserossiiskii Sovet Krest'ianskikh Deputatov*, pp. 326–27, 402–4 (Appendix 20).
[82] *Nash Vek*, December 5, 1917; Gaisinski, *Bor'ba za krest'ianstvo*, p. 252. The *Delo Naroda*, significantly, omits any mention of this vote.
[83] Bykhovskii, *Vserossiiskii Sovet Krest'ianskikh Deputatov*, pp. 328–29; *Delo Naroda*, No. 224 (December 5, 1917); Gaisinski, *Bor'ba za krest'ianstvo*, p. 246; *Revoliutsiia 1917 goda*, VI, 264–65.

Army committee, and the subsequent resignation of Spiridonova as presiding officer,[84] the delegates reassembled late in the evening with their nerves on edge, for the question of permanent organization was coming up and with it a supplementary report from the credentials commission. That body complained of not being able to keep abreast of its duties because of the large number of dubious credentials— there were tens of these, it said, implying that too many delegates of the left had been supplied with them. Whether because of the un- seating of some of its delegates [85] or because of the hope of unseating some on the other side or—more fundamentally—because of a fear that Spiridonova and Kalegaev might fail of reelection,[86] the left desired to postpone the question of permanent organization until all contests had been settled and still other delegates had arrived. The right or "center," on the other hand, contended that with the con- gress already in its ninth day it was time to elect the permanent presidium, and announced that Chernov would be its choice for pre- siding officer. Bedlam broke loose when a vote on whether to pro- ceed with the election was taken and yielded the incredible result of 332 in favor and 362 abstaining. To the indignation of the right, Kamkov had signaled his followers from the platform not to vote and then to raise their cards when the abstentions were called for. The presiding officer, Ovchinnikov, an old guard stalwart, questioned the accuracy of the count in view of the fact that the SR scorekeepers had been prevented by imminent danger of physical violence from checking the number of abstainers. Feeling themselves to be insulted, the soldiers rushed the chair, men from the other side likewise sprang upon the platform, and such a scene ensued as had not yet been wit- nessed, even at this congress. The restraint which the SR's are said (by their own organ) to have exhibited up to this point now vanished completely, and they shouted at their opponents: "You mean to tear Russia to pieces!" Under the fire of the left Ovchinnikov relinquished the chair to Karelin, who was immediately set upon by the right with cries of "We don't trust you!" and likewise prevented from bringing order into the proceedings.

[84] See *Delo Naroda*, No. 224.   [85] *Nash Vek*, December 6, 1917.
[86] O. Ch., "Krest'ianstvo raskololos'" (The Peasantry Has Split), *Delo Naroda*, No. 229 (December 10, 1917); Chernov, manuscript commentary on the minutes of the Central Committee, p. 76.

For a time there were two congresses meeting under the same roof. Each ignored the other's presence. Then the SR's proposed a recess until the next day, since no business could be transacted with the delegates in so beastly a mood. The left voted this down while the right held aloof. And that was the end of the Second All-Russian Congress of Peasants' Soviets. The SR's arose and marched out of the hall, singing the *Marseillaise*. The right repaired to the headquarters of the Executive Committee on the Fontanka, where henceforth it sat as a separate congress. Many of the Left SR's watched it go with dismay as they realized that the peasant movement that once had promised so much was now falling apart, leaving them with but one leg to stand on in their dealings with the high priest of proletarian socialism. Venetsianov of Kazan mounted the tribune to deplore a rupture with the SR's over such a trifle: "Let us give them a pitched battle over the question of war," he said, striking himself on the breast, "and then, if need be, we shall put away from ourselves all enemies of the people and peasantry!" Similarly A. A. Shreider, who asked the left whether it wanted to dispatch to all corners of Russia three hundred couriers of civil war.[87]

The following day Spiridonova returned to her theme of the need for unity. Her friend Anastasia A. Bitsenko, member of the Russian peace delegation at Brest Litovsk, had informed her over the direct wire that when the Germans learned of the serious division of opinion in Russia over the peace question they began to speak in quite a different language. Consequently, it was of the utmost importance to have an authoritative expression of opinion from the peasants' congress in support of the peace negotiations. A delegation was sent to the other side with an invitation to return and take part in the peace discussions, the purpose being more to attract wavering sons of the soil away from their leaders than to heal the breach itself.[88] Indeed, it could not be otherwise, for Spiridonova knew well enough how adamant the SR leaders were against a separate peace. The simple

[87] *Delo Naroda*, No. 225 (December 6, 1917); Bykhovski, *Vserossiiskii Sovet Krest'ianskikh Deputatov*, pp. 330–31; *Novaia Zhizn'*, No. 194/188 (December 6, 1917).

[88] See Gaisinski, *Bor'ba za krest'ianstvo*, p. 253. This account is based on the unpublished minutes of the congress and suggests that the action referred to was in the nature of a political maneuver.

peasants on both sides were deeply troubled by the split in their ranks and inclined to blame the intellectuals who led them—one sailor even went down on his knees to implore the right to come back and restore the broken front. The SR leaders thought they might be able to capitalize on this sentiment and win peasants away from the left if only they could break down the partisan principle and organize the congress along regional or geographical lines. Accordingly, they drafted a set of conditions for reunion which included the election of a presidium on a regional basis, the acceptance of the resolution on the Constituent Assembly as passed on December 2, the right of their scorekeepers to operate freely, and so on. These conditions were presented to the left congress by a counterdelegation in the form of an ultimatum, according to the Left SR organ,[89] but in the form of a bid for further negotiations, according to Bykhovski.[90]

In any event the left, while welcoming the thought of reconciliation, declared it to be inadmissible for one part of the congress to confront the other with demands. The "comrades who had gone away" should simply come back without posing conditions. But the SR delegation announced that no common tongue had been found and withdrew. The split was now definitive. Both sides had been trying to raid the other's sheepfold and had gotten nowhere. Bykhovski says the Bolsheviks stiffened the backbone of the Left SR's on this as on other occasions,[91] but since it is his constant endeavor to portray the Left SR's as tools of the Bolsheviks, he is not convincing. The SR's had first broken up their own household and now they extended their separation to their respective peasant followings.[92]

Which side actually had the majority at the Second Congress? How many delegates marched out with the SR's and how many remained in the hall? The fluid state of the congress resulting from the continued arrival of some delegates and the departure of others

[89] *Znamia Truda*, No. 89 (December 7, 1917).
[90] *Vserossiiskii Sovet Krest'ianskikh Deputatov*, p. 333.   [91] *Ibid.*
[92] *Delo Naroda*, Nos. 225, 226 (December 6, 7, 1917); O. Ch., "Krest'ianstvo raskololos'," *ibid.*, No. 229 (December 10, 1917); Bykhovski, *Vserossiiskii Sovet Krest'ianskikh Deputatov*, pp. 331–33; Gaisinski, *Bor'ba za krest'ianstvo*, pp. 252–54.

makes it impossible to determine with exactitude the size of its fragments, but an approximation can be arrived at. Right after the walkout the presidium asked those who remained to raise their cards and it was found that 332 delegates were still in their seats—at that time somewhat less than half the congress, as Bykhovski points out.[93] The vote on whether to continue the session produced 171 in favor, 128 opposed, and 34 not voting, for a total of 333.[94] The other part of the congress, the right or seceding part, in manifestoes to the peasantry on the cause of the split, placed its own strength at 347 or 351.[95] As the credentials commission had reported a total of 789 delegates with right to vote on December 1, more than a hundred members of the congress are unaccounted for, without considering late arrivals. The attendance at the left congress seems to have increased as time went on and at the right congress to have shrunk. In order to give its peace resolution as much prestige as possible the left held a roll call vote; the result was 424 in favor and 4 not voting.[96] On the other hand, a count at the right congress on December 7 showed only 212 voting and 25 nonvoting delegates. Comparing these figures, our Soviet source arrives at the conclusion that the left congress had twice the strength of the right.[97] The left had apparently gained 91 to 92 delegates since the schism, whereas the right had lost 135 to 139. Now the Bolsheviks had turned on the heat and succeeded in having 50 delegates from army units recalled for having gone with the right,[98] and if we add this number to the apparent gain of the left, we get a figure of 141 or 142, which is very close to the apparent loss of the right.

There are too many uncertainties, however, for us to have confidence in these figures. For one thing, nowhere in the records is

[93] *Vserossiiskii Sovet Krest'ianskikh Deputatov*, p. 331.

[94] *Delo Naroda*, No. 225 (December 6, 1917).

[95] See Bykhovski, *Vserossiiskii Sovet Krest'ianskikh Deputatov*, Appendixes Nos. 24 and 25, p. 409.

[96] M. Kh[aritonov], "Itogi 2-go Vserossiiskago Krest'ianskago S"ezda" (The Results of the Second All-Russian Peasants' Congress), *Izvestiia TsIK i petrogradskago soveta*, No. 253 (December 16, 1917). In addition, there were 60 without voting rights who favored the resolution.

[97] Gaisinski, *Bor'ba za krest'ianstvo*, p. 255.

[98] M. Kh., "Itogi 2-go Krest'ianskago S"ezda," *Izvestiia TsIK i petrogradskago soveta*, No. 253 (December 16, 1917).

there any claim that close to a hundred delegates switched sides after the split. The large number of delegates unaccounted for at the time of separation, together with the substantial number of arrivals and departures, does not admit of calculation but only of speculation. The left could have swelled its ranks by a liberal policy on credentials, and the right may have sustained much of its loss through the homeward drift of peasant adherents who were less heated up and less footloose than the soldier element constituting the bulk of the strength on the other side. And if there were any such marked preponderance on the left why was it not evidenced in the voting before the schism took place? We are forced to conclude with Bykhovski [99] that the Second All-Russian Congress split about evenly into a left half of Left SR's and Bolsheviks and a right half of centrist and right SR's.

On a qualitative basis the SR's claimed to have a decisive advantage.[100] They had the mass of the real peasantry behind them, together with the brains and organizing personnel of the peasant movement, while the opposition consisted of uprooted peasants in an army that was falling apart and a motley crew of intellectuals who had grafted themselves onto the movement without any organic ties with the class in whose name they presumed to speak. The SR's were supremely confident that their social base was firm and enduring in contrast to the shifting foundations of the opposition, which would become a staff without an army when demobilization had run its course and the peasant soldiers had been reabsorbed by the peasant matrix. The SR's were partly right in their analysis of the existing situation and wholly wrong in appraising its future effects. In the whole catalogue of errors compiled by them in 1917 there is not another miscalculation so dire in its consequences as this contempt for peasants in uniform.

Nothing brings out more clearly the line of fracture at the Second Congress than the roll call vote of December 2 on the question of the Constituent Assembly. To be sure, this occasion marks the high-

[99] "K raskolu krest'ianskago s"ezda" (On the Schism of the Peasants' Congress), *Delo Naroda*, No. 230 (December 12, 1917); *Vserossiiskii Sovet Krest'ianskikh Deputatov*, pp. 331, 337.

[100] Gaisinski, *Bor'ba za krest'ianstvo*, pp. 255–57; Bykhovski, "K raskolu krest'ianskago s"ezda," *Delo Naroda*, No. 230 (December 12, 1917).

water level of the right and the low-water level of the left,[101] but the deviation from the average in either case is not great enough to deprive the analysis which Bykhovski has made [102] of its value as an illustration of how social status and political predilection were linked in the peasant movement. The breakdown of the vote by social category is as follows.

Origin of Delegates	For SR Resolution		For Left SR Resolution	
	Number	Percent	Number	Percent
The village *	270	75.2	107	33.3
The army	82	23.4	206	66.3
National organizations	7	1.6	1	0.3
Total	359	100 (*sic*)	314 **	100

* Provincial and district (*uezd*) soviets.
** Figure reduced from 321 because seven delegates voted twice.

The left congress, after the departure of the right, is said to have been embarrassed at its own appearance. These figures show why; it was largely a soldiers' convention. Two-thirds of its strength on this vote had come from the army, three-fourths of the right's from the village. No better illustration could be given of the war's effect on the peasantry. That class had been divided, deeply and disastrously divided. At the same time it would be a mistake to think of Left Social Revolutionism as exclusively a phenomenon of the military environment or of the other SR's as being completely washed out in the armed forces. A nonconforming minority on either side modified to some extent the cleavage between the front and the rear. One hundred and seven provincial delegates out of fewer than four hundred had gone with the Left SR's, while about the same proportion —upwards of a fourth—of the representatives in uniform still adhered to the party whose sway had once been unchallenged in the army and navy. If it were possible to get back of Bykhovski to the

[101] The left always maintained that the adverse majority was accidental in character. A greater proportion of its strength may have been absent and some of the wavering Left SR's may have gone over to the other side on this occasion. See Gaisinski, *Bor'ba za krest'ianstvo*, p. 245; M. Kh., "Itogi 2-go Krest'ianskago S"ezda," *Izvestiia TsIK i petrogradskago soveta*, No. 253 (December 16, 1917).
[102] *Vserossiiskii Sovet Krest'ianskikh Deputatov*, pp. 333–34; this is based on his earlier analysis in the article "K raskolu krest'ianskago s"ezda," *Delo Naroda*, No. 230 (December 12, 1917).

basic sources, we might learn where these army delegates who stood
out against the mass contagion came from—probably the more remote fronts, Southwestern, Rumanian, and Caucasian, which the SR's
had carried in the election to the Constituent Assembly. It was only
a question of time, however, until the contagion spread to these
sectors as well, virtually extinguishing SR influence in the army. The
Left SR influence in the provinces, on the other hand, was waxing
rather than waning and the growth of this minority would gradually
lessen the contrast between front and rear.

A geographical analysis of the vote of December 2 is unfortunately
not possible. Bykhovski tells us only in general how the provinces
voted. Thirty-seven provinces supported the SR resolution and
fifteen sided with the opposition. The SR's had all the votes from
seventeen provinces and majority support from twenty more; only
six provinces went solidly for the Left SR's and nine others gave
them a majority. No information is given in respect to individual
provinces. However, the three major Left SR strongholds of Kharkov, Ufa, and Kazan presumably gave them solid support, and they
must have gotten all or most of the votes from Kherson, Kaluga,
Pskov, Tomsk, and—less certainly—from Riazan. The SR's no doubt
derived the bulk of their strength from the populous black-earth
provinces, as in the election to the Constituent Assembly, which had
been held in most parts of the country on the eve of the congress.
Voronezh province probably gave them all thirty [103] of its votes and
Kursk, Tambov, Saratov, Penza, and Samara must have contributed
heavily to their victory.

The Second All-Russian Peasants' Congress reflected only too well
the disunity of the class.[104] The soldiers had identified the older
party and, even more, the Peasants' Executive Committee, with the
prolongation of the war. As between the soviets and the Constituent

[103] Twenty-five of these had been chosen at the provincial congress (see
above, pp. 227–28, and below, pp. 271–72).
[104] The congress affords other illustrations of the preponderance of the
soldier element on the extremist benches. Of the 424 delegates who signed
the peace resolution of the left, only 150 came from the provinces (Bykhovski,
Vserossiiskii Sovet Krest'ianskikh Deputatov, p. 334). Our Soviet source, however, materially lessens the disparity by placing the number at 182 from forty
provinces (Gaisinski, *Bor'ba za Krest'ianstvo,* p. 247). A contemporary Bolshevik source merely says "over 150" (M. Kh., "Itogi 2-go Krest'ianskago
S"ezda," *Izvestiia TsIK i petrogradskago soveta,* No. 253 [December 16, 1917]).

Assembly, they definitely preferred the former. The soviets had freed them from the hated discipline of the prerevolutionary army and in them they could feel their own immense power. The soviets, moreover, were free from any taint of bourgeois contamination, being purely organs of the lower classes, whereas the Constituent Assembly represented the whole nation, including the propertied element. The very fact that the Constituent Assembly embodied in the fullest sense the democratic principle cursed it in the soldiers' eyes. Quite different was the outlook of the peasants back home in the village. The horrors of the front meant little or nothing to them even though many were tired of the war. They had been taught to look to the Constituent Assembly as the final arbiter in agrarian relations and the outcome of the election had convinced them that it would decide in their favor. Whether they had already seized the land or were still waiting to get it, they valued the sanction of the assembly as the most authoritative as well as the most peaceful means of confirming title. They were frightened by the iconoclasm of the left, by its aggressiveness and penchant for violence, and, being constantly berated on the floor of the congress as "kulaks," those of them who were middle peasants—and Bykhovski would have us believe all of them were—not unnaturally concluded that they would be treated like the kulaks if civil war erupted in the village. The Left SR's sought to preserve the unity of the peasantry with as much zeal as the SR's, but their association with the Bolsheviks, who favored civil war in the village, and the propaganda of the Narodnik intellectuals, who did their utmost to tar the Left SR's with the Bolshevik brush, had rendered the entire left suspect in the eyes of the moderate peasantry.[105]

Not until after they had parted company did the factions at the Second Congress settle down and begin to transact business. But once these subcongresses become deliberative, they lose their interest, and everything that happens after the session of the 4th of December is by way of an anticlimax to the sterile but stirring events of the first ten days. With a self-righteousness such as only moralists like Spiridonova can muster and a willful disregard for realities that must

[105] Bykhovski, *Vserossiiskii Sovet Krest'ianskikh Deputatov,* pp. 334–36.

have made even the SR's envious, the left arrogated to itself all the
prerogatives of a plenary congress and employed all the official means
at its disposal to create the impression that the other half was but a
recalcitrant minority unworthy of further consideration. In the
manifestoes and resolutions of the left, the right half figures as "not
a large part" or as "the less conscious part" of the Second Congress,
which had been induced to bolt by a discredited leadership determined to disrupt the congress rather than admit defeat.

The work of the left half-congress proceeded swiftly and smoothly
in view of the disinclination of the Bolsheviks to dispute at this time
the dominant position of their allies. First on the order of business
was the question of peace, which was settled the very next day after
the schism in favor of the policy of the Soviet government in arranging a separate armistice and pressing forward toward an "honorable
and democratic" peace, to be realized with the help of the suffering
masses of all the belligerent powers. The congress sent its own delegation to the peace negotiations. The resolution on the Constituent
Assembly declared it should meet as elected, with a full staff of
members, and should address itself to giving life to the decisions of
soviet congresses, within the framework of the soviet order. Any
attempt to counter those decisions or supplant that order would be
viewed as a threat to the conquests of the revolution, and for the
purpose of keeping the assembly within bounds, its membership was
to be subject to recall and reelection upon the initiative of local
soviets. No wonder the Bolsheviks did not object to this formula.
There was nothing in it for them to object to. The resolution on
the agrarian problem approved the steps taken by the Soviet government to satisfy the aspirations of the peasantry in accordance with the
principles of the Socialist Revolutionary program—and enjoined continued adherence to these principles. The resolution on the Ukraine
—then a burning question because of the conflict between the
Sovnarkom and the Rada—recognized the full right of self-determination, even to the extent of separation, but demanded free passage
for Soviet troops in striking at the nucleus of counterrevolution on
the Don. With the right's obstruction removed, the left could get
back to its favorite scapegoat, the Executive Committee, and it threw
the book at that body, accusing it of consorting with the class enemy,

prolonging the war, supporting the "criminal adventure" of June 18, betraying the peasantry in its quest for the land, delaying the Second Congress, stifling the voice of rural Russia at the most crucial moment of the October Revolution, and striving to make the peasantry a counterrevolutionary force opposed to the urban workers. Having overlooked nothing in this indictment, the left confirmed the deposition of the Executive Committee and elected a new one, equally large and unwieldy, from which 108 members, 81 of them Left SR's and 20 Bolsheviks, were detailed to sit on the supreme soviet organ of the republic. Such were the major actions of the left in its separate congress.[106]

The right, in its half-congress, exhibited a certain degree of restraint in styling itself the "Second All-Russian Congress—Part Standing for the Defense of the Constituent Assembly." It organized with Chernov in the chair and proceeded to deal in its way with the same basic questions that confronted the left. It strove to counteract the effect of Lenin's land decree by trying to convince the peasantry that the Constituent Assembly alone could give full body to the SR agrarian program, and by fanning suspicion of Bolshevism as the party that pinned its hopes on large-scale economies and the agricultural laborer class while stubbornly resisting the equal-use, right-to-land-through-labor tenets of the Populist faith. The right (or center) sought in every way to link the cause of the rural toilers with the Constituent Assembly, stressing the presence of a large peasant majority in that body and its sole ability to solve the land and peace problems in the manner desired by the peasantry; for by now it was clear that only if the rural masses came out actively in defense of the assembly could it be saved and the fruits of the SR electoral triumph preserved. In respect to peace the SR's at this congress moved forward ever so slightly. They complained of the inadequate support given the new Russia by other peoples, recognizing for the first time the obstruction of the possessing classes of all countries, and not just those of the Central Powers, and they "took into account" the fact of a separate armistice. But they hastened to add that this was a step which injured rather than helped the cause

[106] *Ibid.*, pp. 336–40; Gaisinski, *Bor'ba za krest'ianstvo*, pp. 238–39, 245, 247–48, 263–64.

of a general peace and that it would lead to a separate peace fraught with the possibility of a new war and the economic enslavement of Russia. The proceedings of this congress showed that they were as dead set as ever against a separate peace and left up in the air the question of what they would do if the general armistice to be proposed by the Constituent Assembly should be turned down by the Allies. Whether they would rescind the separate armistice, as they undoubtedly longed to do in their hearts, was something about which they refused to say a word.

In respect to the Ukrainian question the right congress assumed a position of sheer demagoguery. These foes of separatism now suddenly came forward as champions of the Ukrainian Rada in the conflict with the people's commissars, asserting, in blind disregard of manifestations of a separatist spirit in Kiev since long before the October Revolution, that its moves to sever ties with Great Russia were a consequence of the establishment of the Soviet regime in St. Petersburg,[107] but giving no indication of how they themselves would have coped with this problem had they been responsible for the government of Russia. In their eagerness to team up with any force hostile to Bolshevism, the SR's were spared the embarrassment of joining hands with Kaledin's movement on the Don by the discovery that it was not so much directed against Bolshevism as toward the continued repression of the non-Cossack part of the population.

The Executive Committee elected by the May Congress had been a millstone around the neck of the moderates as long as they formed one body with the extremists. In order not to risk defeat in the election of a permanent presidium, the SR caucus had decided to put up an entirely new list of names in which not one member of the Executive Committee would figure and to back Chernov for the chairmanship as one who would be acceptable, it was thought, to the Left SR's.[108] With the split in the congress it was not necessary to go through with this self-denying ordinance, and the Executive Com-

---

[107] A member of the Central Committee writing in the official organ at this very time recognized the element of chauvinism that had always been present in the policy of the Rada and spoke of the struggle which SR workers in the Ukraine had been forced to wage against excesses of the national spirit. See I. Prilezhaev, "Verolomnye moskali iz Smol'nago" (Faithbreaking Muscovites from Smolny), *Delo Naroda*, No. 229 (December 10, 1917).

[108] *Volia Naroda*, No. 186 (December 6, 1917).

mittee emerged from behind the cloud to bask in the favor of its own faction. Some of its members, including wheel horses like Bykhovski, Martiushin, Rakitnikov, Gurevich, Ovchinnikov, and the patriarch Chaikovski, were elected along with new blood from the provinces to the new Executive Committee which this half-congress set up parallel to the one chosen by the left. The real face of the right or "center," as it insisted on being called, was shown in the clean bill of health voted the retiring committee, with only now and then a gentle slap on the wrist for "sometimes" having lagged behind the demands of the revolutionary peasantry, or for having failed to display enough energy in the matter of turning over privately owned lands to the care of the land committees. These timid reproaches were perhaps inserted to gain Chernov's acquiescence in a record that should have been more offensive to him, because pitched even further to the right of center, than the policy of the Gotz-Zenzinov faction in the Central Committee, against which he had continually struggled. But either out of deference to the precarious position of the moderates, which made it inadvisable to rock the boat, or because this half-congress was what the Left SR's said it was—more right than center and hence not subject to his control—Chernov raised no objection even to a blanket endorsement of the peace policy of the Executive Committee, which had followed the line of the First Congress in "indignantly" rejecting a separate peace and had failed to further the cause of a general peace only because of "objective conditions." (Was it because of an objective condition that the committee had backed Tereshchenko and his watered down version of Miliukov's program?) Once more Chernov had an opportunity to give a new turn to the course of his party and once more he capitulated to its gravediggers. With the action on the Executive Committee the moderate half of the disrupted congress concluded its labors.[109]

The left half finished a day earlier than the right, adjourning on December 10. The congress that had not known how to keep from going on the shoals had spent ten days in fruitless though united labor and then a week more in fruitful but divided labor. In its wake

[109] Bykhovski, *Vserossiiskii Sovet Krest'ianskikh Deputatov*, pp. 340–46; Gaisinski, *Bor'ba za krest'ianstvo*, pp. 254–60.

it left a disintegrating peasant movement and two Executive Committees. Spiridonova decided not to put up with this situation—her terrorist past had accustomed her to swift and decisive action and, now that the Left SR's were a government party, she had the machinery of state at her disposal. So on December 11, the day the right adjourned, she signed an order to clear the premises of all members of that congress and of the former Executive Committee. Armed soldiers appeared to enforce the decree, and in this manner the headquarters of the peasant movement passed into the hands of her party. The dispossessed SR's sent a delegation the next day to arrange a modus vivendi until a new congress could be convened, but Spiridonova would not receive it and replied only in writing: "The presidium of the Executive Committee elected by the left part of the Second Soviet Congress of Peasant Deputies considers itself the embodiment of the majority will of said congress as determined by a series of votes on basic questions; the presidium considers it superfluous to enter into any further explanations." Spiridonova could have found an even shorter formula: "Woe to the vanquished!" Henceforth from cramped quarters in an abandoned hospital on a back street the old guard struggled under conditions of semilegality to keep some life in its organization, but with less and less success. The peasants' *Izvestiia* suspended publication in mid-December, the ties with the provinces weakened, as much from transportation difficulties as from official disfavor, and activity in general slackened until only a flicker of life remained in the once imposing organization.[110]

What was lost on the one side was not made up on the other. It was one thing to dispossess the SR command in Petersburg and quite another to take over its following in the provinces, not so much because of the active resistance of that following as because of its lapse into passivity. In other words, disunion did not simply divide the peasant movement but tended to destroy it in both its parts. The Left SR's did not succeed in claiming the inheritance of the PSR, partly because they had no legal title to it in the light of what had happened at the Second Congress, and partly because their ally did not want a strong peasant movement under any auspices. Observers

[110] Bykhovski, *Vserossiiskii Sovet Krest'ianskikh Deputatov*, pp. 347–48.

reported that the net result of the schism and of having two Executive Committees was a creeping paralysis in both. The web of organization was disintegrating. Personnel sent to the provinces spent its energy in agitation and counteragitation and personnel remaining in Petersburg devoted its time to general political questions, with the result that the practical work of maintaining a far-flung organization was neglected on every hand.[111] Worst of all was the effect of this bickering and confusion upon the peasantry itself. Already at the time of the breakup of the Extraordinary Congress Martiushin had warned, on the basis of observations in the provinces, of the evil consequences of the failure to understand what was going on.[112] Now, with the repetition of the fiasco on a grander scale and the much greater volume of charges and countercharges, the rural masses were more hopelessly at sea than ever. They failed to grasp the causes of the schism and had lost their bearings in the flood of manifestoes and recriminations stemming from the rival Executive Committees. Confusion bred frustration and frustration bred resignation.[113]

It was almost as if the two Populist parties were following the master plan of the Bolsheviks, which called for dividing the peasantry and turning it upon itself so that the sway of the proletariat should be unchallenged. For the Bolsheviks were the big winners of this second and last of the peasant congresses.[114] It had resulted in a drawn battle for the two Populist parties, which, under the circumstances, was equivalent to a defeat for both. For the peasantry itself it was a catastrophe, but for the Bolsheviks it could not have been more beneficial unless they had controlled it in their own right. With the new regime not yet firmly seated in the saddle and facing tasks that staggered the imagination, the congress had divested the SR's of the right to speak in the name of the rural toilers without conferring that right on the Left SR's. The enemy had been weakened, the ally strengthened, but not too much, and the way lay open for the Bol-

[111] *Delo Naroda*, No. 239 (December 22, 1917).

[112] Bykhovski, *Vserossiiskii Sovet Krest'ianskikh Deputatov*, p. 310.

[113] *Ibid.*, p. 348. Gaisinski's assertion (*Bor'ba za krest'ianstvo*, p. 266) that the "rank-and-file peasants understood the causes of the schism at this congress and sided wholly with the Bolsheviks and Left SR's" is merely another example of what happens to history at Communist hands.

[114] For the so-called Third Congress or Congresses, see below pp. 275-76, 440 ff.

sheviks to enter the Populist stronghold, dispatch the feuding defenders, and impose their will on a leaderless class. Meanwhile the
Second Congress had cloaked their power with some sort of peasant
sanction, which with their customary zeal for distortion they proceeded to blow up into a full-fledged endorsement. All official means
were employed to hound the rival body into oblivion while representing the Executive Committee elected by the left half-congress as
the embodiment of the peasants' will.

Why had the two Populist parties pursued their fratricidal struggle
to the end when they knew what the consequences of a split would
be and were in fact desirous of averting it? All the sources, regardless
of political coloration, with a single exception, agree that the quarrel
over the election of a presidium was merely the occasion for the
breakup of the congress and that the real reason was the deep-seated
difference of opinion regarding the Constituent Assembly.[115] But is
this a correct analysis, or did something else even more deep-seated
impel the kindred parties to engage in their duel to the death? The
Left SR's had never been as hostile to the Constituent Assembly as
the Bolsheviks and while it is true that the election returns were
making it clearer every day that the partisans of the soviet order
would not control the assembly, the main body of the Left SR's had
gone no further than to adopt a wait-and-see attitude, while the
Karelin wing still attached no reservations to its stand in support of
the assembly. It would seem, therefore, that the feeling in Left SR
circles was not strong enough to make them willing to wreck the
congress by an adamant stand on this issue. Now, if we examine the
program of the congress we find that the next order of business after
the matter of a permanent presidium was the question of war and
peace. In fact, the left took up this question and disposed of it on
December 5, the day following the secession of the right.

That is where the dog is buried, in the opinion of the author. True,
there is no supporting evidence beyond the mute testimony of the
agenda—except for one thing. In opening discussion on the peace
policy of the Soviet government, Spiridonova gave as the reason for

---

[115] Bykhovski, *Vserossiiskii Sovet Krest'ianskikh Deputatov*, pp. 331, 342;
Gaisinski, *Bor'ba za krest'ianstvo*, p. 252; In. Rakitnikova, "S Krest'ianskago
S"ezda" (From the Peasants' Congress), *Delo Naroda*, No. 228 (December 9,
1917).

the breach of the peasant front on the preceding day the steps that had been taken in the direction of peace, observing that the leaders of the right could never forgive the left-wing socialists their initiative in putting an end to the war.[116] The inference is that the right had been forestalled, and sought to take the initiative into its own hands.[117] Again, in the opinion of the author, it was not the initiative in the matter of peace that the right found intolerable but peace itself. The SR leaders had mustered their maximum strength in support of the resolution on the Constituent Assembly and had no assurance of being able to hold it on the next crucial vote. Going on with the war meant less to the peasant delegates than to the intellectuals who led them. Nothing could equal the patriotism in the abstract of these embattled intellectuals nor the intensity of their partisanship for Great Britain and especially for France. Rather than risk having a movement they had founded and fostered sanction steps pointing in the direction of a separate peace, they may have preferred to split the congress, regardless of consequences. Moreover, their consistently erroneous appraisal of the staying powers of Bolshevism would lead them to minimize the dangers of a divided movement. It may well have been, therefore, the impending vote on war and peace rather than the controversy over the Constituent Assembly or exasperation at the barren results of ten days of attempted cohabitation which provoked the schism. The war had divided the SR's in the first place and continued to divide them and everything associated with them. The war may have wrecked the Second Congress, and with it the peasant movement, even as it certainly wrecked, as a liberating movement, the revolution of which these were a part.

The hostility of the soldier element had made it impossible for the SR's to control the Second Congress. But what of the millions of ordinary peasants whom the congress had revealed as standing behind their party? Were they not the rock on which the soldiers' fury would spend itself, and did not their loyalty guarantee that in the long run the party would become once more the dominant factor in Russian political life? Even if the Constituent Assembly, the fruit of

[116] *Znamia Truda*, No. 89 (December 7, 1917).
[117] Gaisinski, *Bor'ba za krest'ianstvo*, p. 246.

its greatest triumph, should be "trampled under the heavy boots of an enraged soldiery," as Gotz feared, there were other ways in which a determined peasantry under skillful leadership could render untenable the power of a regime that was not to its liking. And when the SR's in their half of the congress rejected a proposal to address an appeal to the peasants against curtailing in the spring of 1918 the acreage sown to crops,[118] they may have been acting on an idea that seems to have been in Chernov's mind [119]—to starve the Soviet regime into submission. With a hostile Executive Committee in the field, backed by official favor, the SR's had lost their monopoly control of the peasant movement, but as long as the bulk of the provincial soviets, reflecting the will of the civilian peasantry, continued to back them, they remained a formidable force.

The state of the provincial soviets in the last two months of 1917 thus requires our attention. As always, it is not easy to follow developments outside the main centers of population, but enough material exists to disclose at least the base line of development in three regions of widely varying character: White Russia, where the peasantry lay under the shadow of the front; the central industrial region, where agriculture was intermingled with industry; and the black-earth region, where the rural population was least affected by extraneous influences. Most of the information concerns Minsk province in White Russia, Moscow province in the central region, and the provinces of Saratov and Voronezh in the black-earth zone.

The history of the peasant movement in White Russia is marked by vicissitudes which set it off from other parts of the country. Minsk seems to have been the only province in Russia where the Bolsheviks got to the peasants ahead of the SR's, assuming leadership at the first congress and placing their man, M. V. Frunze, later chief of the armed forces of the Soviet Union, at the head of the provincial soviet of peasants' deputies. By summer, however, the normal pattern had asserted itself and the July congress gave the SR's a majority, their leader, I. P. Nesterov, succeeding to Frunze's position. The sources say that the better-to-do peasants had taken things in hand, but as the sources are Communist and as they explain everything in terms of class conflict within the peasantry, this may or may not be true. But

[118] *Ibid.*, pp. 258–59.   [119] See above, pp. 236–37.

the coming of fall saw the trend reversed once more, with the Bolsheviks unfolding an intensive activity on behalf of their candidates for the Constituent Assembly. Immediate peace and Lenin's land decree were their chief talking points, and soldiers their most effective propagandists. The proximity of the front, in fact, was reckoned as the decisive influence, for nowhere did the burden of the war weigh more heavily or war weariness attain greater proportions than here immediately behind the firing line.[120] The villages were inundated with soldiers preaching the message of Bolshevism and in White Russia the peasants did not stand firm, as Chernov had predicted, but reelected their district soviets to bring these into line with what the soldiers were saying. Thus moderate SR's were ousted by extremist SR's or Bolsheviks. The process of replacement had gone so far by the time of the next provincial congress, November 18–20, that of 335 delegates only 8 voted in favor of the SR leader whom the preceding congress had chosen as soviet chairman. As the Left SR's had no ticket of their own, the congress unanimously called on the peasantry to back the Bolshevik candidates for the Constituent Assembly, and they did so in convincing fashion, giving that party 579,087 votes to 181,673 for the SR's,[121] a result that removes any doubt as to the right of this congress to speak for the class, despite the SR refusal to recognize its validity. The new soviet organ elected by this congress merged with its workers' and soldiers' counterparts, and the paramount influence of the PSR in this main part of White Russia had come to an end in country and city alike.[122]

In neighboring Vitebsk province the same forces must have been at work, reinforced by fifty agitators from the Bureau of Propaganda of the Military Revolutionary Committee in St. Petersburg. Vitebsk ranked second among the provinces of Russia in point of attention from Molotov's bureau.[123] It has not received as much attention in

[120] *Novaia Zhizn'*, No. 201 (December 14, 1917) (report of the Minsk correspondent).

[121] Radkey, *The Election to the Russian Constituent Assembly*, p. 78.

[122] Knorin, *Revoliutsiia i kontr-revoliutsiia v Belorussii*, I, 5–9, 47, 54–56, 61, 63; A. Kirzhnits, "Sto dnei sovetskoi vlasti v Belorussii" (A Hundred Days of Soviet Power in White Russia), *Proletarskaia Revoliutsiia*, LXXIV (III, 1928), 63–64; *Revoliutsiia 1917 goda*, VI, 172, 184.

[123] Trenogova, *Bor'ba petrogradskikh bol'shevikov za krest'ianstvo*, p. 125 (Table of Distribution, pp. 125–26; map facing p. 126).

revolutionary literature, however, being overshadowed by its larger neighbor; but since the Bolshevik success at the polls was only less impressive than in Minsk, the conclusion is inescapable that the SR grip on the agrarian movement must have been broken in the same manner and at about the same time.

A startling exception to the onward march of Bolshevism and the recession of Social Revolutionism in White Russia is to be noted in the case of the third province, Mogilev, where the SR's seem to have been as strong in November as previously, electing twelve men to the Constituent Assembly against only one for the Bolsheviks.[124] No explanation is offered for this discrepancy (Bolshevik sources can be as silent as Socialist Revolutionary in the face of embarrassing circumstances, and while much is said about the factors producing success in Minsk, nothing is said about the reasons for failure in Mogilev). Minsk and Vitebsk lay immediately behind the front, and Mogilev behind them. The soldier influence would not have been so all-pervasive, it is true, but neither would it have been negligible, with General Headquarters at Mogilev-on-the-Dnieper. Furthermore, Smolensk province was still further removed from the front and yet it yielded a Bolshevik majority. The network of peasant soviets in Mogilev is said to have been the handiwork of Golman, an effective organizer of great personal popularity,[125] who may have laid a more solid foundation for partisan power than less gifted workers in the other two provinces. It seems safe to conclude, also, that Mogilev was a garden which the Bolsheviks did not try overly hard to cultivate. Molotov's bureau, for example, sent thither only nine agitators as against fifteen to Minsk and fifty to Vitebsk.[126]

Whatever the reason, the peasants of Mogilev province continued to follow the SR banner after those of Minsk and Vitebsk had gone over to the extremists, and more to the Bolsheviks than to the Left SR's. At the Extraordinary Peasants' Congress in November the representatives of the Minsk and Vitebsk executive committees had sided with the SR's,[127] creating the illusion of support without any sub-

---

[124] See list of provinces in Sviatitski, "Fraktsiia P.S.-R. Uchreditel'nago Sobraniia," *Partiinyia Izvestiia,* No. 5 (January 20, 1918), pp. 32–36.

[125] Bykhovski, *Vserossiiskii Sovet Krest'ianskikh Deputatov,* pp. 170–74.

[126] Trenogova, *Bor'ba petrogradskikh bol'shevikov za krest'ianstvo,* pp. 125–26.

[127] Bykhovski, *Vserossiiskii Sovet Krest'ianskikh Deputatov,* p. 293, n. 2.

stance behind it. We do not know whether the fiction was maintained at the Second Congress or whether these superior soviet organs had already been brought into line with the changed mood of their peasant constituents. In any event the SR's could count on only a part of their former support in White Russia in the struggle to keep their heads above water, and the chief reason for their loss of ground in this locality was that same soldier element which at the Second Congress had denied them a renewal of their mandate for leadership of the All-Russian agrarian movement.

The central industrial region around Moscow could be expected to be less under the boot of the soldiery but on the other hand it would have a strong proletarian influence equally inimical to SR leadership in the village. The peasantry of this cradle of the Great Russian nationality, hard put to wrest a living from the indifferent soil, had either itself become enmeshed in industrial occupations or had relatives who worked in factories, making it unusually sensitive to urban developments.[128] Industrial establishments were not confined to the cities; they studded the countryside, and peasants and proletarians were all mixed up with one another. In Moscow province the main propagandist force was not the intellectuals but the workers themselves. Scores, even hundreds of them were sent out by factory committees or local soviets to beat the bushes for Bolshevism.[129] The soldier influence, however, must not be discounted, even here. Besides the swollen garrison at Moscow there were sizable concentrations of troops at Mozhaisk and other points in Moscow, Vladimir, and Kostroma provinces.

It will help to bring things into clearer focus if we take a cross section of Moscow province and examine developments in two *uezds* or districts for which detailed accounts are available. Volokolamsk *uezd*, in bygone centuries the citadel of Byzantine orthodoxy under Joseph Sanin, had become in 1917 the banner district of Social Revolutionism, with the strongest and most numerous organization in the entire province. It was a peasant *uezd*, uncontaminated by factory influence save in one canton (volost) where there was a textile mill.

[128] For an informative sketch of conditions in Klin *uezd* see *Moskovskaia provintsiia v semnadtsatom godu*, pp. 161–64, 167.

[129] See article of N. Meshcheriakov in *Izvestiia moskovskago soveta*, No. 217 (November 29, 1917).

The SR's had a firm nest in the local teaching staff, which disseminated the idea that the Bolsheviks were German agents if not simple bandits. The "social chauvinism" of the SR intellectuals clashed with the "defeatism" of the Bolshevik organizers, and the war was the main subject of controversy. The Bolsheviks, of course, went after the textile workers in the first instance, and having won them over, as invariably was the case, proceeded to use the mill as the base for conversion of the peasantry. Presently the SR's split and the left wing made common cause with the Bolsheviks, helping to hollow out the once imposing edifice of SR strength until by the October Revolution that party could not offer the armed resistance which the Bolsheviks were prepared to encounter in overawing the soviet organs still in SR hands. The peasants received the Bolshevik emissaries cordially and hearkened to the decrees they read, particularly the land decree, sometimes asking the protesting SR's to leave the village assemblies. The former political influence lingered on in the liberalized zemstvos or local organs of self-government until a soviet district congress in January of 1918, said to have been well attended by the peasants, put an end to such bodies and even approved the dissolution of the Constituent Assembly. The Populist intellectuals, here as everywhere, had clung to the Allied cause at the cost of surrendering the Russian peasantry to the internal enemy, and the peasants, like obedient horses, had suffered the Bolshevik halter to be fastened around their necks. Even those who had registered as members of the PSR had no clear understanding of what they were doing, and the sort of backing they gave their party was of one piece with the low level of political consciousness. Whether in signing up with the SR's or, later, in swinging over to the Bolsheviks, the peasants were governed more by instinct than by conviction or conscience.[130] Such was the mournful end of the struggle for freedom in Volokolamsk *uezd*, where once the SR's had seemed to have everything their way.[131]

They had been no less firmly intrenched in Mozhaisk *uezd*, only to suffer a similar fate. Here again was a peasant district in which there

---

[130] Reminiscences of the peasant E. K. Kuzmichev, in *1917 god v derevne*, pp. 211–13.

[131] *Moskovskaia provintsiia v semnadtsatom godu*, pp. 14, 117–27, 154, 156, 159; see also Mukhin's report to the preliminary conference of members of the Fourth Congress of the PSR in *Delo Naroda*, No. 220 (November 30, 1917).

were but a few hundred workers. The SR's had been organized, as so often was the case, by an army physician, whose strongly defensist views were in harmony with those of the peasants, one of whom declared he would kill his own son if he deserted. Absurd rumors, such as the one that Kornilov and Lenin were comrades and both came from Germany, found ready acceptance. The SR's dominated all public bodies and Bolshevism had not risen as yet from an individual to a corporate status. Only one troublesome feature marred this idyllic scene, for which the Provisional Government itself was responsible—a garrison of elephantine proportions. It seems scarcely credible, even by Russian standards of ineptitude, that the sleepy provincial town of Mozhaisk should be host to 20,000 disgruntled reservists on top of a big garrison in Moscow not many miles away, but there they were, becoming more and more receptive to Bolshevism and passing the contagion on to the civilian population, which would have contracted it in any event from other soldiers returning from the front. By October, Bolshevized peasants were already in evidence—not many, but some—and thereafter the pressure from the soldiery greatly increased, until by the end of the year only the kulak stratum and the monarchist peasants held out against the new order. The soldiers had cracked open the village, the shift of the peasants had given the Bolsheviks control of the district soviet, and this in turn dissolved the democratic organs of self-government. By the new year the fortress had fallen.[132]

Elsewhere in Moscow province the task was made easier by the presence of an industrial proletariat whose efforts were conjoined to those of the military. The situation in October was so favorable to Bolshevism that the SR's could not think of taking up arms as they did in the city.[133] For the Bolsheviks the normal order of things was reversed, with the province coming to the aid of the city instead of the city to the aid of the province, as would be expected in a proletarian revolution. The middle class within the city proved far more resistant to Bolshevism than the peasantry without. The lesson of October was repeated in the elections for the Constituent Assembly, when the Bolsheviks beat the SR's much more decisively in the

[132] *Moskovskaia provintsiia v semnadtsatom godu*, pp. 102–14, 155.
[133] *Ibid.*, pp. 5, 10–12, 14.

province than they beat the Kadets in the city. The SR's had not realized how badly they had slipped or what inroads had been made on their peasant following, and were disheartened by the better than two-to-one margin for their opponents. Seeking to explain what had happened, the delegate from Moscow told his part of the Second All-Russian Peasants' Congress that the election had been held under the fresh impression of bloodshed in the city. "Drunk with the destruction of Moscow, the Bolshevik garrison scattered over the countryside with Lenin's decrees in their hands and slander on their lips. That explains, to a large extent, the unexpected success of the Bolsheviks in our province." [134] But a good deal of spadework had preceded this final burst of activity. The SR's were not the only sufferers; everything was flattened out before it. The inability of religion to curb the instincts of man, especially greed, is seen in the results of the poll at Guslitsy, one of the most backward areas, where the Old Believers earlier in the year had organized a boycott of the election to the innocuous cantonal council (zemstvo) on the ground that it was a trick of the Anti-Christ, only to have Guslitsy vote, and vote Bolshevik, in the November election.[135]

Here in Moscow, as in Minsk, the SR's owed their continued control of the provincial peasants' soviet to the fact that it had not recently been reelected, and in such instances the opposition was justified in saying that their support at the Extraordinary and Second All-Russian Congresses was fictitious. The Moscow Bolsheviks announced that the peasants' soviet must be reelected under the auspices of the workers' and soldiers' soviet in order to bring it into harmony with the will of the peasants as revealed in the election of the Constituent Assembly.[136] The intent was quite clearly not only to harmonize a representative organ with the changed outlook of its constituents, and eliminate SR influence in the process, but even more to subordinate the rural to the urban soviets, the peasantry to the proletariat. Accordingly, a new peasants' congress for the whole province was convened on December 17–18, at which the Bolsheviks and Left SR's, acting in such close agreement that it is not possible

[134] *Delo Naroda*, No. 231 (December 13, 1917).
[135] *Moskovskaia provintsiia v semnadtsatom godu*, p. 153.
[136] *Izvestiia moskovskago soveta*, No. 214 (November 25, 1917).

to determine their respective strength,[137] held a better than two-to-one advantage over the SR's. On the second day the SR's bolted when the congress expressed a clear preference for the soviets over the Constituent Assembly, but enough of them had been present, and in about the same proportion as their strength in the general election, to establish the authentic character of the congress. The old executive committee gave way to one nominated by the victorious bloc, and the congress approved the fusion of the peasants' with the workers' and soldiers' soviets.[138] So ended the SR reign in Moscow province.

The situation in other provinces of the central industrial region bears a close resemblance to that in Moscow province. In all of them the SR's had been in a dominant position outside of the towns and in all of them this position was now being undermined. The SR's still stood at the head of the peasants' soviets in Tver, Vladimir, and Kostroma, and controlled the delegations from these provinces at the Extraordinary Congress [139] and presumably also at the Second All-Russian Congress, but Tver and Vladimir yielded decisive majorities for the Bolsheviks in the election of the Constituent Assembly, and Kostroma but a slender margin for the SR's. The local soviets were passing into the hands of the enemy, either by will of the peasants themselves or, where they were balky, by force and distortion on the part of the authorities. The peasants' congress in the Alexandrovsk *uezd* of Vladimir province which opened on November 8 turned against the SR's and placed the Bolsheviks in power, giving its sanction to the October Revolution and voting to merge with the workers' and soldiers' soviets. Reports from the localities disclosed that nearly all of the peasants had decided to vote the Bolshevik ticket.[140] A similar congress in Pereslavl *uezd* on October 26, however, had remained steadfast in its allegiance to the SR's,

---

[137] The Bolsheviks seem to have had an edge in this extensively industrialized province. The presidium of a congress usually reflected the ratio of strength of at least the parties in the dominant bloc, and in this instance it consisted of three Bolsheviks and two Left SR's. There were around seventy delegates, of whom upwards of forty were members of the extremist bloc and about twenty were SR's.

[138] *Revoliutsiia 1917 goda*, VI, 362, 367–68; *Delo Naroda*, Nos. 236, 238 (December 19, 21, 1917).

[139] Bykhovski, *Vserossiiskii Sovet Krest'ianskikh Deputatov*, p. 293, n. 2.

[140] *1917-i god vo vladimirskoi gubernii*, pp. 124, 126.

causing the Pereslavl Workers' and Soldiers' Soviet to "take steps" to hold a new congress, one of which was the organization of cantonal soviets under Bolshevik control.[141] In the Murom district the town soviet called a peasants' congress over the head of the peasants' soviet. The SR chairman protested this action as illegal [142] but was powerless to prevent the usurpation. Passing from Vladimir province to its neighbor, Kostroma, we find that a similar process of wresting the local soviets from SR control culminated in a victory for the opposition at the December congress, which ended the reign of the "right" SR's by electing a new executive committee of thirteen Left SR's and six Bolsheviks.[143] The ratio indicates that in a province where the proletariat was much less numerous and its influence correspondingly weaker, radicalism tended to run in a Left SR instead of a Bolshevik channel.

The work of undercutting and destroying the SR position in the central industrial region had been greatly facilitated by the presence of a numerous and aggressive proletariat imbued with the Bolshevik spirit. A rule with few if any exceptions was that remoteness from industrial development spelled persistence of SR influence.[144] But if there were communities where working-class agitation had little or no effect, there were none where the soldiers did not make themselves felt.[145] From every locality some unwilling sons had marched off to this unwanted war and now they were coming back with rifles in their hands and rage in their hearts against anything or anyone connected with the war, from the tsar and his generals to the socialist opponents of a separate peace. An observer, speaking of conditions in the rural parts of Kostroma province, said that scenes reminiscent of tsarist times had been enacted: soldiers arrived in the village and behaved in challenging fashion, going about armed and resorting freely to threats.[146] The soldiers were the backbone of radicalism in

[141] *Ibid.*, pp. 114, 132.   [142] *Ibid.*, pp. 123, 128.

[143] *Izvestiia TsIK i petrogradskago soveta*, No. 259 (December 23, 1917), p. 6.

[144] For a concrete example see my book, *The Election to the Russian Constituent Assembly*, p. 25.

[145] See the brief report from Vichuga and two other villages of Kostroma province under the heading, "Iz provintsii" (From the Provinces), *Izvestiia TsIK i petrogradskago soveta*, No. 259, p. 11.

[146] See report to the preliminary conference of members of the Fourth SR Congress, *Delo Naroda*, No. 220 (November 30, 1917).

rural Russia. As a result of their efforts the Bolsheviks harvested votes in unlikely places, but of much greater significance was the physical power derived by the extremist parties from their support.

If the SR's had rough sledding in White Russia because of the proximity of the front, and in the heart of Great Russia because of industrialization, then they should have had things their own way in the central black-earth and Volga regions, where their roots went deepest and the peasant population was denser and more homogeneous than anywhere else outside of India and China. Here, it would seem, they certainly should have kept their hold on the peasant movement. The November election seemed to indicate that they were doing just that. The Bolsheviks had beaten the SR's in Minsk, 579,087 to 181,673, and in Moscow, 337,492 to 153,458, but in Saratov province the SR's beat them, 564,250 to 225,000, and buried them in Voronezh, 875,300 to 151,517.[147] As most of our material for the black-earth region bears on these latter two provinces, we shall look into each and see how it was that the fruits of these splendid victories shriveled and died on the vine.

Hardly anywhere had the Socialist Revolutionaries been so firmly entrenched as in Saratov, the cradle and hearth of their movement. Accounts differ as to whether partisan allegiance was more than skin-deep—one man says that his village had no understanding for political shadings and acted by instinct [148]—but all agree that in so far as the peasantry had accepted any political guidance it was all but exclusively Socialist Revolutionary. To some extent this was due to the fact that the Social Democrats had made no effort to cultivate the peasantry until after the October Revolution. But the Bolsheviks had given plenty of attention to the Saratov garrison, reversing its initially overwhelming sentiment in favor of their adversaries, and from it as a base, with Lenin's land decree and the barren record of the SR's as their talking points, they launched a campaign to conquer the village. The Saratov SR's, who are described as being animated by a "dull and bovine hatred" of Bolshevism, fought back to the best of their ability, though weakened by the schism in their

---

[147] The returns from Voronezh are complete and from Minsk substantially so, but for each of the other two provinces a whole *uezd* is missing.

[148] Reminiscences of A. V. Shabanov, in *1917 god v derevne*, pp. 124–25.

ranks, which seems to have drawn off rather more strength than in the average black-earth province. They incited the populace against the Bolsheviks, raising in Atkarsk *uezd* the familiar cry that they were German agents and seeking to persuade peasants to withhold grain from the Saratov market in order to starve out the center of sedition—a maneuver that attained enough success for the Bolsheviks to answer it by introducing the class war into the village.[149] The response of the Saratov peasantry, while not as vigorous as the SR's might have hoped, was nevertheless more spirited than in other regions. Individual soldier agitators had earlier been lynched like common horse thieves;[150] with their appearance in droves such direct action became less feasible, and peasant displeasure expressed itself in indignation meetings and threats of social ostracism. In Fedorovka village the peasants resolved "not to receive into their midst those mad sons and brothers from the army who had joined the Bolsheviks and betrayed their country."[151] One always has to be wary, in cases like this, of intellectuals speaking through peasant mouths, but it seems quite likely that these words represented the true sentiment of a village which gave only 58 out of 847 votes to the Bolshevik Party.[152] Other peasant communities merely reaffirmed their faith in the PSR and their mistrust of its adversary.

To coordinate the resistance movement the SR's called a new congress of peasants' soviets at the provincial level. The members of this congress were chosen by the volost committees or soviets. Although the SR's controlled the congress they had to make certain concessions to the temper of the times. They acknowledged the error of the Provisional Government and the need for a speedy peace—in agreement with the Allied powers. The Bolsheviks did their best to disrupt this congress and then, to offset its effects, got up one of their own. Making skillful use of soldier-peasants as propagandists

---

[149] Antonov-Saratovski, *Pod stiagom proletarskoi bor'by*, I, 133–34, 160–61, 213 ff.; *1917 god v Saratove*, pp. 78–82.

[150] Antonov-Saratovski, *Pod stiagom proletarskoi bor'by*, I, 223.

[151] Report of Inna Rakitnikova, *Delo Naroda*, No. 215 (November 21, 1917).

[152] Radkey, *The Election to the Russian Constituent Assembly*, p. 68. Although Rakitnikova does not mention the *uezd* in which the village was located, it is probably the large settlement by that name in Khvalynsk *uezd*, for which, by rare fortune, the vote is available.

and parading their virtue in having delegates chosen directly by the peasants in village meetings—the purpose being to bypass the volost soviets—they assembled a pliant congress, three-quarters Bolshevik and one-quarter Left SR, which did their bidding in all respects.[153] It had been their contention that the soviets no longer reflected the will of the peasantry, since many had been elected before October 25, but one would have to know more about the village meetings than we are told to judge whether the Bolsheviks got their delegates through the conscious desire of the peasants or by manipulation, cajolery, and intimidation.

In any event, the Bolsheviks with the aid of this congress had cloaked their authority with a semblance of peasant approval. The wolf had put on a fleece, and now it moved on the fold. The rural organs of self-government, elective bodies, land committees, and soviet organs were all either abolished or purged of their former personnel, stripping the SR's of every last office of power. One after another the weapons were struck from their hands, without evoking any flare-up from their rural following. The peasants had talked of forming armed bands to defend their rights, of shutting Bolshevik agitation out of their districts, of "arresting these criminals," if any appeared in the villages, intent upon seizing power.[154] Yet they did nothing. Either they were too inert and inchoate, too doughlike and soft, or they had been overawed by the soldier missionaries of Bolshevism, or their fighting spirit had been impaired by the land decree that Lenin had issued—why resist a regime that gave them the land? Yet if the yokels had inspected more closely the proceedings of the Bolshevik-dominated congress, and if they had understood something of Marxian theory, they might have discerned what lay in the offing in two attitudes of the Bolshevik leaders— their obvious disinclination to do anything about forming a peasant "red guard," and their tender solicitude for the agricultural laborers on the estates of the nobility.[155] But the peasants, for all their

---

[153] Antonov-Saratovski, *Pod stiagom proletarskoi bor'by*, I, 222–30; Gaisinski, *Bor'ba za krest'ianstvo*, pp. 174–75.

[154] Report of Inna Rakitnikova, *Delo Naroda*, No. 215 (November 21, 1917).

[155] Antonov-Saratovski, *Pod stiagom proletarskoi bor'by*, I, 230, 303. His Bolshevism had not stifled the Russian frankness of this author.

religious background, could not recognize a cloven hoof when they saw one, and quite failed to sense the new technique of which they were to be the victims: today the candy, tomorrow the stick.

The Bolsheviks hastened to set the capstone on their triumph by combining the peasants' soviets with the workers' and soldiers', thereby securing to the more articulate class the hegemony that in their eyes was its due. The Saratov SR's, with more foresight than some other sections of the PSR, had always resisted a fusion.[156] The Left SR's raised no objections—the Bolsheviks had their way in all key matters. Saratov province lay at their feet. The "impregnable stronghold" of Social Revolutionism had first been invested, then sapped and destroyed. In White Russia and the Moscow region the Bolsheviks had actually won over the majority of the rural population, as attested in a general election. It is difficult to believe they had done so in this instance. And yet, to all practical intents and purposes, the result was the same. What was the secret of their success? The soldiers, of course, here and everywhere else.

Voronezh outranked even Saratov on the scale of SR influence. It was the only province of Russia, besides Samara, where that party claimed one hundred thousand members. At first there was no element of the population for which it was not the mouthpiece: workers and soldiers followed its banner in the towns, and its writ was law in the rural areas. It dominated alike the elective organs of government and the soviets, which in this province were merged into one general organization instead of being separated into workers' and soldiers' soviets and peasants' soviets, as in Saratov. But after the July Days the garrison in the city swung over to Bolshevism and by October the workers had either gone the same way or become Left SR's, so that power passed to the extremist bloc with the aid of a machine gun regiment. The SR's, seeing that they were fighting a losing battle in the provincial center, detached the peasants' section from the united soviet, erected it into a separate organization, and prepared to make a stand with the peasant mass behind them. The leader of the Voronezh SR's and chairman of the peasants' soviet, K. S. Sopliakov, who preferred to be known as Klim Burevoi, was himself a thoroughgoing revolutionary, somewhat to

[156] *Ibid.*, pp. 229–30, 265; Gaisinski, *Bor'ba za krest'ianstvo*, pp. 175–76.

the left of Chernov, with enough radicalism in his make-up to appeal to peasants who might otherwise have felt attracted to the Left SR's. At any rate the Voronezh party members went into battle with their ranks still substantially intact and with the conviction that they were defending the cause of several millions of peasants against a group of usurpers who in fact and by choice represented only a small urban element. Thus they displayed considerable fighting spirit as they cast about for "muzhik means" of bringing the cities to their senses.[157]

To mobilize their support and demonstrate their hold on the rural populace, the SR's called the third provincial congress of peasants' soviets (November 21–23). It was a mammoth affair with 552 delegates in attendance, 35 of whom were Bolsheviks and 3 Left SR's, one a Menshevik, one a Popular Socialist or Trudovik (Kerenski's group in the Fourth Duma), 24 nonpartisans, and 487 Socialist Revolutionaries.[158] With their customary shamelessness the Bolsheviks denounced their rivals for having perverted the will of the peasantry,[159] and one of their leaders says in his memoirs that the representation at the congress was dubious and in some cases stacked, but gives no evidence to support his charge.[160] The first Voronezh peasants' congress in April had contained a sprinkling of clergy and a fair number of village intellectuals; the second or July congress, however, had already been almost purely a peasant affair, with not a single priest among the more than 600 delegates and only a handful of intellectuals.[161] There seems no reason to doubt that the November congress was as representative a peasant body as could be gotten together. Neither the Bolsheviks nor the Left SR's had as yet made any impression on the dense mass of the Voronezh peasantry, centrist SR in its outlook or else politically unorganized.

The congress hotly condemned the October Revolution and all its works. It demanded the dissolution of all military revolutionary committees and the conveyance of all power to the Constituent As-

---

[157] *1917i god v Voronezhskoi gubernii*, pp. 121 ff.   [158] *Ibid.*, pp. 148–49.
[159] *Ibid.*, p. 159.
[160] I. Vrachev, "Oktiabr'skaia revoliutsiia v Voronezhe (Zametka uchastnika)" (The October Revolution in Voronezh [Notes of a Participant]), *Proletarskaia Revoliutsiia*, XXXIII (X, 1924), 190.
[161] *Sovety krest'ianskikh deputatov*, I, Part II, 59–60.

sembly. There was nothing indecisive about the vote: 450 to 30 with 19 abstentions. The "broad masses" of this fertile heartland of Russia —it was no exaggeration to speak of the Voronezh peasantry in these terms—had repudiated the new order, and V. Kobytchenko had rubbed salt in the wound with a "flaming speech" which brought matters to the verge of civil war—or so it seemed. The faces of the Bolsheviks may have been red but they were not greatly perturbed by these bucolic blasts, for when propaganda failed they were always in the position of being able to say, with Goethe's *Erlkönig:*

Und bist Du nicht willig, so brauch' ich Gewalt!

In fact, it was not necessary to say anything—the soldiers acted for them, spontaneously, without prompting. Fed up with admonishments from village "fathers" to their erring "children" in the army and enraged by Kobytchenko's oratory, the soldiers descended on the congress. Part of them rounded up the public outside the theater where the sessions were being held and drove them all, men, women, and children, with shots into the hall, while the rest burst onto the floor of the congress and began to beat the delegates with fists and rifle butts, shouting, "We will show you bastards how fathers and children are divided!" Some of the prominent SR's came off badly, and Kobytchenko was sought after, high and low (the public had been driven into the hall so that he would not be able to slip through the soldiers' fingers). Before anything could come of the threats so liberally made to shoot up the congress, members of the local military revolutionary committee arrived and put a stop to the pogrom, but not until the Voronezh SR committee could telegraph to St. Petersburg that the congress had been "half broken up." [162]

This shattering experience showed what the SR's were up against in their struggle to hold on even to their black-earth patrimony. Of course, had the peasants stood firm, had they been willing to accept the blood sacrifice, they could have prevented the consolidation of the Soviet regime. But they did not stand firm, and could not, because their unity was less real than it seemed. The rock

[162] *Delo Naroda*, No. 220 (November 30, 1917); Lev L_____n, "Provintsial'nyia kartinki" (Scenes from the Provinces), *ibid.*, No. 228 (December 9, 1917); *1917i god v Voronezhskoi gubernii*, pp. 148–49.

looked solid but was inwardly seamed, and the water that trickled along the seams, preparing the rock for disintegration, sprang from the war. In the months of SR hegemony the only active element in the village had been the intellectuals and perhaps the kulaks, while the flower of the village manhood was away at the front. By fall the boys were coming home, and the political consequences of their return soon manifested themselves, as we have indicated. Voronezh may well have been the banner SR province, and Valuiki *uezd* the banner district in the province, with 20,000 party members or one fifth of the total number.[163] In Pogrom canton of this district the population is described as being politically adrift, with no attachment to any party and simply falling in with the SR predilections of the local committeemen, until soldiers returning from the front formed a core of opposition to the dominant clique, disputed with it in village meetings, and brought Bolshevism to the attention of the people by calling for immediate seizure of the estates and re-election of the committees. Up to that time the people are said not to have been aware of the existence of such a party.[164] In the village of Sinie Lipegi ("blue knolls"),[165] Nizhne-Devitsk *uezd*, a Bolshevik peasant back from the war by the name of Kochetov broke the monopoly of the SR's by setting himself up as chairman of the volost soviet. That organ already had a chairman who was an SR, so now there were two heads for one body. Each sought to simplify matters by arresting the other, but in the end Kochetov got rid of his rival and made over the committee, no doubt with the help of other armed men like himself. By December a local branch of the Bolshevik Party was being organized, and such was the effect of the educational work of the soldiers that during December and January of 1918 two hundred peasants from this one village are said to have joined the party.[166]

Here are two specific instances in which returning soldiers pried open the SR shell with bayonets and got to the soft flesh of the

[163] Alekseev, *Oktiabr' i grazhdanskaia voina v TsChO*, p. 38.
[164] Reminiscences of the peasant D. Bondarenko, in *1917 god v derevne*, pp. 80–82.
[165] A *lipiag* in the dialect of Tambov means a forested elevation, not necessarily of linden trees (see Dal's dictionary).
[166] Reminiscences of the peasant F. F. Kartashov, in *1917 god v derevne*, pp. 88–89. Kochetov was executed by the Cossacks in 1919, during the civil war.

peasant clam within. Though our information is fragmentary, the broader effects of such activity in the localities are readily illustrated. At first the only Bolshevik-minded villages were those in the neighborhood of Voronezh city,[167] a proletarian center of some consequence because of war industry and railroad shops, but with demobilization such villages could be found elsewhere and the peasantry as a whole, confused and intimidated, began to back away from the PSR without, of course, becoming Bolshevik. There is a bare statement to the effect that a peasants' congress in Bobrov *uezd* agreed to the soviet assumption of power [168] (presumably the town soviet of workers and soldiers). More definite and significant information comes from Zemliansk *uezd*, where a peasants' congress was held on December 12–13, three weeks after the eventful provincial congress discussed above. This *uezd* congress was well attended, 250 delegates being present. The presidium refused to allow a Bolshevik motion to be considered, and the delegates did not demur; but when an SR resolution bespeaking the sovereignty of the Constituent Assembly and demanding the exclusion (!) of Bolsheviks from that body came to a decision, only 50 votes were cast in its favor.[169] Here for once the true face of the Russian peasantry shows itself, free of partisan influence. The peasants for a brief moment were acting on their own, having emancipated themselves from SR tutelage without as yet having succumbed to Bolshevism; they were wavering between the two partisan influences and above all, with true muzhik caution, they were playing it safe, refusing to commit themselves to either side. And that in an *uezd* where the SR's claimed 10,000 members.

The Bolsheviks trumpeted the fall of the fortress when they convened a peasants' congress of their own at the end of December and proclaimed it to be the authentic voice of Voronezh province.[170] We are not told how it was put together and it is not necessary

---

[167] Vrachev, "Oktiabr'skaia revoliutsiia v Voronezhe," *Proletarskaia Revoliutsiia,* XXXIII (X, 1924), 184; *1917i god v Voronezhskoi gubernii,* pp. 124, 140, where two villages (Ivanovka and Latnoe) are cited, both in Voronezh *uezd.* However, one such village is mentioned in Zemliansk *uezd* (*1917i god v Voronezhskoi gubernii,* p. 141).

[168] *1917i god v Voronezhskoi gubernii,* p. 131.

[169] *Ibid.,* p. 160. Four-fifths of the congress abstained on this vote.

[170] *Proletarskaia Revoliutsiia,* XXXIII (X, 1924), 190–91.

to ask, for it was obviously a travesty with its 120 members, hardly a fifth of the number that had attended the third congress and less than half even of the Zemliansk *uezd* congress. One wonders why the dominant party bothered to put on this sorry spectacle and whom it fooled with the farce, yet it went solemnly ahead to cloak its actions with the sanction of this assembly of stooges. The SR's held a countercongress of unknown size in Valuiki. There was little they could do—they had no bayonets. Apparently the bulk of the peasantry sank into apathy, satisfied with the expropriation of the estates, while a considerable number turned to the Left SR's as a medium of political expression, making them for the first time a serious factor in the Central Black-Earth Region.[171] But neither group of SR's could stir a vigorous agrarian movement in opposition to the Communist government before both fell under its guns in the second half of 1918 and were shot to pieces. The Populist plant, however, had deep roots in the fertile chernozem and put forth shoots again when nourished by the excesses of Communism in its militant period. The agrarian movement that had failed to materialize in late 1917 and 1918, when it might have succeeded, came with a vengeance three years later, only to encounter coercive instruments forged in the fire of the civil war that were more than sufficient to deal with Antonov's and Kolesnikov's bands.

The fading away of their support in Voronezh and Saratov, their failure to hold even the strongest positions, meant that the SR's had been vanquished in the fight for the peasantry and were doomed to political extinction. How much ground they had lost in a short interval is seen in the episode of the so-called Third All-Russian Congress of Peasants' Soviets. Each of the Executive Committees growing out of the ruptured Second Congress undertook to freshen its mandate by convening a new congress, the left on January 12, 1918, and the right on January 8.[172] The left congress existed for but a single day before voting to merge with the Third All-Russian Congress of Workers' and Soldiers' Deputies then in session. Once more, and now for the last time, the Left SR's offered no objection to having the peasants' soviets yoked to the workers' and soldiers'

---

[171] Alekseev, *Oktiabr' i grazhdanskaia voina v TsChO*, pp. 34 ff.
[172] Actually they met on January 13 and 10, respectively.

in a single system. The right or SR congress had an equally short duration, but that was not by choice. Hardly had the three hundred-odd delegates assembled—the left congress drew over four hundred, but in the absence of information concerning the basis of representation a comparison would be meaningless—than an armed body of sailors and Red Guardsmen appeared to command their dispersal. The delegates tried fraternization, but after both sides had gone down on their knees to sing "Vechnaia Pamiat' " (Eternal Memory) and touching scenes had been enacted, the ban was enforced and the delegates had to leave the premises. The harried congress led a clandestine existence for a week longer, drew up a declaration of protest and a set of minutes, and then disbanded. Maria Spiridonova blocked the reading of the declaration on the floor of the official congress. She was like a dragon at the door and displayed "particular intolerance and fanaticism" in suppressing the opposition, going so far as to order the sequestration of funds coming in by mail to the SR Executive Committee. Denied access to its premises, with its archives confiscated and its funds shut off, that committee dragged out a precarious existence until spring, then turned up its toes and died.[173]

The broad stream of the peasant movement running through the months from March to November had flowed into the swamp of the Second All-Russian Congress, from which issued two smaller streams, the one on the right ending in sand, the one on the left merging with the mainstream of the October Revolution. Henceforth the peasants' movement had no corporate identity. The Left SR's had not striven to maintain that identity in the soviet system; the SR's had tried but had failed. The peasants themselves remained inactive. Instructions drafted for the guidance of delegates to the Third Congress (right) had proclaimed the readiness of their constituents to rise en masse in support of the Constituent Assembly if the congress could not protect it.[174] But this threat represented nothing more

[173] Rakitnikova, *Kak russkoe krest'ianstvo borolos' za Uchreditel'noe Sobranie,* pp. 45–58; Bykhovski, *Vserossiiskii Sovet Krest'ianskikh Deputatov,* pp. 346, 352–55, 362, and Appendix, Nos. 30–32, pp. 417–19; Gaisinski, *Bor'ba za krest'-ianstvo,* pp. 265–66. Further information on these congresses will be found in ch. 8.

[174] Rakitnikova, *Kak russkoe krest'ianstvo borolos' za Uchreditel'noe Sobranie,* p. 55.

than the vaporings of the intellectuals who wrote the instructions. There was no rising to protect either the assembly or the congress. And there could be none because, as we have seen, the provincial support of the PSR was dissolving.

There were a number of reasons why the SR's lost their fight for the peasantry. For one thing, their peasant empire had rested on shallow foundations. A certain political tradition had been created, particularly in the black-earth region, but it had only relative and not intrinsic strength, being derived from the absence of any other tradition rather than from a tempering process in the fire of competition. There was an undetermined number of peasants who were dyed-in-the-wool partisans, but most members of the class could feel only a perfunctory loyalty to the PSR, simply because political conditions in the past had not permitted the development of a deeper loyalty. Another factor was the split in the party, draining it of much of its vitality and turning the energies of Socialist Revolutionaries against one another instead of permitting them to be directed against the common foe. So bitter did the internecine struggle become, in fact, that the Left SR's made common cause with the Bolsheviks and allowed them to annex the rural to the urban soviets, thereby destroying the basis for an independent peasant movement that would have enabled them to retain some bargaining power in dealing with their voracious ally. Lenin's agrarian policy, combining great flexibility in tactics with a Byzantine rigidity of dogma, was another weighty factor. It robbed the peasantry of any incentive to oppose the new regime while it was still vulnerable and unsteady, denaturing the SR-Bolshevik quarrel of economic content and leaving only abstractions which meant nothing to the peasantry. At the same time it left Lenin or his heirs free to come back on the orphaned class with the instruments of a consolidated state in an effort to deprive it of the fruits of this initial and purely tactical departure from Bolshevik theory. Even at the SR peasants' congress voices had been raised in favor of working with the other side, since both would give land to the peasantry.[175]

Yet the chief reason by far for the SR debacle was the soldier-

---

[175] Bykhovski, *Vserossiiskii Sovet Krest'ianskikh Deputatov*, pp. 360–61.

peasant. Frederick the Great once said that the peasant was "the beast of burden of human society." Truer words were never spoken. In Russia the two foremost attributes of the class are its hugeness and helplessness. Individual peasants may know their own mind but the class on the whole is a formless mass, fated to be dominated and abused by some minority. In the past officials of church and state had kneaded the dough; the rural intelligentsia—scribe, clerk, agronomist, and teacher—kneaded it from March to November. But by fall a new yeast had appeared in the dough, more potent by far than any that had been there before. An army twelve million strong was breaking up, flooding the countryside with peasants in uniform who were returning in bad humor to the villages they had left in bewilderment and despair. In their overwhelming mass they were either Bolsheviks or Left SR's or nonpartisan extremists. They brought back with them a bitter animus against the party whose influence was paramount in the village, and a strong prejudice in favor of the man who had released them from the army, or from the consequences of deserting it. From a remote corner of the Volga region come words that express their sentiments in a quaint synthesis of Bolshevism and Tolstoian teachings: "He [Lenin] alone has given us land while your SR friends made us go into battle to slay our brothers." [176] The SR intellectual behind the counter or in his study watched them go with mixed feelings. Publicly he wrung his hands at their desertion, but secretly he consoled himself, saying, "Since they won't fight, let them go home and be reabsorbed by the peasant matrix, still sound and unspoiled, leaving the Sovnarkom as the political expression of a self-demobilizing army stranded like foam on a landscape that had been inundated and then dried up." So he reasoned. No grosser miscalculation was ever made by people who had miscalculated every step of the way. The soldier-peasant went home—and shattered the matrix. He established his authority in the village and wrenched it out of the age-old ruts, imparting to it a leftward twist which served the Soviet power well for years to come. Probably he became the backbone of the Red Army and of the Communist Party in rural Russia.

[176] Reminiscences of the peasant A. V. Zumorin, in *1917 god v derevne*, p. 119.

At any rate he destroyed in a few short months the shallow foundations of the PSR.

The soldier-peasant's relatives and neighbors deferred to him—usually to his judgment, always to his rifle. The foreigner will never understand the October Revolution unless he disabuses himself of the notion that the village was a torpid nest of reaction presided over by elders with flowing white beards. This stereotype is not unpleasing to the Communists, who have always been loath to recognize the peasantry as a revolutionary force in its own right. It was not the bearded patriarch honoring the Mother of God and hankering still in his heart for the tsar, but the youthful or middle-aged peasant back from the war, accustomed to violence and not loath to use it, who during the last months of 1917 and long thereafter dictated the course of affairs in the village. Age conferred no distinction in these circumstances but only physical debility, and a flowing beard served no other purpose than to be pulled by an angry soldier. Bykhovski, who was in a position to hold a stethoscope to the heart of rural Russia—though oftentimes he did not wish to believe what the instrument was saying—has acknowledged the mighty influence of the deserting or demobilized peasant.[177] When the SR's lost the soldiers, they lost the peasants too, and so the revolution.

[177] *Vserossiiskii Sovet Krest'ianskikh Deputatov*, p. 360.

VI

The Background of the Constituent Assembly

The effort to straighten out the party line, culminating in the fuzzy decisions of the Fourth Congress, and the struggle to maintain control of the peasants' soviets were alike subordinated to the primary objective of the SR's in the era of the October Revolution: the safeguarding and the exploitation of their victory in the election of the Constituent Assembly. Generations of Populists had dreamed of the day when this body would meet and lay the foundations of socialism, securing forever the triumph of the people's cause through the action of the people itself. No doubts disturbed their fresh and simple faith. Neither a sober assessment of the problems confronting the assembly nor a critical appraisal of its capacity to solve them obscured the vision of an earthly paradise at the end of the road. A party member says that for the SR's democracy had become, not a means to an end, as for the classical liberals, but an end in itself.[1] The supreme embodiment of popular sovereignty was the Constituent Assembly, but the SR's strove to make it a perfect embodiment, wasting time in the process and misleading no one but themselves in the quest for an immaculate conception. They developed the cult of an idol, and when the electorate cast the idol in the SR image, their idolatry surpassed all bounds. As one plows through their literary outpourings of the latter part of 1917, one is struck by the adulation of the Constituent Assembly. In this abnormal approach, there was, of course, an element of artificiality: the SR's knew that the Bolsheviks worshiped other gods, and they knew that their own mistakes had given their enemies the weapons with which to pry loose and overthrow their idol.

Desperation thus strengthened their devotion. The Constituent Assembly offered the last hope of escaping a partisan dictatorship.

[1] Sokolov, "Zashchita Vserossiiskago Uchreditel'nago Sobraniia," in *Arkhiv Russkoi Revoliutsii*, XIII, 15.

Only a broad popular movement in its defense could save it from dissolution. So the SR's agitated on every possible and impossible occasion for "all power to the Constituent Assembly." "No matter what the question discussed in that period, it was invariably connected with the Constituent Assembly." [2] At the reconstitution of the shattered Petersburg organization one leader exclaimed that "for us there is no solution of the basic questions of life outside the Constituent Assembly." [3] A consideration for us to keep in mind as we move down this road of gloom is whether there would have been any solution of basic questions *inside* the Constituent Assembly.

The election had been spread out over a period of several months, owing to postponements in various districts, but in most of the country it was held on November 12–14 (November 25–27) and resulted in a great victory for the SR's.[4] The Bolsheviks got less than a fourth of the votes, though they were now the governing party, whereas the SR's achieved a clear majority, both of the popular vote and of seats in the assembly. The circumstances of the election make it impossible to give exact figures, but the SR's polled about 22,000,000 votes out of a total of 41,686,876 in the districts for which returns are available, and they secured approximately 440 seats of the slightly more than 800 provided for by law and the slightly more than 700 actually chosen. It has, therefore, been generally assumed that they would have controlled the Constituent Assembly and endowed the new Russia with institutions of their own choosing had the Bolsheviks not possessed the physical force to violate the majority will and impose a proletarian dictatorship upon a peasant land. This assumption of clear sailing for the SR's in an assembly immune from force rests, however, upon two further assumptions which too often have been taken for granted: that the SR delegation was as one with the voters behind it, and that it would act as a unit. The first assumption is debatable, and the second, definitely erroneous.

For this imposing total of 440 deputies—438 by Sviatitski's count [5]

[2] Bykhovski, *Vserossiiskii Sovet Krest'ianskikh Deputatov*, p. 286.
[3] *Delo Naroda*, No. 205 (November 10, 1917).
[4] The election has been discussed and analyzed in my study, *The Election to the Russian Constituent Assembly*. Here we shall be concerned only with the assembly itself.
[5] *Kogo russkii narod izbral svoimi predstaviteliami?*, p. 11.

—was anything but a solid bloc. Three hundred deputies—299 is his exact figure—constituted the hard core of party strength, another hundred represented nationality groups which had adopted the Narodnik agrarian program, and 40 were Left SR's. The latter, of course, now belonged to a different party and were at feud with the regulars on every major issue, but the nationality groups likewise had branched off on their own, and the big Ukrainian party with 80 seats in this assembly viewed every effort of the majority to provide for a federal authority as a manifestation of "Great Russian chauvinism." The Moslem SR's were hardly less suspicious, their religious distinctiveness compensating for any lack of national consciousness in setting them off from the Russian SR's. The Moslems, moreover, were disposed to throw in their lot with the Left SR's because they came largely from the same regions and found the extremists more amenable to their demand for self-determination. Some of the Ukrainians leaned in the same direction, and for the same reasons, but in the mass they were divided from their Russian comrades by the hypernationalism which was all too prevalent among Populists in general.

The prospects for SR control of the assembly can best be determined with figures in view. The breakdown of the membership by the SR statistician Sviatitski[6] differs only slightly from that later made by Soviet investigators.[7]

Party or Group	Sviatitski		Soviet Source
SR's	299 ⎫		370
Ukrainian SR's	81 ⎭ 380		
Left SR's	39		40
Bolsheviks	168		175
Mensheviks	18		16
Popular Socialists	4		2
Constitutional Democrats	15 ⎫		17
Rightists	2 ⎭ 17		
Cossacks	9 ⎫		
Armenians	10		
Jews, Poles, Letts, Esths	9 ⎬ 77		86
Moslem national groups	28		
National SR groups	19		
Ukrainian SD's	2 ⎭		
Unknown			1
Total	703		707

[6] *Ibid.*, pp. 10–11.
[7] *Vserossiiskoe Uchreditel'noe Sobranie*, p. 115.

To round out the picture, it should be pointed out that voting never took place in some parts of the country and that a hundred-odd seats were left vacant, mainly from districts in Central Asia.

With these figures in mind it can readily be seen that the SR's in the strict sense of the term had no majority in the Constituent Assembly, and that even if they had resurrected the Kerenski coalition with the Mensheviks and Kadets, they still would have had no majority, so puny were these pillars of the Russian state. Even with the Armenians and several other national splinters, they would barely have crossed the line, and this combination would have been no Rock of Gibraltar. There was only one way in which the SR's could firmly have dominated the assembly, and that was in union with their Ukrainian offshoot. Even this would scarcely have sufficed had the full complement of seats been realized with the advent of a large number of Moslem deputies from Turkestan. The conclusion is inescapable: the SR's could have drafted a constitution for Russia only in firm alliance with national groups. Their strategy cannot be understood apart from this consideration. Any attempt to play with the Kadets would have gotten them into hot water, for the partisans of "Russia one and indivisible" would have mixed with the Ukrainian and Moslem delegates like so many spitting wildcats.

Yet such was the character of the SR delegation that this attempt would likely have been made if circumstances had been more favorable to the existence of the assembly. The right SR's could no more put distance between themselves and the Constitutional Democrats than the latter could free themselves of foreign tutelage, and there were a lot of right SR's in the Constituent Assembly. It was not simply that there were fifteen regular SR's for every two Left SR's—that circumstance in itself will bear examination. But within the regular party core of 300 deputies the right of center definitely predominated over the left of center. M. V. Vishniak, secretary of the assembly and himself an SR of the far right, has estimated that V. M. Chernov did not have more than fifty followers in the party delegation [8]—a remarkable circumstance in view of Chernov's victory at the Fourth Congress and the fact that the

[8] Interview in New York (January 2, 1952). The estimate seems low, but no one was in a better position to make it than Vishniak. His opinion is worthy of serious consideration, though subject to some discount on the score of prejudice.

party machinery had there passed into his hands. How are we to explain that the organization leaned to the left and the party delegation in the assembly to the right? Why were they not in harmony, and why should the elected representatives have been drawn so disproportionately from an element that had only an even break at the Third Congress and was decidedly in the minority at the Fourth?

The Left SR's together with the Bolsheviks always maintained that the electoral lists had been loaded by the party bureaucracy, and particularly by the Central Committee which had emerged from the Third Congress with a right-of-center cast. Before examining these charges, it is necessary to have the sequence of events firmly in mind and to understand the process by which the SR's nominated candidates for the Constituent Assembly. The country was divided into sizable electoral districts, corresponding to provinces, instead of single-member constituencies, and the voter chose a party list instead of marking his ballot for an individual candidate. The lists were made up in September and the first part of October,[9] after the leftward trend had set in but before the party schism, which occurred at the time of the October Revolution. The election followed hard thereafter, on November 12 in most parts of the country, affording no time for the Left SR's to disentangle themselves from the general party ticket or for the schism to register upon the voting public's consciousness. As Karelin said in announcing the Left SR bolt from the assembly, the electoral setup did not permit breaking the lists at a moment when the correlation of political forces in the country was undergoing a fundamental change. Consequently, the majority in the assembly was the product of accident and did not reflect the will of the toilers.[10] And Lenin argued that since the SR lists had been completed about October 17, before the people had seen through the situation, the results of the election were invalid.[11] The matter is important, for it placed a club in the hands of the extremists with which to beat the assembly to death.[12]

The party lists were made up on two levels, at the center and in

[9] See article of N. V. Sviatitski in the *Delo Naroda*, No. 245 (December 31, 1917).
[10] *Vserossiiskoe Uchreditel'noe Sobranie*, p. 109.
[11] *Sochineniia*, XXII, 118.
[12] See text of the decree dissolving the Constituent Assembly (*Vserossiiskoe Uchreditel'noe Sobranie*, p. 145).

the provinces. On the theory that leaders living in the capital and specialists who were not widely known might experience difficulty in getting on provincial tickets,[13] the Central Committee decided to draw up a list of candidates who would have to be accepted by the provincial organizations according to a fixed ratio and placed on their tickets, generally in the first position, after which these organizations would be free to complete the ticket as they saw fit. Each district, therefore, would have one or more candidates imposed from the center, while the others would be chosen locally on the basis of an agreement between the provincial conference of party members and the provincial congress of peasants' soviets. This was in conformity with the decision made in July not to offer an independent class ticket of peasant representatives but to bloc with socialist parties accepting the land program of the peasants' soviets (equalized use of socialized land, expropriated without compensation),[14] a formula that quite effectively restricted the fusion to the Socialist Revolutionary Party, since Social Democrats favored nationalization and regarded equalization as utopian, Popular Socialists favored compensation, and Constitutional Democrats were not socialists at all. The decision for fusion was only natural in view of the fact that virtually everywhere except in Little Russia the SR's stood at the head of the agrarian movement. The nominations were made on the basis of parity between the party organization and the peasants' soviet, the one condition being that the candidates of the soviet must be members of the party. A nomination could be vetoed by any one of three agencies: the provincial party organization, the provincial peasants' soviet, or the Central Committee. The democratic principle was safeguarded by providing that the nominations were not to be made by the provincial party committee or provincial soviet executive committee but were to be submitted to a provincial conference (convention) of party members and a provincial congress of peasant deputies.[15]

[13] Chernov, manuscript commentary on the minutes of the Central Committee, p. 51.

[14] Bykhovski, *Vserossiiskii Sovet Krest'ianskikh Deputatov*, p. 158. An interesting sidelight is that even if a nonsocialist party had accepted the program, it would not have been admitted to fusion. Miliukov's party had no standing in the villages of Russia, which is another way of saying that political conservatism had no chance in Russia in 1917.

[15] *Partiinyia Izvestiia*, No. 4 (December 10, 1917), pp. 30–31; article by

So much for the nominating process. Now to seek to determine, first at the center and then in the provinces, whether it was impartially applied, or carried out in such a manner as to stack the lists in favor of the element of the party standing to the right of center—that is, favoring class collaboration and continued prosecution of the war, either for purely defensive reasons or in order to aid the British and French. The sources we draw upon are exceedingly rare but eminently satisfactory in that they afford a cross section of party opinion: statements on behalf of the extreme right;[16] a printed statement and oral testimony by Zenzinov,[17] who stood at the head of the whole business; some remarks by Chernov[18] and the detailed apologia of his factional comrade, Sviatitski,[19] who in this instance was acting as defendant for the Central Committee; and a substantial article from the pen of Karelin, spokesman for the extreme left.[20] Various local reports also shed some light on the problem. As the party expert on matters pertaining to the election, Sviatitski would ordinarily be accorded the preference, but in his account there are no less than four serious misstatements of fact, leading one to wonder whether there may not have been something to conceal after all. The first is that the Central Committee did not compile any list of obligatory candidacies but left this task to the Seventh Party Council (August 6–10, 1917).[21] But the committee did prepare such a list and Zenzinov reported on the matter to the council in executive session, right after Sviatitski had given a report on the subject of election blocs. Discussions followed, and that is as much as was officially disclosed.[22]

Karelin makes it clear that these "discussions" took the form of another heated controversy at a conclave that was one long wrangle

---

Sviatitski in *Delo Naroda*, No. 245 (December 31, 1917); Sviatitski, *Kogo russkii narod izbral svoimi predstaviteliami?*, pp. 9–10.

[16] See controversy with Pitirim Sorokin in *Delo Naroda*, No. 169 (October 1, 1917), and Breshkovskaia's declaration at the Seventh Council in *Volia Naroda*, No. 98 (August 22, 1917).

[17] "Iskusstvennyi podbor" (Artificial Selection), *Delo Naroda*, No. 236 (December 19, 1917); interview in New York (December, 1949).

[18] Manuscript commentary on the minutes of the Central Committee, pp. 52, 80.

[19] Article in *Delo Naroda*, No. 245 (December 31, 1917).

[20] "Iskusstvennyi podbor," *Znamia Truda*, No. 109 (January 3, 1918).

[21] On the council, see my book, *The Agrarian Foes of Bolshevism*, pp. 374–85.

[22] *Delo Naroda*, No. 121 (August 8, 1917).

from beginning to end. The Central Committee had introduced its recommendations in the expectation that their acceptance would be a formality, but the council refused to act as a rubber stamp and, at the insistence of the left, set up a special commission to go over the recommendations. The council also reversed the committee by reducing the ratio of compulsory candidacies. Instead of reserving one out of every three places on the lists for such nominees, it provided that only one need be taken per district (province). The Central Committee was not pleased by the lack of confidence in its handiwork and had its feelings hurt. Sviatitski says the special commission had nine members, of whom five stood to the left of center. Actually, it had eleven members, only three of whom leaned to the left, according to Karelin, or only four, by the reckoning of this author. As the composition of the commission was officially announced,[23] there is no question of Sviatitski's error. On the right were the chairman, Zenzinov, and Gendelman, Rosenblum, Vishniak, Sokolov, Minin, and Frumin; on the left, Karelin, Vysotskaia, and Ratner, the latter two being moderates; the eleventh member, Sviatitski himself, ordinarily was left of center but in this instance he was at pains to whitewash the work of the commission in order not to weaken the case of the Constituent Assembly. Zenzinov is thus correct in saying that the commission represented various currents in the party, but he studiously avoids telling us in what ratio they were represented.[24]

With a commission of this cast, it is not surprising that the handiwork of the Central Committee should have undergone no drastic alterations. Nominations from the left sector of party opinion were as scarce as hen's teeth and became hardly less so as a result of the labors of the commission. With rare exceptions a vote of eight to three overrode the left minority. That was the vote by which Kamkov was rejected. Spiridonova got through with only four votes in her favor, three against, and three abstaining. An inspection of the final revised list of 57 names[25] reveals only four that figured later in the Left SR Party, although some of the names

[23] *Ibid.*, No. 122 (August 9, 1917). Compare also the roll-call vote in No. 124 (August 11, 1917).

[24] "Iskusstvennyi podbor," *Delo Naroda*, No. 236 (December 19, 1917).

[25] This list and others were printed in the *Partiinyia Izvestiia*, No. 2 (October 5, 1917), pp. 29 ff.

are unfamiliar and cannot be identified by faction. Of course, the youth and inexperience of the left militated against the choice of candidates from its midst, but even so it was grossly underrepresented. One service which the commission did perform, according to its left-wing member and critic, was to weed out a number of party hacks who were distinguished by nothing except their sycophancy in relation to the Central Committee. The evidence is conflicting as to whether the Seventh Council had time to pass on the work of its commission, but the Central Committee subsequently did not scruple to juggle things a bit, introducing a new category of candidacies being advanced by local organizations, into which it hastened to transfer some of the left-wing candidacies approved by the commission. That such action was not entirely one-sided, however, is attested by a protest from the opposite extreme, by Pitirim Sorokin against this same kind of treatment.[26] The strong showing of the left at the Seventh Council did not change the fact that it was still a minority, without the means of controlling the commission that revised the work of the Central Committee or of altering in any basic sense the type of candidacy dictated from the center of party life.[27]

Yet the decision of the council to reduce the ratio of obligatory candidacies from one out of every three to only one per district made it certain that the bulk of SR candidates for seats in the Constituent Assembly would be chosen locally in the manner already described. According to a count made by Sviatitski, out of 325 SR deputies, only 50, or 15 percent, had been chosen from the center.[28] What of the other 85 percent, selected, as Zenzinov and Sviatitski assure us, without any form of pressure or restraint from the "party bureaucracy," in conformity with the outlook of the provincial organizations? [29] The first thing to note is that the assurance is false, for in two respects the Central Committee very definitely influenced nominations in the provinces. It could veto any candidate put up by a subordinate authority, anywhere in Russia, and it had the power to

---

[26] *Delo Naroda*, No. 169 (October 1, 1917).

[27] Karelin, "Iskusstvennyi podbor," *Znamia Truda*, No. 109 (January 3, 1918); proceedings of the council in *Delo Naroda*, No. 125 (August 12, 1917).

[28] Article in *Delo Naroda*, No. 245 (December 31, 1917).

[29] *Ibid.*; "Iskusstvennyi podbor," *Delo Naroda*, No. 236 (December 19, 1917).

adjudicate disputes growing out of the choice of a ticket—that is, it decided which side in an organizational split had the right to act in the name of the party and place its candidates on the party list. The minutes of the Central Committee, in so far as they are available, disclose no tendency on the part of that organ to abuse the power of veto, since it specifically cleared the candidacies of Ustinov, Algasov, and Kogan-Bernstein when local challenge arose,[30] and only once disqualified a partisan of the left, Shishko, for reasons that were not disclosed.[31]

The power to intervene in local squabbles, however, gave the Central Committee a more subtle means of influencing the character of the party representation in the Constituent Assembly. Nominations were a fruitful source of dissension in party circles throughout the country,[32] and factions fought ferociously to place their men on the ticket. Only the war did more to inflame feeling and prepare minds for the break that was coming. The chief complaint of the left seems to have been the unwillingness of the committee to uphold the principle of proportional representation which had been tacitly accepted in party circles, yet was persistently flouted in provincial organizations with a rightist majority but with a leftist minority large enough to claim a substantial portion of the places. For example, in Kostroma province the party congress convened to deal with this matter consisted of seventeen delegates to the right of center and fifteen to the left; yet only rightist candidates were presented and all four of the SR's elected represented the faction that was only a bare majority in the province. A similar situation prevailed in Petrograd province and a number of others, with no effort on the part of the Central Committee to bring about an equitable allotment of places on the ballot.[33] While the minutes of that body are far too cryptic to give a clear picture of what was going on, they disclose that an emissary was sent to Kostroma to settle the conflict[34] and that the threat of rival slates in Petrograd

[30] Protokol Zasedaniia Tsentral'nago Komiteta PSR, September 17, October 1, 9, 1917.

[31] *Ibid.*, October 15, 1917.

[32] See *Partiinyia Izvestiia*, No. 4 (December 10, 1917), pp. 30–31.

[33] Karelin, "Iskusstvennyi podbor," *Znamia Truda*, No. 109 (January 3, 1918).

[34] Protokol Zasedaniia Tsentral'nago Komiteta PSR, September 30, 1917.

province was averted by recognizing the one put forth by the majority and forbidding the other one [35]—a procedure that was likewise adopted in Petrograd city,[36] where the shoe was on the other foot. But it was not followed in the case of Kharkov province, where the dissident list of rightists was not disqualified, because it was headed by Breshkovskaia, against whom Gotz declared that "he would never raise his hand." [37] Sentiment rather than calculation no doubt explains the one-sidedness of the committee on this occasion, but the deep feeling over the war issue generally made it callous to minority rights and unwilling to be more than formally correct in its dealings with the wing of the party whose views it abhorred. To be sure, the committee was not legally bound to enforce the principle of proportional representation in the choice of party candidates, and the left appears to have been just as intolerant of dissent in provinces under its control as the right was when it abused a superior position or even a bare majority to exclude the left from the lists entirely. The over-all effect, however, was to favor the right. Here, undoubtedly, is one explanation of the fact that the SR's in the Constituent Assembly were a much more conservative lot than the party organization itself.

The other and more substantial explanation lies in the type of candidate sought by the party as its representative in the Constituent Assembly. Men of prestige and experience with years of service behind them, experts in agronomy or administration, peasants who were looked up to by their communities, or would have been in normal times—these were the people from whom all sections of party opinion save the extreme left wished to select their candidates, and such people were very likely, by the fall of 1917 if not before, to have moved to the right under the influence of the war, the satisfaction of their political demands, and the prospect of a general breakdown that threatened their station in life. The cult of the Revolution had given way to the cult of the State or the Nation, conceived more and more in the conventional bourgeois sense; the claims of the Western or Southern Slavs enlisted more sympathy

---

[35] *Ibid.*, October 12, 14, 1917.   [36] *Ibid.*, October 12, 14, 15, 1917.

[37] Chernov, manuscript commentary on the minutes of the Central Committee, p. 53; Karelin, "Iskusstvennyi podbor," *Znamia Truda*, No. 109 (January 3, 1918).

than those of the Little Russians; and the liberating aspects of the war received more attention than the sufferings of the workers and peasants brought on by that same war. In short, many of these people had developed a Kadet mentality and were Kadets in everything but name.

Imperfect understanding of this transformation of many SR's lessened the opposition to their being placed on the ballot, but a more fruitful reason for their success was the lack of unity on the left between the moderates and the extremists, or between the left unionists and the left schismatics. Even the latter did not always see clearly where their interests lay, but the confusion of thought and slavish leadership of the element in the party to the left of center rendered it totally unsuited to grapple with the problem of securing representation in conformity with its point of view. It prided itself on its breadth of vision and on doing what was best for the party; so the left center went along with the right center in selecting dignitaries and experts and local pundits, leaving the left in isolation. Time after time when a provincial organization objected to someone as being too far to the right or too deferential to the Central Committee, pointed reminders of party discipline would come by telegraph over the signatures of half a dozen leaders with the name of V. M. Chernov at the head of the list.[38] Years later, he as well as the Left SR's would accuse Zenzinov—obliquely, of course—of loading the lists,[39] but at the time he helped him load them.

The left had made its strong showing at the Seventh Council with some help from the left center, though not from Chernov, but in the matter of selecting candidates for the Constituent Assembly it had stood quite alone. This circumstance, together with the special psychology of the type of SR who ran for the assembly, accounts for the startling divergence between the organization, 40 per cent leftist at its August conclave, and the delegation in the assembly, with 40 Left SR's out of a total of 339. The right sector of party opinion had more cohesion and was more conscious of what it

[38] Karelin, "Iskusstvennyi podbor," *Znamia Truda,* No. 109 (January 3, 1918).
[39] Manuscript commentary on the minutes of the Central Committee, pp. 52, 80.

was doing, even though friction between the right center and right was not lacking, as is evidenced by Breshkovskaia's attack on the Central Committee for its arbitrary and clandestine operations in preparing the lists.[40]

From what has been said about the type of candidate selected for the assembly, it might be inferred that the white-collar element predominated numerically as well as intellectually. But a primary source assures us that the delegation consisted about half of real peasants who were spiritually as one with the intellectual contingent.[41] That would accord with the dual source of the lists and the principle of parity upon which the party and the peasants' soviets had agreed. The fragmentary evidence at our disposal, however, of the professional or occupational make-up of the lists would strongly indicate that the sons of toil had been passed over in favor of the more articulate layers of the population. Perhaps these two military constituencies and two provinces for which we have data are not typical, and perhaps the balance between intellectuals and toilers was redressed in the many areas for which we do not possess information.

In any event, the four examples now to be examined afford some coverage and reveal lists top-heavy with intellectuals. Six hundred delegates of the VII Army had come together to choose the party candidates. They named three officers, including two lieutenant colonels, two physicians, three officials, the army commissar, and one soldier(!).[42] On the Southwestern Front the party offered the voter a list with four physicians, eight officers, three military officials, one gunner, two privates, and two candidates of unspecified occupation.[43] Even the two privates were intellectuals, and the Bolsheviks took delight in contrasting this list with their own, on which there was nothing but ordinary soldiers. Their propaganda, in the opinion of one of these SR physicians, planted a seed in the soldiers' minds, or rather linked the prejudice against intellec-

---

[40] See her speech at the council in the toned-down version published in the *Volia Naroda*, No. 98 (August 22, 1917).

[41] N. Oganovski, "Dnevnik chlena Uchreditel'nago Sobraniia," *Golos Minuvshago*, IV–VI (April–June, 1918), 152. See also p. 240.

[42] *Delo Naroda*, No. 166 (September 28, 1917).

[43] *Ibid.*, No. 169 (October 1, 1917); *Partiinyia Izvestiia*, No. 2 (October 5, 1917), p. 34.

tuals that was already there with the Socialist Revolutionary Party.[44]
In Petrograd province, of the twelve candidates put up by the PSR,
seven were party functionaries, two were teachers, two physicians,
one a soldier and one a peasant.[45] Here the countryside was semi-
industrialized and the peasantry of no great weight, but in the
opulent farming province of Kharkov, with the opposite wing of
the party in control, it was no different; the thirteen SR deputies
on the morrow of the election were split three ways in respect to
partisan affiliation, but the intellectual cast of the representation was
as pronounced as in other instances. Because of the prominence of
this electoral district, it will not be amiss to give the names of the
deputies, their partisan affiliation and occupational status: [46]

V. M. Chernov (SR). Party functionary; author
V. M. Kachinski (LSR). Party functionary; journalist
N. V. Sviatitski (SR). Jurist; writer
A. S. Severov-Odoevski (USR). Public official
P. V. Mikhailichenko (USR). Soldier
V. A. Karelin (LSR). Party and public official; journalist
N. N. Alekseev (LSR). Party worker
A. I. Streltsov (LSR). Jurist; zemstvo worker
N. M. Popov (LSR). Jurist; provincial commissar
N. A. Shkorbatov (USR). Agronomist
A. N. Ovcharenko (USR). Farmer
I. G. Kravchenko (LSR). Teacher
V. G. Diakonov (USR). Factory worker

It is regrettable that a breakdown for more provinces is not available. At the request of the author, M. V. Vishniak, secretary of the

[44] Sokolov, "Zashchita Uchreditel'nago Sobraniia," in *Arkhiv Russkoi Revoliutsii*, XIII, 19.
[45] *Delo Naroda*, No. 181 (October 15, 1917). The SR's, and not the author,
are responsible for this arithmetic.
[46] *Russkiia Vedomosti*, No. 261 (November 29, 1917). Chernov is not included
in this list. Probably he had not yet chosen his constituency. He is listed for
Tambov province in the Soviet compilation (*Vserossiiskoe Uchreditel'noe
Sobranie*, p. 134). But in Sviatitski's (*Partiinyia Izvestiia*, No. 5, pp. 32–36), he
is assigned to Kharkov. His own version should be definitive: he says he was
elected in five districts and chose Kharkov (manuscript commentary on the
minutes of the Central Committee, p. 53). Kharkov province had fifteen seats
in the assembly. In addition to the six Left SR's, five Ukrainian SR's, and two
SR's elected on a joint ticket, two Bolsheviks were returned. In this list some
of the initials differ from those given in the Soviet compilation.

Constituent Assembly, agreed to run through a roster of members [47] and single out the SR's known by him to belong in the intellectual category. His search [48] yielded 103 names out of a total of 360 SR deputies. But since he failed to include five of the nine or ten intellectuals in the list above, it is evident that a great many of the provincial delegates were not known to him and that the ratio of intellectuals was much higher. Whatever it may have been, it was large enough to impregnate the SR delegation with the spirit of the Populist intelligentsia as it had come to be by 1917—with the nation in the place of humanity, the Russian state in the place of the Russian toiler, the war in the place of revolution, a new-found zeal for the status quo and an abhorrence of extremism in every form. The social preeminence of these people, dictating their choice as candidates, together with their special psychology, explains much better than any element of manipulation the astounding paradox of a revolutionary party with conservative representation in the parliament that marked its greatest triumph.[49]

Presentation of joint lists with the peasants' soviets in virtually every district might lead to the conclusion that the conservative rural influence had operated against the admission of extremists to candidacy. Perhaps in certain instances it did, but no generalization can be made on the basis of the meager information at our command, nor does the temper of the Russian peasantry in the fall of 1917 support such a hypothesis. In at least one instance peasant influence worked in the opposite direction: two left SR's, A. N. Ustinov and G. K. Ulianov, were placed on the ticket in Saratov province at the insistence of the provincial peasants' congress after the party organization had refused to recognize the claims of the minority and had even carried Ustinov's case to the Central Committee.[50] With a farsightedness only too rare among Russian intellectuals, the economist Tugan-Baranovski had warned the public as far back as July that it had better awaken from its comforting illusion about the

[47] Printed in *Vserossiiskoe Uchreditel'noe Sobranie*, pp. 116–35; supplemental list, pp. 135–38, not included.

[48] At the Hoover Library, summer of 1955.

[49] Compare Bykhovski's analysis of the SR representation at the Second Peasants' Congress above, pp. 212 ff.

[50] *Protokoly pervago s"ezda PLSR*, p. 9; Protokol Zasedaniia Tsentral'nago Komiteta PSR, September 17 and October 9, 1917.

innate conservatism of the Russian peasantry and realize that in some respects it was more radical than the organization that claimed to represent it.[51] There were other penetrating observations in his article which both the SR's and the bourgeoisie could with profit have taken to heart. But both were as blind as bats. And foreign opinion has scarcely been more perspicacious. However difficult it may be for Americans of the twentieth century to understand, the fact remains that in the Russia of 1917 the people were far more revolutionary than the intellectuals who presumed to speak in their name. Not, of course, that the people were socialists, actual or potential. The old English term Leveler would have fitted them much better.

The Left SR's had rarely been so fortunate as in Saratov province in gaining minority representation on the lists of candidates for the Constituent Assembly. Besides the two successful candidates from that district, they secured one seat in Vladimir province (Spiridonova), one in Kursk, one in Penza, and one in Perm. They got an even break in Riazan province, claiming three of the six SR deputies from a district where the unyielding spirit of the landowners had bred extremism on the other side.[52] Most of their scanty representation, however, came from districts where they controlled the party organization and could make up the lists as they saw fit, aside from some interference by the Central Committee. There were eight such districts, one metropolitan and seven provincial. The September triumph of the left in the Petersburg organization brought only one seat in the assembly, since the Central Committee had saddled it with the candidacies of Gotz and Mayor Shreider, and Chernov had been adopted as a compromise to overcome the impasse in respect to the head of the ticket.[53] Consequently, Kamkov was the only Left SR elected in Petersburg. Control of the Poltava organization likewise brought little benefit, owing to the sweep of the Ukrainian SR's, which left the Russian party with but a single seat.[54] In the West Russian provinces of Pskov and Kaluga the Left SR's were in the

---

[51] "Derevnia i Uchreditel'noe Sobranie" (The Village and the Constituent Assembly), *Russkoe Slovo*, No. 163 (July 19, 1917). This man understood his country.

[52] Interview with Chernov in New York, January 4, 1950.

[53] Manuscript commentary on the minutes of the Central Committee, pp. 51–52.

[54] See my book, *The Election to the Russian Constituent Assembly*, pp. 29–31.

ascendancy, but heavy competition from the Bolsheviks and sparseness of population held their gains to four and three seats, respectively. The major strongholds of Kharkov and Kherson in the Ukraine, Kazan on the Volga, and Ufa in the Urals, on the other hand, had a large population that was Russian only in part, compelling the Left SR's to share the seats allotted to these provinces with nationalist parties of like inclination. Nevertheless, the Left SR's won six seats in Kharkov province, six in Kherson, four in Kazan, and four in Ufa, with the added assurance that most of the Ukrainian, Tatar, and Chuvash deputies would make common cause with them. Half of their representation was secured in these four provinces. In all, they won 38 seats and picked up an additional one at the end of the year when an SR deputy from Voronezh (A. P. Blizniuk) went over to them.[55] Sviatitski leaves them with 39 but the Soviet compilation credits them with yet a fortieth seat of unspecified origin.[56]

SR apologists have always argued that the election revealed the weakness of the left wing through its inability to win more than this modest number of places, and these only on the general ticket which had been drawn up before the schism and could not be changed in the short interval before the election. They have pointed to what happened in the six districts where the left minority actually did break away in time to enter splinter lists, and where it achieved a grand total of 26,028 votes without electing a single deputy.[57] From the failure of the right wing to fare any better in the six other districts in which it presented separate lists, these apologists have argued that neither deviation had any strength of its own apart from the general organization of the PSR and the good will which it had accumulated. The Left SR's as an independent party, therefore, were not underrepresented but, if anything, overrepresented in the Con-

[55] Oganovski, "Dnevnik chlena Uchreditel'nago Sobraniia," *Golos Minuvshago*, IV–VI, 156.

[56] Sviatitski, "Fraktsiia partii S.-R. Uchreditel'nago Sobraniia," *Partiinyia Izvestiia*, No. 5 (January 20, 1918), pp. 32–36; Sviatitski, *Kogo russkii narod izbral svoimi predstaviteliami?*, p. 11; Sviatitski, "Itogi vyborov vo Vserossiiskoe Uchreditel'noe Sobranie," in *God russkoi revoliutsii*, pp. 112–13; *Vserossiiskoe Uchreditel'noe Sobranie*, p. 115.

[57] See article entitled, "Failure of the Left and Right SR's" (Russian title inaccessible), *Delo Naroda*, No. 2 (January 4, 1918).

stituent Assembly, since they owed the few seats they possessed to their presence on the general party ticket.

Let us subject this contention to a critical examination, using for that purpose the one district with a Left SR splinter ticket for which we have information. In the black-earth province of Voronezh their ticket drew only 11,871 votes, and even this paltry figure was not all theirs, since they had formed a bloc with the Ukrainian SR's and the Polish Socialist Party (one wonders what Joseph Pilsudski would have thought of this?). The SR list, on the other hand, received 875,300 votes. Apparently, the contention is justified. But let us look at that list with the massive vote, and what do we see? At the very top comes the name of V. M. Chernov, whose backsliding behind the scenes was not known to the people but whose reputation as a radical in respect to land and peace was well known and had been freshened by his break with Kerenski. Then come the names of K. S. Burevoi-Sopliakov, chairman of the provincial soviet of peasants' deputies, and M. L. Kogan-Bernstein and S. P. Postnikov, editor of the *Delo Naroda*, all three of them SR's of a leftist inclination, the first two very decidedly so. Farther down on the list one encounters the name of the peasant Blizniuk, soon to declare himself a Left SR. The obscurity of most of the other names precludes further analysis, but the conclusion is obvious: there was enough radicalism on this list to confuse even a thinking peasant. Why should he vote with a tiny dissident group in the city, recruited from the war factories and railroad shops,[58] when the main list seemed to reflect his peasant radicalism? Left-wing Social Revolutionism was a rural, not an urban, phenomenon, and the process of differentiation within the party, always slower in the village than in the town, had not as yet progressed far enough for radical-minded elements to seek independent expression. Hence the few thousands of votes for a Left SR splinter group does not begin to measure the strength of radical sentiment in Voronezh province.

Furthermore, in evaluating this attempt to belittle extremism in the PSR, it must be remembered that in eight districts there was no need for the left to offer its own slate, since it was the party in those

---

[58] *1917i god v Voronezhskoi gubernii, passim; Protokoly pervago s"ezda PLSR,* p. 5; Protokol Zasedaniia Tsentral'nago Komiteta PSR, October 11, 1917.

districts, and that in a number of others it had secured at least a
measure of representation, though certainly not as much as faithful
adherence to the principle of minority representation would have
warranted, either in these districts or in those where it had been shut
out completely. There were provinces like Kharkov where peasant
radicalism had achieved political form, but in most it was still groping for expression when the election was held, and so cannot be
measured by the results. The Left SR's elected deputies where they
already were in control of the peasant movement; elsewhere they
elected few or none, but the mood from which their movement
sprang was far more prevalent than their lack of success would
indicate.

Finally, there is a factor in the apparent weakness of the Left SR's
which has been completely ignored in the literature of the revolution. Among the ten million votes recorded for the Bolshevik Party,
many more of them from peasants and peasant soldiers than from
proletarians, there was an indeterminable number that belonged to
the Left SR's or would have gone to them, had the schism in the PSR
occurred in time for the new party to stand forth clearly in opposition to the old, with its own candidates and its own publicity campaign. Dissatisfaction even with mixed tickets, not to speak of those
without leftist representation, had impelled some people, with a
greater or lesser degree of reluctance, to cast their vote for the only
thoroughly revolutionary and antiwar party in the field, even though
they regarded it—correctly, as the sequel would show—as a dubious
champion of peasant rights. To attempt to estimate what portion of
Boshevik strength really belonged to the Left SR's would be pure
guesswork. But it is a matter of record that Left SR's voted the
Bolshevik ticket. In Baku, an SR assembly in the Surakhan district
went over to the left and called for support of the Bolshevik slate in
the election.[59] In the Taganrog area, the worker SR's who composed
the organization refused to support a ticket with the names of
Kerenski and S. P. Shvetsov and gave their suffrage to the Bolsheviks.[60] Information from Tver province is fragmentary, but the PSR
was rent with dissension and at the September peasants' congress fell

[59] *Revoliutsiia 1917 goda v Azerbaidzhane*, p. 212; see also pp. 205-6, and
Rathauser, *Revoliutsiia i grazhdanskaia voina v Baku*, I, 49.
[60] *Protokoly pervago s"ezda PLSR*, p. 8.

apart into two hostile camps. After the left in union with the Bolsheviks had lost out on the test vote, 170 to 75, a rightist slate of candidates was adopted,[61] but the heavy defeat it sustained in the November election leads to the conclusion that the victorious Bolsheviks
must have had a whole lot of support from dissident SR groups, and
more particularly, from their peasant following. There is no doubt
at all about Novgorod province, where the Left SR's and their
following rejected the party list headed by Avksentiev and threw
their support to the Bolsheviks.[62] But the most striking example of
Bolshevism's harvesting of votes that in part, at least, were not
properly its own is offered by the November peasants' congress in
Minsk province, which decided that, since the Left SR's had no list
of their own, the peasants should back the Bolshevik slate.[63] And
they certainly did, inflicting upon the SR's the most signal reverse
in any province of Russia, 579,087 to 181,673, or better than three
to one.

Seemingly, there is another way of illustrating the Left SR contribution to the Bolshevik poll, less conclusive but more tangible.
Two widely separated provinces of European Russia, Pskov and Ufa,
presented radical SR lists in competition with Bolshevism, whereas
the surrounding provinces in both instances offered SR lists that
were right-centrist or even rightist in cast. Let us see what happened by comparing the SR and Bolshevik polls in each of these two
provinces with those of its neighbors.[64]

NORTHWESTERN			EASTERN		
	SR	Bolshevik		SR	Bolshevik
Pskov	269,267	139,690	Ufa *	627,397	48,135
Petersburg	119,761	229,698	Perm	664,883	267,577
Novgorod	220,665	203,658	Viatka **	300,503	78,278
Tver	186,030	362,687	Samara	690,341	195,132
Smolensk	250,134	361,062	Orenburg	110,172	163,425
Vitebsk	150,279	287,101			

* 322,276 for SR list plus 305,121 for Moslem SR's.
** Partial returns only.

[61] *Volia Naroda*, Nos. 124, 129 (September 21, 27, 1917).
[62] *Protokoly pervago s"ezda PLSR*, p. 12.
[63] Knorin, *Revoliutsiia i kontr-revoliutsiia v Belorussii*, I, 55; see also above,
p. 259.
[64] Radkey, *The Election to the Russian Constituent Assembly*, appendix.

A very clear pattern emerges from these figures: an abnormally low vote for the Bolsheviks in the two districts controlled by the Left SR's, and a very large increment of strength for them in the neighboring provinces where the SR organizations combated land seizures and opposed any practical step toward ending the war. Whether this increment of strength came from dissident SR's and their peasant following, or whether it was produced by other factors, is the question. Unfortunately, social phenomena are not subject to isolation and accurate measurement, and other factors, too, cannot be ignored—the relative strength of party organizations, reflected in the intensity of the campaign they staged; the comparative economic structure of the provinces involved, particularly the degree of industrialization; the ethnic make-up of their populations; the degree of soldier influence; and so on. The formidable Bolshevik organization in the city of Samara with its 4,000 disciplined zealots,[65] and the relative weakness of this party in Ufa province,[66] undoubtedly were of some influence, though it could be argued in rebuttal that the presence of a thoroughly radical SR alternative in Ufa province had operated to take the wind out of the sails of Bolshevism, in contrast to the situation in Samara province, where the dominant right-centrist faction of the PSR had stimulated opposition by its war on extremism. Industrialization is not a significant factor except in relation to Perm; Ufa embraced the southern Urals, and must have had a larger proletariat than the other three provinces, which nevertheless gave many more votes to the Bolsheviks. The evidence is even more convincing in the case of the northwestern region, for with the exception of suburban, semi-industrialized Petersburg province, the other five are all very much alike and the divergence between Pskov and its neighbors can scarcely have other than a strictly political explanation. Our thesis that the substantial Bolshevik poll in the country at large includes a component of agrarian radicalism that really belonged to the Left SR's would appear to be sustained by the facts, and one would be justified in concluding, on the basis

[65] *Istoriia grazhdanskoi voiny v SSSR*, II, 81.

[66] Podshivalov, *Grazhdanskaia bor'ba na Urale*, pp. 50–51, 109; G. Kotov, "Partiinaia i sovetskaia rabota v Ufe v 1918 g." (Party and Soviet Work in Ufa in 1918), *Proletarskaia Revoliutsiia*, LXXVII–LXXVIII (VI–VII, 1928), 296–97.

of the areas studied, which alone are suitable for analysis, that the component was a sizable one.

The question of the choice of candidates by the Socialist Revolutionaries has been thoroughly examined, for on it hinges the whole controversy over the fate of the Constituent Assembly. There undoubtedly is some substance in the Bolshevik claim, which is also the claim of the Left SR's, that the candidates elected under the SR label did not reflect the will of the voters behind them. The deputies, they contended, were far more conservative than those who elected them, owing to the belated schism in the ranks of the PSR, which had deprived the voters of a clear-cut choice between left and right. The common party lists had been manipulated by the party bureaucracy in the interest of the nonrevolutionary, pro-war wing, and the following had accepted these lists because the peasants had not yet learned to distinguish between left and right SR's, or between those who defended their interests and those who only claimed to do so. The mass of right-wing deputies had thus gotten into the assembly as contraband, rather than through the conscious will of the electorate.[67] However, we have seen that the element of manipulation is not the key to the make-up of the SR delegation, though it cannot altogether be ignored. After all, the Central Committee had allowed Natanson's candidacy to fall to the ground, making no effort to place him elsewhere after he had been rejected in one district (Omsk?),[68]

[67] This line of argument may be found in the statements of Sverdlov, Skvortsov, Raskolnikov, and Karelin in the Constituent Assembly (*Vserossiiskoe Uchreditel'noe Sobranie*, pp. 5, 60, 89, 109; see also text of the decree of dissolution, p. 145); Vladimirova, *God sluzhby "sotsialistov" kapitalistam*, p. 111, n. 1; T. Remezova, "Vybory v uchred. sobranie v 1917 godu" (The Election to the Constituent Assembly in 1917), *Istoricheskii Zhurnal*, XI (November, 1937), 46–47.

[68] Karelin, "Iskusstvennyi podbor," *Znamia Truda*, No. 109 (January 3, 1918); Protokol Zasedaniia Tsentral'nago Komiteta, October 11, 1917. It would be interesting to know whether Natanson failed of acceptance because he was a radical or because he was a Jew. The latent anti-Semitism in the lower reaches of this party came out in the cases of A. Iu. Feit and Saker. When Feit's candidacy was proposed, the Kuban organization countered with a request for someone with a "Russian name," and Saker was turned down in another district. Whether in the end they succeeded in being adopted, and by whom, we are not told, but in any event they both failed of election to the Constituent Assembly. See *Delo Naroda*, No. 169 (October 1, 1917); Protokol Zasedaniia Tsentral'nago Komiteta PSR, October 4, 5, 1917; Chernov, manuscript com-

and it had not even advanced the candidacy of N. S. Rusanov.[69] The failure of a leader with Natanson's record to gain a seat in the assembly while one was being provided for Oganovski, an intellectual who was not even a party member, is as clear a case of prejudice against the antiwar faction as can be imagined.

In his public statements as well as in private conversation,[70] Zenzinov denied that there had been any discrimination in selecting candidates for seats in the assembly. About his honesty there can be no question, just as there can be none about his prejudice against the whole left element in his party. Doubtlessly he drove his prejudice down into his subconsciousness, whence it exerted a powerful though indirect influence upon his decisions and those of like-minded colleagues, in both the electoral commission of the Seventh Council and the Central Committee. These men strove for impartiality and thought they had achieved it, for it was not difficult to bring their subconscious prejudice into harmony with an honest conscience in view of the youth and immaturity of the Left SR's as contrasted to the record of service and experience of their opponents, or in view of what seemed to be the state-wrecking clamor for peace on the one side as contrasted to sober acceptance of war on the other, which to Zenzinov and his friends seemed the epitome of statesmanship.

Lest anyone misjudge the depth of feeling which made true impartiality impossible, let it be illustrated by an incident that took place. Zenzinov possessed in full measure the Populist reverence for the Constituent Assembly as the embodiment of popular sovereignty, and more than anyone else he had determined the character of his

---

mentary on the minutes of the Central Committee, p. 52. There must also have been friction on the upper levels of the organization. In the secrecy of the Central Committee Avksentiev protested the appointment of Feit as mayor of Odessa, for reasons that were not stated, yet Feit was not a left SR or even a left-centrist SR, and the Central Committee regularly entrusted him with the most confidential missions. Arkhangelski drew up an appeal to the Jews which the Central Committee suppressed. Cryptic references to these actions are contained in the minutes for September 12, 18, and 22, 1917.

[69] Chernov, manuscript commentary on the minutes of the Central Committee, p. 52.

[70] Interview in New York, December 19, 1949; "Iskusstvennyi podbor," *Delo Naroda*, No. 236 (December 19, 1917).

party's representation; yet when the time came to bring these plans to fruition, he did not even vote! The deadlock between the Central Committee and the local organization over whether Gotz or Kamkov should head the ticket in St. Petersburg had been broken by placing Chernov in first position, followed by Kamkov, Gotz, and Mayor Shreider. It was an arrangement that satisfied no one, one of those hybrid lists that faced in two directions while moving in neither. The public was in no greater quandary than the party official who had overseen the nominating process, yet had not been able to satisfy even himself, let alone the public. Like many people who work all their life to attain an objective and then cannot enjoy it when it is won, Zenzinov found himself torn between a desire to join with the millions of his fellow-citizens in their march to the polls and his aversion to supporting a ticket with a candidate whose stand on the war outraged his deepest feeling.[71] It was a conflict between Populist tradition and the nationalism that had grown out of it, and nationalism won. Only the closing of the polls put an end to his mental anguish. Perhaps no other incident illustrates so well the futility of the election or the ravages of war within the SR fold.

The same absurd bracketing of incompatible elements occurred in Moscow,[72] where the slate contained the names of Mayor Rudnev and Anastasia Bitsenko, one of whom had said the Russian people lived only for the war and the other one of whom would go in the name of the Russian peasantry to Brest Litovsk. Even more ludicrous was the situation in Saratov province. Kerenski had consented to run on the SR ticket if in return Gotz and Zenzinov would undertake not to embarrass him by the inclusion of any extremists,[73] but the Saratov Peasants' Soviet, as we have seen, had intruded on this touching entente and the minister-president was incensed to find himself

[71] Interview in New York, December 31, 1951. Denying any personal antipathy to Kamkov, Zenzinov did not attribute his political antipathy to the war—he simply passed over the matter without further comment. It is certain, however, that the war was at the root of the trouble.

[72] See comment of Boris Voronov in *Vlast' Naroda*, No. 164 (November 18, 1917).

[73] Statement to the author in Palo Alto, November 17, 1956. For the mix-up in respect to Kerenski's candidacy in Simbirsk province, see *Volia Naroda*, No. 151 (October 22, 1917). The version here does not entirely correspond to reality, but this author is not at liberty to reveal the reality.

in the company of two left SR's, one of whom, Ustinov, he had clapped into prison in connection with the July disorders.[74] Not only Kerenski felt a sense of frustration; at the opposite extreme radical voters in the industrial center of Tsaritsyn took it out on him and other rightists by scratching their names from the SR list, of course at the cost of invalidating their ballots.[75] Besides revealing the character of this party, these episodes also show that the degree of manipulation by the party bureaucracy in choosing candidates was not as great as the Bolsheviks like to depict; indeed, the impression one carries away is not so much one of manipulation as of anarchy.

If, as is generally conceded, the SR representation in the Constituent Assembly stood well to the right of the party organization and was not nearly so revolutionary as its peasant constituency, the cause of the discrepancy is to be sought in the transformation of the Populist intelligentsia, from which a very large part of the representation had been drawn. All of these intellectuals and "half-intellectuals," [76] as Zenzinov calls them, from the cooperative societies, zemstvos, and schools, had begun to gravitate to the right in the wake of the disillusionment of 1905. The war had greatly accelerated the swing by awakening the latent nationalism which had given birth to Populism in the first place. By the time of the Provisional Government these people were willing to keep the peasants waiting in the villages and the soldiers cursing in the trenches, they were willing to keep the nationalities in a state of uncertainty at the expense of feeding the fires of separatism, if only they could maintain the front against Imperial Germany in unison with the West. The interests of war far outweighed those of revolution, but since they continued to use the traditional revolutionary phraseology after the flame had died in their hearts, their constituents did not realize how far to the right they had moved. And so when their experience and training caused them to be nominated, the peasants elected them to the Constituent Assembly. It was all the harder for the peasants to realize what they were doing because mixed in with these intellectuals were a number of left unionists and more than a few authentic peasants, as our

---

[74] See Lebedev's comment in *Kratkii otchët*, p. 121.
[75] *Pravda*, No. 3 (January 5, 1918).
[76] A way of distinguishing between those who had completed a higher education and those who had fallen short of attaining degrees.

inspection of the Voronezh list has disclosed. Thus the SR delegation in the assembly was not wholly a distorted image of the mass of voters behind it.

Considering all factors, how could the distortion have been prevented and what would the true image have been? If the schism had occurred a little sooner, or the election a little later, so that the two SR parties could have competed throughout the country, it is unlikely that the results would have been very different. The Left schismatics would have elected their men in areas where they already stood at the head of the peasant movement but elsewhere would have suffered from the continued adherence of the left unionists (moderate left and left center) to the party standard and from the attachment of the peasants to the party label regardless of what that label concealed. In fact, a clear-cut and vigorous campaign by the Left SR's might have pulled more votes away from the Bolsheviks than from the PSR. Only a lengthy interval between the schism and the election would have produced an appreciable displacement of strength within the Constituent Assembly. The Left SR spokesman is undoubtedly correct in saying that the millions of votes for the PSR were cast for the old party with the old ideals,[77] which were truly revolutionary, whatever one may think of their socialist quality. But before he and his comrades could convince the Russian peasantry outside of certain limited areas of the justice of their claims to be the heirs of that tradition, it would have been necessary to conduct a lengthy campaign of exposure against the element in the old party which furnished the bulk of the SR candidates for the Constituent Assembly yet consisted of burnt-out revolutionaries who were Kadets in everything except in name.[78] Such a campaign, in fact, was launched, and there are indications that it was producing an effect, even in the Central Black-Earth citadels of Social Revolutionism, in the first months of 1918, shortly before the Left SR's themselves were entombed with the Constituent Assembly and the party from which they had sprung. Had the election been postponed until then, many of these backsliders would have been knocked out

[77] Karelin, "Iskusstvennyi podbor," *Znamia Truda*, No. 109 (January 3, 1918).
[78] That is what Tsereteli, a very moderate Menshevik and their ally in 1917, later called them (interview in New York, December 23, 1949).

of the assembly, without, however, reducing the PSR to the status of a small party, perhaps even without depriving it of its status as the largest single party. For it must be remembered that it consisted, even after the schism, of a great deal more than this highly articulate faction of right SR's, which filled so many seats of power only because of the inept leadership of the central mass of the party. All we can say with certainty is that had there been no confusion and had the vote of the Russian peasantry accorded precisely with its mood, there would have been many more Left SR's in the Constituent Assembly, and many fewer right SR's, but also fewer Bolsheviks.

A perfect assembly has never been elected, and the people had unmistakably bestowed their favor upon the political movement that championed the peasantry, even though they had neither the experience nor the time to distinguish shadings within that movement. It was now up to the SR's to show what they could do with the mandate the people had given them. Their entire effort would take the form of a desperate struggle to make up for lost time, redeem past mistakes, and overcome the handicap which in large measure they themselves had imposed. It will be seen that adversity had introduced a certain flexibility into their decisions and had moved them, if ever so slightly, away from the moral perch on which they had squatted so long. Yet their nature did not change, and beneath the tactical deviations from former positions could be found the same blind devotion to shibboleths. Adversity had not brought the right a sense of reality nor cured the center of its flabbiness. But the party was less hidebound in its stand on burning issues, now that its cause was hopeless, than it had been in the days when greater openmindedness might perhaps have saved that cause. In their endeavor to preserve the fruits of their electoral triumph, the SR's pursued simultaneously three basic objectives: they sought allies to bolster their cause inside and outside the Constituent Assembly, they set to work on a program that would strengthen their cause with the people generally, including those who had turned away, and they laid plans to defend the assembly, arms in hand. Let us see what they accomplished on each of these fronts.

The search for allies involved a break with the past, less because of the will of SR strategists than through force of circumstances. There is no question as to what the element which had been dominant up to the Fourth Congress, and continued to be dominant in the delegation to the Constituent Assembly, would have liked to do. With unerring instinct, it would have made for the Constitutional Democrats and cloven to them, though the heavens should fall and the Russian people be immolated on the altar of war. The resurrection of the Kerenski coalition would have been completed by calling in the Mensheviks (perhaps the Mensheviks would not have responded, owing to their turn to the left, late in the year), and once again the bankrupt heirs of revolutionary Populism would have found comfort in association with the socialist party that wanted a bourgeois revolution, and the bourgeois party that wanted no revolution at all. But, alas, fate had ruled otherwise. There were only fifteen Kadets in the Constituent Assembly—fifteen deputies out of more than seven hundred. The Russian people had done what the Populist intelligentsia would never do: it had taken the measure of the party which had equated the first revolution of 1917 with an outburst of war fever, the second with a plot of German agents, chauvinism with statesmanship, peace with treason, servility to one's allies with service to one's nation, a multinational empire with a unitary nation-state, Slavonic brotherhood with Ukrainophobia, and so on through the catalogue of errors compiled by a political movement that might have stood unrivaled as a monument of folly had it not faced such determined competition from its Narodnik emulators. Not only the workers and soldiers, but also the peasants, had passed it by. Adding the Mensheviks would have helped little, for they also numbered less than twenty, nearly all from Georgia. From Kadets and Mensheviks taken together, the SR's would have derived less support than from the badly underrepresented schismatic wing of their own movement. But, of course, there was no thought of reconciliation with the Left SR's; they had served as a ladder for the Bolshevik ascent to power and they must be shunned and even punished. Blinded by moral indignation, the SR's would not see that the Left SR's were casting about for a means of braking the party of the proletariat, and they would not admit that what they really held against them was their stand in favor of peace.

There was an iron logic about the arithmetic of the assembly's membership: no majority with the Kadets and the Mensheviks, and no stable majority even with the addition of small splinter groups such as the Cossacks and Jews—an unlikely combination in itself. Only in one way could the Socialist Revolutionaries put together a stable majority bloc—by turning to the daughter movement in the Ukraine.

The daughter was not on good terms with the parent and was giving every indication of desiring to live by herself, in a house of her own fabrication. The child had inherited from the parent certain congenital weaknesses in respect to organization, sense of direction, and, above all, leadership. Another trait shared in common, and certainly a weakness as far as family relations were concerned, was an excess of nationalism. With commendable frankness an eminent Ukrainian socialist has acknowledged that "we who belonged to the ruling parties in the Ukraine were not socialists, but only democrats, republicans and *national* revolutionaries." Though called socialists, they were not so in fact. They had adopted the name as a matter of course. In the reaction against tsarism they had gone the whole way and would not be satisfied with anything less than the latest in revolutionary fashions.[79] What Vinnichenko says about socialism in the Ukraine applies to socialism in general in less advanced countries, and notably to Russian Populism, which had never been strong in powers of self-analysis and lacked a spokesman of comparable candor. The excess of nationalism so characteristic of Populism in both its All-Russian and Ukrainian aspects, and so provocative of trouble between them, was nevertheless an attribute of the intelligentsia, and was much less marked at the peasant base of these movements than in the directing spheres. It was also less evident on the left bank of the Dnieper, where the strife of nationalities was submerged in a common dedication to social revolution. Throughout 1917 Kharkov is the symbol of national harmony and social strife, whereas Kiev is the arena of national contention, if not of social truce.

The Ukrainian Socialist Revolutionaries had won some eighty seats in the Constituent Assembly, and together with the Moslem SR's, who reacted in much the same manner to the issues of the day, they

[79] Vinnichenko, *Vidrodzhennia natsiï*, II, 89 ff.

could muster a hundred deputies, six or seven times as many as the Constitutional Democrats and thrice as many as both the allies cherished by the right SR's. Whatever one may think of their organization and leadership—and both were miserable—the Ukrainian SR's were a democratic force to be reckoned with, and their alliance a prize to be sought after. But sacrifices would have to be made. The very first and much the heaviest, as far as the right SR's were concerned, was the Kadet connection. Here no temporizing was possible, for the centralism, imperialism, and peculiar Pan-Slavism of Miliukov's party were wholly incompatible with the chauvinism of the village intellectuals in the Ukraine. There was much talk in SR circles, late in 1917, about hewing to the party line and letting the chips fall where they might, regardless of the attitude of other parties and alliance possibilities, but this talk served as a smoke screen to conceal the maneuver of turning away from former combinations and moving in the direction of a bloc with related national parties.

Giving up the Kadet ties for the time being was only one of the reversals of policy which the SR's now felt impelled to make. In the ceaseless conflict between the Provisional Government and the Ukrainian Rada the dominant clique had never wavered in support of Petrograd, but now, with the establishment of the Soviet government, it completely reversed itself and loudly proclaimed its sympathy for the Rada. The central organ now discovered that the majority in the Rada was socialist; it branded fratricide among socialists as a crime before the International, and announced that in the "war" between the Soviet government and the Ukraine the body of opinion for which it spoke was "not on the commissars' side." [80] Yet it had been on Kerenski's side, usually if not always. It would be difficult to say whether calculation in seeking Ukrainian allies or hatred of Bolshevism had done more to inspire this change of front. In any event it had been made, and we witness the spectacle of a delegation from the SR wing of the peasants' congress trooping in protest to the Commissariat of Nationalities. The line taken by the Soviet government toward the Central Rada, it declared, flagrantly contravened the principle of national self-determination. Stalin told them

[80] "Mezhdousobnaia voina" (Internecine Warfare), *Delo Naroda*, No. 227 (December 8, 1917).

off in language that should forever lay the legend of Bolshevism as the disinterested champion of subject nationalities:

Vam zhe izvestno, chto my stremimsia k revoliutsii v mezhdunarodnom masshtabe, i potomu, esli etogo potrebuiut obstoiatel'stva, my, ne schitaias' s interesami otdel'nykh natsional'nostei, smetëm vsë na svoëm puti (You know well enough that we are out to make a revolution on the international scale, and therefore, if circumstances demand, we shall pay no heed to the interests of individual nationalities but shall sweep everything from our path).[81]

So strong was their new-found zeal for national rights that the SR's now came to favor the reconstitution of the army on a nationality basis. This was something they had always opposed under the Provisional Government on the ground that it would disorganize the army in time of war, an objection no longer valid since the conclusion of an armistice (the SR's were not above using the armistice for their own purposes while denouncing it on every other occasion).[82] The SR's even adopted a charitable attitude toward Ukrainian separatism, viewing it as a natural reaction against the violence of the Soviet regime, and as a transitory phenomenon that would vanish with that regime.[83] One SR theorist even reasoned that regional patriotism, which had proved itself stronger than Russian patriotism, could serve as the basis for reunification of the country after the centrifugal process had run its course and the need for an over-all authority to secure constitutional rights had become generally recognized.[84]

All of this was far removed from the attitude of the SR's in the later days of the Provisional Government, when a whole procession of conflicts had marked, or marred, the relations between the Russian and Ukrainian SR's. The Central Committee had dumped the thorny problem of these relations into the lap of its nationalities

[81] *Delo Naroda*, No. 227 (December 8, 1917).

[82] "Nasiliia nad natsional'nostiami" (Coercion of Nationalities), *ibid.*, No. 237 (December 20, 1917).

[83] Sviatitski, " 'Staroe' ili 'novoe' Uchreditel'noe Sobranie?" ("Old" or "New" Constituent Assembly?), *Narodovlastie*, No. 3, pp. 28–29; Prilezhaev, "Verolomnye moskali iz Smol'nago" (Faith-breaking Muscovites from the Smolny), *Delo Naroda*, No. 229 (December 10, 1917).

[84] Stalinski, "Novyi etap revoliutsii" (A New Stage of the Revolution), *Volia Naroda*, No. 189 (December 9, 1917).

commission,[85] but the SR's in the Ukraine, who were on the spot in a double sense, had taken the bull by the horns and brought matters to an open break by recalling their representative, Zarubin, from the General Secretariat (the executive organ of the Rada). They had also boycotted the two commissions preparing for the Ukrainian Constituent Assembly on the ground that the affirmation of sovereignty for this body contravened the basic SR principle of subordinating the parts to the whole in the form of the All-Russian Constituent Assembly.[86] Negotiations for a bloc between the two parties in the coming election had ended in failure on the Southwestern Front, and the SR conference which made the decision had accorded an ovation to Colonel Oberuchev when he firmly opposed as destructive to discipline demands for the creation of army units on a nationality basis.[87] The land question, extolled as the chief bond of union among Narodnik parties, itself served as a divisive factor, with the SR's opposing on the last day of the Provisional Government any regional initiative in tackling a problem which for eight months they had done nothing to solve. No wonder the Ukrainian SR's had proposed going ahead on a regional basis, and Tkachenko for the Ukrainian SD's had fiercely attacked the Russian SR's as a party which styled itself revolutionary and democratic, yet dragged its feet every time legislation in the interest of the people came up for consideration.[88] Contrasting these actions with those that came after October, we are forced to conclude that prejudice had triumphed over principle, and that for the SR's it was a question of whose ox was being gored, the Provisional Government's or the Council of People's Commissars'? [89]

The PSR was not the only suitor for the hand of the Ukrainian maiden. The Left SR's likewise put in a bid, thinking that perhaps it would be possible to effect a combination of the Ukrainian SR's, the Bolsheviks, and themselves which would serve the dual purpose of controlling the Constituent Assembly and adding to their braking

[85] Protokol Zasedaniia Tsentral'nago Komiteta PSR, October 1, 1917.

[86] See report of the action of the Ukrainian Regional Committee in *Delo Naroda*, No. 187 (October 22, 1917).

[87] *Partiinyia Izvestiia*, No. 2 (October 5, 1917), p. 46; *Delo Naroda*, No. 165 (September 27, 1917).

[88] *1917 god na Kievshchine*, p. 308.

[89] State's attorney Krylenko played up the contrast at the SR trial in 1922; see the report in *Pravda*, No. 169 (July 30, 1922).

power upon the actions of the Bolsheviks. Actually, such a combination would have had around three hundred seats and would only have matched the SR's, but amid the chaotic conditions in this immense and wretchedly administered country no one could be sure what the final outcome of the election would be or how many deputies, and of what persuasion, would get through to Petersburg. The fact that a section of the Ukrainian party was itself leftist in proclivities, particularly in the Kharkov region, and that the party as a whole at its third congress stressed the social side of the revolution more than the national,[90] whetted the expectancy of the Left SR's.[91] They had always pandered to the nationalist sentiment of the Ukrainian comrades and seem, after long vacillation, to have come to the conclusion that Kharkov province could be included in the corpus of the new state.[92] As a final bid for the alliance, the Left SR's at a conference of members of the Constituent Assembly at Kiev accepted the Ukrainian thesis that federal institutions must rest upon a nationality basis instead of upon All-Russian parties or agencies that crossed the lines of nationality.[93]

The marriage between the Left and Ukrainian SR's was never consummated. In an interesting statement, the USR deputy from Kharkov, Ignatius V. Mikhailichenko, pointed out that before October these two groups had marched shoulder to shoulder and that after October they continued to agree on the competence of the Constituent Assembly, whereas relations with SR's of the center, which had previously been strained, could be put on a good footing if the SR's were sincere in favoring the federal reconstruction of Russia. In that case, there would be no reason why all SR groups could not work together in the assembly.[94] His statement is more significant for what it leaves unsaid than for what it says. Implicit in it is a cooling-off between the Left and Ukrainian SR's and a certain drawing together of the latter with the regular SR's. What had happened? The answer seems to be that the numerically predominant

[90] *1917 god na Kievshchine*, p. 404.

[91] Steinberg, *Als ich Volkskommissar war*, pp. 64–65; Oganovski, "Dnevnik chlena Uchreditel'nago Sobraniia," *Golos Minuvshago*, IV–VI (April–June, 1918), 156.

[92] *1917 god v Khar'kove*, p. 57.

[93] *Delo Naroda*, No. 237 (December 20, 1917).   [94] *Ibid.*

right-bank or Kievan faction, more conservative in economic matters and more radical in national, had taken over the helm from the left-bank or Kharkov faction and had given it a turn to the right. Kievan circles are quoted as saying that the voters would not approve an alliance with the left.[95] There were three points of disagreement: over the principle of all power to the soviets, over the nationalization of banks and industry, and over the annulment of state indebtedness, all three of which had been embraced by the Left SR's and enacted by the Soviet government, at least in part.[96] The Ukrainians balked particularly at the omnipotence of the soviets because of the experience in their homeland, where the personnel of these organs had been recruited largely from the Russian and Jewish segments of the population, predominant in the towns. As a consequence, the soviets had been notably unresponsive to the claims of particularism and were suspected of centralizing tendencies.[97] The slogan of ALL POWER TO THE SOVIETS is said to have meant nothing to the Ukrainian peasants, who were organized in their own peasants' union or Spilka and regarded the soviets simply as class organs in the towns, essentially alien to themselves, with no right to the exercise of public functions.[98] Certain statements indicate that the soviets would have been acceptable if they were made Ukrainian, but only as governing agencies in the localities, not on any higher level, which presumably would have been reserved to organs elected on the basis of universal suffrage.[99] All in all, by the late fall of 1917 the controversy over the role of the soviets in the revolution had erected a barrier between the Left and Ukrainian SR's and spoiled their chances of collaboration.

Disappointment also attended the Left SR hopes of detaching from the Ukrainian Socialist Revolutionary Party the considerable wing which shared their social radicalism. Later on there would be a schism in the ranks of the Ukrainian party, just as there already had been in the Russian party, but for the time being nationalist

[95] *Ibid.*, No. 242 (December 28, 1917).
[96] See report in *ibid.*, No. 243 (December 29, 1917).
[97] Prilezhaev, "Verolomnye moskali iz Smol'nago," *ibid.*, No. 229 (December 10, 1917).
[98] See statement of a Ukrainian SR in defense of the Rada, *ibid.*, No. 238 (December 21, 1917).
[99] See declaration of the USR spokesman in the soviet executive committee in *1917 god na Kievshchine*, p. 388.

sentiment prevailed and the left wing of the PUSR decided to go along with the majority in the struggle to uphold the autonomy of the homeland against Soviet encroachments, even though this wing of the party favored the same solution of the land and peace problems that was put forward in the name of the Soviet government.[100] The Left SR's did not win the hand of the Ukrainian party or even of its radical elements, and the deputy from Ekaterinoslav province, Ivan K. Mitsiuk, no doubt appraised correctly the sentiment among his comrades when he said that the Ukrainians stood closer to the Chernov faction of the main party than to the extremists on the left.[101]

Yet the main party was to be no more successful than the Left in its quest for the Ukrainian alliance. Perhaps if Chernov's faction had dominated the delegation in the assembly as it had the Fourth Congress, or if it had known how, or had had the courage, to subordinate the delegation to the directives of the congress, the result would have been different, but the PSR and its Ukrainian offspring continued to be divided by certain issues that were in the open as well as by a carefully veiled issue of still greater significance. The respective attitudes toward the Soviet government diverged widely. While the SR's continued their stand of implacable hostility, the Ukrainian SR's opposed the new regime only in so far as it threatened the autonomy of their homeland, and were quite prepared to recognize it as the "government of Great Russia" if only it would confine its attention to Great Russia. At the third congress of the USR Party, which opened on November 21, Shapoval as reporter on the present situation asserted that the Soviet regime, having been established by the will of the Great Russian people, must be recognized in that capacity and not combated, except when it pretended to power over all of Russia.[102] Similarly with respect to the war: while the SR's were beating their breasts over the Soviet move toward an armistice,

---

[100] *Delo Naroda*, No. 235 (December 17, 1917); see also statement of A. I. Streltsov of Kharkov in *Vserossiiskoe Uchreditel'noe Sobranie*, p. 110.

[101] *Delo Naroda*, No. 224 (December 5, 1917).

[102] *1917 god na Kievshchine*, p. 402; see also report of deputies' conference at Kiev in *Delo Naroda*, No. 237 (December 20, 1917); Sviatitski, " 'Pravitel'stvo Velikorossii' (vopros delegatam iz Ukrainy)" (The "Government of Great Russia" [A Question Addressed to the Delegates from the Ukraine]), *ibid.*, No. 240 (December 23, 1917).

the Ukrainian SR's with their allies in the Rada were preparing to take over negotiations for an armistice on the sections of the front of immediate concern to them (Southwestern and Rumanian),[103] not so much because they shared the antiwar position of the Bolsheviks and Left SR's as because they automatically opposed the foreign policy of the Provisional Government [104] and were less concerned about Slavs under Austrian or German oppression, particularly the Poles, their hereditary enemies, than about those under Russian oppression. Here was a point of deep cleavage between the related parties that undoubtedly would have wrecked their collaboration in the long run, even in the absence of a more basic issue that spoiled the chances of collaboration at the very beginning.

It was the question of sovereignty that divided the Russian and Ukrainian SR's most fundamentally,[105] and continued to divide them even after the October disaster had chastened the PSR and made it eager to contract an alliance with Ukrainian Populism. Because of their peasant constituency, favorable to Ukrainization but unreceptive to the separatism already spreading among the intellectuals, the Ukrainian SR's had never renounced the idea of a "free federation" of all the nationalities inhabiting the former empire,[106] but they meant to have no restrictions on the right of self-determination except what they would yield of their own free will. And the federal authority that came from their hands would be a pale thing, indeed. Theirs was undoubtedly a democratic movement—for example, they would have no truck with the revival of the hetmanship as proposed by the *samostiiniki* (separatists)[107]—but mixed in with the democracy was more than a little chauvinism, the contribution of the intellectuals at the head of the movement. A people that has been stepped on through history is bound to compensate for its harsh destiny with chauvinism unless its spirit be utterly broken. For the Ukrainians in 1917 sovereignty took the form of a free and untrammeled constituent assembly in their part of Russia. Spokesmen

[103] *1917 god na Kievshchine*, pp. 396–97.
[104] See Erde, *Gody buri i natiska*, I, 42. Erde is speaking of the Ukrainian SD's, but his observation could with equal validity apply to the Ukrainian SR's.
[105] See my book, *The Agrarian Foes of Bolshevism*, pp. 269 ff.
[106] Rafes, *Dva goda revoliutsii na Ukraine*, p. 78.
[107] See statement of Kovalevski in *1917 god na Kievshchine*, p. 302.

for the Ukrainian segment of Populism made it abundantly clear that no interference would be tolerated in the preparations for this assembly or in the conduct of its business or the execution of its decisions.[108]

Back of this truculence lay the fear that the power of intervention vested in an All-Russian authority, whether the Provisional Government, the Soviet government, or the Constituent Assembly, would be exercised to narrow the territorial limits of the Ukraine and undermine the political unity of what was left by according the Great Russian, Jewish, Polish, and other minorities broader privileges than the Ukrainians themselves were willing to concede or believed consonant with the interests of the newly founded state. The fears were not groundless, for already there had been passages at arms between the related parties over these issues, one Russian SR going so far as to assert that the Ukrainians could claim as their territory only that which was purely Ukrainian "or at least 80 to 90 per cent so." [109] As for the rest, referendums would decide, the SR view being that, not residence in a given territory, but the wish of the individual citizen freely to inscribe himself in a national union should be the test of nationality.[110] The SR's sought extraterritorial autonomy for minorities, in the Ukraine and elsewhere, particularly for the Jews, the most dispersed people and always the one most befriended by the Narodnik intellectuals, with the exception of the Armenians. The Ukrainian claims to Bessarabia specifically had aroused controversy.[111]

To clear up these differences and ascertain the possibility of an alliance in the Constituent Assembly such as the SR's had come to

[108] See declarations of Maevski, Shapoval, and Kovalevski, in *1917 god na Kievshchine*, pp. 287–88, 297, 342; Steinberg, *Als ich Volkskommissar war*, p. 78.

[109] N. Briullova-Shaskolskaia, "K ukrainskomu voprosu" (On the Ukrainian Question), *Delo Naroda*, No. 110 (July 26, 1917).

[110] I. Sklovski, "K ukrainskomu uchreditel'nomu sobraniiu" (On the Ukrainian Constituent Assembly), *ibid.*, No. 224 (December 5, 1917).

[111] See article of *Privat Dozent* A. V. Boldyr, "Ukraina i Bessarabia" (The Ukraine and Bessarabia), *ibid.*, No. 119 (August 5, 1917), and the letter of protest from the Petrograd Committee of the Ukrainian SR Party in *ibid.*, No. 129 (August 17, 1917). Boldyr had pointed out that on the basis of the only available statistics Ukrainians constituted but 19.6 per cent of the population of the province, with a majority in but one district (*uezd*), Khotin.

favor, the Central Committee of the Ukrainian Socialist Revolutionaries addressed an inquiry to the Bureau of the SR Delegation in the assembly, as well as to the SR Central Committee, asking for their views on the future organization of Russia and on the limits of competence of the All-Russian Constituent Assembly in dealing with nationalities, particularly the Ukrainian nationality. This communication, sent in the form of a telegram, was, in effect, an ultimatum without time limit. It will be noted that the inquiry was addressed both to the bureau and the Central Committee, and not just to the Central Committee. After all, the Ukrainians were SR's, too, and knew the SR system, of which nothing was more typical than divided authority. The bureau busied itself with the matter. It came to an agreement with the delegation itself and with the Central Committee, and wired back to Kiev that the SR's wished to begin by proclaiming Russia a federation, in which the Ukrainian constituent assembly would be free to work out the internal order of the Ukraine on the basis of principles laid down by the All-Russian assembly. Because of the community of viewpoint (!) of the two parties and also because of the way regions differ from one another, it was considered inexpedient to settle beforehand the limits of competence of the All-Russian Constituent Assembly.[112] Once again the SR's had side-stepped the issue, and now for the last time. The Ukrainian SR's drew the logical conclusion from this noncommittal reply. They gave up the thought of an alliance, and went their own way. An excess of nationalism on both sides had destroyed the chances of a combination which alone could have given the SR's a firm hold on the Constituent Assembly. The Populists could not stand together, and so they would hang separately.

A second line of SR endeavor after October was to fashion a program that would captivate the public mind and teach the people to look to the Constituent Assembly for the fulfillment of their desires. In fact, the second effort was to overshadow the first, for, as Rakitnikov proudly told the Fourth Congress, the SR's should act as though they had an absolute majority and, without thought of

[112] *Delo Naroda*, No. 234 (December 16, 1917).

coalition, march straight toward the realization of their program, letting other parties adhere or not as they saw fit.[113] Actually, the SR's had been by no means so independent-minded, yet in their bid for the Ukrainian alliance they had been unwilling to make concessions that would have endangered the economic union of Great and Little Russia, the maintenance of which one member termed a matter of life and death.[114] The nationalities section of their program had been neither altered nor made more definite, and was characterized as before by the endless reiteration of stereotyped phrases. Since the basic SR strategy was to impress the program upon the public consciousness before proceeding in the assembly to the constitution of the executive power,[115] which would inevitably entail a showdown with the Soviet regime, and since nothing new was proposed in respect to the nationalities problem, it is obvious that the play of the party for active public support would stand or fall with its policy in respect to the other two burning issues of the day: land and peace.

The PSR now at last faced the "colossal task" of putting flesh on the ethereal concepts of its agrarian program, of proceeding from the realm of "bare slogans" and "general formulas" to the world of harsh realities. The words in quotation marks are taken from Chernov's inaugural address as president of the Constituent Assembly,[116] and illustrate the quandary, or even the panic, of a society of theorists brought down from the clouds onto earth. But further evasion was impossible, and when a substantial number of deputies assembled in Petersburg after the election, an agrarian commission was set up, representative of all three currents in the delegation on agrarian matters. On one side, and holding the fort, as always, for a "castrated revolution" (the expression is Chernov's), were the "realists" or "state-minded" element, as the right SR's styled themselves in their struggle to contain the agrarian upheaval within limits which would not undermine the productivity of agriculture, as they conceived it, or unsettle the foundations of the state. In their fear of the *okhlos* or mass which in the past they had sought to arouse, and in their

---

[113] *Kratkii otchët*, p. 131.

[114] A. Eliashevich, "Razrushenie promyshlennosti i rabochii klass" (The Ruin of Industry and the Working Class), *Narodovlastie*, No. 2, p. 40.

[115] See the resolution on the Constituent Assembly in *Kratkii otchët*, p. 158.

[116] *Vserossiiskoe Uchreditel'noe Sobranie*, pp. 16–17.

devotion to a state that already had foundered, they were prepared to throw overboard some of the shibboleths of Populism, leaving only a shell of national exaltation into which they would infuse a Kadet substance. On the other side were the "orthodox" or "old believers" who clung to the shibboleths imbedded in the agrarian program and wished to deviate neither from the letter nor the spirit of the promises made to the people. And in between was the "swamp" of dirt-soil deputies, headless and unsure of direction, but determined to shake up the agrarian order and have no foolishness about it.

They were not all of one mind as to how to proceed. The bulk of the peasant deputies came from the congested areas of the Central Black-Earth Region and the Volga, and were animated by an intense egalitarianism which would level everything—peasant holdings as well as *pomeshchik* estates. All lands would go into one crucible and out of it would come equalized holdings, never mind what better-to-do peasants might wish or economists might think. On the other hand, peasants from the more generously endowed regions like Kherson and the North Caucasus had been led to think that their larger holdings would be immune from the leveling process, in so far as these were cultivated by their own labor. But all peasant deputies were as one when it came to despoiling the landowners.

No sooner had the commission assembled than the battle began. As a basis for the agrarian legislation to be enacted by the Constituent Assembly, the "state-minded" people succeeded in having adopted the Maslov land project of October, in preference to the Vikhliaev plan or the SR bill submitted to the Second Duma, but they were not successful in preserving the emasculated features of this typical right-wing Narodnik document, either in respect to the inequalities it would have countenanced in the use of the land, or in respect to the loopholes it left for compensation and hired labor. Under the pressure of the "old believers" and the dirt-soil deputies, compensation was ruled out, the hiring of labor prohibited, save in exceptional cases, and all citizens were to have a right to land, although the "state-minded," battling tooth and nail to hold the positions the Kadets themselves were too weak to man, succeeded in preventing the insertion of "equal" before "right to land." But worse was to come in the plenum of the delegation, much worse, indeed. Here the fierce heat of the revolution could be felt in the temper of the men from Tambov, Saratov, Riazan, and elsewhere, men who were social revolutionaries if not Socialist Revolutionaries, and who had come to Petersburg to put through the *chërnyi peredel* (black redistribution) demanded by the village, without which they dared not return, for, as Deputy Ivan Vasilevich Mamkin of Voronezh told the Constituent Assembly in confused but classic language, the intellectuals were free to pack up and go home, whereas he faced the prospect of swinging from an aspen bough.[117]

After a month's labor—and wrangling—on January 2 the agrarian commission reported back to the plenum. All day the delegation sat on the land question, and far into the night, till two o'clock in the morning. The die-hard right-wing Populist intellectuals, feeling the whole weight of the Russian state on their shoulders, were driven from one position to another, fighting tenaciously every step of the way against the fulfillment of demands to which their party had been pledged for a dozen years. Grossly overrepresented as they were, they did not have the numbers to overcome both sets of adversaries. Perhaps with their education and powers of deception they would have succeeded in climbing back into the saddle had the inarticulate peasants not found a spokesman from the intellectuals (unfortunately his name is not given) who turned back all the arguments of the "state-minded" with the rejoinder that unless these points were inserted, the Bolsheviks and Left SR's would take them over and win the masses to their side. The peasant deputies, having already ruled out compensation for the landowner's property, now forced through a provision confiscating his equipment and livestock and the improvements on his property, all with the assertion that they had paid many times over in sweat and blood for the means of production that would come into their possession. At the same time they evinced a desire for legality, for an equitable distribution of the land and the collective utilization of livestock and implements. The "old believers" were most interested in upholding the principle of the equal right of all citizens to land. Now they had their way, but not until these Rakitnikovs and Chernovs had displayed a firmness quite un-

[117] *Ibid.*, p. 87; Oganovski, "Dnevnik chlena Uchreditel'nago Sobraniia," *Golos Minuvshago*, IV–VI (April–June, 1918), 159.

usual for them—they demanded a roll call and threatened to black-list the backsliders. The "state-minded" had had a bad time; they had been overborne in the commission and routed in the plenum. They could only wring their hands and wail that "the comrades have ruined the land reform." Actually it had been ruined long before, by the whole past of Russia and by people who posed as "state-minded" when they let all pressing matters, agrarian and otherwise, be deferred to the Constituent Assembly, and then let the Kadets defer the assembly.[118]

If the "state-minded" had tried so strenuously to curtail the land reform, would they not fight ten times harder to block any concessions to the public clamor for peace? Their devotion to France and respect for Great Britain, their dislike and dread of Germany, amounting to Germanophobia (one of their distinguishing characteristics), their solicitude for Slavs not under Russian rule, their Turkophobia—in fact, their whole essence—would have suggested an unbending attitude on the war, as would also the full-throated cry of the SR pack in the days following the October overturn. When the Soviet government initiated action toward a separate armistice, the SR's went into a convulsion, the left center because of the unilateral character of the initiative, and the right because of any initiative at all. An editorial had appeared in the central organ accusing the Soviet leaders of open treason and, in one and the same breath, both bewailing the danger to the Allies as a result of the free hand given Germany and predicting that these same Allies might now turn around and conclude a peace at Russia's expense. Particularly reprehensible, in the opinion of the editor, was the disregard for the millions of lives lost in the war—the logic here being, apparently, that many more must be lost to redeem their sacrifice.[119] Still more authoritative was the voice of the Central Committee, lifted

---

[118] Oganovski, "Stikhiia i razum" (Mass Pressure and Reason), *Volia Naroda*, No. 198 (December 20, 1917); Oganovski, "Dnevnik chlena Uchreditel'nago Sobraniia," *Golos Minuvshago*, IV–VI (April–June, 1918), 145–47; see also reports on the proceedings of the delegation in *Delo Naroda*, Nos. 234, 242 (December 16, 28, 1917). Oganovski, who was in the front ranks of the "state-minded," attributes the ruin of land reform to the failure to achieve a "strong government." He was going to get a strong government, though not of his choosing, and he was going to serve it, though with his mouth closed, which for him must have been very nearly its worst feature.

[119] "Bezumie ili predatel'stvo?" (Madness or Treason?), *Delo Naroda*, No. 205 (November 10, 1917).

in condemnation of a separate armistice, the responsibility for which, it declared, must rest solely upon the usurpers without in any way binding the Russian nation.[120] Fraternization horrified the SR's, who could see at the end of the road only a separate peace, which to them was a "foul peace." [121] Not only the external effects of stopping the war but the internal ones upset the SR's, and one editorial very definitely betrays the fear that demobilization would let the soldiers loose like locusts on the land.[122] The prospect of Allied vengeance on Russia, either by war or by abandoning her to Germany, the helplessness of Russia before German imperialism, her degradation to the status of a colony, the territorial losses to be anticipated, including Courland and Lithuania and perhaps even more, were recurring themes in the SR propaganda of the period, together with the promise that the Constituent Assembly could bring Russia a real peace in the form of a general cessation of hostilities instead of the disastrous isolation toward which the usurpers were heading.

Yet intermingled with these variations on the song of war, from the end of November onward, a different note was sounded. On December 6 the right half of the Second All-Russian Peasants' Congress, in reaffirming the SR position that the only road to peace lay through collective action, tacitly acknowledged Russia's exit from the war with the statement that a separate armistice was now an accomplished fact, which must be taken into consideration.[123] And a few days later, Chernov, while noting the protruding claws of German imperialism in the negotiations at Brest, nevertheless approved of carrying them on because it is "our duty always to do everything possible to bring peace." [124] He did not, of course, approve of the way they were being carried on, for he decried the ludicrous diplomacy of the Bolsheviks, whose actions in engaging in civil war and subverting the army placed them at the mercy of the crowned heads of Central Europe.[125]

---

[120] See the joint manifesto in *ibid.*, No. 219 (November 26, 1917).

[121] "Stupen' k spaseniiu ili skachëk v propast'?" (A Step Toward Salvation or a Leap into the Abyss?), *ibid.*, No. 210 (November 15, 1917).

[122] "Anarkhiia po . . . Leninu" (Anarchy According to Lenin), *ibid.*, No. 206 (November 11, 1917).

[123] *Ibid.*, No. 228 (December 9, 1917).

[124] "Delo mira" (The Cause of Peace), *ibid.*, No. 233 (December 15, 1917).

[125] "Ch'ia pobeda?" (Whose Victory?), *ibid.*, No. 235 (December 17, 1917).

At the same time that the SR's were moving toward new positions in respect to war and peace, they showed a tendency to admit past mistakes. In the Constituent Assembly they would solemnly pledge themselves to open diplomacy, concealing nothing from the people.[126] This undertaking needs to be interpreted in the light of the admission at the half-congress of peasants' deputies mentioned above that the diplomats of the Provisional Government had worked against efforts to promote peace (and not only the diplomats, we might add). The big break in SR policy on the war, however, came at the end of December when the Central Committee instructed the delegation in the Constituent Assembly to bring in a bill for the formation of a new army on a volunteer basis, to replace the old army, which would be demobilized.[127] For once, the instructions of the new or Chernovian Central Committee coincided with the will of the delegation, and the measure was included in the program to be submitted to the assembly in the name of the party.

The immovability of the Socialist Revolutionaries on the question of war and peace had at last been overcome. Ten months after it had destroyed the monarchy and two months after it had engulfed the moderate revolution, they recognized war fatigue as a factor that must be taken into consideration, and with a solicitude never shown under the Provisional Government, conceded that those who had borne the burden of war for three and one half years had discharged their duty to the fatherland and should be allowed to go home, leaving the task of defense to those who consciously wished to perform it. Six months or even three months previously, when such a concession might have saved the first revolution, the pro-war element in the party would have recoiled in horror before it, and the left-centrist element favoring peace would not, in the name of a non-existent unity, have lifted a finger to put it across. Now, of course, the army was in full tide of self-demobilization. The SR's had also brought themselves to recognize, post facto and de facto, the armistice with the Central Powers—there was little else for them to do if they wished to convert the army from a conscript to a volunteer basis. Instead of breaking off the peace negotiations with the enemy,

---

[126] *Vserossiiskoe Uchreditel'noe Sobranie*, p. 84.
[127] *Delo Naroda*, No. 1 (246) (January 3, 1918).

they proposed to guide them into the channel of a general peace under the authority of the Constituent Assembly. All of this represented real progress on the part of the SR's, progress which but a short time before would have been inconceivable. But in relation to the acknowledged need for an immediate peace,[128] they were still treading water, thinking to achieve the ideal of a general peace on equitable terms which none of the belligerents save Russia desired.

That the SR's had moved, or rather had been moved, from their immobile position is a tribute to the strength of the tide running in favor of peace. Yet the real masters of this party, the Gotzes and Zenzinovs and the men to the right of them, had been swept along by an irresistible current and had not moved of their own volition. There was as little understanding as ever between them and the soldier-peasants. How little they had changed is seen in the words of the SR spokesman in the Constituent Assembly when he said that "our allies now see that we are deprived of the possibility of continuing the war." [129] But it was necessary outwardly to bend before the storm, for the Constituent Assembly had to be convened in the capital if its authority were not hopelessly to be compromised, and to convene an assembly that promised to renew the war in the Petersburg atmosphere of January, 1918, was a physical impossibility. To promise demobilization cost nothing, now that the fate of the old army was obvious to all.

It is reasonably certain, however, that the SR's were not simply bending before the storm but that there was an element of calculation in their decisions. Demobilization of the existing army would in their eyes undercut the basis of Bolshevik power, since their weak faculties of social analysis permitted them to see behind the Soviet regime only the bayonets of a demoralized and disintegrating army. A volunteer army by its very nature would be proof against Bolshevism and would serve as a dependable support for SR rule through the Constituent Assembly—or so they thought, till the experience of 1918 proved that recourse to the hereditary fighting caste of Russian

[128] See especially "Smysl proisshedshago" (The Sense of What Has Happened), *ibid.*, No. 202 (November 7, 1917), an editorial in the left-centrist vein which conceded the strength of Bolshevism and viewed it as a reflex of an organism exhausted by war.

[129] *Vserossiiskoe Uchreditel'noe Sobranie*, p. 80.

society would not only swallow up an SR regime but was incompatible with any form of democratic government. But at the time they could think that they were outsmarting the Bolsheviks by taking up their program for the relief of the fighting man and turning it into a program for the extinction of Soviet power. In promising not to disturb the armistice the SR's probably thought to strengthen their cause with the people without cost to their inner convictions, since they may well have expected the armistice to collapse under the weight of German imperialism.

Land and peace were placed in the forefront of the SR program for the Constituent Assembly. Only after a full-bodied land reform and outward deference to peace were connected in the public mind with the majority position in the Constituent Assembly would the SR's proceed to the question of power, the most ticklish of all, since it involved a collision with the Soviet government and the soviet system itself. The SR's wished to be in a better position than that in which the collapse of the Provisional Government had left them before tackling this problem. First entrenchment, then attack, was their strategy. It was not only inevitable but also legitimate that the showdown should come over power, for the SR's were now talking much the same language as the Bolsheviks on land and peace, the common revolutionary phraseology concealing the profound difference in spirit on both these issues. The chief outward distinction between the two warring camps was now the method of governing, whether by parliamentary or dictatorial means, the SR's depicting themselves as the party of revolutionary freedom and the Bolsheviks as the party of revolutionary violence.[130] The SR's had never wavered in their stand that only the four-point formula of equal, direct, secret, and universal suffrage could be the source of power, and that the soviets must yield their lawmaking functions to the Constituent Assembly, becoming merely class organizations of the toiling masses without public functions, in which reduced status they would enjoy the approval and even the protection of the SR's.[131] Under the slogan of ALL POWER TO THE CONSTITUENT ASSEMBLY that

[130] Oganovski, "Dnevnik chlena Uchreditel'nago Sobraniia," *Golos Minuvshago,* IV–VI (April–June, 1918), 148, 150, 159.
[131] See the declaration of the delegation concerning its program, published in the *Delo Naroda,* No. 245 (December 31, 1917).

body would also divest the Council of People's Commissars of the executive authority and gather the plenitude of power into its hands.

Assuming that the SR's had regained enough popularity through the land and peace core of their program actually to take over the executive power, or that the Bolsheviks had despaired of the situation and tossed it into the lap of the assembly, as the SR's once believed, or affected to believe, might happen, what kind of a government would they have set up? A commission on government had been created by the delegation to consider just this problem. The SR's seemed to be of one mind that the government set up by the assembly should be homogeneous in composition, that is, only socialists should be members. Since more than 600 of some 700 elected deputies were "socialists" of one type or another and there were only fifteen Kadets, two rightists, and nine Cossacks in the assembly, this was scarcely a heroic decision. But no sooner had this daring zig been made than the zagging began. While the executive authority would emanate exclusively from the majority groups in the assembly, the drafting of basic legislation should admit of a certain give and take in view of the fact that numbers alone did not determine the social weight of elements in the population [132]—a clear intimation that the influence of the Kadets on legislation would be far greater than the ratio of 15:700 fixed by the Russian people, which was now to be modified not so much by the "social weight" of the Kadet constituency as by the scores of hidden Kadets in the SR ranks.

There was virtually no sentiment in the SR delegation for an independent executive based on the principle of separation of powers, and none at all for a presidency that might become a point of crystallization for monarchist sentiment. Evidently the members' intuition warned them of the vulnerability of the Populist theory about the peasant's "toiling conscience," while their own pro-war myopia blinded them to the effects of the war on traditional loyalties in the village. Nearly all were prepared to accept Vishniak's plan of a ministry responsible to the assembly. But there was a joker in this plan, conceived by a man who was an SR in political affiliation

[132] Gendelman, "Organizatsiia pravitel'stvennoi vlasti pri Uchreditel'nom Sobranii" (Organization of the Governmental Power in the Constituent Assembly), *ibid.*, No. 225 (December 6, 1917).

but Kadet in spirit. The assembly would choose by ballot a prime minister, who would then fill out the ministry at his discretion. The carte blanche given the prime minister in the matter of selecting his colleagues encountered strenuous objection from many deputies, before whose eyes rose the specter of the Kerenski cabinet with its months of motionless progress in all directions. These deputies wanted to entrust the formation of a government to the president of the assembly or to a special commission.[133] The warmth of the argument over how to constitute the parliamentary ministry which all desired can be understood in the light of developments concerning the presidency of the assembly, which we shall discuss further on.[134] For the time being, however, a decision on the executive power had to be put off, and the whole matter trails off into uncertainty as the central organ ceases to report the deliberations of the commission on government or to say what, if anything, it accomplished. The snag that had developed over the discretionary powers of the prime minister apparently held up the formulation of that part of the program which would have required more skillful handling than any other.

Other aspects [135] of the program to be offered the Constituent Assembly in the name of the party occasioned little controversy because they aroused no interest. They are not, however, without interest for the student of history. Subsoil resources would be nationalized along with sources of water power and private railroads. There would be state control of banks and state regulation of industry with the "broadest participation" of labor unions. Banks and business, then, would not be nationalized; they would merely be throttled, unless, indeed, Kadet influence succeeded in emasculating the control and regulation. Quite interesting was the SR stand on war indebtedness. Instead of annulling the loans from the Allies, as the Bolsheviks and Left SR's had done, the SR's would recognize them as valid but shift the incidence of service and repayment onto the shoulders of the "possessing classes." Here we have an example

---

[133] See report of the session of the commission on government, December 12, in the *Delo Naroda*, No. 231 (December 13, 1917).

[134] See below, pp. 381 ff.; see also p. 462.

[135] See the statement of the delegation on the program to be followed in the *Delo Naroda*, No. 245 (December 31, 1917).

of sheer demagogy. Nothing was more unlikely than for the SR's to follow through on a promise that would have made the Kadets pay for their devotion to war. Furthermore, the "possessing classes" could not have borne this crushing burden, which must have weighed for many years to come upon the Russian nation as a whole. Long before the folly of this promise had been demonstrated, Kadet influence over the fellow-travelers in SR ranks and servility before the Allies would have sufficed to shift the burden back upon the Russian people, who in any event were doomed to be the goats of Allied greed. The Bolsheviks and Left SR's took the short cut of annulment, and paid through intervention. The SR's would some-where have lost themselves in the desert of fulfillment.

More than a search for allies and the formulation of a program would be necessary to sustain the SR bid to govern Russia through the Constituent Assembly. Each passing day made it clearer that the jeopardy in which the October Revolution had placed the assembly was not diminishing but rather growing more acute. At first the SR's seemed to have hoped that the Soviet regime would fall of its own weight or that the objective circumstances which had so dismayed the important people of Russian society, inside and outside the Kadet Party, would sober these fanatics and cause them to steal away abashed. Nothing was so incomprehensible to the SR mentality as people who actually craved power and had the will to use it. A recurring theme in their journalistic or forensic outpourings was that the fate of the Paris Commune awaited the Council of People's Commissars, which had isolated the proletariat by its mad venture and could only lead it to destruction at the hands of the rest of Russia unless it repented in time, stopped the civil war, and surrendered power to the Constituent Assembly.[136] If the civil war ran its course, it would see the SR toiling peasantry pitted against the Bolshevik working class, the cold and hungry industrial north against the rich and populous south.[137] Petersburg would be Paris, and the Russian peasantry would re-enact the role of the French peasantry in

[136] See, for example, the editorial, "Tri sily" (Three Forces), *Delo Naroda*, No. 226 (December 7, 1917).

[137] "5 ianvaria i federativnaia respublika" (January 5 and the Federal Republic), *ibid.*, No. 242 (December 28, 1917).

1870–71, first constricting and then overwhelming the Red fury of the Neva. This reasoning ignored the peasant soldiers who had cast down the monarchy and raised the Bolsheviks to power, presumably because these soldiers would soon be at home and become again like the other peasants, forgetting their war experiences. It ignored the Left SR's, who had divided the peasant movement and arrayed a considerable part of the class behind the new regime. Above everything else, it ignored the core of Populist teaching, which had always emphasized the weakness of the Russian bourgeoisie and the special character of the Russian peasantry, so little comparable to the peasant proprietors of France and other Western lands. Before their eyes these latter-day Populists could see only Kadets and Cossacks. Fixation on the war and rage at the extremists' coup had crowded every other consideration out of their minds, even their own theory.

Yet a different view of Bolshevism was not wanting in party circles. It found expression in the *Delo Naroda*, that organ of many keys, in an editorial which sought to explain events in terms of the strength of extremism rather than its weakness. It was useless to deny the popular character of Bolshevism, declared this editorial, because it was essentially a reflex of an organism overstrained by war. By implication, it condemned those whose loud talk about the interests of the state deafened them to cries for peace. Peace must come; not only the interests, but the existence, of the state depended on it.[138] Weeks passed, and the Soviet regime did not fall of its own weight, nor was it overturned. The time for the Constituent Assembly to meet was approaching, if it were ever to meet. It became steadily more apparent that if the Council of Commissars sent down an order to dissolve the assembly, there would be enough force at its command to execute the order, unless the SR's were able to oppose that force with greater force. Activist elements within the PSR, with some encouragement from the leadership, began to look around for means of accumulating such a force. The defense of the Constituent Assembly could assume various forms, and each of these became the object of intensive though clandestine study in the expiring weeks of 1917.

One form, of course, would be a resort to the "old, time-tested"

[138] "Smysl proisshedshago," No. 202 (November 7, 1917).

tactics of Social Revolutionism in keeping with the grim warning once addressed to the officials of Nicholas II: "You will get it according to your deeds." Both Chernov [139] and Gotz [140] used this language with broad implications of terrorism. Some years later, when he was on trial for his life, Gotz denied this interpretation of his words and said they implied merely an armed struggle to defend the Constituent Assembly.[141] His colleague, Gendelman, asserted that the party had in mind a mass uprising, which had always been for it the highest form of resistance to oppression.[142] But a youthful member of the party who had turned informer maintained that such phrases did refer to terrorism and were so understood by the membership, which had discussed the matter both in private and at party gatherings, before the convocation of the assembly and especially after Brest Litovsk.[143] And when Chernov declared it to be his party's duty to defend the will of the people against ravishers "with all the force at its disposal, as in the days of yore," [144] what else could spring to mind but the spectacular campaign of assassination between 1902 and 1907? Or when Saakian at the opposite end of the country assured the Bolsheviks that "all means without exception" would be used against them? [145] Or when the organ of the right wing summoned the party to close ranks and prepare for war in an upsurge of the old spirit that alone could save it from the Girondins' fate? [146]

A threat to engage in terrorism was not yet the deed. After three years of struggle with Bolshevism the Central Committee would declare that the PSR had never resorted to this expedient,[147] and there is no reason to question the truth of this assertion. The party had moved so far from its underground past in the direction of legality and parliamentarianism that a reversion to a conspirative footing was neither psychologically nor organizationally possible.

[139] See his speech at the Tenth Petersburg Conference in *Delo Naroda*, No. 212 (November 17, 1917).
[140] See his letter to the Fourth Congress in *Kratkii otchët*, p. 11.
[141] Report of the SR trial in *Pravda*, No. 156 (July 15, 1922).
[142] *Ibid.*, No. 170 (August 1, 1922).
[143] *Ibid.*, No. 156; testimony of Semenov in *ibid.*, No. 158 (July 18, 1922).
[144] *Kratkii otchët*, p. 35; *Obvinitel'noe zakliuchenie*, pp. 85–86.
[145] Rathauser, *Revoliutsiia i grazhdanskaia voina v Baku*, I, 97–98.
[146] "Novyi zagovor" (A New Conspiracy), *Volia Naroda*, No. 199 (December 21, 1917).
[147] Izveshchenie Ts. K. Partii Sotsialistov-Revoliutsionerov, December 5, 1920.

The evolution had been particularly marked on the upper levels, less so in the ranks, where a residue of activism could be noted.[148] There was also the feeling in circles to the left of center that since Bolshevism was sustained by part of the population, it would be neither proper nor efficacious to combat it with the same weapons that had been used against tsarism, at least not for the present, so long as it retained the confidence of its popular following. Related to this consideration, but further in the background, was the knowledge that Bolshevism had established a plebeian regime, using plebeian methods and imbued with an animal vigor, without the legal fastidiousness that had sometimes restrained the old regime, and without its sloth and corruption. The creation of the Extraordinary Commission, the embryo of the Red Terror, indicated clearly enough what a resort to violence would entail, and *Pravda* spoke of reprisals in the ratio of one hundred to one. For a variety of reasons, therefore, a resumption of terrorism did not enlist much support in SR circles. Only two or three members of the new Central Committee favored such tactics, one of whom is identified as N. N. Ivanov, while at the other extreme M. I. Sumgin wanted the party to renounce terrorism under any circumstances, a stand that eventually led to his resignation from the Central Committee. Most agreed with Chernov that the weapon should be held in abeyance but that it might be used in the future against "rabid commissars" divested of any shred of public favor. Once more Chernov had found a middle course, but this time there was little need for him to balance off conflicting segments of opinion, for the right wing, also, had no desire to engage in terrorism. He must have acted from conviction, or at least from force of habit.[149]

Late in 1917, however, a plot was hatched under the wing of the PSR which was of a rather serious nature. A small but determined band of men, imbued with the idea that in a struggle with Bolshevism all means were admissible, gathered at the end of November on the

---

[148] Sokolov, "Zashchita Vserossiiskago Uchreditel'nago Sobraniia," in *Arkhiv Russkoi Revoliutsii*, XIII, 31–33.

[149] See testimony of Burevoi in *Pravda*, No. 157 (July 16, 1922); see also testimony of Timofeev and Ivanov in *ibid.*, No. 156 (July 15, 1922), and statements of Gendelman and State Prosecutor Krylenko in *ibid.*, No. 170 (August 1, 1922); *Obvinitel'noe zakliuchenie*, pp. 88–89; Chernov, manuscript commentary on the minutes of the Central Committee, pp. 79, 85.

fringe of a party agency, the Military Commission of the Central Committee. The initiative in forming this group belonged to F. M. Onipko, who was a right SR, a veteran of the French Army,[150] and apparently the most enterprising member of the commission, but others in the group were nonpartisan and disposed to operate accordingly, concealing their plan from the commission as a whole. The conspirators were all military men: Second Lieutenant Ushakov, Chairman Osminin of the Union of the Knights of St. George, army physician Nekrasov, Captain A. M. Zenkevich, Onipko himself, and others. Only Onipko was a party man. After their arrest in January, Osminin, Ushakov, and Nekrasov would say that their sympathies lay with the center SR's [151] (a euphemism at the time for any kind of SR except a left schismatic), but whether this confession revealed their true convictions or served as a blind for views much farther to the right is a matter of conjecture. The impossibility of operating in the Russian capital at the time without a revolutionary coloration may well have made the SR's hosts to elements that in other circumstances would have been their mortal foes.

Less doubt attaches to what these men proposed to do. They planned to abduct Lenin and hold him as a hostage against any further outrages such as the murders of Shingarev and Kokoshkin, which they believed to have been inspired by the Soviet authorities. Such was their stated purpose.[152] But since the two Kadet leaders were killed on the night of January 6–7, and since the plan, at least in general outline, had been submitted to the Central Committee in mid-December, apparently on or before December 12, the falseness of the claim is easily established. While Onipko's plan, according to a colleague on the Military Commission, envisaged Lenin's removal from the scene as a hostage, it did not exclude his "more definitive" removal as a corpse. The concrete plan of abduction appears to have been worked out by Ushakov and Osminin, and whatever Onipko's intent may have been, there is little doubt that the hard core of

[150] For information on Onipko, see V. I. Lebedev, *Iz riadov frantsuzskoi armii*, pp. 22–24 and *passim*.
[151] "Popytka uvoza V. I. Lenina (Ul'ianova) iz Petrograda" (An Attempt to Abduct V. I. Lenin [Ulianov] from Petrograd), *Izvestiia TsIK i petrogradskago soveta*, No. 20 (284) (January 26, 1918).
[152] *Ibid.*

nonpartisans entrusted with the execution of the plan meant to kill Lenin. Such was their purpose, according to Ia. N. Spiridonov, the soldier who gave the plot away, and such would have been the outcome, according to Kerenski, who knew or became acquainted with one or more of the principals involved.[153] Nor was Lenin the only intended victim. Trotski, also, was slated for "removal," and beyond these immediate objectives lay a shadowy plan to eliminate the whole Bolshevik hierarchy. In simplest terms, therefore, the aim was to behead the Bolshevik Party.

The enterprise failed for want of a sponsor, after earnest efforts had been made to carry it out. The movements of the Bolshevik leaders were studied, a web of death woven about Lenin, another about Trotski—how tightly woven, we cannot be sure, as the sources do not agree. An attempt was made to plant one of the conspirators as a chauffeur in the Smolny and another as a janitor in an apartment building frequented at night by Lenin; various other dispositions were also made. The war had inured these men to violence. They meant business, but stood in need of a sponsoring organization, which they expected to find in the party that once had practiced terrorism. Toward the middle of December the time had come to lay their cards on the table, and the plot was disclosed to the Military Commission, which gave its sanction on the ground that in a struggle with Bolshevism the rule to follow was "pomen'she miloserdiia, pobol'she zhestokosti"—a minimum of mercy and a maximum of harshness. But when the matter came before the Central Committee, it met with a different reception. Only two or three members were inclined to favor it. The rest agreed with a "very prominent leader whose opinion carried especial weight" (V. M. Chernov?) that to employ the same means of struggle as against the old autocracy would be absurd and even criminal. The members felt that a wave of terror would be the result, that the rage of workers and soldiers over the disappearance or death of Lenin would overflow in a pogrom of intellectuals. Lenin had a popular following. The four hundred thousand Bolshevik votes in the general election and again in the municipal election could not be explained away by wishful thinking.

---

[153] Statement to the author in 1956. Kerenski also called my attention to the two articles on the topic in *Izvestiia*.

With near unanimity the Central Committee turned down the plan.
While such particulars, unfortunately, could not be expected to
appear in the minutes, there is a brief notation for the session of
December 12 to this effect: [154]

> 2. It is called to the attention of all comrades through the bureau of
> the delegation in the Constituent Assembly that the Central Committee
> considers that such means of combating Bolshevism as terrorism are at
> the present moment wholly inadmissible.
> 3. A special commission is entrusted with the duty of supervising the
> work of those comrades who are engaged in organizing the defense of the
> Constituent Assembly.

There is no doubt that these measures were evoked by the affair
in question, whether or not this was the session at which the abduction plot received the *coup de grâce* at the hands of the Central Committee. That organ went even further, and ordered Onipko to disband his terrorist group. But though Onipko himself was bound by
party discipline, his nonpartisan associates were not, and though the
abduction of a man in Lenin's position required the services of an
elaborate organization, there were simpler means of attaining the
same end which did not.

The incident on New Year's Day, 1918 (O.S.), was doubtlessly
the muffled echo of this affair in place of the major detonation that
had been planned. On that day Lenin delivered a speech of welcome
to volunteers who were leaving for the front. According to the contemporary Soviet account, he was planting the seed of the "mighty
Socialist Army" of the future—truly a remarkable forecast of things
to come, for never has a prophecy been more justified in the light
of future developments nor less justified by the circumstances of the
hour. As he was being driven away, four shots were fired at his car.
Lenin did not even hear the shots. "He was sitting in deep thought,
meditating upon the construction of proletarian happiness." But
Fritz Platten, the Swiss Social Democrat who was riding with him,
lacked such powers of concentration and heard the shots; with a
swift motion, he pulled Lenin's head down and saved his life.

[154] Protokol Zasedaniia Tsentral'nago Komiteta PSR. These points are omitted
from the minutes printed in *Partiinyia Izvestiia*, No. 5 (January 20, 1918), pp.
45–46.

"However, a traitorous bullet grazed a finger on the hand that had bent the head of the people's leader." [155] Whether or not Lenin had as close a call as the Soviet press makes it out to be, it was a serious incident, and one that opens up a broad avenue of speculation as to what would have happened to his party had Lenin been removed from the scene while Sverdlov and Stalin were still upon it. Both SR and Soviet sources treat the shots on New Year's Day as an outgrowth of the frustrated plot of abduction. But when the Soviet press spoke of a "black coalition" between Gotz and Purishkevich to sustain the activities of hired murderers, it went far afield. The PSR as such was no more responsible for the attempted assassination of Lenin than for the actual assassination of Stolypin.[156]

Terrorism had been firmly rejected, alike by party opinion and the Central Committee, as a means of saving the life of the Constituent Assembly. There was another method, less open to objection, more worthy of a party with mass support, and hallowed in revolutionary tradition, the general strike. Strange to tell, the new left-of-center Central Committee chosen at the Fourth Congress proved more receptive to the idea than the right-of-center delegation in the assembly, whose defense the strike was to aid. At its first meeting the new Central Committee set up a subcommittee of four to feel out sentiment in workers' quarters and get in touch with public organizations, preparatory to initiating such action, which might be adjudged inopportune at the moment but could become in the near future an indispensable means of struggle.[157] The committee also sent a representative to the interparty conference held

---

[155] "Pokushenie na tov. Lenina" (An Attempt on Comrade Lenin's Life), *Izvestiia TsIK i petrogradskago soveta*, No. 1 (265) (January 3, 1918).

[156] *Ibid.*; "Popytka uvoza V. I. Lenina (Ul'ianova)," *Izvestiia TsIK i petrogradskago soveta*, No. 20 (284) (January 26, 1918); Sokolov, "Zashchita Uchreditel'nago Sobraniia," in *Arkhiv Russkoi Revoliutsii*, XIII, 46–48; Vladimirova, *God sluzhby "sotsialistov" kapitalistam*, pp. 115–19. A vague report of the arrest of a "rather prominent SR of the left center" who had been promised 25,000 rubles to kill Lenin and Trotski is printed in the *Delo Naroda*, No. 231 (December 13, 1917). Where this fits into the picture, if at all, is anybody's guess.

[157] Protokol Zasedaniia Tsentral'nago Komiteta PSR, December 8, 1917; Chernov, manuscript commentary on the minutes of the Central Committee, p. 79. Again, this portion of the minutes was omitted in the version published in the *Partiinyia Izvestiia*, No. 5 (January 20, 1918), pp. 43–44.

on December 12 to discuss the question of a strike in defense of the assembly.[158] The All-Russian Employees' Union had offered through Berkenheim and Chaikovski, Populists of the far right, to support a general strike, but the SR delegation in the Constituent Assembly would not espouse this course of action: "We do not object to a general strike, but we will not lead it and consider it undesirable even to be directly connected with it"—a decision, it is true, which had not been reached without a stormy discussion.[159] The general strike never eventuated, for reasons more basic than the delegation's want of enthusiasm.

As it turned out, the Socialist Revolutionaries neither resorted to terrorism nor fomented a general strike but centered their attention on providing an armed defense for the Constituent Assembly. To coordinate their activities along these lines with those of other groups, an interparty Committee to Defend the Constituent Assembly was set up, consisting of SR's, Mensheviks, Popular Socialists, and some Kadets. In addition to the parties, various public bodies sent representatives. The SR contingent was drawn from the right wing of the party. But it was the Popular Socialists under Chaikovski who constituted the backbone of the committee, and the cooperative societies which provided it with funds. The PSR as such did not operate through the Committee of Defense but had its own organ in the Military Commission of the Central Committee, which entered into relations with the Committee of Defense at the suggestion of Likhach and received money from it to help organize the defense of the assembly.[160]

The Military Commission, therefore, is the key organ in respect to PSR plans to save the assembly. We have already encountered the commission in dealing with the October Revolution, and particularly the cadet uprising in the capital. Now we must follow its subsequent history amid the new conditions created by the triumph of Bolshevism. If, as all accounts agree, the commission had languished before October, being the stepchild of the party and the

---

[158] Protokol Zasedaniia Tsentral'nago Komiteta PSR, December 12, 1917.

[159] Sokolov, "Zashchita Uchreditel'nago Sobraniia," in *Arkhiv Russkoi Revoliutsii*, XIII, 35.

[160] *Ibid.*, pp. 36–37; testimony of Likhach in *Pravda*, No. 131 (June 15, 1922); Vladimirova, *God sluzhby "sotsialistov" kapitalistam*, pp. 88–89.

butt of constant ridicule, stinted in funds and personnel, with a permanent staff of three or four, virtually cut off from the army and having only the most tenuous of ties with the garrison, one does not see how it is possible to speak of the shattering effect of the October Revolution upon an organism that scarcely breathed, or of a worsening of the situation, after the cadet rising, as a result of the flight of its most active members—Colonels Krakovetski and Bruderer, and Secretary Rakitin-Broun.[161] At any rate, it was certainly a wreck after October, if not before, and the remaining personnel was not capable of any serious work in the military or conspirative sense.

Critics seemed to hold Vladimir Utgof—certainly now, if not before, the main personality in the commission—in low esteem, citing his half-literary studies of the war as a symbol of the futility of an organization that was supposed to reach out to the soldier mass and not just the military intelligentsia. But this son of a general of the gendarmerie—his real name was Deriuzhinski—was a sincere and intelligent man, distinguished among Socialist Revolutionaries by his ability to think clearly. His remarks at the Third Congress, analyzing the predicament in which the party found itself, though offering no solution (there may have been none), had set him apart in a society of wishful thinkers.[162] By conviction an SR of the left center, he suffered from the same frustration as V. M. Chernov; he was unable to march with the right because he was against war, and unwilling to throw in with the left because he harbored no illusions about Bolshevism. At the trial in 1922 he bore himself well, his tragedy being that of an honest but open-eyed revolutionary who sees his ideals corrupted from the hour of their triumph. But as a member of the Military Commission—that is, as an organizer of civil war—he was not an effective worker, since he could never be wholeheartedly with either side, realizing only too well the drawbacks of both.

The parlous condition of the commission must be viewed in its

[161] See report of Nikanorov (Nikiforov?—name varies) to the Fourth Congress in *Partiinyia Izvestiia*, No. 5 (January 20, 1918), pp. 14–15; Sokolov, "Zashchita Uchreditel'nago Sobraniia," in *Arkhiv Russkoi Revoliutsii*, XIII, 39; Semenov, *Voennaia i boevaia rabota PSR*, p. 9; Vladimirova, *God sluzhby "sotsialistov" kapitalistam*, p. 105.

[162] See *The Agrarian Foes of Bolshevism*, p. 481, n. 72.

context, as a natural consequence of the party's basking in the sun of legality after long years of molelike existence. But now with a great electoral victory to defend and a predatory regime on the prowl, this state of affairs had to end. The Fourth Congress shook up the moribund commission, gave it a transfusion of new blood, and charged it with gathering an armed force on which the Central Committee could rely in defending the assembly. The commission was also to propagate the idea of defense among the soldiers generally. It was to consist of two members from the Central Committee (actually there were three—the SR's rarely paid attention to their own stipulations), four from the SR delegation in the assembly, and ten from the military section of the Fourth Congress.[163] The military element held the ascendancy over the civilian, and communicated to the commission its will to action and its penchant for violence, as is attested by its stand on the abduction plot mentioned above. Among the most active recruits taken from the army were the physician Boris F. Sokolov, who became chairman of the commission; his colleague from the Southwestern Front, Dmitri P. Surguchev, who is listed as a commissar; and still another, better-known, commissar, G. I. Semenov, who had served in that capacity with the Ninth Army and then with the celebrated Third Cavalry Corps, which had moved on Petersburg in the days of Kornilov's rebellion. Kerenski had advanced Semenov, with Gotz's approval,[164] their faulty judgment again being displayed in this instance, for in the years of despair Semenov ratted on the PSR and turned state's witness in the great trial of 1922. Sokolov belittles the role of Semenov, asserting that he was not at the time a member of the commission but merely a collaborator entrusted with secondary tasks,[165] whereas other sources make it clear that not only was he a member, but that he directed the work of the commission in Petersburg.[166]

When Semenov came in, Utgof went out, displeased at the direction the work had taken at the hands of Semenov and I. S. Dashev-

---

[163] *Partiinyia Izvestiia*, No. 5 (January 20, 1918), p. 15.

[164] *Izvestiia*, No. 134 (June 18, 1922).

[165] "Zashchita Uchreditel'nago Sobraniia," in *Arkhiv Russkoi Revoliutsii*, XIII, 40.

[166] See testimony of Likhach in *Pravda*, No. 131 (June 15, 1922); testimony of Gotz in *Izvestiia*, No. 136 (June 22, 1922); Vladimirova, *God sluzhby "sotsialistov" kapitalistam*, p. 103, n. 3; Semenov, *Voennaia i boevaia rabota PSR*, p. 9.

ski,[167] another informer in the days of adversity. Gotz speaks of Semenov's "energy" in performing the "responsible" work entrusted to him. What was gained in energy and decision was lost in character and stability. Semenov's assumption of leadership also resulted in the elimination of Dr. Paevski, a member of the party since 1904, who had arrived from serving as a physician in the French army, and who would claim that he became the victim of an intrigue in the commission, which Semenov denied.[168] Since enlistment in the French army argues that Paevski was not of the same factional allegiance as Utgof, the fact that both fell out of the commission is evidence that jealousy as well as politics played a role, or else that the new leadership ran roughshod over the feelings of members who did not belong to the clique. Just where Onipko fitted into this combination is not entirely clear. Presumably he found to his liking the dominance of the front element, at whose insistence the reorganization of the commission had taken place,[169] and in any event there is evidence of his collaboration with Semenov.

The relations between the Military Commission of the Central Committee and the Central Committee itself reveal the inner workings of this party with its diffused authority and general formlessness. The Central Committee salaried the members of the commission at 300 rubles a month and the three of its own members who sat with the commission were to direct its activities. Some accounts point to Gerstein as the key figure in this relationship, others to Likhach, and there is a faint suggestion that either may have regarded the presence of the other as superfluous. The third member of the Central Committee set over the commission, Teterkin, had less to do with determining policy. Yet at the same time that it took steps to keep a halter on the commission, the Central Committee endowed it with "a certain autonomy" and permitted it to work in sections independently of one another, in clandestine fashion. Where supervision left off and autonomy began, we do not know, nor, in all probability, did the members of the Military Commission. Gotz

---

[167] *Pravda*, No. 136 (June 22, 1922).

[168] *Ibid.*, No. 130 (June 14, 1922) [due to a printer's error, apparently, the page is marked No. 129 (June 13, 1922)]; *Izvestiia*, No. 129 (June 13, 1922).

[169] Sokolov, "Zashchita Uchreditel'nago Sobraniia," in *Arkhiv Russkoi Revoliutsii*, XIII, 39–40.

made the remarkable statement that Semenov carried on "responsible work" in the commission without being accountable to the Central Committee. How could that be? Any member of the party was accountable for his actions to the Central Committee as the highest authority between congresses—this point had been made at the Fourth Congress with reference to Kerenski [170]—and if Semenov were not a party member, as it is virtually certain he was and as he was indicted for being, then how did he come to be a member of the Military Commission, in charge of its work in the capital? Here we have an example of how the SR's conducted their affairs, from the days of Azef to the final disasters of 1918.

Besides the Central Committee, the SR delegation in the Constituent Assembly also had a tie-in with the Military Commission through two of its members (the plan called for four),[171] presumably Sokolov and Surguchev. Though the delegation was predominantly right of center and the new Central Committee left of center, neither shared the militant spirit of the commission and repeatedly found it necessary to dampen its ardor. Gotz says that the commission was given to adventure, with a tendency to exaggerate the forces at the party's disposal and with a dangerous misconception of the relationship between the minority of initiative and the mass of toilers. Whereas the commission acted on the principle that it was only necessary to organize some action in order to win mass support, the Central Committee preferred to wait until the masses moved on their own accord before standing at their head with whatever forces the party could mobilize, either through the Military Commission or otherwise. Gotz summarized the relationship by saying that "the Central Committee acted as a strong brake on the Military Commission." [172]

Such was the machinery for the defense of the Constituent Assembly. Among the possible sources of an armed force, the most obvious was the Petersburg garrison. But there the prospects were

[170] See *Kratkii otchët*, p. 95 and *passim*.

[171] See Dashevski's statement in *Pravda*, No. 131 (June 15, 1922).

[172] Testimony of Gotz in *Izvestiia*, No. 136 (June 22, 1922); testimony of Likhach in *Pravda*, No. 131 (June 15, 1922); testimony of Paevski in *Izvestiia*, No. 129 (June 13, 1922); Sokolov, "Zashchita Uchreditel'nago Sobraniia," in *Arkhiv Russkoi Revoliutsii*, XIII, 39-40; Vladimirova, *God sluzhby "sotsialistov" kapitalistam*, pp. 26, n. 2, 103, n. 3, 107-8; *Obvinitel'noe zakliuchenie*, pp. 60-61.

bleak, indeed. Work in the garrison had virtually ceased after the October overturn and party cells had either been destroyed by the Bolsheviks or had died out "under the circumstances"—that is, had withered in the fierce heat of the soldiers' aversion for anything connected with the Provisional Government, and so with the war.[173] Now it was the duty of the reorganized Military Commission to re-knit ties with the garrison units and reestablish party cells in them as support for the assembly.[174] It was not an easy task. The garrison may not have been committed to Bolshevism, but that party had the inside track, and the last thing the soldiers wanted to hear about was anything in the way of fighting.[175] Orators defending the Constituent Assembly were howled down at a meeting of the Volynian Regiment, and the right SR Gizetti was even struck.[176] Nevertheless, the work continued and by December 20 had borne fruit in the Fourth Petrograd SR Military Conference, at which representatives from most garrison units were present.[177] The conference elected a Petrograd Military Commission of twelve to share with the Central Committee's Military Commission the work of winning over the garrison. But regaining a foothold in the garrison did not mean moving it to action in the interest of the assembly. In so demoralized a condition, the garrison was a force only in the absence of any other force; its weight in the scales was comparable to that of an armed mob.

When a group of activists from the front, among them Sokolov, made the rounds, looking for elements of the garrison that were least demoralized and most responsive to the message of the Military Commission, they discovered that unit after unit must be written off as a total loss. Nothing could be done with the Jäger or Pavlovski Regiments, or with the Volynian. Only three units could conceivably be swung into action, having preserved some discipline

[173] See report of the Fourth Petrograd SR Military Conference in *Delo Naroda*, No. 243 (December 29, 1917).

[174] Testimony of Keller in *Izvestiia*, No. 131 (June 15, 1922).

[175] For SR appraisals of the mood of the garrison, see I. Dashevski, "Voennaia sektsiia IV-go s"ezda" (The Military Section of the Fourth Congress), *Partiinyia Izvestiia*, No. 5 (January 20, 1918), pp. 13–14; Sokolov, "Zashchita Uchreditel'nago Sobraniia," in *Arkhiv Russkoi Revoliutsii*, XIII, 25–26, 40.

[176] *Delo Naroda*, No. 222 (December 2, 1917).

[177] *Ibid.*, No. 243 (December 29, 1917).

and a certain immunity to "scarlet fever." These were the Semenov-ski and Preobrazhenski Regiments and the armored car division. To these on Sokolov's list, Likhach added the Izmailovski Regiment (in part) and several special units.[178] The Military Commission decided to concentrate its attention upon the first three mentioned as the most promising base upon which to build. Though largely non-partisan, the regimental and company committees of these units were anti-Bolshevik in sentiment, relations were satisfactory between officers and men, and there were a fair number of Knights of St. George, as the holders of decorations for wounds at the front were called.

It now became the endeavor of the Military Commission to raise the specific gravity of the anti-Bolshevik elements in the two regiments and the armored car division by drawing in reliable elements from the front.[179] For this purpose the Military Commission brought in over 600 officers and soldiers during December from the more remote fronts, where the election had revealed a relatively small degree of Bolshevik penetration. The ringleaders of the new commission, Sokolov and Surguchev, themselves came from the South-western Front and for personal as well as political reasons found it more feasible to recruit men there and on the neighboring Ru-manian Front. The soldiers thus brought to the capital were distributed among the companies of the two regiments, more in the Semenovski than the Preobrazhenski, and some specialists, mainly ex-students, were introduced into the armored car division. But in order to have an immediate striking force at hand, not all of the arrivals were so dispersed. Some were placed in a dormitory secured with the aid of a "public-spirited citizen from the Red Cross" as "students" in a new "soldiers' university," which was opened in mid-December with the sanction of the Soviet government. The "students" arrived from the front well armed with hand grenades as well as rifles. Though only a handful in number—some "tens" in the Russian phraseology—their resolution is said to have made them a force to be reckoned with. The Central Committee, however,

[178] *Pravda*, No. 131 (June 15, 1922).
[179] Sokolov, "Zashchita Uchreditel'nago Sobraniia," in *Arkhiv Russkoi Revo-liutsii*, XIII, 41–42.

stopped this build-up as a risky adventure, and in the end nothing came of the enterprise except the arrest of a number of unusually frustrated students.[180]

It would have been nice, of course, to bring not individuals, but whole units from the front to defend the assembly. And that is what the Central Committee had in mind when it conducted a desperate search for some substantial force, any force, that could be used in place of units from the Petersburg garrison, which, in the opinion of the committee, was so riddled with Bolshevism as to be irredeemable. It did permit the Military Commission to go ahead and see what it could do by way of organizing support in the garrison, but without great expectations.[181] Meanwhile the committee itself looked to the front for salvation. And on the face of things, not without reason. In the November election the SR's had carried the Southwestern Front decisively, and the Rumanian and Caucasian Fronts overwhelmingly. An inspection of these sections of the army a few weeks after the election, however, would have revealed a very different situation from that which existed on paper. The soldiers' soviets or committees were still in the hands of the moderates, but down below, in the rank and file, the same ferment was going on as on the Northern and Western Fronts, only more slowly and without the same degree of infiltration from the industrial centers. Delegates from the Petersburg garrison managed to get through to these fronts in December and found the SR defenses easy to penetrate. One of their specific reports concerns the XXIV Corps of the IV Army, located at Kumaneshty on the Rumanian Front. They found an amorphous mass of soldiers whose mood had not crystallized. The isolation of the Rumanian Front was such that news arrived two weeks late, and the insulation devised by the defensist elements entrenched in the soviets was such that the news came from like-minded outlets in Kiev and Odessa or the Black Sea naval centers, while literature from Petersburg was shut out entirely. Once agitation had started, however, most of the soldiers rallied to the platform of the Petersburg Soviet, the Ukrainians as well as the Russians. The delegates were everywhere welcomed, the officers took

[180] *Ibid.*, pp. 41, 44–45; *Obvinitel'noe zakliuchenie*, pp. 12, 60.
[181] Testimony of Likhach and Dashevski in *Pravda*, No. 131 (June 15, 1922).

refuge under the Rada's wing, and the soldiers regretted that they had had so little contact with Petersburg. A shift in political sentiment followed: "Very many are disillusioned in their vote for the SR list." [182]

On the Caucasian Front, seemingly the other chief reservoir of SR strength in the army after October, the same process was taking place. At first the Bolsheviks were strong only in the Baku garrison, where they received 2,675 of the 3,093 soldier votes in the October municipal election. The next month for the front as a whole they elected only one deputy against five for the SR's. But the crumbling process went on rapidly and in December the regional army congress threw out the SR's and chose a new soviet, Bolshevik in majority. The mood of those soldiers who had passed over can be judged from a communication addressed to the old soviet by the committee of an infantry regiment on December 8. The members of the regional soviet, it declared, were scoundrels of the worst kind, engaged in fighting those who did much for the soldiers, especially Lenin, in order to thwart their efforts for peace. It was warm in the soviet, warm for these scoundrels. "If you were in the trenches, you would not go against Lenin, but would do all you could to strengthen his power so that peace could be concluded as quickly as possible." Lenin was a "savior on earth" whose thoughts were centered on saving human life, as those of the regional soviet were on continuing the war. If peace were not made by New Year's Day, the soldiers in the regiment would desert, and the first thing they would do would be to kill the members of the regional soviet. "Think it over. . . . and live—else death awaits you." [183]

The conclusion is inescapable that only time was needed to make the more remote fronts resemble the Petersburg garrison. For the Central Committee it was a bitter experience, this belated realization of how costly the experiment in coalition and the party's stand on the war had been. More than once Likhach traveled to the front,

[182] "Delegaty Petrogradskogo garnizona na fronte" (Delegates of the Petrograd Garrison at the Front), in *Krasnyi Arkhiv*, LXXXV (VI, 1937), 55. For similar reaction in the XII Corps of the VII Army on the SW Front, see p. 48. A re-election of the soviet in the XII Division of the VIII Army, however, kept the right SR's in power (p. 50).

[183] G. Khachapuridze, "Pobeda Velikoi sotsialisticheskoi revoliutsii v Zakavkaz'e" (The Triumph of the Great Socialist Revolution in the Transcaucasus), *Istoricheskii Zhurnal*, X (October, 1937), 100–1.

looking for support in likely and unlikely places. Other members did likewise, especially Gerstein. No stone was left unturned, no rumor unexplored. A report came in that the garrison at Luga, a town south of Petersburg on the line to Pskov, showed antipathy to Bolshevism and was ready, at least in part, to move into Petersburg to guard the assembly. The Military Commission, ever sanguine in temperament, wished to take advantage of this mood, but the Central Committee sent one of its own to investigate. His appraisal was different from that of the commission, and doubtlessly more accurate: he advised against the "current adventure" of the hotheads in the commission; and the attitude of Vikzhel, which spoke fair words but denied the use of the railroads to troop movements directed against the Soviet government, also helped to kill the project.[184]

Even more pathetic was the Wesenberg venture of the Central Committee. It had caught wind of a rumor that a Ukrainian division in that Estonian town burned with a desire to get to Petersburg so that it could fight under the SR banner. The Central Committee should have known that there was scarcely a division in the Russian army which desired to fight under any banner, but hope springs eternal in Populist breasts, and Gerstein sent Paevski to Wesenberg, and also to Pskov, to ascertain the mood of the troops, giving him his overcoat to conceal Paevski's French uniform.

"What did you find in place of this burning desire?" asked state's attorney Krylenko at the trial in 1922.

"I found," replied Paevski, "that the division, in truth, burned with a desire to get to Petersburg, but only as a means of returning sooner to the Ukrainian homeland." [185]

Pskov was no better. Likhach also went to the front, only to discover that hopes invariably were based on illusions. He returned empty-handed with the conviction that if conditions in the Petersburg garrison were hopeless, those at the front were even worse.[186]

Grasping at any straw, the SR's turned to the national minorities

[184] Sokolov, "Zashchita Uchreditel'nago Sobraniia," in *Arkhiv Russkoi Revoliutsii*, XIII, 45–46. The identity of the committeeman is not clear from the cryptic reference in the text to "G . . . . . ch." Before the reelection of the committee at the Fourth Congress, only Gurevich's name would fit; after the reelection, no one's would. The best guess is that the author was inaccurate, and that Gerstein was the emissary.

[185] *Pravda*, No. 129 (June 13, 1922); *Izvestiia*, No. 129 (June 13, 1922).

[186] *Pravda*, No. 131 (June 15, 1922).

in the hope that these might make a contribution to the defense of the Constituent Assembly. Some of them maintained armed bands in the capital or elsewhere, probably in the form of splinters from the demolished structure of the old army. The hopes of Peter Shaskolski were centered on these armed bands—he is quoted as saying "all his hopes." He arranged a conference of minority groups to discuss the matter. It was well attended. Only the Poles and the Finns did not come—they did not consider themselves national minorities, but independent nationalities. The separatists of other nationalities, however, were well represented. At the question, "How many armed men can each nationality provide for the defense of the assembly?" they wanted to know, first, what would be its stand on self-determination—would that principle be limited to federation or extended to embrace independence? Until satisfaction was secured on this score, declared the Russophobe representative of the Lithuanians, not one bayonet would be placed at the service of the assembly. The SR's, of course, were not prepared to commit themselves to independence, and the conference ended in failure. A second one was held with the separatists, including the Ukrainians, absent. But only the Armenians and the Jews volunteered any assistance. The old bond between Populists and Armenians, rooted in a common dislike for the Turks, still held, and the Armenians were relatively well armed, having two machine guns. Not so the Jews, who could put 200 men in the field, armed with an order for rifles, but without the rifles themselves, since the Provisional Government had gone out of business before filling the order. The second conference proved no more fruitful than the first, and the effort to find support in the national minorities ended in fiasco.[187]

The Petersburg proletariat had once given strong backing to the SR's. Had the wells of sympathy dried up so completely that now the SR's could not emulate, even on a reduced scale, the work of the Bolsheviks in organizing the Red Guard? In the opinion of Boris Flekkel, secretary of the Petersburg organization, the working masses of the capital had shaken loose from SR and Menshevik influence without becoming Bolshevik, however willing they might

[187] Sokolov, "Zashchita Uchreditel'nago Sobraniia," in *Arkhiv Russkoi Revoliutsii*, XIII, 37–38.

be to follow that party for the time being. The SR's refused to write off the proletariat as a total loss and decided to complement their work in the garrison by forming in each city district an armed squad of workers. Paevski was placed in charge of this work under the general supervision of Gerstein, and a head man was named in each district. But an army physician in a French uniform was not a happy choice, and soon Paevski was superseded by C. G. Kononov, a worker active in the class movement since 1898 and a member of the PSR since 1902. Yet little was accomplished. In a city swimming in arms, these were hard to obtain except with the approval of the soviet, which under the energetic leadership of Trotski had pretty well cut off the supply to the counterrevolution. Moreover, the workers opposed to Bolshevism had no desire to fight against it, partly because of the general loathing for further bloodshed and partly because they looked upon Bolshevism as a proletarian movement with which it might yet be possible to come to terms. So in a great industrial center with hundreds of thousands of workers the most optimistic estimate of the yield of this effort is 2,000 SR guardsmen, the majority without arms, many absent from muster, and the rest low in spirit—admittedly a paper strength that was not to be relied upon. A more meaningful figure, as best it can be deduced from the press version of Paevski's testimony, is a core of sixty to seventy old-line party fighters with up to 300 auxiliaries in the districts, armed with bombs, Mausers, and Brownings—all that the party could cull, in the way of armed support, from the Petersburg proletariat. Much of this weakness, of course, stemmed from the schism, which had taken away from this party at least half, and probably more than half, of its proletarian following, and had sapped it of the youthful elements which would have borne the brunt of armed resistance.[188]

In the Russian capital, of course, lived many people who were neither workers nor soldiers. It was a great business and administra-

---

[188] The SR's found it most difficult to recognize the ravages of the schism or to concede a measure of popular strength to the Left SR's. Their sources ignore or brush over this cause of weakness. On the effort to organize armed support among the workers see Sokolov, "Zashchita Uchreditel'nago Sobraniia," in *Arkhiv Russkoi Revoliutsii*, XIII, 26–27, 43–44; *Izvestiia*, No. 129 (June 13, 1922); *Obvinitel'noe zakliuchenie*, pp. 12, 65; Vladimirova, *God sluzhby "sotsialistov" kapitalistam*, p. 106.

tive as well as industrial center, with a large bourgeoisie and a host of civil servants. The Constitutional Democrats in November had polled a quarter of a million votes. If the SR's could not rally enough support among the workers and soldiers to defend the Constituent Assembly, could they not borrow strength from outside the socialist camp? The city was seething with hatred of Bolshevism—a much stronger motivation for action than love of the Constituent Assembly—and the party was censured by the head of the Military Commission for failing to take advantage of this powerful negative sentiment in the interest of the assembly.[189] The officers of the garrison are described as being passively hostile even to the assembly,[190] but their much greater hostility to Bolshevism would have induced them to accept it as the most feasible means of ending the Soviet regime. Some concessions to conservative feeling would have been necessary, however, the anti-Bolshevik slogans would have had to be more pointed and less equivocal, and differences of principle stressed as well as of method. As it was, the radical slogans of the socialist parties offended people who had trouble in distinguishing moderates from extremists and who were disposed to consign all socialists to one pit of perdition. But had the SR's bid for conservative support, they would have had to renounce all hope of assistance from the workers and soldiers, and this they were not yet ready to do. One part of them would never be ready, and the other part would discover later, when it had a free hand, that one could not invite in the reactionaries and remain master of the house. The earthquake of the revolution had opened a rift in Russian society, and the SR's, unable to move to either side, fell in between.

It was natural that plans for defending the assembly should center in Petersburg, since it would meet there, and had to meet there if it were not to be discredited in the eyes of a nation long accustomed to look to the capital as the center of all authority. Elsewhere little was done to protect the assembly. A proposal to form armed peasant bands received no encouragement from the SR leaders. Both Vishniak from the right and Chernov from the left poured cold water on the

---

[189] Sokolov, "Zashchita Uchreditel'nago Sobraniia," in *Arkhiv Russkoi Revoliutsii,* XIII, 28, 36, 65–66.
[190] *Ibid.,* p. 40.

idea as an ineffective answer to the Bolshevik and Left SR campaign to undermine the faith of the masses in the assembly. Only vigorous counteragitation could preserve that faith and lead the masses to see that their welfare was bound up with the preservation of the assembly, which stood between them and a tyranny that masked its real designs and came to them with lying phrases. So instead of armed bands the peasants were to organize demonstrations, adopt resolutions, and write their relatives at the front and in the garrisons.[191] Unfortunately for the SR's, those relatives, as we have seen, influenced the peasants more than the peasants influenced them. In any event the peasants could not have protected the assembly, even if the Left SR's had not been royally confusing them by splitting their soviets. And in the towns the Bolshevik garrisons acted as a fearful drag. In the one place where something conceivably could have been done, in Moscow, the opponents of Bolshevism had not recovered from the shattering defeat of October. No one wanted to move, not even Rudnev, over whom a strange passivity had settled.[192] Moreover, he was now in Petersburg directing the activities of the SR membership in the assembly. With neither the will nor the means for resistance, the Moscow organization simply marked time and, during the whole period from October to the Eighth Party Council in May, engaged in no military activity.[193]

Preparations for defense of the Constituent Assembly were thus restricted to three military units and a trickle of civilian recruits in a single city of Russia. In addition, there were to be demonstrations of unarmed people, in Petersburg and elsewhere. Before noting the outcome of these preparations, however, we must turn to the state of affairs at the party helm and also examine the attitude of the Left SR's. After that, we shall return to the defense of the assembly, and then deal with the assembly itself and its fate.

[191] Bykhovski, *Vserossiiskii Sovet Krest'ianskikh Deputatov,* p. 306; see also speech of Chernov to the right half of the Second Peasants' Congress and the resolution based thereon in *Delo Naroda,* Nos. 230, 231 (December 12, 13, 1917).

[192] Chernov, manuscript commentary on the minutes of the Central Committee, p. 81; Sokolov, "Zashchita Uchreditel'nago Sobraniia," in *Arkhiv Russkoi Revoliutsii,* XIII, 35.

[193] *Izvestiia,* No. 136 (June 22, 1922); *Pravda,* No. 136 (June 22, 1922) (testimony of Gregory Ratner and Shestakov, member of the Moscow Committee).

VII

On the Eve of the Assembly

In the fateful year of 1917, disunity had never ceased to curse the Socialist Revolutionaries, at the end of the trail as in the rosy dawn of the revolution. The shearing off of the left wing had not restored harmony but merely reduced disharmony, and only the experience of one great disaster and the threat of another imparted a semblance of unity as the party prepared for the showdown that must end either in the demise of the Soviet government or the dissolution of the Constituent Assembly. Just below the surface three currents were visible. There were the right activists who thought they were assembling a force which would not only insure the existence of the assembly but liquidate the October Revolution. Theirs was the mentality of the officers' corps in the army, transmitted through Sokolov and his associates at the head of the Military Commission, and also of right-wing Populists of the type of S. S. Maslov, who were more wedded to war than the tsar had ever been. Then there were the right-wing passivists, led by Mayor Rudnev of Moscow, who did not believe it feasible to stop the process of self-demobilization or overturn the regime which was its expression short of anarchy and a disastrous peace, the onus of which they were quite willing to leave to the Bolsheviks. The third current around V. M. Chernov shared neither the counterrevolutionary zeal of the first nor the lassitude of the second. It thought that something could be done, but not at once, and not by force of arms. Above everything else it wished to avoid forcing the pace of developments, on the ground that time was on the side of the SR's; for the masses would sober up when they saw the emptiness of Bolshevik promises and it would then be possible to proceed with all available means, not excluding terrorism, against the Soviet regime without having to fight a considerable part of the Russian people to the benefit of the counterrevolution.

Common to all three currents was the conviction that Bolshevism was an ephemeral phenomenon with which it was unnecessary as well as immoral to compromise. The SR's often referred to their opponents as the "party of the rear garrisons," a description that lost its edge when Bolshevism engulfed the front as well. So Chernov broadened it to "elements of disintegration and decay in the revolution," and foretold the doom of a movement that rested on "the declassed sailordom and soldiery, which can only destroy the state and create chaos but can do nothing more." [1] The area of agreement, however, did not extend further than damning the Bolsheviks and rejecting any thought of compromise, which, of course, was also the policy of the Bolsheviks. In the task of winning back the sympathy of the masses with the aid of the negative manifestations of Bolshevism, particularly in the international and economic fields, the Chernov faction was determined not to play into the hands of the counterrevolution. A new armed struggle before the people had become disillusioned with Bolshevism would inevitably have that effect. What was needed was to take advantage of the difficulties of the regime, educate the people to distinguish between demagogy and performance, and gradually isolate the Bolsheviks from their allies, the Left SR's and the Menshevik Internationalists, not, indeed, by coming to terms with the general staffs of these groups but by seducing their popular followings. In order to pursue these tactics successfully, however, the SR's must leave no doubt as to their own devotion to revolutionary principles and must keep their distance from elements which as partners in coalition had emasculated their program under the Provisional Government. Here lay one main difference between Chernov's group and the other two currents, unwilling as always to stand alone without seeking support further to the right. It was simply a new passage at arms over the old issue of war before revolution or revolution before war which had wracked this party since 1914.

The other main difference, purely tactical in nature, concerned the convocation of the assembly. Chernov's faction was in no hurry for it to meet, believing that a delay would result in more favorable circumstances. The more evident the catastrophe toward which Bol-

[1] *Pravda,* No. 136 (June 22, 1922).

shevism was heading, the more likely the country would be to turn to the assembly for salvation. The other two currents pressed for the assembly to meet as soon as possible. They refused to consider the Soviet regime in their calculations. Their principles demanded that they absolutely ignore its existence and go ahead as though the assembly were the government of Russia, instead of the bunch of political bandits who had usurped the functions of state. To delay convocation might lessen the people's interest or cause them to regard the assembly as unworkable, and might demoralize the deputies who would gather in Petersburg, waiting for the assembly to open. Without any faith in the assembly's ability to defend itself, the right-wing passivists nevertheless were sustained, as they pressed for convocation, by a mystical faith in the people's willingness to defend its cause, and also by doubt that the Bolsheviks would really raise their hands against this supreme manifestation of popular sovereignty. It was a peculiar psychology that animated these people, and one closely akin to their stand on war: they would not yield an inch, yet they could not fight at all. And so they sat with passive heroism and waited to see what fate would bring.[2]

The cleavage in the ranks of the party which would manifest itself all too clearly in 1918 and 1919 was at first veiled by a reluctance to admit discord in the camp of those who championed the Constituent Assembly. Yet almost immediately it assumed an institutional aspect with the muted conflict between the Central Committee and the SR membership of the assembly. The views of Chernov naturally prevailed in the new Central Committee elected at the Fourth Congress, which hastened to adopt his strategy of waiting for the effects of Bolshevik policies to appear and avoiding exceptional measures to force the convocation of the assembly.[3] After losing out in the Central Committee and surrendering control of the party machinery,

[2] Chernov, manuscript commentary on the minutes of the Central Committee, pp. 81–85, 88; Chernov, "Iz itogov proshlogo opyta" (From the Results of Past Experience), *Revoliutsionnaia Rossiia*, No. 23 (December, 1922), pp. 4–5, 12; statement of Gotz in *Pravda*, No. 171 (August 2, 1922); Sokolov, "Zashchita Uchreditel'nago Sobraniia," in *Arkhiv Russkoi Revoliutsii*, XIII, 56, 59–60; see also editorials in *Volia Naroda*, especially "Protiv novago samoderzhaviia" (Against a New Autocracy), No. 197 (December 19, 1917), and "Medlit' nel'zia" (There Must Be No Delay), No. 198 (December 20, 1917).

[3] Protokol Zasedaniia Tsentral'nago Komiteta PSR, December 12, 1917.

the right SR's retired into the parliamentary arena and organized the delegation as a rival center of authority.[4]

The temper of the SR deputies can best be judged by what happened on December 9 when they elected a Bureau of the Delegation to act as its executive organ. By December 7 the delegation consisted of 134 deputies who had arrived in Petersburg,[5] a number sufficient to justify organization, of which the chief feature was the election of a bureau of twenty-five members. The results are most revealing. The successful candidates with the votes they received are as follows.

1.	V. V. Rudnev	83	14.	D. S. Rosenblum	54
2.	M. V. Vishniak	77	15.	M. Ia. Gendelman	52
3.	S. S. Maslov	76	16.	I. I. Fundaminski	51
4.	Ia. D. Dedusenko	69	17.	I. N. Kovarski	49
5.	A. N. Sletova	67	18.	V. G. Arkhangelski	48
6.	A. A. Argunov	66	19.	M. A. Likhach	44
7.	S. M. Lotoshnikov	66	20.	M. L. Kogan-Bernstein	44
8.	V. M. Zenzinov	66	21.	V. P. Bykov	43
9.	V. A. Kolerov	62	22.	F. M. Onipko	41
10.	G. K. Pokrovski	61	23.	S. L. Maslov	39
11.	A. R. Gotz	58	24.	B. N. Moiseenko	36
12.	A. B. Eliashevich	56	25.	V. K. Volski	36
13.	G. I. Shreider	55			

Then came the runners-up, or "candidates" or alternates: Sviatitski with 36 votes, Filippovski with 35, Merkulov with 33, and—finally—Chernov with 33.[6] The leader of the party had not only failed to place among the twenty-five successful candidates, but had drawn only one-half the vote given Argunov, whose position on the right fringe of the party had made him since the early days of the revolution a virtual outcast in the organization. Not only was Argunov spokesman for the extreme right, but he was open and above board about it, so that his position high on the list was as much a demonstration as the blackballing of Chernov. In the face of this scandal the SR's simply preserved their customary silence. The *Delo Naroda* omitted the vote, while Argunov's *Volia Naroda* gave it, but without comment. The Left SR's, now a separate party, were less reticent. They seized upon the incident to embarrass their

---

[4] *Obvinitel'noe zakliuchenie*, p. 71.
[5] *Delo Naroda*, No. 227 (December 8, 1917).
[6] *Volia Naroda*, No. 190 (December 10, 1917); *Delo Naroda*, No. 229 (December 10, 1917).

enemies and Chernov in particular.[7] From a provincial organ of Kadet leaning comes the information—if any were needed—that the strongly pro-war delegation was determined to have no taint of Zimmerwaldism among those entrusted with leadership.[8] And it must be admitted that it had been remarkably consistent: of the twenty-five members of the bureau, one was a left-wing unionist, four were of uncertain allegiance, and twenty were in favor of war, with the center of gravity more on the right than the right center.

This result, of course, could not be suffered to stand. It was too revealing and too vindictive. Such a gulf between the party organization and the party representation in the Constituent Assembly had to be bridged over. Besides, the pro-war SR's had need of Chernov. He was to be the revolutionary camouflage behind which they would make their bid for power. So his docility had to be assured and the sting of his blackballing soothed. Twice subsequently the bureau was reelected as more deputies arrived in the capital, and on December 23 Chernov's name appeared at the head of the list of victorious candidates,[9] which otherwise was little if any less right than before. He certainly became a member of the presidium, and may even have replaced Rudnev as chairman, though a definite assertion to this effect in one source [10] is not confirmed in another.[11] In any event, he now figured in the leadership of a body from which his continued exclusion would have occasioned a scandal, yet without disturbing the grip of the party faction opposed to his own.

[7] Selianin (pseudonym?), "33," *Znamia Truda,* No. 93 (December 12, 1917).
[8] *Severnoe Ekho* (Vologda), No. 99 (December 20, 1917).
[9] See N. V. Sviatitski, "Fraktsiia P.S.-R. Uchreditel'nago Sobraniia," *Partiinyia Izvestiia,* No. 5 (January 20, 1918), p. 37; *Delo Naroda,* No. 242 (December 28, 1917); *Volia Naroda,* No. 203 (December 28, 1917); Vladimirova, *God sluzhby "sotsialistov" kapitalistam,* p. 107, n. 1. No source gives the vote, not even the *Volia Naroda,* which had done so when the bureau was first chosen.
[10] *Delo Naroda,* No. 242 (December 28, 1917). Vladimirova's statement is based on this source.
[11] The presidium mentioned by Sviatitski is, with the exception of a single name, the same as the one originally chosen on December 10 (see *Delo Naroda,* No. 230 [December 12, 1917] and *Volia Naroda,* No. 191 [December 12, 1917]). As Chernov logically would have become chairman when the presidium was revised by virtue of running at the head of the list—and the *Volia Naroda* concedes that he did (No. 203 [December 28, 1917]), thereby removing any doubt—the presumption is that the central organ is correct in assigning him the position originally held by Rudnev.

Of course, the dualism that persisted in the soul of this party, even after the amputation of its left wing, could not be overcome by gestures of this kind, and the parliamentary representation of the party and its Central Committee continued to be at odds, becoming rival centers of authority with conflicting claims and divergent policies. One would have thought the Central Committee would make its will prevail. But not in this party. The right wing, in surrendering control of the party machinery at the Fourth Congress, had merely retired into the parliamentary arena. There it put forth a claim to autonomy and went its own way. An SR deputy maintains that the degree of influence exercised by the Central Committee over his colleagues was not less than in most European parties and that in the majority of instances they heeded its injunctions.[12] But by his own admission he took little part in their deliberations,[13] and he was thinking primarily of the community of viewpoint between the right-wing passivists and Chernov's left center in renouncing for the present the use of violence against the Soviet regime. The need for presenting a united front to the dangers of the hour also operated to obscure the cleavage within the party, but the conflict was irrepressible and had, in fact, already begun at the Fourth Congress with the refusal of voting privileges to members of the assembly [14]—a very clear indication of the difference between the party organization and its parliamentary representation, the former reflecting the turn to the left in the post-October period and the latter the conservatism of the Gotz-Zenzinov era.

The congress also undertook to subordinate the parliamentary delegation to the Central Committee by writing into the statutes of the party the principle of responsibility to the organization as well as to the constituency. It was expressly provided that all members of SR delegations, in the soviets as in the parliament, must heed the injunctions of the party leadership and that the work of the parliamentary group must proceed under the direct supervision of the

[12] Sokolov, "Zashchita Uchreditel'nago Sobraniia," in *Arkhiv Russkoi Revoliutsii*, XIII, 60.

[13] *Ibid.*, p. 50.

[14] *Kratkii otchët*, pp. 4, 6. The proposal to confer voting rights was made by Argunov (R) and opposed by Kogan-Bernstein (left unionist) and Utgof (LC). The congress turned it down, 29 to 63.

Central Committee.[15] In this manner the left-of-center majority had thought to settle the issue with those who argued for parliamentary autonomy on the ground that the Central Committee was too narrowly representative to give orders to men elected by the people, a contention that ignored the character of the electoral system under which the voter expressed a preference for a party list rather than an individual candidate, thus rendering valid the claim for party control of the deputies who rode into parliament on its back.[16] Rakitnikov had declared at the congress that deputies must either follow party instructions or resign their mandates.[17] No opposition is recorded to the decision of the congress, perhaps because it was made under pressure at the end of the session, but the absence of controversy does not mean that the element in the party which had lost out at the congress but controlled the delegation had accepted the principle of subordination or was disposed to alter its course accordingly.

The right-wing majority of the delegation went its own way, pushing for speedy convocation of the assembly without regard for the left-centrist line of waiting for the people to become disillusioned with the Soviet regime before provoking a showdown. The parliamentary leaders had no confidence in the judgment of the Central Committee.[18] The members of the committee all had mandates but were too busy to attend the caucus. When they found its line diverging from their own, they decided to "submit to group discipline" [19]—that is, to abdicate as the governing authority in party affairs. What became of the decision of the Fourth Congress we are not told. Perhaps Chernov had forgotten about it when he wrote these words, but he could scarcely have forgotten about it at the time when he and his colleagues executed this shameful climbdown, the superior authority bowing before the inferior, the victors before the vanquished, against their own better judgment and in defiance

[15] *Ibid.*, pp. 136, 158.
[16] M. K-b. (M. Kogan-Bernstein?), "Partiia i parlamentskaia fraktsiia" (The Party and the Parliamentary Delegation), *Partiinyia Izvestiia*, No. 5 (January 20, 1918), pp. 21–22.
[17] *Kratkii otchët*, p. 134.
[18] Chernov, manuscript commentary on the minutes of the Central Committee, p. 88.
[19] *Ibid.*, pp. 85–86.

of the clearly expressed will of the body which had given birth to their committee. Nothing really had changed in this party: the right continued to make policy, even after it was no longer in control of the machinery, because it had will as well as purpose, whereas the majority under Chernov had only purpose but no will.

The semblance of unity in the PSR on the eve of the Constituent Assembly was primarily the work of Chernov, under whose "leadership" the majority abdicated in favor of the minority. But discerning observers commented on the motley character of the SR representation and predicted that it would likely fall apart into two groups if not into three.[20] With the right SR's still so influential, the prospects for any form of cooperation with the group that already had split off were more remote than ever, and it became daily more obvious that in defending the assembly the SR's would be without the help, and might even encounter the hostility, of the Left SR's, whose influence in the country was not to be measured by their weakness in the assembly.

An inspection of the Left SR record on the Constituent Assembly would convey an impression of irresponsibility, yet behind their gyrations on the subject there was a definite logic. Even in the heyday of their collaboration with Bolshevism, the Left SR's were looking for a means of restraining their ally, for some counterbalance that would increase their weight in Soviet councils and afford added protection to themselves and the class they represented. At the same time they were determined not to play into the hands of the right SR's, whom they regarded, and not without reason, as the worst enemies of the revolution. Depending on which consideration was uppermost, they drew closer to or backed away from the Constituent Assembly. And in the final analysis their attitude was dictated by the fact that their hatred of the right SR's was greater than their fear of Bolshevism.

At first they showed solicitude for the assembly. The Kazan city organization adhered to the October Revolution with the stipulation that its first task should be to convene the assembly,[21] and on

---

[20] *Russkiia Vedomosti*, No. 263 (December 1, 1917).
[21] *Kazanskii Oktiabr'*, pp. 224–25, 227–28.

the Southwestern Front the Left SR's fell in with the idea, reputedly of Bolshevik origin, that the soviets would merely exercise power in the interval between the downfall of the Provisional Government and the convocation of the assembly [22]—in this manner they were being led a step at a time toward the Bolshevik position. In the negotiations over their admission to the Soviet government, the Left SR's had insisted on freedom for the assembly to meet in the form the electorate had given it, without excision or mutilation.[23] They had protested the decree excluding the Kadets [24] and continued to demand immunity for the membership, aside from a few individuals like Kaledin who were notoriously guilty of counterrevolutionary activities.[25] If the convocation of the assembly was assured, said Karelin, the credit belonged to the Left SR's, who also had toned down the decree providing for the recall of members so that it could not be used as an instrument for disrupting the assembly.[26]

The initially tolerant attitude toward the Constituent Assembly was based in part on the calculation that it might be possible to construct a majority that would effect a synthesis of the democratic principle exemplified in the assembly and the toilers' dictatorship realized through the soviets. Parliamentary legislation and soviet administration would have been an ideal solution for the Left SR's [27] in their search for something intermediate between the pre-October era with its constraint of revolutionary action and the existing situation with plenty of revolutionary action but no constraint of the Bolshevik Party. A painless settlement of the October conflict and the creation of a further counterweight to Bolshevism beyond their own inadequate strength in the soviets beckoned to the Left SR's as they strove to make the best of both the democratic and

[22] Sokolov, "Zashchita Uchreditel'nago Sobraniia," in *Arkhiv Russkoi Revoliutsii*, XIII, 21–23.

[23] Steinberg, *Als ich Volkskommissar war*, p. 61.

[24] *Revoliutsiia 1917 goda*, VI, 384.

[25] See answer of the Left SR delegation to an SR inquiry in *Delo Naroda*, No. 232 (December 14, 1917).

[26] "Perspektivy bol'shevistskoi vlasti (Zaiavleniia V. A. Karelina)" (A Perspective of Bolshevik Power [Statement of V. A. Karelin]), *Novaia Zhizn'*, No. 206 (December 20, 1917); brief summary of this part of the interview only in *Revoliutsiia 1917 goda*, VI, 377.

[27] See Kamkov's formula in *Protokoly pervago s"ezda PLSR*, p. 64.

soviet worlds. But how to put together a majority in the Constituent Assembly?

For one thing, the Left SR's anticipated a much larger representation of their own. They reckoned in terms of a hundred deputies.[28] These would effect a combination on the one side with the Bolsheviks and on the other with national minority groups of a revolutionary persuasion, above all with the Ukrainian SR's. For a time the Left SR's might think they were getting somewhere with the brethren from Little Russia. Certainly they did everything possible to cultivate good relations. They condemned the abruptness of the Soviet authorities in dealing with the Rada, preferring to avoid any appearance of coercion from the center which would only solidify the popular support of the Rada, and preferring to stake their hopes on a further differentiation of classes within the Ukraine as a means of anchoring the new regime. The Kharkov Rada had already recognized Soviet authority, and the prospects seemed bright, if not for an agreement with all the Ukrainian SR's, then at least for a deal with some of them by promoting a split in their ranks.[29] A press report in the second half of December suggested that the Left SR's had succeeded beyond their expectations. It was announced that full agreement had been reached with the Ukrainian SR's over basing the federal authority on the component republics and reducing the role of the All-Russian Constituent Assembly to the enactment of general principles underlying the social and political reconstruction of Russia, after which it would be dissolved to make way for the regional or national constituent assemblies.[30] The prospects of collaboration, however, soon proved illusory.[31]

The most daring aspect of the Left SR plan was the effort to raid the SR delegation itself and pull out of union with the right SR's the center under Chernov. Even at this late date the Left SR's are represented as hankering after their lost mentor, whose name inscribed on their banner would give them the drawing power they

[28] "Levye s. r. na vyborakh" (The Left SR's in the Election), *Delo Naroda*, No. 244 (December 30, 1917).

[29] See Karelin interview in *Novaia Zhizn'*, No. 206 (December 20, 1917).

[30] See report in *Novaia Zhizn'*, No. 210 (December 24, 1917); see also Steinberg, *Als ich Volkskommissar war*, pp. 64-65, and above, p. 312.

[31] See below, p. 362.

had previously lacked in the village. Whether the Left SR's actually hoped or wanted to make Chernov their leader may be doubted, but in any event they would have welcomed a special parliamentary group under his leadership with which they could have worked in constructing a revolutionary order less subject to Bolshevik domination. The land question seems to have been the lever they would use to spring the SR delegation. If the right would not consent to full-scale socialization, Chernov might be induced to break away and either form a new majority on the ruins of SR unity or head a rump parliament of radicals which would act in the spirit of the French Convention of 1792. It was inevitable that the Left SR's should speculate on the differences within the SR camp, for these were real enough and had even assumed organizational form with the cleavage between the Bureau of the Delegation and the Central Committee. The delicate soundings involved and, indeed, the execution of the whole plan had been entrusted to Karelin, who reckoned on a bloc of around 350 delegates, or about half of the assembly, which could be converted into a majority if Chernov and his following or at least some waverers from the SR center would come over.[32]

While the relatively moderate wing under Karelin was seeking a combination that would reconcile the democratic and soviet orders, another group of Left SR's remained firmly planted in the soviet camp. The two currents were plainly visible at their First, or November, Congress. One line of argument was that, apart from the chance of an accommodation between the assembly and the soviets, the Left SR's could not afford to proceed without more ado against an institution in which so many people still believed, unless they were prepared to set themselves up as masters of the people. Numerous delegates attested to the hold of the assembly upon the affec-

---

[32] "Sredi levykh 's.-r.' " (Among the Left "SR's"), *Volia Naroda,* No. 193 (December 14, 1917); "Perspektivy bol'shevistskoi vlasti," *Novaia Zhizn'*, No. 206 (December 20, 1917); report on negotiations with the Ukrainian SR's in *ibid.,* No. 210 (December 24, 1917); Steinberg, *Als ich Volkskommissar war*, p. 64. The Left SR's were a bit too sanguine in their calculations: instead of 350 delegates, a bloc with the Bolsheviks and the radical national groups would have yielded only a little over 300 (see above, p. 312), and for a bare majority it would have been necessary to pull out about 50 SR's of the left center, or all the strength that Vishniak concedes to Chernov.

tions of the populace; expediency as well as principle cautioned against any highhanded action.[33] Let the assembly meet and show its colors. If it made war on the revolution and sought to undo the conquests of October, the people would become disillusioned and it could painlessly be put away. Let the people learn from experience, as in the case of the Kerenski coalition. The pace of their political development could not be forced unduly.

The opposing current could not deny that in the past the Left SR's had loudly championed the Constituent Assembly, but between that past and the present lay the October Revolution. Power now rested in the hands of the toilers and nothing must be permitted to jeopardize this situation. The toilers already had what it had only been hoped the assembly would give them, and in the soviet system they possessed the best safeguard of their emancipation. At best the assembly was unnecessary, and at worst, a serious danger. Though the radicals did not voice the formula applied by the caliph to the library at Alexandria, something like it was in their minds. They viewed a counterrevolutionary majority as assured, the right SR's as in no way different from the Kadets, and a clash between the soviets and the assembly as inevitable. They raised a cry against fetishism, particularly in respect to an institution whose make-up had been determined by slipping in a host of counterrevolutionaries under a revolutionary label. In their zeal to cut down the tree of the Constituent Assembly, these people laid the ax at the root of the whole democratic system. Arguing that the fruits of October must be preserved from impairment at the hands of the assembly, the younger Shreider asserted that Narodnik tradition had always held that the highest criterion for evaluating a policy or course of action was the interest of the people, not its opinion, and that in order to preserve certain values the subjective "I" could impose limitations upon the will of the people.[34]

This was the same young man who only two months before, at

---

[33] According to an SR observer, the Left SR's had begun to lose their peasant following in Perm province when it was rumored that they had adopted the same stand on the assembly as the Bolsheviks. See report of the deputy Tarabukin in *Delo Naroda*, No. 242 (December 28, 1917).

[34] *Protokoly pervago s"ezda PLSR*, p. 107. For debate at the congress on the assembly, see pp. 63–110, with breaks here and there.

the Seventh Petersburg Conference, had seen the root of evil in post-
poning the Constituent Assembly, the convocation of which he defined as "our first aim." [35] Principle may govern political action, but
if so, the principle is rooted less in abstruse ideology, Populist or
otherwise, than in the old adage about whose ox is being gored.

Out of the welter of scrambled views and heated words at this
congress, one fact clearly emerges: even those Left SR's like Karelin
who wished to give the assembly a try were prepared to tolerate it
only so long as it operated within the framework of the October
Revolution. The resolution adopted at the congress was drawn up in
this spirit. Little of basic import was left to the discretion of the
assembly, either in legislation or in administration, and its task
was simply to make effective the rule of the workers and peasants.
Any attempt to enter into a conflict with the soviets "as organs of
power" would encounter the "decisive opposition" of the Left SR's,
and while a threat of dissolution was not openly voiced, as a Soviet
source would lead one to think,[36] it was implied in the text of the
resolution.[37] The more moderate faction had averted a death sentence but only on condition that the assembly do its bidding.

Very soon, however, events transpired to strengthen the hand of
the extremists. The prospects for a combination that could muster a
majority in the assembly all proved illusory. Instead of the hundred-
odd seats they had originally counted on having, the Left SR's saw
their hopes reduced to seventy-five,[38] and finally to forty. The
Ukrainian SR's proved wholly unreliable, dickering now with the
Left SR's and now with the regular SR's,[39] and in the end throwing both of them over. And Chernov evinced as little will as ever to
free himself from the clutches of the right SR's, who were now
preparing for this bird a gilded cage.

As their hopes sank, the Left SR's turned more and more against
the assembly. Already before the results of the election were known,

[35] *Znamia Truda*, No. 17 (September 12, 1917).
[36] Vladimirova, *God sluzhby "sotsialistov" kapitalistam*, p. 113, n. 1.
[37] See *Protokoly pervago s"ezda PLSR*, pp. 110–11.
[38] "Levye s. r. na vyborakh," *Delo Naroda*, No. 244 (December 30, 1917).
[39] *Novaia Zhizn'*, No. 213 (December 30, 1917); see also above, pp. 311–17. As
stated above, the *Novaia Zhizn'* had only a few days before announced the
complete agreement between the Left and Ukrainian SR's (No. 210 [December
24, 1917]).

they had taken out insurance against an unsuccessful outcome by starting a campaign to disparage the assembly. An article had appeared in their press entitled "Take Not unto Thyself an Idol," whose theme was that the SR's were promoting idolatry of an institution accidental in make-up, the product of a confused and fleeting mood among the voters, with no just claim upon the abiding loyalty of the toilers. The latter should look behind the fetish, and then they would see that the idol was being set up and its wonder-working powers proclaimed by the same people who had promised to turn the land over to the land committees but had defaulted on this pledge as on so many others.[40] Kalegaev had declared amid applause at the peasants' congress on November 30 that if the assembly did not give the people peace, land, and bread, if it went against the will of the toiling masses, "I shall fight against it and I believe all of you will, too." [41] No one did more to sustain the campaign than Proshian, who repeatedly urged the needlessness of the assembly and saw in it a blind for the restoration of the Kerenski regime. Only by cleaving to the soviets could the toilers frustrate the designs of a "small politician" and would-be Napoleon, who had ordered an offensive instead of seeking peace, repressed the land committees instead of giving out the land, and decreed the death penalty instead of upholding freedom.[42]

The theme of Kerenski's return was picked up by others as the Left SR's backed away from their equivocal stand on the assembly into a position of outright hostility. Even Karelin moved with the others. While in public he still spoke of the inadmissibility of force in dealing with the assembly,[43] in private he and Kalegaev are quoted by Zenzinov as saying that it would be dissolved at an advantageous moment.[44] On the eve of the convocation we find Ustinov decry-

[40] N. Arefev, "Ne sotvori sebe kumira," in *Vokrug Uchreditel'nago Sobraniia*, pp. 12-15.

[41] *Znamia Truda*, No. 86 (December 2, 1917).

[42] "Nesbytochnyia mechtaniia" (Dreams That Can Never Be), in *Vokrug Uchreditel'nago Sobraniia*, pp. 11-12; *Protokoly pervago s"ezda PLSR*, pp. 108-9; see also Proshian's pronouncement in the All-Russian Executive Committee as reported in *Delo Naroda*, No. 240 (December 23, 1917).

[43] "Perspektivy bol'shevistskoi vlasti," *Novaia Zhizn'*, No. 206 (December 20, 1917).

[44] "Oproverzhenie" (A Refutation), *Delo Naroda*, No. 240 (December 23, 1917).

ing the existence of two centers of authority and revealing that the Left SR's, in their search for a body that would water down Bolshevik power, had shifted their hopes from the assembly itself to a convention of its radical elements with the All-Russian soviet organs.[45] Only a small push was needed to bring the Left SR's over to the Bolshevik position on the assembly, and that push came with the election of a presiding officer.

The convocation of the Constituent Assembly was preceded by a tussle between the SR's and the Bolsheviks over control of the arrangements. There is no need to go into this protracted and tedious conflict: the result was preordained, the Bolsheviks had the armed force and kept the arrangements in their own hands, appointing M. S. Uritski as commissar of affairs relating to the assembly or, as the SR's chose to call him, commissar over the assembly. The date of convocation was fixed for the fifth of January (January 18, N.S.), 1918, as a result of compromise between the Bolsheviks and the Left SR's. The Ukrainian SR's having accepted this decision of the "existing order in Great Russia," the SR's had no choice but to go along.[46]

Their efforts to provide a defense for the assembly, already noted, now had to be stepped up and given final form. Before seeing what they were able to accomplish, however, it is necessary to say a word about their psychology, which by any other standards than their own would have to be pronounced strange indeed. At one and the same time they knew the assembly to be in mortal danger yet somehow could not believe that the blow would really come.

Ever since the October overturn the SR press had been filled with dark forebodings as to the assembly's fate. By December it was clearly intimating that dissolution would lead to civil war.[47] The action of the Soviet government in convening a Third Soviet Congress only three days after the opening of the assembly left no

[45] "K otkrytiiu Uchreditel'nago Sobraniia" (On the Opening of the Constituent Assembly), in *Vokrug Uchreditel'nago Sobraniia*, pp. 18–20.

[46] *Delo Naroda*, No. 240 (December 23, 1917); Zenzinov, "Predparlamentskiia deistviia" (Preparliamentary Maneuvers), *ibid.*, No. 243 (December 29, 1917).

[47] "5 ianvaria i federativnaia respublika" (January 5 and a Federated Republic), *ibid.*, No. 242 (December 28, 1917); Zenzinov, "Oproverzhenie," *ibid.*, No. 240 (December 23, 1917).

doubt of its intent to provide a substitute for the parliament it meant to destroy.[48] "Criminals do not give up power," observed the central organ of the PSR, as it summoned the people to defend the assembly.[49] Yet hope for a peaceful solution never entirely disappeared in SR circles, not even in those most conscious of the danger. The paradox can be explained only in terms of the excessive idealism of these people, in their propensity for seeing things, not as they were, but as they wished them to be. Just because the assembly meant so much to them, both as the highest form of popular sovereignty and as the embodiment of their greatest triumph, they imagined that it must mean as much to the Russian people, and something even to the Bolsheviks, perhaps enough to restrain them from attempting its ravishment. The Constituent Assembly had become a sacred thing to the SR's, like the person of the sovereign to monarchists, an institution set high above the arena of political contention, to assault which seemed an incredible crime.[50] Zenzinov himself compared the effect on the SR's of the violence done the assembly to the smashing of an icon for a religious-minded person.[51] Many party members were inclined to leave its defense to the people, who had created it and would not allow it to be destroyed. Apparently the expectation was that either the Bolsheviks would hesitate to incur the odium of a dissolution, or the people would stay their hand in the act, or the wave of public indignation would hasten the inevitable downfall of their regime.[52]

With the SR's in this frame of mind, it is not hard to understand their reluctance to accept the prospect of bloodshed or their failure to develop a do-or-die spirit, which has led their opponents to accuse them of faintheartedness or even cowardice. In general, the delegation in the assembly, dominated by right-wing passivists of the Rudnev type, held aloof from preparations for armed defense,[53] the Central Committee under Chernov felt the need for preparations but

---

[48] Zenzinov, "Oproverzhenie," *ibid.*, No. 240 (December 23, 1917).
[49] See appeal to the country in *ibid.*, No. 241 (December 24, 1917).
[50] Sokolov, "Zashchita Uchreditel'nago Sobraniia," in *Arkhiv Russkoi Revoliutsii*, XIII, 56.
[51] Interview in Paris (September, 1935).
[52] Bykhovski, *Vserossiiskii Sovet Krest'ianskikh Deputatov*, p. 349.
[53] See Sokolov, "Zashchita Uchreditel'nago Sobraniia," in *Arkhiv Russkoi Revoliutsii*, XIII, 34–35, 55.

hesitated to push them to the limit, while only the right-wing activists about the Military Commission were prepared to accept with equanimity the logical conclusion of their labors. Yet this is not to say that the delegation was impractical and the Central Committee timorous, while the military elements were brave and realistic; the latter may only have been foolhardy, as the sequel will show.

Whether hesitatingly or wholeheartedly, however, the SR's were engaged in preparations for armed defense, and for this purpose money was needed. The party coffers were empty.[54] Where was it to come from? At their trial in 1922, the Soviet government exerted itself to prove that the SR's worked on Allied gold, in the period immediately following the October Revolution as well as in 1918. The effort was not a success. It does seem that toward the end of 1917, down in the Ukraine, Gerstein tried to get hold of some of the French money which had been turned over to Krakovetski, now representing a Siberian "regime," but only for a very limited purpose and in any event without success.[55] The choice of a culprit had been a poor one, for Gerstein was a left-centrist of the Chernovian stripe who by no conceivable stretch of the imagination would have stooped to the role of Allied agent. The records of the party—in so far as they are available—disclose that the SR's tried to raise money for the general purposes of the party through a loan from the trades unions,[56] and for the specific purpose of defending the assembly, through public collections.[57] In both cases the results are unknown, but they could not have been brilliant; for the unions were already or soon would be under Bolshevik control, and it seems unlikely that a party gasping for breath could have staged a fund-raising campaign

[54] See *Obvinitel'noe zakliuchenie*, p. 106.

[55] On this matter see testimony of Krakovetski in *Izvestiia*, No. 147 (July 5, 1922), and *Pravda*, No. 147 (July 5, 1922); testimony of Gerstein in *Pravda*, No. 149 (July 7, 1922); summation of Krylenko in *Pravda*, No. 169 (July 30, 1922). The effort to link Gerstein with the Allies was effectively disposed of by Burevoi; see his testimony in *Pravda*, No. 149 (July 7, 1922). Later, in 1918, the SR's seem to have received some money from the Allies, but for the most part indirectly and not in significant amounts. As A. V. Lunacharski was constrained to admit, "The Entente did not give . . . or if it gave, then little, as if it were giving tips." See *Pravda*, No. 167 (July 28, 1922). For the later period, see also below, p. 453. For right SR's, see pp. 492–93.

[56] Protokol Zasedaniia Tsentral'nago Komiteta PSR, December 8, 1917.

[57] *Ibid.;* see appeal for contributions printed in the *Delo Naroda*, No. 242 (December 28, 1917).

of any consequence. Some money was contributed by the front organizations from which the heads of the reorganized Military Commission had been drawn,[58] but the man who connected up that commission with the Central Committee was doubtlessly correct when he attributed the bulk of the financial support to those same cooperative societies which throughout 1917 had used their funds in an endeavor to tame the revolution and get on with the war.[59] It is not possible to say how much support the party derived from the cooperatives through the nonpartisan Committee of Defense, but it is possible to say that factors of finance did not determine the fate of the enterprise.

The main lines along which the SR's proposed to organize the defense of the assembly have already been described.[60] Outside of St. Petersburg very little was done, either because of the organizational weakness of the party, or because the garrisons were everywhere against it, or because of the virtual impossibility of mobilizing the peasantry for any purpose other than the seizure of land. Chernov had started off on the tack of disclosing to the peasants what Bolshevism held in store for them,[61] but his effort would have had to be much more sustained, and the time at his disposal much greater, for him to have achieved any practical effect. For the most part the SR's in the provinces contented themselves with arranging demonstrations on behalf of the Constituent Assembly. Sometimes these passed off without incident, sometimes they led to tragic consequences, but always they did little to change the situation. At Kaluga on December 10, forty thousand people are said to have taken part in such a demonstration, evidently to the alarm of Soviet sympa-

[58] See Sokolov, "Zashchita Uchreditel'nago Sobraniia," in *Arkhiv Russkoi Revoliutsii*, XIII, 40.

[59] Testimony of Likhach in *Pravda*, No. 131 (June 15, 1922); Vladimirova, *God sluzhby "sotsialistov" kapitalistam*, p. 89. The question of expropriating funds for the need of the party arose at the end of 1917, but neither the Central Committee nor the delegation would sanction such methods. See *Obvinitel'noe zakliuchenie*, pp. 106–7.

[60] See above, pp. 336 ff.

[61] See his speech and the resolution based on it at his half of the Second Peasants' Congress as reported in the *Delo Naroda*, Nos. 230, 231 (December 12, 13, 1917). Of course, Chernov had spoken in this vein on a number of occasions in 1917 but he had never campaigned systematically on the issue. Other members of his party had not done so because they so consistently underrated the Bolsheviks.

thizers, whose counteraction resulted in a score of casualties.[62] At Saratov an attempt to stage a demonstration had to be postponed until the end of the month because of an armed Soviet counter-demonstration. When the adherents of the Constituent Assembly at length took to the streets, they were set upon by the soldiers and again there were casualties.[63] In both these instances white-collar employees seem to have formed the backbone of the manifestations in favor of the assembly. There was nothing the SR's could do on the fronts nearest the capital where support would have counted most—they were washed out on the Northern and Western Fronts —but on the Southwestern they tried hard to convene army conferences not later than December 28 and a front conference on January 3,[64] obviously in an effort to muster support for the Constituent Assembly.

As so often before, the fate of the revolution would be settled in St. Petersburg. The heart of the SR plan to defend the assembly was the demonstration to be staged in the capital on January 5, the day the assembly was to meet. Was the purpose to overthrow the Soviet government, as the Bolsheviks have charged, or merely to insure the life of the assembly, as the SR's have maintained? In other words, was it primarily an offensive or a defensive move?

As usual, the SR's were not of one mind regarding the action to save the assembly. The Central Committee had confided the task not only to Boris Sokolov and his co-workers on the reorganized Military Commission, but also to Sergius S. Maslov,[65] a party member of the right, strongly pro-war in sentiment. Evidently it was the old Central Committee—the one issuing from the Third Congress—which made the appointment, for his biography [66] speaks of Maslov as being active for two months before the assembly met, and the new committee had not been chosen by the Fourth Congress until one month previously. Chernov made no change after taking over the helm—he

[62] *Delo Naroda*, Nos. 235, 236 (December 17, 19, 1917).

[63] Antonov-Saratovski, *Pod stiagom proletarskoi bor'by*, I, 239.

[64] *Volia Naroda*, No. 197 (December 19, 1917).

[65] Interview with Zenzinov in Paris (September, 1935). This Maslov is not to be confused with Simon L. Maslov, minister of agriculture in the third coalition of the Provisional Government.

[66] *Vozrozhdenie Severa* (Rebirth of the North) (Archangel), No. 2 (August 13, 1918), cited by state's attorney Krylenko at the trial in 1922; see *Pravda*, No. 131 (June 15, 1922).

was not in the habit of disturbing the arrangements of the right wing of his party. Little is known of Maslov's activities, but he should doubtlessly be thought of as the strategist or master planner behind the scenes, and Sokolov and his associates merely as the technicians immediately concerned with the work. All of them, Maslov as well as the military men, were right-wing activists, so that there was little room for disharmony among them, except perhaps of a personal nature. With them the minority of initiative came first, and only then, and at some distance, the people. Maslov's purpose was to gather a striking force of 11,000 men [67] as the decisive element in success. The magnitude of the popular response was a secondary consideration.

On the other hand, the leaders of the party, Gotz, Chernov, the right-wing passivists, and the centrists of all shades, thought in terms of a mass outpouring of people which the party must be prepared to protect against dispersal. Idealistic democrats that they were, they hoped that the spontaneous action of the people would rescue the assembly with such armed assistance as the party could provide. They also had to weigh the chances of failure, and what that would entail, for they were the custodians of a great though damaged cause and of whatever was left of the democratic principle in Russian public life. The soberness and sense of responsibility on their side contrasted with the optimism and impetuosity on the other. The difference in temperament as well as in political outlook produced more and more friction as events moved toward a climax, with Maslov and the Military Commission pressing for vanguard action and the party leaders willing to move only in conjunction with the populace.[68]

Ostensibly the SR's were engaged in a peaceful enterprise. Their press announced that the Central Committee at its sessions of December 26 and 29 had decided to organize a peaceful demonstration in support of the Constituent Assembly on the day of its opening.[69]

[67] *Pravda*, No. 131 (June 15, 1922).

[68] See testimony of Gotz in *Izvestiia*, No. 131 (June 15, 1922), and No. 136 (June 22, 1922); testimony of Likhach in *Pravda*, No. 131 (June 15, 1922), and in *Izvestiia*, No. 134 (June 18, 1922) (this information is not contained in the *Pravda* issue of the same date); see also Sokolov, "Zashchita Uchreditel'nago Sobraniia," in *Arkhiv Russkoi Revoliutsii*, XIII, 55.

[69] *Delo Naroda*, No. 1/246 (January 3, 1918). The minutes of the Central Committee placed at the disposal of the author by V. M. Chernov have a gap between the sessions of December 12, 1917, and January 30, 1918.

On January 4 appeared the manifesto of the Central Committee affirming the peaceful character of the demonstration and accusing the Bolsheviks of attempting to provoke bloodshed as an excuse for proceeding against the assembly.[70] But behind the scenes the Central Committee long debated the advisability of armed or unarmed action without coming to any hard and fast decision.[71] In effect it left the question open for circumstances to decide while allowing those charged with the task of defense to go ahead as though armed action had been approved.[72]

Preparations had been in full swing ever since the reorganization of the Military Commission. As we have seen, that body followed the policy of bringing in reliable elements from the front to stiffen the more dependable units in the garrison, principally the Fifth Armored Division and the Semenovski and Preobrazhenski Regiments.[73] By the end of December the process had gone far enough, and ties with the divisional or regimental committees (soviets) had been knit firmly enough, for the sponsors to feel that the units could be swung into action. It must be especially emphasized that for that purpose they relied upon the commitments, or perhaps it would be better to say the promises, of these representative organs. How representative they were of the soldiers beneath them—that, of course, was the question. To build up anti-Bolshevik sentiment in the garrison as a whole, a newspaper was founded called the *Seraia Shinel'* (The Gray Coat), which ridiculed the Soviet government and its leaders and attacked their tenets. Bolsheviks are not noted for a sense of humor and the authorities took measures to rid themselves of this gadfly, only to meet with disobedience on the part of the regiments under whose auspices the sheet was appearing. The *Seraia Shinel'*, selling ten thousand copies or more an issue, continued to come out in the first days of January and was a factor in the growing uncertainty as to what the troops might do when the showdown came.[74]

[70] *Delo Naroda*, No. 2 (January 4, 1918).

[71] Interview with Zenzinov in Paris (September, 1935).

[72] One of the Central Committeemen who supervised the work of the Military Commission has conceded that the party was preparing for a fight. See testimony of Likhach in *Pravda*, No. 131 (June 15, 1922).

[73] See above, p. 342.

[74] Sokolov, "Zashchita Uchreditel'nago Sobraniia," in *Arkhiv Russkoi Revoliutsii*, XIII, 42–43.

For the most part, however, the work of the Military Commission was done underground. On a conspiratorial footing since undertaking the task of defense,[75] its members went in for counterespionage and succeeded in planting one of their number on the staff of the Red Guard, in the post of assistant to K. A. Mekhonoshin. This officer gave them reports on Soviet movements so that they need not act in the dark.[76] The Military Commission was assisted by its local counterpart of the same name, operating under the authority of the Petersburg SR Committee and having as its main function the establishment of party cells in various garrison units.[77] The city committee itself sought to mobilize the ward or district organizations behind action in support of the assembly.[78] The Military Commission of the Central Committee also coordinated its activities with the military section of the nonpartisan Committee to Defend the Assembly, and at a joint session two days before the opening of the assembly a staff was set up to draw things together and guide the action on January 5. Present were Sergius S. Maslov, Onipko, Semenov, Surguchev, and several others. Onipko and Semenov were named to the staff, along with a nonpartisan expert, N. N. Poradelov, a colonel of the General Staff, reputedly of democratic leanings, whose function seems to have been to lend a professional touch to this amateur enterprise. The staff had its quarters in the apartment of N. V. Chaikovski,[79] the veteran Populist and inveterate "defensist," who now, as a Popular Socialist, was one of the leaders of the national organization of cooperatives and head of the Committee to Defend the Constituent Assembly. On the basis of the preparations already made and the hopes entertained, the newly appointed staff worked out an operational plan which must now be examined.[80]

It should be said at the outset that to reconstruct this plan is a task

---

[75] Testimony of Semenov in *Pravda*, No. 131 (June 15, 1922).

[76] *Obvinitel'noe zakliuchenie*, p. 60.

[77] *Ibid.*, pp. 59–60; on the Petersburg Military Commission see also above, p. 341.

[78] *Delo Naroda*, No. 245 (December 31, 1917).

[79] See Semenov's statement in *Pravda*, No. 131 (June 15, 1922).

[80] On the staff, see Keller's testimony in *Pravda*, No. 130 (June 14, 1922); Likhach's testimony in *ibid.*, No. 131 (June 15, 1922); Paevski's testimony in *Izvestiia*, No, 129 (June 13, 1922); *Obvinitel'noe zakliuchenie*, p. 61; Vladimirova, *God sluzhby "sotsialistov" kapitalistam*, p. 108. Colonel Poradelov commanded respect as a military figure. In addition to his role on this occasion, he seems to have had a hand in the cadet uprising at the end of October. The spelling of his name varies and also his rank: the name sometimes appears as

of exceptional difficulty. The evidence at the trial of 1922, upon which any study must rest, is not infrequently contradictory and nearly always confusing. Each witness had his own slant if, indeed, he did not consciously strive to create a different impression. The plan had changed in its basic aspect before the staff undertook to formulate it specifically, and would change again after the staff had completed its labors. Yet the basic outline is clear and the results all too evident. The plan was to be built around the same three units of the garrison—the Fifth Armored Division and the Semenovski and Preobrazhenski Regiments—upon which the SR's had pinned their hopes all along. Other units received some attention [81] but without serious expectation that they could be brought into action.

Of the three units viewed as saviors of the assembly, the Armored Division occupied the first position, both because of the special nature of its equipment, which made it a formidable force in street fighting, and because of the good fortune of the SR's in having one of their number in a post of authority. The officer Keller had figured in the October events as the owner of the vehicle in which Kerenski escaped from Gatchina, although Keller claimed at the trial in 1922 that it had been used by another officer without his knowledge. He was still the commander, either of the whole division or of one of its sections,[82] and so in a position to make his party affiliation count. The Russian army was not favored with tanks in the World War and the armor in question consisted merely of motor vehicles, some fourteen to seventeen of them, of which eight or nine, perhaps more, were thought to be at the disposal of the party through Keller. Similarly with respect to the Semenovski Regiment—it was not expected that the whole force could be brought out but only that about 3,000 of the 4,000 men would take to the streets, bringing their

---

Paradelov and the rank as lieutenant colonel. Apparently the latter rank is correct.

[81] For mention of such units see *Obvinitel'noe zakliuchenie*, p. 60, and Chernov's manuscript commentary on the minutes of the Central Committee, p. 87. In this respect, also, the sources are not in agreement. In one place a certain unit will be written off as impervious to argument, whereas in another the same unit is said to have shown interest in the survival of the assembly.

[82] The sources refer to him as commander of an armored detachment (*otriad*) without making it clear whether this term is synonymous with "division" or is a component thereof. That somewhat more than a dozen armored cars should be dignified by the name of "division" is in itself surprising.

machine guns with them. Plans were more vague and hopes less sanguine in relation to the Preobrazhenski Regiment, for which the lever of action would be more the example of the other two units than its own resolution.[83]

In addition to these elements of the garrison, the SR's counted on the armed workers' detachments of their party to supply some strength as a partial offset to the Red Guard of the Bolsheviks. The failure of these detachments to make a showing in the October Revolution could be attributed to the paralyzing effect of the schism and their unwillingness to aid the Provisional Government, the unpopularity of which in proletarian circles contrasted to the still prevalent faith in universal suffrage, which would make it feasible to rally workers in support of the Constituent Assembly who would not lift a finger on behalf of the Kerenski regime.

The armed strength which the SR's calculated on having at their disposal cannot be determined with certainty. The disclosure about Maslov's work, made during the civil war in the relative security of the Allied occupied zone of the north, reveals that it yielded about 5,000 of the 11,000 men the "staff of the insurrection" insisted on having.[84] But Keller testified some years later that the Military Commission made no accurate count of the force at its command, and that in his opinion it amounted to very little, with only the Armored Division a serious quantity, and the rest a dubious asset of the "maybe yes, maybe no" variety.[85] His statement seems plausible.

Whatever the figure may have been, it was not large enough for the SR's to hold to their original plan, and another one had to be adopted with little time to spare. The original intent had been to stage an armed uprising both to overthrow the Soviet regime and to safeguard the assembly, and for weeks all preparations had been made with this end in view.[86] But by the new year it was evident

---

[83] See testimony of Keller in *Pravda*, No. 130 (June 14, 1922); Sokolov, "Zashchita Uchreditel'nago Sobraniia," in *Arkhiv Russkoi Revoliutsii*, XIII, 49–50; Vladimirova, *God sluzhby "sotsialistov" kapitalistam*, p. 108.

[84] *Vozrozhdenie Severa*, No. 2 (August 13, 1918), as quoted in *Pravda*, No. 131 (June 15, 1922).

[85] *Pravda*, No. 130 (June 14, 1922).

[86] Vladimirova, *God sluzhby "sotsialistov" kapitalistam*, pp. 108–9, citing Dashevski's testimony in 1922. Evidently his testimony was not fully reported in the press accounts of the trial.

that a strictly military coup could not succeed and the emphasis was shifted to a mass demonstration with armed support. The people would march through the streets toward the Taurida Palace in a demonstration of loyalty to the assembly, inspiring sympathetic elements of the garrison to come out and act as a cover in case of a clash with Bolshevik forces. It would be easier and more effective, in other words, to mobilize armed strength through civilian initiative than under its own steam. A plan along these lines was drawn up by Semenov and presented to the newly constituted staff, which adopted it in preference to a second plan submitted by Colonel Poradelov. That officer was then commissioned to work out the details of the action, presumably because of his military skill. His design took the form of a chain reaction. First the people would fetch out the armored cars and then would come the turn of the Semenovski Regiment, after which the Preobrazhenski Regiment might feel emboldened to take to the streets. The whole mass then would move on the Taurida Palace, the military and civilian elements along different routes, according to the Soviet indictment,[87] probably to keep the soldiers from losing themselves in the crowd. As one member of the SR Central Committee testified, it was desired that the soldiers go in formation to demonstrate that the assembly had army support.[88] In any event the demonstrants would arrive before the meeting place of the assembly as masters of the situation, prepared to exploit the developing crisis beyond the limits of a purely defensive action. Arrangements were concerted, it should be noted, between the planners and the soldiers' committees, and the understanding was that things would move strictly in sequence, first the armored vehicles and then the two regiments in the order of the firmness of their convictions. The idea might be summed up in the parlance of American children: "You go first, and then I'll go." [89]

[87] See the sentence pronounced at the end of the trial in *Izvestiia*, No. 177 (August 9, 1922). State's attorney Krylenko made much of the hidden intent behind the dual line of march; see press accounts of his speeches in *Izvestiia*, No. 131 (June 15, 1922) and in *Pravda*, No. 169 (July 30, 1922). His argument was not too successfully developed, nor was it free of contradiction.

[88] See statement of Likhach in *Pravda*, No. 131 (June 15, 1922).

[89] This sketch of the plan and its features is based mainly on the press accounts of the testimony at the SR trial in 1922; see especially statements of Likhach in *Pravda*, No. 131 (June 15, 1922), and in *Izvestiia*, No. 134 (June 18, 1922); of Semenov in *Pravda*, No. 134 (June 18, 1922); of Krylenko in *Pravda*, No. 131

The last few days before the opening of the Constituent Assembly witnessed feverish efforts on the part of the SR's and their allies to arouse the populace while secretly preparing to act in accordance with the plan. For some time garrison conferences on the premises of this or that party organization had been a feature of the agitation, and now on January 3, seemingly on the same day that the staff was constituted, Semenov presented its plan to 210 delegates from the garrison without revealing all of the implications but with the plain intimation that an armed clash might result.[90] There seem to have been no serious objections, and things went ahead as planned.

Meanwhile the Soviet government, with its own plan for dealing with the assembly, was moving to thwart the SR's. One source claims that as a group in contact with both sides, the Left SR's listened to the plans of the defenders and betrayed them to the Bolsheviks.[91] But it is likely that the regime, despite its administrative weakness, had other informers. Secrets could have leaked through the garrison conferences or the soldiers' committees, and the Extraordinary Commission, the Cheka, was already in process of formation. Like a baby rattlesnake, this institution had poison from the start. It set energetically to work, with very little at its disposal, to behead the opposition and wall off the assembly from its defenders. At Moscow its action succeeded when 63 SR's were caught in the dragnet, including the city committee, but in St. Petersburg the SR and Menshevik leaders eluded the order of arrest issued on December 31 and hid out in the city, although their movements were impeded by the necessity for going underground.[92] Among those specifically sought were Gotz and Chernov of the Central Committee and Sokolov of the Military Commission. A state of siege was proclaimed in the capital, the regime readied its "praetorian guard" of soldiers and sailors, called up the Red Guard, and generally took measures to keep the

(June 15, 1922); see also *Obvinitel'noe zakliuchenie po delu tsentral'nogo komiteta PSR*, p. 12; Sokolov, "Zashchita Uchreditel'nago Sobraniia," in *Arkhiv Russkoi Revoliutsii*, XIII, 49; Vladimirova, *God sluzhby "sotsialistov" kapitalistam*, pp. 108–9.

[90] Testimony of Likhach and Semenov in *Pravda*, No. 131 (June 15, 1922); of Keller in *ibid.*, No. 130 (June 14, 1922); *Obvinitel'noe zakliuchenie*, p. 61.

[91] Sokolov, "Zashchita Uchreditel'nago Sobraniia," in *Arkhiv Russkoi Revoliutsii*, XIII, 62.

[92] See Gotz's remark in *Izvestiia*, No. 131 (June 15, 1922).

deputies at its mercy when they assembled in the Taurida Palace. Announcing that no armed demonstrants would be permitted near the meeting place, it blocked off the approaches to any kind of demonstrants favorable to the assembly, since even an unarmed crowd would not preclude the danger of fraternization with the guard and the weakening of its resolution to deal with the deputies as the regime had in mind. A previous experience when SR deputies with their supporters had taken possession of the palace and fraternized with the Lettish Guard only to disperse because no quorum was at hand is said to have so alarmed the government that it decided, first, to keep sympathizers away from the assembly and, second, to replace the Lettish guards with Kronstadt sailors under the leadership of the anarchist A. G. Zhelezniakov, a man of hatred and violence, who would not wince or waver in disposing of a threat to the regime which at the time he was serving.[93]

A tense situation had developed in the capital. A common revolutionary phraseology masked only partially an irreconcilable clash of opinion between the partisans of ALL POWER TO THE CONSTITUENT ASSEMBLY and those of ALL POWER TO THE SOVIETS. Two placards were posted everywhere, oftentimes side by side, the one by the Committee to Defend the Assembly, urging the people to come out into the streets, the other by the Petersburg Soviet, warning them to stay off.[94] The All-Russian Soviet Executive Committee published in *Pravda* on January 4 a decree to the effect that all power inhered in the soviets and that any effort on the part of a person or institution to encroach on this power would be considered a counterrevolutionary action which would be dealt with by armed force if necessary.[95] One of the Bolshevik commanders is said to have estimated the strength on his side at no more than 3,500 to 4,000 trustworthy sailors and soldiers, plus 5,000 armed workers of the Red Guard,

[93] Chernov, manuscript commentary on the minutes of the Central Committee, pp. 86–87; *Vserossiiskoe Uchreditel'noe Sobranie*, pp. 213–14, n. 22; Vladimirova, *God sluzhby "sotsialistov" kapitalistam*, pp. 110–11; Sokolov, "Zashchita Uchreditel'nago Sobraniia," in *Arkhiv Russkoi Revoliutsii*, XIII, 45. Other sources view the Letts as entirely reliable; Chernov may be in error in imputing softness to them.

[94] Oganovski, "Dnevnik chlena Uchreditel'nago Sobraniia," *Golos Minuvshago*, IV–VI (April–June, 1918), 149; Vladimirova, *God sluzhby "sotsialistov" kapitalistam*, pp. 106–7.

[95] Lenin, *Sochineniia* (2d ed.), XXII, 179, 597–98, n. 84.

many of whom did not know how to shoot.[96] As the defenders of the assembly thought they could count on an armed force of around 5,000,[97] the disparity was not so great but that a bloody affair could have been in the making.

Several things must be borne in mind, however, as we turn from the preparations to defend the assembly to the assembly itself and its fate. The men of the Military Commission had made their arrangements with the soldiers' committees on the divisional, regimental, or company levels in the expectation that these could swing their soldier constituents into action. All through 1917 these organs had been making commitments only to have the troops refuse to honor them. The explanation, of course, is simple—the committees were filled with intellectuals and the ranks with common men. Even among the activists there was skepticism as to whether promises would or could be made good in a setting where men would say yes in the morning and no in the evening.[98] How much greater the doubt in the minds of the leaders, who had been sobered by the shattering defeats in October and had never shared the sanguine hopes of the young army men immediately concerned with the task of defense. All SR's wished to save the assembly, but there was no unity among them as to how it could be done and no plan which all of them could back wholeheartedly. Finally it must be remembered that the "you go first" principle underlying the marching sequence of January 5 betrayed the absence of a do-or-die spirit on the part of the armed forces supporting the assembly, and carried with it the danger that, if some unit failed to go first, the others waiting for their cue might not go at all.

SR strategy had to be planned without knowing what the outcome of the popular demonstration would be and without knowing how the Bolsheviks would proceed against the assembly. Despite the uncertainty, party members now began to exhibit in the hour of adversity all the energy, purpose, and sense of urgency which had

[96] Sokolov, "Zashchita Uchreditel'nago Sobraniia," in *Arkhiv Russkoi Revoliutsii*, XIII, 41. But see also below, p. 428.
[97] See above, p. 373.
[98] Sokolov, "Zashchita Uchreditel'nago Sobraniia," in *Arkhiv Russkoi Revoliutsii*, XIII, 50.

been so sadly lacking when they were in power. Already at the Fourth Congress the question of strategy had received attention. There were those who would have an immediate showdown with the Soviet government, the very existence of which was in derogation of the assembly, its rights, and its duties. There were others who would first assert the legislative authority of the assembly in the form of enactments that would clarify for the public the issues at stake before attempting to wrest from the soviets executive power. As Rakitnikov put it, the people must first understand what the struggle was about before the assembly majority could enter into the struggle itself.[99] Soon the second point of view prevailed among Socialist Revolutionaries, supported as it was by a part of the right as well as by the center generally.

The responsiveness of the Constituent Assembly to the will of the electorate was another matter of concern to the SR's in the face of the invidious comparisons the Bolsheviks were drawing between the frozen composition of the assembly and the flexibility of the soviets, which could be reelected at any time and hence reflected the present rather than the past mood of the voters. The regime had, in fact, decreed the right of recall after the Left SR's had been successful in transferring the power of decision from soviet executive committees to soviet congresses or to the electorate itself.[100] In the Bolshevik conception representatives were out of harmony with the people's will if they were Socialist Revolutionaries.[101] Many members of the latter party did not reject out of hand a renewed test at the polls in order to preserve the authority of the assembly, but for them such a test must be in accordance with the democratic principle, not at the will of the soviets. Peasant deputies wanted first a referendum to determine whether the majority of the voters in a given district favored a recall.[102] Chernov would have committed his party to all three of the advanced democratic devices so much in vogue in the

[99] *Kratkii otchët*, pp. 132–34. I. A. Prilezhaev, a member of the Central Committee not identified with any faction, even advocated leaving the Soviet decrees in effect, partly as a tactical move to wrest the initiative from Lenin's regime, partly because of their intrinsic merit. Needless to say, his was a point of view which found little favor in party circles.

[100] See Lenin, *Sochineniia*, XXII, 92–97, 586, n. 43.

[101] *Delo Naroda*, No. 236 (December 19, 1917).

[102] *Ibid.*, No. 227 (December 8, 1917).

earlier years of the twentieth century—to the initiative, referendum, and recall [103]—and both he [104] and Rakitnikov [105] favored resolving a deadlock between the assembly and the soviets over the executive power by an appeal to the electorate with the lines tightly drawn between the adherents of democracy and those of dictatorship. In advocating this course, as in his over-all concept of strategy in the post-October era, Chernov was counting on disillusionment with the promises and performance of the Bolsheviks to produce reverses for them at the polls and reaffirm the verdict of November. Some of the right-wing SR's opposed the idea of reelections as an approach to mobocracy,[106] but even in that sector of party opinion the view was gaining ground that the best way out of the difficulties confronting the assembly might be to let the country decide between it and the soviet system. Mark Vishniak, who would be chosen as secretary of the Constituent Assembly, favored doing the most essential things and then holding a new election.[107]

But how much time would the SR's have? Few of them were optimistic in this respect, and the opening day came to assume quite exceptional importance in their thinking. The greater their concern about it, the stronger their resolve to use it well, so that all their preparations came to be centered on this single day. A commission of five, known as the "commission of the opening day," was set up to act as a general staff in planning the program for that day and marshaling the deputies behind it. The whole delegation was pledged to follow its instructions, quickly and without argument or individual deviation, like an army on the battlefield. It is not certain who were members of this key commission.[108] But E. M. Timofeev and

---

[103] *Kratkii otchët*, p. 34.

[104] Speech of December 29 to the All-Russian Railwaymen's Congress, reported in *Delo Naroda*, No. 245 (December 31, 1917).

[105] *Kratkii otchët*, p. 134.

[106] See Podvitski's opinion in *ibid.*, p. 46.

[107] Statement to the author in 1955.

[108] Vishniak does not name the five in his book. When this author raised the question many years later, he at first mentioned Gotz and Rudnev; then, reconsidering, he named Fondaminski, Kovarski, Gendelman, Eliashevich, and Timofeev (interview in New York, 1952). Zenzinov also named Fondaminski and Timofeev but not the other three; instead, he mentioned P. A. Sorokin and Vishniak himself without being able to recall a fifth member (interview in New York, December 19, 1949).

Fondaminski seem to have been on it, and its rightist cast was entirely in harmony with the group out of which it was formed.[109] In any event the personnel of the commission is not a matter of great importance—the SR's were always carefree in organizational matters, as is illustrated in this instance by the fact that Zenzinov, who was not a member of the commission, participated freely in its work.

What is of much greater moment is the plan the commission drew up, embodying the strategy of the Socialist Revolutionary Party in the hour that could have been its greatest opportunity and was to mark the nadir of its fortunes. It was framed in a mood of quiet dignity, neither militant nor yielding, by people who were armed mainly with a faith in democracy, for purposes laudable in themselves but no longer corresponding to reality. Basically the plan was to infuse as much content as possible into the first day's work so that if it were also the last, there would be something to stand on in the ensuing struggle which the SR's now regarded as inevitable. If the physical existence of the Constituent Assembly could not be guaranteed, at least its moral authority must be elevated and preserved. The toiling masses of Russia must be convinced by solid acts of legislation on their behalf that in defending the assembly they were defending their own cause. Everything that was abstract and secondary was set aside in favor of issues that were concrete and primary. Under the pressure of peasant deputies, who would not hear of a declaration of principles but demanded action the people could understand, the SR intellectuals at last abandoned the abstractions which had been their refuge from reality and came to grips with the basic issues of the day. The bills to be presented to the assembly were carefully worked out and majestically worded. Land, peace, and the structure of state received precedence over the question of executive power, in keeping with the decision to get something substantial on the record before challenging the soviet system —first entrenchment and then attack was to be the strategy. The

---

[109] Vishniak at first described the commission as entirely rightist in cast but later conceded that Timofeev would more properly be characterized as a right centrist. Zenzinov also stated that Timofeev stood somewhat to the left of the others. Zenzinov had the Central Committee appointing the commission, but Vishniak is doubtlessly correct in saying that it was chosen by the Bureau of the Delegation (see his *Vserossiiskoe Uchreditel'noe Sobranie*, p. 105).

SR delegation proposed to whip the measures through the first day's session, if necessary unloading all ballast such as the bills deposing the Romanovs and establishing the deputies' immunity. The determination to accomplish at least this much amounted to an obsession with these unfortunate people, now striving to do in one day what they had failed to do in eight months of power.

Besides the legislative content of their program, the SR's had to decide their tactics for the opening day. They were pledged to go unarmed to the Taurida Palace, entrusting their personal safety to the people. They were enjoined not to respond to provocation but to invest themselves with the dignity of Roman senators, sitting out in grim silence insults, threats, and even the appearance of Lenin. In their concern for bigger things, they did not overlook the possibility of petty sabotage: if the electricity were cut off, candles were to be provided by Anastasia N. Slëtova, sister of Stephen Slëtov and first wife of Chernov; if the deputies were deprived of food, she was to have ready hundreds of sandwiches. The SR's displayed considerable intuition in their plans for a protracted first session, at which they did not count on doing everything they had in mind but were determined to make a gesture in the direction of peace, demonstrate their acceptance of federalism, and, above everything else, put through the whole land law, all eighty sections of it, with a roll call at the end. The common sense of danger and the solemnity of the occasion left no room for factional dissension as they resolved to do their duty even in the face of death.[110]

Only in the light of this submergence of factionalism is it possible to understand the SR decision in respect to their candidate for the presidency of the assembly, the most thorny of all the problems confronting the delegation save only that of the executive power, since it would have to be resolved at the outset in a manner that would neither strike the colors of the majority nor terminate the life of the assembly. And, of course, it was necessary to have a candidate who would hold together all elements of the party representation. If the

[110] Bykhovski, *Vserossiiskii Sovet Krest'ianskikh Deputatov*, pp. 350–51; Oganovski, "Dnevnik chlena Uchreditel'nago Sobraniia," *Golos Minuvshago*, IV–VI (April–June, 1918), 148–50, 159–60; Vishniak, *Vserossiiskoe Uchreditel'noe Sobranie*, pp. 104–7; Sokolov, "Zashchita Uchreditel'nago Sobraniia," in *Arkhiv Russkoi Revoliutsii*, XIII, 58–59.

majority of the SR deputies had been free to follow their wishes, if the delegation had been in character, it would have chosen Avksentiev or perhaps Breshkovskaia, Rudnev, or even Kerenski. But it had no freedom of choice, and even if it had had, would not dared have used it. Either the candidates of its choice were unavailable or they were politically impossible, not simply from the standpoint of the physical safety of the assembly, but even more in the sense that the selection of any one of them would have exposed all too clearly the true character of the SR representation. What was needed in the circumstances of the hour was a leftist decoy, and what better decoy could be devised than V. M. Chernov?

In an astonishing reversal of front the deputies who had at first blackballed the party leader as a candidate for their bureau, where he would have been one among twenty-five, now proposed him for the lonely eminence of president of the assembly, in preference to one of their own and even to a presidium in which he would have shared his functions with others. They did this, we are told, "after long hesitation . . . knowing full well how little, either in the political or the technical sense, his candidacy met the requirements for this most responsible of positions." [111] As a matter of fact, any less prejudiced source would have conceded that because of his voice, stage presence, experience (he had presided over the Third Congress of his party at its most tumultuous session),[112] oratorical ability, and knowledge of the situation, Chernov was well qualified to serve as presiding officer. Politically, of course, he was dreadful in the eyes of those who put him up—even "odious," to borrow a term from the *Novaia Zhizn'*.[113] More than half his party comrades, according to a hostile source, were fed up with his rhetoric. At a New Year's meeting only perfunctory applause had greeted the speech of this "provincial tragedian," whereas another deputy had brought down the house by drawing a parallel between the image of Pleve's carriage as a symbol of autocracy and this deputy's vision of a new carriage rumbling through the streets of Petersburg, with the kaiser's bristling mustaches at the window, Hindenburg in the

[111] Vishniak, *Vserossiiskoe Uchreditel'noe Sobranie*, p. 107.
[112] See my book, *The Agrarian Foes of Bolshevism*, pp. 227 ff.
[113] Quoted in Vishniak, *Vserossiiskoe Uchreditel'noe Sobranie*, p. 109n.

driver's seat, Lenin and Trotski on the footboards, bent over, and an Okhrana guard running alongside. Here we have the essence of the SR delegation laid bare.

But if Chernov was a "provincial tragedian" to these Populist intellectuals whom the revolution had terrified and the war enraged, he was still the "village minister" to millions of peasants. His backbiting "comrades" had no one to match his popularity and so he was chosen to grace the assembly as he had the Second All-Russian Peasants' Congress, for the same reasons and against the same opponent. The Bolsheviks, on the other side, were being equally crafty, and equally hypocritical. They were uniting with the Left SR's behind the candidacy of Maria Spiridonova, whom they would later cast into prison. In the absence of a counterbalance such as Chernov alone could provide, the pull of her name might lead to defections among the peasants on the SR side of the fence, one of whom, A. P. Blizniuk of Voronezh province, actually did go over before the voting took place.[114] The designation of V. M. Chernov must be viewed as a concession to reality, as a maneuver dictated by tactical considerations in line with the "Vikzhel" policy then being followed by the leadership of the delegation, not because it wanted to but because it had to. It must also be viewed as a confession of weakness on the part of the right SR's.

Whether there were other considerations involved in the choice of Chernov is a matter of conjecture. Vishniak claims he had been less touched by slander than other party leaders. But the Bolsheviks had given it to Chernov hot and heavy, probably more than to Avksentiev, who was much less influential with the rural masses. The partisans of Chernov in the delegation argued that his flexibility befitted him for the role of chairman—a by no means idle consideration, for violence came easily to the Kronstadt sailors, and was it not conceivable that Bolshevik discipline might rest lightly on the anarchist Zhelezniakov, and that the assembly might be shot up before anything had been accomplished? A critic of the party from its own ranks has suggested that the right-wing majority wished to commit Chernov to the defense of this institution cast in its image by according him a distinction that would forever raise a barrier between him

[114] See above, p. 296.

and the Soviet system,[115] but as Chernov had always opposed the soviets as governing institutions, he might have refused in any event to come to terms with the Bolsheviks or the Left SR's.[116]

Once committed to the Chernov candidacy, the right SR's had next to make him speak their language. The custom of having a presiding officer deliver an oration when he entered upon his duties presented them with an opportunity for a keynote address that would distinguish clearly between the opposing principles of democracy and dictatorship as embodied, on the one hand, in the Constituent Assembly and, on the other, in the Council of Commissars. They seem to have wanted something in the way of a declaration of war on the revolution in its extremist phase, yet without disrupting the assembly and without commissioning a spokesman who believed in what they wanted. They demanded that Chernov be as much out of character in delivering his speech as they had been in selecting him for this position. To do a rightist deed with leftist hands was only a variant of the technique used during 1917 of attempting to foist a revolutionary program upon a nonrevolutionary government. Small wonder that neither variant worked.

In the present instance there are two quite different versions of how the right SR's went about the task of making Chernov speak their language. The first is that he agreed to do their bidding in a prolonged conference with the commission of the first day, at which the ground was gone over in detail and he was coached in the performance of a task that could not have been to his liking. The content, if not the rhetoric, of his speech had been a matter of prior agreement. And when he gave it, according to this version, he did not improvise but spoke from notes.[117] The second version is more charitable to Chernov, though scarcely more flattering to his party. After repeated demands for the text of his speech had brought no results,

[115] Burevoi (Sopliakov), *Raspad 1918–1922*, p. 128.

[116] It is significant that Chernov does not discuss this affair. The information in the foregoing paragraphs has been drawn from interviews with Zenzinov in 1949 and Vishniak in 1952, and from the following printed sources: Oganovski, "Dnevnik chlena Uchreditel'nago Sobraniia," *Golos Minuvshago*, IV–VI (April–June, 1918), 143–45, 155–56; Vishniak, *Vserossiiskoe Uchreditel'noe Sobranie*, pp. 106–7; Burevoi (Sopliakov), *Raspad 1918–1922*, p. 128.

[117] Interview with Zenzinov in New York (December 19, 1949); interview with Vishniak in New York (January 2, 1952); Vishniak, *Vserossiiskoe Uchreditel'noe Sobranie*, pp. 108–9.

the Bureau of the Delegation asked him for at least his theses. But toward midnight on the day before convocation Chernov appeared in an exhausted state from five or six meetings, muttered some platitudes to which no one could take exception, and got them accepted without discussion. His speech was delivered "virtually impromptu." [118] Either version is plausible. The first accords with the nature of Chernov, the second with the business methods of the SR's, and both with the character of this party.

[118] Oganovski, "Dnevnik chlena Uchreditel'nago Sobraniia," *Golos Minuvshago,* IV–VI (April–June, 1918), 156. All these sources are unfriendly to Chernov, who himself says nothing. Oganovski's account may be closer to the truth because it was written soon after the events in question. And Vishniak in his memoirs, published twenty-two years after his treatise on the Constituent Assembly, somewhat modifies his earlier statement. He says in one place that Chernov agreed to speak in the spirit of the plan worked out by the commission but would not divulge the general content of his speech. See *Dan' proshlomu,* p. 344. But further on Vishniak more or less returns to his original position with the assertion that in general terms the content of the speech had been agreed on (*ibid.,* p. 369).

VIII

Agony and Aftermath

And now for the session itself—for the tense afternoon and the "terrible night" that would mark the life span of the All-Russian Constituent Assembly. The SR deputies were due to assemble at ten in the morning on January 5, 1918 (January 18 by the Western calendar), in a place not far from the Taurida Palace. "But the Russian public is incurable"—not even on such a day could it be on time.[1] By noon the SR procession got under way, some two hundred deputies marching six abreast through streets that resembled more an armed camp than a city.[2] Many of these armed workers and sea-going peasants had once been theirs. But the hypnosis of war had been overpowering, the loyalty to the Allies unswerving, and now the strength that had been wantonly wasted would put an end to their dreams. All of these marching SR's were convinced that violence might befall the assembly, and many did not expect to return alive to their homes.[3]

The occasion had brought together the cream of the Populist intelligentsia from all over Russia. But though the right-wing "infantry" was well represented—overrepresented as we have seen—not all of the "generals" were there. Kerenski was in St. Petersburg and sent a letter to the Central Committee, seeking permission to attend the opening session. Preoccupied as always with the "unbroken" succession of power, he wished to lay down his mandate before a legally constituted authority. In other circumstances he might have been chosen as executive head, if not as president of the assembly, but not under these. He was asked not to appear at the

[1] Oganovski, "Dnevnik chlena Uchreditel'nago Sobraniia," *Golos Minuvshago,* IV–VI (April–June, 1918), 151.

[2] For impressions of the setting, see also O. S. Minor, "Odin den' Uchreditel'nago Sobraniia: Ocherk" (One Day of the Constituent Assembly: A Sketch), in *Perezhitoe,* I, 126–27.

[3] Zenzinov, *Iz zhizni revoliutsionera,* p. 99.

session.[4] Probably he was swayed less by the decision of the Central Committee than by the entreaties of his friends, whose finesse in setting up Chernov would have been ruined by an explosion at the outset. The whereabouts of Avksentiev are uncertain. An SR source has him under lock and key in Petropavlovsk Fortress, and qualifies the report of his release as a rumor,[5] whereas the press account not only sets him at liberty but has him appearing at the SR caucus amid the plaudits of his friends.[6] But about Gotz and Rudnev there is no doubt. They were both there, Gotz with the charge of fomenting the cadet uprising hanging over him, and Rudnev in a similarly precarious situation as a result of the fighting in Moscow. They were safe for the time being, however, for Lenin had decided to respect the immunity of deputies who were sought by the police.[7] But they were inhibited in their movements and could not play a prominent part in the proceedings.[8]

The session did not begin at noon as scheduled because the Bolsheviks and Left SR's were in caucus, awaiting the outcome of the street demonstrations and the return of key figures before deciding on their strategy.[9] But around 4 P.M. the delegations and the public at last filled the hall and hostilities could begin. Scarcely less resplendent than in the days of the Enlightened Empress and even more comfortable than in those of the Duma, the great hall had been neatly picked up and newly decorated. The Bolsheviks had provided a magnificent setting for the assembly, as if in deference to the democratic principle (among their many talents, not least has been the undertaker's art). The SR's occupied the center and right of the hall with a thin screen of non-Russian representatives, mainly Moslem, be-

[4] Ishchushchim A. F. Kerenskago" (To Those Who Are Looking for A. F. Kerenski), *Delo Naroda*, No. 6 (March 28 [N.S.], 1918); *Novaia Zhizn'*, No. 4/218 (January 6, 1918); Vishniak, *Vserossiiskoe Uchreditel'noe Sobranie*, p. 106; Vishniak, *Dan' proshlomu*, p. 365, where Kerenski's idea is called "crazy."
[5] Vishniak, *Vserossiiskoe Uchreditel'noe Sobranie*, pp. 99–100, 106; Vishniak, *Dan' proshlomu*, p. 365.
[6] *Novaia Zhizn'*, No. 4/218 (January 6, 1918).
[7] Bonch-Bruevich, *Na boevykh postakh*, pp. 246–47.
[8] *Ibid.*, pp. 235, 246; Steinberg, *Als ich Volkskommissar war*, p. 71; Vishniak, *Vserossiiskoe Uchreditel'noe Sobranie*, p. 106; Vishniak, *Dan' Proshlomu*, p. 365.
[9] Steinberg, *Als ich Volkskommissar war*, pp. 71–73; Vishniak, *Dan' proshlomu*, pp. 358–60; Chernov, *Pered burei*, 358–59. But for a different version, see Mstislavski, *Piat' dnei*, p. 141. This second Left SR source is less credible because one may infer from Steinberg that the two SR sources are correct.

tween them and the Left SR's. Then came the Bolsheviks, their leaders in the front rows noticeably older than those of the Left SR's. Further back on the left were the beardless youth in uniform. The SR's varied less in age but more in dress, the intellectuals in business suits with buttoned jackets, the peasants in sheepskin and jerkins, while the soldiers among them were conspicuously fewer in numbers.[10] Only a handful of deputies sat to the right of the Socialist Revolutionaries—the Constitutional Democrats had been outlawed and not many had been elected, anyway—while only the anarchists could have outflanked the Bolsheviks on the left, and anarchists are not at home in parliaments. Mstislavski is wrong in asserting that Irakli Tsereteli was the only Menshevik present,[11] for there is record of a speech made by A. A. Troianovski, but nearly all of the small Menshevik delegation had been elected from Georgia, and, except for Tsereteli, the Georgian Mensheviks had stayed in Georgia.

But the main gap in the membership of the Constituent Assembly, aside from the Moslem contingent from Turkestan, where the election was never held or at least never completed, resulted from the decision of the Ukrainian Socialist Revolutionaries not to attend the session but to go their own way, with their own constituent assembly, the sovereignty of which they asserted with increasing truculence. At its session of December 30 their central committee had forbidden their representatives to go to St. Petersburg because of the hostilities between the Ukraine and the Soviet government, because of the disorders in the Ukraine, and because their services were needed at home.[12] Of their eighty-odd deputies, only a handful appeared at the session of January 5 to read a declaration and announce that, while the delegation was not coming, it reserved its

---

[10] Oganovski, "Dnevnik chlena Uchreditel'nago Sobraniia," *Golos Minuvshago*, IV–VI (April–June, 1918), 154; Mstislavski, *Piat' dnei*, p. 141. Comparing these two sources, both highly prejudiced, one may conclude that eyewitnesses saw what they wanted to see. Oganovski does not even mention workers, nor Mstislavski peasants. Of course there were more soldiers on the left than on the right or in the center (that is why the SR's had lost the revolution!), but there were peasants among the Left SR's and even among the Bolsheviks, while workers and intellectuals who were not in uniform must have been rather numerous in the left sector of the hall. All of the sources must be used with caution, for they all are prejudiced in one way or another.

[11] *Piat' dnei*, p. 142.

[12] *Narodnia Volia* (Ukrainian newspaper), No. 193 (December 31, 1917).

right to come.[13] In other words, if the assembly were a failure, they did not wish to be involved, but if it succeeded, and came to wield authority, then they would take their seats. Not only did this position of the third largest delegation betoken lack of dignity—honest conviction was also lacking.

The total number of deputies who attended this first and only session of the All-Russian Constituent Assembly is variously given: 427 by Bykhovski,[14] 402 by Vladimirova,[15] around 500 by Steinberg.[16] The absenteeism was enormous and seriously detracts from the validity of the assembly as constituted on January 5, 1918, since the law had provided for slightly in excess of 800 members.[17] But if virtually half the membership was absent, either through failure to get there or failure to be elected, there were plenty of "guests" in the galleries. Uritski had seen to that. In his capacity as commissar of matters pertaining to the assembly, or, as the SR's liked to call him, "commissar over the assembly," with control of admissions, he had packed the galleries with workers, soldiers, and sailors to assure a "public" hostile to the assembly and favorable to the existing regime.[18] The Bolsheviks had dredged up the depths of the city and unloaded them on the galleries, according to a hostile observer, who speaks of the drunkenness of half the audience, the vomiting in the lunchroom, and the dreadful language everywhere.[19] One pastime was to draw a bead on a deputy, and the unsteadiness

---

[13] *Vserossiiskoe Uchreditel'noe Sobranie*, pp. 85–86; Steinberg, *Als ich Volkskommissar war*, p. 78; Oganovski, "Dnevnik chlena Uchreditel'nago Sobraniia," *Golos Minuvshago*, IV–VI (April–June, 1918), 156. The first source, which was published under the auspices of the Soviet government, is not to be confused with Vishniak's book of the same title.

[14] *Vserossiiskii Sovet Krest'ianskikh Deputatov*, p. 415.

[15] *God sluzhby "sotsialistov" kapitalistam*, p. 111.

[16] *Als ich Volkskommissar war*, p. 70.

[17] *Vserossiiskoe Uchreditel'noe Sobranie*, p. 115; Vishniak, *Vserossiiskoe Uchreditel'noe Sobranie*, p. 86.

[18] Steinberg, *Als ich Volkskommissar war*, p. 64. Since the author was a member of the government, one could not wish for better testimony. The technique of gallery-packing, of course, is not restricted to Bolsheviks. One is reminded of the 1940 convention of the Republican Party in the United States, when an organized claque in the galleries helped to put across a whipped-up candidacy never before tested in public life.

[19] Sokolov, "Zashchita Uchreditel'nago Sobraniia," in *Arkhiv Russkoi Revoliutsii*, XIII, 66–67; see also Minor, "Odin den' Uchreditel'nago Sobraniia," in *Perezhitoe*, I, 129, 130–31.

of the bead in no way diminished the concern of the deputy or of his neighbors. A shot, whether accidental or deliberate, might have set off a whole round of shooting and could conceivably have led to a massacre. A more unpromising setting for parliamentary proceedings could not well be imagined. "We, the deputies, were surrounded by an enraged crowd ready at any moment to throw itself upon us and tear us to pieces." [20]

After the Constituent Assembly had been opened twice, first by the SR's and then by Sverdlov in the name of the government, the Bolsheviks proposed that the International be sung. The SR delegation now found itself between the devil and the deep blue sea, or between the rifles and the music, for if it refused to sing, it would expose its essence, and if it sang, it would violate the sentiment of the majority of its members against ending the war. A minor matter can sometimes pose a dilemma more forcefully than a major issue, merely because it is so simple that it offers no room for evasion. The delegation rose to its feet hesitatingly, raggedly, with obvious aversion. Chernov turned around to face it and, opening wide his mouth and gesticulating, sought to lead it in the singing, but he could no more evoke music from this band of war-inebriated intellectuals than from the "quartet" in Krylov's fable. Only some of them sang— Chernov himself, Sukhomlin, perhaps Zenzinov, his glasses glittering in the light as he tried to make the best of an awkward situation.[21] In the cruel language of a former comrade on the left, Chernov took the very highest notes—until his voice cracked on one of them, the offensive of June 18.[22] Everything about this assembly was ill-fated, even the attempt at music.

After the song came the showdown. The assembly had now to choose under whom it would function, and the choice would provide

[20] Zenzinov, *Iz zhizni revoliutsionera*, p. 9.

[21] Interview with Vishniak (New York, 1952); Vishniak, *Dan' proshlomu*, p. 363; Steinberg, *Als ich Volkskommissar war*, pp. 76–77; Mstislavski, *Piat' dnei*, p. 146. Once more, the sources divide according to their political bias. The author's uncertainty about Zenzinov springs from the fact that the information is drawn from Mstislavski, apparently a bitter and even a poisonous enemy.

[22] Ligovski, "Vsia vlast' ushedshim!" (All Power to Those Who Have Left!), in *Vokrug Uchreditel'nago Sobraniia*, pp. 46–47. Reference is to the military offensive of 1917, which Chernov as a member of the Provisional Government had not opposed and which in general terms he had excused in the press. See my book, *The Agrarian Foes of Bolshevism*, pp. 335–36, 369.

a clear-cut test of strength. With so many elected representatives absent, and with the SR's by no means sure that their peasant deputies would withstand the blandishments of the left or the pull of Spiridonova's name, there was some uncertainty about the outcome or at least about the margin of victory, even with Chernov as their standard-bearer. It was a sad spectacle, this confrontation of the teacher with his pupil, both devoted to the revolution, to peace, and to the peasantry, since the major force behind either had other ends in view. The force behind Chernov aimed to turn back the revolution and find still further victims for the bloody god of war; the force behind his pupil meant to impose a superstructure of industrial socialism upon a foundation of peasant individualism, remaking the foundation in the process, a stupendous undertaking, as destructive as a second war. The unenviable situation of the principals in this drama reflected the plight of the class they represented—divided, confused, and constrained to serve an alien purpose. Despite the affinity of their points of view they had been pulled apart and now were pitted against each other, not because of Spiridonova's seduction by Bolshevism, as is so often and so ignorantly claimed, but because Chernov never could bring himself to stand up against the small but willful wing of his party which had torn it to pieces, paralyzed its will to action, dissipated its following, thwarted his initiative (when he had shown any), and even now was using him as revolutionary window dressing. The maneuver of putting up Chernov was successful in preventing defections on the part of peasant deputies. He was elected with 244 votes in his favor and 151 against, whereas Spiridonova's candidacy drew 153 affirmative and 244 negative votes. According to Chernov, the results were much more favorable than expected. The total vote, it will be noted, was less than half the total membership. Sverdlov relinquished the chair with equanimity—he was still chairman in the soviet system, and had the soldiers with him.[23]

Chernov now delivered his inaugural address. We have already spoken of its background, of the false position in which he was

[23] Chernov, *Pered burei*, p. 362; Oganovski, "Dnevnik chlena Uchreditel'nago Sobraniia," *Golos Minuvshago*, IV–VI (April–June, 1918), 155–56; Bonch-Bruevich, *Na boevykh postakh*, p. 249; Mstislavski, *Piat' dnei*, p. 149.

placed by accepting this "honor" from people who loathed him, at
the price of speaking their language. That very noon, on the way to
the Taurida Palace, he had been prompted by Vishniak,[24] the future
president of the assembly by the future secretary, the superior by
his subordinate, a reversal of roles quite typical of the PSR. But now
a miracle happened. This bird, thought safely caged and taught to
sing strange notes, escaped the cage and sang according to its nature.
The sources differ as to the quality of the speech but all agree as
to its tone and content. One of Chernov's most poisonous detractors,
the "comrade" elected with him as secretary, thought the speech a
humdrum affair, in no sense outstanding, "even for Chernov" [25]
(the truth is that Chernov was a fine speaker,[26] though long-winded
and given to embroidery). An enemy from the left speaks of its
pale monotony.[27] To judge from the stenographic record, it suffered from wordiness and loose construction; the orator ranged too
widely, even within the framework of his sentences, and permitted
the torrent of words to drown the force of his argument.[28] But
oratory cannot be judged through stenography. Chernov was a
cunning man and even better than other SR's he had mastered the
art of purposeful obfuscation. It may be that he did not want his
argument to be too forceful. In his private memoirs he says that
great coolness was needed to avert a catastrophe in opposing the
Constituent Assembly to the Council of Commissars.[29] And Steinberg pays him the tribute of saying: "Das war eine kunstvolle Rede,
eine Rede, die viele Köpfe in diesem Moment verwirren konnte"
(It was an artful speech, a speech which at this juncture could lead
many astray).[30]

Chernov laid emphasis on his revolutionary past and his record

[24] Interview in New York (1952); *Dan' proshlomu*, p. 355.

[25] Vishniak, *Vserossiiskoe Uchreditel'noe Sobranie*, p. 108.

[26] S. P. Postnikov ranked Chernov with Kerenski, Trotski, and Tsereteli in this
respect. The finest orator of the revolution, in his opinion, was Irakli Tsereteli.

[27] Mstislavski, *Piat' dnei*, pp. 149–50.

[28] Text of the speech in *Vserossiiskoe Uchreditel'noe Sobranie*, pp. 9–23.

[29] Manuscript commentary on the minutes of the Central Committee, p. 88.
According to Minor, Chernov also sought to create the possibility of legislative
collaboration with the Bolsheviks and Left SR's, who after all represented a
sizable segment of the population. See his "Odin den' Uchreditel'nago Sobraniia," ih *Perezhitoe*, I, 128.

[30] *Als ich Volkskommissar war*, p. 78.

of opposition to the war. In dealing with the questions of land, peace, nationalities, and renewed consultation of the people, he skirted so near the position of the left that its partisans, who had listened attentively at first, broke in upon him with cries of astonishment and irritation: "That's the Bolshevik program!"; "We know—all that has been done already!" Thinking to pin him down, they yelled at him: "Talk about power!" but this skater was not to be gotten onto such thin ice, and Chernov evaded the issue, remarking obliquely in another connection that the assembly embodied the majority will and was based on the most perfect electoral system.[31] As Chernov performed his balancing act with bows in the direction of his enemies, a chill settled over his "friends" on the other side of the hall. They were taken aback by these "acrobatic exercises on a Bolshevik trapeze," by this praise of the Zimmerwald spirit which "cut the heart like a dull knife." [32] In the cruel words of another witness, "even Zenzinov, with all his—shall I say—incapacity for passion, shuddered visibly" at some of his colleague's phrases.[33] If not Zenzinov, then certainly those Populist intellectuals farther to the right must have writhed inwardly when Chernov declared that the "Russian Revolution was born with peace on its lips," [34] when he named as "our allies . . . the socialist toilers of all countries," [35] and when he called on the assembly to stand in honor of those who had fallen in defense of the "borders of the Russian Revolution." [36]

Yet there was nothing in Chernov's speech to which more reasonable members of his party should have taken exception: he unequivocally rejected any thought of a separate peace,[37] he obviously meant to hold the tsarist empire together in a fraternal federation of peoples,[38] and he cautiously set the Constituent Assembly above the soviets in language that was veiled and circumspect, yet fully in keeping with the circumstances of the hour.[39] But he had in no way

[31] *Novaia Zhizn'*, No. 5/219 (January 7, 1918).

[32] Oganovski, "Dnevnik chlena Uchreditel'nago Sobraniia," *Golos Minuvshago*, IV–VI (April–June, 1918), 157.

[33] Mstislavski, *Piat' dnei*, p. 150.

[34] *Vserossiiskoe Uchreditel'noe Sobranie*, p. 9.   [35] *Ibid.*, p. 11.

[36] *Ibid.*, p. 23.   [37] *Ibid.*, pp. 10–13.   [38] *Ibid.*, pp. 13–15.

[39] *Ibid.*, pp. 19–21; Steinberg, *Als ich Volkskommissar war*, p. 80; see also citation above from the *Novaia Zhizn'*. Chernov's boiled-down version in his memoirs (*Pered burei*, pp. 362–63) is essentially correct but conveys the impression of more vigorous language than he used.

satisfied the right wing of his party, which censured him for having blurred the lines between Bolshevism and the assembly majority instead of making them sharp and clear.[40] One wonders whether he could have satisfied these people by any action short of singing the Marseillaise. A left-centrist leader of a party with a left-centrist majority had made a left-centrist speech. What was reprehensible or out of place about this? If the Populist intellectuals were disgruntled with his failure to heed their instructions, which were not those of the party, why had they not entrusted the task to one of their own number? The answer is obvious, and requires no comment.

Under heartbreaking circumstances Chernov had performed a service for his party and for the assembly. If he had done nothing else, he had gotten the session under way without a breakdown and had preserved for his party the opportunity of getting on the record acts of legislation that ought to have been there long before. He speaks without exaggeration when he says that a reading of the official record does not convey even a remote impression of what it was like to carry on under the torrent of abuse that broke loose now and then or in the face of the dozens of insults, catcalls, and shouts that accompanied every phrase.[41] Even his most heartless critic concedes—after thirty-six years—that he showed courage.[42] His words could have influenced the intellectuals on the left; they had not the slightest effect on the crowd in the galleries or down below, in the entrances to the hall, on the churned-up plebeian elements who were swayed solely by their class instinct. While he was speaking, two of the Kronstadt sailors, cleverly screening themselves behind their companions, had brought him under the sights of their rifle. They may, of course, merely have been bored and seeking a

---

[40] Vishniak, *Vserossiiskoe Uchreditel'noe Sobranie*, pp. 107–9; Oganovski, "Dnevnik chlena Uchreditel'nago Sobraniia," *Golos Minuvshago*, IV–VI (April–June, 1918), 157; interview with Zenzinov (New York, December 19, 1949); interview with Vishniak (New York, January 2, 1952). Not even in his private writings does Chernov say anything about this friction—a striking example of his meekness in the face of criticism from the minority wing of his party. Vishniak speaks of his "openhearted lack of understanding" for the dissatisfaction with his speech. In this author's opinion, it was not his understanding, but his will that was at fault.

[41] *Pered burei*, p. 362; Steinberg, *Als ich Volkskommissar war*, pp. 79–80; Minor, "Odin den' Uchreditel'nago Sobraniia," in *Perezhitoe*, I, 129.

[42] Vishniak, *Dan' proshlomu*, p. 369.

diversion, but it is also possible that their caution sprang from grim intent, and that, in the absence of other game, they had determined to get themselves a "lord." Lenin, informed of what was happening, sent down a commissar to frustrate their design. "If papa says no, then no it must be," they said, and lapsed into passivity. But they were "fed up" with this hapless man, and in allowing himself to become the focal point of social hatred mixed with drink, Chernov had no assurance but that he was entering upon his last assignment.[43]

After the election of president and secretary came the question of procedure. Chernov had side-stepped the issue of power only to have it posed squarely and belligerently by Sverdlov and Bukharin. Sverdlov brought it to the fore when he demanded assembly approval of the Soviet declaration of the rights of toilers—a twentieth-century, socialized imitation of the French Declaration of the Rights of Man—and Bukharin, when he declared war in the name of his party on the "bourgeois-parliamentary" or "imperialist" republic to which the SR's were no less committed than in the days of Kerenski. Only if the state power remained in Soviet hands, he argued, could the toilers be assured that the measures now being advocated by the SR's would not be perverted into traps through the readmission of the class enemy into positions of power.[44] It was clear that the Bolsheviks meant to fight it out on the naked issue of power and were not going to permit their opponents to build up their popularity with other measures before coming to grips with this most basic of issues. As for the Left SR's, they were once again fighting on the right flank against their erstwhile comrades and struggling on the left flank to preserve their identity against their present allies. They would not single out any one issue to provoke a showdown, as the Bolsheviks were doing, but took their stand on the Soviet program as a whole, making its acceptance or rejection by the SR's the test of their intentions. Pointedly the Left SR spokesman reminded his opponents that the Constituent Assembly faced a sterner task than meeting the demands of the February Revolution, which for eleven months the people had been realizing through the

[43] Bonch-Bruevich, *Na boevykh postakh*, pp. 249–50.
[44] See text of Bukharin's speech in *Vserossiiskoe Uchreditel'noe Sobranie*, pp. 25–31.

soviets.[45] The contention advanced in later years that the Left SR's
were seeking middle ground when they invited adherence to the
Soviet declaration without making an issue of the ultimate source
of power [46] simply does not hold water, for the very first point of
the declaration stated that "all power at the center and in the localities belongs to the soviets."

The SR's, however, were determined not to pick up the gauntlet
until they had done all in their power to convince the people that
the assembly meant to give them what they wanted, and until they
themselves had reclaimed some of the ground lost in 1917 through
failure to take action on the problems of the hour. Their plan for
the opening day, as we have seen, had been worked out carefully
beforehand, and in urging its acceptance upon the assembly the SR's
cloaked their strategy in virtuous talk about taking up first what was
uppermost in the minds of the people. The land question was the
mainspring of the Russian Revolution as well as the heart of the SR
program, but since peace was needed for its solution, measures for
the "speediest termination" of the war should first be considered,
then the solution of the land problem, the question as to the form
of the state, and other matters. Zenzinov as spokesman for his party
expressly disclaimed any intent to evade the issue of state power—
the SR's wished to settle it at the present session, he said—but first
they wanted to satisfy the aspirations of the people for peace, land,
and national autonomy.[47] By a vote of 237 to 146 the SR order of
the day prevailed over the Bolshevik motion to take up the Soviet
declaration of the rights of toilers.[48] Before noting the effect of this
decision upon the fortunes of the assembly, let us see how the SR's
utilized their victory in respect to the priority of peace, land, and
federation.

That the SR's should have proposed to deal first with the problem
of peace was in itself a startling reversal of form, for in the whole
compendium of their inactivities in 1917 there was no subject in rela-

[45] See Steinberg's speech in *ibid.*, pp. 34–36.
[46] See Steinberg, *Als ich Volkskommissar war*, pp. 82–83.
[47] See text of Zenzinov's statement in *Vserossiiskoe Uchreditel'noe Sobranie*,
pp. 54–55; see also prior speech of N. P. Pumpianski in *ibid.*, pp. 32–33.
[48] *Ibid.*, p. 64.

tion to which they had been more inactive. Their language seemed to indicate a desire for action—Zenzinov, their floor leader, used the phrase "quickest ending of the war," [49] and Tsereteli, the Menshevik mentor of this headless herd, spoke of the "immediate conclusion of peace." [50] But as soon as their spokesman on peace, E. M. Timofeev, took the floor, the usual backing and filling began. Peace must not be understood in the vulgar sense of leaving the war, for it must be 1) universal and 2) democratic, that is, it must be in accordance with the ideals of the revolution. A separate peace not only would lead to the isolation of Russia, to her prostration at the feet of German imperialism, and to the abandonment of the border peoples, but also it would violate the conscience of the nation, for even under the tsar, the mere rumor of a separate peace had "convulsed the whole country." [51] The Central Powers must be made to understand that peace proposals were acceptable only in so far as they were conducive to a general peace. The talk about immediate peace, then, did not mean at all that peace would be immediate, or even that it was in the offing. As the party spokesman assured his audience, a "long and persistent struggle" was necessary to unite the toilers of all the countries and "make all peoples democratic" before peace as the SR's conceived it could be realized.[52] Thus peace was some distance away—some distance, indeed.

In his denunciation of Soviet initiative in the matter of peace, the SR spokesman showed great concern for the Western borderlands of the Russian empire, for the peoples of Latvia, Lithuania, and Poland, "already virtually in the German maw," and also for the Armenian people in their dismembered and helpless condition.[53] Implicit in his condemnation of the continued exposure of this people to pogroms was the chagrin of his party at the abandonment of its ideal of a Greater Armenia. SR solicitude for the Armenians, of course, did not spring from the knavery of the Soviet government, rooted as this solicitude was in the Turkophobia of the Populist intelligentsia, nor did the concern over the Western borderlands grow out of German pretensions at Brest Litovsk, for already in the early

---

[49] *Ibid.*, pp. 54–55. [50] *Ibid.*, p. 51.
[51] *Ibid.*, p. 74. This figure of speech is a remarkable tribute to the powers of social analysis of the "Populist" intelligentsia.
[52] *Ibid.*, p. 77. [53] *Ibid.*, pp. 76, 83.

days of the October Revolution, before the peace conference opened, the SR press had raised a hue and cry about the possible loss of Courland and Lithuania.[54] The embittered resistance to a separate peace concealed behind talk of national self-determination an unwillingness to see the tsarist empire reduced by even one of the outlying, non-Russian provinces, although the SR's would gladly have seen it augmented by the Armenian-inhabited districts of Turkey and perhaps much more.

Having seen what peace did not mean to the SR's, let us now see what positive steps they proposed to take in order to make their vision of peace a little less remote. A positive program of peace meant to them above everything else the restoration of a united front with the Western Allies. To listen to the refrain in their press,[55] one would have concluded that the Constituent Assembly possessed some magic power to move the Allies toward the acceptance of the peace formula which the Petersburg Soviet had long since advanced in the name of the revolution and to which the SR's now renewed their allegiance,[56] after having done virtually nothing to realize it in the days of their power. So the first point in their program was an appeal to the Allies to work out jointly with Russia the conditions of a "democratic" peace "acceptable to all belligerents" which would then be submitted in the name of the whole coalition to the enemy powers. The text of the note to the Allies is interesting: the Constituent Assembly was "filled with unshakable faith that the effort of the people of Russia to end this ruinous war will meet with the unanimous response of the peoples *and governments*[57] of the Allied states and that through common efforts a speedy peace will be attained which will secure the well-being and dignity of all the warring peoples."[58]

[54] "Bezumie ili predatel'stvo?" (Madness or Treason?), *Delo Naroda*, No. 205 (November 10, 1917).

[55] See especially the editorials of Chernov, "Delo mira" (The Cause of Peace), and "Ch'ia pobeda?" (Whose Triumph?), *Delo Naroda*, Nos. 233, 235 (December 15, 17, 1917).

[56] See statements of Pumpianski and Timofeev in *Vserossiiskoe Uchreditel'noe Sobranie*, pp. 32, 77, 80.

[57] Italics are mine.

[58] "Obrashchenie Uchreditel'nogo Sobraniia k soiuznym derzhavam" (Appeal of the Constituent Assembly to the Allied Powers), in *Vserossiiskoe Uchreditel'noe Sobranie*, p. 113.

The SR's had done two things in drafting the note: they had returned to the idea of the Paris conference of Allied powers to concert war aims, which had been interrupted by the October Revolution, and they had recommitted themselves to the original soviet formula of peace, but without its specific rejection of annexations and indemnities and without its espousal of the right of all peoples to self-determination. What lay behind this switch to vaguer and more elastic language has never been explained, but it is quite possible that it sprang from the desire of the right SR's to leave the door open to territorial alterations and certain reparations without binding the Russian empire to the observance of a principle that could prove only less embarrassing to it than to Austria or Turkey.

In addition to renewed supplication of the Allied powers and renewed allegiance to the Soviet formula, the SR's had recourse to still another peace measure from the "heritage of the past," [59] as their spokesman termed these exhumations in the graveyard of their earlier hopes: they befriended the Stockholm Conference. Once before they had favored this socialist assembly on behalf of peace, but without enthusiasm or apparent regret when the plan had been frustrated with the obvious connivance of the government they were supporting.[60] Now, however, they were willing to waive formalities and have the Constituent Assembly stand forth as the sponsor of Stockholm, even though it was a public institution and the conference was of a partisan or class character. They had advanced a step beyond the legalism of the Kerenski regime. Nay more, they had even become daring: "We act in revolutionary times, so let our decisions also be fiery and also be revolutionary," they said in proposing that the assembly take the initiative in calling the conference, which might even meet in the Russian instead of the Swedish capital, if the Austrian and German socialists were willing.[61]

So far the SR's had been merely reheating uneaten food from the past. What new bill of fare could they offer, in view of the changed and greatly worsened conditions? There were only two new departures in their peace program, both imposed by circumstances,

[59] See Timofeev's speech in *ibid.*, pp. 77–78, 80.
[60] See my book, *The Agrarian Foes of Bolshevism*, pp. 336 ff.
[61] See speeches of Chernov and Timofeev in *Vserossiiskoe Uchreditel'noe Sobranie*, pp. 11–12, 82.

neither proceeding from their own volition. The first was in respect to the situation at the front, where the fighting had now ceased, not only in reality, but also by formal agreement. However great their repugnance, the Populist intellectuals dared not move to overturn the armistice. The current was too swift for them to swim openly against it. They proposed that the Constituent Assembly continue the armistice while taking over the conduct of negotiations with the enemy, regretfully begun without prior agreement with the Allies, in order to safeguard Russian interests and guide these negotiations into the channel of a general instead of a separate peace.[62] It is obvious that the aversion to a separate peace had in no way abated. But the SR's were at pains to show that they did not demand a resumption of hostilities. They even sent Bunakov-Fondaminski to the tribune to reiterate their willingness to continue the armistice that was already in effect [63]—a convincing demonstration, since of all the drumbeaters for war, this ex-commissar of the Black Sea Fleet may well have been the most extravagant.

The second new feature in the SR program for war and peace was the issuance of a death certificate to the old army and a birth certificate to the new. The intention to move along these lines has been noted in connection with the preparations for the assembly.[64] Here it remains to be seen what specifications were added in the assembly itself. The SR's had rather suddenly become aware of the "superhuman burden" imposed on the men at the front and of their "legitimate right" to rest after three and one-half years in the trenches. They promised to introduce shortly a law for the demobilization of the army, for "we know that the present Russian army must be sent home without delay," a conviction undoubtedly reinforced by the spectacle in the galleries of the Taurida Palace. They would also introduce a law for the creation of a new volunteer army on a territorial basis. Apparently the same administrative confusion would attend the new birth as in the case of other SR enterprises, since all the peoples of Russia were to concern themselves with defense and the new army would be under both the territorial con-

---

[62] See text in *ibid.*, p. 113. Here this proposal is put under the note to the Allies, whereas it is clear from Timofeev's speech that it was intended as a separate resolution (see *ibid.*, p. 84).

[63] *Ibid.*, p. 107.   [64] See above, p. 323.

stituent assemblies and the All-Russian Constituent Assembly, with the latter institution establishing the rules for its organization and use. Chernov had treated the volunteer army as an expedient which would yield in time to a socialist militia, and had defined its purpose as "safeguarding the work of reconstruction against intervention," [65] but the other and more authoritative spokesman in the assembly had nothing to say about a socialist militia, nor did he choose to specify the purpose of the new army, aside from protecting "our boundaries." [66] It was not surprising that Chernov should be a shade cooler about a volunteer army than his right-wing colleagues, but in any event it was a party decision, for the Central Committee at its session of December 26–27 had instructed the delegation to bring in a bill to this effect.[67]

Such was the peace program of the Socialist Revolutionaries in the All-Russian Constituent Assembly. Comparing it to the program in 1917, which had been so wholly unrealized that it could all be repeated in the new program, one can only say that this party was still being dragged at the tail of events, only now it was being dragged much faster. Had the SR's really made any progress down the road to peace on their own volition? One is tempted to say, none at all. It is true that the proceedings of the assembly enshrine certain admissions and pledges on their part which could perhaps be taken as evidence of a change of heart. The note to the Allies contained a formal acknowledgment of the will to peace of the Russian people: it was their "unalterable" purpose that the war end "immediately" and a "just and general" peace be concluded.[68] The mistakes of the past were admitted to a certain extent, in respect to the efforts of "more than a few" to pervert the ideal of a democratic peace into a blind for aggressive designs,[69] and in respect to the failure to do then what had to be done now under far more grievous conditions.[70] For the

[65] *Vserossiiskoe Uchreditel'noe Sobranie*, p. 13.   [66] *Ibid.*, pp. 81–82.
[67] *Delo Naroda*, No. 1/246 (January 3, 1918).
[68] *Vserossiiskoe Uchreditel'noe Sobranie*, pp. 84, 113.
[69] *Ibid.*, pp. 79–80. This belated recognition of the attempt on the part of adherents of "war to victory" to undermine the concept of a peace of reconciliation raises the question of whom the spokesman (Timofeev) had in mind— the Kadets and their allies within the Provisional Government or the right wing within his own party.
[70] *Ibid.*, p. 82.

future, certain pledges were given. The SR's promised to work unremittingly at the task of peace—a tacit admission that in 1917 their efforts had been somewhat less than unremitting—and they promised to do everything in the open, hiding nothing from the Russian people.[71] Would this renunciation of secret diplomacy have carried with it a repudiation of its devotees in the diplomatic corps, who had preserved without interference from the SR's not only the forms but the spirit of the old diplomacy during the lifetime of the Provisional Government in complete harmony with the latter's dogma of the unbroken succession of power?

But if the letter of their statements indicates a willingness to work toward peace, the tone of those statements betrays an unrepentant spirit. The SR spokesman assured the assembly that "our Allies now see that we are deprived of the possibility of continuing the war" but they must also see that "our every effort is directed together with theirs toward a general peace." [72] The concern for the Allied countries themselves had in no way diminished with the passage of time nor even with the desperate situation into which the homeland had been cast as a result of the foolhardy insistence upon carrying on a war which the Russian people had not wanted in the first place—as the SR's now officially conceded [73]—and to which in 1917 they had clearly demonstrated their repugnance. The peace initiative of the Soviet government drew the fire of the SR spokesman because it endangered the "human existence" of the Allied countries [74] and because it brought "us into closer contact with our enemies than with those to whom our history has bound us," a novel interpretation of Russian history, extending as far back as the Anglo-Russian Convention of 1907 or the Franco-Russian Alliance of 1893. Above all else the Populist intelligentsia desired to restore the united front with the Allies, "to reknit the ties that have recently been broken against the will . . . of the majority of the Russian

[71] *Ibid.*, pp. 72, 84.   [72] *Ibid.*, p. 80.   [73] *Ibid.*, p. 72.
[74] *Ibid.*, p. 76. It may be that the SR spokesman meant to differentiate in favor of these countries as having, "as it were, put aside imperialism," but his language at this point is so muddy that it is not safe to impute to him a point of view that would be either incredibly naive or willfully misleading in the light of secret treaties reposing in the files of the foreign ministry, about which the SR's either knew or had no excuse for not knowing.

people." [75] The enemy was warned that Russia, though wounded and wracked, was still a lion and that peoples who constituted the Russian state (the plural was a concession to the times) would "bristle with bayonets" in defense of their free lands.[76] The talk was of peace, but the tone of the speeches in the assembly reveals clearly enough that, while these Populist intellectuals may have desired peace in the abstract, emotionally they were as wedded as ever to war—if only the people could be made to fight it for them.

The Socialist Revolutionaries, of course, never presented a united front on any question. In this "motley gypsy camp," as Ivan Maiski calls it,[77] there were divergent elements which, as he complains, did not diverge but spent their time in neutralizing one another. And in the course of the debate on peace the Constituent Assembly was treated to the spectacle of a deputy arising to announce that the left deviationist group from Tomsk province [78] did not agree with the party's position in rejecting a separate peace.[79] "We Russians, who have seized one-sixth of the globe, can we say, comrades, that we will not conclude peace merely because the German takes something from us?" Straightforward language is always welcome, and doubly so in dealing with this party.[80] As a soldier who had spent two and one-half years in the trenches, L. A. Grigoriev, in the name of the peasants' soviet of Tomsk province, proclaimed the solidarity of his segment of the party with the Bolsheviks on war and peace while continuing to differ from them in respect to the land question. His words bring us close to the heartbeat of the populace, for he spoke for the very numerous but virtually headless social elements who might have preserved Russia from Bolshevism—had the anti-revolutionary and pro-war intellectuals not usurped the leadership within his party—and who did determine, in the opinion of this au-

[75] *Ibid.*, p. 83. [76] *Ibid.*, pp. 83–84.

[77] *Demokraticheskaia kontr-revoliutsiia*, pp. 115–16. See pp. 111–25, 327–28 for his flagellation of the Socialist Revolutionaries, perhaps the most merciless to be found anywhere. A Menshevik who knew them well from the days of the Samara episode, Maiski eventually went over to the Bolsheviks, partly, no doubt, because of disgust with his allies.

[78] See above, p. 128.

[79] *Vserossiiskoe Uchreditel'noe Sobranie*, pp. 95–96.

[80] "Who does not know," asks Maiski, "that words were given them to conceal their thoughts?" (*Demokraticheskaia kontr-revoliutsiia*, p. 123).

thor, the outcome of the civil war by preferring the Red to the White minority while actually desiring the triumph of neither. The very loud noise in the galleries accompanying this short speech betrayed the dismay of the Bolshevik public at this kind of competition. Scarcely less must have been the chagrin of the Populist intellectuals, yet little noise came from their ranks, as they were sitting like "marble statues," in emulation of "Roman senators." [81] No sign of life came from Chernov's group of the left center; it was as "still as water and low as grass" in the presence of this painful drama.

The Moslem SR's, however, made common cause with their Russian comrades from Tomsk province in endorsing the peace initiative of the Soviet government, while criticizing it for failure to move even faster in that direction.[82] Neither the lopping off of the left wing and its erection into a separate party nor the subservience of the left-centrist majority in the rump party to the rightist majority in the parliamentary delegation had restored unity in the ranks of the PSR on this most fateful of all issues, and the division along lines of nationality deepened with the tendency to divide on other matters, as evidenced by the Moslem SR's stand on war and peace.

The nationalities problem was not debated in the Constituent Assembly; it was only touched on now and then. Peace had been the first subject of discussion, and, though the debate on it had been inconclusive, no other subject was fated to have as much attention. The SR's managed to place on the record in the dying minutes of the assembly the bare principle of reorganization of the Russian state into a "Russian Democratic Federated Republic, joining in an indissoluble union peoples and regions whose sovereignty is exercised within limits established by the federal constitution." [83] Here was a typical SR concept: sovereign components of an indissoluble union. But what if a people or a region of Great Russia stood on its sovereignty and rejected the union? In the dream world of the Socialist Revolutionaries, separatism did not exist in Russia, but only "regional movements" in reaction to Bolshevism, and these would

[81] These phrases are used by Oganovski in his diary. See "Dnevnik chlena Uchreditel'nago Sobraniia," *Golos Minuvshago*, IV–VI (April–June, 1918), 154.

[82] See declaration of Sunchaliaev or Sunchalias, deputy from Ufa province, in *Vserossiiskoe Uchreditel'noe Sobranie*, p. 100.

[83] "Postanovlenie o gosudarstvennom ustroistve Rossii" (Decree on the State Structure of Russia), in *ibid.*, p. 113.

not become separatist unless Russia continued without a generally recognized authority.[84] Just as the Constituent Assembly possessed in their eyes some magic to incline the Western Allies toward a just and democratic peace, so it could somehow still the passions of the subject nationalities whose rights either had never been recognized or had been trampled on by a succession of conquerors and oppressors.

We have seen how, in a startling reversal of form from the days of the Kerenski regime, the SR's had taken the side of the Ukraine against Soviet Russia, and now they proposed to use the authority of the assembly to halt all further troop movements in connection with the civil war. In the words of Chernov, no longer would the hands of the Great Russian soldier be stained with his brother's blood. The president of the assembly also made obeisance to other ethnic or social groups: to the toiling Cossacks, the great majority of the population on the "free Don," when he assured them that they had nothing to fear from the Great Russian soldiery; to the Moslems, "hitherto one of the most downtrodden" groups, when he promised that, whether living in ethnically homogeneous areas or mixed in with others, they should have their "sovereign rights"; and to the Jews, when he pledged that they would no longer be scapegoats but would enjoy the right of self-government though living in the midst of others. In the conception of Chernov, and also in that of his party, national or regional constituent assemblies were as compatible with the All-Russian Constituent Assembly as organs of local government with these lesser assemblies. The function of the All-Russian authority was to complete and harmonize the work done in the national and regional areas.[85] No fears of ethnic separatism or economic selfishness marred this conception of concord and magnanimity.

The absence of most of the deputies from the Ukraine prevented that problem from being fully aired at this All-Russian forum, but the Moslem socialists spoke their mind in a formal declaration read to the assembly.[86] Both the Provisional and Soviet governments were

[84] See report of a speech by Chernov in *Delo Naroda*, No. 226 (December 7, 1917).

[85] *Vserossiiskoe Uchreditel'noe Sobranie*, pp. 13–15; see also the delegation's outline of its program in *Delo Naroda*, No. 245 (December 31, 1917).

[86] *Vserossiiskoe Uchreditel'noe Sobranie*, pp. 57–59.

censured for having pursued an unsatisfactory nationalities policy. The Constituent Assembly must proceed to make Russia over into a federal republic, in reality and not on paper, sanctioning the creation of federal units not only where these were already indicated but also where they were still in gestation, as in the case of a state on the Volga, another in the south Ural region, and one in Turkestan. With unerring instinct the Moslems went to the heart of the problem with a demand for nationalization of army units. They permitted their hopes to range freely. Hardly more than on the threshold of their own national awakening, these long-submerged nationalities with a common religion were already beginning to think of their brothers in Asia and Africa when they demanded for them the same right of self-determination as was being proposed for European peoples. They would broaden the concept, both of the soviet peace formula and the Stockholm Conference, by securing representation at the latter for the submerged peoples not only of Russia but of all three continents. Here is a clue to their divergence from the Russian SR delegation on the question of peace. These Moslem socialists, all of whom were nationalists with a Populist agrarian slant, instinctively reacted against the Francophile and Anglophile sentiments of the majority of the Russian Populist intellectuals. Their own nationalism, of course, would even sooner have brought them into collision with these intellectuals.

Like the nationalities problem, the land question was not debated in the assembly. The features of the agrarian order which the SR's would have had the assembly enact into law have already been noted,[87] and appear without significant change in the text of the final draft, of which only ten sections actually went through the assembly; [88] the remaining seventy were referred to a commission for presentation at a later session which never was held.[89] In his inaugural address Chernov made certain interesting remarks about agrarian legislation. His reference to the "colossal task" confronting

---

[87] See above, pp. 319–21.

[88] See "Zakon o zemle" (Land Law), in *Vserossiiskoe Uchreditel'noe Sobranie*, p. 112.

[89] Oganovski says there were eighty sections in all; see "Dnevnik chlena Uchreditel'nago Sobraniia," *Golos Minuvshago*, IV–VI (April–June, 1918), 160. Chernov states that only six basic points were enacted (*Pered burei*, p. 365); Vishniak says ten (*Dan' proshlomu*, p. 379).

those who would give Russia a new agrarian order betrayed the fear
that always gripped the SR's when they faced the necessity of transforming their slogans into reality. Now, indeed, they had to move
out of the "realm of bare slogans and general formulas into the realm
of realization." At this point from the left benches came cries of
"late!" Chernov's party had constantly boasted that it would give
the country real laws instead of the half-baked, ineffective decrees
of the Soviet regime, and now it plumed itself on the land law,[90]
forgetting that the peasants for some time already had been settling
things in their own way with as little heed for what the SR's had in
mind as for the prescriptions of their rivals. As a nonsocialist critic
observed, between the beginning of the revolution and the convocation of the assembly stretched long months of an elemental process
which had brought about the dissipation of the land fund, burying
the hope for an orderly land reform regulated from the center [91]
along with the privately owned estates. This process would go
blindly on and end far from the socialist utopia.[92] The SR's were
late, indeed.

After confessing the magnitude of the task before it, Chernov
tried to make capital for his party out of the provisions of the proposed legislation. He played up the abolition of private property in
land without compensation; its conversion into free land open to
everyone rather than into state property on which users would have
to pay rent (here he was striking at Social Democrats in general); its
unencumberance by anything save an equalization tax to put the
users of good land and those of inferior land on the same footing; its
equitable distribution throughout the country. In typically Chernovian fashion, softly and obliquely, he announced the exclusion of
the soviets from the land reform, which would be entrusted in the
localities to the land committees, "inspired by the slogans of the
peasants' soviets." But the anvil chorus in the galleries broke in upon
his words, robbing them of their effect. At one point in his exposi-

[90] See statements of Eliashevich and Bunakov in *Vserossiiskoe Uchreditel'noe
Sobranie*, pp. 95, 107.
[91] Actually, the land reform was to be worked out in harmony between the
center and the regions (Ukraine, Siberia, and so on)—a still more utopian idea.
[92] L. Litoshenko, "Sotsializatsiia zemli" (Socialization of the Land), *Russkiia
Vedomosti*, No. 9 (January 17, 1918).

tion he was warned that "you won't get off without a bullet!" Try
as he might, he could not recover for his party the ground it had
lost.[93]

An interesting feature of the Constituent Assembly was that the
land reform program was not being left exclusively to the intellectuals. The rather numerous peasant contingent in the SR delegation had made its weight felt in the party caucus in the direction of
more radical solutions than the Populist intelligentsia had desired.
The minutes of the proceedings reveal that this restiveness over-
flowed onto the floor of the assembly in the form of incidents that
betokened the stirrings of a class interest transcending partisan lines.
The SR's and the Left SR's had been maneuvering to raid one another's peasant support only to discover that a developing sense of
solidarity on the part of the peasants threatened the hold of both.
The peasant delegate [94] whom the Left SR's had commissioned to
read their declaration suddenly announced at its conclusion that he
would now say something on his own, and proceeded to appeal to
all the peasants who were there to stand together in the task of
getting for the village what it craved above all else. They had been
sent there for that purpose and they must fulfill their mission to the
end. When it came to land there were no differences among peasants;
the left and right were all alike. The SR's were jubilant, and applauded vigorously, while from the confused ranks of the Left SR's
came cries of "sabotage." [95]

The SR's naturally seized on this incident as evidence of weakness
in the enemy camp,[96] but with characteristic one-sidedness they fail
to point out that one of their own peasants made a similar statement
at their expense. Deputy Ivan V. Mamkin, center SR from Voronezh
province, arose to address the assembly on behalf of a group of
peasants, SR by affiliation but nonpartisan in spirit, who had delegated him to demand "in the name of Russia" a solution, here and
now, of the questions of land and peace, for "we have had enough of

[93] *Vserossiiskoe Uchreditel'noe Sobranie,* pp. 16–18.
[94] His name was Sorokin, initials not given. As there were four Sorokins
listed as deputies, it is not certain who he was—perhaps E. I. Sorokin of
Riazan province.
[95] *Vserossiiskoe Uchreditel'noe Sobranie,* pp. 63–64.
[96] Oganovski, "Dnevnik chlena Uchreditel'nago Sobraniia," *Golos Minuvshago,*
IV–VI (April–June, 1918), 158; see also Chernov, *Pered burei,* p. 364.

living like this, of having our strength frittered away, of having the people lose faith in the revolution and freedom." In confused but forceful language Mamkin declared that "we have come together not as parties but as representatives of the people for the purpose, not of deciding the fate of this or that party, but of deciding the fate of our freedom and the revolution." Impatient with partisan divisions, he was equally impatient of language barriers, and his warning to the assembly not to fall apart like the builders of the Tower of Babel reflected both the leveling tendency of the Great Russian peasantry and his personal irritation at the Ukrainian delegate who had just used his own native language. Evidence of an awakening class consciousness could be found in his assertion that laws should now come from below, from the peasants and workers, and in his reference, laden with scorn, to Populist intellectuals, who were now invited to transmute their protestations of love for the people into action on measures desired by the people. Proudly the orator told how the land reform had been prepared in Voronezh province, leaving no room for doubt that it had not only been "prepared" but already carried out through the action of the peasants in lighting on land not their own like a swarm of locusts, turning it up with spades where horses were lacking to pull the plows, until virtually every piece had been sown. It was an interesting speech,[97] and one is left with the impression that had this country undergone an even course of development, unimpeded by the ills of the past or the machinations of mail-fisted minorities, the result might well have been the emergence of an agrarian interest group that would have been neither reactionary nor socialist but broadly democratic in character.

So much for what the SR's did in the assembly, for the back-stage illumination of their actions as well as for the actions themselves. Now to see how they fought to preserve the assembly from the fate closing in upon it. The adoption of the SR order of the day, shunting aside the Soviet declaration to which the assembly had been invited to subscribe, was to entail the bolt of the Bolshevik delegation for the purpose of undermining the authority of the assembly and baring

[97] *Vserossiiskoe Uchreditel'noe Sobranie*, pp. 86–88.

its breast to the blow that was now certain to fall. But first the Bolsheviks with Left SR support had demanded an intermission to discuss in caucus their further plans. In the midst of this situation the attempt of a Ukrainian deputy to address the assembly in his own tongue had caused exasperation, curiously enough, in the left sector of the hall, whence came shouts of "speak in Russian!" Chernov observes that the Bolsheviks, for all their internationalism, did not wish to hear any other language than Russian. The SR's now had a chance to demonstrate their concern for other nationalities, particularly one that had eighty seats in this assembly, and the plaudits of his party accompanied Chernov's ruling that "the citizen member of the Constituent Assembly has full right to make use of his language in the assembly." [98]

Since withdrawal under these circumstances had already been decided upon, and the fate of the assembly itself predetermined in their Central Committee, the Bolsheviks appear to have been seeking common ground with the Left SR's in asking for an intermission. But their allies were not yet ready to bolt the assembly. When Lenin asked them, either at a joint meeting of the Central Committees or within the Council of Commissars, whether the situation were not sufficiently clear and whether they had not had enough, they rejected his proposal of a joint declaration of withdrawal with the argument that the break should not come over formal grounds, such as the refusal to discuss the Soviet declaration, but over a tangible issue lifted from the content of that declaration which the people could understand. The Left SR's wished to give battle over the question of peace, using it as a means of forcing the regular SR's to take off their mask and disclose their true countenance to the people.[99] Perhaps the Left SR's were sincere in their political calculations, or perhaps they were motivated primarily by a desire to show their independence of the Bolsheviks and do things their own way. In any event the paths of the allies parted and the Bolsheviks withdrew

[98] *Ibid.*, p. 66; Chernov, *Pered burei*, pp. 363–64. Chernov errs in stating that the deputy in question was Severtsov-Odoevski (he means A. S. Severov-Odoevski); from the minutes it appears that I. V. Mikhailichenko was the Ukrainian spokesman on this occasion.

[99] Steinberg, *Als ich Volkskommissar war*, pp. 83–84; "K izbirateliam" (To Our Electors), in *Vokrug Uchreditel'nago Sobraniia*, p. 43; Bonch-Bruevich, *Na boevykh postakh*, p. 250.

from the assembly while the Left SR's remained in their seats. In reading the declaration which Lenin had written, Raskolnikov denounced the SR majority as representing the "yesterday of the revolution" in its endeavor to stand in the way of the workers' and peasants' movement. He accused it of having become the focal point of the counterrevolution in combating the achievements of October, including the distribution to the peasantry of land taken over without compensation—a charge that stung the SR's to fury and provoked cries of "lie! lie!" from their side.[100] The Bolsheviks now disclosed their strategy of splitting the assembly, reducing its prestige by making it appear to be a rump parliament, and thus softening it up for the final blow.

Either fearing the imminence of this blow, or desiring to give the lie to Raskolnikov's charge in graphic form, or thinking to compel the Left SR's to remain in the hall, the SR's now decided to change the order of the day. The question of peace was still under discussion and it would have been logical to hold a vote at the end. But immediately after the young naval officer had read the Bolshevik declaration, Chernov announced from the chair that the SR delegation had brought in the bill on the basic land law.[101] This threat to their freedom of action, however, did not deter the Left SR's from posing their own ultimatum. On the ground that the majority was evading the issue in the hope of becoming entrenched with its own machinery of state and subverting the Soviet order, while deluding the public with talk of doing as much for it by different means, the Left SR's now proposed to smoke out the enemy. They tried inviting him to subscribe to at least the peace section of the rejected Soviet declaration, thereby forcing him to disclose his hand on a concrete issue,[102] just as they had suggested to the Bolsheviks. But once more the SR's bent away from an ultimatum. When the list of speakers on peace had been exhausted, they pledged themselves to a decision on the peace question by a roll-call vote, but not until the end of the session, after the land bill had been debated—first all the issues

---

[100] *Vserossiiskoe Uchreditel'noe Sobranie*, pp. 88–90, 216, n. 27; Steinberg, *Als ich Volkskommissar war*, pp. 84–85.

[101] *Vserossiiskoe Uchreditel'noe Sobranie*, p. 90.

[102] See speech of Steinberg, *ibid.*, pp. 91–94; Steinberg, *Als ich Volkskommissar war*, p. 85.

would be successively discussed, and then all the votes taken. Each set of SR's was trying to pin the other down, and in addition the regulars were trying to hold the rump assembly together. Bunakov-Fondaminski went the length of denying any difference in substance between the SR and Left SR proposals for peace (!), and threw out the added concession of representation for all parties on the peace deputation to be chosen by the Constituent Assembly. This was a far cry from the days of the Kerenski era when he had been the most stalwart of all right SR's in combating the slightest advance in the direction of peace. He now quite clearly revealed at least one of the purposes in the minds of his colleagues in bringing up the land question when he intimated that their peasants would not let the Left SR's leave with this matter under discussion, or would let them go only at the cost of a schism.[103]

The Left SR's, however, had reached the end of their indecision. They must act to preserve the united front of the October Revolution, and they could act, now that they had established their position independently of the Bolsheviks. They were ready for the definitive break with the moderate or conservative wing of the Populist movement—not only organizationally, but also in the sense of being willing to fight it out, for they felt that they had made their final effort to force the traitors back into the trenches of the revolution.[104] The sidetracking of the effort to force a vote on peace brought Karelin to the platform with the announcement that the maneuver of the majority in bringing up a new question before the one under discussion had been decided marked a continuation of the policy of cowardice and hypocrisy which it had pursued from the outset. The Left SR's were unwilling to cover any longer by their presence the conversion of a parliamentary position resulting from outmoded electoral lists into a base of operations against the Soviet regime, and were transferring the scene of their activities to the soviets with the intention of defending there the interests of the toilers in the conflict that had now become irrepressible.[105] With

[103] *Vserossiiskoe Uchreditel'noe Sobranie*, pp. 106–8.
[104] Ligovski, "Vsia vlast' ushedshim!" in *Vokrug Uchreditel'nago Sobraniia*, p. 47.
[105] *Vserossiiskoe Uchreditel'noe Sobranie*, pp. 108–10; "K izbirateliam," in *Vokrug Uchreditel'nago Sobraniia*, pp. 42–43. The latter citation reveals that the Left SR's had a precise understanding of the enemy's strategy.

these words the leader of the more moderate wing of his party took leave of his hopes of building a bridge between the two Narodnik camps, between the soviet and parliamentary systems, between February and October. The Populist intelligentsia of Kharkov province had always been as much opposed to war as the Populist intelligentsia of Samara or Penza or Moscow provinces had been in favor, and it was only logical that it should have been this issue which impelled the head of the Kharkov municipality to abandon his search for a compromise. The fetish of unity around which the Populists had worshiped so fervently and so foolishly, to their mutual undoing, had in the end, like everything else, been corroded by the poison of war.

The duel between the Bolsheviks and the SR's had given way to the duel between the latter and the Left SR's. Both partners in the Soviet coalition had now abandoned the parliamentary field though not the arena of conflict. For the "public" was still there, more menacing than ever, and now it came right down onto the floor and sat in the abandoned chairs, drawing tighter the ring round the embattled SR's. It was long past midnight. The agony of the assembly had begun, according to Steinberg, but the closing scene differed only in degree from the opening. From the bolt of the Left SR's to the end there were two hours and ten minutes. The president began to whip through legislation, reading rapidly and unintelligibly, the promised roll calls gave way to voice voting, the absence of opposition made things seem unreal as the SR's hastened onward in a desperate attempt to do in minutes what they had failed to do in months under the Provisional Government. Meanwhile the fate of the assembly was being arranged—one can hardly say decided—at an informal meeting of the Council of Commissars within the Taurida Palace. It was decided not to interrupt the session but to let it run down, to prevent resumption on the morrow, and then to proclaim the assembly dissolved. The sailors, having seen to the inviolability of the deputies, were to let them leave freely and then lock them out.

But the sailors were tired and wanted to sleep. They decided to speed things up a bit. Zhelezniakov approached Chernov, called to his attention the fatigue of the guard, and invited him to close the session.[106] Chernov was engaged in reading the land law at the moment. He was taken aback but recovered to say that "all members of the Constituent Assembly are also very tired but no amount of fatigue can stop the reading of the land law for which Russia is waiting." An uproar followed his words, and he added that the assembly would disperse only if force were used. Chernov then held snap votes on the more important legislation, overwhelming the Baltic sailor with his volubility. The declarative part of the land law, the measures on peace, and the proclamation of a federated republic went through in some fashion. One would have thought that the impetus for the last-named piece of legislation would come from the desire to placate the nationalities, but Chernov in his memoirs says that he wanted particularly to have Russia declared a republic so that the Bolsheviks could not say on the morrow that the assembly had left the door open to a return of the monarchy. At any rate, the laws tumbled over one another in the last-minute jam and the president even succeeded in having the next session scheduled for 5 P.M. It was 4:40 A.M. when he proclaimed the session closed—then and forever, as one source observes.[107]

Did the circumstances of the closing reflect discredit upon the SR's and particularly upon the chairman, as some Bolshevik and even some SR sources would have us believe? Was the characterization of the SR's as "rabbit-like" justified,[108] and did Chernov "obediently" close down the session at the dictation of Zhelezniakov, "without the slightest resistance?"[109] It seems indisputable that the intervention of the "citizen sailor" shortened the session and that the deputies lost

[106] Details will be spared the reader. Chernov says the sailor pulled at his sleeve, another source states that he clapped his hand on the chairman's shoulder, and a third, that he pounded on the table. Dybenko's account of how he and Zhelezniakov circumvented Lenin's will in closing things down does not ring true. It seems unlikely that Lenin remained that long in the palace, and Dybenko's version may reflect self-magnification.

[107] *Vserossiiskoe Uchreditel'noe Sobranie*, pp. 110–11, 216, n. 28, 217, n. 31; Lenin, *Sochineniia* (2d ed.), XXII, 598–99, n. 87; Chernov, *Pered burei*, pp. 364–66; Steinberg, *Als ich Volkskommissar war*, pp. 85–86; Sokolov, "Zashchita Uchreditel'nago Sobraniia," in *Arkhiv Russkoi Revoliutsii*, XIII, 67–68; Bonch-Bruevich, *Na boevykh postakh*, pp. 250–53; Vishniak, *Dan' proshlomu*, pp. 376–79; Dybenko, *Miatezhniki*, pp. 110–11; Minor, "Odin den' Uchreditel'nago Sobraniia," in *Perezhitoe*, I, 131–32.

[108] Bonch-Bruevich, *Na boevykh postakh*, p. 232.

[109] *Ibid.*, p. 253; Dybenko, *Miatezhniki*, p. 111.

little time in leaving the building. Oganovski speaks of "our running crowd" and asserts that the chairman, in terminating the session, dealt irreparable harm to the assembly, to his party and the land reform, which in any event was hanging by a thread.[110] But according to the official Soviet source, Chernov did not act until the "guiding three" (actually five) of the SR delegation sent him a note suggesting that the proceedings be suspended.[111] At any rate, the session had been going on for more than twelve hours, and it had been a strenuous one. The Petersburg dawn was breaking, and it was time to go to bed, even for Russians. The chairman had been the object of the derision and hatred of the onlookers, many of whom were men of action and more than a few of whom were drunk. For twelve hours he had been a target, literally as well as figuratively. Even as he was leaving the chamber, his secretary and detractor overhead the remark: "How nice it would be to run a bayonet into his side!"[112] And Chernov himself states that a Bolshevik party member warned him not to go to his automobile, where a band of murderers were awaiting him.[113] There was logic in the rumor abroad in the city that it was all over with the Constituent Assembly, and that Chernov and Tsereteli had been killed. That no bullet or bayonet had found its mark testifies less to Chernov's failure to flaunt the SR banner than to the discipline of the Baltic sailors and Lenin's technique of smothering rather than assaulting the assembly. Chernov had been brave enough on this occasion, and if any dishonor reflects upon him, then it is solely for accepting this "honor" at the hands of people who could have been satisfied only if he had died at his post—and they had lived on.[114]

As for discredit to the party as a whole, some deputies later told the Peasants' Executive Committee (the SR one) that they had been prepared to die, and that if they had nevertheless felt impelled to leave, it was not to save themselves but the honor of the assembly.

[110] "Dnevnik chlena Uchreditel'nago Sobraniia," *Golos Minuvshago*, IV–VI (April–June, 1918), 160.
[111] *Vserossiiskoe Uchreditel'noe Sobranie*, p. 217, n. 31.
[112] Vishniak, *Dan' proshlomu*, p. 380.
[113] *Pered burei*, p. 366.
[114] It is significant that Minor does not reproach Chernov for closing down the session. His account leaves no doubt that there was nothing else to do. See "Odin den' Uchreditel'nago Sobraniia," in *Perezhitoe*, I, 132.

"Out of a feeling of our own dignity, out of respect for the place where we were, we could not permit ourselves as representatives of the people to be subjected to violence and ousted by force from the Taurida Palace." [115] This was spinning it out a bit finely. But to bring the argument down to a less exalted plane, there was no reason to undergo martyrdom. The deputies had accomplished what they could; the "laws" had been written into the record. And if it had been a ragged performance, it was no more irregular than for 250-odd deputies to arrogate to themselves the functions of 815. Would the farce have become any less a farce through the shedding of blood? Discredit does not attach to failure to die in a hopeless cause. Discredit attaches to the eight months' record of unfulfilled promises under the Provisional Government which had brought things to this pass. The party that in the days of its power and influence had given the Russian people nothing except empty words and war could not have redeemed the situation by mock heroics at the end of the road.

No better fate attended the effort to save the assembly from without, through action of the people. The plans of the SR activists on the eve of convocation and the misgivings of the SR leaders have alike been noted. The events in the streets of St. Petersburg on January 5/18, 1918, will now be discussed in the following manner: first, what actually happened on that day; second, what the SR's intended should happen; third, why the outcome was so little to their liking.

The SR's and their allies were successful in setting on foot demonstrations in support of the Constituent Assembly. In the later forenoon of the day of convocation groups of people with banners began to converge from various parts of the city on the Liteiny Prospect, the central thoroughfare that led to the river in the vicinity of the Taurida Palace, with which it was connected by several side streets that were short and straight (Kirochna, Furshtadt, and others). The natural flow of a demonstration heading for the palace would carry it off the thoroughfare onto these streets, at the corners

[115] Rakitnikova, *Kak russkoe krest'ianstvo borolos' za Uchreditel'noe Sobranie,* pp. 44–45.

of which, accordingly, strong detachments of sailors and Red Guardsmen had been posted. From all accounts [116] it was a large and even an imposing demonstration—one source estimates the turnout in the tens of thousands.[117] But testimony differs in respect to the make-up of the crowd. SR sources stress the working-class component, Bolshevik sources play it down. The wife of Rakitnikov says that workers predominated,[118] Dr. Paevski says there were no workers,[119] yet both marched in this procession. It is possible, however, to abstract the area of agreement or near-agreement from sources of divergent tendencies and arrive at a composite picture that should be reasonably accurate.

There were certainly workers in this demonstration, yet it was primarily an affair of the average citizenry apart from the working class, of students and other intellectuals, of government employees and office workers, of shopkeepers and burghers in general. There were a number of party henchmen and some peasants who had arrived for their Third All-Russian Congress, which the Executive Committee set up by the right half of the divided Second Congress was now trying to convene in support of the Constituent Assembly.[120] The red banners of LAND AND LIBERTY and ALL POWER TO THE CONSTITUENT ASSEMBLY mingled with the green and white flags of Kadet organizations and the insignia of the Poalei Zion. It was basically a counterrevolutionary demonstration, certainly in the sense of October if not of February, although revolutionary elements were present. The commissar riding with Steinberg thought the faces of the crowd betrayed an ugly mood,[121] and its spirit is said to have risen rather than fallen after it was fired upon. One of its instigators admits that the true friends of the Constituent Assembly probably formed only a small part of the crowd, that the motivating force was not love of the assembly but hatred of Bolshevism.[122] The SR's had no illusions about majority sentiment

[116] Except the Bolshevik press. But Bolshevik eyewitnesses in their memoirs concede that the demonstration was "good-sized."

[117] Sokolov, "Zashchita Uchreditel'nago Sobraniia," in *Arkhiv Russkoi Revoliutsii*, XIII, 36, 64.

[118] *Kak russkoe krest'ianstvo borolos' za Uchreditel'noe Sobranie*, p. 40.

[119] See his testimony at the SR trial in *Pravda*, No. 130 (June 14, 1922).

[120] See below, pp. 440 ff.   [121] *Als ich Volkskommissar war*, pp. 72–73.

[122] Sokolov, "Zashchita Uchreditel'nago Sobraniia," in *Arkhiv Russkoi Revoliutsii*, XIII, 65.

among the Petersburg workers. They knew that only a relatively small segment supported them—the most conscious, the most advanced segment, as they conceived it.[123] And the nonproletarian part of the population had moved further to the right. The November election had left no doubt on that score. The SR's had assembled some strength in setting on foot this demonstration, but the bulk of it was not their strength.[124]

Almost none of it was the kind of strength that counted. If the demonstration had not been conspicuously successful in attracting workers, it had failed completely to attract soldiers. Where were the armored cars, the backbone of the whole enterprise, and where were the Semenovski and Preobrazhenski Guardsmen, who had so often passed resolutions demanding all power for the Constituent Assembly? They were not there. Not a single armored car appeared, and as for the Semenovski Regiment, which was to have furnished the main contingent of soldiers, several hundred came out of the barracks to banter with the marchers, but only a score or so joined the procession. The rest declined the invitation. At the barracks of the Petrograd Regiment a crowd of soldiers showered abuse upon the marchers as "hirelings of the Entente." [125] As the marchers themselves abused the Red Guard along the way as "traitors," it is obvious that the cleavage induced by the war between the upper and lower levels of Russian society is as basic to an understanding of the events of this day as to that of the revolution in general. The reaction of the soldiers on January 5 seems to have been one of indifference where the SR's were expecting support and open hostility where they were not. The only armed element in the whole procession, or series of processions, was a small number of workers who

---

[123] Minor, "Odin den' Uchreditel'nago Sobraniia," in *Perezhitoe*, I, 125; see also admission of P. D. Klimushkin, quoted in A. Koroleva, "Razgon Uchredilki," *Bor'ba Klassov*, XI (November, 1934), 35; see also Chernov, *Pered burei*, pp. 356–57

[124] Bykhovski, *Vserossiiskii Sovet Krest'ianskikh Deputatov*, pp. 349–50; *Obvinitel'noe zakliuchenie*, p. 13; testimony of Paevski in *Pravda*, No. 130 (June 14, 1922); Sokolov, "Zashchita Uchreditel'nago Sobraniia," in *Arkhiv Russkoi Revoliutsii*, XIII, 36, 62–63, 65; Bonch-Bruevich, *Na boevykh postakh*, p. 240; Rubinstein, *Bol'sheviki i Uchreditel'noe Sobranie*, p. 82; *Istoriia grazhdanskoi voiny v SSSR*, III, 93. Many of the marchers were women—students, party workers, zealots for democracy.

[125] Sokolov, "Zashchita Uchreditel'nago Sobraniia," in *Arkhiv Russkoi Revoliutsii*, XIII, 63.

belonged to the fighting squads maintained by the party in some of the city districts or wards.[126] These had been ordered up to provide a measure of protection for the demonstration. The response was disappointing. Only a few score of these squadsmen appeared, and only some of them had arms. From the Moscow ward about forty came, half with arms and half without.[127] From the Kolpino district came either eighteen or thirty men (both figures are from the same source), of whom seven were armed with revolvers.[128] The squadsmen from the Vasileostrov district carried no weapons at all, expecting to get them from the Semenovski Regiment.[129] At least one other district, the Alexander Nevski, contributed something, but the sum total of armed participants in the demonstration was so small that even the most foolhardy leadership could not think of fighting it out.

While the demonstration led to incidents in other parts of the city, the main trouble occurred at the intersection of the Liteiny with the streets leading to the Taurida Palace. Here was the focal point of the demonstration, and here further progress was barred by sailors and Red Guardsmen in strength. Emboldened by its numbers or by its sense of frustration, and disregarding the disparity in arms, the crowd moved on the obstruction. One Bolshevik source has it turned back by speechmaking,[130] another by a volley fired overhead,[131] but the SR sources insist that the Red Guard fired without warning, straight into the crowd. It is certain that shooting occurred, attended by casualties. The SR party worker Gorbachevskaia lost her life, as did also the Siberian peasant G. I. Logvinov, a member of the right-wing Peasants' Executive Committee. One source puts the number of dead at seven, another at eight, a third at nine, while SR estimates of the total number of casualties for the day run as high as one hundred.

[126] See above, p. 347.

[127] See Kononov's testimony in *Pravda*, No. 130 (June 14, 1922). Paevski's estimate is somewhat higher; see the same issue of *Pravda* and *Izvestiia*, No. 129 (June 13, 1922); see also *Obvinitel'noe zakliuchenie*, p. 12; Vladimirova, *God sluzhby "sotsialistov" kapitalistam*, p. 109.

[128] Testimony of Usov in *Pravda*, No. 131 (June 15, 1922), and No. 133 (June 17, 1922).

[129] Testimony of Morachevski in *ibid.*, No. 133.

[130] Bonch-Bruevich, *Na boevykh postakh*, p. 241.

[131] Dybenko, *Miatezhniki*, p. 109.

There is also no agreement as to the cause and details of the shooting. Bolshevik accounts have the first shots coming from the crowd, whereas SR accounts have the enemy firing without provocation— usually the Red Guard, though one of their publications blames it on the sailors.[132] From the limited number of casualties, one would gather that the Red Guard did the shooting—the sailors would have been more effective. The measures taken against the demonstration were denounced on the floor of the assembly by Skobelev, the right-wing Menshevik who had been one of the mainstays of the Provisional Government. Although his description of it as a "working-men's demonstration" did not correspond to reality, it helped to arouse indignation and led to the setting up of a special commission of investigation which the SR's felt should do its work as speedily as possible.[133] It might be pointed out that while the measures had been effective in discouraging further attempts to reach the Taurida Palace, the crowd was not intimidated to the extent that it fled in panic. It recoiled from the shooting but milled about in an angry mood for some time before breaking up into small groups and gradually dispersing. The handful of armed party squadsmen waited around for instructions and, when none came, went home feeling that they had been left in the lurch by the party leadership.[134] The demonstration had been a failure but those who took part had behaved bravely.[135]

In the light of what actually had happened, it can be said that the Russian capital had witnessed a peaceful demonstration in favor of the Constituent Assembly rather than an attempt to enthrone it by armed force. What, then, had happened to the original plan of

[132] *Dvenadtsat' smertnikov*, p. 113.

[133] *Vserossiiskoe Uchreditel'noe Sobranie*, pp. 67–71.

[134] Testimony of Paevski in *Izvestiia*, No. 129 (June 13, 1922), and in *Pravda*, No. 130 (June 14, 1922).

[135] Rakitnikova, *Kak russkoe krest'ianstvo borolos' za Uchreditel'noe Sobranie*, pp. 41–42; Bykhovski, *Vserossiiskii Sovet Krest'ianskikh Deputatov*, p. 350; *Vserossiiskoe Uchreditel'noe Sobranie*, pp. 68, 213–14, n. 22; Sokolov, "Zashchita Uchreditel'nago Sobraniia," in *Arkhiv Russkoi Revoliutsii*, XIII, 64; Oganovski, "Dnevnik chlena Uchreditel'nago Sobraniia," *Golos Minuvshago*, IV–VI (April–June, 1918), 153, 156; Rubinstein, *Bol'sheviki i Uchreditel'noe Sobranie*, pp. 82–83; Vladimirova, *God sluzhby "sotsialistov" kapitalistam*, p. 110; Koroleva, "Razgon Uchredilki," *Bor'ba Klassov*, XI (November, 1934), 35–36; Chernov, *Pered burei*, p. 359; Vishniak, *Dan' proshlomu*, pp. 357–58. Oganovski's figures of 25 dead and 200 wounded represent a rumor rather than an estimate.

coming out in force with an armored division and two regiments, either to overawe the Soviet regime or to compel it to yield to a higher authority? And why had the party leadership left the handful of armed workers without instructions, after calling them up to stiffen the manifestation? There is no need to grope for an answer: the SR's had abandoned their plan at the last moment. Always skeptical of its feasibility, the leaders had taken stock of the situation and had decided that the effort to assemble a striking force under the direction of Maslov and the members of the Military Commission had not yielded results commensurate with the task at hand. Accordingly, on the night of January 4–5, Gotz in the name of the Central Committee ordered the Military Commission not to initiate armed action the next day but to leave the issue to the people, stepping in only to assume direction of a spontaneous upsurge from below. The virtues of an armed versus an unarmed demonstration had long been debated in the Central Committee,[136] so that the decision was not a snap judgment but the considered opinion of the leadership—apparently of the entire leadership, irrespective of faction. The fact that the question had been left open as long as possible may be explained as readily by the desire to take into account any last-minute change of circumstances as by vacillation or procrastination. Published accounts that the Central Committee had decreed the peaceful character of the manifestation at its sessions of December 26 and 29,[137] and its proclamation of January 4 to the same effect,[138] are without question purposeful misrepresentations of the situation, for it was not until the night before convocation that Gotz called off the plan for armed action.

Two aspects of the decision to countermand are thoroughly characteristic of the Socialist Revolutionary Party. First, it was Gotz who had given the order, albeit in the name of the Central Committee. Second, in backing away from a projected course of action, the SR's had not renounced it entirely but clung to certain of its features in

---

[136] Interview with Zenzinov in Paris (September, 1935).

[137] *Delo Naroda*, No. 1/246 (January 3, 1918).

[138] *Ibid.*, No. 2 (January 4, 1918). The proclamation accused the Bolsheviks of seeking to provoke bloodshed through imputation of aggressive intent to the friends of the assembly in order to have an excuse for proceeding against the assembly itself.

the hope that, in a different manner, it might yet be realized. This party never made clean decisions. The explanation that the Central Committee had acted as it did because of aversion to fratricidal strife, because of pessimism over defeats in October, because of faith in the triumph of democracy, because of resignation to Bolshevism as an inevitable though transitory phenomenon,[139] was exploded at the trial of 1922, when it was established that the SR's, by their own admission, had been just as desirous of overthrowing Bolshevism by force of arms on January 5/18, 1918, as on any other day but had desisted because they saw no prospects of success, without by any means abandoning hope of achieving their purpose on some more auspicious occasion. Even on this occasion, moreover, they had not despaired entirely, calling out the members of the armed workers' squads in case the popular wave of indignation should mount high enough to sweep over the enemy's positions. In respect to the soldiers who might be induced to join the demonstration, the situation is not clear. Sokolov speaks of the dismay and indignation aroused in the Semenovski Regiment by the injunction to come unarmed,[140] but if the SR leadership deemed it necessary to make this request, it was solely because it had given up any hope that the regiment could be brought out *in corpore*, in full military trappings. When the Central Committee prevailed upon Likhach not to address the regimental assembly, as he had been invited to do in an attempt to overcome its wavering mood, it was not because of an unwillingness to fight it out with the Bolsheviks but because in all probability Likhach would succeed only in stirring up trouble without being able to overcome the basic disparity of forces.[141]

If circumstances made the SR's earthbound in their calculations, their fancy was free to soar, and they accepted no limitations upon the action that might grow out of the demonstration of January 5, if it assumed massive proportions and was imbued with the requisite spirit. In probing for the ultimate intent of the SR's on January 5,

[139] See Sokolov, "Zashchita Uchreditel'nago Sobraniia," in *Arkhiv Russkoi Revoliutsii*, XIII, 60–61.

[140] *Ibid.*, pp. 61–62.

[141] *Izvestiia*, No. 134 (June 18, 1922). This information does not appear in the *Pravda* issue of the same date. The reporting of the trial in the two Soviet newspapers makes it necessary to read the miserable print of both.

the Soviet prosecutor finally elicited the answer that if things had gone well, not only would the Soviet guard at the Taurida Palace have been ousted and resistance offered to Soviet troops hastening to its assistance, but the SR forces would have gone over to the offensive and stormed the Smolny Institute, the seat of Lenin's government.[142] Everything depended on the reaction of the populace. If it were vigorous enough and sustained enough, the SR's would not have shrunk from exploiting the ultimate possibilities of action against the existing regime, in addition to providing for the safety of the Constituent Assembly. They had not enough strength of their own to initiate the overthrow of the Soviet system but they would have enthusiastically rallied to any upheaval from below—an inevitability if only the people had shared their adulation of the assembly—and would have striven to provide it with purposeful direction.[143]

There remains the question of why the SR's had to seek cover behind the people instead of standing in the foreground, as originally planned, and leading the people in an assault upon the bastions of Bolshevism. The question concerns the absence of armed support for the demonstration and, specifically, the default of the Armored Division and the Semenovski and Preobrazhenski Regiments, since the whole plan hinged on the armored cars for striking power and the Semenovski Regiment for infantry support. Surely, one could expect to find in the sources a relatively simple and clear-cut explanation for a development of such significance, yet the impression one carries away is as scrambled as for matters of lesser import.

To take first the default of the Armored Division, Oganovski has the cars immobilized for want of gasoline, and leaves them without

[142] See Timofeev's statement in *Pravda*, No. 131 (June 15, 1922). At least *Pravda* attributes such a statement to him. But see also No. 134 (June 18, 1922) for his evasive answer to a similar question.

[143] On the last-minute change in plans from something like a coup to a peaceful demonstration, see above all the testimony of Likhach in *Pravda*, No. 131 (June 15, 1922), and *Izvestiia*, No. 134 (June 18, 1922); see also testimony of Gotz in *Pravda*, No. 171 (August 2, 1922); Krylenko's summation in *ibid.*, No. 169 (July 30, 1922); text of the sentence pronounced in *Izvestiia*, No. 177 (August 9, 1922); *Obvinitel'noe zakliuchenie*, pp. 12, 61; Vladimirova, *God sluzhby "sotsialistov" kapitalistam*, p. 109; Sokolov, "Zashchita Uchreditel'nago Sobraniia," in *Arkhiv Russkoi Revoliutsii*, XIII, 60–62. The last-named source gives January 3 as the date of the switch in plans, but the other accounts state unequivocally that it occurred on the night of January 4–5.

gasoline.[144] Chernov, on the other hand, has them disabled by the workers of the repair shops, Bolshevik in sentiment, who through skillful sabotage had converted them by morning into "masses of motionless metal." The crews themselves, according to Chernov, had been ready to roll.[145] Now the accounts of Chernov and Oganovski, though primary sources in general, are not so in this instance, for Populist intellectuals would never think of going to the garage where the cars were stationed. So let us listen to two members of the armed workers' squads whose function it had been to bring out the armored cars. Usov had been told that a group of worker revolutionaries was needed, either to entice the soldiers out by providing a cover for them or to seize the machines before morning—both courses of action are to be inferred from his testimony.[146] But nothing happened, and Usov's colleague, Kononov, informed him that the cars had not been seized (why should it have been necessary to seize them if, as Chernov asserts, the Armored Division had kept faith with the SR's?). Kononov himself is more specific. He actually went with his handful of armed men to the garage of the Armored Division, where he found thirteen machines in a state of "full repair," though without any gasoline. This deficiency was soon remedied, and all was in readiness. But the cars did not move—as Kononov explained, soldiers came and surrounded the garage.[147] Now back to Likhach, the superior of Usov and Kononov as contact man between the Central Committee and the Military Commission. According to his testimony, the armored cars at first could not move for lack of gasoline. When fuel was provided, the workers did not come for them, and without the workers the crews did not wish to act.[148] Likhach partly agrees with Kononov and partly contradicts him with testimony that brings us partly back to Oganovski, and partly not. And if the reader's head is swimming at this point, then he has been duly initiated into the affairs of the Socialist Revolutionary Party.

Fortunately, in the testimony of Keller we have a corrective for

[144] "Dnevnik chlena Uchreditel'nago Sobraniia," *Golos Minuvshago*, IV–VI (April–June, 1918), 153.

[145] Manuscript commentary on the minutes of the Central Committee, p. 87; *Pered burei*, p. 359.

[146] *Pravda*, No. 131 (June 15, 1922).

[147] *Ibid.*, No. 130 (June 14, 1922), and No. 133 (June 17, 1922).

[148] *Ibid.*, No. 131.

this state of affairs, a means of escape from the morass of uncertainty into which a study of this movement so often trails. The explanation given by this officer of the Armored Division is terse, matter-of-fact, and obvious. After pointing out that his command was the only serious hope of the SR's besides their workers' squads, he concedes that this hope, also, had proved false when the whole division went over to the Soviet side.[149] All other promises of support he considered unreliable, and correctly so, and he apparently had not foreseen the meager result of the attempt to mobilize the workers' squads, a force poorly organized and badly decimated by the October schism, more a misfortune than a source of strength, according to one of its leaders.[150]

The Semenovski Regiment presents much the same picture of willingness in words, slackness in spirit, and default in deed. There is less information concerning its failure to march, but a similar diversity of explanations, all skirting the obvious one that the troops did not have their heart in redeeming the pledge they had made, or had permitted to be made in their name, to defend the Constituent Assembly. Paevski has the regimental committee or soviet sitting all day, awaiting an order that never came because of the timorousness of the Central Committee,[151] whereas the Soviet indictment based on his testimony states that the regimental committee flatly refused to instruct the troops to take part in the demonstration.[152] Sokolov speaks of the indignation aroused in the regiment by the instruction of the Central Committee to march unarmed, the effect of which, according to the soldiers, would be to have the Bolsheviks shoot them like rabbits.[153] The soldiers are represented as being fed up with the shilly-shallying of the SR's, whereas it is apparent from Sokolov's own account of a related matter that the regimental committee yielded to no one when it came to shilly-shallying.[154] Likhach explained the default of the Semenovski and Preobrazhenski Regiments by the prior default of the Armored Division, in accordance

[149] *Izvestiia*, No. 131 (June 15, 1922); *Pravda*, No. 130 (June 14, 1922).

[150] See Kononov's statement in *Pravda*, No. 130.

[151] See his statement in *ibid.*   [152] *Obvinitel'noe zakliuchenie*, p. 13.

[153] "Zashchita Uchreditel'nago Sobraniia," in *Arkhiv Russkoi Revoliutsii*, XIII, 61–62.

[154] See episode of the *Seraia Shinel'* in *ibid.*, pp. 42–43.

with what we have termed the "you go first" psychology, but his blanket confession that the SR's lacked the strength to undertake serious action on January 5 covers the situation much better.[155] In the last analysis, the soldiers did not march because they did not want to march, and all the fault-finding and shifting of blame onto other factors are mere rationalizations of this underlying attitude.

With this confession we come to the heart of the problem of the debacle that overtook the efforts to defend the All-Russian Constituent Assembly. Critics of the PSR from its own ranks and from the enemy camp maintain that it did not have the will or the courage to follow through with its plans. They have not hesitated to accuse it of cowardice and of desertion of the rank and file whom it had stirred up and then left leaderless in the face of danger.[156]

A more charitable but still condemnatory opinion is that of Sokolov, who feels that the demonstration would have succeeded had it been armed and who sees in the failure of his party to capitalize upon the anti-Bolshevik sentiment of the Petersburg populace the basic cause of its downfall.[157] What he means, in effect, is that the SR's had not sharply enough marked themselves off from the Bolsheviks with slogans that would have appealed to the counter-revolutionary segment of the Petersburg populace which had cast a quarter of a million votes for the Kadet ticket in the November election. But suppose that the SR's had followed the wish of these officers in their Military Commission and made an open play for the support of the right: would not their admitted gains in this respect have been offset, and more than offset, by the consolidation of the still larger radical element behind the Soviet power, since in that event the Constituent Assembly in its existing form would have been divested of its revolutionary vestments and would have stood forth as what it was, a body dominated by Populist intellectuals revo-

---

[155] *Pravda*, No. 131 (June 15, 1922).

[156] This theme is repeated with variations by the "students" of the fictitious "university" (see above, p. 342) in Sokolov, "Zashchita Uchreditel'nago Sobraniia," in *Arkhiv Russkoi Revoliutsii*, XIII, 45; by Semenov in *Pravda*, No. 131 (June 15, 1922); by Paevski in *Izvestiia*, No. 129 (June 13, 1922), and *Pravda*, No. 130 (June 14, 1922); by Ignatiev in *Pravda*, No. 135 (June 20, 1922); by state's attorney Krylenko in *Pravda*, No. 171 (August 2, 1922).

[157] "Zashchita Uchreditel'nago Sobraniia," in *Arkhiv Russkoi Revoliutsii*, XIII, 28, 36, 65–66.

lutionary in words but Kadet in sentiment? The radical element was not solidly behind the Bolsheviks or the Left SR's in proceeding against the assembly—witness the attitude of the worker Usov, who had been with them against the Cossacks in October yet opposed them on January 5 because of "excessive faith in universal suffrage"[158]—but it would have been put solidly behind them if the SR's had followed the prescription of their youthful officers and gone out after the counterrevolutionaries.[159] One could not have it both ways—to have rallied enthusiasm on the right would have forfeited support on the left.

The party leaders defend themselves against these charges by saying that they did their best, but their best was not enough. They simply could not assemble the armed force that would have justified their making a fight of it. Most authoritative are the words of Gotz, who testified at his trial that the military units did not want to come out and would not follow the party lead: "We had no armed force."[160] And both Gotz and Zenzinov make clear their disbelief in the claims of the Military Commission to have put together a reliable striking force. The propensities of Boris Sokolov and S. S. Maslov for boasting were such as easily to lead them to exaggerate their achievements, and the SR high command did not so much reject their plans as it refused to take them seriously.[161] Chernov saw no hope unless the party could be sure of the Armored Division; without its intervention there would only be bloodshed without any serious chance of victory.[162] And Likhach reaffirms the position of the leadership when he declared at the trial that "there was no attempt at force on January 5, not because we did not wish it, but because we had no strength."[163]

[158] *Pravda*, No. 133 (June 17, 1922). See above, pp. 16–17.

[159] These were stirring, even without their encouragement. Reports reached the Petersburg Soviet of anti-Soviet agitation in the churches and among employees and students, and also of the handing out of broadsides inciting to pogroms—probably a reference to anti-Semitic agitation. See Erykalov, *Krasnaia gvardiia v bor'be za vlast' sovetov*, p. 83, citing archival material.

[160] *Pravda*, No. 171 (August 2, 1922); see also Krylenko's summation in *ibid.*, No. 169 (July 30, 1922).

[161] Statement of Gotz in *Izvestiia*, No. 136 (June 22, 1922); interviews with Zenzinov in Paris (September, 1935) and New York (December 31, 1949).

[162] Manuscript commentary on the minutes of the Central Committee, p. 87.

[163] *Pravda*, No. 131 (June 15, 1922).

The SR leaders merely attest to the absence of strength. They do not go into the problem of why there was none—it would have been too embarrassing for them. But others make the reasons clear. For one thing, it was too hard to swim against the tide of Bolshevism in the Petersburg garrison.[164] For another, it was too hard to buck the authority of the Petersburg Soviet in enlisting support among the workers in competition with the Red Guard,[165] dominated by the Bolsheviks and blessed by the soviet, then a powerful institution with weight of its own, in contrast to its later degradation as an instrument of one-party rule. Underlying everything else as a factor working in favor of Bolshevism was the war-weariness, the immense thirst for peace which had killed all SR sentiment in the armed forces, according to the admission even of Eliashevich, one of the inveterate proponents of marching with the Allies "at no matter what cost" [166]—a cost that he and his party were now paying and would continue to pay until no breath was left in the corpse. The disparity of forces in the Russian capital in January of 1918 was too great for the SR's to make headway even with a cause such as defense of the Constituent Assembly, which still commanded a measure of popularity. No better statement of the situation can be found than the sailor Dybenko's words of reassurance to a nervous commissar, Bonch-Bruevich (nervous, that is, by Dybenko's account, not by his own), who had just been frightened by rumors that Petersburg regiments were joining the demonstration: "Comrade Bonch-Bruevich, that is all nonsense. What are Petersburg regiments worth at present? Their condition is such that not one of them can fight. But there are 5,000 sailors in the city who can." [167]

On top of the sailors would come various other units and also the Red Guard, numbering thirty to forty thousand, of whom, it is true, only three to four thousand were as a rule under arms.[168] Now, however, it had been brought into a state of readiness because of the tension in connection with the opening of the Constituent As-

---

[164] See Dashevski's statement in *ibid.*

[165] See reply of Kononov in *Pravda*, No. 130 (June 14, 1922), to Bukharin's query as to why it should have been so hard for the SR's to enlist workers when the Red Guard recruited them so easily.

[166] See above, p. 189.   [167] Dybenko, *Miatezhniki*, p. 108.

[168] E. Pinezhski, *Krasnaia gvardiia*, p. 122.

sembly.[169] The Red Guard was not a trained fighting force but neither was it the rabble the SR's like to depict, for it was even more aggressive than the Populist intellectuals, and much less careful of its skin.

When individual members of the party drifted back on the morrow to the scene of the night's engagement, to the park surrounding the Taurida Palace, they found the doors locked and the building under heavy guard, complete with machine guns and field artillery. The Council of People's Commissars dissolved the Constituent Assembly on January 6, and the next day the All-Russian Soviet Executive Committee, having absorbed the two bolting delegations, ratified this decision. The Left SR's did not obstruct the course of the Soviet government. Their delegation in the Constituent Assembly approved the decree of dissolution, its own absorption into the Executive Committee with voting rights, and the text of a statement to their constituents explaining their action. For several days they busied themselves with justifying their new position after having occupied a somewhat equivocal position in the preceding weeks. It is apparent that with them the hours of the assembly were numbered from the moment it rejected the candidacy of Spiridonova. The brief session had been long enough to arouse their ire with its spectacle of the "Mogilevian Zimmerwaldist," Chernov, riding the crest of a wave of sabotage into the president's chair.[170]

The Left SR's attainted the assembly on the grounds of its origin, its attendance, and its work. The "accidental majority" against the soviets they attributed to the fact that the candidates' lists had been made up before the October Revolution had fully awakened the class consciousness of the toilers and before the schism had destroyed the illusion that the PSR was a revolutionary party. The assembly as constituted on January 5 they decried as unrepresentative, even within the framework of a defective election, because only 400 of the 800 members had appeared, and of the half who did, over 150 had withdrawn as the result of the secession of the two Soviet

[169] *Ibid.*, pp. 137–38.
[170] Ligovski, "Vsia vlast' ushedshim!", in *Vokrug Uchreditel'nago Sobraniia*, p. 46.

parties. The majority had demonstrated a sneaking desire to leave the door open to compensation for landowners by refusing to nationalize the banks, which held mortgages on the estates; it had demonstrated a readiness to saddle the people with crushing indebtedness by refusing to annul the loans contracted by the Kerenski and tsarist regimes; and it had even evinced a willingness to continue the war by refusing to undertake action independently of the Allies. The rightist majority had betrayed its purpose of returning to the outworn, generally execrated, and altogether baneful policy of A. F. Kerenski. An obstacle in the path of October since its inception and rendered wholly so by the departure of the radical delegations, the rump assembly could only serve as a base for counterrevolution and could not be left in existence lest it endanger the revolution. The Constituent Assembly had already fallen apart; the decree of dissolution did little more than attest an accomplished fact.[171]

The inevitable had happened, said the Left SR's, as they burned their bridges behind them and took a firm stand on Soviet ground: "The Constituent Assembly has died, long live the Soviets!" [172] With these words they took leave of their search for a political order intermediate between the soviet and parliamentary systems, between the principle of suffrage on a class basis, confined to the toilers, and the principle of universal suffrage exemplified in the Constituent Assembly. They now discovered virtues in the soviets of which those among them who were less ochlocratically inclined had not been fully aware. The soviets represented a higher form of political development in which the functions of administration in every phase of economic as well as political activity were placed in the hands of the toilers themselves, to the exclusion of the "lords," who would be in no position to impede, confuse, or subvert the genius of the people in working out its own form of society. Institutions based on class collaboration were outmoded in an era of

---

[171] See text of the decree of dissolution in *Vserossiiskoe Uchreditel'noe Sobranie*, pp. 145–46; A. Ustinov, "Konvent" (The Convention), in *Vokrug Uchreditel'nago Sobraniia*, p. 44; "K rospusku Uchreditel'nago Sobraniia" (On the Dissolution of the Constituent Assembly), in *ibid.*, p. 42; "K izbirateliam," in *ibid.*, pp. 42–43; "Pochemu my ushli?" (Why Did We Leave?), in *ibid.*, p. 44.

[172] "Neizbezhnoe" (The Inevitable), *Znamia Truda*, No. 113 (January 7, 1918).

acute class conflict with the future form of society at stake. "There should be no hesitation in breaking the old when it cramps the development of the new." One idealistic Left SR even saw in decentralization the primary feature of the soviet system.[173] The Left SR's may have intended to break with the centralized pattern of government but they failed to reckon with the purpose of the other and far stronger party represented in the soviets. Yet the Left SR's were not as utopian as their enemies like to make them out to be. Already they were predicting that this Republic of Toil would decide the fate of the world, if not at the present, then at least in the future, and in laying so much emphasis upon creativeness from the depths, they realized something which the right SR's in their intellectual conceit have never realized—that a major social upheaval brings to the top talent with a power of achievement far exceeding that of the system it displaces.[174]

Not all of the Left SR's found it possible to make this transition. Although the less radical wing under Karelin had moved along with the others, less because of adulation of the soviets, in all probability, than because of rage at the right SR's, and although Karelin himself had announced the break with the assembly, the Left SR ranks in his home city of Kharkov began to crumble with the secession of a moderate element under Agabekov, Ivanitski, and the majority of the delegation in the city council. These joined hands with the enemies of the new order to put through a resolution condemning the dissolution of the assembly, which promptly entailed the dissolution of the city council itself at the hands of the struggling but resolute Soviet power.[175] The disaffection in the city does not seem to have carried over into Kharkov province, for in February the sixth congress of peasants' soviets decided that the Constituent Assembly had lost its significance with the establishment of soviets and its

[173] Leonid Venetsianov, "Sovetskaia respublika" (The Republic of Soviets), in *Vokrug Uchreditel'nago Sobraniia*, pp. 49–50.

[174] For appraisal of the soviets as a higher form of political organization, see especially Al. Ustinov, "O novoi vlasti" (About the New Power), in *ibid.*, pp. 47–48.

[175] *1917 god v Khar'kove*, pp. 61–62. The crumbling had, in fact, set in before the November election, when the Chernovich group had split off from the others. It now coalesced with the new splinter groups. No measure of strength is indicated.

inability to work with them in harmony.[176] Elsewhere the Left SR's seem to have moved over to a position of full-throated acclaim of Soviet power without splitting up in the process.

While the Left SR's were drawing the logical conclusion from their weak parliamentary position by assenting to the abolition of the Constituent Assembly and the investiture of the soviets with power, the regular SR's were writhing in rage and frustration. They were now back on the Bolotnaia (swampy), a street name as descriptive of their thoughts and emotions as of the condition of the ground before Peter's work of reclamation. In their search for a culprit they turned on one another. Some blamed the Bureau of the Delegation; the bureau blamed the president who had not heeded its instructions; and others blamed themselves, not, however, for having failed to be revolutionary in 1917 but for having seemed to be revolutionary on January 5. They beat on their breasts and swore to be true to themselves in the future, which for a good many of them would have meant a general assault on the revolution all along the line. Panic reigned on the one hand, and defiance on the other. A sense of utter defeat gripped some, while others announced proudly that "we shall die, but recover our honor." Actually they had no idea of what should be done, and looked to the populace for succor.[177]

There were many citizens of the capital, even among the working class, who found the dissolution of the assembly not to their liking. The Bolsheviks had maintained that it was necessary for the assembly to meet and show its true colors before the people became disillusioned with it, and many of its supporters, no doubt, would have been disillusioned by the policies of the right SR's, but a one-day session had not been enough to produce this disillusionment. In the factories and plants, in barracks and assembly halls, meetings

[176] *Ibid.*, p. 268. Caution must be used with reference to peasant conventions in the post-October era. Even in provinces where it commanded little support, the Soviet government was quite capable of rounding up an assorted bunch of bumpkins and holding a fake congress which in the printed records will be invested with all the dignity of a regularly constituted congress. In the present instance, however, it would seem that we have to do with a bona fide congress, for the tone of its language is Left SR, as was befitting in Kharkov province.

[177] Oganovski, "Dnevnik chlena Uchreditel'nago Sobraniia," *Golos Minuvshago,* IV–VI (April–June, 1918), 162.

were held to discuss the situation. At these meetings Bolshevik orators attempted to win approval for the government's action while the SR's sought to have it condemned, though not as vigorously as one would have expected. In fact, Sokolov remarks on an inexplicable tendency to leave the platform to the Bolsheviks.[178] The fact that the SR's were organizing mass protest meetings of their own made it less essential for them to appear at other gatherings not of their calling, but the effort to rally sentiment against the act of dissolution does not seem to have been as determined as it might have been. The SR press claimed success in respect to the large number of workers who turned out in protest, with 4,000 estimated for the Nikolaevski railroad shops (that is, the line connecting Petersburg with Moscow) and 8,000 for the Obukhov plant.[179] The burial of the victims of repression during the demonstration of January 5 gave the SR's another opportunity to embarrass the regime. According to Chernov, the funeral procession on January 9, the thirteenth anniversary of Bloody Sunday, exceeded anything of the kind ever seen before,[180] but according to Oganovski, it got off to an unimpressive start and the marchers scattered like sheep in sudden panic at some baseless rumor.[181]

The mood of the populace in a great city is never easy to determine because of the crosscurrents, which may be either visible or hidden from view. The Bolsheviks did not always have clear sailing in addressing assemblies in the barracks or factories. Their attacks on the war, the Entente, and the Provisional Government everywhere met with approbation, leaving no doubt as to sentiment on these points, but when they assailed the Constituent Assembly, they might be listened to in silence or even encounter shouts of disapproval. The Preobrazhenski Regiment greeted them in silence on January 6 after having refused to listen to their spokesman, Piatakov, on January 2, but the Izmailovski Regiment, upon which the SR's

---

[178] "Zashchita Uchreditel'nago Sobraniia," in *Arkhiv Russkoi Revoliutsii*, XIII, 35, 68.

[179] *Delo Naroda*, No. 5 (January 12, 1918).

[180] Manuscript commentary on the minutes of the Central Committee, p. 89; *Pered burei*, pp. 366, 368; see also Rakitnikova, *Kak russkoe krest'ianstvo borolos' za Uchreditel'noe Sobranie*, p. 46.

[181] "Dnevnik chlena Uchreditel'nago Sobraniia," *Golos Minuvshago*, IV–VI (April–June, 1918), 163, 165–66.

had not depended, reacted adversely to denunciations of the assembly. On the other hand, the workers of the Franco-Russian plant, in their majority opposed to violence against the assembly, acclaimed Zinoviev on the morrow of dissolution. Though the workers and soldiers generally had not been willing to take the offensive against the assembly, and even had viewed it with a certain hope and expectancy, their tolerance did not admit of any positive action on its behalf or any sustained indignation against its ravishers. Rather, there was evidence of a certain primitive tendency to judge right and wrong in terms of strength and weakness: no one had defended the assembly, so right was not on its side. The Bolsheviks had won easily, and "victors are not judged." The idea of coexistence had also cropped up in certain quarters. The Bolsheviks have often made skillful use of a suggestion of compromise to undermine an opponent's position without in the least intending to compromise. So in the present instance, the notion of coexistence to a certain extent helped to soften the will to resist aggression until the assembly had been safely disposed of. The mood of the populace, moreover, interposed no barriers to measures against the majority party in the assembly, and the SR's had their headquarters raided, both the delegation's on the Bolotnaia and the Central Committee's on the Galernaia, their publications hounded or closed down, and their garrison gazette, *The Seraia Shinel'*, terminated through the withdrawal of protection by the host regimental committees.[182]

Obviously, the prospects in Petersburg were not promising as the SR's faced up to the question of what to do next. A group of them who gathered before the Taurida Palace during the day of January 6 sent an "order" to the commandant to admit them, but the doors did not open.[183] Then they assembled at the Gurevich high school to decide on the advisability of reopening the sessions in some factory building where the workers were friendly and where they would be in a position to claim that the Constituent Assembly had resumed

[182] *Ibid.*, p. 162; Sokolov, "Zashchita Uchreditel'nago Sobraniia," in *Arkhiv Russkoi Revoliutsii*, XIII, 43, 50–54, 68–69; Rakitnikova, *Kak russkoe krest'-ianstvo borolos' za Uchreditel'noe Sobranie*, pp. 45–46; for Bolshevik version, see Rubinstein, *Bol'sheviki i Uchreditel'noe Sobranie*, p. 100. Both Rubinstein and Sokolov state that only two SR members of the assembly appeared at the public meetings to defend their cause.

[183] Rubinstein, *Bol'sheviki i Uchreditel'noe Sobranie*, p. 99.

its work under the protection of proletarian Petersburg. Apparently there were two invitations, one from the Semiannikov foundry, extended through A. Vysotski, and the other from the Obukhov steel mill and cannon foundry. But the SR delegation "did not exhibit the needed unity." While one group, including Chernov, thought the moment favorable for an attempt to keep the assembly alive under the sheltering wing of an irreproachably proletarian sponsor, another and larger group, the core of which must have been the right-wing "passivists," argued against exposing the workers to the fire of a gunboat anchored near by in the river or, if the Bolsheviks did not resort to force, against launching a futile experiment without the means of enforcing decisions or even of bringing them to the attention of the public. Such an exhibition of impotence would destroy the assembly's prestige and militate against the chances of revival on a more favorable occasion. The majority turned down the offer, the decision being made, it will be noted, by the delegation, and not by the Central Committee.[184]

No doubt it was the right decision. It is a safe conjecture that many of the workers had not acceded to the invitation, for Bolshevism had strength here, also, and the Red Guard had drawn many recruits from the Obukhov mill. The Bolsheviks would not have found it necessary to shell the plant; they would simply have appeared within its walls with the approval of part of the workers and the passivity of the rest, and the deputies would either have been arrested or again have found themselves without a roof over their heads. When the worker Kononov, who had proposed to bring three hundred armed comrades to the Obukhov mill as a guard for the assembly, was asked at the 1922 trial whether the assembly could have relied on the protection of the Obukhov workers, he replied amid the laughter of the courtroom that, yes, the promise of protection had been made, but whether it would have been honored or not he could not say.[185]

If not in St. Petersburg, then where could the assembly reconvene with at least some prospect of being able to continue its labors? Certainly not in Moscow. There the Bolshevik contagion was not

---

[184] Chernov, manuscript commentary on the minutes of the Central Committee, pp. 88–89; Chernov, *Pered burei*, pp. 367–68; Koroleva, "Razgon Uchredilki," *Bor'ba Klassov*, XI (November, 1934), 41.

[185] *Pravda*, No. 130 (June 14, 1922).

less strong than in the capital, according to Chernov, and the "sobering up" process even slower.[186] The feebleness of party enterprise
there has already been noted in connection with the plans to defend
the assembly.[187] The act of dissolution had occasioned only a ripple
of dissent in Moscow,[188] and when the delegation moved its headquarters there at the end of January by decision of the Central
Committee, it decided, after feeling out the situation, that nothing
could be done.[189] Nearly all the SR deputies now concluded that
the cause had been lost in the big cities of Russia,[190] and that they
must look farther afield in the search for a place of refuge.

Two possibilities that came readily in view had to be rejected for
political reasons. Though many of the Populist intellectuals in their
hearts abominated the revolution and were blind partisans of the
Allied Powers, they could not think of accepting hospitality in the
Don Cossack Region, where the need of the chieftains for democratic window dressing was stronger than their detestation of Socialist Revolutionaries,[191] or of following the advice of Kilchevski and
going to Archangel in the hope of being able to operate in the
shadow of Allied intervention. Kerenski had already thrown himself upon the Cossacks—with results that did not invite repetition
—and later the SR's would have their fling on the Volga with borrowed strength from the Czechoslovaks, but at the present stage
reliance on Cossack or Allied bayonets did not beckon to them with
all that it would entail in the way of a confession of bankruptcy.
The Archangel proposal drew fire not only from Kogan-Bernstein
on the left but also from Gendelman on the right,[192] and the extreme partisans of the Allies were not yet ready to disclose their
hand.

[186] *Pered burei*, p. 368.   [187] See above, p. 349.

[188] See Vladimirova, *God sluzhby "sotsialistov" kapitalistam*, p. 110; testimony
of Gregory Ratner, in *Izvestiia*, No. 136 (June 22, 1922); for arrest of the city
committee, see above, p. 375.

[189] Testimony of Gregory Ratner in *Pravda*, No. 136 (June 22, 1922).

[190] Chernov, manuscript commentary on the minutes of the Central Committee, p. 89; V. Garmiza, "Iz istorii Samarskoi uchredilki" (From the History of the Constituent Assembly Affair at Samara), *Istoricheskii Zhurnal*,
VIII (August, 1940), 33.

[191] Chernov, manuscript commentary on the minutes of the Central Committee, pp. 89–90, but see also below, p. 474.

[192] Testimony of Gregory Ratner in *Izvestiia*, No. 136 (June 22, 1922), and in
Pravda of the same date.

More attractive at first glance seemed the prospect of finding shelter with the Rada in Kiev. Already before January 5, a delegation consisting of two members of the Central Committee, Richter and Gerstein, had been sent thither to negotiate with the corresponding organ of the Ukrainian SR's and the Rada authorities concerning cooperation within the Constituent Assembly, the creation of a favorable climate for its work, and the reconstitution of a central government to replace Kerenski's (in the make-believe world of these people, the Soviet government was mentally exorcised).[193] The veiled language of the published report did not reveal the main purpose, which was to explore the possibility of a change of venue for the Constituent Assembly if a fair trial could not be had in Petersburg. Special SR military organizations were at work assembling an armed force out of units withdrawn from the front (the Southwestern and Rumanian Fronts, no doubt, since these were near the Ukraine and were much less pervaded with Bolshevism than those further north). The hand-picked units were then to be brought together and formed into larger ones.[194] If the mission to Kiev succeeded, and it proved possible to conclude a fighting alliance with Ukrainian federalism, the SR's are said to have planned to assemble in Kiev on February 1.[195]

Ukrainian federalism, however, was fast becoming Ukrainian separatism under the spur of the conflict with Moscow and the need for German support. No great spur was needed, of course, for it had long been tending in that direction as a result of the excess of nationalism which the Little Russian Populists shared with the Great Russian. With an eye toward keeping on the good side of the Germans, the Ukrainian authorities refused to permit the scattered military units to be drawn together.[196] The declaration of Ukrainian independence on January 16, 1918, met with SR disapproval, expressed, however, in language of exceptional mildness, wholly unlike

[193] From the minutes of the Central Committee of the PSR, session of December 26–27, 1917, as published in *Delo Naroda*, No. 1/246 (January 3, 1918).

[194] Testimony of Gerstein in *Pravda*, No. 149 (July 7, 1922).

[195] Koroleva, "Razgon Uchredilki," *Bor'ba Klassov*, XI (November, 1934), 41; Rubinstein, *Bol'sheviki i Uchreditel'noe Sobranie*, p. 99.

[196] Testimony of Gerstein in *Pravda*, No. 149 (July 7, 1922). On Gerstein's activities in Kiev, see also testimony of Colonel Krakovetski in *ibid.*, No. 147 (July 4, 1922).

the fulminations that would have ensued had this step been taken under the Provisional Government. The resolution of the Central Committee held a declaration of full independence to be inexpedient while social reforms were pending which were of equal concern to toilers in all parts of the former empire. Such action sacrificed the general interests of the class struggle to minor and temporary considerations and still further dislocated the strength of democracy.[197]

By this time relations were back to the starting point; the sweet milk had all turned sour. Nothing came of the effort to reopen the Constituent Assembly in Kiev; [198] an alliance between the two sets of Populists had proved as little feasible for the purpose of salvaging the assembly as it had for the purpose of saving it from dissolution.

Other possibilities received less attention.[199] Apparently the thought of Finland no sooner crossed the mind of the SR's than it was crossed out. A body dominated by people who had steadily backed the Provisional Government in its steady refusal to concede anything to the Finns beyond the restoration of the old constitution would not have been welcome in Finland, and the SR's decided not to court a certain and well-merited rebuff. Siberia was their territory, industrially undeveloped and with only knots of Bolshevik strength in isolated mining centers, aside from the garrisons that were melting away. But it was far removed from the main part of the country, and had the party fallen so low that it could not find a foothold in European Russia that would prevent the All-Russian Constituent Assembly from sinking to the level of a Siberian council? In the wake of dissolution the SR deputies had proudly proclaimed: "The Constituent Assembly is not dead. . . . At the call of its president, on the day set by him, the Constituent Assembly will gather again to continue its work." [200] On January 13, in the bulletin of the Committee to Defend the Assembly, Chernov had informed "all citizens of Russia" that the use of armed force would not suffice to

---

[197] *Partiinyia Izvestiia*, No. 6 (March 8/21, 1918), pp. 41–43. This issue of the party news bulletin is of very great rarity.

[198] Chernov, manuscript commentary on the minutes of the Central Committee, p. 90; brief mention of the matter in Oganovski, "Dnevnik chlena Uchreditel'nago Sobraniia," *Golos Minuvshago*, IV–VI (April–June, 1918), 162.

[199] Sokolov, "Zashchita Uchreditel'nago Sobraniia," in *Arkhiv Russkoi Revoliutsii*, XIII, 68–69.

[200] *Obvinitel'noe zakliuchenie*, p. 13.

prevent the reopening of the assembly at a time and place that would be the subject of a special announcement.[201] But the days and weeks went by without any indication of this time and place. There was this or that detraction to meeting on the outskirts of Russia, and the heart of the country, the region around Moscow and the industrial northwest, continued firmly in the grasp of the workers' and soldiers' government.

In their desperation the SR's reverted to their homeland, to the valley of the Volga and the provinces around Saratov, where their roots went deepest and their majorities in the November election had been most impressive. Surely all this strength had not been dissipated, even though the soviets might hold sway in the cities and the soldiers be introducing Bolshevism into the villages. Chernov mentions as an element of encouragement the psychological reaction that had set in among the peasants as a result of friction between the stay-at-homes and the returning soldiers, each armed with a different political faith. No doubt the antagonism arising from differences of age, outlook, war experience, economic interest, and political influence did afford a certain handle for the SR's to grasp. The few urban centers did not relieve to any marked degree the agrarian complexion of the region; the proletariat existed only as islands at Samara, Saratov, and Tsaritsyn (Stalingrad); and the proportion of kulak enterprises is said to have been quite high in comparison to central Russia. The center of activity would be Samara rather than Saratov province, and it is true that many kulaks nested in Samara province. Another consideration was the remoteness from the zone of German operations, which might conceivably be extended to much of central Russia in answer to the re-creation of an Eastern Front such as the Populist intelligentsia already had in mind and actively promoted after Brest Litovsk. The Volga was the logical base for an attempted comeback of this kind. But exclusive significance should not be assigned to post-treaty military considerations. Already before Brest Litovsk, Rudnev in Moscow had raised the question of the best place to reconvene the assembly with the Volga in mind, especially Saratov, where, it was hoped, not only the sympathy but the active support of the peasantry might be en-

---

[201] Quoted in Rubinstein, *Bol'sheviki i Uchreditel'noe Sobranie,* p. 100.

listed.[202] As it turned out, Samara province became the center of the attempt to subvert the Soviet government, with preparations for a counterblow already under way in the period immediately following dissolution of the assembly, and with the first try at subversion taking place in February of 1918. No doubt the greater aggressiveness of the Samara SR's is to be accounted for by the right-centrist tone of the organization, in contrast to the centrist or even left-of-center tone of the organization in the home province of Rakitnikov and Chernov. But in both provinces, of course, speculation was based on peasant antipathy to Bolshevism.[203]

The peasants had elected the Constituent Assembly; how did they react to its dissolution? It was inevitable that the split in the national peasants' organization at its Second All-Russian Congress (see chapter 5) should be deepened by the conflict over the Constituent Assembly. Both the SR's and the Left SR's resolved to mobilize their peasant followings in support of their stand on the question by convening a Third All-Russian Peasants' Congress separately from one another. So the calls went out from the rival Executive Committees, the one chosen by the 359 delegates who had sided with Chernov in the memorable division at the Second Congress, and the other by the 314 who had followed Maria Spiridonova. The SR Executive Committee notified all soviets standing for defense of the assembly that its congress would open on January 8, the earliest feasible date after convocation. The Left SR Executive Committee, being less pressed, fixed on January 12. Actually, these congresses opened on January 10 and 13 (or 14), respectively. And to make matters still more complex, Lenin's government convened the Third All-Russian Congress of Workers', Soldiers', and Peasants' Soviets on January 10. If the uninitiated foreigner becomes confused at this point, he will have a better understanding of the impact of all this on the Russian peasantry. We have two congresses of rural soviets, one SR and the other Left SR, and a mainly Bolshevik congress of urban soviets, though with a certain peasant admixture, all

[202] Testimony of Gregory Ratner in *Pravda*, No. 136 (June 22, 1922).
[203] Chernov, manuscript commentary on the minutes of the Central Committee, pp. 90–91; Garmiza, "Iz istorii Samarskoi uchredilki," *Istoricheskii Zhurnal*, VIII (August, 1940), 33.

with the same numeral and all meeting at about the same time.[204]

The SR or right-wing Congress of Peasants' Soviets was attended by some 300 delegates with more to come. But its deliberations were destined to be even shorter than those of the Constituent Assembly. In fact, even before it opened, the sailors and the Red Guard had already descended upon it under the command of a red Kornilov—a name that adds the final touch of confusion. The congress got under way, however, despite its uninvited escort, and soon a torrent of words bewildered the guard and overwhelmed the Soviet regime with denunciations. Touching scenes were enacted: a sailor, seeing peasants in the congress arrayed against peasants in the armed guard and wondering how they had gotten separated, broke down and bawled, saying it were better that he end his life; the peasants got down on their knees and intoned the anthem "Vechnaia pamiat' " (Eternal Memory), in honor of Logvinov, the member of the Executive Committee who had lost his life in the demonstration of January 5; the sailors also kneeled and sang. But the Soviet command pulled itself together and the troops made ready to clear the hall. Having just paid deference to one victim, they were obviously not averse to creating others, returning to questions of "Why do you do this?" the age-old answer: "Tak prikazano—nechego razgovarivat' " (It is so ordered—there's no use talking about it). The delegates were turned out onto the street in driblets, to wander aimlessly about or head for the railroad station or the Workers' and Soldiers' Congress (the address of which was given them), but not before they had been searched and relieved of their victuals, and some of their leaders arrested, including Chairman Ovchinnikov, Inna Rakitnikova, and the veteran Populist O. S. Minor. The literature destined for distribution in the villages was sequestrated, as were the premises generally, and machine guns were posted at the entrance. Apparently the peasants had seen before them only armed workers and sailors, but the Populist intelligentsia had more fertile imaginations. Later

[204] Plans for still a fourth congress did not materialize. The defensist bloc in control of the workers' and soldiers' soviets until the Second All-Russian Congress in October tried to assemble a congress of its own in January to offset the official one being convened by the Soviet government, but the attempt ended in a fiasco with only fifteen delegates responding to the call (according to a Soviet source; see Vladimirova, *God sluzhby "sotsialistov" kapitalistam*, pp. 113-15).

on, witnesses were interrogated, and it was learned that among
the guard there had been German and Austrian prisoners of war
dressed in Russian uniforms (one wonders where the Turks were,
and it seems that the Mongols were yet to come). Here was the
sure touch of the Populist intellectuals, perpetually in search of some
artificial and non-Russian explanation for the strength of Bolshevism.[205]

This right-wing peasants' congress struggled against death longer
than the Constituent Assembly. For some days it maintained a
clandestine existence, meeting in various places, until it had made
certain decisions, confirmed its Executive Committee in office, and
drawn up an account of its travails together with an arraignment
of the "new autocracy." It decided that, with socialization of the
land now legally if only partially enacted, the execution would have
to be left to the localities, especially to the land committees.[206] It
acclaimed the Constituent Assembly as the only safeguard against a
swift transition from pseudo-socialism to dark reaction; its mandate
could be extinguished only in the same broad manner in which it
had been conferred. The peasantry must defend the Constituent
Assembly and the local organs of self-government—zemstvos, city
councils, land committees—against usurpation by the soviets; for
the soviets did not rest on universal suffrage but were imperfectly
elected on a class basis in a grossly disproportionate manner, since
election was indirect, by open vote, on a basis of parity between the
rural and urban toilers, whereas in reality there were sixty times as
many peasants as workers in Russia.[207] It was inevitable that partisans

---

[205] Rakitnikova, *Kak russkoe krest'ianstvo borolos' za Uchreditel'noe Sobranie*,
pp. 46–48, 52, 54–57; Bykhovski, *Vserossiiskii Sovet Krest'ianskikh Deputatov*,
pp. 352–55; Oganovski, "Dnevnik chlena Uchreditel'nago Sobraniia," *Golos
Minuvshago*, IV–VI (April–June, 1918), 167, 169; Vladimirova, *God sluzhby
"sotsialistov" kapitalistam*, pp. 114–15. Vladimirova has most of the delegates
leaving when the guard explained that they had come to the wrong place. The
SR sources make it clear that it was not the explanation but the rifles that
induced them to leave. Later Soviet sources do not even mention this congress. Bykhovski states that it was on this occasion that the archives of the
All-Russian Peasants' Soviet were lost. Either they were classified as counterrevolutionary and destroyed or else they were used as fuel.
[206] Bykhovski, *Vserossiiskii Sovet Krest'ianskikh Deputatov*, Appendix No.
31, sec. IV, pp. 418–19.
[207] *Ibid.*, secs. I and II, pp. 417–18; Rakitnikova, *Kak russkoe krest'ianstvo
borolos' za Uchreditel'noe Sobranie*, pp. 51–52, 57.

of the peasantry should lay their finger on the Achilles' heel of Soviet democracy, but the disproportion existed, of course, only where the soviets were merged according to the Bolshevik formula. The original soviets in the country were purely peasant. Certainly, too, the ratio was inaccurate. There were not sixty times as many peasants as workers in Russia, even in 1918. Having voiced no confidence in the soviets as governmental organs, however, the right-wing peasants' congress acknowledged their usefulness otherwise and laid down a line of conduct to be pursued in them that entailed no bolting if they would not divest themselves of public functions but did entail refusal to serve on their executive committees. Here is an example of compliance with the general SR line, subsequent to the October disaster, of combating the Soviet regime from a minority position within the soviets. It was the hope of the congress that a firm stand by the peasantry for the Constituent Assembly and against the soviets might bring the latter to their knees, since the villages were most of Russia and the source of its food [208]—another indication of a vague intent to starve out the proletariat.

But things did not go that way. The congress had sounded a note of desperation, plaintive and pathetic, in its manifesto to the peasantry on the subject of its own dissolution. There was no end, it said, to what the peasants were called on to endure; tsars, *pomeshchiks,* bureaucrats, and now the Bolsheviks—"all have scoffed and mocked at us." [209] Of the things said at the congress, none was so true as this. And why had the class been the butt of oppression for a thousand years, and why was it still being oppressed? Because it was so weak —imposing in numbers, and in no other way. The peasant delegates are said to have gone home with "great hatred" of Bolshevism in their hearts.[210] It probably would be more accurate to say they went home in confusion while the Populist intellectuals nursed the hatred. The delegates had pledged themselves to fight against the "new autocracy" and its crimes, to convene a new congress in a safe place, and to expose the nature of Bolshevism in the provinces, so that the peasants would call to account the regime and their own

[208] Bykhovski, *Vserossiiskii Sovet Krest'ianskikh Deputatov,* p. 356.
[209] *Ibid.,* Appendix No. 30, p. 417.
[210] Rakitnikova, *Kak russkoe krest'ianstvo borolos' za Uchreditel'noe Sobranie,* pp. 57-58.

"erring sons" in the armed forces who were supporting it.[211] None of these pledges were redeemed. It was the "erring sons" who went home and called the peasants to account. The war had reversed the pattern of village authority.[212]

The right-wing or SR Executive Committee issuing from this congress had to struggle desperately to stay alive, without hope of assembling a new congress. The SR's now began to experience the full effects of the schism which had resulted in part from the radicalism of the Kamkov-Spiridonova faction but even more from the on-with-the-war, coalition-at-any-cost tactics of the small but extremely articulate right wing with Chernov fast in its clutches. No matter what they tried to do, the Left SR's were there to do the opposite, also in the name of the peasantry and also with the SR trademark. A congress of land committees had been scheduled at this same time, amid all the others, but no sooner had the remnants of the Supreme Land Committee set things in motion than Kalegaev seized the initiative from it and convened the congress on January 14. It surrendered its identity almost immediately by acceding to fusion with the peasants' section of the Third Congress of Workers', Soldiers', and Peasants' Soviets, its members having been won over, according to Oganovski, by the prospect of receiving shoes and galoshes.[213] At every turn the SR's encountered the baneful influence of Maria Spiridonova, head of the "uniformed peasantry," who distinguished herself by her intolerance and fanaticism in warring on the other branch of the peasant movement. Spiridonova, of course, was no more intolerant or fanatical than the right SR's, nor was her influence confined to the peasants with bayonets, for she had behind her a sizable segment of the civilian peasantry and was in a position to hurt her foes. She blocked the reading of their protest on the floor of the official Soviet congress; she expropriated the funds of the right-wing Executive Committee; she smothered its initiative on behalf of the Constituent Assembly, in the provinces as at the

---

[211] *Ibid.*, p. 53.

[212] See development of this train of thought above, pp. 278–79.

[213] "Dnevnik chlena Uchreditel'nago Sobraniia," *Golos Minuvshago*, IV–VI (April–June, 1918), 167–68, 171; Rakitnikova, *Kak russkoe krest'ianstvo borolos' za Uchreditel'noe Sobranie*, p. 58.

center.[214] All this she did, not to serve the Bolsheviks, as the SR's like to say, but in an effort to re-create the unity of the peasant movement by eliminating the rivalry of the older party.

Deprived of its funds and twice deprived of its quarters and belongings, the right-wing or SR Executive Committee managed to keep alive for several more months. It engaged in no significant activity, though it did attempt to propagate the idea of resurrection of the Constituent Assembly. Part of its membership followed the Soviet government to Moscow, the rest dispersed to the provinces. It was, therefore, already falling to pieces. In the spring of 1918 it ceased to exist. So ended the SR or right-wing branch of the peasant soviet organization.[215]

The Left SR branch had ended with the fusion of the urban and rural soviets at the Third or January Congress. The left-wing Executive Committee had convened its congress on January 14, only on that same day to merge with the congress of workers' and soldiers' soviets. This step, inevitable in any event, becomes more readily understandable in the light of the Bolshevik claim that half of the 422 delegates to the left-wing peasants' congress were members of that party (163) or sympathizers with it (48). It is a little bit suspicious that these added up to exactly half the total number of delegates, as is also the circumstance that the Bolsheviks as early as January of 1918 should have pulled up to parity with the Left SR's in a peasants' congress. Perhaps Bolshevik delegates got through more easily to Petersburg, or were more easily provided with mandates, or perhaps the change-over of the soldiers from the extremist Populist to the extremist Marxist party was taking place more rapidly than the correlation of strength at the Second or December Congress would suggest. In any event the Left SR's were in no position to withstand Sverdlov's motion for a merger, even if they had not been impelled by other considerations to agree to it. And so what was in effect half of an All-Russian peasants' congress with a large Bolshevik contingent among its 400 members was swallowed up in

[214] Bykhovski, *Vserossiiskii Sovet Krest'ianskikh Deputatov*, pp. 355, 361; Rakitnikova, *Kak russkoe krest'ianstvo borolos' za Uchreditel'noe Sobranie*, p. 58.
[215] Bykhovski, *Vserossiiskii Sovet Krest'ianskikh Deputatov*, p. 362.

a congress of urban and army soviets more than twice its size with a strong Bolshevik majority.[216] The more articulate character of the urban population is graphically represented in these figures. Manifestly, neither the Left SR's nor the class they represented were going to enjoy parity at the base of Soviet power, and in the new Executive Committee for the combined soviets, 160 of the 306 members were Bolsheviks and 125 Left SR's.

The disadvantage of the Left SR's manifested itself even in relation to the formal law of land socialization presented by their commissar of agriculture, A. L. Kolegaev. The soviet congress was not exclusively an extremist affair; small numbers of SR's and Mensheviks were also present. The SR Central Committee elected in December had rescinded the boycottist tactics practiced in October and enjoined participation in the soviets in an effort to get them back on the "right path" as soon as the toilers began to be disillusioned in Bolshevik promises.[217] But the SR's had a long way to go to recover even a measure of their former influence in the soviets. At the beginning of the Third Congress only sixteen of them were present; after fusion with the peasants' congress the figure rose to twenty-seven; and at the end it reached forty-three.[218] Marching as always

[216] There were 1,046 delegates. Neither the figures on party allegiance nor the minutes of this congress have been preserved. See Lenin, *Sochineniia* (2d ed.), XXII, 601, n. 92.

[217] Instructions of the Central Committee of the PSR, January 17, 1918, to _____ Committee of the PSR (manuscript of four pages in possession of Boris Nikolaevski); see also Rakitnikova, *Kak russkoe krest'ianstvo borolos' za Uchreditel'noe Sobranie*, pp. 58-59; Chernov, manuscript commentary on the minutes of the Central Committee, pp. 82-83. Following dissolution of the assembly, the SR press, when it could appear, summoned the workers to demand the reelection of the Petersburg Soviet (*Delo Naroda*, No. 5 [January 12, 1918]). The Fifteenth Petersburg SR Conference decreed a struggle to reintroduce democracy into the soviets through securing proper representation in these organs. See *Delo Naroda*, No. 4 (new series) (March 26 [N.S.], 1918).

[218] *Partiinyia Izvestiia*, No. 6 (March 8/21, 1918), p. 55. These were SR's of the center and right—probably the best description would be SR's of the center in captivity to the right. There were four kinds of SR's at the congress: these two, the Left SR's, and the SR Maximalists. Of the 306 seats in the new Executive Committee, 125 went to the Left SR's, 7 went to the regular SR's (i.e., of the center and right, called always "right SR's" in Soviet sources), and 7 to the SR Maximalists. There is a distinction, often ignored in literature of the revolution, between Left SR's and SR Maximalists; the latter verged close to the anarchists. Although several of the more prominent Mensheviks attended this congress, no SR of consequence was there. By this time, if not

in closed ranks with the Mensheviks, there were enough of them on hand to cause trouble. They decided to break the Soviet spear at its most vulnerable spot—where the proletarian spearhead fits on to the peasant shaft—by forcing debate on the measure for land socialization. Sverdlov blocked this maneuver by having the congress accept the law in principle without debate and referring the details to the presidium and the peasants' section of the congress for later submission to the new Executive Committee. The Left SR's evidently assented to this shrewd method of shutting off debate if only because their hated rivals favored the opposite course. They gave further ground in committee, where the Bolsheviks secured preferential treatment for the agricultural laborers or hired hands (*batraki*), weighted the scales in favor of collective use of the land, and deprived the zemstvos and land committees of their functions, vesting administration of the land fund exclusively in the soviets.[219]

The Left SR's could not wage war on two fronts, and if a choice had to be made, then better to yield to the Bolsheviks than to be forced into any kind of common action with the pro-war zealots who in effect dominated the old party. The evil fruits of the schism were now apparent: the split in the party had entailed a split in the peasant movement, reducing both segments to impotence and making it impossible for the SR's to muster behind the Constituent Assembly more than paper support or for the Left SR's to defend either their own or the peasants' interests in the face of their ally's relentless drive toward the goal of a proletarian dictatorship in a peasant land. When the Left SR's surrendered the independence of the peasants' soviets, they surrendered whatever base of power they possessed. They had called on their ally for help in the fight over the family house. The help had been given and the SR's were out

---

before, the SR's were much more counterrevolutionary, at least in the October sense, than the Mensheviks.

[219] On the Third Congress see *Istoriia grazhdanskoi voiny v SSSR*, III, 94–100, especially 98–99; T. Remezova, "III Vserossiiskii s"ezd sovetov 10–18 (23–31) ianvaria 1918 g." (The Third All-Russian Congress of Soviets, January 10–18 [23–31], 1918), *Istoricheskii Zhurnal*, XII (December, 1937), 16–28; Lenin, *Sochineniia* (2d ed.), XXII, *passim*, especially p. 601, n. 92. It is regrettable that the issues of the Left SR organ, the *Znamia Truda*, are not available for this period. Bykhovski does not deal with the Left SR congress—only bare mention of it is made in his *Vserossiiskii Sovet Krest'ianskikh Deputatov*, p. 362.

in the cold, but the Left SR's got only the back room, while the ally had the rest of the house. Yet the two sets of snarling SR's never thought of composing their quarrel—too much moral indignation had been mixed in with the political differences. Relations had been embittered to the point of a blood feud as the Left SR's proclaimed their intent of breaking forever with the "pseudo-socialists" and warring to the knife on the "rotten hierarchy" of the PSR.[220]

Efforts to stir up active support in the provinces for the Constituent Assembly met with no greater success than at the apex of the peasant structure. Information is exceedingly meager and based for the most part on prejudiced sources, but the conclusion is inescapable that the Russian peasantry had no particular reaction to the dissolution of the Constituent Assembly. Even in Perm province, where the SR's had received a massive vote, attempts to foment uprisings or organize strikes of protest seem to have been confined to the towns, to agitation among white-collar workers and public employees in Ekaterinburg, Verkhoture, and Shadrinsk.[221] In Mogilev province, scene of another electoral triumph, a body which the Soviet press called the Fourth Provincial Peasants' Congress approved the act of dissolution and favored the creation of a new constituent assembly out of the Third All-Russian Soviet Congress and the left part of the old [222]—an example of the bridge-building technique of the Bolsheviks in spanning the gap between institutions based on universal suffrage and those resting on a frankly class basis. But this congress may have been an *ad hoc* improvisation of the Bolsheviks instead of a bona fide peasants' congress.[223]

We are better informed regarding Kazan province. It was, of course, a Left SR stronghold and had been all along—that is to say, a mass of nonpartisan peasants followed a Populist intelligentsia which for some reason was here predominantly leftist in tone. But the idea of the Constituent Assembly had been quite popular in Kazan province, and its dissolution had come as a surprise, especially since no agitation had been conducted against it. Yet the Fourth

---

[220] "Pochemu my ushli?" (Why Did We Walk Out?), in *Vokrug Uchreditel'nago Sobraniia*, p. 44.

[221] *Rabochii klass Urala v gody voiny i revoliutsii*, III, 7–8.

[222] *Pravda*, No. 17 (January 23 [N.S.], 1918).

[223] See cautioning statement above, p. 432, n. 176.

Provincial Peasants' Congress there, a fully democratic body of 700 delegates that was convened in March of 1918, refused to defend it. No pressure on this mass was feasible. Moreover, the debate was open and two-sided, with the Left SR spokesmen (Maiorov, Sukhanov, Mokhov, and others) opposed by G. A. Martiushin, a pillar of the old right-wing All-Russian Executive Committee and a man of peasant background from Chistopol volost. Martiushin delivered a speech warmly defending the Constituent Assembly. It had no effect whatever. As one man the 700 peasant delegates adopted a resolution that ran as follows:

In view of the fact that the phase of the revolution which Russia is now passing through [March, 1918] represents a higher stage than the one in which the idea of an all-national, classless Constituent Assembly prevailed, new elections to the Constituent Assembly as well as convocation of the old and now defunct assembly are to be considered unnecessary, and efforts to convoke such an assembly, from whatever quarter they may emanate, are to be considered a counterrevolutionary action.[224]

For some reason, perhaps through absenteeism or misrepresentation at the polls, the zemstvos in this radical stronghold had fallen into the hands of the right SR's and their liberal allies, and so resembled miniature constituent assemblies which served as rallying points for elements opposed to the October order. They had entered into conflict with the soviets, and this dualism, in the absence of directives from the center, the peasants' congress now determined to end. On its own initiative it decreed the dissolution of the zemstvos, transferred their economic functions to the peasants' soviets, and established the political monopoly of the latter, except for the town soviets, which were still separate in this province in line with the original agreement at the time of the October Revolution by which the Bolsheviks took the towns and the Left SR's the villages.[225]

Going farther down the Volga, we come to the provinces of Samara and Saratov, the old stamping grounds of the Socialist Revolutionaries, where they already were thinking of staging a comeback

[224] K. Shnurovski, "Kazanskii Sovet Krest'ianskikh Deputatov i levye es-ery pered chekhami" (The Kazan Soviet of Peasants' Deputies and the Left SR's before the Czechs Came), in *Bor'ba za Kazan'*, I, 62.

[225] *Ibid.*, pp. 61–64.

and actually would make their bid for power in the summer of 1918. The Soviet archives contain a document purporting to show that the Fifth Peasants' Congress of Samara Province, held in January of 1918, favored the dissolution of the Constituent Assembly.[226] Now the SR's were hard pressed everywhere, but their fortunes had not yet sunk so low that the Samara kulaks would be applauding the death of the Constituent Assembly. Almost certainly this was not an authentic peasants' congress convened in the regular manner but a spurious gathering put together by the Bolsheviks to create the semblance of peasant assent and to produce delegates for themselves at the left-wing All-Russian peasants' congress, which, it will be remembered, rather surprisingly consisted half of Bolsheviks. Samara was unquestionably still an SR province.

The SR's thought of themselves as even stronger in Saratov province. Its peasant organizations, numerous and militant in spirit, as well as its geographical position made it a natural choice for a base of operations.[227] Yet essentially nothing happened there—no uprising nor even a spasm in answer to the assembly's dissolution. A Bolshevik observer describes class reactions in this province with essential accuracy when he says that the workers greeted the failure of the class enemy's latest attempt to regain power, the soldiers rejoiced at the downfall of an SR majority suspected of desiring to bring back Kerenski, while only the peasantry showed any displeasure—since it already had the land, however, it did not lift a finger to save the assembly.[228] An SR leader assigns weight to disgruntlement among the Saratov peasants over the electoral system, which condemned them to vote for a party list studded with names that meant little to them, instead of for candidates of their own choosing in whom they had confidence and whose mandates they would have known how to defend.[229] Yet it may be doubted whether closer personal ties between deputies and constituents would materially have altered the situation.

[226] "K dvadtsatiletiiu III Vserossiiskogo s"ezda Sovetov" (On the Twentieth Anniversary of the Third All-Russian Congress of Soviets), in *Krasnyi Arkhiv*, LXXXV (VI, 1937), 28.

[227] *Pravda*, Nos. 141, 142 (June 28, 29, 1922) (testimony of Timofeev, Altovski, and Donskoi).

[228] Antonov-Saratovski, *Pod stiagom proletarskoi bor'by*, I, 238.

[229] Minor, "Odin den' Uchreditel'nago Sobraniia," in *Perezhitoe*, I, 133–34.

Neither in Saratov province nor elsewhere did the Russian peasantry rise in defense of the Constituent Assembly. A leading nonsocialist newspaper has observed that it was idle to expect a defense of the assembly's prerogatives from voters who in some places did not know the difference between a Bolshevik and a Kadet.[230] It is possible, however, that in this judgment we encounter less the ignorance of the Russian electorate than the snobbishness of the Russian intelligentsia, which was not least among the factors accounting for the debacle of the Provisional Government. Russia is not Abyssinia, as a lady once remarked to the author, and there were many peasants who could distinguish between Bolshevism and Constitutional Democracy, certainly enough to enlighten the others. Bykhovski has explained the failure of the peasants to react to the dissolution of the Constituent Assembly. Let us listen to his words.

First, the principle of democracy meant far less to the Russian peasant than to the intellectual. Elements of democracy were not wanting in the village, but the peasant simply could not grasp the essence of the conflict between the Constituent Assembly and the soviets—even at the right-wing congress, voices were heard asking why the rival organs could not work together, since both favored giving land to the peasants. Political rights were an abstraction, possession of the land was everything. Here, Bykhovski is only confirming in other words Durnovo's masterful analysis of Russian society, written on the eve of the war. Second, there was the all-pervasive influence of the soldiery, now streaming home from the trenches in which for months it had been held with growing exasperation while being told that nothing could be done before the Constituent Assembly, itself a vision that was becoming a mirage through chronic delay. This circumstance had bred irritation at the assembly and a strong predilection for the soviets, so that when the soldiers returned to the village they assured the peasants that they could get more from the soviets, unencumbered as these were by the presence of the bourgeoisie. Third, the peasants already had the land, thanks to their own seizures, confirmed by the Soviet decree of October 26 with the addition of the landowners' livestock and farm equipment,

---

[230] "Rospusk Uchreditel'nago Sobraniia" (Dissolution of the Constituent Assembly), *Russkiia Vedomosti*, No. 4 (January 11, 1918).

which they had then hastened to take over. They still desired a clearer title and regulations insuring equalized distribution but they were gaining confidence through the demonstrated weakness of the class enemy and felt that in a pinch "we ourselves can level." And, finally, with the satisfaction of their demands in the absence of laws enacted by the assembly, the peasants reverted to their habitual passivity, out of which they could be roused only by something more drastic than the suffocation of the ill-fated assembly. There was simply no reason as yet for them to struggle against the Soviet government.[231]

From this passivity the Socialist Revolutionaries never succeeded in stirring the peasants. The fate of the Constituent Assembly had convinced the SR's, according to their most authoritative spokesman, of the need for armed overthrow of the Soviet regime and henceforth all their energies were directed to this end.[232] Actually, the SR's never ceased working for its overthrow, from the days of Kerenski's Cossack band at Gatchina to the final catastrophe at the hands of Kolchak, and always with strength borrowed from someone else, since they had so little of their own. Only its exclusively military character distinguished their work after the Constituent Assembly from that of the preceding period, with attention centered on intelligence activities, formation of cells, infiltration of the nascent Red Army, and so on. From all accounts little was accomplished.[233] The mass desertion of the PSR by the soldiers imposed the severest kind of a handicap on this type of work. Zenzinov, who, with Dr. Feit, followed the affairs of anti-Bolshevik military organizations on behalf of the Central Committee from February to May, 1918, says

---

[231] *Vserossiiskii Sovet Krest'ianskikh Deputatov*, pp. 359–61. A press report, commenting on the all-pervading apathy which made it so difficult to organize the defense of the Constituent Assembly, found the explanation in Bolshevik measures which distracted public attention, in the universal craving for peace, and in the colossal drunkenness that afflicted the village, where private stills under prohibition were doing much greater harm than state-regulated distilleries. See "Vserossiiskaia apatiia" (All-Russian Apathy), *Vechernii Chas*, No. 22 (December 22, 1917).

[232] Testimony of Gotz in *Pravda*, No. 136 (June 22, 1922), and No. 171 (August 2, 1922). Here the SR chieftain reviews party policy during the whole period from October of 1917 to the Ninth Party Council in 1919.

[233] See the testimony of various members or ex-members of the PSR in *Pravda*, Nos. 130, 131, 132 (June 14, 15, 16, 1922); *Obvinitel'noe zakliuchenie*, pp. 61 ff.; Vladimirova, *God sluzhby "sotsialistov" kapitalistam*, pp. 186 ff.

there were all kinds of them, invariably shot through with provocation and characterized chiefly by their lightheadedness. In the midst of these plottings was the proto-Fascist Savinkov, with whom the SR's maintained relations, though only of an "informational" character.[234]

The type of work in which it was now engaged forced a transformation in the character of the party, from a mass organization to a small clandestine society, through the liquidation of its visible assets, chiefly its large printing press, and acceptance of an underground existence.[235] The party was reverting to form as it had been in tsarist times. But for these sacrifices it had little to show. The officers' group around General Verkhovski, which it might call its own or at least consider trustworthy from the democratic standpoint, numbered only about a hundred, whereas the monarchist group under General Suvorov numbered a thousand.[236] But the SR's could no more escape dependence upon such organizations than upon the spiritual home of too many Populist intellectuals—the French Republic. Weak in numbers and without money, the SR's came to accept money from the Allies, either directly or indirectly through the Union of Regeneration, and to accept or even solicit Allied intervention on condition that Russia's sovereignty be respected.[237] Their concept of grand strategy took the form of a siege and the gradual constriction of Soviet Russia by outlying regional "democratic" regimes drawing encouragement—and more than encouragement—from the Allies. How they expected the heterogeneous borderlands to coalesce against the homogeneous center is one of the mysteries of SR thought.[238]

By May of 1918 trouble was banking up for the Bolsheviks in the

[234] Interview with Zenzinov in Paris (September, 1935).

[235] Chernov, manuscript commentary on the minutes of the Central Committee, p. 91.

[236] *Pravda*, No. 136 (June 22, 1922).

[237] See testimony at the SR trial in the summer of 1922 in the columns of *Pravda* and *Izvestiia, passim.* Timofeev denied that the party got money from the Allies, but witnesses affirmed the contrary. It is certain that SR's received funds indirectly, and probable that they received them directly. Japan was not in the charmed circle of "friends"—her intervention was not favored. And it seems that the SR's heroically mustered a faint suspicion of French disinterestedness, for they preferred that the main force be American.

[238] Testimony of Timofeev, citing a circular of the Central Committee to this effect at the end of January, 1918, in *Pravda*, No. 149 (July 7, 1922); Chernov, manuscript commentary on the minutes of the Central Committee, p. 91.

east, and the SR's, stung to fury by the Treaty of Brest Litovsk, directed all of their meager forces to the Volga.[239] The Constituent Assembly, it seemed, might at last find a place of refuge. But even in their home territory, it was not really to be their show. They had planned to have the flame go up in Saratov province; it was ignited in Samara province, and not by their modest force of somewhat over 500 men but by the Czechoslovak Legion, unexpectedly, and with the party forces not yet in position.[240] The committees of the poor, the food detachments and grain requisitions of the Soviet regime had alienated the peasantry, and at first it seemed that the SR's might succeed in grounding their Committee of the Constituent Assembly (Komuch) upon a broad popular base, but they ruined everything by decreeing the reestablishment of the Eastern Front and subjecting the peasants to the recruitment and training techniques of an officers' organization with a mentality not too different from that of Alexander III. The excesses of the Bolsheviks were counterbalanced by the war craze of the Socialist Revolutionaries. Once again, they had failed to stand on their own feet, once again they had turned to the shades of the past, and once again they would be beaten into the dust, never to rise again.[241]

The Constituent Assembly is a sad episode in Russian history. With it to the grave went whatever hope there was for self-government in Russia, for an outcome to the revolution that would have meant less glory for Russia but more repose for the rest of the world, less consideration for colonial peoples but more tranquillity for individuals in Western lands. Responsibility for the failure is generally attributed either to the dastardliness of the Bolsheviks or to the pusillanimity of the SR's. Yet in one sense the Bolsheviks were only the executors of fate and the Socialist Revolutionaries its hapless victims. The grave had been prepared long before, by the whole course of Russian history, by the evolution of Russian society, and more immediately by the accursed war and the invincible wrong-

---

[239] Interview with Zenzinov in Paris (September, 1935).

[240] Testimony of Timofeev in *Pravda*, No. 141 (June 28, 1922); testimony of Rakov in *ibid.*, No. 172 (August 3, 1922); Garmiza, "Iz istorii Samarskoi uchredilki," *Istoricheskii Zhurnal*, VIII (August, 1940), 35.

[241] For a merciless exposé of their regime by one who worked with them, see Maiski, *Demokraticheskaia kontr-revoliutsiia*.

headedness of the Provisional Government, which had refused either to try to give the Russian people what they wanted or to make way in time for the body which could perhaps have legislated on their behalf with a measure of success. When Kerenski deferred to the Constitutional Democrats, the right SR's to Kerenski, and the center SR's to the right SR's, these people were compromising more than their own future: they were cutting down the stalk of the February Revolution, on which the Constituent Assembly was to have been the fairest flower.

IX

The True Face of the SR's

It is hard to see how the All-Russian Constituent Assembly could have been a success even if the Bolsheviks had not so abruptly ended its life after a single session. The image of the assembly that has gone down in history is that of a body with a solid SR majority, the product of a decisive triumph at the polls. It is a false image. For many years the basic study of the election was that of the SR specialist N. V. Sviatitski, and Sviatitski gave Populism 57 percent of the vote and about the same proportion of seats in the assembly.[1] Yet one need look only a little more closely at what Sviatitski has done and one will find that instead of a solid phalanx of 400 seats, only 299 are claimed for his party, while 81 go to the Ukrainian Socialist Revolutionaries and 19 to smaller SR national groups— Moslem, Chuvash, Moldavian, and Buriat.[2] It is these hundred deputies from dissident nationalities that are so important in any speculation about what might have been. Enough has been said in the foregoing study to show how meaningless it is to lump Ukrainian and Moslem with Russian SR's, not only because the parties were separate organizations but also because they had been feuding throughout 1917 over the question of sovereignty and were divided on other matters as well, above all the question of war and peace. Ukrainian and Moslem SR's did not share the antipathy for Germans, Turks, Magyars, and Finns or the adulation of France and of Slavdom that is the distilled essence of right-wing Populism, certainly by 1917 if not before. The excess of nationalism that cursed all segments of Populism save those that were truly social revolutionary had imposed divergent friendships and antagonisms, and in the end had caused the Populists to turn upon one another. It is not excluded, though by no means is it certain, that the national SR groups

[1] *Kogo russkii narod izbral svoimi predstaviteliami?*, p. 5.
[2] *Ibid.*, pp. 10–11.

could have found a common tongue with the Chernov faction, but the domination of the right wing within the assembly meant that no agreement was possible.

Another consideration to be borne in mind is that in twelve districts the election never came off. Two of these were in the North Caucasus (the Kuban-Black Sea[3] and Terek-Dagestan areas) and ten in Central Asia. Eighty-six seats were thus left vacant,[4] or 81, if we accept the 5 deputies from Fergana listed in a Soviet source despite its assurance that no election was held in that district.[5] Of these seats that were never filled, some would have gone to the SR's, as in the Kuban Region (though here, presumably, the Ukrainian SR's would also have claimed a share), but the bulk of them would have gone to Moslem nationalists in the homeland of the Turks.

Then there are the deputies who were elected but lost in the shuffle, their names not inscribed on the rolls and their partisan affiliation a matter of inference from less direct evidence. Soviet research places the total number of seats in the assembly at about 815; Sviatitski gives the exact figure of 817.[6] As the most complete list[7] carries only 707 names (including the five from Fergana), adding the residue of 81 vacant seats to obtain a total of 788 would still leave 27 to 29 deputies to be accounted for. Apparently they were from Podolia and Volynia, districts from which no names are listed but which had been allotted 29 representatives. Nearly all of these would have been Ukrainian SR's.[8]

The final make-up of the Constituent Assembly, therefore, cannot be determined with exactitude since here and there an estimate must be made. But in the caricature assembly that convened on

---

[3] Only in the town of Ekaterinodar is the election said to have taken place—in February of 1918, a month after the death of the assembly. See *Vserossiiskoe Uchreditel'noe Sobranie*, p. 115.

[4] See list of districts with number of seats allotted to each in *ibid.*, p. 142.

[5] See my book, *The Election to the Russian Constituent Assembly*, p. 19, n. 14. Of the five, one was a very radical SR, V. A. Chaikin, and four were Moslems.

[6] *Kogo russkii narod izbral svoimi predstaviteliami?*, p. 10.

[7] In the Soviet study, *Vserossiiskoe Uchreditel'noe Sobranie*, pp. 116–38.

[8] Sviatitski reports 9 USR's and 1 Pole as elected from Volynia. He had no information of any kind concerning Podolia. See his *Itogi vyborov vo Vserossiiskoe Uchreditel'noe Sobranie*, p. 38, and the tables; see also his article, "Itogi vyborov vo Vserossiiskoe Uchreditel'noe Sobranie," in *God russkoi revoliutsii*, pp. 106, 108–9.

January 5, 1918, and died the next day, the test of strength between Chernov and Spiridonova had not involved even half the membership. The third largest political organization in the country had so little regard for the assembly that its deputies did not even make an appearance. If the prospects had been more favorable and the sovereignty of the assembly more generally respected, it is reasonable to assume that the full membership would have been elected and present. In that case the struggle for mastery between the SR's and their allies and the social and national opposition would have been desperately close with the issue in doubt. The Bolsheviks and the Left SR's held 215 places (175 plus 40).[9] If we assume that 60 of the 86 seats in Central Asia and the North Caucasus would have gone to the Moslems (and it might have been more), then the Ukrainian and Moslem nationalities would have had at a minimum 185 seats in the assembly.[10] That would have meant a powerful if negative bloc of 400 votes arrayed against the sway of the right SR's, against their inevitable attempt to encompass federalism within narrow limits, and against their foreign policy.

On the other side, guarding the integrity of the Russian empire with all its non-Russian territory, would have been the 299 deputies whom Sviatitski counts for his party, plus all 26 of the remaining un-

[9] *Vserossiiskoe Uchreditel'noe Sobranie*, p. 115.

[10] For the Moslems, 60 plus the 25 elected elsewhere on nationalist lists, according to my reckoning (Sviatitski assigns them 28), plus 7 Moslem SR's (8 according to Sviatitski)—a total of 92 deputies. For the Ukrainians, the 81 USR's and 2 USD's found by Sviatitski, whose figures check out correctly but do not include Podolia province. Subsequent research by this author (see *The Election to the Russian Constituent Assembly*, p. 5, n. 13) unearthed substantial though still incomplete returns for the district in question. Of 830,260 votes, the USR's had 656,116, or enough to have given them about 10 seats in the assembly. Actually, the way the vote was running indicates that the Jews would have secured at most 2 seats and the Poles 1, leaving the USR's with 16 of the 19 seats. But since this involves an estimate, and since the fate of the assembly apparently prevented the compilation of definitive returns, I will give them only the 10 seats they were certain to have. Accordingly, 93 Ukrainian seats and 92 Moslem, for a total of 185. It might well have been more. The two groups had a joint list in Saratov province which attracted 53,000 votes with Kamyshin *uezd* missing. One of the 15 seats here may have been theirs, although it seems to have been assigned in the reigning confusion to the SR's. Besides the prospective six or more additional seats in Podolia province, the USR's might have picked up one more in Kiev and several in the Kuban-Black Sea Region, and the Moslems likewise might have exceeded my conservative estimate. In fact, it is quite possible that the enemies of the right SR's might even have had a majority in the full assembly.

filled seats, which we will allow them, almost certainly with an excess of generosity.[11] To these 325 SR deputies should be added their natural allies, the 10 Armenians and 2 Popular Socialists. Then would come the resurrected Kerenski coalition with 18 Mensheviks and 15 Constitutional Democrats, all that these pillars of the Russian state would have been able to contribute. Thus the strength of the SR's with their traditional allies would reach the figure of 370, still thirty votes short of the opposition and thirty-nine short of a one-vote majority in a Constituent Assembly that would really have been All-Russian. Of the remaining 47 places, 38 were claimed by small groups of whom the Cossacks with 15 were the most sizable. The two rightists elected to the assembly, Sergius, Archbishop of Nizhni Novgorod, and a solitary landowner from Poltava province, would have made common cause with the Cossacks. There were five Jewish nationalists, four Esths, one Lett,[12] and the Pole from Volynia. There were three Chuvash SR's from Kazan, five Moldavian SR's from Bessarabia, one Buriat and one Cossack SR from eastern Siberia. How these little groups would have gone is a matter of conjecture, probably some one way and some the other,[13] but they would all have had to go with the SR's for these to have even a chance of controlling the assembly. Finally, there were the remaining nine deputies from Podolia, most likely six or seven Ukrainian SR's, one or two Jews, and one Pole.

If every other group or individual in the assembly had supported the SR's, they would have had 411 or 410 votes against 406 or 407 for those who would have countered their unannounced policies on peace and the structure of state. And if men who called themselves socialists and revolutionaries had dispensed with the services of the archbishop and the landowner from Poltava, they at best would have controlled the assembly by a margin of one vote. But one can-

[11] The USR's, as stated, might have been expected to have some success in the Kuban–Black Sea Region, and the Bolsheviks in the cities and garrisons of Central Asia, while the Moslems might have won more than 60 seats.

[12] German military occupation of Courland and of the Riga district in Livonia meant no election in the most populous part of Latvia; Lithuania also was occupied.

[13] The Chuvash SR's came from a province where even the Moslem SR's leaned to the left. Sviatitski himself concedes one Moldavian SR to the left. See his list of 282 SR deputies in "Fraktsiia P. S.-R. Uchreditel'nago Sobraniia," *Partiinyia Izvestiia*, No. 5 (January 20, 1918), pp. 32–36.

not figure that closely. Besides the several estimates in our calculations, the list itself is not free of error in that sometimes it contains
more names from a certain district than there were seats allotted (for
example, the Transcaucasus) and at other times does not give enough
names to fill the quota (for example, Bessarabia). Even if one were
in the Archives of the October Revolution with all the materials at
his disposal, incomplete returns would still thwart his quest for accuracy. It is possible that the SR's might have put together a somewhat larger majority. It is equally possible that no combination
they could have devised would have given them any kind of
majority.

Whatever the margin might have been, whether by a hair or the
breadth of a little finger, the basic facts are clear. Just over a fourth
of the assembly was claimed by the Soviet coalition—Bolsheviks and
Left SR's. Just under a fourth consisted of representatives of the
two great dissident nationalities, Ukrainian and Turko-Tatar, together with minor Moslem groups (Bashkirs, peoples of Dagestan,
and so on). And the coalition behind the Provisional Government—
Constitutional Democrats, Mensheviks, SR's, and Popular Socialists,
to name the components in the order of their importance—with
everything else in the assembly had about half of the total number
of seats. It will be claimed that nothing held together the opposition
to the traditional conception of Russian patriotism. It is perfectly
true that there was little in common between Nicholas Bukharin or
Maria Spiridonova and Simon Petliura or a bigoted Moslem from
Central Asia. But there was a negative bond, pronounced and powerful, of sharing neither the fervor for war nor the phobia against
Turks and Germans nor the infatuation for a Russia one and indivisible, or at least for an undiminished Russian empire, which
linked the dominant right-wing Populist intelligentsia with the last
phase of tsarist diplomacy and the Constitutional Democratic Party.

On the SR side, also, there would have been no monolithic structure. The arithmetic of the assembly leaves no doubt that the SR's
would have needed not only the Kadets but also the Cossacks and,
while the right SR's were fully equal to collaborating with both,
they could not have done so without serious dissension in their own
caucus. If there were no limits to the subservience of V. M. Chernov,

the same was not true of the left-unionist faction, centering in the Tomsk delegation with scattered support elsewhere, and this element would likely have flown off on the left at the prospect of having to work with the Cossacks or even with the Kadets. The right SR's would thus have lost on one flank what they gained on the other. The correspondent of the *Russkiia Vedomosti* had something like this in mind when he wrote of the possibility of the SR delegation's disintegrating into two or even three parts.[14] Trouble would also have arisen with the peasant members of the delegation, who were determined to have a sweeping, egalitarian land reform and who had imposed their will on the right SR's in the caucus.[15] Then there were the Mensheviks, all eighteen of them, fourteen of whom came from Georgia. The Menshevik role in the assembly would likely have been different from what it had been in the Russian soviets in 1917, for Irakli Tsereteli, architect of soviet support of the Provisional Government until the extremist upheaval, was not boss in his native land. He was overshadowed by Noah Zhordaniia, the patriarch of Georgian Menshevism, who had been quarreling with the SR's in 1917 [16] and who would likely have insisted in 1918 upon some real federalism, less because of Social Democratic theory than because of Georgian nationalism. With Zhordaniia holding sway in the Transcaucasus and Dan on the All-Russian scene, the Mensheviks might no longer have been content to follow the Kadets around, hat in hand, as in the palmy days of Tsereteli's ascendancy. Only the negative bond of antipathy for Turkey would have held the Armenian Dashnaktsutiun and the Kadets together, and not even that would have availed to induce the touching spectacle of Judeo-Cossack collaboration. If the enemies of the right SR's had no bond of union except the negation of what the right SR's stood for, there was no excess of the spirit of positive achievement on the other side: the SR crazy-quilt coalition could at any moment have come loose at the seams—assuming that, in the first place, it could have been stitched together.

With such weaknesses on either side and with voting strength so

[14] See p. 357.   [15] See ch. 6.
[16] See, for example, *The Agrarian Foes of Bolshevism*, pp. 347–48. See also above, p. 190.

evenly balanced, there is the possibility or even the likelihood that
the assembly would have proved unworkable. At best it could have
drafted for Russia a constitution in general terms. To have attempted
more would have been to invite a breakdown. And the breakdown
would have come over the question of executive power. The right
SR's were as determined not to leave this power in the hands of the
Bolsheviks as the partisans of the soviet order were determined not
to brook interference from the assembly. The right SR's had been
maneuvering in caucus to lodge the executive power in the hands of
someone cast in their own image—if not Kerenski or Avksentiev
personally, then at least some other choice of like views. They could
cherish the illusion of success only because of their distorted conception of the assembly arising out of the absence of half the membership. It is clear that the full assembly would never have elected
Kerenski or Avksentiev premier, that it would never have restored
the Provisional Government to power. To have won any support
among the Ukrainians and Tatars and to have kept their own party
ranks intact, the dominant right SR clique would have had to put
up Chernov, and it is possible, in this author's opinion, that they
made him presiding officer—aside from the tactical reasons already
examined—just to remove him from consideration for a more responsible position, even as in 1917 they may well have designated
him minister of agriculture in order to shut him up on the war. Only
in desperation would they have made such a choice, and our whole
line of argument in considering what might have been is predicated
upon the assumption that the assembly would have had a fair chance
of life. Yet even if the right SR's could have brought themselves to
take the bitter medicine, there is nothing in Chernov's record as a
party leader to suggest that he could have succeeded on a wider
stage. He would either have incurred the wrath of his right-wing
colleagues or, more probably, have continued his long record of
subservience to them at the expense of forfeiting whatever support
he might have enlisted on the left or among the dissident nationalities.
In any event the fateful question of the executive power would
sooner or later have disrupted the assembly. In striving to erect the
assembly into a governing as well as a constituent body the SR's
were displaying their customary utopian approach to a problem.

Hence in dissolving the Constituent Assembly, Lenin was putting an end to a body that would likely have fallen of its own weight. But he was scarcely destroying a nest of counterrevolution, as he and his comrades have so often proclaimed. He had hastened to strike down the specter of right SR control arising out of the half assembly of January, 1918, without waiting for the full assembly to convene. In such an assembly, with all members elected and present, there would have been a majority for peace and one for recasting the conquered empire of the tsars along lines of broad national autonomy. There would have been no majority for restoring the discredited Provisional Government. The right SR's with their contraband Kadetism would not have ruled this assembly, grossly overrepresented as they were. With all of its imperfections, chief among them this Trojan horse of counterrevolution in SR trappings, the Constituent Assembly was nevertheless an authentic expression of the hopes and hatreds of the populations residing within the Russian empire. To say that it was probably unworkable is not in the least to detract from its representative character. The Russian state was unworkable on democratic principles. It had been put together by force, without consultation of the populations within it, and could be maintained only by repressing the free interplay of divergent social and ethnic factors. The assembly was the product of this free interplay and as such it was destined to die, either from internal causes or as a result of an external blow which would have come from the right had it not come first from the left.

The opprobrium that has descended on Lenin's government because of its abrupt termination of an experiment in democracy has obscured the situation on the opposite extreme, where a sentence of death was hanging over the ill-fated assembly, as certain as Lenin's, if less immediate. The Kadets were not pleased with the outcome of the election. Naturally they were not pleased, with 15 seats out of 817. The party which had presumed to govern Russia with the aid of the right SR's behind the all too transparent screen of the Provisional Government had suddenly been illuminated in all its naked impotence. The discomfort was only partly relieved by the knowledge that it could rely on the large group of fellow travelers safely tucked away in the SR delegation behind a front of revolutionary phraseology and the indulgence of V. M. Chernov. Dimly, perhaps, yet with growing uneasiness, the Kadets realized that even this hidden support might not be enough to insure control of a body in which there were altogether too many Great Russian radicals, too many kinsmen and co-religionists of the Turks, and far too many Little Russian nationalists. So in their circles the view gained ground that if the assembly should somehow begin to function again, it should do no more than decree its own dissolution and the holding of new elections. This view found an echo in SR circles.[17] When had the right SR's failed to echo what their mentors were thinking? And the SR's of the center to defer to the right SR's? Hence it is not hard to predict the course of events if the assembly had not been dispatched by leftist hands. The more its true face was revealed, the greater would have been the revulsion in rightist circles. The Kadets would have decreed dissolution, the right SR's would have hastened to comply with their demand, V. M. Chernov would have "submitted to discipline," and the deed would have been done with the help of partisans of the soviet system. The "friends" of the Constituent Assembly were no better than its enemies.

At first glance it seems strange that the right SR's, for all of their subservience to the Kadets, would likewise have entertained the thought of a new election. In what election could they have done better, or as well, as in this one? Self-interest, if nothing else, ought to have helped them to display some independence on this occasion. Yet even before the abortive session of January 5/18, there is evidence of wavering in their ranks in respect to a last-ditch stand. The remark of Vishniak has been quoted to the effect that it was necessary to do only the most indispensable things and then disband and call a new election. Desperation in the face of the January situation might explain this attitude, and subservience to the Kadets on a later occasion, when it was a question of reviving the moribund assembly. But on both occasions, before the Bolshevik blow had fallen and afterwards, when it was a question of keeping the idea of the assembly alive, the guiding consideration in the mind of the right SR's may have been that the outcome of the first election was in reality

[17] See O. S. Minor, "Odin den' Uchreditel'nago Sobraniia," in *Perezhitoe*, I, 133-34, and especially Argunov, *Mezhdu dvumia bol'shevizmami*, pp. 4-5.

not nearly so favorable to themselves as they made it out to be, and that the assembly, if finally constituted with all members present and voting, would have escaped their control. Hence their willingness to contemplate a new election, a measure that was all the more acceptable to them since their Kadet friends had decreed it. The elevation of Chernov to the presidency had been on their part a confession of weakness, and the play for an alliance with the Ukrainian SR's, which had come to naught, pointed in the same direction. Endless reiteration of the boast that the assembly was theirs does not mean that the right SR's may not have examined the realities of the situation, only to conclude that it may not have been theirs and that it might be as little amenable to their will in matters of war and peace or of federation as it obviously was going to be in respect to the agrarian problem. Such considerations may have softened their determination to stand by the results of the November election in which they had done much better than they had any reason to expect or deserved to do.

It is remarkable that for forty years the fiction of SR control of the Constituent Assembly has remained unexploded. It is remarkable that no one has looked beyond the caricature assembly of January 5/18, 1918, to discover the true face of the All-Russian Constituent Assembly as it was supposed to be and would have been, had conditions promised life instead of death. An excursion into what might have been can be enlightening and at times even profitable. But now our excursion must end. The assembly died, not only without having constituted a new Russian order, but without having fully constituted even itself. In words so beloved by Chernov, it had withered away without ever having come to bloom. To have had a real chance of fulfilling its mission it would have had to be convened not later than August of 1917. Even then its work might have crumbled, as in the case of its counterpart in the French Revolution which had controlled the country, completed its labors, and created a new order, only to have it swept away by further tremors of a social earthquake. Yet this possibility can in no way exculpate the Provisional Government for its policy of negligence or purposeful delay. Technical difficulties are no explanation—Russia was not Abyssinia. In the last analysis, the prospects of the Constituent As-

sembly were ruined by the same combination of Kadet obduracy
and SR obsequiousness which had doomed whatever chance there
may have been for a moderate outcome of the Russian Revolution,
and all in the name of continuing a war which the Russian people
had not wanted in 1914 and were desperately determined to escape
in 1917. The Kadets had not wanted the election before the late fall,
when the front would be quiet, and late fall it was. "Late" was also
the word inscribed on the shroud of the Constituent Assembly.
It had been kept in labor so long that when the new life finally appeared the conditions necessary for its nourishment and growth had
passed away. Neither the men at the head of the Provisional Government, nor the ministers beneath them, nor the parties that kept them
in power will ever be able to explain away this least excusable of all
their mistakes.[18]

We have now to consider what basically was wrong with the
Socialist Revolutionary Party, in the heyday of its power as in the
depths of its disaster. Here was a question the SR leaders could not
ignore. In answering it, Gotz was specific.[19] Explaining the failure
on the Samara front in 1918, he attributed it to the organizational
weakness of his party in contrast to the powerful apparatus of
Bolshevism, which had enabled the latter to create an army adequate
at least for domestic purposes and police power that would have
aroused the envy of Joseph Fouché. There is some validity in Gotz's
contention, although it also betrays the shallow perception so characteristic of his kind: the SR's never tired of imputing cowardice to
the Bolsheviks in their dealings with foreign enemies, as though
everything could be done in a few years' time. Even in the courtroom on trial for his life Gotz could not restrain a sneer. Yet given
time, the same animal vigor and the same knowledge of human

[18] Bykhovski ascribes the passiveness of the population in the face of dissolution to the belatedness of the assembly (*Vserossiiskii Sovet Krest'ianskikh
Deputatov*, p. 352). And Tsereteli in his speech before the assembly conceded
that for the eight months of the Provisional Government revolutionary Russia
had been cursed by the absence of a body that would have commanded general
recognition (*Vserossiiskoe Uchreditel'noe Sobranie*, p. 49). Why, then, had he
battled at every turn to keep in power the government that had imposed this
curse?

[19] See his testimony at the SR trial in *Pravda*, No. 171 (August 2, 1922), and
in *Izvestiia*, No. 171 (August 2, 1922).

weakness which had overborne the domestic opposition would wreak havoc on foreign foes as well. The SR's were as bad prophets of the future as actors in the present. Gotz conceded that the Bolshevik Party functioned with clocklike precision [20]—a natural, if unwilling, tribute of a politician whose own party mechanism worked not at all. But he went far afield when he contended that the PSR had had no time to put together a strong organization and had been compelled to assemble its armed forces only after taking the battlefield. As Lunacharski observed, this was a ridiculous argument.[21] The SR Party was two years older than the Bolshevik, had held power for eight months before the October Revolution, and had disposed of abundant resources. If it failed to utilize them, the cause must be attributed to factors other than lack of time. Furthermore, when the SR's did assemble a force on the field of battle, it was not their own. They had forfeited their fighting strength to the Left SR's and the Bolsheviks and now could gather under their banner only rightist elements desirous of a protective coloration until it was safe to show their true colors. When that time came, these elements roughly dispensed with the services of their hosts. Hence the succession of SR debacles at Archangel, in Siberia, and on the Volga. Nowhere did they make a creditable showing because nowhere could they operate with strength of their own. Gotz's explanation does no more than scratch the surface of the problem.

Other explanations offered by prominent members of the party are equally unsatisfactory. Rakov conceded the slow pace of legislation on behalf of the peasantry but sought to excuse it on the ground of his party's concern for productive forces, which had to be left undisturbed by agrarian reform.[22] An obvious rejoinder would have been: had those forces not been disturbed by the war, about which his party had done virtually nothing? Gendelman maintained that the PSR had lost the confidence of the masses because of its refusal to make false promises.[23] But the party had made notoriously false promises in 1917—for example, it had pledged to turn the land over to the land committees, and had then let the matter go by default

---

[20] See Bukharin's reference to Gotz's testimony in *Pravda*, No. 174 (August 5, 1922).

[21] *Pravda*, No. 173 (August 4, 1922).   [22] *Ibid.*, No. 172 (August 3, 1922).
[23] *Ibid.*, No. 170 (August 1, 1922).

through unwillingness to precipitate a crisis with its partners in coalition. And at the time of the Constituent Assembly it was doing everything it could to convey the impression that it favored a speedy peace, whereas in reality it knew the chances for the only kind of peace it would accept were remote, and secretly favored continuance of the war. Furthermore, the inference in Gendelman's statement is that the Bolsheviks achieved success through false promises. But the Bolsheviks promised peace, and made peace—a bad peace, yet the only kind that was feasible. They promised land, and gave land, without by any means committing themselves always to honor the carte blanche which at first they had given the peasants. They enjoyed a freedom of maneuver unknown to their opponents because they were not democrats. But in the initial stage they fulfilled their promises, and that is more than can be said for Gendelman's party. What they did later, of course, is another story.

Such explanations as those of Gotz and Gendelman represent either self-deception or refusal to face up to the true cause of their party's disaster. The organizational weakness mentioned by Gotz undoubtedly was a source of woe, but not nearly so much as the SR record in 1917. And for that record there is one simple explanation: the PSR had ceased to be revolutionary at a time when the country was becoming so in the broadest and deepest sense of the term.

Much has been said from the Marxist side about the nonsocialist character of the PSR. Maybe it was nonsocialist, although the SR's considered themselves collectivists, but whether or not theirs was a bona fide socialist movement is not important for the purposes of an inquest. Russia was not a socialist country in 1917, and an aggregation of revolutionary democrats masquerading as socialists need not have suffered unduly. But Russia was most certainly a revolutionary country in 1917, with a backlog of unsolved problems extending into the distant past, and an aggregation of ordinary democrats masquerading as revolutionaries would sooner or later find themselves in trouble. While it may be doubted that the Socialist Revolutionary Party was socialist, it definitely was not revolutionary, and this discrepancy between its name and its essence, its claims and its actions, is the source of its misfortune. Professor M. N. Pokrovski was not unduly swayed by Bolshevik prejudice when he said at the trial in 1922 that for the whole twenty years of its existence the PSR had never been a socialist party and that it had been a revolutionary one only before 1917.[24]

On the face of it, it seems absurd to say that the PSR was not a revolutionary party. Its constituency was revolutionary, revolutionary also its organization; yet the presence on the right of a willful minority and the character of the centrist majority combined to make it a nonrevolutionary party after February and, in effect, a counterrevolutionary one after October. The metamorphosis of the right-wing Populist intelligentsia from insurrectionaries in 1905 to jaded democrats in the period between the revolutions and then to fervent patriots, partisans of the Entente, and devotees of the cult of the state with the coming of war, accounts for the character of the delegation in the Constituent Assembly, as we have seen, and constituted a ball and chain on the revolutionary initiative of the party as a whole. It was a logical transformation. Many of these intellectuals in the trough of the revolutionary movement had gone into public service or social work as civil servants in the zemstvos and municipalities or as functionaries in the cooperative societies, where the daily routine and the outlook induced were alike deadly to the revolutionary spirit. Others had entered the professions. And all were getting older. Yet they still had to embrace a cause, and since the old one no longer warmed their hearts, they took up the new one of the war, all the more easily because nationalism was the root of Populism, and with all the greater fervor because they were at pains to conceal how completely spent they were in the revolutionary sense. Why customary Russian frankness should have been so notably lacking in this instance is hard to say, but the fact is that a large segment of the Populist intelligentsia had become Kadets without admitting it. They clung to the old SR label even though the old faith was gone, aside from a residue of interest in political liberties. When these were conceded by the Provisional Government, the Populist intellectuals were satisfied and asked for nothing more, not even for the election which that regime was notoriously slow in calling. The last thing wanted by these people who continued to call themselves

[24] *Pravda*, No. 168 (July 29, 1922).

Socialist Revolutionaries was a social revolution, for it would halt the war, jeopardize their status in life, and enrage the Kadets, to whom they looked up in worshipful admiration. Asking nothing for themselves except more war and the preservation of the status quo under the Provisional Government, they were determined to keep their party from asking for anything.

Here the center played into their hands. By every test except that of will power the center should have dominated the party. But it had lost its unity because of the war, which had erected a bridge between the right and the right center over the flood of imperialism below. A right centrist like Zenzinov was a loyal adherent of the revolution and an enemy of imperialism—any brand of imperialism —but his feeling of nationalism and his dread of Germany were so strong that he could tacitly tolerate Entente imperialism without approving of it. Hence the community of feeling between the right center and the extreme right, which not only swallowed Entente imperialism but had its own particular, Pan-Slavist brand. Numerically the largest component of the PSR was probably the left center but it was so badly served by its leadership that in the party scales its weight counted for little. The left center had only Chernov, and Chernov thought only of avoiding a fight.

The Fourth Congress had ended any excuse for default of leadership on his part by placing the organization in the hands of himself and his faction. His success may have been less sweeping than he likes to depict—he claims E. M. Timofeev as a left centrist whereas Timofeev's speech on peace in the assembly was distinctly right of center in tone—but as to the displacement of strength in his favor there can be no doubt, just as there can be no excuse for his failure to use it. Not only did Chernov henceforth have the upper hand in the Central Committee but the Fourth Congress had specifically armed him with a decree subordinating the delegation in the assembly to the instructions of the Central Committee.[25] Far from making any effort to enforce this decree, he himself "submitted to discipline" by deferring to the will of the delegation's right-wing majority in an abject abdication of his responsibilities of leadership, in contradiction to his own better judgment, and in defiance of an

[25] See pp. 199, 355–56.

ordinance enacted by the highest party instance—the same instance that had placed him at the helm. Here was no respect for discipline nor consideration for unity but only human weakness carried to a point that is difficult to believe and sad to record.

As to why Chernov presented this spectacle, to his own detriment and the ruin of his party, there is no ready explanation. He obviously had no will, yet he might have been expected to have some pride. Had the right SR's so thoroughly cowed him with their defamation on the score of Zimmerwaldism that he could in no wise stand up to them? How could he, the leader of his party, bring himself to accept instructions on the way to the Constituent Assembly from M. V. Vishniak, one of his most active enemies, a member of the extreme right and a partisan of French nationalism, who could not have mustered more than a small number of votes for election to high party office outside of this warped delegation? What stick did these people hold over Chernov, that he would always fade before them? He was personally an honest man and his devotion to the revolutionary cause has never been questioned, so that apparently in his private life or public record there was nothing for them to seize upon and use as a club. At Mogilev and elsewhere we have seen that Gotz represented authority in Chernov's eyes. During the war in exile Natanson is said to have occupied that position, and before the war, in the era of the first revolution, it was Gershuni who would lock Chernov in the office when he wanted an editorial out of him, to keep him from going fishing.[26] Chernov seems to have sought out authority in order to defer to it. Always he was "submitting to discipline." One of his favorite figures of speech was the "stern stepmother" (*surovaia machikha*). Chernov had a stepmother in childhood. Whatever the explanation, the fact is incontestable. He continually abdicated in the presence of the right SR's, stepping down from the throne to which the December congress had elevated him, rather than contest it with a willful opposition. And the right SR's themselves continually abdicated in the presence of the Kadets. The process of self-effacement—we are tempted to say, the prostration tendency—ran always to the right; never was there a willingness to yield to Bolshevism, which had literally to beat this

[26] Related to the author by Zenzinov (Paris, 1935).

party into the dust to end its opposition. Seemingly it was not a matter of cowardice but of a strange perversion which found satisfaction in prostrating the revolutionary will to a weaker, nonrevolutionary source of authority.

Chernov's role in the revolution remains baffling, even after every allowance is made for the difficulties of the situation, the defects of his character, and the depths of his party patriotism. Granted that he was weak, weak to the point of self-abnegation. Granted that he underestimated the strength of Bolshevism, though less so than most of his colleagues. Granted that he sought to preserve the unity of his party and awaited with patience the verdict of the Fourth Congress, even if the country would not. Yet when the verdict had been given and the power placed in his hands, he still could not bring himself to coerce this willful minority whose course he himself had pronounced to be ruinous. No longer could he plead party patriotism for his failure to proceed against an element in the party which had dragged it athwart the course of the revolution in the name of a war that in his heart he abhorred. He found his party prostrate at the feet of a clique which long since had renounced the revolution to find a spiritual home in the Progressive Bloc of the Fourth State Duma, and he did virtually nothing to lift up his party and stand it on its own feet. It is perhaps not enough to say that he was weak. After all, he had found the strength to break with Kerenski after the Kornilov affair. Some other explanation may be needed to account for his conduct, an explanation that would lead away from the field of history into the realm of psychoanalysis. Or it may be that the answer could be found in some hidden personal relationship. In any event Chernov's position and prestige make him primarily responsible for a situation in which a revolutionary party was made to serve nonrevolutionary and even counterrevolutionary ends.

It was the misfortune of Chernov, of his party and the class it represented, that in his left-centrist faction there was nowhere to be found a strong-willed comrade who could have stiffened his backbone and led him down the path of his own choosing, since he could not move down it of his own volition. Aside from him there was not a single outstanding personality on his side of the fence (or for that matter, in the party as a whole), and Chernov himself was strictly a literary and intellectual quantity. There was, for example, the colleague from his home province of Saratov, N. I. Rakitnikov, highly respected in party circles and often honored with high party office —he placed second in the poll for Central Committeemen at the Third Congress and first at the Fourth—yet one has only to read a speech or an article by Rakitnikov to grasp the hopelessness of his leadership and the inferiority of his mind. Chernov could think clearly, but he could not act; his comrades could neither think clearly nor act—they could only feel. They had sentiments rather than convictions; they could produce words in endless quantity, but scarcely a single deed. The essence of Chernov's strategy after taking over the helm was to correct the course of the party in the sense of causing it to stand forth as a revolutionary alternative to Bolshevism in the belief that only thus could it hope to reclaim the strength it had lost. By failing to subordinate the right wing of his party to the projected course of action, he made it impossible for the party as a whole to present a new image of itself to the country. And there was no one at his side to supply the resolution which he lacked for the salvation of the policy which he had formulated. By no means the worst description of this party was given by the SR worker Usov, when he said that "at the sides there were two wings, and in the middle Chernov without wings." [27]

As a result of the default of the left center, the pattern of power existing before the Fourth Congress remained unchanged, with the nonrevolutionary wing of the party not only entrenched in the delegation to the Constituent Assembly but also making decisions of crucial importance in the organization itself, where it occupied a distinctly inferior position. Thus an SR of the far right, S. S. Maslov, continued in charge of the effort to assemble an armed force for defense of the Constituent Assembly or even for the overthrow of the Soviet government, while Gotz made the all-important decision on the night of January 4 as to whether the demonstration should be armed or unarmed.

Similarly with respect to a change of venue for the Constituent Assembly. In his private memoirs Chernov says that his party virtuously put away any thought of seeking refuge on the Don in line

[27] Quoted by Lunacharski in *Pravda*, No. 167 (July 28, 1922).

with Kaledin's offer of Cossack protection, and this version we have
followed in our account.[28] Yet in a conversation with Boris Nikolaevski some twenty years after the events in question [29] (the private
memoirs, also, must have been written a number of years later),
Chernov asserted that the Bureau of the Delegation, without in-
forming the Central Committee, had sent an emissary to the Don to
investigate the feasibility of such a step. The emissary had returned
with a favorable report, but Chernov did not know whether any
decision had been taken. Naturally he did not know. He, the leader
of the party, was not privy to decisions of grave import. In fact, he
had come into the session of the bureau at which the report was
being made and witnessed the hushing up of the emissary so that
vital information would not be divulged. Now the official representatives of the Central Committee in the Bureau of the Delegation
were Gotz and E. M. Timofeev, and Chernov says that either they
did not know about the bureau's action or were themselves in sympathy with it. Either way it was a disgraceful state of affairs and
one all too typical of this party. It also throws light on the quality
of Chernov's leadership, first, because he initiated no action to clear
up this situation, damaging to the authority of the Central Committee and humiliating to him personally, and, secondly, because he cannot escape responsibility for the choice of representatives on whom
he himself could not rely. Why had he not caused the committee to
select agents of liaison—since agents of control in keeping with the
decision of the Fourth Congress were not to be thought of under
his dispensation—who would faithfully reflect the left-centrist point
of view and certainly challenge a decision to go to the Don? Nothing came of the negotiations, it is true, more because the Don failed
the delegation than the delegation the Don, since a short time later
the prospective host committed suicide. Even the Cossacks had had
enough of war.

The willingness to take up with the Cossack chieftains reflects
the temper of the right SR's. It was no new departure, for already in
the early days of the October Revolution Gotz had been angling
for Cossack support.[30] With their stock at zero in the Russian army,

[28] See above, p. 436.
[29] The author is indebted to Nikolaevski for reading to him the notes of this
conversation (New York, June, 1959).
[30] See above, p. 87.

once the patrimony of their party, and facing the inevitable consequences of their course in 1917, these people were turning for support to the old order, even as the German Majority Socialists would do at the end of 1918. They claimed to be acting in the name of national defense. That this claim does not bring us to the heart of the matter, however, is seen in their actions after peace had returned to Europe, though not yet to Russia because of the civil war. In this struggle the right SR's evinced an unmistakable fondness for the White cause, and the other SR's did little or nothing to curb them. It is true that when E. P. Riabtsev, the SR mayor of Kiev, delivered a speech of welcome to General Denikin, he was expelled from the party.[31] But there is no evidence of disciplinary action in the case of Nezlobin, a printer by trade and a party worker in Kiev, who despite his working-class origin favored the Volunteer Army and defended it against charges of reaction with the argument that any excesses committed were born of the circumstances and were natural and transitory.[32] Whether or not the party organization reacted to such incidents, they reveal the spirit of the right SR's. Argunov took the same basic line as Nezlobin in contending that the Siberian reaction, to which his party had fallen victim and which he treated as a kind of Bolshevism in reverse, could not be compared in depth of depravity or enduring damage to the Bolshevism of the left.[33]

Another note is sounded by the Czech observer Major Kratochvíl, who implies that in the east, in the zone of operations of the Czechoslovak Legion, the SR leaders fanned the Czech antipathy for Germans and Magyars with talk of Slavic solidarity and of Bolshevik betrayal of Slavic interests.[34] And if one listens to the speech of Breshko-Breshkovskaia before the convention of the legion, one

[31] Statement made by Ivanov at the SR trial; see *Pravda*, No. 148 (July 6, 1922).

[32] Kh. Tokar, "Kievskie esery i dobrarmiia" (Kievan SR's and the Volunteer Army), *Pravda*, No. 152 (July 11, 1922). The defense was contained in a speech made on the anniversary of the army. Extracts from the *Kievskaia Zhizn'* (Kievan Life) were cited to show Nezlobin's friendliness for the White cause and his hatred of the Reds.

[33] *Mezhdu dvumia bol'shevizmami*, pp. 46–47.

[34] A. Platonov, "Chekho-slovatskii legioner ob eserakh" (A Czechoslovak Legionary on the SR's), *Izvestiia*, No. 175 (August 6, 1922), evidently referring to the passage on p. 151 of Kratochvíl's *Cesta revoluce*. Unequivocal corroboration of this point will be found in Kennan, *Soviet-American Relations*, II, 401.

hears a veritable hymn to Slavonic unity: "You are laying a broad
and firm foundation for the unification of Slavic peoples, and may
this God-given mission strengthen your spirit, your patience and
courage. Long live the unity of the Slavs!" [35] These words from one
of their authoritative spokesmen bring us close to the soul of the
right SR's. From the enthusiasm with which they served this cause,
one would think that they were only doing what the Germans and
Italians had done before. Actually they were attempting something
comparable to Latin or Teutonic unification—a task that was as
utopian as it was presumptuous.

A very clear indication of the nature of the right SR's as well as
of the illness of this party is afforded by the events in the southeastern region during the years of civil war. Here on the Kuban, as in
most parts of the country, the bulk of the membership adhered to
the center, although there was a rightist current and the organization
at Ekaterinodar, the chief town of the region, stood to the left of
center. A general party conference had elected a regional bureau
which was centrist in tone. But the right SR's were no more inhibited here by considerations of party unity than elsewhere in the
country. They set up a Southeastern Committee of Members of
the Constituent Assembly and went their own way. Overwhelmingly right SR in composition, the Southeastern Committee showed
its true colors by supporting the White cause and calling for recruits
for the Volunteer Army, against the will of the party organization
and in defiance of its instructions. These party members had laid
aside the SR label to assume a position above parties and above classes
in order to serve the interests of the Russian state, as they said, against
German aggression; yet the collapse of Imperial Germany brought
no change in their policy. They merely shifted their ground a bit
and went right ahead, posing now as their supreme objectives the
constitution of an All-Russian government and admission to the Paris
peace conference. Above all else they wished to represent Russia at

[35] "Babushka na s"ezde chekho-slovakov," *Vestnik Uchreditel'nago Sobraniia*
(Samara) (Messenger of the Constituent Assembly) (August 22, 1918). The
address is of high literary quality. The "grandmother of the revolution" (or of
the counterrevolution, according to the Bolsheviks) departed from the Pan-Slav
pattern only in cautioning her listeners that in breaking the will to domination
of other peoples, the Slavs would not wish them grief or humiliation.

the peace conference. Having inveighed on every occasion against the "shameful" Brest Litovsk Treaty, they were now desperately desirous, as a former SR leader says, of taking part in the framing of an even worse treaty.[36]

Nothing was done to bring them to heel. The representative of the Central Committee in the southeast was Eugenia Ratner, the friend of Chernov and his factional colleague. This lady viewed indulgently the conduct of the right SR's, imposing no veto on their actions and taking no steps to end the chaos in party affairs. Prominent among the right SR's were Shreider and Rudnev, the mayors of St. Petersburg and Moscow in 1917. Eugenia Ratner shielded Shreider from party censure when, as she admitted, he lent his support to the recruitment campaign of the Volunteer Army; he had merely a weakness for Alekseev as a "peasant general," she said. So the ex-mayor of Petersburg did not share the fate of the mayor of Kiev in being expelled from the party—a rare fate in this party, it must be said. Ratner attempted to defend the SR's against the charge of counterrevolution by citing the action of Ataman Krasnov in hanging the whole town council in Iuzovka (later Stalino, a city in the Donets Basin), which was exclusively SR in membership. It was not, however, so much the antediluvian views of this Don Cossack chieftain as his pro-German orientation which repelled the right SR's. Here on the Kuban in 1918 and 1919 we have the same dualism, the same working at cross purposes, and the same incapacity for setting in order the affairs of this party that we observed on the All-Russian scene in 1917. Here were recapitulated all the evils that had previously cursed the party, with Ratner in the role of Chernov. It was not a question of an immature organism being overwhelmed by the problems of war and revolution, as apologists like to claim; it was a question of a chronic disease affecting the nerve centers of the organism and paralyzing its will to action.[37]

Whenever the right SR's had been challenged on their independ-

[36] Burevoi (Sopliakov), *Raspad,* p. 130.

[37] The events in the Kuban region are sketched from the proceedings of the trial and particularly from the testimony of Gregory and Eugenia Ratner in *Pravda,* No. 149 (July 7, 1922). Gregory had turned state's evidence, but his sister was as she had been.

ent course, they had invariably raised the cry of national defense.
But legitimate fear of German imperialism was obviously not the
mainspring of their conduct, for with Germany out of the picture,
they in no way altered their tactics but continued to cleave to the
Allies abroad (and in Russia) and to the domestic bourgeoisie.
Eugenia Ratner saw them in a ceaseless quest for an "honest" bourgeoisie such as the French Revolution had produced, in blind disregard of the fact that the Russian Revolution not only was not
dominated by the bourgeoisie but was directed against it. Populist
doctrine would have told them that, but no one paid any attention
to Populist doctrine, least of all the Populists themselves. Tied to the
Allies abroad and the Kadets at home, these SR's could not have
been revolutionary even had they wanted to be, and by the end of
1917 nothing came lower on the scale of their loyalties than the
revolution. Bukharin made an effort, in line with Marxist ideology,
to explain their conduct in economic terms, asserting that no other
pseudo-revolutionary movement had so many millionaires at the top:
Zenzinov came from a family that owned extensive tea planta-
tions, Fondaminski from one engaged in the diamond trade, Rabino-
vich (Rubanovich?) from one that dealt in furs, while Gotz drew
his wealth from a commercial-industrial firm.[38] The SR leaders were
not drawn from nondescript families of the democratic intelligentsia
but from those that were at the center of the capitalist web. Hence
their attraction to the Kadets was no accidental matter but the
consequence of a community of economic interest.[39] It would be in-

[38] The SR hierarchy comprised a network of families linked by marriage. The
Gotz, Fondaminski, Vysotski, and Gavronski families were all interrelated and
all Jewish. Not long before his death Zenzinov related to the author how he
as a Gentile friend would on certain occasions perform a service for them from
which they were debarred by religious considerations. The phenomenon of
"fathers and sons," or the gulf between generations, could be observed in these
circles. The elders failed to understand the revolutionary zeal of the children
and looked upon them as "touched." For various reasons Chernov did not fit
into this setting, and so was somewhat removed from the center of things until
the Fourth Congress.
[39] *Pravda*, No. 173 (August 4, 1922). Bukharin approved Vandervelde's comparison of the SR's to the Girondins in the sense that the French party had in
reality represented the upper level of the bourgeoisie instead of the lower level
and the peasantry. The French ex-army officer Jacques Sadoul also endorsed the
comparison with the observation that just as London had made use of the
Girondins, so the SR's had become puppets of the Entente.

teresting to follow out Bukharin's line of reasoning and in particular to see what connections these businesses had with the outside world.[40] But since Bukharin did not do it, and we cannot, the matter must be left to speculation.

These men, however, were not dominant enough personalities to impress their stamp upon the right SR's as a whole, most of whom were not people of wealth and doubtlessly were motivated by other reasons in casting their lot with the Kadets. As intellectuals who had found a place in Russian society, either in the zemstvos, schools, cooperatives, or government service, they could feel their station in life endangered by the hazards of revolution. In this sense they were, indeed, motivated by economic considerations. The residue of nationalism that remained after the rest of Narodnik socialism had evaporated has been stressed throughout this study as a major influence in determining their political conduct, as has also the aspect of Pan-Slavism into which that nationalism readily passed as a result of the Slavophile heritage.

Less tangible but scarcely less important was the pro-French sentiment of these people, altogether surprising in its intensity and not to be explained solely in terms of war experience, since pro-English sentiment was so much less marked. Probably one factor was the knowledge that France as the mortal foe of Germany would give carte blanche to Pan-Slav aspirations, as England would be less apt to do because of balance of power considerations, imperialist rivalries in the Near and Middle East, and a less deep-seated antagonism toward Germany, coupled with a certain favoritism for Austria. The French Revolution had captivated the minds of Populist intellectuals, all the more so since it was a bourgeois revolution and less earth-shaking than what they faced, and the French Republic seemed much more advanced in its political life than other countries. The combination of wishful thinking and half-baked minds did not permit them to perceive that the French are not an evangelical people and that Clemenceau thought monarchy quite good enough for Russians. The hold that French culture had on these people,

[40] Members of the Vysotski family who figured in the party record for 1917 were not pro-war and adhered to the Chernov faction. And one of the Gavronskis had returned from exile through Germany.

however, must have had more than a political explanation—something in the educational environment, perhaps the greater ease of learning the language, or some more intangible factor that is hard to fix upon but harder to deny.[41] The author does not know of a single exception to the rule that a right SR was pro-French and Pan-Slav in sentiment. As though with uneasy consciences for having turned away from the revolution while still styling themselves revolutionists, the right SR's threw themselves with abandonment into a curious sort of nationalism which combined continued sacrifice on the part of the Russian people with unquestioning loyalty to France and fulsome friendship for all segments of Slavdom except the Little Russians.

These were the people who dominated the destinies of their movement. Yet they were only a minority, even a small minority, as every record of that movement shows. But they had a purpose, even though it was not the purpose of their movement, and they had a will, which made them a force to be reckoned with in this mass of human jelly. More than any other element, they imparted to the activity of their movement the specious quality of intellectualism which was its gravest handicap. For them Russia was experiencing a political revolution which ought to end with the conferring of political liberties. Since they cherished this boon above all else, they felt that the people also must cherish it and not go in for social revolution, which would subvert their way of life, offend the Kadets, and make impossible the prosecution of the war. Before the October Revolution they had closed their eyes to evidence that the Russian people would not accept their prescription for the revolution. A. N. Sletova had tried to get influential members of the old Peasants' Executive Committee to go to Tambov province and view that scene of disorders for themselves, but she had found these leaders engrossed in politics and devoid of any historical perspective—hopelessly devoid of it, as she frankly admits.[42] And Inna Rakitnikova speaks of people lost in words who were gradually walling them-

---

[41] Some of the SR leaders had attended German universities. Such an experience could, of course, have produced either a positive or a negative reaction, depending on the individual and his experiences.

[42] "Komu na pol'zu?" (Who Stands to Gain?), *Delo Naroda*, No. 163 (September 24, 1917).

selves off from the "dark, hungry people." [43] This testimony of the two lady SR's is important, for they were typical organizational figures—sister and wife of two of the party's founders—whose strictly centrist position leaves no room for suspicion of radical deviation. Essentially they were saying the same thing as ex-Colonel Krakovetski and Professor Pokrovski when these observers defined the PSR as a party of the intelligentsia which stood aloof from the mass of the toilers.[44] The revolutionary element left in the party after the schism now and then raised its voice in protest against the preoccupation of the intellectuals with political liberties and nothing more,[45] but in its leaderless state it could not hope to get the party off the track of political reform and onto that of social revolution. Thus the default of the party in the realm of social change was in large measure the consequence of Chernov's default as leader of the center, which at any time had the votes to bring the right wing into line or amputate it from the party.

The intellectualism of the party betrayed it most grievously in respect to the army. Boris Sokolov comments on the lack of vision of the democratic intelligentsia concerning the role of the army in the revolution, which led them to concentrate their attention on other, less crucial matters, a mistake that the Bolsheviks did not make.[46] His observation is all the more pertinent in that he himself was a right SR. Neglect of the soldiers and callousness to their suffering are indisputable. The only question is whether it was lack of discernment or lack of willingness to discern. Certainly there were individuals who understood clearly enough the situation at the front, even in the early days of the revolution. The words of a junior officer about the relations between officers and men, contained in a letter to his family of March 11, 1917, deserve to be quoted at length:

Between them and ourselves is a gulf which cannot be crossed. However well disposed they may be to individuals among us, we remain lords in their eyes. When we speak of the people, we mean the nation; when they speak of it, they mean the democratic depths. From their point of

---

[43] *Delo Naroda*, No. 184 (October 19, 1917).
[44] *Pravda*, No. 168 (July 29, 1922).
[45] See especially *Kratkii otchët*, pp. 44–45, 64 (speeches of Utgof and Berezin).
[46] "Zashchita Uchreditel'nago Sobraniia," in *Arkhiv Russkoi Revoliutsii*, XIII, 38–39.

view it is not a political but a social revolution that has taken place, from which we have lost and they have gained. Under the new order it will be better for them and worse for us—of that they are convinced. Therefore they do not believe in the sincerity of our profession of good will for the soldiers. Formerly we governed; now they wish to govern themselves. In them are speaking the unavenged wrongs of the ages. We shall not find a common tongue—that is the accursed heritage of the old order.[47]

This young man should not have been buried in a guard regiment on the Southwestern Front; he ought to have been in the Provisional Government, where he would have supplied some of the good sense and also the human feeling lacking in the deliberations of men who had set themselves high above the Russian people in their conviction that the interests of the State transcended those of the population beneath it.

What this officer had said from above at the beginning of the revolution was said later from below by a sailor in the corridors of the Taurida Palace when E. E. Lazarev[48] engaged him in a heated argument in an effort to influence the guard against dissolution of the Constituent Assembly:

We all the same will put a bullet into anyone who deceives us. We don't care whether it is Kerenski, Lenin, or some one else! We are fed up with living as we did, we don't want our life again to be as it has been! Maybe you are a peasant and a good man, but the right SR's have done nothing for us and now they don't want to recognize our authority! Enough of this! Now we are going to take everything into our own hands![49]

In the interval between these two statements, the SR's cannot say they were not warned. The editorial offices of the *Delo Naroda* were flooded with letters from unknown authors. In them breathed a

---

[47] "Iz zapisnoi knizhki arkhivista: iz ofitserskikh pisem s fronta v 1917 g." (From the Archivist's Notebook: From Officers' Letters from the Front in 1917), in *Krasnyi Arkhiv*, L–LI (I–II, 1932), 200.

[48] Member of the assembly from Samara province, long-time exile, and SR of the far right. An extremely loquacious person.

[49] Minor, "Odin den' Uchreditel'nago Sobraniia," in *Perezhitoe*, I, 132. Although the words are in the form of a direct quotation, Minor could scarcely have reproduced them exactly as they were spoken. But as he was a person of balance and veracity and himself inclined to the right of center, there is no reason to assume that he has taken liberties with what the sailor said.

fierce egalitarian spirit and hatred of all officers. In them were no subtlety and little rationality, according to the editors, yet in their bluntness and their stark simplicity they reflected the minds of those who had never been anything but now were becoming something. A quick peace was the ever-recurring theme. "Our patience is breaking down. . . . Autumn has come, it rains, and outside winter has already set in. The men are cold and hungry." Where was Stockholm, and why did not France and England say what they wanted? "Where is the promised equality and fraternity, when the capitalists have the power and the people the death penalty?" The editors shrank from these letters. They knew the March mood had vanished and thought they could discern in the army seeds of reaction that were beginning to sprout. They measured faith in the revolution by their own, without asking themselves how they could gauge the strength of a revolution when one had yet to be made. The letters were filed away or more often put in the wastebasket of unwanted materials.[50] And there the matter ended—except for the October Revolution.

These letters mirror a state in dissolution. But the right-wing Populist intellectuals continued in their trance of "state-mindedness," telling themselves they were virtuous because they turned a deaf ear to the demands of the Russian people while keeping their hearing attuned to the martial music in London and Paris. And the other Populist intellectuals with Chernov at the head sat with folded hands, waiting for the December congress of their party and somehow assuming that everything else would wait with them. The propensity for self-destruction seems to have been stronger than the instinct of self-preservation. They were left only with their hope that these "depraved" elements at the front and in the garrisons would go home and be reabsorbed into the peasant matrix, which they considered sound and healthy, without asking themselves whether it might not be well to reexamine this matrix and without reflecting that the soldiers, by age and training, by physical strength and angry disposition, were the most important peasants in Russia, the yeast of every village. The right SR's in their hearts hated these

---

[50] Iv. B_____ov, "Pis'ma" (Letters), *Delo Naroda*, No. 186 (October 21, 1917). Four days after this report was published, the Bolsheviks took power.

soldiers who refused to die at the intellectuals' bidding. They welcomed their exodus from the party or from the orbit of party influence. One of the more extreme partisans of France and zealots for war had greeted the defection of seven soldier members of the PSR with the observation that they would make no better Bolsheviks now than SR's in the past or anarchists in the future.[51] This judgment exhibits the two basic features of many right SR judgments—venom and shallowness. It was not necessary for these soldiers to be good Bolsheviks. Average men have never perfectly understood nor fully conformed to the faith they embrace. It was necessary only for these soldiers to serve the Bolsheviks, giving them the physical power to deal with their opponents, whether SR's at the time or anarchists and others in the future.

If the right SR's were mainly responsible for the specious intellectualism which dominated the counsels of this party and wrought such havoc with its soldier following, all SR's shared certain failings that go far to explain the debacle in 1917 and the inability to redeem the situation in the earlier, plastic months of Soviet rule. One of their leaders in 1917 who later broke with the movement, K. Burevoi (Sopliakov), chairman of the peasants' soviets of Voronezh province, singles out two aspects of wrongheadedness on their part which remained with them throughout their public career. They never were able to part with one another, and they never could bring themselves to abandon a position once taken, which he regards as an attribute of petrified thought.[52] Certainly no features of the movement were more marked than these. Even the Left SR's had formed their party only as a consequence of expulsion from the parent organization, to their own undoing in the contest with Bolshevism for the allegiance of the soldier mass. And as late as 1922, if not later, despite everything that had happened, Chernov was still meeting with Kerenski and Avksentiev for a wake in the German capital, there to contend once more in hopeless disagreement over the question of coalition or no coalition with the shadows of the past.[53] For a long while the SR's reenacted the farce of the

[51] M. V. Vishniak, "Moskovskie pobediteli" (The Victors in Moscow), *Delo Naroda*, No. 167 (September 29, 1917).

[52] *Raspad*, pp. 130–31.

[53] See report of the SR conference in December of 1922 in *Revoliutsionnaia Rossiia*, Nos. 24–25 (January–February, 1923), pp. 21 ff.

imminent resurrection of the body that marked their greatest triumph. Over and over again the organ notes sounded for the bridal procession of the PSR and the Constituent Assembly, though the bride had long since passed away. The only progress the SR's made was to be dragged at the tail of events from one position to another. "Vsiakoe deistvie my vosprinimaem *post factum*" (every action we accede to after it has taken place) was the verdict of a youthful member of the party.[54] And Chernov expressed it in peasant language when he said, "We ought not to have let things slip through our hands when everything was coming our way; if you can't hold on by the mane, you certainly won't hold on by the tail."[55]

The question of war and peace best illustrates the frozen thought of the SR's, their incapacity for abandoning a position once taken except through intervention of a superior force. We have seen how in their desperation they accepted the armistice and demobilization of the army in an effort to save the Constituent Assembly. But in a short time they were back at their old positions. Writing in May of 1918, in the seventh month of Lenin's ascendancy and after Skoropadski had been installed in the Ukraine, with even the Kadets wavering in their stand on the war, the most authoritative SR spokesman could say:[56]

And the democracy alone remains true to its old positions and is as irreconcilably opposed as ever to all the machinations of German imperialism.

In a military union with the Western democracies it beholds the only outlet for Russia onto the broad highway of national development; in the renewal of armed conflict with Germany it sees the only possible means of state resurrection.

Here it all is: the "old positions," the irreconcilable opposition to *all* manifestations of German imperialism, the unexpressed but self-evident determination to preserve *all* fruits of Russian imperialism, the impossibility of national development apart from military union with the Western powers, the "state-mindedness" of this party, and,

[54] *Kratkii otchët*, p. 80.
[55] *Stranitsy iz politicheskago dnevnika* (Pages from a Political Diary), a rare and unavailable publication, cited in Burevoi (Sopliakov), *Raspad*, p. 125.
[56] A. R. Gotz, "Politicheskie bliznetsy" (Political Twins), *Delo Naroda*, No. 45 (May 5/18, 1918).

above all, the renewal of armed conflict, the supreme goal of the democratic element in Russian society, which, as the Czech major points out, was obsessed with the notion of driving the jaded Russian peasantry back into war in a crusade of Slavs against Germans.[57] It would soon have its chance on the Volga, where it achieved perhaps the most miserable of all its failures.

It is true that these words of Gotz were written after Brest Litovsk, when the German presence in the Ukraine threatened the existence of Russia as a great power and when the danger of German-sponsored reaction in Russia proper was no longer a mere figment of the imagination.[58] Yet in essence his words are as applicable to 1917 as they are to the post-treaty period. And it will be noted that he himself speaks of the "old positions." Long before the terms of peace were known the design of the right SR's, which in due time would be communicated to the other SR's, had been outlined in their paper. Conceding at last that the Russian people wanted an end to war, they said that the Constituent Assembly would try for a general peace but that if it failed, a separate peace was out of the question and the war would be continued with a volunteer army (here was the genesis of the SR proposal in the assembly a few weeks later). The likelihood was foreseen and accepted that this army would have to retreat deep into Russia, abandoning large areas to the enemy on the principle that occupation of parts of the country was preferable to enslavement of the whole. The old scarecrow so often used by the right SR's that the Allies would make peace at Russia's expense was suddenly scrapped in favor of the argument that German domination of Russia was not to the Allied interest and that in the West the war would be fought out to victory.[59] The net result of this right SR design would have been at best the same as Brest Litovsk—a German occupation of extensive portions of the former Russian empire. And it might have been much worse if the million volunteers envisaged did not present themselves—and who can seriously be-

[57] Kratochvíl, *Cesta revoluce*, p. 152.
[58] Eugenia Ratner stressed this danger as a major factor in determining her party's reaction to the peace treaty. See her testimony in *Pravda*, No. 171 (August 2, 1922).
[59] "Uchreditel'noe Sobranie i mir" (The Constituent Assembly and Peace), *Volia Naroda*, No. 191 (December 12, 1917).

lieve that they would have? The lower classes were sick of war and the Populist intellectuals did not fight. Lenin's plan was far more realistic, for it at least preserved the nerve centers of the country from occupation and afforded a breathing spell during which the elements of statehood could be reassembled and a fresh start made.[60]

The SR's never tired of declaiming against the "shameful" peace of Brest Litovsk, even after it had lapsed and been supplanted by the not less iniquitous system of Versailles, against which their main grievance seems to have been that they were not consulted in its making.[61] Such is the indictment of a party member from the left of center. And one from the right of center has admitted in retrospect that a will to peace on the part of the Russian government in the summer of 1917, when the Russian army was still not a negligible quantity, would have found Germany in a reasonable mood and far removed from any thought of a Romanov restoration. But the old SR utopianism crops out again in the further assertion that "a firm will to peace on the part of the revolutionary Russian government of that time would probably have also forced our Allies to consent to peace negotiations." [62]

Here, in fact, is a double dose of utopianism, for the Russian government of the time was revolutionary only in the sense that it stood in the place of the tsar, and nothing that it could have done would have inclined the Allies to peace after America's entrance into the war. This negative aspect of American intervention the SR's never realized, just as they never realized its positive aspect—that America's entrance made possible Russia's exit from the war. Be-

[60] It is interesting to note that, at about the time Gotz was mounting the horse of war, one of the most prominent of the right SR's was holding back. V. V. Rudnev seems to have feared that if the Bolsheviks were overthrown prematurely and the war renewed Russia might go completely to pieces. The SR's could not accept peace and so would face a German offensive. He considered a separate peace inevitable under the circumstances and counseled waiting for clarification of the struggle in the West before proceeding against the Bolsheviks (from Chernov's report of a conversation with Rudnev in early May, 1918; notes in the possession of Boris Nikolaevski). Chernov's account seems entirely plausible, for it is merely a projection of Rudnev's attitude at the time of convoking the Constituent Assembly. One of the right SR's had at last stumbled onto the track of waiting for the West to win, which could have led somewhere had he and his colleagues entered upon it early enough.

[61] Burevoi (Sopliakov), *Raspad,* p. 130.
[62] Bykhovski, *Vserossiiskii Sovet Krest'ianskikh Deputatov,* p. 249.

fore October they had moved not at all in relation to this problem. After October they only seemed to move before the storm, accepting the armistice in the expectation that it would break down under the weight of German demands, and accepting demobilization in the hope that they could raise a volunteer army, which either would have been a dismal failure or would have put power back into the hands of the nobility, the hereditary fighting caste of Russian society. Neither before nor after October did they make any real progress in solving this problem, since the only feasible solution was a separate peace or at least that separate suspension of hostilities which nature had already effected. But they set themselves with stonelike stubbornness against either peace or nature's handiwork. And since they would not solve this problem, they could not solve any other.

They had only one thing to fall back on—words. Endless palaver was for them the substitute for action. "And we always talked and talked and talked. And in the end nothing came of all our talk." These were the words, not of some enemy, but of an eminently qualified observer, a member of the Central Committee.[63]

But the war would not yield to a barrage of words. The war was the nemesis of Russian Populism. It was the major cause at once of the Populists' backsliding and the country's convulsion. The war had aroused all the latent nationalism in Populism and had mercilessly exposed the sham intellectualism behind the assertion of independence from Western tutelage. At the same time it had brought to a head all the long-standing grievances of the lower orders of Russian society and had shaken the peasants in the army out of their village torpor while having an only less pronounced effect upon the village itself. Between the Populist intellectuals and the masses for whom they presumed to speak a rift was growing which only seemed to be patched over by the results of the November election; when the Populists tried to stand on the patchwork in their war on Bolshevism, it collapsed beneath their weight. Nowhere would the peasants rally to their standard, and only later, when these Populists had found a natural refuge in Paris and in Prague, did the peasants band

---

[63] V. Lunkevich, *O nashikh dniakh* (About Our Days), quoted in Burevoi (Sopliakov), *Raspad*, p. 125.

together in the green movement in an effort to give the revolution the cast they wanted, as if in conscious recognition of the fact that the Populist cause was not their own.

For the ruin alike of Populist pretensions and peasant aspirations all segments of the PSR must bear the blame, though not in equal measure. The left was at fault for having allowed Bolshevism to wax too strong before putting distance between itself and the rest of the party, the right center for the inferior leadership of Abram Gotz, the left center under Chernov for having no leadership, and the right for deserting the party shrine and worshiping other gods. It is true that the French Republic had all along occupied one niche in the Populist pantheon and the Slavonic brethren another, but now the cult of these lesser divinities had come to overshadow the chief object of veneration, the Russian people itself, all the more so since the actions of that people in 1917 seemed anything but god-like to the Populist intellectuals. Obviously deficient in "state-mindedness" and with a penchant for anarchism, the Russian people responded not at all to the pleadings of the "neo-Slavists" but fixed their gaze on social problems. The exasperation of the pro-war, right-wing Populist intellectuals at the Russian people found public expression in the pronouncements of S. L. Maslov, the minister of agriculture with whom A. F. Kerenski had found it so congenial to work. Naturally these intellectuals could not worship too openly before the French and Pan-Slav shrines but in their cult of the state they went the limit, setting the abstraction of the state above the reality of the people in precisely the same manner as the German intellectuals. Here, at last, was something that did not emanate primarily from France and certainly not from the soul of the Russian people. Only their well-developed inability to face unpleasant facts prevented these intellectuals from seeing the Made in Germany label on their new object of veneration. Nothing illustrates better the fraud of an ideology which combined hatred of a nation with thralldom to its thought.

It is not easy for an uninitiated observer to understand how this ideology could have been communicated to an organization in which by every test save that of nominations for the Constituent Assembly—an exceptional procedure—these right-wing Populist in-

tellectuals were a minority and not even a strong minority. Outwardly, of course, it was not communicated to the organization.
The party remained in words both socialist and revolutionary, it
claimed to place the interests of the Russian people above all other
considerations, condemned even French imperialism, and accepted
the war only in so far as it was necessary to resist German imperialism. It continued to proclaim its devotion to the peasantry.
Yet in reality it followed a course that sacrificed the peasantry to the
dictates of the Western Allies and the preservation of the Russian
empire with every jot and tittle of its non-Russian territories. It
turned a deaf ear to the will of the most active elements in the village and drove these elements into the embraces of a political organization which had other interests than the peasants' at heart. It could
not break with the hypnosis of war nor would it attempt to co-
operate with its own schismatics even at a moment when they were
becoming receptive to the idea of a war of revolutionary defense.
The majority of this party was held in chains by the minority and
led down the road, not merely of disaster, but of multiple disaster.
Of the two centrist leaders responsible for this fateful captivity,
A. R. Gotz on the right and V. M. Chernov on the left, the latter's
role is all the more difficult to understand in that he had the vision
to foresee the disaster and the grace to grieve for the dead.

The right SR's were a key element in Russian society. They did
not advertise their role in the revolution and others have failed to
detect or have not wished to acknowledge that role. Yet without
understanding it, one can explain neither the paradox of the strength
of conservative influence in the early years of the revolution, despite
the apparent weakness of conservative sentiment, nor the paradox
of the eventual triumph of a proletarian dictatorship in a peasant
land. It is a great mistake to identify conservatism with the Constitutional Democratic Party, as has so often been done, and to
attribute the Kadet debacle in the November election of 1917 to
the deficiencies of the election, the ignorance of the people, or to
some other similar factor. It is a great mistake to measure conservative strength by the 15 out of 815 seats won by the Constitutional
Democratic Party. Even allowing for the retarded development of
Russian society and the traditional weakness of the middle class, the

Kadets ought to have done much better than that, had they been the sole representatives of the conservative cause. They were not the sole representatives, of course. The main contingent of conservatism was to be found on the SR benches. Instead of there not being enough conservatives in the Constituent Assembly, as its detractors have claimed, there were too many, as this study has demonstrated. It is merely a case of a label concealing reality, in this instance not only from Russian peasants but from investigators of all nationalities. All of these public welfare people, these functionaries, state employees, agronomists, cooperative officials, and others might, indeed, have contributed to the coming of revolution, but after it came, a few months of observing the people in action sufficed to convert them into one of the most conservative elements in Russian society; the war did the rest by inflaming their latent nationalism. By any rational test, these right-wing Populist intellectuals should have been in one camp with the Constitutional Democrats.

Why were they not? Why did they dissemble their convictions under the flag of Social Revolutionism? Sentiment might be one reason, though A. A. Argunov assured the author that sentimental ties among the SR's had been dissolved by the war. If not sentiment, then inertia helped to hold them where they were. Personal interest also may have had some influence. They may have realized that they would never achieve the position of power in the Kadet Party that they held in their own. There they would merely be foot soldiers, whereas here they were generals. But doubtlessly the main consideration was how best they could serve the cause of war. Not without reason they may have concluded that it would be more efficacious to stay in the PSR and neutralize the strong but amorphous sentiment for peace which pervaded its ranks.

Emotion or passion swayed the right SR's much more than reason. Not that they were wholly lacking in a sense of realism or that their position was always wrong. Their willingness to grant compensation for land to be alienated in the peasant interest contrasted favorably to the belief of other SR's that somehow the hereditary fighting caste of Russian society could be pauperized without forfeiting many peasant lives in the process. The right SR's were also justified in fearing the pretensions of Imperial Germany. But hate beclouded their reason, even more than fear, and they could not see or did not wish to see that the power of Germany no longer matched its pretensions and that what Bismarck had said about the big appetite and bad teeth of Italy could now be applied to the ruling elements of his own country. Transatlantic intervention in the European conflict meant nothing to the right SR's except a welcome source of revenue. How different the view of Lenin as he began to prepare his party for the acceptance of an outwardly onerous peace which he knew, and others should have known, Germany would never have a free hand to exploit:

19. I germanskaia revoliutsiia vovse ne zatrudnitsia, po ego ob'ektivnym osnovaniiam, esli my zakliuchim separatnyi mir. Veroiatno, na vremia ugar shovinizma oslabit eë, no polozhenie Germanii ostanetsia kraine tiazhëlym, voina s Angliei i Amerikoi budet zatiazhnoi, agressivnyi imperializm vpolne do kontsa razoblachën s obeikh storon. [19. And the German revolution will in no basic sense be hampered if we conclude a separate peace. For a while the flare-up of chauvinism may weaken it, but Germany's *position will remain extremely grave, the war with England and America will be long drawn out,* and aggressive imperialism will be from both sides completely unmasked.] [64]

Such vision was denied the SR's, and even if granted, would have been repressed with moral indignation, in the case of the right SR's because of partisanship for France, as well as concern for the Western and Southern Slavs and for the preservation of Russian control over populations that were neither Russian nor Slav. Right SR denunciations of Left SR's as German dupes or agents came with bad grace. We know that the right SR's received money from American sources. [65] We do not know whether there was a material basis for

---

[64] "Tezisy po voprosu o nemedlennom zakliuchenii separatnogo i anneksionistskogo mira" (Theses Concerning the Immediate Conclusion of a Separate and Annexationist Peace), in *Sochineniia*, XXII, 198 (written on the 7/20 of January, 1918, and printed in *Pravda* on February 24, 1918). Italics in the translation are mine. Thesis No. 20 relates to the creation of a powerful workers' and peasants' red army. It is noteworthy that Lenin does not even mention France. The impending German offensive on the Western Front, the terrors of which have been played up by apologists for the suicidal course of the pro-war elements in Russian society, did not obscure from Lenin, and should not have obscured from others, the certainty of continued war in the West regardless of the fate of France. The right SR's were like the Ludendorff clique in the Reich: neither could see the world beyond Paris.

[65] See Kennan, *Soviet-American Relations*, I, 47, 49, 56 ff.; II, 325. This admirable study makes it clear that the money came from Wall Street sources

their championship of French interests. Investigations of the German archives by hostile sources have indicated that the Bolsheviks may have received some financial aid from the Reich. But in this case German gold did not make German agents, as the Germans themselves would be the first to admit. History has relieved the right SR's of the obligation to demonstrate their independence of foreign patronage. But a thoroughgoing investigation of the archives in Paris, were that ever possible, might also yield some interesting results.

Independently of French influence or in obedience to it, the right SR's labored mightily to stoke the fires of war. They tied their party in knots over the war and over every problem directly or indirectly connected with it, including the land problem. Weak in respect to numbers, they were highly articulate, they knew how to write, speak, and manipulate, were masters of the art of political dissimulation, and occupied many of the key positions in rural society. In normal times they would have pulled many peasants after them, and even in these times they exercised an influence from which the peasants only gradually emancipated themselves, and the party—not at all. They were the chief roadblock in the path of the agrarian revolution and no one did more than they to bring about the triumph of Bolshevism save the Bolsheviks themselves. Lacking any means of sabotaging the Bolshevik organization, they could not turn back the whole army of revolution, but they quite effectively hamstrung its agrarian component. They could not defeat the revolution, but they did much to change its character. By throwing a dam across the natural course of the agrarian revolution, with the center SR's standing nervelessly by, they deflected the torrent into Marxist channels. The peasantry, left leaderless by the default of the SR's, lapsed into anarchy and then into passivity or else followed after the extremists, in whom it had at first reposed little confidence.

When all is said and done, it was only natural that the Bolsheviks should win and the SR's should lose. The contrast between the two parties could not have been greater, and not merely in respect to the

close to the American government, though not from the government itself, as the Bolsheviks have always intimated (see, for example, *Petrogradskie bol'sheviki v Oktiabr'skoi revoliutsii*, p. 356).

war. To take first the matter of organization. Every manifestation of a spirit of compromise in the Bolshevik Party, every tendency toward moderation, was rigidly subordinated to the intransigence of the Central Committee. Lenin knew that his party's delegation in the Constituent Assembly was not free of democratic illusions and forced it to toe the line.[66] The SR delegation not only pursued its own course of action but dragged the Central Committee behind it. From the writings of Chernov and others we know of the cleavage that existed, yet Zenzinov asserted that there had been no conflict behind the scenes.[67] Here is a contradiction that can easily be resolved when one understands the nature of the Socialist Revolutionary Party. There was no conflict because Chernov surrendered the authority conferred upon him by the Fourth Congress. The higher instance yielded to the lower, the majority bowed to the minority will, as it had throughout 1917. Nothing had changed in a party in which everything was as it should not be.

Nor would it change. We have already mentioned the immunity from expulsion enjoyed by Shreider, ex-mayor of Petersburg, in backing the Whites in the civil war, and the indulgence shown him by Eugenia Ratner, the high commissioner of the party in the southeastern realm. Now Eugenia was the friend of Chernov and like him a member of the left-centrist majority of the Central Committee; hence her attitude is revealing. When the Soviet judge with a show of incredulity asked her whether a party worker were free to embrace a nonparty cause, she answered, yes, that the "broad liberty" enjoyed by Socialist Revolutionaries had prevented their being subjected to the severe discipline and enforced unity of the Bolshevik Party. When members adhered to organizations in which no party work as such was carried on, they were free to act according to their discretion.[68] The organization in question was the Southeastern Committee of Members of the Constituent Assembly, nearly all of whom were Socialist Revolutionaries, yet its nonpartisan character entitled them to act as they pleased, even in respect to the civil war. It is not surprising that Eugenia's brother should have spoken of the

[66] *Sochineniia* (3d ed.), XXII, 130, 134 (Point No. 17 of Theses on the Constituent Assembly), 593, n. 62.
[67] Interview in New York (December 19, 1949).
[68] *Pravda*, No. 149 (July 7, 1922).

PSR as a political community in which the members generally spat on the Central Committee.[69] The discipline of the rival party, its centralism, tautness, and repression of dissent, would in time present grievous problems, and not least for the Bolsheviks themselves, but the point here is that in a contest for power in 1917 these features constituted a very great advantage.

Equally startling was the contrast between Bolshevism and Social Revolutionism in respect to their vision of the future, the former having remarkable perspicacity and the latter none at all. Even as it struggled for breath in a world of enemies, the Soviet regime discerned a potent ally for the future in the awakening nationalisms of Asia and Africa, manifestations of which were not wanting in the All Russian Constituent Assembly. Asia and Africa might as well have been the lost continent of Atlantis as far as the SR's were concerned. The youthful Left SR, V. E. Trutovski, did have a presentiment of their importance for the fortunes of the Russian Revolution, but he was a lonely figure. The dominant clique in the PSR was so blinded by the light from Paris that it could see nothing in the outer darkness. Nor could it foresee the European constellation that would have resulted from the triumph of its own war policy. In a Europe with France and Russia victorious, with the Western and South Slavs free, and all rewarded with slices of German, Magyar, and Turkish territories, Great Britain beyond any reasonable doubt would have picked up a cut-down Germany that she had ceased to fear and sought to use it as a counterbalance to the Franco-Russian combination which would not have been to her liking, either in Europe or in the Near East. The Kadets and their SR echoes, assuming that they had survived the embraces of allies still further to the right, would then have faced a cruel choice. There is no doubt what their choice would have been—1893 would have been repeated, but 1904 and 1907 reversed—and the old game would have started all over again, with as little benefit as ever to the Eastern Slavs in Tambov and Voronezh provinces, ostensibly first on the scale of Populist solicitude, yet actually last.

The Socialist Revolutionaries had constituted themselves defenders of the rural toilers. They might have made a brave and earnest effort

[69] *Ibid.*, No. 175 (August 6, 1922).

to discharge their duty and still have ended in defeat, for the rule seems to be that no matter what happens in Eastern Europe, the rural toilers always lose. But the SR's made no brave and earnest effort, either before the October Revolution or belatedly, after it had taken place. Twice they failed the peasantry, the second time after the October explosion had illuminated the scene for them. In the case of the dominant minority, failure was the consequence of having subordinated peasant interests to the preservation of the tsarist empire and the needs—or fancied needs—of other peoples. This subordination arose in part from the vexation of the Populist intellectuals at a people devoid of "state-mindedness" and loath to defend their country, and also from willful disregard of such considerations as what the Russian state had done to merit devotion on the part of the people, and where in 1917 did the enemy stand on truly Russian soil. If the Russian people failed to comprehend the need for genuine revolutionary defense, the fault lies with those who had done so little for them and who had perverted the slogan of defense into a cover for aggressive warfare on behalf of alien as well as domestic imperialism. In the case of the self-effacing majority of Socialist Revolutionaries, failure was the consequence of weakness developed into a system, of doing nothing while knowing better. Just as the Varangians had assumed sway over the Eastern Slavs, so had the right SR's fastened their rule on this party, and if the analogy is imperfect, then not merely because the Varangians belonged to the accursed German breed but also because they were far better leaders. As a result of this combined dereliction of duty, by the minority and the majority, willfully and without will, a proletarian-centered party had triumphed in a peasant land with strength that came to it out of the peasant camp. The Bolshevism of the early years of the revolution is a much broader term than the Communism of later times. It was the SR's who made it broader and its triumph inevitable. There would be little use in seeking to determine whose is the primary responsibility, the minority which produced this result or the majority which cowered before it. In any event, the gravestone over their movement is not heavier than the blame that both must bear.[70]

[70] Burevoi considered all the sacrifices of Social Revolutionism to have been in vain (*Raspad*, p. 131). There is no reason to dissent from his verdict.

List of Sources

Sources of little significance with one or two citations have not been included.

Society publications and edited works or compilations are listed by title rather than by editor or sponsoring agency.

Only lengthy articles of exceptional importance are listed separately from the journals in which they appear; newspaper articles are not listed separately, as there are too many of them.

Sources have been grouped under three headings: manuscripts, printed sources, and oral information.

MANUSCRIPTS

Babushka na s"ezde chekho-slovakov (Grandmother at the Czechoslovak Congress). [Typed copy of an article that appeared in the *Vestnik Uchreditel'nago Sobraniia* of Samara, August 22, 1918. Preserved in the Dzvonkevich-Wagner Collection in the Hoover Library on War, Revolution, and Peace, Stanford University, California. Placed at author's disposal along with other materials through courtesy of Witold S. Sworakowski. The "grandmother" is E. K. Breshko-Breshkovskaia.]

Chernov, V. M. Izbiratel'naia statistika (Election Statistics). 8 pp. [Appendix to the minutes of the Central Committee. Typewritten manuscript of unnumbered pages. Analysis of elections to the Central Committee at the Third and Fourth Party Congresses, invaluable for the light it sheds on factionalism.]

—— Manuscript commentary on the minutes of the sessions of the Central Committee of the PSR. 100 pp. [Manuscript on typed, legal-size sheets without a title but with corrections and insertions in author's handwriting. Used in Prague in 1934 by courtesy of the author and returned to him. Indispensable source, affording backstage illumination of the SR scene. Accurate on the whole, it contains some misrepresentations of Chernov's role in 1917, so that it must be taken in conjunction with the party press and publications of the time. Deals with the whole range of the author's experience in 1917 and early 1918, not just with the period covered by the fragmentary minutes of the Central Committee in his possession. Equivalent to a book, but much franker because of its private character.]

Instructions of the Central Committee of the PSR, January 17, 1918 to . . . . . Committee of the PSR. 4 pp. [Manuscript in the possession of Boris I. Nikolaevski.]

Izveshchenie Tsentral'nogo Komiteta Partii Sotsialistov-Revoliutsionerov (Communication of the Central Committee of the PSR), dated December 5, 1920. [Included in Documents of the S.-R. Party, 1917–1923, Received from V. Chernov, a collection in the vault of the Hoover Library, Stanford University, California.]

Protokol Zasedaniia Tsentral'nago Komiteta Partii Sotsialistov-Revoliutsionerov Sentiabria mesiatsa 2 dnia 1917 goda (Minutes of the Session of the Central Committee of the Socialist Revolutionary Party Held on September 2, 1917) . . . and minutes for succeeding sessions through that of January 30, 1918, followed by minutes for three sessions of subsidiary bodies in 1918. 38 pp. [Typewritten manuscript of terse notes arranged in three columns with some entries in hand of V. M. Chernov. Inspection permitted by Chernov in 1935 in Prague. This fragmentary record of the proceedings of the Central Committee has three breaks even for this limited period. It is largely duplicated by the published record in the *Partiinyia Izvestiia* (Party News) though some items were there suppressed. A basic though fitful source of information.]

Steinberg, Dr. J. [I. Z.]. The Events of July, 1918. 23 pp. [Typed copy in English of the original manuscript; in the Hoover Library, Stanford University, California.]

PRINTED SOURCES

Alekseev, V. *Oktiabr' i grazhdanskaia voina v TsChO* (October and the Civil War in the Central Black Earth Region). Voronezh, 1932.

Antonov-Saratovski, V. P. *Pod stiagom proletarskoi bor'by: Otryvki iz vospominanii o rabote v Saratove za vremia s 1915 g. do 1918 g.* (Under the Banner of Proletarian Struggle: Extracts from Recollections of Work in Saratov for the Period from 1915 to 1918). Moscow and Leningrad, 1925. Vol. I. [No further volume published. One of the fuller and more objective provincial accounts.]

Argunov, A. A. *Mezhdu dvumia bol'shevizmami* (Between Two Bolshevisms). Paris, 1919.

Arkhiv Russkoi Revoliutsii (Archives of the Russian Revolution). Edited by I. V. Gessen. 22 vols. Berlin, 1921–1937. [Most extensive and substantial of the émigré collections.]

Bonch-Bruevich, Vladimir D. *Na boevykh postakh fevral'skoi i oktiabr'skoi revoliutsii* (At Combat Positions in the February and October Revolutions). 2d ed. Moscow, 1931.

Bor'ba za Kazan': Sbornik materialov o chekho-uchredilovskoi inter-ventsii v 1918 (The Fight for Kazan: A Collection of Materials on the Intervention of Czech and Constituent Assembly Forces in 1918). Kazan, 1924. Vol. I. [All that was published?] [Valuable information contained in a source of great rarity; is not limited to 1918 but extends back into 1917.]

Boris Savinkov pered voennoi kollegiei verkhovnogo suda S.S.S.R.: Polnyi otchët po stenogramme suda (Boris Savinkov before the Military Collegium of the Supreme Court of the USSR: Complete Account According to the Court Stenographic Record). Notes by I. Shubin (Samarin). Moscow, 1924.

Bosh, Eugenia. *God bor'by: Bor'ba za vlast' na Ukraine s aprelia 1917 g. do nemetskoi okkupatsii* (A Year of Struggle: The Struggle for Power in the Ukraine from April, 1917, to the German Occupation). Moscow and Leningrad, 1925.

Buchanan, George. *My Mission to Russia and Other Diplomatic Memories*. 2 vols. London and Boston, 1923. Vol. II. [The British ambassador does not tell everything, but what he does tell is truthful and enlightening.]

Burevoi, K. [K. S. Sopliakov]. *Raspad 1918–1922* (The Breakup, 1918–1922). Moscow, 1923. [An examination of the party fortunes by a disillusioned left-centrist SR. Valuable for insight as well as for information.]

Bykhovski, N. Ia. *Vserossiiskii Sovet Krest'ianskikh Deputatov 1917 g.* (The All-Russian Soviet of Peasant Deputies in 1917). Moscow, 1929. [Rarest of all the sources, and one of the most important. Belonging to the inner ring of the dominant right-centrist faction of the Executive Committee of Peasant Soviets, and editor of the peasants' *Izvestiia* (News), Bykhovski was in a splendid position to observe the political aspects of the agrarian movement. His sober account, conceding the errors that were made in 1917, but reaffirming the fact that the PSR as a whole had spoken for the middle peasants instead of the kulaks, proved highly unpalatable to the Soviet government, which caused his book to be torn from the press after only a single copy is said to have found its way abroad. The appendix contains a number of important and otherwise inaccessible documents.]

Byloe (The Past). New series, 35 nos., Petrograd, 1917–1926 (irregular numeration); 13 nos., 1917–1918. [A journal devoted to the history of the revolutionary movement. Significant articles and records.]

Chernov, V. M. *The Great Russian Revolution*. Translated by Philip E. Mosely. New Haven, 1936. [Valuable both for the information it contains and for the author's judgments. Merits more attention than it has received.]

Chernov, V. M. *Pered burei* (Before the Storm). New York, 1953. [Last of the author's many books, these memoirs contain some information not to be found elsewhere.]

Delo Naroda (The People's Cause). 245 nos. for 1917; irregular for 1918, owing to repression (Nos. 246–250 or 1–5 [January 3–12] and Nos. 4–48 of new series [March 26–June 20] have been consulted, aside from missing numbers). Petrograd, 1917–1918. [Daily newspaper; central organ of the PSR. Edited by S. P. Postnikov, V. M. Chernov, V. M. Zenzinov, and others. Most basic of all the sources. Reticent on scandal and conflicts within the party, the *Delo Naroda* is nevertheless a storehouse of information. Editorials are anonymous but Chernov has signed those of his composition in the file preserved in the Russian Archives Abroad at Prague.]

Dvenadtsat' smertnikov: Sud nad sotsialistami-revoliutsionerami v Moskve (Twelve Condemned to Die: Trial of the Socialist Revolutionaries in Moscow). Berlin, 1922.

Dybenko. P. E. *Miatezhniki: Iz vospominanii o revoliutsii* (The Rebels: From Reminiscences of the Revolution). Moscow, 1923.

Erde, D. *Gody buri i natiska* (Years of Storm and Stress). Kharkov, 1923. Book I: *Na levoberezh'i 1917* (On the Left Bank in 1917).

Erykalov, E. *Krasnaia gvardiia v bor'be za vlast' sovetov* (The Red Guard in the Struggle for Soviet Rule). Moscow, 1957.

Gaisinski, M. *Bor'ba bol'shevikov za krest'ianstvo v 1917 g.: Vserossiiskie s"ezdy Sovetov krest'ianskikh deputatov* (The Bolsheviks' Struggle to Win the Peasantry in 1917: The All-Russian Congresses of Soviets of Peasant Deputies). Moscow, 1933. [Apparently intended as replacement for Bykhovski's study, this Soviet product falls short of the suppressed book in content and objectivity, although it is rather substantial and has some use.]

Gins, G. K. *Sibir', soiuzniki i Kolchak: Povorotnyi moment russkoi istorii 1918–1920 g.g.* (Siberia, the Allies and Kolchak: A Turning Point in Russian History 1918–1920). 2 vols. Peking, 1921.

God russkoi revoliutsii (1917–1918 g.g.): Sbornik statei (A Year of the Russian Revolution [1917–1918]: A Collection of Articles). Moscow, 1918. [Several important articles.]

Ignatiev, V. I. *Nekotorye fakty i itogi chetyrëkh let grazhdanskoi voiny (1917–1921 g.)* (Some Facts and Results of Four Years of Civil War [1917–1921]). Moscow, 1922. Part I: (*Oktiabr' 1917 g.–Avgust 1921 g.*) *Petrograd, Vologda, Arkhangelsk (Lichnye vospominaniia)* ([October, 1917–August, 1921] Petrograd, Vologda, Archangel [Personal Memoirs]).

Istoricheskii Zhurnal (Historical Journal). Moscow, 1936–1945. [The articles in this journal are usually thin, superficial, and warped, but sometimes archival materials are cited.]

Istoriia grazhdanskoi voiny v SSSR (History of the Civil War in the USSR). Edited by Maxim Gorki [M. Gor'kii] *et al.* 5 vols. (with different subtitles). Moscow, 1935–1960. Vols. II and III. [The second volume is particularly useful.]

Izhevsk v ogne grazhdanskoi voiny: 1917–18 gody: Iz istorii revoliutsionnogo dvizheniia izhevskikh rabochikh (Izhevsk in the Fire of the Civil War: The Years 1917–18: From the History of the Revolutionary Movement of the Izhevsk Workers). Izhevsk, 1927.

Izvestiia moskovskago soveta rabochikh i soldatskikh deputatov (News of the Moscow Soviet of Workers' and Soldiers' Deputies). Moscow, 1917. Nos. 194–233 (October 22–December 19).

Izvestiia Tsentral'nago Ispolnitel'nago Komiteta petrogradskago soveta rabochikh i soldatskikh deputatov (News of the Central Executive Committee and the Petrograd Soviet of Workers' and Soldiers' Deputies). Petrograd, 1917–1918. [Scattered numbers consulted for latter part of 1917 and early 1918.]

Izvestiia Vserossiiskogo Tsentral'nogo Ispolnitel'nogo Komiteta Sovetov krest'ianskikh, rabochikh, soldatskikh i kazachikh deputatov (News of the All-Russian Central Executive Committee of Soviets of Peasants', Workers', Soldiers', and Cossacks' Deputies). Moscow, 1918–. [All numbers for 1922 covering the SR trial from June 8 to August 7 were consulted. They contain a vast amount of information about the PSR, its operations and personnel, from 1917 onward. The reports of the trial do not fully duplicate those in *Pravda,* making it necessary to bear up under the abominable print of both to get the whole story. One of the basic sources for information on the SR movement, 1917–1921.]

Kamkov, B. V. *Kto takie levye sotsialisty-revoliutsionery* (Who Are the Left Socialist Revolutionaries). Petrograd, 1918.

Kazanskii Oktiabr': Materialy i dokumenty (The October Revolution in Kazan: Materials and Documents). Edited by E. Grachev. Kazan, 1926. Part I: *Mart–Oktiabr' 1917 goda* (March–October, 1917).

Kennan, George F. *Soviet-American Relations, 1917–1920.* Vol. I: *Russia Leaves the War* (Princeton, 1956). Vol. II: *The Decision to Intervene* (Princeton, 1958). [An admirable study, with insight and a sense of reality too seldom found in the productions of the American academic community. Even in relation to Social Revolutionism, for him a matter of subsidiary significance, the author reveals real understanding.]

Kerenski, A. F. *Izdalëka: Sbornik statei (1920–1921 g.)* (From Afar: A Collection of Articles [1920–1921]). Paris, 1922. 249 pp. [The best of Kerenski's writings. Written after the bitter lesson of 1917 but before the bitterness tarnished his judgment, these newspaper articles reflect credit on their author and are well worth reading. They are the product of a statesman rather than a politician.]

Khronika grazhdanskoi voiny v Sibiri (1917–1918) (A Chronicle of the

Civil War in Siberia [1917–1918]). Edited by V. Maksakov and A. Turunov. Moscow and Leningrad, 1926.

Knorin, V. *Revoliutsiia i kontr-revoliutsiia v Belorussii (Fevral' 1917–fevral' 1918)* (Revolution and Counterrevolution in White Russia [February, 1917–February, 1918]). Smolensk, 1920. Part I [all that was published].

Knox, A. *With the Russian Army 1914–1917: Extracts from the Diary of a Military Attaché.* 2 vols. London, 1921.

Koroleva, A. "Razgon uchredilki" (Dispersal of the So-called Constituent Assembly), *Bor'ba Klassov* (The Class Struggle), XI (November, 1934).

Krasnyi Arkhiv (The Red Archives). 106 vols. Moscow, 1922–1941. [Scattered information of exceptional importance in the form of documents and shorter commentaries, dealing with revolutionary as well as diplomatic matters.]

Kratkii otchët o rabotakh chetvërtago s"ezda Partii Sotsialistov-Revoliutsionerov (26 noiabria–5 dekabria 1917 goda) (Brief Account of the Work of the Fourth Congress of the Socialist Revolutionary Party [November 26–December 5, 1917]). Edited by V. M. Zenzinov. Petrograd, 1918. [An exceedingly important source, and exceedingly rare. The function of this congress was essentially to hold an inquest and it did not pass without violent scenes which Zenzinov has greatly toned down, making it necessary to supplement his edited version of the proceedings by reports in the *Delo Naroda* (The People's Cause) and, especially, the *Volia Naroda* (The People's Will). Even the press versions, however, do not re-create the incandescence of this congress.]

Kratochvíl, Jaroslav. *Cesta revoluce* (The Course of Revolution). 2d ed. Prague, 1928. [Memoirs of merit, free of the Pan-Slavist taint].

Lebedev, V. *Iz riadov frantsuzskoi armii: russkie volonteri vo Frantsii* (From the Ranks of the French Army: Russian Volunteers in France). Moscow, 1916.

—— *Souvenirs d'un volontaire russe dans l'armée française 1914–1916.* Paris, 1917. [French translation of above with special introduction.]

Lelevich, L. [Kalmanson, L. G.]. *Oktiabr' v stavke* (October at General Headquarters). Gomel, 1922. [Valuable source with an appendix containing documents of great rarity.]

Lenin, V. I. *Sochineniia* (Works). 2d ed. 30 vols. Moscow and Leningrad, 1926–1932. Vol. XXII. [3d ed. used when 2d unavailable.]

—— *Leninskii Sbornik* (Lenin Collection). 29 vols. Moscow and Leningrad, 1924–1936. Vol. XXI (Moscow, 1933), edited by V. V. Adoratski et al.

Maiski, I. *Demokraticheskaia kontr-revoliutsiia* (The Democratic Counterrevolution). Moscow and Petrograd, 1923. [An entertaining and well-written book, merciless in relation to the SR's.]

Makarov, F. P. *Oktiabr' i grazhdanskaia voina v Udmurtii* (October and the Civil War in Udmurtia). Izhevsk, 1932.

Maliantovich, P. N. "V Zimnem Dvortse 25–26 oktiabria 1917 goda: Iz vospominanii" (In the Winter Palace, October 25–26, 1917: From Memoirs), *Byloe*, VI (June, 1918) (No. 12 of new series), 111–41.

Melgunov, S. P. *N. V. Chaikovskii v gody grazhdanskoi voiny (Materialy dlia istorii russkoi obshchestvennosti 1917–1925 g.g.)* (N. V. Chaikovski during the Years of Civil War [Material for a History of Russian Public Life 1917–1925]). Paris, 1929.

Miliukov, P. N. *Istoriia vtoroi russkoi revoliutsii* (History of the Second Russian Revolution). Sofia, 1921–1924. Vol. I, Parts I, II, III. [Reflecting the author's strongly conservative point of view in 1917 and his inadequate knowledge of SR affairs, Miliukov's history nevertheless is a basic source for the period.]

Morokhovets, E. A. *Agrarnye programmy rossiiskikh politicheskikh partii v 1917 godu* (The Agrarian Programs of Russian Political Parties in 1917). Leningrad, 1929. [Useful study.]

Moskovskaia provintsiia v semnadtsatom godu (Moscow Province in the Year 1917). Edited by E. Popova. Moscow and Leningrad, 1927.

Mstislavskii, S. *Piat' dnei: Nachalo i konets fevral'skoi revoliutsii* (Five Days: Beginning and End of the February Revolution). Berlin, St. Petersburg, and Moscow, 1922.

Muratov, Kh. I. *Revoliutsionnoe dvizhenie v russkoi armii v 1917 g.* (The Revolutionary Movement in the Russian Army in 1917). Moscow, 1958.

Nabokov, V. D. "Vremennoe Pravitel'stvo" (The Provisional Government), in *Arkhiv Russkoi Revoliutsii* (Archives of the Russian Revolution), I (2d ed.), 9–96. [Basic contribution.]

Narodnia Volia (The People's Will). No. 193 (December 31, 1917). [Ukrainian newspaper.]

Narodovlastie: Sbornik statei chlenov uchreditel'nago sobraniia fraktsii sotsial.-revoliutsionerov (Sovereignty of the People: A Collection of Articles by SR Members of the Constituent Assembly). 3 nos. Moscow, 1918. [These articles do not contribute very much.]

Nash Put': Organ revoliutsionnago sotsializma (Our Way: An Organ of Revolutionary Socialism). 2 nos. St. Petersburg, 1917. [Edited by M. A. Spiridonova. A rare and valuable source, containing information not to be found anywhere else.]

Nash Vek (Our Age). Petrograd, 1917. Issues for December 5 and 6, 1917.

Niessel, H. A. *Le Triomphe des bolchéviks et la paix de Brest-Litovsk: souvenirs 1917–1918.* Paris, 1940. [The French general tells little.]

Noulens, J. *Mon Ambassade en Russie soviétique 1917–1919.* 2 vols. Paris, 1933. [The French ambassador does not tell much.]

Novaia Zhizn' (New Life). 214 nos. for 1917 (Nos. 179 [November 12, 1917]–214 [December 31, 1917] were used; also some of the early numbers for 1918). Petrograd, 1917–1918. [Maxim Gorki's newspaper, independent, radical, and antiwar.]

Obvinitel'noe zakliuchenie po delu tsentral'nogo komiteta i otdel'nykh chlenov inykh organizatsii partii s.-r. po obvineniiu ikh v vooruzhënnoi bor'be protiv Sovetskoi vlasti, organizatsii ubiistv, vooruzhënnykh ograblenii i izmennicheskikh snosheniiakh s inostrannymi gosudarstvami (Final Statement of the Prosecution in the Trial of the Central Committee and Individual Members of Other Organizations of the SR Party on Charges of Taking up Arms against the Soviet Regime, Instigating Murders and Armed Robberies, and Having Treasonable Relations with Foreign States). Moscow, 1922. [A major source.]

Oganovski, N. "Dnevnik chlena Uchreditel'nago Sobraniia" (Diary of a Member of the Constituent Assembly), *Golos Minuvshago* (Voice of the Past), IV–VI (April–June, 1918), 143–72. [A key article.]

Oktiabr' na Odeshchine: Sbornik statei i vospominanii k X-letiiu oktiabria (October in the Odessa Area: A Collection of Articles and Reminiscences for the Tenth Anniversary of October). Odessa, 1927.

Oktiabr' v zapadnoi Sibiri (October in Western Siberia). Edited by E. I. Petrova. Novosibirsk, 1948.

Oktiabr'skoe vooruzhënnoe vosstanie v Petrograde (Velikaia Oktiabr'skaia sotsialisticheskaia revoliutsiia: Dokumenty i materialy) (The October Armed Insurrection in Petrograd [The Great October Socialist Revolution: Documents and Materials]). Moscow, 1957.

Oktiabr'skoe vooruzhënnoe vosstanie v Petrograde (Vospominaniia aktivnykh uchastnikov revoliutsii) (The October Armed Insurrection in Petrograd [Recollections of Active Participants in the Revolution]). Leningrad, 1956.

Oktiabr'skoe vosstanie v Moskve: Sbornik dokumentov, statei i vospominanii (The October Insurrection in Moscow: A Collection of Documents, Articles, and Reminiscences). Edited by N. Ovsiannikov. Moscow, 1922. [Recommended to the author by V. V. Rudnev in 1935 as the most reliable source.]

Parfenov, P. S. *Grazhdanskaia voina v Sibiri 1918–1920* (The Civil War in Siberia 1918–1920). 2d ed. Moscow, n.d.

—— "Predoktiabr'skie dni v Sibiri" (Pre-October Days in Siberia), *Sibirskie Ogni* (Siberian Lights), III (June–August, 1924), 107–37.

Partiinyia Izvestiia (Party News). 6 nos. Petrograd, 1917–1918. No. 1 (September 28, 1917); No. 2 (October 5, 1917), 64 pp.; No. 3 (October 19, 1917), 64 pp.; No. 4 (December 10, 1917); No. 5 (January 20, 1918), 72 pp.; No. 6 (March 8/21, 1918). [Published by the Central Committee of the PSR. Edited by V. M. Zenzinov and others. Indispensable source. Exceedingly rare. Yields more information on the party than any other source save the *Delo Naroda* (The People's Cause). Certain valuable material can be found only in the *Partiinyia Izvestiia*, which was supposed to be a weekly but did not make the grade. Though scattered in libraries from Moscow to California, all six numbers have been used.]

Perezhitoe (V god revoliutsii) (What Has Been Experienced in a Year of Revolution). Moscow, 1918. Vol. I. [All that was published. Brief recollections of various public figures; a rare and valuable source.]

Petrogradskie bol'sheviki v Oktiabr'skoi revoliutsii (Petrograd Bolsheviks in the October Revolution). Leningrad, 1957. 456 pp.

Pinezhski, E. *Krasnaia gvardiia* (The Red Guard). 2d ed. Moscow, 1933.

Piontkovski, S. *Oktiabr' 1917 g.* (October, 1917). Moscow and Leningrad, 1927.

Podshivalov, I. *Grazhdanskaia bor'ba na Urale 1917-1918 gg.: Opyt voenno-istoricheskogo issledovaniia* (The Civil War in the Urals 1917–1918: A Study in Military History). Moscow, 1925.

Poincaré, Raymond. *Au Service de la France: neuf années de souvenirs.* 10 vols. Paris, 1926–1933. Vol. IX: *L'Année trouble, 1917.*

Pokrovski, M. N. *Chto ustanovil protsess tak nazyvaemykh "sotsialistov-revoliutsionerov"?* (What Has the Trial of the So-called "Socialist Revolutionaries" Established?). Moscow, 1922. [The noted Marxist historian adds something to the account of the trial published in the Soviet press and does not simply rake over what is to be found there.]

Pravda. St. Petersburg, Moscow, 1917–. 1917: various numbers late in the year; 1918: various numbers early in the year; 1922: all numbers covering the SR trial, June 8 to August 7. [See remarks under *Izvestiia.*]

Proletarskaia Revoliutsiia (Proletarian Revolution). 113 vols. Moscow, 1921–1931.

Protokoly pervago s"ezda Partii Levykh Sotsialistov-Revoliutsionerov (Internatsionalistov) (Minutes of the First Congress of the Left Socialist Revolutionary Party [Internationalists]). N.p., 1918. [One of the two main sources of information concerning the movement that is the dark province of the revolution.]

Rabochii klass Urala v gody voiny i revoliutsii (The Ural Working Class in the Years of War and Revolution). 3 vols. Sverdlovsk, 1927. Vol. III: *Oktiabr'skii perevorot na Urale* (The October Revolution in the Ural Region).

Radkey, O. H. *The Agrarian Foes of Bolshevism: Promise and Default of the Russian Socialist Revolutionaries, February to October 1917.* New York, 1958.

—— *The Election to the Russian Constituent Assembly of 1917.* Cambridge, Mass., 1950. Harvard Historical Monograph No. XXI.

Rafes, N. *Dva goda revoliutsii na Ukraine: Raskol "Bunda"* (Two Years of Revolution in the Ukraine: The Split in the Bund). Moscow, 1920.

Rakitnikova, Inna. *Kak russkoe krest'ianstvo borolos' za Uchreditel'noe Sobranie: Doklad Mezhdunarodnomu Sotsialisticheskomu Biuro* (How the Russian Peasantry Fought for the Constituent Assembly: Report to the International Socialist Bureau). Paris, 1918.

Rathauser, Ia. *Revoliutsiia i grazhdanskaia voina v Baku* (The Revolution and Civil War in Baku). Baku, 1927. Part I: *1917–1918 g.g.*

Revoliutsiia 1917 goda (Khronika sobytii) (The Revolution of 1917: A Chronicle of Events). Compiled by N. Avdeev and others. 6 vols. Moscow and Petrograd, 1923–1930. [Valuable for source material as well as for reference.]

Revoliutsiia 1917 goda v Azerbaidzhane (khronika sobytii) (The Revolution of 1917 in Azerbaidzhan: A Chronicle of Events). Edited by S. Belenky and A. Manvelov. Baku, 1927.

Revoliutsionnaia Rossiia (Revolutionary Russia). New series. 78 nos. Dorpat, Berlin, and Prague, 1920–1931. [Some longer articles by Chernov and others in which they look back on the debacle.]

Rubinshtein, N. *Bol'sheviki i Uchreditel'noe Sobranie* (The Bolsheviks and the Constituent Assembly). Moscow, 1938.

Russkiia Vedomosti (Russian News). Moscow, 1917–1918. 1917: Nos. 248–279 (November 12–December 31); 1918: Nos. 1–21 (January 3–31) (some missing). [Perhaps the best Russian newspaper; sober and factual.]

Russkoe Slovo (Russian Word). Moscow, 1917. No. 163 (July 19, 1917).

Samoupravlenie (Self-Rule). Edited by G. I. Shreider. Petrograd, 1917. No. 14–15 (November 5, 1917).

Sef, S. E. *Revoliutsiia 1917 goda v Zakavkaz'i (Dokumenty, materialy)* (The Revolution of 1917 in the Transcaucasus [Documents and Materials]). Tiflis, 1927. [An important regional source.]

Semenov, G. [Vasil'ev]. *Voennaia i boevaia rabota Partii sotsialistov-revoliutsionerov za 1917–1918 g.g.* (Military and Combat Activity of the PSR in 1917–1918). Moscow, 1922.

—— "Vospominaniia byvshego esera" (Memoirs of a Former SR), *Prozhektor* (The Projector), No. 8 (May 31, 1923), No. 9 (June 17, 1923).

Severnoe Ekho (Northern Echo). Vologda, 1917. No. 99 (December 20, 1917).

Sokolov, Boris. "Zashchita Vserossiiskago Uchreditel'nago Sobraniia" (Defense of the All Russian Constituent Assembly), in *Arkhiv Russkoi Revoliutsii*, XIII, 5–70. [A long and detailed account, considered by Zenzinov to be unreliable and replete with bombast, but valued by this author both for the mass of information and the sociological insight it contains. Sokolov was rather too sanguine in his hopes of offering armed resistance to the Bolsheviks, but an underlying sense of realism prevented his fancy from soaring too high.]

Sovety krest'ianskikh deputatov i drugie krest'ianskie organizatsii (Soviets of Peasants' Deputies and Other Peasant Organizations). Edited by A. V. Shestakov. Moscow, 1929. Vol. I, Part II.

Stankevich, V. B. *Vospominaniia 1914–1919 g.* (Memoirs 1914–1919). Berlin, 1920. [Though an army commissar of the Provisional Government from the right fringe of Populism, the author is independent in thought and objective in judgment. A significant contribution.]

Steinberg, I. Z. *Als ich Volkskommissar war: Episoden aus der russischen Oktoberrevolution.* Munich, 1929. [Entertaining and enlightening memoirs.]

—— *Ot fevralia po oktiabr' 1917 g.* (From February to October of 1917). Berlin and Milan, n.d. [Brief survey of the revolution from an unusual (Left SR) point of view, and hence very useful.]

Sukhanov, N. (pseud. of N. N. Gimmer). *Zapiski o revoliutsii* (Notes on the Revolution). 7 vols. Berlin, St. Petersburg, and Moscow, 1922–1923.

Sviatitski, N. V. "Fraktsiia P.S.-R. Uchreditel'nago Sobraniia i eia deiatel'-nost'" (The SR Delegation in the Constituent Assembly and Its Activity), *Partiinyia Izvestiia* (Party News), No. 5 (January 20, 1918).

—— *Itogi vyborov vo Vserossiiskoe Uchreditel'noe Sobranie* (The Results of the Election for the All-Russian Constituent Assembly). Moscow, 1918.

—— *Kogo russkii narod izbral svoimi predstaviteliami?* (Whom Did the Russian People Choose as Their Representatives?). Moscow, 1918.

Trenogova, T. *Bor'ba petrogradskikh bol'shevikov za krest'ianstvo v 1917 godu* (The Struggle of the Petrograd Bolsheviks to Win the Peasantry in 1917). Leningrad, 1946. [Based on archival material; weak in analysis.]

Trotski, L. *The History of the Russian Revolution.* 3 vols. New York, 1932. [Trotski informed the author that these volumes contained all that he had to say about the SR's. He did not say much.]

—— *Oktiabr'skaia revoliutsiia* (The October Revolution). Moscow and Petrograd, 1918. [A sketch, simple and clear, without the embroidery to be found in his history of the revolution.]

1917 god na Kievshchine: Khronika sobytii (The Year 1917 in the Region of Kiev: A Chronicle of Events). Edited by V. Manilov. Kiev, 1928. [A massive compilation. Not as well organized as some provincial sources.]

1917 god v derevne: vospominaniia krest'ian (1917 in the Village: Reminiscences of Peasants). Compiled by I. V. Igritski. Moscow and Leningrad, 1929. [Though the peasants were hand-picked, their geographical distribution is satisfactory and they record experiences that illuminate the village scene. One of the most interesting and rewarding sources.]

1917 god v Khar'kove: Sbornik statei i vospominanii (The Year 1917 in Kharkov: A Collection of Articles and Reminiscences). Edited by V. Morgunov and Z. Machulski. Kharkov, 1927.

1917 god v Saratove (The Year 1917 in Saratov). Saratov, 1927.

1917-i god vo vladimirskoi gubernii: Khronika sobytii (The Year 1917 in Vladimir Province: A Chronicle of Events). Edited by N. Shakhanov. Vladimir, 1927.

1917i god v Voronezhskoi gubernii (Khronika). (The Year 1917 in Voronezh Province: A Chronicle). Edited by V. M. Lavygin. Voronezh, 1928. [Material well chosen and well edited.]

Vechernii Chas (The Evening Hour). No. 22 (December 22, 1917).

Vinnichenko, V. *Vidrodzhennia natsii: Istoriia ukraïnskoï revoliutsiï (marets 1917 r.–gruden 1919 r.)* (Resurrection of a Nation: History of the Ukrainian Revolution [March, 1917–December, 1919]). 3 vols. Kiev and Vienna, 1920. [Only slightly used because of language difficulty.]

Vishniak, Mark V. *Dan' proshlomu* (To the Past Its Due). New York, 1954.

—— *Vserossiiskoe Uchreditel'noe Sobranie* (The All-Russian Constituent Assembly). Paris, 1932.

Vladimirova, Vera. *God sluzhby "sotsialistov" kapitalistam: Ocherki po istorii kontr-revoliutsii v 1918 godu* (One Year's Service of "Socialists" to Capitalists: A Study in the History of Counterrevolution in the Year 1918). Moscow and Leningrad, 1927. [A very useful and rather reliable Soviet survey, incorporating a great deal of material, some of archival character.]

Vlast' Naroda (People's Rule). No. 164 (November 18, 1917).

Vokrug Uchreditel'nago Sobraniia: Sbornik statei i dokumentov (Around the Constituent Assembly: A Collection of Articles and Documents). Petrograd, 1918. [A reprint in book form of selected articles from the Left SR press, the *Znamia Truda* (Banner of Toil) (*see below*) and the *Golos Trudovogo Krest'ianstva* (Voice of the Toiling Peasantry).]

Volia Naroda (The People's Will). 206 nos. Petrograd, 1917. No. 1 (April 29, 1917)–No. 206 (December 31, 1917). [Edited by A. A. Argunov and others. Indispensable source, the right-wing complement to the left-centrist *Delo Naroda*. Despite the fervor of his convictions, Argunov practiced good journalism and set high standards for himself and his paper.]

Vompe, P. *Dni Oktiabr'skoi revoliutsii i zheleznodorozhniki* (Days of the October Revolution and the Railway Workers). Moscow, 1924. [A book containing unique and valuable material on the revolution.]

Voprosy Istorii (Questions of History). Moscow, 1945–.

Voznesenski, A. N. *Moskva v 1917 godu* (Moscow in 1917). Moscow and Leningrad, 1928. [Interesting and well-informed memoirs, written without slavish deference to the victorious regime by a city official who had not been on its side in 1917.]

Vserossiiskoe Uchreditel'noe Sobranie (The All Russian Constituent Assembly). Edited by I. S. Malchevski. Moscow and Leningrad, 1930. [Contains the stenographic report of the session together with important documents, tables, notes, and statistics. A publication of the Central Archives, Archives of the October Revolution.]

Vtoroi Vserossiiskii S"ezd Sovetov Rabochikh i Soldatskikh Deputatov (The Second All-Russian Congress of Soviets of Workers' and Soldiers' Deputies). Edited by K. G. Kotelnikov. Moscow and Leningrad, 1928. [Another publication of the Central Archives, Archives of the October Revolution.]

Zenzinov, V. M. *Iz zhizni revoliutsionera* (Out of the Life of a Revolutionary). Paris, 1919. [Reminiscences of the revolution and civil war, unfortunately all too brief.]

Znamia Bor'by (Banner of Struggle). 21 nos. Berlin, 1924–1927. [Organ of the Delegation Abroad of the Left SR's (not many of them got abroad) and of the Union of SR Maximalists.]

Znamia Truda (Banner of Toil). Petrograd, 1917–1918. No. 1 (August 23, 1917)–No. 108 (December 31, 1917). [Beginning with No. 109 (January 3, 1918) issues for January of 1918 were also consulted in so far as available. Central organ of the Left SR's. One of the rarest and most important of sources.]

ORAL INFORMATION

Chernov, V. M. Left-centrist SR; member of Central Committee; chief intellectual force of revolutionary Populism. Interviews in Prague, 1934–1935; in New York, January 4, 1950.

Kerenski, A. F. Right SR; Russian premier, 1917. Statement in California, November 17, 1956.

Nikolaevski, Boris. Menshevik; student of the revolution. Conferences in New York, 1949–1959.

Postnikov, S. P. Left-centrist SR; chief editor of *Delo Naroda*. Talks in Prague, 1934–1935; interviews there, August and September, 1935.

Rudnev, V. V. Right SR; mayor of Moscow, 1917. Interview in Paris, September, 1935.

Tsereteli, I. G. Menshevik; member of presidium of Petrograd Soviet, 1917. Interview in New York, December 23, 1949.

Vishniak, M. V. Right SR; editor of *Delo Naroda*. Interview in New York, January 2, 1952; conversations in California, summer of 1955.

Zenzinov, V. M. Right-centrist SR; member of Central Committee; editor of *Delo Naroda* and *Partiinyia Izvestiia*. Interviews in Paris, September, 1935; in New York, December 19, and December 31, 1949, December 31, 1951.

Index

Activists, and passivists, 181, 350-52
Africa, 406, 495
Agrarian movement, 250, 275, 318 ff.; schism in, 171, 203-79 *passim*; revolution, SR's and, 480, 493; *see also* Peasants
Agriculture, Commissariat of, 148; collectivization of production, 150
Alekseev, M. V., 13, 477
Alekseev, N. N., 293
Alexander III, 454
Alexandróvich, Peter, 149, 153
Alexandrovsk *uezd* (Vladimir province), 265
Algasov, V., charges against, 134; re Military Revolutionary Committee, 147
Allies, and peace negotiations, 84 ff., 146; SR adherence to, 180, 321 ff., 490; armistice proposal and, 193 f.; withdrawal of missions, 211 ff.; and war debts, 327 f.; financial aid to SR's, 366 ff., *passim*, 453, 492-93; Paris conference, 399
All-Russian Congress of Peasants' Soviets, *First*, 208; *Second*, 76 ff., 139, 383; proposed, 204 ff.; delegates, 211 ff., 226 f.; constituency, 225; strategy of major political groups, 230 ff.; major controversies, 232 ff.; credentials commission, 237 f., 242, 245 f.; resolutions, 240 f.; split into two congresses, 243 ff., 440; vote on the Assembly, 246 ff.; on war and peace, 250, 251-52, 253, 256 f., 322; new Executive Committee, 253 f., 417; outcome, 255 f.; *Third*, SR, 275 ff., 440 ff.; Left SR, 445 ff.
All-Russian Congress of Workers' and Soldiers' Soviets, 206; *Second*, 3, 8, 69, 188 f.; formation of new party, 96 ff.; Left SR's re, 101; *Third*, 444

All-Russian Constituent Assembly, *see* Constituent Assembly
All-Russian Employees' Union, and general strike, 336
All-Russian Executive Committee (Workers', Soldiers' and Peasants'), 52, 139, 144; Military Revolutionary Committee transferred to, 145; formation of, 220 f.; decree re power, 376; and dissolution of the Assembly, 429
All-Russian Executive Committee of Peasants' Soviets, 10, 109, 221*n*, 417, 440; and formation of a new government, 68 ff.; on transfer of second congress to Mogilev, 76 ff.; new, 148; old, 150; controversy, 204 ff.; party factions in, 206 ff.; soldiers re, 210, 248 f.; deprived of right to vote, 210 f.; criticisms of, 235 ff.; SR, 415 f.
All-Russian Executive Committee of Railway Employees (Vikzhel), 345; intervention in Moscow, 57 f., 65 f.; peace negotiations during October Revolution, 70 ff., 144; policy, 92, 383
All-Siberian Soviet Congress, 125 f.
All-socialist government, 63 f., 69, 77, 223
Altai province, 126, 127
Amur Region, 127
Anarcho-syndicalism, 139 f.
Anglo-Russian Convention of 1907, 402, 407
Anokhin, Bolshevik leader, 238
Anti-Semitism, 159 f., 218, 241, 301*n*
Antonov, leader of green movement, 275
Archangel, 436, 467
Argunov, A. A., 167, 353 ff., 475, 491
Arkhangelski, V. G., 81, 185

DATE DUE

APR 9 '65			
MAY 6 '66			
GAYLORD			PRINTED IN U.S.A.